372
374
376

Console and Classify

certezze positivite

CONSOLE AND CLASSIFY

The French Psychiatric Profession
in the Nineteenth Century

JAN GOLDSTEIN
University of Chicago

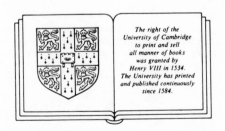

The right of the
University of Cambridge
to print and sell
all manner of books
was granted by
Henry VIII in 1534.
The University has printed
and published continuously
since 1584.

CAMBRIDGE UNIVERSITY PRESS

CAMBRIDGE

NEW YORK   PORT CHESTER   MELBOURNE   SYDNEY

Published by the Press Syndicate of the University of Cambridge
The Pitt Building, Trumpington Street, Cambridge CB2 1RP
40 West 20th Street, New York, NY 10011, USA
10 Stamford Road, Oakleigh, Melbourne 3166, Australia

First published 1987
First paperback edition 1990

Printed in the United States of America

Library of Congress Cataloging-in-Publication Data
Goldstein, Jan.
Console and classify.
Revision of thesis (Ph.D.) – Columbia University.
Bibliography: p.
Includes index.
1. Psychiatry – France – History – 19th century.
2. Psychiatrists – France – History – 19th century.
I. Title.
RC450.F7G65   1987   616.89'00944   86-26831

British Library Cataloging in Publication Data
Goldstein, Jan
Console and classify: the French psychiatric
profession in the nineteenth century.
1. Psychiatry – France – History –
19th century
I. Title.
616.89'00944   RC450.F8

ISBN 0-521-32279-0 hardback
ISBN 0-521-39555-0 paperback

Parts of Chapter 9 of the present work appeared in a slightly different version as "The Hysteria Diagnosis and the Politics of Anticlericalism in Later Nineteenth-Century France," *Journal of Modern History* 54 (1982): 209–39, and are reprinted by permission of the University of Chicago Press. © 1982 by the University of Chicago.

TO MY PARENTS

Contents

Contents

Illustrations

Plates

Figures

Acknowledgments

DURING this book's long passage into print, I have had a great deal of moral and material support. Robert Paxton, Fritz Stern, and Isser Woloch read the book in its original form – as a Columbia University doctoral dissertation covering the period 1820–1860 – and I am indebted to each of them for generous encouragement and sound advice. My dissertation research in France was funded by the Foreign Area Fellowship Program of the Social Science Research Council. Upon my return to the United States, a fellowship from the Section on the History of Psychiatry and the Behavioral Sciences of the Department of Psychiatry at Cornell University Medical College placed me in the company of practicing American psychiatrists and familiarized me with their perspectives, as "insiders," on the growth of their professional specialty.

I soon realized that writing the book I had in mind would require not a revision of my dissertation but a full-scale metamorphosis of it. In carrying out that latter project, I was not, fortunately, left entirely to my own devices. I am grateful to George Stocking, who invited me to join the Chicago Group in the History of the Social Sciences when he founded it in the winter of 1979, during my first year at the University of Chicago. The papers presented at the CGHSS broadened my conceptual horizons, and I benefited as well from the camaraderie and from the discussions of my own work, including early versions of two chapters in this book. Peter Novick listened sympathetically but critically to some of the ideas in the book when they were still too inchoate to be committed to paper. And in what shall always seem to me an exemplary act of friendship, Keith Baker read and commented on the entire manuscript at an especially critical point in its development.

Joan Scott's enthusiasm for this project over the years has been a boon. Charles Rosenberg, who read the manuscript for Cambridge University Press, made judicious suggestions for revision, almost all of which I (eventually) adopted. Two loyal and generous friends, Mary Gluck and Priscilla Clark – both writing books of their own at the time – shared the ups and downs of this one and helped to ensure that it was finally brought to completion.

Much needed leaves of absence from teaching to work on this project full time were provided by a Research Fellowship for Recent Recipients of the Ph.D. from the American Council of Learned Societies and, later, by a Fellowship for Independent Study and Research from the National Endowment for the Humanities. Each of these fellowships also made possible a research trip to France, as did a grant from the Social Sciences Divisional Research Committee of the University of Chicago. A variety of expenses incidental to the project were covered by Biomedical Research Support Grants from funds made available to the University of Chicago by the U. S. Public Health Service.

I owe many thanks to librarians and archivists on both sides of the Atlantic and a special debt of gratitude to the interlibrary loan departments of Butler and Regenstein Libraries; to Mme Florence Greffe, curator of the archives of the Assistance Publique de Paris; and to M. Evrard, curator of the departmental archives of Ille-et-Vilaine, who managed to locate the then-uncatalogued Chambeyron papers for me during my hurried visit to Rennes in the late summer of 1982. As assistant to the dean of the Social Sciences Division, Steven Wheatley watched over my computer account with a benevolent eye. Therese Chappell typed the manuscript and its successive revisions with good humor and impressive accuracy. Michael Conzen graciously volunteered to serve as my consultant in matters of map and chart design, and Katherine Sellers of the Cartographic Services Unit of the University of Chicago executed the map and chart that appear in these pages. At the final stage of the process, John Brooks and my sister, Arlene V. Ashley, helped with the proofreading.

One final acknowledgment is due. In a very real sense, the patients of nineteenth-century French psychiatrists made this book possible. They are shadowy figures, known to me only through the words of their doctors, who recorded their tenaciously held delusions, their "agitated" and "laborious" periods, their despairing leaps into the Seine. They deserve a book of their own, but in this book they appear only as the objects from which a science of psychiatry was drawn.

Abbreviations

AAP	Archives de l'Assistance Publique de Paris, Paris
ADIV	Archives départementales d'Ille-et-Vilaine, Rennes
AN	Archives Nationales, Paris
Ann. d'hyg. pub.	*Annales d'hygiène publique et de médecine légale*
Ann. m.-p.	*Annales médico-psychologiques*
APP	Archives de la Préfecture de Police de Paris, Paris
Arch. gen. de med.	*Archives générales de médecine*
Arch. parl.	*Archives parlementaires de 1787 à 1860*, 1st ser.: 1787 à 1799, 82 vols. (Paris: Paul Dupont, 1879–1913); 2d ser.: 1800 à 1860, 127 vols. (Paris: Paul Dupont, 1862–1913)
BN	Bibliothèque Nationale, Paris
Bull. Hist. Med.	*Bulletin of the History of Medicine*
Cabanis, *O.P.*	*Oeuvres philosophiques de Cabanis*, ed. Claude Lehec and Jean Cazeneuve, 2 vols. (Paris: Presses universitaires de France, 1956)
Dict. des sci. med.	*Dictionaire des sciences médicales*, 60 vols. (Paris: C.L.F. Panckoucke, 1812–22)
Encyclopédie	Denis Diderot and Jean le Rond d'Alembert, *Encyclopédie, ou dictionnaire raisonné des sciences, des arts et des métiers*, 36 vols. (Lausanne and Berne: Société typographique, 1778–81)
Gaz. hebd. de med.	*Gazette hebdomadaire de médecine et de chirurgie*
J. de med. ment.	*Journal de médecine mentale*
M.S.M.E.	*Mémoires de la Société médicale d'émulation de Paris*
Pionniers	René Semelaigne, *Les pionniers de la psychiatrie française avant et après Pinel*, 2 vols. (Paris: J.-B. Baillière, 1930–32)

Introduction

A ROUND 1800, investigators claiming scientific status and authority began to fasten their attention on the ordinary activities and the internal processes of human beings. Among the many "human sciences" thrown up by this far-reaching development was psychiatry, the medical study and treatment of the disorders of the mind. It arose almost simultaneously in France, Britain, America, and the German lands and, despite considerable mutual borrowing, soon bore in each setting the marks of a distinctive national tradition. From the closing decade of the eighteenth century, when they pledged to outdistance their English rivals, to the closing decade of the nineteenth century, when they began in turn to be overtaken by the Germans, French physicians played the single most vigorous role in constituting and legitimating a psychiatric science. In this book I have traced their largely successful participation in that venture.

As will soon become apparent, the history of French psychiatry in the nineteenth century is really a set of concurrent histories. There is an intellectual history of the elaboration of a body of scientific knowledge. There is a social history of the formation, within the relatively fluid society created by the Revolution, of a new profession that came to impart elite status to its members. And there is a political history of the articulation and pursuit of administrative goals by a modern bureaucratic state. I have sought to reconstruct each of these histories and to bring them together, in order to restore the "text" of psychiatric theory to the specific social and political contexts from which its full historical meaning is inseparable. In doing so, I have focused on three central elements of that long and multi-authored "text": the psychiatric therapy called by contemporaries the moral treatment, and the disease entities of monomania and hysteria.

Since the history of psychiatry, once a scholarly backwater, has become an active and populous field during the past two decades, the place of my work within this growing literature – or at least the portion of it concerning France[1] – needs a few words of comment. As is

<hr />

[1] Thus far, all book-length studies of the history of French psychiatry have been written

1

well-known, the attacks on the modern psychiatric system that began in the 1960s and were first associated with the names of Thomas Szasz and R. D. Laing sparked a good deal of the recent interest in unearthing psychiatry's past. In France, where attacks of this sort have been so fully elaborated that they have acquired the status of a genre, and bookstores contain whole sections labeled "Anti-Psychiatry," it is hardly surprising that studies of the history of psychiatry have been especially strongly influenced by this ongoing, policy-oriented controversy – or that they have often been produced by men and women who are not primarily historians. These are features not only of the writings of Michel Foucault (who may be counted among the initiators of the anti-psychiatry movement) but of the other important general contributions to the field as well: *L'ordre psychiatrique: L'âge d'or de l'aliénisme,* by the sociologist Robert Castel, which reviews the period 1790–1860; and *La pratique de l'esprit humain: L'institution asilaire et la révolution démocratique* by Marcel Gauchet, a political philosopher, and Gladys Swain, a practicing psychiatrist, which treats the first ten years of the nineteenth century.

Castel's leftist critique of psychiatry is contained in his account of its genesis in France: The new science arose, he argues, not in direct response to the problem of mental illness itself but in response to a strictly legalistic problem posed by the bourgeois revolution – how to justify incarceration in a society ideologically committed to operating on a "contractual" model. By contrast, Gauchet and Swain (though no more partisans of the present-day asylum than is Castel) are intent upon portraying the impetus behind the medical specialty of psychiatry in a favorable and idealistic light. For them 1789 is the "democratic" rather than the "bourgeois" revolution; and in their liberal rejoinder to Castel, psychiatry appears as the form in which that revolution extended itself into the individual's mental make-up, through a normative concept of "self-possession." The latter – the opposite of "mental alienation," as insanity was then called – had arisen naturally in the course of the scientific exploration of insanity. As our stake in ourselves, self-possession corresponded to the democratic placement of sovereignty in the hands of the people, which gave us a stake in the polity.[2]

by French scholars. Among American scholars, Dora B. Weiner has published important articles on Philippe Pinel and is working on a Pinel biography; and Robert A. Nye's *Crime, Madness and Politics in Modern France: The Medical Concept of National Decline* (Princeton, N.J.: Princeton University Press, 1984) includes discussions of late nineteenth-century psychiatry as part of its argument. Several younger scholars also have works in progress.

2   Robert Castel, *L'ordre psychiatrique: L'âge d'or de l'aliénisme* (Paris: Minuit, 1976); and Marcel Gauchet and Gladys Swain, *La pratique de l'esprit humain: L'institution asilaire et la révolution démocratique* (Paris: Gallimard, 1980). For a commentary on Castel's work, which distinguishes it from the anti-psychiatry it so much resembles, see Peter Miller, "The Territory of the Psychiatrist," *Ideology and Consciousness* 7 (1980): 63–105. Gauchet and Swain, *Pratique* is reviewed by Claude Quétel in *Clio Medica* 16 (1981): 149–51.

Such brief summaries can only hint at the richness and sophistication of these books, whose interest is further heightened by their involvement in current political debates. But inevitably, such involvement also has its drawbacks when these books are considered as works of history, for it has constrained the historical inquiry, largely determining the questions asked. Thus, for example, Castel and the team of Gauchet and Swain have both placed a high priority on explaining the failure – so evident from the vantage point of our own day – of the nineteenth-century asylum experiment.

The case of Foucault – though obviously special – offers a variation on the same theme. Certainly Foucault used historical material to great advantage, and his historical sense was extraordinarily acute. The brilliant global conceptualization in *Discipline and Punish* of "disciplines" such as psychiatry, clinical medicine, pedagogy, and penology and their role in sustaining the nineteenth-century liberal state is not merely suggestive; it is frequently borne out by detailed research.[3] At the same time, Foucault always considered himself at least as much a philosopher as a historian, whose epistemological and political project required that he challenge the ordinary canons of history-writing. In particular, Foucault questioned the necessary continuity of history. Even after he abandoned the focus on radical epistemic ruptures that marked his "archaeology," and began in the 1970s to call his investigations of the past "genealogy," historical time still moved for him in a kind of staccato fashion. He continued to suppress those gradual processes of historical transition and transformation through which the components of modern rational civilization, including psychiatry, had come into existence.[4] With its Nietzschean overtones, Foucauldian "genealogy" was, after all, a deliberately polemical use of the past designed to debunk the most cherished values and institutions of liberal culture by showing that they had originated in mere historical contingency. To locate them at the end of a long, continuous development would have been, for Foucault, only to dignify them.[5]

---

[3] See, for example, my article, "Foucault Among the Sociologists: The 'Disciplines' and the History of the Professions," *History and Theory* 23 (1984): 170–92; and, with the qualifications indicated, Chapters 8 and 9 of this book.

[4] For example, while he identified the direct antecedents of the "disciplines" – namely, the monastic regimen and the quarantine in time of plague – he remained silent about the process connecting antecedent to end product. Michel Foucault, *Discipline and Punish: The Birth of the Prison*, trans. A. Sheridan (New York: Pantheon, 1977), pp. 137, 143, 197–98.

[5] On "genealogy," see Allan Megill, *Prophets of Extremity: Nietzsche, Heidegger, Foucault, Derrida* (Berkeley and Los Angeles: University of California Press, 1985), pp. 232–36; Hubert L. Dreyfus and Paul Rabinow, *Michel Foucault: Beyond Structuralism and Hermeneutics* (Chicago: University of Chicago Press, 1982), pp. 104–10; and Jeffrey Minson, *Genealogies of Morals: Nietzsche, Foucault, Donzelot and the Eccentricity of Ethics* (New York: St. Martin's Press, 1985), pp. 7–13 and Ch. 2. There is, of course, disagreement

Thus, despite all that these authors have accomplished, work on the history of nineteenth-century French psychiatry has remained, in certain respects, insufficiently historical. Many of the distinctive features of this book can be viewed, by contrast, as the result of a thoroughgoing exploitation of the specifically historical nature of its subject matter. By this I mean, first of all, that the participation of French psychiatry in some of the broadest and most characteristic themes of modern history – professionalization, bureaucratization, secularization – has not yet been explored. In this book, I have reconstructed the story of psychiatry, from both archival and printed sources, in such a way as to add substance and specificity to our knowledge of each of these long-range trends. Second, while Foucault and, following him, Castel preferred to remove human agency from the plot of history and to speak instead of a faceless and ubiquitous "power" working to satisfy abstract, systematic requirements, I have filled my canvas with historical actors – primarily psychiatrists, but also bureaucrats and legislators. Treating them both as individuals and as members of social and political groups, I have connected historical outcomes to their motives and initiatives. While power is, in other words, central to my analysis, I have chosen always to speak of it in embodied form.[6] Third, writing as a historian rather than as a Foucauldian "genealogist," I have followed carefully the emergence of psychiatry out of its antecedents. Because religious antecedents loomed large, I have come to emphasize a process of secularization virtually ignored in other accounts of psychiatry's entrance upon the scene.

As many Frenchmen were well aware by the early nineteenth century, professionalization coincided with and entailed secularization. Contemporaries sometimes alluded to a declining church, whose spoils would inevitably be divided among the secular professions. Professional rivalries could even take the form of arguments about which occupational group was most qualified to inherit the mantle of cultural authority that had so long cloaked the priest. Thus the dean of the Paris medical faculty told the assembled student body in 1836 that, contrary to a commonplace which held that lawyers stood to gain "the influence that the ministers of the altar have lost," physicians were the true and rightful successors to the clergy. For, he asked, "what are the

---

about the definition of Foucault's projects and their mutual relationships; for a view somewhat different from my own, see Arnold I. Davidson, "Archaeology, Genealogy, Ethics" in David Couzens Hoy, ed., *Foucault: A Critical Reader* (Oxford: Basil Blackwell, 1986): 221–33.

[6] For a lucid analysis of Foucault's concept of power without a subject – and one which justifies the historical reconstruction of purposeful human action even if Foucault's point about the "undesigned systematicity" of history is conceded – see Charles Taylor, "Foucault on Freedom and Truth," in *Philosophy and the Human Sciences: Philosophical Papers*, Vol. 2 (Cambridge University Press, 1985), esp. pp. 170–71.

concerns of wealth as compared to the concern for preservation?" The physician was "the family's most intimate confidant. Before him fall all the veils of the private life. To him are revealed all the aches of the soul, so frequently the source of their bodily counterparts."[7]

In the case of psychiatry, the line of succession from cleric to physician was especially clear. An important element in the psychiatric therapy known as the moral treatment was the technique of "consolation," which derived most immediately from Catholic pastoral care. Though they had shorn it of explicit religious content, the psychiatrists nonetheless referred to this soothing and empathic therapeutic intervention as consolation; and the name's religious connotations advertised more loudly than they had intended the partially religious inspiration for the new professional function they sought to establish at the expense of the clergy. Thus the psychiatrists found themselves in the uncomfortable position of simultaneously repudiating and adapting religious practice in full public view.

This hybrid, scientific-cum-religious nature of French psychiatry so marks its nineteenth-century development that my title is intended to suggest it. *Console and Classify* refers, on the one hand, to the imperfectly severed religious roots of the early psychiatric practitioner and, on the other, to his strong scientific persona and main activity as a scientist. The classification of data under clear and distinct rubrics was the sine qua non of enlightened scientific method in France at the end of the eighteenth century. With respect to psychiatry, this meant–and continued to mean throughout the nineteenth century–drawing up and periodically overhauling nosologies, or classificatory systems of mental disease, in which each disease was defined by the cluster of symptoms it regularly presented and the ensemble was presumed to exhaust all the pathological possibilities.[8] If "classify" has an appropriately Foucauldian ring, suggesting the claim to power inherent in the act of creating a set of diagnostic labels, "console" stands as a reminder of the quite un-Foucauldian investigation of the dynamics of historical change that is an equally essential part of the story that follows.

A final difference between my approach and that of my French predecessors is the different aspects of psychiatry that we have chosen to highlight. For Foucault, Castel, Gauchet, and Swain, that aspect is the

---

[7] J. Cruveilhier, *Des devoirs et de la morale du médecin. Discours prononcé dans la séance de la Faculté de médecine de Paris, 2 novembre 1836* (Paris: J.-B. Baillière, 1837), p. 23.

[8] On the place of classification in scientific method at the end of the Enlightenment, see Keith Michael Baker, *Condorcet: From Natural Philosophy to Social Mathematics* (Chicago: University of Chicago Press, 1975), pp. 118–25; on its place in eighteenth-century medicine, see Lester S. King, *The Medical World of the Eighteenth Century* (Chicago: University of Chicago Press, 1958), Ch. 7, and Michel Foucault, *The Birth of the Clinic: An Archaeology of Medical Perception*, trans. A. M. Sheridan Smith (New York: Vintage, 1975), Ch. 1.

incarcerative practice of psychiatry as epitomized in the asylum. In keeping with my intent to write an intellectual history of psychiatry in social and political context, I am more interested in psychiatry as a set of categories, a way of looking at and making sense of human behavior that can be applied outside the asylum as well as within. How this new interpretive framework gained authority in our culture, and what some of the consequences of its ascendancy were in the nineteenth century, are the problems that I have sought especially to illuminate.

These introductory remarks would be incomplete without some mention of the semantics of our subject. Not until the last decade of the nineteenth century – the very end of the period covered here – was the medical study and treatment of insanity and related aberrations regularly called *psychiatrie* in France. This word, which appears to have been taken over wholesale from a German coinage of 1808, found its way into French as early as the 1840s. But despite its availability, it was used only sporadically in French writing during most of the nineteenth century, initially by physicians conversant with the German medical literature.[9] Curiously enough, a variety of compound terms and circumlocutions were long preferred to the succinct option offered by *psychiatrie:* "the medicine that has for its object the lesions of the functions of the understanding," to cite a very early one, and more routinely later on, "the medicine of the insane" or "mental medicine." Thus the first two French psychiatric journals, founded in 1843 and 1861 respectively, were the *Annales médico-psychologiques* and the *Journal de médecine mentale.* Not until 1891 did the *Annales de psychiatrie* begin publication.

The person now called a psychiatrist – that is, the certified physician occupied with psychiatry full time and to the exclusion of other medical concerns – took even longer to acquire a concise, one-word name in French. *Psychiatre* was (for all practical purposes, if not technically) an early twentieth-century neologism derived from the newly victorious *psychiatrie.*[10] Its nineteenth-century counterparts included the "physi-

---

[9] On the German coinage of *Psychiatrie,* see "The Word 'Psychiatry,' " *American Journal of Psychiatry* 107 (1951): 628–29, 868–69. The first French usage of *psychiatrie* I have found is in a quotation translated from the German by J.-P. Falret, "De l'enseignement clinique des maladies mentales," *Ann m.-p.,* 1st ser., 10 (1847): 247. Similarly, an early adjectival usage occurs in a review of the German periodical literature; see Emile Renaudin, *Ann m.-p.,* 3d ser., 2 (1856): 279. During the 1860s, the term became somewhat more common in French medical writing and also made its way into legislative debate; see the report on civil liberties and lunatic asylums by the senator Victor Suin, July 2, 1867, *Annales du Sénat et du Corps législatif,* Vol. 8, p. 116. It is of course possible that the term was coined in German and French independently, both languages drawing upon the Greek roots meaning "medicine of the psyche."

[10] In fact, *psychiatre* (formed directly from the Greek roots meaning "physician of the psyche") was first listed in a French dictionary in 1802 as a term reserved solely for scholarly discourse; see Paul Robert, *Dictionnaire alphabétique et analogique de la langue*

cian of the insane," the "physician who lives among lunatics and observes them," the "physician-alienist" and, more colorfully if far less frequently, the "physician of the Pinelière,"[11] a backhanded tribute to Dr. Philippe Pinel, whose innovations in the care of the insane were for a time regarded by supporters and detractors alike as identical to the nascent psychiatric science. Language has its reasons, and the general adoption of a simplified and more distinctive designation for the enterprise of psychiatry and its practitioners awaited the full professional consolidation of that enterprise. In my translations and often in my discussions, I have preserved the later discarded, multiword usages of the nineteenth century as an emblem of a psychiatry still in the making.

française; and *Complément du Dictionnaire de l'Académie,* 1842. Since I have not come across the word in any text before the early twentieth century, I have assumed that it was essentially "reinvented" at about that time, when it also entered the nontechnical vocabulary.

[11] For this last, as well as the one-word appellation "Pineliste," see the satirical *Supplément au voyage en France de M. Leigh* (Montpellier: Impr. Tournel, 1826), pp. 1, 5, 35, BN: Te⁶⁶ 3.

1

"Profession" in context

O N an afternoon in 1778, the dean of the Paris Faculty of Medicine accompanied by four of his doctors-regent arrived at an obscure private house in the capital. The ground floor was occupied by a certain sieur Dufour, an assistant surgeon at the Royal Military School, and the eminences of the faculty were paying him an official and prearranged visit to "verify the effects of a secret treatment employed by [him] for curing madness (*folie*)." In one room, partitioned by boards, they found three patients confined to bed. The first, whose "delirium" was his belief that he was a monarch, was talkative and cheerful. The second, thin and of a melancholic complexion and bearing, replied aptly to all their questions, sighed a great deal, and recognized himself to be ill. The conversation of the third revolved wholly around his conviction that he was Christ; he, like the first, was cheerful and "of a gentle humor." Their interviews with the patients completed, the men of the faculty turned their attention to the sieur Dufour. In response to their interrogation, the surgeon stated that these three manifestly peaceable patients had, before his treatment of them, been "in a habitual and extreme furor." He had selected them from among the inmates at the municipal detention house of Bicêtre and had brought them to this lodging at his own expense to try to improve their condition. He now revealed the rudiments (though not the details) of his mode of treatment – bleeding followed by purgings ("they had swallowed beverages which had cleaned them out above and below"). The faculty deputies returned a week later and then eight months after that but, in the final analysis, were unable to reach a conclusion. Not having seen the patients in their original condition at Bicêtre, they could not, they stressed, judge the degree of difference that the treatment had produced and pronounce on its efficacy; they would neither "approve nor proscribe it absolutely." They recommended more extensive, public, and controlled experiments, "that the method used by the sieur Dufour be applied on a larger number of maniacs of different types under the eyes of doctors . . . , that the recovery of the patients be confirmed by a sufficient lapse of time." Though equivocal, the surgeon's "several trials with happy results" still held out promise for "greater success than has heretofore been obtained with a malady that is common today."[1]

Some eighty years later, in 1861, one Dr. Berthier arrived by railroad in the town of Auxerre, where "the first object to catch the attention of a voyager" as the train neared the station was "the architectonic harmony of an edifice . . . , the Asylum." Auxerre was only the first of dozens of stops that Berthier would make over the next several years in what he called his "scientific excursions" to the lunatic asylums of France. The "itinerary map" appended to his book graphically illustrated the profusion of these institutions. From one end of France to the other, in small villages and in Paris, Berthier guided his readers through each asylum, reporting its history and sometimes describing the personality of the supervising doctor. Though he stripped his prose of "technical terms" so as to lend it "a literary allure" – apparently he hoped to include the general public among his readers – Berthier, chief doctor of the asylum of Bourg in the department of the Ain, dedicated his book "to my colleagues." He wanted in his scientific travelogue "to do justice to those among us who have made an apostolate of their career." And while he would not shrink from "voicing moderate criticism" of those efforts which seemed to have fallen short of their goals, it was emphatically not his intention to wound the pride of any individual colleague. He declared his willingness to take all criticism upon himself, "regarding psychiatrists (*médecins-aliénistes*) as members, by sentiment and by *esprit*, of an elite family, to which one is proud to belong."[2]

Placed side by side, the figures of Dufour and Berthier bear witness to a historical shift: They bracket the period in which the study and treatment of insanity was transformed in France. Beginning as an occasional pursuit – here, the avocation of a military surgeon who experimented alone in makeshift quarters with a "secret" remedy, and who seems to have analogized his enterprise to that of the hawkers of "secret" medicinal potions and concoctions operating on the fringes of official medicine[3] – it became the full-time occupation of a national cadre of specialist physicians who manned a large and conspicuous

---

[1] *Commentaires de la Faculté de Médecine de Paris, 1777 à 1786*, ed. A. Pinard, H. Varnier, H. Hartmann, F. Widal and G. Steinheil, 2 vols. (Paris: Steinheil, 1903), Vol. 2, pp. 127–31. This source, over a thousand pages in length, is a printed version of portions of the faculty archives for the years indicated.

[2] Pierre Berthier, *Excursions scientifiques dans les asiles d'aliénés*, 1st ser. (Paris: Savy, 1862), p. 20 and dedicatory letter, n.p.

[3] "Persons with secrets" was a contemporary term quite similar in meaning to "charlatans" and "empirics"; see the wording of a 1790 government *enquête* cited in Toby Gelfand, "Medical Professionals and Charlatans: The Comité de Salubrité *Enquête* of 1790–91," *Histoire sociale/Social History* 11 (1978): 67. On hawkers of secret remedies generally, see Charles Coulston Gillispie, *Science and Polity in France at the End of the Old Regime* (Princeton: N.J.: Princeton University Press, 1981), pp. 219–26.

network of special institutions and could speak of themselves as a solidary "family" of "colleagues." The study and treatment of insanity was, in other words, professionalized.

Labeling the transformation in this way, though almost inevitable, is not without problems. Because this book is intended as a consideration of the emergence of psychiatry in France – construed on one level as the professionalization of the study and treatment of insanity – this chapter will address what seems to me the most important of those problems: the transfer of the idiom of "profession" into the context of late eighteenth- and nineteenth-century France.

The explicit concepts of a profession and of a process of professionalization are the products of twentieth-century Anglo-American sociology – although sociologists have rarely contended that the phenomena themselves are confined to the twentieth-century social world but have usually regarded them as having distant medieval origins, and as having begun to proliferate in the West in nearly recognizable form in the late eighteenth and nineteenth centuries. In providing a definition of "profession," the sociologists have not been especially consistent or rigorous.[4] Constructing the concept as a refinement of ordinary usage, trying to turn muddy nontechnical into lucid technical language, they have come up with different if partially overlapping lists of formal defining attributes. All have been struck by the prestigious position of "professions" in the hierarchy of gainful employments, and one of the functions of the attributes they have adduced is to account for this prestige. A composite list, reflecting at least some degree of sociological consensus about the nature of a profession, would include: (1) a body of esoteric knowledge, mastery of which is the indispensable qualification for practice; (2) monopoly – that is, recognition of the exclusive competence of the profession in the general domain to which its body of knowledge refers; (3) autonomy, or control by the profession over its work, including who can legitimately do that work and how the work should be done; and (4) a service ideal – a commitment or ethical imperative to place the welfare of the public or of the individual client above the self-interest of the practitioner, even though the practitioner is earning a living through exercise of the profession. This ideal fundamentally separates a commercial occupation from a profession, for in the latter "*caveat emptor* cannot be allowed to prevail."[5] The prestige of

---

[4] See, e.g., the overview of the literature in Howard M. Vollmer and Donald L. Mills, eds., *Professionalization* (Englewood Cliffs, N.J.: Prentice-Hall, 1966), p. vii.

[5] The caveat emptor prohibition is T. H. Marshall's full definition of a profession, cited in Vollmer and Mills, *Professionalization*, p. 64. Different sociologists have stressed these four attributes differently. Thus, e.g., while Marshall stressed the altruism of the service ideal, Eliot Freidson, *Profession of Medicine: A Study of the Sociology of Applied Knowledge* (New York: Dodd, Mead, 1970) has made autonomy the central defining

professions also underlies most sociological concepts of professional-ization, which impute to members of middle-class occupations con-scious motivation for a "collective effort to improve the place [of their occupation] and increase its power in relation to others," "to turn . . . themselves into professional people." Professionalization is a collec-tively organized act of social climbing wherein benefits accrue to indi-vidual careers through the shaping of the "career of an occupation" as a whole.[6]

While the everyday twentieth-century English word "profession" corresponds roughly but adequately to the social scientific concept of the same name, there is no comparable word in eighteenth- and nine-teenth-century French. *Profession* carried a much more general signifi-cation. It was, according to the *Encyclopédie* of Diderot and d'Alem-bert, any "station (*état*), service (*condition*) or trade (*métier*) that one embraces" for the purpose of acquiring "the necessities of human life" or fulfilling "social functions." "Professions" arranged them-selves in three categories: those that were "glorious" (religion, the army, government, arts and letters), those that were merely "honest" (handicraft industry, agriculture), and those that were "base or un-seemly" but nonetheless necessary to society (hangman, butcher, sewer cleaner).[7] When, in 1842, Balzac described himself, as author of *La comédie humaine*, as "the nomenclator of the professions," the meaning he attached to the term was likewise catholic: He would delineate "social species" as discrete as "zoological species," show the marked "differences between a soldier, a workman (*ouvrier*), a lawyer, an idler, a savant, . . . a merchant."[8]

Even at the end of the nineteenth century and in the vocabulary of as acute and theoretically minded an observer of society as Emile Durk-heim, the word remained entirely general, a synonym for "occupation." Durkheim's lectures on professional ethics and, later, his preface to the second edition of *Division of Labor in Society*, did distinguish between "professions" such as law and medicine, in which moral notions of "duty" and "discipline" germane to the work setting (and different from the broader "civic morality") were articulated and enforced, and "pro-fessions" such as "industry" and "commerce," which had since the inauguration of laissez-faire become entirely amoral and anarchic. But this distinction appeared to him as a transient historical one, a social ab-normality or pathology, and he counseled the restoration of "pro-

mark of a profession; and Harold J. Wilensky, "The Professionalization of Everyone?," *American Journal of Sociology* 70 (1964): 138–58, has singled out the body of knowledge *and* the service ideal.

[6] See Everett C. Hughes in Vollmer and Mills, *Professionalization*, pp. 65–66; and Hughes, *Men and Their Work* (Glencoe, Ill.: Free Press, 1968), pp. 9, 44–45.

[7] "Profession," *Encyclopédie*, Vol. 27, pp. 500–501.

[8] "Avant-Propos" *La comédie humaine* (Paris: Gallimard-Pléiade, 1976–81), Vol. 1, pp. 8, 11.

fessional ethics" in the marketplace.[9] Thus, in Durkheimian parlance, all modes of earning a living were "professions," and all were, along the only axis that interested Durkheim – that is, their moral capacity as groups – of a piece. In 1905, Paul Lapie, a member of the Durkheimian school, did attempt to discover a "law" to explain why the " 'liberal' professions" were more highly esteemed than the "economic professions" – an investigation that adumbrated those which Anglo-American sociologists would pursue more intensively beginning in the 1920s, but that still betrayed a more homogeneous concept of occupations than the sharply drawn Anglo-American sociological distinction between "occupation" and profession.[10]

It might seem, from Lapie's terminology, that much of the meaning that eventually came to be compressed into the English "profession" was carried in French by the compound term "liberal profession" (*profession libérale*).[11] The latter term derived from the thirteenth-century meaning of "liberal" as "worthy of a free man," most commonly found in the epithet which opposed *arts libéraux*, those belonging entirely or primarily to the mind and in which manual labor played little or no part, to *arts mécaniques* – the liberal arts of architecture and poetry, for example, as opposed to the corresponding mechanical arts of masonry and typography. This usage of "liberal" thus disclosed the fundamental Old Regime prejudice against manual labor as debasing and servile.[12] By extension, then, "liberal education" referred to an "education appropriate to form the mind and the heart,"[13] and a "liberal profession" was one that relied primarily upon the exercise of the intellectual faculties. These two were closely related. A liberal education meant, in nineteenth-century practice, a classical education culminating in the conferral of the *baccalauréat;* and, likewise, the *baccalauréat* was the prerequisite for entrance into the schools of law, medicine, and engineering, which "hatched" the so-called liberal professionals – who could thus, by dint of their humanistic preprofessional training, hold

[9] Durkheim, *Leçons de sociologie: Physique des moeurs et du droit* (Paris: Presses universitaires de France, 1950), pp. 13–19. The preface to the 2d edition (1902) of *De la division du travail social* is entitled "Quelques remarques sur les groupements professionnels"; for the views indicated above, see pp. i–vii of that text in the 6th ed. (Paris: F. Alcan, 1932).

[10] Paul Lapie, "La hiérarchie des professions," *Revue de Paris* 12 (1905): esp. 400, 406–10.

[11] This suggestion has been made regarding the British context by W. J. Reader, *Professional Men: The Rise of the Professional Classes in Nineteenth-Century England* (London: Weidenfeld & Nicolson, 1966), pp. 9–10. Reader does not specify when either of the two terms gained currency.

[12] *Dictionnaire de l'Académie française,* 5th ed. (1798/Year VI), entry "libéral"; E. Littré, *Dictionnaire de la langue française* (1866), entry "libéral"; "Art," *Encyclopédie,* Vol. 3, pp. 475–76, 481–82.

[13] *Dictionnaire de l'Académie française,* 6th ed. (1835), entry "libéral."

themselves up as estimable men of general culture. A popular practical handbook on choosing a career, the *Guide pour la choix d'un état* of 1842, observed that "Education draws [the crowd of young men] from the milieu of the manual professions and raises them up into the liberal professions." Every liberal profession, it continued, satisfied three criteria: It enabled its practitioner to earn a living; it "develop[ed] his intellectual faculties"; and it was "useful to society."[14] "Liberal profession," then, seems to be the progenitor and rough equivalent of the twentieth-century Anglo-American "profession."

But, significantly, "liberal profession" (like "liberal education") is a nineteenth-century neologism in French, not coming into widespread use until the 1840s.[15] "The liberal professions, as they are called," wrote Michelet in *Le peuple* (1846), tacitly acknowledging the recency and slight awkwardness of the turn of phrase.[16] It came into French via English and ultimately via Adam Smith, who coined it in his *Wealth of Nations* (1776).[17] That the term had this provenance is oddly fitting, because the adjective "liberal" within it could have an ambiguous meaning for nineteenth-century Frenchmen, sometimes referring to the older meaning, "intellectual, non-manual" (which Smith himself intended),[18] sometimes to the newer one, "pertaining to the freedom of the market." Thus a French legislator in 1847 deliberately and emphatically called medicine a "liberal profession" and even a "liberal art" in order to argue that it should not be fettered by excessive state regulation![19]

The relatively late appearance of "liberal profession" in ordinary speech coupled with the nonspecificity of "profession" suggests that,

---

[14] Edouard Charton, *Guide pour le choix d'un état* (Paris: Lenormant, 1842), pp. vi, xii.

[15] According both to Walther V. Wartburg, *Französisches Etymologisches Wörterbuch* (entry "libéral") and Paul Robert, *Dictionnaire alphabétique et analogique de la langue française* (entry "libéral"), the first dictionary to include "profession libérale" is L. N. Bescherelle, *Dictionnaire national* (Paris, 1845–47). Bescherelle merely cites the term under "profession" but gives no definition.

[16] Jules Michelet, *Le peuple*, 2d ed. (Paris: Hachette, 1846), p. 202. See the similarly self-conscious construction, "les professions auxquelles on a donné le nom de libérales," in "Médecine politique," *Union médicale*, May 9, 1848.

[17] See entry "liberal" in the *Oxford English Dictionary*. The first usage I have found in French (apart from French translations of *Wealth of Nations*) is in Sieyès's 1789 pamphlet *Qu'est-ce que le tiers état?* in its opening typology of the "four classes of labor" required for the subsistence and prosperity of a nation (Paris: Corréard, 1822, p. 60). Sieyès's precocious use of the term can be explained either by the fact that he was a relentless neologizer, never hesitating to form new words on logical principles, or by his having drawn the word directly from Smith's *Wealth of Nations*, a book which had made a profound impression on him; see Paul Bastid, *Sieyès et sa pensée*, new ed. (Paris: Hachette, 1970), pp. 312, 343.

[18] See his pairing "the ingenious arts and the liberal professions," *Wealth of Nations* (Chicago: University of Chicago Press, 1976), p. 115.

[19] Montalembert, speech before the Chamber of Peers, *Moniteur universel*, June 6, 1847, p. 1440.

from the Old Regime through at least the early nineteenth century, Frenchmen had in their cognitive mappings of the social world no concept corresponding to the twentieth-century Anglo-American "profession." They knew, to be sure, doctors and lawyers, but different categories shaped their understanding of the work of these persons and of their place in the social scheme. Thus, for example, in Loyseau's early seventeenth-century treatise of social taxonomy, doctors and lawyers are to be found (together with theologians, grammarians, and rhetoricians) under the heading "men of letters" (*gens de lettres*); and the core of their common identity is the fact that they are all degree-holders of the faculties.[20] Loyseau's late seventeenth-century counterpart, the jurist Domat, who included doctors and lawyers under the rubric *profession des sciences et arts libéraux*, likewise focused on the faculty connection; he clearly gave pride of place to the teaching and transmission of useful sciences and arts in the faculties, adding only secondarily those doctors and lawyers who, after taking degrees, had left the faculties and "presently practice [their] sciences among the public."[21] When, before 1789, doctors and lawyers disputed matters of precedence in town ceremonies, the applicable rule of thumb again pointed to the faculty connection as the essential identity of both occupational groups: Medical doctors possessing the *doctorat* were to precede those lawyers who had been awarded only the degree of *licencié*; but lawyers with the doctorate were to precede all medical doctors because the faculty of jurisprudence was superior to the faculty of medicine.[22]

To help lay the foundation for a consideration of the professionalization of the study and treatment of insanity – or, in other words, of the emergence of psychiatry – we would do well to attempt to reconstruct and articulate the concept of "profession" that existed in France at the turn of the nineteenth century, when that process began. For while the concepts of twentieth-century social science are useful for our purposes, while they alert us to the significance of certain details and help us to organize a coherent narrative account, they leave us uncomfortably unsure about the historicity of that account, the degree to which our historical personages experienced events in the terms imputed to them. A reconstruction of the contemporary concept of a profession

---

[20] Charles Loyseau, *Traité des ordres et simples dignitez* (Paris, 1665), pp. 74–75. The work was first published in 1610.

[21] Jean Domat, *Le droit public, suite des loix civiles dans leur ordre naturel*, new ed. (Avignon: De Laire, 1766), pp. 57, 61. Domat's treatise, first published between 1689 and 1697, was highly influential until the Revolution; see Roland Mousnier, *Les institutions de la France sous la monarchie absolue*, Vol. 1 (Paris: Presses universitaires de France, 1974), pp. 33–38.

[22] "Avocat," *Encyclopédie méthodique*, Series: Jurisprudence, Vol. 1 (1782), p. 625.

has another advantage as well: It reveals and explains what will later be recognized as a characteristic proclivity of the nineteenth-century French mode of psychiatric profession building, a proclivity rooted in basic features of French history, society, and polity.

I will reconstruct the contemporary concept of a profession only with respect to the profession of medicine. It was out of the matrix of medicine that psychiatry developed; and furthermore, for Anglo-American sociologists, medicine has always been the profession par excellence, the case that most nearly approximates the ideal type.[23] Looking at the period from the closing decades of the Old Regime to the beginning of the Napoleonic regime, three distinct and to some extent competing models of a medical profession can be discerned, each having a basis in concrete reality and each linked to a parti pris in the intense and continuing debate over society and politics which occupied those years. That there was fundamental disagreement and confusion about how medicine should be organized, about what would be a suitable "medical constitution" for France, illustrates with great clarity the dependence of the concept of "profession" on explicit sociopolitical conditions and its sensitivity to their fluctuation. After the Revolution, legislators seem to have sifted through the three available models and rejoined selected aspects of them to form a new amalgam. The three models were, in order of their appearance on the historical scene, the corporate, the statist, and the laissez-faire.

The corporate model

The corporate organization of medicine in France dated from the thirteenth century[24] and lasted until the Revolution. Over this long period the "art of healing" was, with respect to its organizational structure, no different from most other town-based occupations. Artisans, petty tradesmen, overseas merchants, financiers, lawyers – all belonged to their appropriate corporations. The medical corporation – it referred to itself as a *compagnie*, the most distinguished title in the galaxy of Old Regime occupational associations[25] – took the form of a Faculté de Méd-

---

[23] See, e.g., the comments to this effect in Freidson, *Profession of Medicine*, p. 4: "I assume that if anything 'is' a profession, it is contemporary medicine." See also Magali Sarfatti Larson, *The Rise of Professionalism: A Sociological Analysis* (Berkeley and Los Angeles: University of California Press, 1977), p. xi.

[24] See the introduction to *Commentaires de la Faculté de Médecine de l'Université de Paris, 1395–1516*, ed. E. Wickersheimer (Paris: Impr. nationale, 1915), pp. xi–xiii. The first reference to a faculty of medicine as one of the component elements of the University of Paris occurs in 1254.

[25] On the connotations of the term *compagnie*, see Pierre Goubert, *The Ancien Regime: French Society, 1600–1750*, trans. S. Cox (New York: Harper & Row, 1974), p. 214.

ecine in certain cities and towns and of a Collège de Médecine, a body of more circumscribed powers, in others.[26]

A faculty of medicine claimed exclusive control in a given geographical area over both the teaching and the practice of medicine. It offered the course of study which alone, and at its discretion, could lead to the conferral of a medical degree; and the latter, in turn, carried with it the only legitimate right to set up as a practicing physician. Only graduates of the faculty were permitted to teach medicine. Instruction was not confined to the official curriculum (the "teaching in the schools"); the faculty also claimed the right to inspect all public lessons on medical subjects "outside the schools." It claimed as well the right to censor medical books, construing them as a type of instruction – *par écrit* instead of *de vive voix*.[27] A degree from the faculty of X sufficed for practice in X and the surrounding region; if the doctor were to move to Y, he had to satisfy the idiosyncratic requirements of the faculty there to get his degree validated for practice in Y. In towns lacking a faculty, the college, which was not a teaching or degree-granting body, regulated medical practice in the locality by admitting into its membership applicants who held diplomas from a faculty and whom it judged up to par.

The faculties and colleges, much like their lesser cousins the trade corporations, expended a good deal of energy in the jealous defense of their monopolies, both great and small.[28] Witness the outraged college of medicine in Lyon enlisting support in its lawsuit against an individual who had usurped its right to publish the city's pharmacopoeia, "an affair which appears to us to be of the greatest importance and interest to all medical *corps*" and which could "by its repercussions influence [them] directly."[29] Or the Paris Faculty of Medicine, protesting loudly that the new College of Pharmacy (set up when the royal edict of 1776 ended the corporate union of apothecaries and grocers) had abrogated some of the faculty's customary "honorific" rights of surveillance over this inferior branch of the art of healing, resulting in nothing short of the "crime of *lèze-Faculté* in the eyes of the doctors."[30] Indeed, the faculties

---

[26] General information on the corporate organization of French medicine can be found in François Olivier-Martin, *L'organisation corporative de la France d'ancien régime* (Paris: Sirey, 1938), pp. 366–400. As is so often the case in French historiography, much more is known about the medical corporation in Paris than in the provinces; the one notable exception is the faculty of medicine in Montpellier.

[27] *Commentaires* (1777–86), Vol. 2, p. 331.

[28] On the "ubiquitous intertrade warfare" among artisans' corporations, see William H. Sewell, Jr., *Work and Revolution in France: The Language of Labor from the Old Regime to 1848* (Cambridge University Press, 1980), pp. 28–29.

[29] *Commentaires* (1777–86), Vol. 2, p. 189, letter of the dean of the college of Lyon to the dean of the Paris faculty, August 4, 1778.

[30] Ibid., p. 640. The sarcastic phrase "lèze-Faculté" was used by the apothecaries. See also pp. 124–25, 618–57.

and colleges regarded monopoly as the essence of their mission, as their raison d'être. Speaking of an assault upon its prerogatives at the end of the eighteenth century, the faculty of Paris, which occupied a special place at the pinnacle of the system, depicted its rival as coming

> to devour the patrimony of the Faculty, the patrimony of honor, of esteem. For the existence of the Faculty is glorious only when the Faculty is viewed as the tribunal of the nation for everything that concerns medicine. Remove its right in this regard and nothing remains but to destroy it.

Monopoly was the lifeblood of the medical corporation, its beneficiaries asserted, because it alone was capable of providing adequate protection for the medical art and thus of enabling the corporation to fulfill its social function as the keeper and continuator of that art. Any "conflict of jurisdiction," warned the Paris faculty, detracted from "the glory . . . of medicine," brought "derision and opprobrium" upon it. Eventually deviation from monopoly would produce full-fledged "anarchy, and anarchy will plunge the important art of healing into a disastrous quackery (*empyrisme*)."[31]

Strong ties were supposed to join together the members of the faculty or college, producing a lively esprit de corps. The ties were tantamount to ones of blood, of biological kinship – at least according to the metaphors still typically employed in the late eighteenth century. The *compagnie* was "this common mother"; members of the faculty were "her children, who respect her, cherish her and are inviolably attached to her"; disloyal members were "her own children, forgetting the oaths that bind them to their mother and the duties of the brotherhood (*confraternité*)."[32] Obligatory participation in corporate ceremonies and rites of passage – the faculty masses, the thesis defenses of degree candidates – and the wearing of official robes and caps gave the ties a concrete representation.[33] Membership in such a body was supposed to entail a willing submergence of one's individual preferences and an identification with the common union.

An emotional letter of 1781 by a doctor of the Paris faculty – written after he had been imprisoned in the Bastille by a royal lettre de cachet and the faculty had rallied around him, making concerted efforts to obtain his release – sought, in a peculiarly transitional mixture of traditional and Enlightenment vocabulary, to analyze the relationship of the individual to the medical corporation. What "our happy constitution . . . by its essence procures for each individual" was "the quiet enjoyment of honor," an honor unassailable even in a cell in the Bas-

---

[31] Ibid., pp. 107, 177, 339.
[32] Ibid., pp. 103, 121, 161.
[33] Paul Delaunay, *Le monde médical parisien au dix-huitième siècle* (Paris: Rousset, 1906), pp. 3, 15–16.

tille. Such a "great advantage" was this preservation of individual honor that it meant that

> personal interest, that first motive of all human action, is among us so
> bound up with the general interest that one can do nothing better for
> himself than that which most contributes to the common good.

Hence individual self-expression was acceptable when it coincided with the rules of the faculty and with the policy decisions reached by vote at its periodic assemblies. When it did not, this "freedom" immediately went sour:

> Among us the general opinion is really a verdict; and the freedom to
> think, speak and write which we enjoy becomes a ready punishment for
> those who are unfaithful in their duty – either by violating the statutes,
> meeting clandestinely or fomenting divisions which, more than all else,
> can bring about the dissolution of our order of things.[34]

This relative effacement of the individual, this symbiosis between the individual and the corporate "mother," probably affected the way in which the medical doctor conceived of his work. He did not have an "individual right" to practice that he had won as a result of his schooling at the faculty, the diploma he had received, and the *capacité* he had acquired there. Rather, such a right inhered irremovably in the corporate collectivity, and as an early historian of French medicine has put it, "the practitioner lived a borrowed life, borrowed from the Faculty or College of which he was a part."[35]

The medical corporation was self-governing. Although toward the end of the eighteenth century there was some timely insistence on an abstract "perfect equality" of all members through the protection afforded by the association, and some comments on the democratic nature of a rotating deanship,[36] the obvious fact was that the medical faculty had a highly stratified internal power structure. At the bottom of the ladder were those doctors with degrees from other faculties, allowed to practice but forever barred from teaching of any kind; and the *bacheliers*, candidates who had completed some degree requirements at the faculty and were allowed to teach "outside the schools" but not to practice. The middle-level personnel included the *licenciés*, who had completed additional requirements and were allowed to practice as well as teach; and those, few in number, who held the doctorate but lacked the further distinction of the regency. At the top were the doctors-regent, who alone had the right to train future practitioners by

---

[34] *Commentaires* (1777–86), Vol. 2, letter by Hallot, p. 732.
[35] Paul Delaunay, as cited by Pierre Huard, "L'enseignement médico-chirurgical" in René Taton, ed., *Enseignement et diffusion des sciences en France au XVIIIe siècle* (Paris: Hermann, 1964), pp. 179–80.
[36] *Commentaires* (1777–86), Vol. 2, letters by Hallot, pp. 732, 883.

teaching the official curriculum "in the schools," to attend and vote at all meetings of the assembled faculty, and to hold corporate office.[37] The doctors-regent functioned as the governing board; theirs was "a more intimate brotherhood" within the brotherhood. Admission into the regency, it was said, "incorporates [a person] in a more special manner" into the collective body by "conceding his worthiness to uphold its honor and the execution of its laws and to manage its affairs." Whereas "science" or "knowledge of medicine," as determined by examination, was the sole requirement for the doctorate, admission into the regency depended on more subtle and subjective judgments of character: "One must have that conduct and those sentiments which merit confidence" – that is to say, total loyalty to the *corps* and full acceptance of its jurisdiction, instead of, as one irate dean described it, "trampling [one's oaths] underfoot the moment they are pronounced."[38] In the ordinary course of events, the holder of a doctorate passed quasiautomatically into the regency, but the regents could – and on occasion did – exercise the prerogatives of oligarchy and withhold the promotion. Rejected aspirants might then turn to the royal judiciary for the redress of their grievance; but so firmly established was the principle of medical corporate autonomy that royal officials were reluctant to meddle, except gently and informally, and certainly preferred to refrain from initiating legal proceedings.[39]

Though self-government – and financial independence[40] – were their salient features, the medical corporations were perforce also connected to the state. Their monopolistic spheres of activity had originally been granted them by the Crown in letters-patent; their statutes were officially confirmed by the parlements or by lesser courts; the Edict of Marly, promulgated by Louis XIV in 1707, had ratified their existence once again. But in line with the Sun King's habitual centralizing impulse, the Marly edict also injected a new note: an attempt to introduce greater uniformity into the requirements for the medical degree throughout France and, toward that end, to upgrade the smaller provincial faculties, where an "extreme slackening" in both the quality and duration of instruction had been observed. The Paris faculty was, however, explicitly exempted from this royal intervention and its statutes pronounced fully adequate as they stood, leaving "nothing to add for the sake of good order and public utility." Execution of the statutes of

[37] See the definition of the judicial magistrate Joly de Fleury cited in Caroline C. F. Hannaway, "Medicine, Public Welfare and the State in 18th-Century France: The Société Royale de Médecine of Paris (1776–1793)," Ph.D. dissertation, Johns Hopkins University, 1974, p. 470. The power structure being described here is that of the Paris faculty and is not generalizable in detail to other French medical corporations.

[38] *Commentaires* (1777–86), Vol. 2, pp. 311, 838, 840.

[39] Hannaway, "Medicine, Public Welfare and the State," pp. 462–73, 487–519.

[40] Huard, "Enseignement médico-chirurgical," p. 174.

the other medical corporations – "insofar as they do not contradict our present edict" – was also mandated.[41] Louis XIV was, in other words, walking a fine line, upholding the corporate organization of medicine but taking tentative steps toward state centralization.

Looking at its corporate structure in the late eighteenth century, it would seem that French medicine bore all the formal marks of a "profession" by present-day sociological standards. What was missing, however, was the practical efficacy of its essentially paper monopoly. Not only did it lack the coercive power to prevent the activity of "quacks," "charlatans," and other unlicensed healers,[42] but, even more important, only a tiny elite segment of the population was convinced of the superiority of its "expert" services. It did not command a significant market; and the expansion of its market would have been necessary to give its monopoly true weight. This crucial combination of market expansion and monopolistic control is an implicit but often unstated aspect of the sociological definition of profession.[43]

The statist model

Just as the corporate model of a medical profession had its institutional embodiment – the some thirty or forty faculties and colleges of medicine scattered throughout France and looking to the Paris faculty, "the most steady guarantor of the rights and prerogatives of doctors," for informal leadership[44] – so the much newer statist model had its first, prototypical institutional embodiment in the Société royale de médecine, founded in 1778. In a narrow juristic sense, the Société developed out of the one legitimate noncorporate sector of medical practice in France: the physicians of the King's household, immune to corporate localism and entitled to practice anywhere in France without admission to the relevant faculty or college.[45] In a broader sense, it derived, like so many of the reform projects undertaken during the reign of Louis XVI, from the marriage of the goals and instruments of the absolutist state with the goals of Enlightenment thought.

---

[41]   See the text of the edict in *Commentaires* (1777–86), Vol. 1, Preamble, p. 331, and Article 37, p. 339.

[42]   On the failure of the police to stamp out unlicensed healers in eighteenth-century Paris, see Alan Williams, *The Police of Paris, 1718–1798* (Baton Rouge: Louisiana State University Press, 1979), p. 266.

[43]   See Freidson, *Profession of Medicine*, pp. 19–20; and esp. Larson, *Rise of Professionalism*, Part 1, which develops a theory of professions emphasizing the market context.

[44]   The tally is imprecise because a number of the smaller faculties suspended activity or were absorbed by larger faculties during the course of the eighteenth century; see Huard, "Enseignement médico-chirurgical," p. 172. The phrase quoted is that of the dean of the College of Medicine of Lyon, *Commentaires* (1777–86), Vol. 2, p. 189.

[45]   Hannaway, "Medicine, Public Welfare and the State," pp. 26–28, 45–47.

One of the chief instruments of French absolutism was *police:* that is, public administration in all its aspects designed to foster the well-being of the population and – by rendering the population numerous, productive, and tax-paying, satisfied in its elementary material needs and hence supposedly unseditious – to enhance at the same time the power of the state.[46] The word *police* had, under the Old Regime, none of the pejorative connotations it has since acquired; to call a nation "policed" or "well-policed" was a way of complimenting it, of saying that it was not barbaric but civilized.[47] The ubiquitous and interlacing bureaucratic networks of police included, logically enough, the police of health (*santé*) and sanitation (*salubrité*). A classic early eighteenth-century *Traité de la police* discussed under this heading measures taken to maintain the wholesomeness of air and water; inspection of foodstuffs sold at market; and strategies for coping with epidemic outbreaks of disease. The police of *santé* and *salubrité* was, in this original conception, primarily the job of administrators; the medical profession played a decidedly ancillary role. Thus an article on "Contagion and Plague" in a police dictionary began: "The functions of magistrates and officers of police are very important in this time of calamity. . . . The life of a multitude of citizens is entrusted to their care, their prudence and their activity. . . . Each man who escapes the death which threatens him regards [the magistrate] as a tutelary deity."[48] To this preexisting state commitment to "health police" the Enlightenment brought a new and dynamic perspective: How much more effective this administrative endeavor would be if it made use of the most advanced medical knowledge; and how much, then, in the state's own interest would it be to create conditions conducive to the progress of medicine![49]

This was the "enlightened absolutist" position taken by Turgot when, as chief minister, he founded in 1776 under the presidency of the first physician to the King, a special commission that evolved two years later into the Société royale de médecine. The purpose of the commission and the initial purpose of the Société was to conduct a giant ongoing re-

---

[46] The word *police* was of early modern French coinage, but the principle applied to continental absolutism generally. See Marc Raeff, "The Well-Ordered Police State and the Development of Modernity in Seventeenth- and Eighteenth-Century Europe," *American Historical Review* 80 (1975): 1221–43.

[47] See Lucien Febvre, *"Civilisation:* evolution of a word and of a group of ideas," in *A New Kind of History,* ed. Peter Burke, trans. K. Folca (New York: Harper & Row, 1973), esp. pp. 226–28.

[48] Nicolas Delamare, *Traité de la police,* 3d ed. (Amsterdam, 1729), Vol. 2, passim; N.-T.-L. Des Essarts, *Dictionnaire universel de police* (Paris: Moutard, 1786–90), Vol. 3, pp. 214–15.

[49] Steven L. Kaplan makes a similar point about the lack of reliance on scientific expertise until the late 1760s in the branch of *police* concerned with provisioning and bread supply. See *Bread, Politics and Political Economy in the Reign of Louis XV* (The Hague: Nijhoff, 1976), Vol. 1, p. 336.

search project. Through correspondence with doctors throughout France, it was to gather in a central depot as many on-the-spot observations of epidemic disease as possible. The accumulation of empirical data would, it was believed, eventually lead to breakthroughs in understanding that dread phenomenon and in formulating superior tactics of health police with regard to it. As a state agency, the Société used the channels of the royal bureaucracy to carry out this project. The provincial intendants were called upon to identify local physicians suitable to serve as correspondents and to designate those who would assume regular responsibility for treating epidemics in their regions.[50]

The epidemics project stood alongside the wider function assumed by the Société: It was an academy of medicine. Like the academies of seventeenth-century establishment, including the Academy of Sciences, it was a body under royal protection – and with its upper-grade membership pensioned by the state – devoted to the advancement of a branch of knowledge through such institutional mechanisms as providing regular occasions for the presentation and publication of memoirs, sponsoring prize essay contests, and holding out the powerful lure of admission into the academy as a goad to scholarly accomplishment. As protégés of the state, academies were also required to serve the state in a consultative capacity. "The Society will be concerned with all matters of theoretical and practical medicine," said the letters-patent of the King, indicating that although the label "academy" had not been used, the Société was being invested with an academy's guardianship over French medicine as a whole.[51]

The Paris faculty responded to the Société as a rival of major proportions; in its distress, it went so far as to petition the Parlement to refuse registration of the letters-patent giving the Société a legal existence. The faculty perceived the Société as encroaching upon two of its traditional monopolies: to be regarded as premier repository of medical knowledge in France and to serve as consultant to the government on health matters. (The trip to the house of the surgeon Dufour to evaluate his treatment of madness was one such instance of the faculty's collaboration in health police; it was embarked upon at the request of Lenoir, the lieutenant-general of police in Paris.)[52] The government and the proponents of the Société denied that they were usurping anything of substance from the faculty and maintained that the real – and untouched – prerogatives of the latter were as a teaching body.[53] The

---

[50] See Caroline C. Hannaway, "The Société Royale de Médecine and Epidemics in the Ancien Régime," *Bull. Hist. Med.* 46 (1972): esp. 261, 265.

[51] The quote is from "Lettres patentes du Roi, portant établissement d'une Société royale de médecine," in *Histoire de la Société royale de médecine, 1776* (Paris, 1779), pp. 17–24, Article 9. On academies as institutions, see Gillispie, *Science and Polity,* pp. 75–92.

[52] *Commentaires* (1777–86), Vol. 2, p. 127. On the scope of Lenoir's activities in the area of health, see Williams, *Police of Paris,* pp. 261–77.

[53] See "Lettres patentes du Roi," Preamble, p. 17, and Article 14, pp. 23–24.

faculty for its part maintained that it had always engaged in information-gathering and consultation, that its own institutional structure, though different from that of an academy, was admirably suited for these purposes. It decried the contemporary shallow fashion for academies, the "academic mania."[54]

Even more was at stake here than the loss by the Paris faculty of some of its customary corporate prerogatives. The Société was challenging the faculty on a more fundamental level, for it was presenting, albeit in rough form, a new model of the profession of medicine – something that its intellectually aggressive leadership certainly understood, although they did not express themselves in these terms, and that the defensive and panicky members of the Paris faculty, caught up in a traditional-style struggle, may not have fully grasped. (The latter did, however, in response to the Société, reiterate the corporate ethos of the organic link between the individual doctor and the corporation, indicating that they may have perceived the threat to this very ethos. A doctor-turned-academician was, through this "distinction," "isolated from his Company" and, like "a pineapple . . . transplanted to our country," removed from his "natural climate.")[55] The new model consisted of two basic elements – the state, and a concept of medicine as a progressive body of empirical scientific knowledge. The physician was to derive his identity, self-esteem, and public status not from his membership in a corporation but from his connection to the state and his commitment to an abstract ideal of the integrity and advancement of medical science.[56] The linkage of these two elements is not logically necessary, but historical circumstances in France made it expedient.

The epistemological status of medicine became an issue during the last quarter of the eighteenth century. At a time when such sciences as chemistry, physics, and astronomy were taking great strides forward, medicine seemed to be in a rut, not sharing in this general tendency. But was medicine a science anyway? The Paris faculty of the eighteenth century considered it an "art" surrounded by a loose cluster of affiliated accessory "sciences" – anatomy, chemistry, physics, botany.[57] Such a conceptualization was behind the longstanding *absence* of an academy of medicine: Medicine so-defined could be quite adequately served by the Academy of Sciences, which fostered the development of these individual accessory sciences.[58] Nor did the faculty assume any responsibility for grounding a prospective doctor in the accessory sciences. They

---

54 *Commentaires* (1777–86), Vol. 2, pp. 335–38, 882.

55 Ibid., letter by Hallot, p. 883.

56 Hannaway makes a similar point about the ideal of science replacing the corporate ideal in the context of the Société; see "Medicine, Public Welfare and the State," pp. 526–27.

57 See, e.g., the self-depiction of the faculty in *Commentaires* (1777–86), Vol. 2, p. 335.

58 Félix Vicq d'Azyr, "Notice historique sur les principales académies," in *Oeuvres*, 6 vols. (Paris: Duprat-Duverger, Year XIII/1805), Vol. 2, pp. 147–48.

were not a part of its official curriculum[59] and could be taught on its premises only on the sufferance of the dean. Thus Félix Vicq d'Azyr, who later masterminded the formation of the Société and became its permanent secretary, taught a notably well-attended course in comparative anatomy in the faculty amphitheatre (but technically "outside the schools") during the summer recess of 1773, only to be informed in the fall that he would have to suspend his lectures because of a time conflict with one of the official courses.[60]

To doctors like Vicq d'Azyr, who considered themselves *éclairé*, the faculty's concept of medicine was seriously flawed. Not only was there insufficient commitment to the accessory sciences – Vicq d'Azyr would write caustically of the common "abuse," even in large cities, for doctors to "despise chemistry, . . . know nothing of anatomy and maintain that physics is useless"[61] – but there was no concept of an autonomous science of medicine separate from its various accessory sciences. Vicq d'Azyr and the other doctors who joined in the leadership of the new Société insisted that medicine "exists apart, like an island in the midst of the ocean of human learning."[62] It was not just the centerless sum total of "the application of physics, natural history, anatomy, chemistry and botany to the knowledge of the human body, healthy or diseased." Rather, it had its own independent and fully scientific basis – "observation of the effects of diseases and remedies." And although it was difficult for it to make progress without its accessory sciences, "I say difficult and not impossible":

> It can acquire some measure of perfection by experience alone, without the intermediary of any other study. One must thus distinguish within medicine the accessory sciences and the observation which those sciences illuminate and render more fruitful.[63]

Such a reform in the concept of medicine put a new emphasis on the progress of medicine and on cooperative effort to bring about that result. "All sciences that are perfected through observation," commented Vicq d'Azyr, "need to be cultivated in common."[64]

---

[59] One exception seems to have been chemistry at Paris after 1770; see Delaunay, *Monde médical*, p. 15.
[60] Jacques L. Moreau de la Sarthe, "Discours sur la vie et les ouvrages de Vicq d'Azyr," in Vicq d'Azyr, *Oeuvres*, Vol. 1, p. 12.
[61] "Abus," *Encyclopédie méthodique*, Series: Medicine, Vol. 1 (1782), p. 41.
[62] Vicq d'Azyr, "Idée générale de la médecine et de ses différentes parties," *Oeuvres*, Vol. 1, p. 45.
[63] Vicq d'Azyr, "Principales académies," *Oeuvres*, Vol. 2, p. 147. See also Sergio Moravia, "Philosophie et médecine en France à la fin du XVIIIe siècle," *Studies on Voltaire and the Eighteenth Century* 89 (1972): esp. 1092–98.
[64] Vicq d'Azyr, "Réflexions sur le perfectionnement de la médecine," *Oeuvres*, Vol. 5, p. 80.

Now the traditional-minded faculty hardly seemed a promising locus for this theoretical reform of medicine. Not only had it given half-hearted and merely sporadic support to the teaching of the accessory sciences, but it had, in 1683 and again in 1730, shown itself hostile to the projected foundation of an academy of medicine.[65] This hostility was rooted in corporate jealousy, and its rationalization had locked the faculty into a conception of medicine as a diffuse ensemble of sciences and art rather than an autonomous science with its own unique trajectory. Thus the young *médecins éclairés* (the contemporary perception was that they formed a generational cohort, younger than those doctors who opted for the faculty over the Société)[66] had to look outside the corporate sector for support; and that meant looking to the state. The principled intransigence of the faculty meant, in other words, that an "enlightened" ideology of a progressive medical science would have to be linked to the state. "Slow in its advance, difficult in its researches, complicated in its relationships [with other sciences]," medicine, said Vicq d'Azyr, "languishes without the protection of the government."[67]

The provincial doctors of France were enthusiastically receptive to the idea of participating in a collaborative research endeavor of medicine-as-science and in doing so under state auspices. Over a thousand of them enlisted as correspondents of the Société and cheerfully cooperated in the tasks laid out for them, including even ordering expensive instruments from Paris to enable them to take precise daily meteorological measurements in their regions (data that were supposed to correlate with the epidemiological trends also being monitored by the correspondents).[68] That a great many French doctors preferred an identification with the state to one with the old corporate structure seems evident from an unintentional "poll" that was taken by the Paris faculty: Attempting to undermine the Société, the faculty inaugurated a correspondence of its own, but it attracted few participants.[69] Probably, a representative of the Société volunteered, the manner of the faculty was offputting: "It is impossible for it to treat with provincial doctors on equal terms; it can speak to them only as to schoolchildren."[70]

The mobilization of this body of correspondents was just one aspect of Vicq d'Azyr's conception of a statist medicine. He envisioned the correspondents not merely as data collectors but also as an ad hoc government agency, responsible for the practical education of doctors

---

[65] See Gillispie, *Science and Polity*, pp. 203–204; Delaunay, *Monde médical*, p. 117; and Vicq d'Azyr, "Principales académies," *Oeuvres*, Vol. 2, pp. 147–48.

[66] See *Commentaires* (1777–86), Vol. 2, pp. 144, 149, 164.

[67] Vicq d'Azyr, "Lieutaud," *Oeuvres*, Vol. 3, p. 26.

[68] Gillispie, *Science and Polity*, pp. 226–27.

[69] Hannaway, "Medicine, Public Welfare and the State," p. 417. The effort was made in 1777.

[70] *Commentaires* (1777–86), Vol. 2, p. 121.

(whose bookish studies at the faculties were presumed to have left them ill-equipped for the realities of their job) and for countering folk healing, those "popular errors [which] give rise daily to evils of all sorts."[71] Other suggestions contained in Vicq d'Azyr's printed writings remained more clearly in the planning stage. In light of the dire economic consequences of epizootics, or contagious diseases afflicting farm animals, he imagined that "all doctors might be so good as to familiarize themselves with the veterinary art and not to regard as beneath them a science that can put them in a position to render the most important services to the state." As early as the 1770s, he toyed with the idea of placing physicians in the ranks of the state bureaucracy as an alternative to their corporate organization and particularistic corporate loyalties, going so far as to give the name "health officers" (*officiers de santé*) to these hypothetical medical functionaries.[72] But his full statist vision is elaborated in a long text, the *Nouveau plan de constitution pour la médecine en France*, which had germinated in Vicq d'Azyr's mind during the closing years of the Old Regime and which, reworked in some of its details and rhetoric, was presented by the Société to the National Assembly in 1790.[73]

The *Nouveau plan* proceeds on that double front that typifies the statist model – the concept of medicine as a progressive science, and the centrality of health police. With respect to the former, it recommends the overhaul of the medical curriculum, fully integrating the accessory sciences, and in accordance with Vicq d'Azyr's contention that "observation" is the core of medical scientific autonomy, adding clinical instruction. It also recommends the establishment of an academy of medicine, which is seen as the most effective way to hasten medical advance. The academy is to work "by fixing the attention of doctors on all that can be contributed to the perfecting of their art"; by giving them the incentive to do so in the form of numerous "palms that they can win"; and by creating a correspondence – "liaisons that render common to all the fruits of the observations of each" – converging on "a center" (in Paris) where such observations can be collected and pondered, and where a research design for all of medicine can be drawn up to be tackled seriatim by the "cooperators."[74]

---

[71] Vicq d'Azyr, "Perfectionnement de la médecine," *Oeuvres*, Vol. 5, pp. 85–86, 113.

[72] "Lieutaud," *Oeuvres*, Vol. 3, p. 26. Vicq d'Azyr is restating and commending the view of Joseph Lieutaud as first physician to the King and later president of the Société.

[73] See D. B. Weiner, "Le droit de l'homme à la santé – une belle idée devant l'Assemblée constituante, 1790–91," *Clio Medica* 5 (1970): esp. 213–16. The proposal, which in slightly altered form was also presented to the Constituent Assembly, was never enacted into law.

[74] Vicq d'Azyr, *Nouveau plan de constitution pour la médecine en France*, in Ministère de l'Instruction Publique et des Beaux-Arts, *Enquêtes et documents relatifs à l'enseignement supérieur*, Vol. 28: *Médecine et pharmacie*, ed. A. de Beauchamp (Paris: Impr. nationale, 1888), pp. 8–9, 17–22, 118–20, 124.

With respect to the latter front, the network of observation-gathering correspondents was to be superimposed on a bureaucratic network of practicing doctors. The French countryside, the *Nouveau plan* asserted, was ill served by doctors, especially because the urban-based corporations usually granted the right to practice outside the city walls to men who had completed a shortened course of study: "One would think, to look at these bizarre regulations, that all places are not equally inhabited by men." Thus, especially in light of the importance of "watching over the treatment of epidemics," doctors were to be distributed throughout the countryside, allocated "in a precise manner" by canton, or national administrative unit, and salaried by the state. The cities too would have a number of salaried physicians (*médecins stipendiés*) responsible for the care of the poor. In the event of an epidemic, the full bureaucratic panoply could be activated: The cantonal doctor could turn for advice to the district doctor, and if both were in doubt they could consult the Health Council in the capital of the department; if necessary, the academy in Paris could also be approached. Vicq d'Azyr envisioned an "uninterrupted connectedness" among all parts of the system, insuring that prompt and well-informed aid would be brought wherever the health of the people was endangered.[75]

The would-be penetration of medical expertise into the countryside – that heartland of folk healing and charlatanism – shows the Société's interest in expanding the "market" for the services of bona fide physicians, using the state as a lever. The corporations, with their much more tenuous ties to the state, had no comparable project of total "medicalization," no such aggressively "professionalizing" impulse.

What was implicit in the emergence of the Société in the 1770s and in its early encroachments on the terrain of the faculty became explicit in the *Nouveau plan:* A statist conception of the medical profession was fundamentally incompatible with and stood to supersede a corporate conception. The *Nouveau plan* called for uniformity in medical education, not the curricular variation among faculties (and the marked inferiority of all faculties to those at Paris and Montpellier) that characterized the corporate regime. Uniform training led logically to the insistence that corporate particularism in the sphere of medical practice be ended: "Every doctor . . . ought to be able to exercise his profession over the entire compass of the realm." Corporate monopolies in the two critical areas of teaching and practice were thus declared obsolete. Added to this, as the *coup de grace*, was a damning evaluation of the corporate mentality. It encouraged a stubborn and arrogant attachment to custom which was harmful to science:

> We do not deny that . . . despite the vices of certain schools and the nullity of others, great doctors have been formed [in the faculties of

[75] Ibid., pp. 7–9, 13, 59–62.

medicine]. But it is also beyond doubt that, in a better order of things, an infinitely larger number of them would have been formed, and the medical art, so retarded in its movement, would have made rapid progress. Those people are blind, those people are to be pitied, who regard their corporation as the most perfect thing on earth and who think its ancient usages definitive.

Perhaps even worse was the interpersonal viciousness, the pseudofellowship of corporate life: "Under the pretext of mutual surveillance, [corporations] establish over some of their members an inquisition, and in a free state this must be repressed."[76] The charge, tailored though it was to the Revolutionary political context, had an autobiographical resonance, recalling Vicq d'Azyr's own experience of losing his permission to teach comparative anatomy in the faculty amphitheatre almost twenty years before.[77] Such experiences must not have been unusual, because indirect allusions to them became a staple of medical anticorporate rhetoric.

The laissez-faire model

What I have called the laissez-faire model of the medical profession corresponds to the situation of medicine in France from 1791 to 1803, when the healing art was, by law, an unregulated trade, open to all comers whatever their credentials.

The Société's "statist" attack on corporate medicine certainly never intended or anticipated such an outcome, for it contained no attack upon the principle of regulation per se. According to the *Nouveau plan*, aspiring doctors would still have to pass qualifying examinations, now to be administered by state-run colleges of medicine instead of the self-governing faculties.[78] If anything, the Société wanted a stricter surveillance of entry into the profession than the corporations had provided – or rather, a surveillance based on strictly intellectual criteria whose rigor would not be compromised by the pecuniary needs of the faculties: "Easy and almost nonexistent examinations have so multiplied the number of ignorant doctors . . . that the health of the citizenry is threatened from all sides."[79] The Société, then, stood for a monopoly of the scientifically qualified, and thus it prided itself on the

---

[76] Ibid., pp. 12–13.
[77] Moreau de la Sarthe, "Discours sur Vicq d'Azyr," in Vicq d'Azyr, *Oeuvres*, Vol. 1, p. 12, retrospectively interpreted the episode as an example of faculty "persecution." So did Cabanis, who spoke of the "jealous influence" responsible for closing the course; see "Eloge de Vicq d'Azyr," *O.P.* Vol. 2, p. 372.
[78] Vicq d'Azyr, *Nouveau plan*, pp. 88, 146–47.
[79] Ibid., p. 7. The scandalous leniency of the medical faculties is also alleged in Vicq d'Azyr, "Abus," p. 41, and Julien Offray de La Mettrie, *Ouvrage de Pénélope, ou Machiavel en médecine* (Berlin, 1748), Vol. 2, p. 259.

severity of its campaign against charlatanism, which outstripped that of the Paris faculty: "The Society of Medicine has always been strongly opposed to the progress of charlatanism, that implacable enemy; in the past fourteen years it has approved only four [secret] remedies . . . and has rejected more than eight hundred."[80]

How, then, did total medical deregulation come about? As is well-known, a broad anticorporate sentiment, with roots and justifications in both political and economic theory, was one of the driving forces of the Revolution. Politically, corporations were privileged bodies, their members invidiously protected by special laws, whereas the Revolution stood for a universal law and the equality of all citizens before it. Politically, too – and this was Rousseau's main contribution to the ideology – corporations fostered a collective egoism that detracted from the citizen's identification with the nation and weakened and corrupted his "higher" patriotic nature. It was this Rousseauean attitude that the *Nouveau plan* espoused when it noted, "Since esprit de corps isolates citizens and is, by its nature, contrary to civic-mindedness, the harms to which corporations expose doctors should doubtless be avoided."[81] Economically, corporations were inefficient nuisances. By preventing competition, they raised the prices and lowered the quality of goods; their restrictions on membership deprived able-bodied men of work and encouraged idleness; the fees exacted at various stages of their initiation process and on ceremonial occasions were a wasteful use of funds that could otherwise be channeled into commerce and industry. These economic arguments were so familiar in enlightened circles by the last quarter of the eighteenth century that when the reforming Minister Turgot was about to decree the liquidation of the trade corporations in 1776, he commented to the King, "I daresay that [my] way of thinking is shared by everyone who has reflected a little on the nature of commerce."[82] Turgot's project proved abortive, but eventually the makers of the Revolution, acknowledging Turgot as their predecessor and explaining that in 1776 "the time was not yet ripe," picked up where he had left off.[83] The d'Allarde law of March 2–17, 1791 abolished the corporations and established a new tax, the patent, on all urban profit-making enterprises. Henceforth, the annual purchase of a patent replaced membership in a corporation as the way to legitimize one's practice of an occupation in a town.[84]

---

[80] Vicq d'Azyr, *Nouveau plan*, p. 123. Gillispie, *Science and Polity*, pp. 221–26, discusses the Société's more severe and "professional" (his word) attitude toward charlatans. Manuscripts by Lenoir, the lieutenant-general of Paris police, indicate his perception that the Société was more effective than his own police in controlling charlatanism; see Williams, *Police of Paris*, p. 267.

[81] Vicq d'Azyr, *Nouveau plan*, p. 13.

[82] *Oeuvres de Turgot*, ed. G. Schelle (Paris: F. Alcan, 1923), Vol. 5, pp. 158–59, 238–48.

[83] D'Allarde in *Arch. parl.*, 1st ser., Vol. 23, p. 200.

[84] See ibid., pp. 625–30, for the final text of the law.

The medical corporations – that is, the faculties in their capacity as the grantors of the right to practice, and the colleges – were swept away by this law, together with the corporations of greengrocers, of cobblers, in short, of the entire array of tradesmen and artisans. Whereas the 1776 Turgot edict had been intended for trade and artisanal corporations only, the d'Allarde law cast its net wider, suppressing not only "the rights of admission of all masterships (*maîtrises*) and *jurandes*" – terms reserved for crafts and trades – but also "all professional privileges, under any denomination whatsoever" (Article 2). It boldly declared, "Everyone will be free to carry on such a business, or to practice such a profession, art or trade as he finds advantageous," as long as he "furnishes himself beforehand with a patent" (Article 7).

The law, aiming in good Rousseauean fashion to be as general as possible and to omit enumeration of specific cases,[85] was absolutely silent about medicine. An article on that subject in the original draft bill was quickly struck out during the debates, on the grounds that its content had been adequately subsumed by the revised version of another article. Reconstructing the "editorial" process that took place on the floor of the Assembly, it is clear that the legislators did not intend the d'Allarde law to be the last word on the organization of medicine; once liberated from the corporations, practitioners of the healing art would be required to comply with "rules of police that would be forthcoming at some future time."[86] This proviso was consistent with d'Allarde's general philosophy. While he considered the "police" function of the old corporations, with respect to quality of work as well as entry into the trade, to be for the most part dispensable – "by competition [workers] exercise over one another a kind of inspection that is much more efficacious" – he did acknowledge that there were some "professions" for which market mechanisms would not suffice. His preamble to the draft bill mentioned two of these – pharmacy and the gold- and silversmith's trade – for which "special rules" of surveillance of an indeterminate nature would have to be drawn up;[87] and presumably he placed medicine under this heading as well.

Despite its incompleteness with respect to medicine, the d'Allarde law was indicative of a new conceptualization of that profession: It had been assimilated to the general model and categories of political economy. The destruction of the medical corporations had been enacted as part and parcel of a law devoted primarily to trade and commerce; and that this was not a mere accident or practical exigency, but rather an ideological decision, was demonstrated by the debates. One deputy, raising a fine (and marginal) point that he hoped to turn into an

---

[85] Sentiments of this sort are expressed by the deputy d'André, ibid., p. 226.
[86] Article 7 of the final law, ibid., p. 626. For the article on medicine in the original draft bill (Article 15), see p. 202; for the decision to delete it, pp. 226–27.
[87] Ibid., p. 200.

amendment to the law, happened to characterize doctors and lawyers as practitioners of professions based upon "the arts that are called, after the ancient [definition of] liberty, liberal arts." The spokesman for the committee that had prepared the bill dismissed the point summarily, but he took the time to object most emphatically to the language in which it was couched. The suggested amendment, he said, "would require us to establish a distinction we have not believed ourselves obliged to make: we do not want to separate the arts which are liberal from those which are not."[88] In other words, the ideological intention had been to deny the traditional dichotomy between "liberal arts" and "mechanical arts" that made the one honorable and the other base – to legislate for doctors and cobblers in a single general law as a way of saying that both were simply and essentially men who worked for a living, who were part of the national work force. This "demotion" of doctors by the standards of Old Regime social hierarchy – and by the standards of the current sociological distinction between a profession and a "mere" occupation – was, in the Revolutionary canon, really a positive revaluation of the meaning of work[89] and the placement of useful work at the center of a new conception of society: the economic and laissez-faire conception, which had been most fully articulated in Adam Smith's *Wealth of Nations*.[90]

The legal destruction of corporate medicine begun with the d'Allarde law was completed by the law of August 8, 1792 abolishing the universities. Here it was the teaching monopoly of the medical faculties that was broken, as opposed to their right to certify individuals for medical practice. War and the necessity to train surgeons for military hospitals prompted a reopening of the medical faculties of Paris, Montpellier, and Strasbourg – under state auspices and under the new name of *écoles de santé* – by emergency decree in 1794.[91] But the gap left by the d'Allarde law – that is, any legal criterion beyond the purchase of a patent for setting up as a physician – remained unfilled.

---

[88] Ibid., p. 625.

[89] For an excellent analysis of this process of revaluation in the writings of Diderot and Sieyès, see Sewell, *Work and Revolution*, pp. 64–72, 78–83. See also the pointed comments of a Nantais medical man arguing in 1790 for the abolition of the distinction between physicians (as doing intellectual work) and surgeons (as doing manual work): "He who cures with one means is no less valuable than he who cures with another. The only criterion for preference is efficacy, and it must be avowed that all who are useful are of the same rank." D.-M.-J. Cantin, *Projet de réforme adressé à l'assemblée nationale, où l'on se propose d'établir l'unité et l'art de guérir* ([Paris]: Impr. de Vézard et le Normant, 1790), pp. 12–13.

[90] Two French translations of *Wealth of Nations* appeared before the Revolution (1778–79, 1781); a third appeared in 1790–91.

[91] Fourcroy, "Rapport et projet de décret portant sur l'établissement d'une école centrale de santé . . . " in Beauchamp, *Enquêtes et documents*, Vol. 28, pp. 198–99; and "Décret portant établissement de trois écoles de santé," 14 frimaire Year III, in ibid., p. 213.

No policy-maker seemed to entertain seriously the possibility of a totally "free" medical profession, although a utopian plan for a totally free teaching profession was presented by a noted deputy – in fact, by a physician – to the Convention: "In tasks that should be entrusted only to talent (*génie*), efforts, in order to be sustained and to be crowned with success, should perhaps have as a perpetual stimulus the rival efforts of competitors. . . . Let all intelligent men who feel suited to lecturing be called in all quarters of the Republic and invited to open schools; let the number of students who are faithful to them after a given amount of time be the real measure of their success and their merit. . . . *Laisser faire* is the great secret here."[92] In such an ideological climate, a comparable plan for a free market in healing services was not therefore unthinkable – especially given the primitive state of integration of medical theory and practice in the late eighteenth century, which made "official" accredited medicine and "charlatanism" often indistinguishable at the level of therapeutic procedure.[93] But even in the absence of explicit legislation, individuals were not *supposed* to assume that the purchase of a patent gave a legitimate right of medical practice to those without formal training. Doing so was, according to the Executive Body of the Directory, "abusing the sacred name of liberty and taking advantage of that sort of cloud that enveloped the first moments of our regeneration."[94] Similarly, representatives of the old official medicine were horrified that the populace was construing the d'Allarde law literally with respect to medicine: "Whoever wishes, calls himself a doctor or a surgeon. . . . Circe's wand transformed men into pigs; does the patent have the virtue of working the opposite miracle, of suddenly summoning into existence learned and experienced men?" The influx of unqualified, self-designated practitioners – "this strange brigandage" – had already caused many "respectable" doctors to "abandon a profession whose present state of degradation and debasement can only disgust [them]."[95]

---

[92] Fourcroy, "Rapport et projet de décret sur l'enseignement libre des sciences et des arts," 27 frimaire Year II, in J. Guillaume, ed., *Procès-verbaux du Comité de l'Instruction publique de la Convention nationale* (Paris: Impr. nationale, 1898), Vol. 3, pp. 97–98, 101. This text is cited in Michel Foucault, *The Birth of the Clinic: An Archaeology of Medical Perception*, trans. A. M. Sheridan Smith (New York: Vintage, 1975), which contains (Chs. 3 and 5) an excellent discussion of the period of medical deregulation.

[93] Much recent historical scholarship has pointed to the similarity between accredited and "charlatanistic" medicine at this date. See, e.g., Gelfand, "Medical Professionals and Charlatans," esp. pp. 62–63; and Jean-Pierre Goubert, "L'art de guérir: médecine savante et médecine populaire dans la France de 1790," *Annales E.S.C.* 32 (1977): 908–26.

[94] "Message du Directoire exécutif," 27 nivôse Year VI, in Beauchamp, *Enquêtes et documents*, Vol. 28, p. 332.

[95] "Pétition au Corps législatif," 28 prairial Year V, AN: AD VIII 42. The petition was signed by twenty-eight Paris medical men.

There was, to be sure, some articulate grass roots support for total medical deregulation. The sans-culottes, with their antipathy for aristocracies of intellect as well as those of birth, advocated getting rid of accredited physicians altogether and putting in their place, as one of their petitions read, "a popular medicine, infinitely preferable to and more certain than all the frequently erroneous practices of our physicians," practices whose "qualities of guesswork and blind routinization have caused these alleged healers to be so widely and justly reproached."[96] But this medical populism, which turned the usual meaning of charlatanism upside down, had no resonance in policy-making circles.

Even if total deregulation were rejected, could revolutionary "liberty" have some other, more circumscribed meaning for a medical profession released from the stranglehold of the corporations? Various reports presented to the legislature of the Directory – which had been called upon by the Constitution of 1795 and by imploring messages from the executive branch to supply the medical profession with a mode of police – suggested that it could. "You will not reestablish *jurandes*, but you will require proofs of ability: a person can become a doctor without having attended any school, but you will demand a solemn guarantee of the knowledge possessed by each candidate." In other words, according to this plan, the abolition of the medical corporations would mean the definitive abolition of that minute regulation of preparatory training that was traditionally one of the functions of all trade corporations. By allowing the individual to be an autodidact or to pick up his medical expertise in any other way he saw fit, insisting only that he be able to pass an examination, "you will reconcile the rights of personal liberty with those of the public safety."[97] Another plan, violently hostile to the practice of medicine by "quacks . . . without diplomas" ("They seem to be consorting with our cruelest enemies to destroy the republicans"), nonetheless salvaged enough of the laissez-faire model to resist a proposal for a state-salaried medical corps, touting instead the beneficial effects of competition among doctors: "You will see them piqued by ambition to study fruitfully and to seek to gain over their rivals by merit." If there were "no competition," "laziness would take the place of love of study . . . and the most blind routine the place of the spirit of observation."[98] Other plans sought to

---

96   AN: F^{17}A 1146, d. 4, "Pétition à la convention nationale," by Cardon, citoyen de la section Poissonnière (Impr. Franklin, n.d.), p. 2.

97   Daunou, "Rapport sur l'organisation des écoles spéciales," 25 floréal Year V, in Beauchamp, *Enquêtes et documents*, Vol. 28, p. 257. The same basic proposal is made by J.-F. Baraillon, "Motion d'ordre sur les établissements relatifs à l'art de guérir . . . ," 14 nivôse Year V, in ibid., p. 234.

98   Vitet, "Rapport . . . fait sur les écoles spéciales de médecine," 17 ventôse Year VI, in ibid., pp. 341–42, 346.

retain something of the revolutionary "openness" of the medical profession by making medical education free of charge.[99]

So fully accepted was the new mental habit of inserting medicine into the schema of political economy that even the arguments for the "police" of the profession were cast in such terms. The proposal of the Idéologue P.-J.-G. Cabanis to the Council of Five Hundred in the Year VI (1798) discoursed at length on the "precious" advantages of a "liberty of industry" that was "total, unlimited" and on the logically necessary convergence of private and public interest where "industry" was concerned. But, said Cabanis, one could depart from this principle in certain cases without having in any sense "violated" it, for there were two types of industrial "products." On the one hand were those which the public "can easily evaluate" and concerning which any errors it makes "are of little importance or easily repaired." On the other hand were those products "which the public does not know how to judge competently" and concerning which its errors in judgment, compounded by frauds deliberately perpetrated by certain "producers," were likely to have "baneful" consequences. Here "the legislator, charged with watching over the common safety, establishes rules according to which the talents of the industrious man are certified, his probity recognized, the real value and good quality of the commodities he sells verified by enlightened and unerring inspectors." Healing services fell into this second category, and hence the regulation or "police of medicine," which had thus been shown to be necessary, could not be considered as "obstructing industry [or] constituting an attack on individual liberty."[100]

The legislature of the Directory was paralyzed by disagreement; none of the plans for the reorganization of the medical profession could command a majority. Similar paralysis marked its efforts to reorganize the legal profession, whose corporate structure had been destroyed in 1790 and which had since, like medicine, traversed a period of "anarchy."[101] The failure to legislate in both instances reflects an uncertainty about the nature of a medical or legal "profession," a lack of consensus about the definition of this kind of work in a society which had just radically unsettled itself – which had repudiated corporations and state-sponsored academies (the Société royale de médecine,

---

[99] Daunou, "Rapport," p. 257; Vitet, "Rapport," p. 342.

[100] Cabanis, "Rapport fait au nom de la Commission d'Instruction publique et projet de résolution sur un mode provisoire de police médicale," 4 messidor Year VI, *O.P.,* Vol. 2, esp. p. 391.

[101] See Michael P. Fitzsimmons, "Dissolution and Disillusionment: The Parisian Order of Barristers, 1789–1815," Ph.D. dissertation, University of North Carolina at Chapel Hill, 1981, Chs. 4–6. "Anarchy," traditionally used by the corporations to describe the only alternative to their monopolistic control, was the term applied to legal and medical deregulation by its opponents in the 1790s.

together with all other academies, was abolished in 1793) and had embraced laissez-faire "liberty" with a zeal that, it now believed, needed tempering.

Redefinition

Not until the Napoleonic regime began to lay its "granite blocks" of social order did it prove possible to legislate regarding the medical profession. The Law of 19 ventôse Year XI (1803) almost qualifies, in fact, as one of those "granite blocks," for it governed the practice of medicine for most of the nineteenth century, succumbing to reform only in 1892. It is not my purpose here to describe all of the provisions of the Law but only to extrapolate its definition of a medical "profession," and to see how that definition was formulated within the parameters established by the three models just outlined.

The author of the Law, Bonaparte's councillor of state responsible for public instruction, happens to have had direct personal involvement in all three models. Antoine-François Fourcroy had been a student at the Paris Faculty of Medicine in the 1770s; simultaneously, as a protégé of Vicq d'Azyr, he had been affiliated with the Royal Society of Medicine – allowed, despite his student status, to attend its meetings, entrusted with the care of its library, and clearly influenced by its statist orientation in his youthful project to write a systematic treatise on the diseases of artisans.[102] Probably because of Fourcroy's precocious affiliation with the Royal Society, and perhaps because of his own provocative behavior, corporate medicine showed this young man on the make its most unpleasant side. He was denied the usual pro forma promotion into the Regency after being awarded the doctorate; Fourcroy then proceeded to flout this ruling by calling himself a regent nonetheless. In a detailed and grim memorandum, the dean of the faculty recounted how he summoned Fourcroy for an interview and demanded that he "explain why he fled from the jurisdiction of his *corps*" by failing to seek faculty approval for the hours of his public chemistry course "outside the schools" and, worse still, by arrogating to himself the title of regent on the posters announcing the course. Fourcroy first challenged the dean's right to interrogate him and then wrangled with him over the faculty statutes concerning the Regency; but soon, cowed or chastened, he "consented[ed] to everything," had three hundred copies of the corrected poster printed at his own expense and wrote to the dean renouncing his membership in "any society which is schismatic with respect to [the faculty] and especially in the Royal Society of Medicine."[103] But the

---

[102] W. A. Smeaton, *Fourcroy, Chemist and Revolutionary, 1755–1809* (Cambridge: Heffer, 1962), Ch. 6 and pp. 3–4.

[103] *Commentaires* (1777–86), Vol. 2, pp. 834–35, 842.

renunciation was disingenuous: Fourcroy's primary identification as a medical man was always with the Société, and he was a highly active member – eventually even an officer – from 1780 until its dissolution in 1793.[104] Finally it was Fourcroy, as a deputy to the Convention, whose commitment to laissez-faire was (momentarily) so thoroughgoing that, in the 1793 speech cited above, he recommended a total deregulation of the teaching profession. This is not to suggest, of course, that the Law of 19 ventôse Year XI be read in some fashion as Fourcroy's covert autobiography, but only that in the drafting of the Law, Fourcroy's personal biases meshed with and reinforced the social and political biases of the regime he served.

It is a "statist" element (though not precisely the "statism" of the Société) that preponderates in the Law. The Law in fact illustrates that curious continuity between the absolute monarchy of the Old Regime and the Napoleonic system that Tocqueville discerned and emphasized. The Napoleonic legislators frankly admitted that they had turned to Louis XIV for guidance: "In writing [the bill], we have taken all that was good from the ancient forms prescribed by the edict of 1707, by adjusting these forms to the order of things that exists today." The new "order of things" referred, in part, to the absence of the medical corporations. Far from restoring them (after all, Louis XIV's purpose in 1707 had been to domesticate them, to begin to submit them to central state control), the Law confirmed the Revolution's repudiation of them, and Fourcroy's preamble rehearsed the justification for this in that bitter anticorporate rhetoric that had become standardized by this date but which he, like Vicq d'Azyr, must have understood viscerally:

> Under the pretext of corporate discipline, the members were scrutinized, even persecuted for their medical opinions as well as for their private conduct. Alongside several advantages of this regimen, passions and jealousies were too often covered with the veil of "order" and of "the nobility of the medical estate" for the purpose of tormenting those whose ideas and too prompt successes distinguished them and drew them out above the commonality.[105]

Firmly committed to ending that "most complete anarchy" which had prevailed in the healing art for more than a decade, but unable to look to the corporations for regulation, the Law looked instead to the state. State-run medical schools would administer the examinations that were to be the only gateway to the medical profession (Title II); the state bureaucracy would check the credentials and draw up the lists of certified doctors who wished to practice in each locality (Title IV); state

---

[104] Smeaton, *Fourcroy*, pp. 19–25.
[105] Fourcroy's preamble to the draft bill, *Arch. parl.*, 2d ser., Vol. 4, p. 31. For the draft bill itself, enacted into law unchanged, see pp. 28–29.

tribunals would fine illegal practitioners (Title VI), who were, as it turned out, usually "caught" and denounced by state administrative personnel. On its own initiative, the state bureaucracy also conducted in the early nineteenth century occasional *enquêtes* to assess statistically the extent of "charlatanism" in France.[106]

Modern professions, the sociologists tell us, are always ultimately dependent upon the state, which alone has the power to vouchsafe their monopoly over a given type of work.[107] Still, the solution offered by the Law of 19 ventôse Year XI gave an inordinately large role to the state: The state effectively constituted the profession at that historical juncture, because the earlier structures of medical professional community – the corporations – were gone.

Thus the remarks of Fourcroy and other government supporters of the Law contain nothing about association among doctors; it is the unencumbered individual doctor who receives their attention. The doctor was "to exercise freely," a phrase that apparently meant without the geographical restrictions and annoying intrusions into his affairs that corporate membership had entailed. Success on the examinations gave him the full run of France, with only the slight bureaucratic formality of having his name inscribed on the local list of practitioners. By implication, his professional *capacité* resided in him as an isolated individual; he had no need of a corporate matrix.

His profession continued to be construed in terms of political economy; but all the libertarian and meritocratic connotations of laissez-faire so prominent during the Revolution were now discarded. The proposals for inventive, idiosyncratic ways of learning medicine gave way to the insistence that only students who had completed four years at official medical schools would be eligible for the certifying examinations (Article 8); and the ideal of a medical career open to talent yielded to the decision that medical education would *not* be free of charge, that talented poor boys would be barred de facto and given access only to the inferior status of country "health officer."[108] What now emerged was the more hard-nosed aspect of Smithian theory: a rudimentary cost-benefit analysis, a conceptualization of the doctor's position in society based on a calculation of exchanges in the marketplace. This conceptualization was articulated at length with respect to three provisions of the draft bill that appear to have stimulated some controversy: the fees for the certifying examination, the tuition for medical school itself, and the two-tiered medical system with a superior grade of doc-

---

[106] Matthew Ramsey, "Sous le régime de la législation de 1803: Trois enquêtes sur les charlatans au XIXe siècle," *Revue d'histoire moderne et contemporaine* 27 (1980): 485–97.

[107] See Freidson, *Profession of Medicine*, Ch. 2, esp. pp. 23–25.

[108] The government position papers were very explicit about this; see *Arch. parl.*, 2d ser., Vol. 4, pp. 31, 141.

tors and an inferior one of health officers.[109] Said Fourcroy in defense of the fees: "Justice and reason require that these expenses be borne by the aspirants, who will receive in exchange the right to exercise freely a profession from which they ought to draw a more or less considerable profit." Similarly, Jard-Panvillier justified the *officiat de santé* on the grounds that no one could reasonably expect fully trained doctors to practice in the countryside:

> But how would you bring it about that the sort of man you desire would make the sacrifice of the considerable outlay that his primary education cost him, and of the advantages that he could derive from his higher education, in order to practice in obscurity and without the hope of glory or fortune the abilities that he acquired at great expense? . . . I know that there are philosophers . . . who delight in seclusion and disinterestedness. Unfortunately, they are in short supply.

The same basic proposition was posed starkly when Fourcroy argued for medical school tuition:

> As honorable as the profession of doctor may be, it is accompanied by lucre. It leads to fortune, and it is just that, producing gain for those who practice it, it asks preliminary expenditures of them. Besides, honor is not attached solely to exemption from monetary transactions; and, if it were, that opinion would have to be ranked among the prejudices, especially those that make commerce appear as a degrading occupation.

Fourcroy went on to compress his thinking on the subject into an almost epigrammatic phrase: "The value that one attaches to things is made up in part of the money that they have cost."[110]

The profession of medicine had, in 1803, been "officially" assimilated into the categories of political economy. It was an investment of money, effort, and time on the part of *pères de famille* and their sons,[111] and it was supposed to yield a return in money and in status. The French government rhetoric has the same presuppositions as the arguments of Adam Smith in the chapter of *Wealth of Nations* in which the term "liberal profession" is used probably for the first time. Smith is pondering the question of why the value of some types of work – as measured by "pecuniary wages and profit" – is greater than that of others; and his discussion, crucially, touches indiscriminately upon the "mechanic trades" and what he calls the "liberal professions." That this mixture (which the d'Allarde law replicated) is an innovation on Smith's part is clearly seen in the fact that his chapter is a reworking of sections of Cantillon's *Essai sur la nature du commerce en général* (1755);

---

[109] There was no recorded debate over the bill in the Corps législatif, just three speeches in favor of it; but all three contain replies to anticipated objections.

[110] *Arch. parl.*, 2d ser., Vol. 4, pp. 31, 142, 146.

[111] Ibid., p. 142, mentions the sacrifices of fathers.

yet Cantillon's inquiry is confined to different types of manual labor.[112] Smith seeks – and finds – "natural" market justification for the relatively high remuneration accorded to doctors. (The name "liberal profession" was thus born at almost the same time as the impulse to view the phenomenon so named in fundamentally economic terms.) In the first place, Smith argues,

> We trust our health to the physician. . . . Such confidence could not be safely reposed in people of a very mean or low condition. Their reward must be such, therefore, as may give them that rank in society which so important a trust requires. The long time and the great expense which must be laid out in their education, when combined with this circumstance, necessarily enhance still further the price of their labour.

Furthermore, the risk involved in education for the "liberal professions" is much greater than that for the "mechanic trades": "Put your son apprentice to a shoemaker, there is little doubt of his learning to make a pair of shoes. But send him to study the law, it is at least twenty to one if ever he makes such proficiency as will enable him to live by the business."[113]

At the beginning of the nineteenth century, then, the "profession" of medicine was defined in France in a way that stressed two poles – the state, and the individual doctor in the market economy – and left out the middle term, professional association. Insofar as the doctor became a subspecies of *Homo economicus,* his claim to relatively high monetary and status rewards was recognized. But any higher calling – what twentieth-century sociologists would call a "service ideal" – was severely deemphasized; and especially given the anticommercial prejudice in France, which Fourcroy acknowledged while decrying it, such a situation could only, ironically, erode medical status. Toward midcentury, doctors began to chafe at the medical order established in 1803 and to struggle – against such deterrents as repressive legislation and their own inertia and mutual distrust – toward the formation of a professional association.[114] The most ardent of them would, much like the Paris workers, interpret the Revolution of February 1848 as a mandate for "the freedom of . . . professional association" and for their own

---

[112] The 1904 Cannan edition of *Wealth of Nations* (reprinted by the University of Chicago Press, 1976) notes Smith's reliance on Cantillon and supplies the titles of the relevant chapters in Cantillon's treatise; see p. 111n.

[113] Ibid., p. 118. The chapter also contains an argument against educating doctors and lawyers at the public expense; see p. 147.

[114] The 1845 Medical Congress was the benchmark here; see the account of it in George Weisz, "The Politics of Medical Professionalization in France, 1845–1848," *Journal of Social History* 12 (1978): esp. 7–13.

corporate solidarity.[115] But such hopes were realized slowly and partially, and the state remained the scaffolding and *point de repère* of the collectivity of French medical men. The salience of the state in the nineteenth-century French model of a medical "profession" – and its corollary, the continuity of Old Regime traditions of health police – is especially important to remember when embarking upon a study of the emergence of psychiatry.

[115] See the editorials in *Union médicale*, "Au corps médical," February 26, 1848, and "Association pour la défense des droits et des intérêts du corps médical," March 2, 1848. In the latter, the doctors call for emulation of "the men of letters, the artists [and] the workers of all trades" who, in the aftermath of the February Revolution, "have already constituted themselves in associations."

2

Toward psychiatry

A T the same time that the "profession" of medicine was passing through a period of flux and uncertain definition from the closing decades of the Old Regime to the beginning of the Napoleonic era, the foundations of psychiatry were inconspicuously being laid. These foundations can, with hindsight, be discerned in three areas: in the state bureaucracy; in general medical theory; and in recommendations for and spontaneous developments within the modus operandi of medical practice itself.

The bureaucracy: health police of the insane

The Old Regime category of police was not static. Its inherent logic pushed it toward comprehensiveness, toward ordering and mastering with ever greater efficacy an ever greater number of the contingent details of social life. Hence its subcategory, health police, came to include attention to lunatics – who, as unproductive and frequently disruptive members of the population, readily took on a political significance in the context of bureaucratic absolutism. The interest of the Old Regime state in lunacy was, to be sure, minimal compared to its interest in other health matters, especially epidemics and epizootics; but evidence from the 1780s suggests that this interest was growing. The evolutionary pattern here was the same as in other aspects of police: What began as a purely administrative function was later supplemented and to some degree transformed by reliance upon "enlightened" science.

In the case of lunacy, the purely administrative task had been undertaken in the second half of the seventeenth century by Louis XIV's creation "in each city of his realm" of an institution called the *hôpital-général* and the subsequent "Great Confinement" of a wide assortment of the idle and potentially unruly poor – not only lunatics but also vagrants, beggars, invalids, and prostitutes. Despite its name, the *hôpital-général* was not a hospital; it had no medical aim whatsoever. It aimed only at maintaining political control over urban agglomerations (which had, as Paris had shown, an alarming capacity for growth) by

segregating those elements identified as undesirable and forcibly setting them to work, so that they would earn their own keep and might
even return a profit to the state.[1] About a century later, a second
institution for the expeditious confinement of lunatics was added, quite
inadvertently, to the apparatus of police. The *dépôts de mendicité*, work-
houses intended for the short-term detention and correction of able-
bodied beggars, were created in 1764, when administrators finally acknowledged the inability of the *hôpital-général* to deal adequately with
this group. But the *dépôts*, which recruited their internees from the
countryside as well as from the city, could not in practice stick to such
a neat and narrow definition of them. They soon lapsed into that
heterogeneity of population which was already the hallmark of the
hôpital-général; two additional groups usually sheltered within their
walls were women with venereal diseases (often interned at the request of the army) and lunatics whose families refused to care for
them.[2] By the closing decades of the eighteenth century, however,
mere confinement of lunatics had come to seem insufficient. The state,
in its new liaison with science, began to entertain a more ambitious
aim: cure of madness, the conversion of blighted insane subjects into
sane healthy ones who could safely reenter ordinary society. Simple
police of the insane as one of several groups of perennial trouble-
makers gave way to health police of the disease of insanity.

That the cure of insanity was at least a possibility – if far from a
likelihood – was the assumption that informed late eighteenth-century French medical writing and Parisian administrative practice. The
relevant articles in the *Encyclopédie* (which in this case conveyed accepted wisdom rather than original views) expressed varying degrees
of confidence. The positive outcome of an informed treatment of
"frenzy" seemed more or less assured; treatment of melancholy was
a more elaborate and tricky business, with only relatively good prospects; whereas mania was described as "one of those diseases on
which the most skillful physicians habitually fail," frustratingly un-
predictable because "a remedy that has worked on one maniac only
intensifies the delirium of another."[3] The curability of madness was
taken seriously enough that an attempt to bring it about – attested by
a doctor's or surgeon's certificate – was legally required before an
individual could be locked away indefinitely in Paris in either the

---

[1] See Michel Foucault, *Folie et déraison: Histoire de la folie à l'âge classique* (Paris: Plon,
1961), Part 1, Ch. 2. The first *hôpital-général* was created in Paris in 1656; the king
decreed the creation of its provincial counterparts in 1676. *Grand renfermement* is Foucault's term, the 1656 edict speaking only of a *renfermement*.

[2] Olwen H. Hufton, *The Poor of Eighteenth-Century France, 1750–1789* (Oxford: Oxford
University Press, 1974), pp. 155–57, 219–27, 238.

[3] "Phrénésie," Vol. 25, p. 687; "Mélancolie," Vol. 21, pp. 419–20; "Manie," Vol. 20, pp.
958–59.

hôpital-général or the Petites-Maisons, the pair of custodial institutions catering to *fous incurables.*

For those *fous* and *folles* still deemed (usually by dint of the recency of their condition) curable, a single public facility existed in the capital: two wards of the sprawling, all-purpose, ramshackle Hôtel-Dieu. One of these had space for forty-two men, the other for thirty-four women, the lunatics of both sexes being kept for the most part four to a bed in so-called *grands lits.*[4] The kinds of treatment typically employed in these wards will be discussed later in this chapter. While the rates of cure are unknown, an impressionistic sense of their magnitude can be gained from comments made by some physicians of the Hôtel-Dieu at the very end of the century. "It would be difficult," they said, "to depict the profound depression that this department [i.e., the lunatic wards] inspires in all physicians"; nonetheless, treating the insane of the Hôtel-Dieu caused less "torment" to these medical men than attending the consumptive patients (who typically arrived there "in extremis"), for with the lunatics "at least one reckons *some* successes."[5] In short, the curability of insanity was not in itself a novel idea. The novel idea – and optimistic article of faith – that took root in the state bureaucracy in the 1780s was that, with the diligent application of rational measures, the number of cures could be made to increase, certainly appreciably and perhaps indefinitely; hence both interest and duty dictated that the government promote such measures.

One small indication of this drift in bureaucratic thinking has already been noted: the full-scale investigation in 1781 of Dufour's "secret" treatment of lunatics, instigated by Lenoir as lieutenant-general of Paris police. Since this investigation technically fell within the police power to regulate charlatans and assess secret remedies – an area in which Lenoir, lacking the resources for exhaustive coverage, had to proceed selectively[6] – his selection of the Dufour case represented a deliberate bureaucratic decision to test and foster potential improvements in the treatment of insanity. Another indication was the state's patronage of Nicolas-Philippe Ledru, a scientific showman (he called himself "Comus," after the god of festivals) who employed electricity in the healing of epilepsy, catalepsy, "maladies of the nerves," and, it was sometimes alleged, madness.[7] At the Crown's insistence, communicated

---

[4] See Tenon, *Mémoires sur les hôpitaux de Paris* (Paris: Impr. de Ph.-D. Pierres, 1788), pp. 212–14.

[5] AN: F[15] 1863, "Mémoire lu par les médecins du grand hospice d'humanité ci-devant Hôtel-Dieu, en présence des citoyens . . . composant la Commission administrative des hospices civils de Paris," thermidor Year VI, pp. 4, 8, my italics.

[6] Alan Williams, *The Police of Paris, 1718–1798* (Baton Rouge: Louisiana State University Press, 1979), pp. 266–67.

[7] For references to Ledru's healing of madness (*folie*), see the letter by Lenoir dated December 13, 1783, in *Commentaires de la Faculté de Médecine de Paris, 1777 à 1786*, ed. A. Pinard et. al., 2 vols. (Paris: Steinheil, 1903), Vol. 2, p. 1126; and Ledru's own intro-

through the Ministry of the King's Household, or Maison du Roi (the agency of the royal government which had direct authority over the Paris police and which frequently intervened in health matters), a commission of the Paris Faculty of Medicine subjected Ledru's methods to sustained examination in 1783 and found them effective.[8] The King then bestowed upon Ledru and his son the title of "His Majesty's Scientists (*Physiciens*)" – a title which carried with it the privilege of medical practice in Paris – and urged the faculty (unsuccessfully, as it turned out) to grant them a comparable title. The government went so far as to aid Ledru *père* and *fils* in setting up an electrotherapy clinic in the capital, a purpose for which Lenoir's police budget allocated some 17,000 livres annually.[9]

These pieces of evidence become more significant when we add to them the most extensive and deliberate inclusion of the insane within the workings of Old Regime health police. In 1785 the royal printing house brought out, at the order and expense of the government, an official directive, or *instruction*, on the "way to manage (*gouverner*) lunatics and work toward their cure in the houses of refuge reserved for them." The forty-four page brochure was coauthored by Jean Colombier and François Doublet, both physicians and members of the Royal Society of Medicine. Colombier, the senior author, was a prototypical physician–bureaucrat, an *administrateur éclairé*, as his colleagues at the Royal Society called him, despite his primary medical identity.[10] Having first been drawn into the royal bureaucracy in the 1770s as a consultant to the Ministry of War on military hygiene, he subsequently collaborated with the Paris police lieutenant Lenoir on an experimental hospice for the cure of foundlings afflicted with venereal disease. In 1781, he reached the pinnacle of his career in health police when the reforming Chief Minister Necker appointed him to the newly created post of inspector of civil hospitals and prisons, thus giving him responsibility for a vast bureaucratic domain. It was in this last capacity that,

ductory "Aperçu" to *Rapport de MM. Cosnier, Maloet, Darcet, Philip, Le Preux, Dessartz & Paulet, Docteurs-Régens de la Faculté de Médecine de Paris; sur les avantages reconnus de la nouvelle méthode d'administrer l'électricité dans les maladies nerveuses* . . . (Paris: Philippe-Denys Pierres, 1783), p. 10. General information on Ledru can be found in Jean Torlais, "Un prestidigateur célèbre, chef de service d'électrothérapie au XVIIIe siècle: Ledru dit Comus (1731–1807)," *Histoire de la médecine* 5 (1955): 13–25; and Geoffrey Sutton, "Electric Medicine and Mesmerism," *Isis* 72 (1981): 375–92.

[8] *Rapport de MM. Cosnier* . . . , passim and esp. pp. 109–15. The official examination was confined to the effect of electricity on epileptics.

[9] *Commentaires* (1777–86), Vol. 2, pp. 1128–30, documents the refusal of the faculty assembly to act as "the passive instrument of the King's will" with respect to Ledru; Williams, *Police of Paris*, p. 268, supplies the amount of royal aid.

[10] See *Histoire de la Société royale de médecine, 1782–83* (Paris, 1787), "Ouvrages par les membres de la Société . . . ," p. 225.

in 1785, Colombier drafted a plan for the centralized regulation of all the *dépôts de mendicité* in France. He intended his *Instruction* on insanity of that same year as ancillary to this regulation, as a means of introducing uniformity and enlightened attitudes into an area of policy particularly relevant to the *dépôts* (with their de facto populations of lunatics), though obviously relevant to other public institutions within his purview as well.[11]

In both its provenance and its rhetoric the *Instruction* is unmistakably a document of enlightened absolutism. Its introduction argues that chief responsibility for the care of the insane ought to be assigned to the government: The insane are, together with children, the weakest members of society; but while both groups inspire "pity," the "hope" that children arouse insures that they – "this fertile source of the prosperity of a state" – will naturally be nurtured, while the horror that lunatics arouse routinely leads private persons "to flee them." By default, then, lunatics "require especially the attention and the surveillance of the government." Government policy toward them must meet two goals. First, in order to "prevent [lunatics] from troubling society" and to assuage "public fear" of them, they must be incarcerated. This was the practice already adopted "in all of the civilized (*policé*) countries of Europe, and especially in France." But "pity" demanded more and stipulated a second goal: a concerted attempt to cure them, or at least to diminish their suffering, or at the very least to refrain from exacerbating it. This second, humanitarian goal, which was consonant with "the visions of *bienfaisance* which animate the prince whom it is our happiness to have for master," could be accomplished only with the aid of science, the application of "*lumières acquises.*"[12] Thus the *Instruction* was a compendium of these *lumières*, a succinct scientific handbook for administrators.

The first part, written by Colombier, discussed the design of institutions for curable lunatics. A checklist of specifications of proven therapeutic value was presented: the presence of pure air and water on the site, regularly scheduled promenades in places shaded from the sun, suitable diet.[13] The second part of the *Instruction*, the work of Doublet, reviewed the nosology of insanity and the most advanced forms of treatment devised by the medical art. Doublet identified four basic types of insanity – frenzy, melancholy, mania, and imbecility – the clas-

---

[11] See Thomas M. Adams, "Medicine and Bureaucracy: Jean Colombier's Regulation for the *Dépôts de Mendicité* (1785)," *Bull. Hist. Med.* 52 (1979): 529–41; and P.-L.-M.-J. Gallot-Lavallée, *Un hygiéniste au XVIIIe siècle: Jean Colombier* (Paris: Thèse de médecine, 1913), esp. pp. 56–62.

[12] [Jean Colombier and François Doublet], *Instruction sur la manière de gouverner les insensés, et de travailler à leur guérison dans les asyles qui leur sont destinés* (Paris: Impr. royale, 1785), pp. 1–5.

[13] Ibid., pp. 11–14.

sificatory scheme implicitly used by the *Encyclopédie*[14] and the one generally ratified by seventeenth- and eighteenth-century medical opinion, despite the revisionist efforts of nosologists like Boissier de Sauvages and Linnaeus.[15] Frenzy was a "delirium" – literally a straying from a path, in this case the path of reason – both "furious" and "continuous" and accompanied by fever; mania was the same condition, but without fever; melancholy differed from mania in that the apyretic, or unfeverish delirium was limited to a single subject and was always "pacific" in tone; in imbecility, the delirium was characterized by a virtual cessation of all mental activity.[16]

As for treatment, Doublet delivered authoritative pronouncements on the advantages of bleedings, purgings (the use of hellebore for this purpose, which dates back to antiquity, was especially touted), lukewarm baths and cold showers, and alternations between the two, or daily alternations between baths and purgings. The precise prescriptions varied somewhat for each of the four types of insanity, but the repertory of strategies remained constant. Methods of this generic sort, Doublet noted, were employed in the Hôtel-Dieu in Paris, which had thereby earned its "merited . . . reputation for the treatment of lunatics." The reader will recognize that the surgeon Dufour was very much in the therapeutic mainstream; in fact, Doublet alluded to him, furnishing us with the outcome of his story as well as with a gloss on it: "A surgeon in Paris who advertised himself some years ago as able to cure madmen treated several maniacs at Bicêtre; while some of them experienced very notable relief, it failed to prove durable. The remedy he administered was a strong purgative, and he would perhaps have had more success had he persevered in its administration."[17] In addition, Doublet, who was at this time experimenting with an "electric machine" at the *dépôt de mendicité* of Saint-Denis, expressed a cautious optimism about electrotherapy. "Electric commotion" was endorsed for certain types of imbecility; its effects on maniacs were palpable but could "not yet" be said to have effected any cures.[18]

All in all, the *Instruction* outlined a complete program for the health police of insanity. The government distributed the brochure with a generous hand and with stern admonitions. Each intendant received fifty copies from Chief Minister Calonne and was bidden to deliver them to the various "establishments of this type in your district and to make known to their administrators that the King's intention is conformity [to the *Instruction*] insofar as the facilities and the circumstances permit. You

---

14 Ibid., p. 19; and "Délire," *Encyclopédie*, Vol. 10, p. 593, referring the reader to articles on "Manie," "Phrénésie," "Mélancolie," and "Stupidité."

15 See Foucault, *Folie et déraison*, Part 2, Ch. 1, esp. pp. 243–47.

16 Colombier and Doublet, *Instruction*, pp. 19, 25, 38, 42.

17 Ibid., pp. 24, 29.

18 Ibid., pp. 33, 44; and Adams, "Medicine and Bureaucracy," p. 535.

will be so kind as to inform me of everything concerning its execution."[19] Colombier's personal visits of inspection to *hôtels-Dieu* and
dépôts in all parts of France seconded the enforcement effort.[20] Nor did
Colombier neglect provision for the continuing development of scientific knowledge about insanity. In a supplementary directive of 1788 he
called for the collection and tabulation of medical data from all of the
dépôts de mendicité in France. Now the doctors and surgeons who
served as medical officers at these institutions usually served also as
correspondents of the Royal Society of Medicine and as the epidemic
fighters for their localities, designated by the intendant.[21] Through this
overlap of personnel, Colombier integrated the new insanity project
naturally into the data-gathering network of the Royal Society. In other
words, a statist medicine which included as one of its components
serious treatment of and research about insanity was beginning to take
shape in France on the eve of the Revolution.

Another, simultaneous bureaucratic initiative in the field of health
dovetailed with that of Colombier and deserves to be mentioned here: the
widely publicized reevaluation of the Paris hospital system, sponsored by
the reforming minister of the King's household, the Baron de Breteuil. In
1785 Breteuil appointed a special commission of the Academy of Sciences,
one of whose members, the surgeon Jacques Tenon, set forth his recommendations in the encyclopedic *Mémoires sur les hôpitaux de Paris* (1788).
Tenon advised the "dismemberment" of the unwieldy, overcrowded,
and insalubrious Hôtel-Dieu and its division into four smaller hospitals
"placed at the circumference of Paris," each having both a general service
(for the standard complaints of fevers and wounds) and a single specialized function. He envisioned that one of these four hospitals, Sainte-
Anne, would be devoted to the treatment of the curable insane. Tenon
was, in effect, taking the two wards of the Hôtel-Dieu and magnifying
their capacity almost threefold, for Sainte-Anne was to have space for two
hundred lunatics, a clear indicator of the growing importance of treatment of insanity in the scientific-cum-bureaucratic circles in which he
traveled. As Tenon explicitly remarked after setting forth a list of all the
existing resources of the Paris hospitals for diseases of all kinds: "We still
have virtually no assistance for the treatment of madness."

Tenon happens to give us in the *Mémoires* a vivid informal portrait of
himself at work as an enlightened formulator of public health policy. In
order to plan Sainte-Anne, he wants to know statistics: annual admis-

---

[19] Letter of Calonne dated July 15, 1785, Archives départementales de l'Orne, quoted in
Hélène Bonnafous-Sérieux, *La Charité de Senlis d'après des documents en grande partie
inédits* (Paris: Presses universitaires de France, 1936), p. 6 n2.
[20] See Gallot-Lavallée, *Un hygiéniste*, pp. 76–77. One such visit is mentioned in Colin
Jones, "The Treatment of the Insane in Eighteenth- and Early Nineteenth-Century
Montpellier," *Medical History* 24 (1980): esp. 379 and plate 1.
[21] Adams, "Medicine and Bureaucracy," 536–37.

sions of lunatics into the Hôtel-Dieu, percentage of cures, length of treatment. But to his dismay he discovers that the registers of the ancient hospital are so badly kept and so indifferent to these matters as to be virtually useless to him. To his rescue comes that most familiar figure in this story: Lenoir, the lieutenant-general of the Paris police, who has been systematically recording the relevant admission figures and is easily prevailed upon by the Baron de Breteuil to release them to Tenon. Tenon sizes them up and immediately finds not only the guide to specific institutional reform he had sought, but also grist for theoretical speculation about the incidence of insanity: "It is certain that among furious lunatics, there are more women than men. A new subject for research. Does this difference originate in the sequelae of childbearing, in the nervous sensations accompanying lactation?" Whatever the precise cause, which Tenon admits he cannot readily determine, he knows he has stumbled upon "one more motive" for his concern with the cure of insanity – the need to arrest the "deterioration" of the sex that "perpetuates society." And he concludes that the new Sainte-Anne hospital must be built to reverse the proportions of the Hôtel-Dieu: It must have more space for women than for men, whereas the ward for *fous* at the parent facility was larger than that for *folles*.[22] Tenon's vignette reveals in a few deft strokes the collaboration and even the symbiosis between the scientific and bureaucratic mentalities that was, at the end of the eighteenth century, not only shaping state policy toward the insane but also facilitating the constitution of new knowledge about insanity.[23]

A phrase used by Tenon to describe his new conception of the hospital – *machine à guérir*, or healing machine – expresses the late eighteenth-century fascination with the ideal of rational and efficient medical care, including care of the insane, which had become associated with the bureaucracy and its activities. In fact, "immense machine, astonishing mechanism" were the words by which a 1785 dictionary of jurisprudence characterized the network of Paris police itself.[24]

Tenon's proposed contribution to the health police of insanity very nearly succeeded but ultimately miscarried. The entire plan for the four new hospitals, although adopted by the Academy of Sciences commission and accepted by one government ministry in 1787, was rejected by

---

[22] *Mémoires sur les hôpitaux*, pp. xxxviii–xxxix, xl–xli, 14–15, 217–20.

[23] I have analyzed this vignette in terms of Foucauldian categories in "Foucault among the Sociologists: The 'Disciplines' and the History of the Professions," *History and Theory* 23 (1984): 170–92, esp. 185–86.

[24] For Tenon's usage, see the quotations from his printed works and manuscripts in Michel Foucault et al., *Les machines à guérir (aux origines de l'hôpital moderne)* (Paris: Institut de l'Environnement, 1976), first page of preface (n.p.) and p. 55 n1. The 1785 *Répertoire universel de jurisprudence* by Guyot is cited in Claude Quétel, *De par le Roy: Essai sur les lettres de cachet* (Toulouse: Privat, 1981), p. 109.

another ministry the following year in favor of a refurbished, monolithic Hôtel-Dieu. Yet this outcome, the result of complicated political infighting, seems quite circumstantial.[25] It does not diminish the significance of Tenon's proposal as further confirmation of the trend set in motion by Colombier's *Instruction*. Indeed, Tenon, who criticized the insanity wards of the Hôtel-Dieu according to criteria enunciated in the *Instruction* – the dangers of direct sunlight, the need for fresh air – was an avowed admirer of Colombier.[26]

General medical theory: medicine as "anthropology"

The epistemological crisis of eighteenth-century medicine, which had brought forth Vicq d'Azyr's claim for the autonomy of medical knowledge, was not so simply resolved. The sense of crisis persisted, eliciting much more grandiose claims from Vicq d'Azyr's post-Revolutionary successors. The physicians associated with the circle of the Idéologues – and in particular P.-J.-G. Cabanis – sought to rescue medicine from its putative inferiority by declaring it not merely autonomous from the host of accessory sciences that served it but also tantamount to, or at least the most salient element in, an all-embracing science of man, or "anthropology," a term they borrowed from the Germans.[27] Under the Directory and the Consulate, this bold dictum was explored by the Idéologues in their small Société médicale d'émulation and was also delivered more publicly and from the heights of official culture; for the Idéologues were, at this time, insiders. They controlled the Second Class of the Institut de France – it was there, for example, that Cabanis's most characteristic treatise, the *Rapports du physique et du moral de l'homme*, was first unveiled. One result of the new conception of medicine was to make central to the medical enterprise the investigation of what would later be called "psychiatric" subjects – as will become ap-

[25] See Louis S. Greenbaum, "Jean-Sylvain Bailly, the Baron de Breteuil and the 'Four New Hospitals' of Paris," *Clio Medica* 8 (1973): 261–84.

[26] See letter of Tenon to Necker of July 30, 1780, cited in Louis S. Greenbaum, "The Commercial Treaty of Humanity: La tournée des hôpitaux anglais par Jacques Tenon en 1787," *Revue d'histoire des sciences* 24 (1971): 319 n8.

[27] The most important secondary work on Cabanis, and the one which has in many ways shaped my discussion of him in this chapter, is Martin S. Staum, *Cabanis: Enlightenment and Medical Philosophy in the French Revolution* (Princeton, N.J.: Princeton University Press, 1980). On the filiation between Vicq d'Azyr and the Idéologues, see Sergio Moravia, "Philosophie et médecine en France à la fin du XVIIIe siècle," *Studies on Voltaire and the Eighteenth Century* 89 (1972): 1089–91. Two places in Cabanis's writings that refer to *anthropologie* and its relationship to medicine are *O.P.*, Vol. 1, p. 126 and p. 126 n1, and Vol. 2, p. 77; in both places Cabanis notes that he has borrowed the term from "les Allemands" but fails to be more specific. For his possible German sources, see Mareta Linden, *Untersuchungen zum Anthropologie-begriff des 18. Jahrhunderts* (Bern: Herbert Lang; Frankfurt: Peter Lang, 1976).

parent when the meaning of the Idéologues' "anthropological" assertions is explored.

Cabanis envisioned a "total reform" of medicine in his own day,
comparable in magnitude to that of Hippocrates, to be carried out by
"physicians gifted in philosophy." Medicine, it appears, was to be
philosophized in two senses, one formal and the other substantive. In
the first place, although Cabanis did not dispute Vicq d'Azyr's contention that observation was the true basis of medicine, he saw it as
harboring a distinct peril: A science of observation could readily "lose
itself in the multitude of facts gathered," much like "an inquisitive
traveler overstuffing his baggage" with all the interesting items found
en route. Hence medicine needed philosophy to provide general principles for the arrangement of its data and to undertake periodic revision and simplification of the arrangements adopted. Here was the
characteristic late Enlightenment stress on classification. As part and
parcel of this task, the *esprit philosophique* would renovate medical language, purging it of all that vagueness, imprecision, and ambiguity, all
that "meaningless and ridiculous jargon," which "furnishes an impe-
netrable sanctuary to ignorant charlatanism."[28] Second, and most important for our purposes here, medicine was to be philosophized by
the redefinition of its subject matter in accordance with the basic premise of the dominant epistemology of the Enlightenment, the sensationalist psychology inaugurated by Locke and "improved" by
Condillac.[29] Now Condillac maintained that all mental contents derived
from physical sensation. But not being himself a physiologist, he had,
in Cabanis's view, lopsidedly focused on the mental side of the linkage
and had thus failed to perceive its full and rich implications: to wit,
that since physical sensitivity was the single, irreducible property of
living things; and since the physical man, the intellectual man, and the
moral or volitional man were all manifestations of this same sensitivity,
the study of any one of the three was really but an aspect of a single
science – an omnibus "science of man" which was most nearly ap-
proximated by medicine.

In specifying the nature of the crucial "act of sensitivity," Cabanis
was obliged to emend Condillac's notion of it, to give it the visceral
dimension that was his fitting contribution as a physician and that
helped to stake out the "science of man" for medicine. According to
Condillac, the ultimate source of all ideas and moral resolutions was
the external world as apprehended by the sense organs. But Cabanis
insisted that there were "internal impressions" as well, impressions
which originated deep within internal organs and usually quite outside

---

[28] Cabanis, *Coup d'oeil sur les révolutions et sur la reforme de la médecine, O.P.,* Vol. 2, pp.
68–70, 161–63.

[29] Cabanis, *Rapports du physique et du moral de l'homme, O.P.,* Vol. 1, pp. 111–12.

the conscious awareness of the individual and which, upon reaching the brain, generated ideas or moral propensities just as did sensations, the impressions garnered from the external world by the sensory receptors. Those mental contents dependent on internal impressions, or on "excitations whose stimuli work internally," Cabanis called "instinct," meaning the term in a special sense different from that of "vulgar language" (and remarkably similar to the sense in which Sigmund Freud would use the term a century later).[30] Those mental contents which "are formed about impressions which come to us from exterior objects by the intermediary of the senses" he called reason. The passions were located in this system as derivatives of instinct. The contributions of reason and instinct together constituted the domain of le moral.[31]

A medicine with "anthropological" aspirations, then, was one that spanned the two domains of le physique and le moral and whose task was, in part, to determine the relations obtaining between the two. Traffic, Cabanis stressed, flowed in both directions. Since both domains were ultimately of the same stuff, both rooted in sensitivity, they necessarily existed in mutual enchaînement: The physical condition of individuals affected their passions and ideas; and the passions and ideas in turn affected the physical condition. As a result of this conceptualization, two notions of "medicine" coexisted for the Idéologues. There was medicine in its older, narrow sense, which they continued to refer to as "medicine properly so-called" and which denoted the art of healing sickness through the application of physical remedies.[32] And there were, as Alibert put it to the Société médicale d'émulation, the "new destinies" which awaited medicine now that it had been properly philosophically construed, medicine as the "supreme science of the living man."[33]

Obviously this new medicine of psychophysiological reciprocity pushed the mental realm to the forefront in a way that the older conception of medicine had not. Cabanis's theoretical texts are accordingly

---

[30] Ibid., pp. 113, 165, 174, 178, 188. Both Cabanis and Freud stress that instinct is a borderline psychosomatic phenomenon and an unconscious one—"l'individu n'en a point la conscience," says Cabanis of the internal impressions (p. 179). Freud cited Cabanis's Rapports in the bibliography of The Interpretation of Dreams. Cf. Condillac's concept of instinct, derived exclusively from external impressions; Essai sur l'origine des connaissances humaines in Oeuvres de Condillac (Paris: Impr. de Ch. Houel, Year VI/1798), Vol. 1, pp. 83–84.

[31] Cabanis, Rapports, O.P., Vol. 1, pp. 187–88. On Cabanis's conceptualization of the passions, see Staum, Cabanis, p. 239.

[32] For this usage see, e.g., Jacques Moreau de la Sarthe, "Art de guérir: Traité médico-philosophique sur l'aliénation mentale par Ph. Pinel," Décade philosophique (20 prairial Year IX): 458–59 n1.

[33] J.-L. Alibert, "Discours sur les rapports de la médecine avec les sciences physiques et morales," M.S.M.E. 2 (Year VII): iii–iv.

larded with comments and speculations about mental states and the health or morbidity of mental functions – "the movements, disorderly or regular, of the spirit (*âme*)," in his phrase.[34] Thus, in the course of his refutation of Condillac's exclusive reliance on impressions issuing from the external world, Cabanis considered the nature and etiology of madness (*folie*). Madness, he said, referring to its standard definition in sensationalist psychology, is usually regarded as "nothing but the disorder or failure of accord of ordinary [externally derived] impressions." Yet the sensationalists' account could easily be shown inadequate on empirical grounds, for in many cases of madness "the sentient external extremities of the nerves which comprise the so-called senses are not at all affected." In such cases the disorder of mental contents must have sprung from another, internal source: Cabanis named the "viscera of the lower abdomen" and the "procreative organs" as likely alternate candidates for the bodily seat (*siège*) of madness, the internal impressions emanating from them disrupting, under certain circumstances, the coherent linkage of ideas. An examination of the period of adolescence bolstered this point, for it revealed an analogous pattern of mental peculiarity caused by internal impressions. The adolescent was typically "plunged into deep reveries"; his imagination was ascendant, absorbing him in an "inexhaustible" supply of "vague images." Yet the source of this hyperactive imagination was not a modification of the sensory receptors but rather the sudden awakening of sensitivity in the genital organs, which had until this time been sunk in torpor.[35]

While Cabanis himself never gave systematic or concerted attention to madness and other "disorderly movements of the spirit," he recognized this as a lacuna in his work and emphatically recommended that such a project be undertaken by others. "What a fine part of medicine is the descriptive study (*histoire*) and the treatment of madness," he exclaimed upon one occasion; "well-chosen facts about this subject matter would singularly illuminate the study of man."[36] And in the *Rapports*, after drawing a parallel between madness and dreams, he regretted not having "push[ed] these inquiries as far as they can go," in particular by specifying "each type of delirium" in detail. "How medicine . . . would profit from such a fine study!"[37] The anthropological conception of medicine thus led logically to the validation and cultivation of an explicitly "psychiatric" domain.

That conception had the additional effect, which would also prove relevant to the emergence of psychiatry, of underscoring the psychological dimension of all practice of the healing art. "Woe," intoned

---

[34] Cabanis, *Coup d'oeil, O.P.,* Vol. 2, p. 210.
[35] Cabanis, *Rapports, O.P.,* Vol. 1, pp. 175–77.
[36] Cabanis, "Quelques principes et quelques vues sur les secours publics," *O.P.,* Vol. 2, p. 57 n2.
[37] Cabanis, *Rapports, O.P.,* Vol. 1, p. 599.

Cabanis, "to the physician who has never learned to read in the human heart as well as recognizing the state of fever; who, caring for a sick body, does not know how to discern in features, glances and words the signs of a disordered mind or a wounded heart!"[38] It was when treating patients whose mental life was especially "highly developed" and in whom "the ideas and affections of the spirit [therefore] have an incalculable influence on the condition and direction of the physical forces" that the physician most needed this acuity and the corresponding ability to prevent or reverse, through "consolations," the physical damage wrought by the patient's "cruel anxieties."[39]

This requisite psychological therapy for fundamentally physical diseases was to focus its efforts upon the imagination (in another portion of the passage just quoted, Cabanis equated the patient's "cruel anxieties" with "errors of the imagination"); and the reason for this focus is not difficult to find. Imagination was for Cabanis, as for theorists of both the Cartesian and the sensationalist schools, the largely nonverbal mental operation found in beasts as well as in human beings. Located in the latter at the juncture between *le moral* and *le physique*, it typically functioned as the intermediary between the two domains. Hence, just as Cabanis believed that the maturation of the sexual organs overstimulated the adolescent imagination, so he believed the converse proposition: that an imagination subjected to "vicious excitements" and "set on the wrong course" by environmental factors could accelerate the onset of puberty. Indeed, this stepping up of physical development was almost the rule in large cities, for "bad mores" prevailed there.[40] But the power of imagination over the body was even more wide-ranging: "How many men," Cabanis marvelled, "have been killed, or cured, by imagination!"[41]

It should be noted that psychophysiological postulates of this sort, focusing upon the imagination, were a commonplace of late eighteenth-century French medical discourse. This can be seen quite clearly in a representative text – the report of the royal commission appointed in 1784 to study mesmerism. Rejecting the mesmerists' claims to have effected the cure of illness through magnetic redistribution of some alleged universal fluid, the commissioners contended that when mesmeric procedures worked, the active therapeutic agent had really been the patient's imagination, massively overstimulated by the "fondling" and public spectacle that were integral parts of the treatment. Mesmerism was, they said, nothing but a "medicine of the imagination." But the remark was not intended as a snide or dismissive one. A medicine of the imagination was not an imaginary medicine, and the commission had

---

[38] Cabanis, *Coup d'oeil, O.P.*, Vol. 2, p. 247.
[39] Cabanis, "Discours de clôture pour le cours sur Hippocrate," *O.P.*, Vol. 2, p. 337.
[40] Cabanis, *Rapports, O.P.*, Vol. 1, p. 176.
[41] Cabanis, *Coup d'oeil, O.P.*, Vol. 2, p. 224.

no fundamental objection to it as a form of medical therapeutics. If they recommended that mesmerism be banned it was because they objected to Mesmer's dishonest representation of his healing method and to his use of imagination to provoke convulsions – an unnatural, "violent means" of action which was "almost always destructive":

> Doubtless the imagination of patients often greatly influences the cure of their maladies. . . . It is a well-known adage that, in medicine, faith saves; and that faith is the product of the imagination. In such cases the imagination acts only by gentle means – by spreading calm in all the senses, reestablishing order in the functions, by reviving everything through hope.[42]

Cabanis' point about the reciprocal influence of *le moral* and *le physique* and the special role of imagination in mediating the relationship between the two was thus neither a new nor a particularly controversial one. But it had long been relegated to commonsensical, subscientific status in the medical community; the effect of imagination, observed the 1784 commission, "is known only by general experience and has never been determined by exacting (*positif*) experiments."[43] Cabanis lent legitimacy to the point by anchoring it in a sophisticated medical-philosophical theory about the nature of man, and he thus moved a "medicine of the imagination" from the shadowy periphery to the center of medical orthodoxy.

It was not only by mandating the study of madness and bringing psychological concerns to the fore in all medical therapeutics that the Idéologues' anthropological program for medicine served as a kind of midwife to psychiatry. Because its proponents derived a statist conception of medicine from its premises, it also reinforced the ethos of a bureaucratic health police and, by extension, those proto-psychiatric tendencies contained in the health police of insanity. How did "anthropology" yield up a statist medicine? The grounding of both *le moral* and *le physique* in physical sensitivity meant to Cabanis that the legislator, who "by laws and forms of government . . . tries to perfect nations and their happiness," was beholden to the physician as an indispensable source of knowledge. He "must proceed, if one can use such an expression, with the picture of man in hand," and "as the physical part of it forms the fundamental outline, the healing art, which illuminates and completes that part" will shed necessary light upon the science of governing.[44] For Alibert, too, the fact that man was "a soul and body united by a reciprocal linkage" – and hence was affected morally, emo-

---

[42] *Rapport des commissaires chargés par le Roi de l'examen du magnétisme animal* (Paris, 1784), pp. 43–45. The commission was composed of four physicians of the Paris faculty and five nonmedical members of the Academy of Sciences.

[43] Ibid., p. 44.

[44] Cabanis, *Coup d'oeil, O.P.,* Vol. 2, p. 77; see also p. 210.

tionally, and physically by political arrangements – meant that it fell to the physician to advise the state about whether proposed legislation would conduce to the health and well-being of the population.[45] And if, within this psychophysiological nexus, the political necessarily implicated the medical, statesmen had no reason to fret about their involvement with the healing art. For as Cabanis demonstrated at length, medicine was "founded on a solid [philosophical] base"; it could dispense with dubious final causes and rely only on "facts." "Thus, then," he concluded this approving assessment of medicine's epistemological status, "the healing art merits the attention of any government which is a friend of mankind."[46] To lean upon it was, in other words, only to rest upon the stability of truth.

Specialization

"Anthropological" speculation in medical theory and specialization in medical practice, though in some ways antithetical impulses – the one all-inclusive, the other narrowing – collaborated in the emergence of psychiatry. The first decisively claimed the territory of the mental life for medicine and gave it unprecedented theoretical prominence; the second would eventually make it possible for a physician to concentrate on mental disorders full-time and to the virtual exclusion of other medical concerns. That little exclusive or even focused medical attention had been devoted to the subject of madness by the middle of the eighteenth century is implicit in the wry comments of the *Encyclopédie* article "Folie": "This malady of the mind is so well-known by everyone that, even among the most famous nosographers, no one has believed himself obliged to give a precise idea or a really distinct definition of it; nowhere [in the literature] is it expressly discussed."[47] And the medical men who gave such laudable treatment to the insane in the Hôtel-Dieu of Paris did so on a part-time basis: All the physicians attached to that vast facility rotated among its departments at two-month intervals.[48]

Medical specialization had already been articulated as a concept in the French medical community by the eighteenth century, although it was not yet called by that name. Not until the 1830s and 1840s did Frenchmen speak of "embracing" a "specialty" (*spécialité*) or call the person who did so an *homme spécial*.[49] To call him a *spécialiste* was also possible by this time, but that term still had an awkward, novel ring

---

[45] See J.-L. Alibert, "De l'influence des causes politiques sur les maladies et la constitution de l'homme," *Magasin encyclopédique* 5 (1795): 298–305, esp. 298–301, 303.

[46] Cabanis, *Coup d'oeil*, *O.P.*, Vol. 2, pp. 72–75.

[47] *Encyclopédie*, Vol. 14, p. 843.

[48] "Mémoire lu par des médecins du grand hospice de l'humanité . . . ," esp. p. 6.

[49] Francis Wey, *Remarques sur la langue française au XIXe siècle* (Paris: Firmin Didot, 1845), pp. 255–57.

and was less frequently heard.[50] In this instance the appearance of the words accurately reflected the appearance of the thing: Medical specialization did not become a well-established phenomenon in France until the 1830s and 1840s. But at least a century before, referred to by various descriptive phrases such as "obliging physicians to cultivate specially a small number of diseases,"[51] it had been regarded by some as a desideratum. Such specialization of function within medicine was, it should be stressed, fundamentally different from the tripartite division of the healing art into medicine, surgery, and pharmacy which already obtained during the Old Regime. This latter division assumed a hierarchical superiority for medicine, as a liberal art marshaling knowledge, over the other two, as merely mechanical arts. Modern medical specialization would, by contrast, assume intellectual parity among the specialties.[52]

Specialization within medicine, its eighteenth-century advocates believed, would conduce to the improvement of medical care and eventually to the scientific progress of medicine. The Lyonnais physician Gilibert presented the full argument in 1772. "However vast and extensive the mind of man, it loses its force in proportion as it multiplies the objects to which it attends." Thus, if physicians would renounce their pretensions to "universality of practice" and confine themselves to a small number of diseases, "their method would always be sound, they would acquire that penetrating glance, that instinct so precious to all artists." Insistence upon universal practice, on the other hand, left practitioners "devoid of the factual principles that can guide them" and consigned them to adherence to blind "routine"; thus they became a "scourge" to their countrymen.[53] On much the same grounds, Diderot, in a letter of 1748, applauded certain tendencies he observed in surgical practice and predicted analogous developments in medicine:

> The surgeons, trained in the common principles of surgery, have distributed the various operations amongst themselves, and the operations are the better for it. The physicians, armed with the fundamental maxims of the healing art, will divide the various diseases amongst themselves. Each will master one branch of medicine; and when this science undergoes in Paris the same number of divisions as in Peking, we will be better served by it.[54]

---

[50] See Jean Raimond (pseudonym for Amédée Latour), feuilleton in *Union médicale*, March 14, 1848, p. 125, who takes credit for introducing the neologism *spécialiste*.

[51] J.-E. Gilibert, *L'anarchie médicinale, ou la médecine considerée comme nuisible à la société* (Neuchatel, 1772), Vol. 3, p. 200.

[52] On this point see the excellent article of Toby Gelfand, "The Origins of a Modern Concept of Medical Specialization: John Morgan's *Discourse* of 1765," *Bull. Hist. Med.* 50 (1976): esp. 512–15.

[53] Gilibert, *Anarchie médicinale*, Vol. 3, pp. 220, 224–25.

[54] Letter to M. De Morand, maître en chirurgie, December 16, 1748, in Denis Diderot, *Correspondance*, ed. G. Roth (Paris: Minuit, 1955), Vol. 1, pp. 68–69.

This program for medical specialization was put forth in advance of actual structural changes in the way medical work was carried on, although Diderot does note and draw inspiration from rudimentary manifestations of *surgical* specialization. Where, apart from surgery, did the idea come from?

Very probably, it came from the example of craft industry,[55] where specialization of function in the production of commodities had evolved naturally and, in the early eighteenth century, was raised to a theoretical plane and converted by philosophically minded observers into a recommended principle of industrial organization and a key to both material and intellectual progress. This dual trend – of spontaneous economic developments coupled with a philosophical gloss on them – was well under way before Adam Smith labeled the principle "division of labor," giving it canonical status.[56] In his *Encyclopédie*, Diderot was already a great advocate of the as yet unnamed principle. At about the same time that he wrote in praise of a would-be medical specialization, he wrote of the mechanical arts:

> The speed of work and the perfection of the result depend entirely on the number of workers assembled. When an item is manufactured in large quantities, each operation occupies a different man. Such a worker does and will do during his lifetime only a simple and unique thing; another one, another thing: whence it comes to pass that each thing is well and properly executed and that the best wrought product is also the cheapest.[57]

And he furthermore specified division of intellectual labor as the overriding principle in the compilation of the *Encyclopédie* (that project could "never be brought to completion without the cooperation of a large number of men endowed with special talents"), contrasting this procedure to the retrograde way the French Academy went about compiling its dictionary by assuming that all academicians possessed the same, universal knowledge of things.[58] By the mid-eighteenth century, then, the virtues of specialization were well appreciated, and it was only logical to want the same arrangement extended to the healing art. Occasionally, arguments for specialization in medicine were made by explicit reference to the obviously beneficial use of that practice in craft production. Having a doctor who ministered to any and all diseases, wrote the Abbé de Saint Pierre in 1725, was like having but a single

---

[55] This suggestion is made in Gelfand, "Origins of Modern Medical Specialization."

[56] The Cannan edition of *Wealth of Nations,* Book 1, Ch. 1, notes that Smith was probably the first to use the phrase "division of labor" but that the component elements of the concept were already present in Mandeville's *Fable of the Bees* (1714).

[57] "Art," *Encyclopédie,* Vol. 3, p. 481.

[58] "Encyclopédie," *Encyclopédie,* Vol. 12, p. 342.

worker on wood who performed by turns as a carpenter, joiner, cooper, and wheelwright.[59]

No smooth and easy victory was to be had for medical specialization. Clear perils attached to its advocacy and affected the way the principle was represented. In the first place, the craft analogy could not be pressed too far or taken too literally, for eighteenth-century medicine regarded itself most emphatically as a liberal and not a mechanical art. Advocates of medical specialization needed to find a way to capitalize upon the positive and progressive attributes of craft specialization while avoiding the implication that medicine itself was a craft. Second, the eighteenth-century medical world was, in fact, already flooded with "specialists"; but these were charlatanistic, not official accredited practitioners. Itinerant oculists and "cataract couchers," lithotomists (who "cut for the stone" in the urinary bladder), hernia operators – all hawking their services in town and countryside – were familiar figures in early modern Europe. The trade in these selected procedures had fallen to them because the procedures were dangerous and seldom successful, and hence regular surgeons, chary of their reputations, deliberately excluded them from their repertory. These charlatan-specialists, branded "ignorant laborers and rustics," were disdained and ostracized by the official medical community.[60] Together with other unlicensed medical practitioners, they came to be known as "empirics" by their detractors, precisely to underscore the improper disjunction between their practical skills and any theoretical considerations. This usage, which began in the seventeenth century, betrayed the assumption of the seventeenth-century *esprit de système:* that a true medical theory must be derived speculatively, that induction from accumulated empirical data was procedurally incorrect.[61]

This deeply ingrained association of medical specialization with quackery made it highly suspect to many eighteenth-century medical men. Hence the insistence of its advocates that the specialists they envisioned would be not throwbacks to a pretheoretical state but rather the more sophisticated and effective products of a full medical education: The distinction between the "new" specialist and the atheoretical charlatan had to be drawn with utmost clarity. Insisting upon a full

---

[59] "Mémoire pour perfectionner la médecine," *Mémoires pour l'histoire des sciences et des beaux-arts, ou Journal de Trévoux* (May 1725): esp. 860–61.

[60] George Rosen, *The Specialization of Medicine* (New York: Froben, 1944), p. 50, quotes the phrase from a seventeenth-century professor at the Montpellier Faculty of Medicine.

[61] Thus the surgeon and physiocrat Quesnay, arguing for an inductive method in surgery, felt obliged to point out that this popular usage of "empiricism" was based on a misunderstanding of the original ancient term, which had made observation and experience the source but not the sum total of all knowledge. *Recherches critiques et historiques sur l'origine, sur les divers états et sur les progrès de la chirurgie en France* (Paris: Osmont, 1744), p. 38 and p. 38 note b.

medical education and a thorough immersion in medical theory as prerequisites to specialization also neutralized the negative rhetorical effect of the analogy between craft and medical specialization. Thus Tenon, discussing care for the "curable blind" in his hypothetical renovated Paris hospital system, specified "a skillful Parisian surgeon versed in the study of anatomy, surgery, and medicine as well as optics," for, he noted, "the diseases of the eye do not proceed simply from local causes." The trustworthy special practitioner that Tenon had in mind was fundamentally different from an empiric: "Now never will those who are called oculist-experts, confined to the exclusive study of the eye," be able to "advance this essential part of the art."[62] Similarly, in the passage from his 1748 letter cited above, Diderot stipulated that the new medical specialists come "armed with the fundamental maxims of the healing art"; and the 1791 report of the Talleyrand committee on public instruction to the National Assembly, enumerating the benefits of a proposed measure situating medical schools in hospitals, noted that "in that way those [students] headed especially for one of the branches of the medical art will nonetheless be sufficiently instructed in all."[63]

Division of labor in craft production had occurred spontaneously. But the eighteenth-century French advocates of medical specialization did not always expect the same for it. At least one expressed the hope that "in a century in which enlightened princes never cease working for the destruction of obstacles to the happiness of peoples," the state could be counted upon to introduce medical specialization; and he cited in support of this view the state's recent role as patron in the creation of a serious veterinary medicine.[64]

Was rational-philosophic advocacy of medical specialization instrumental in achieving that result? Probably it exerted a positive influence; for as we will see, the birth of specialties in France was often monitored at the institutional level, and hence beliefs and values shaped the outcome. But other forces acting indirectly were perhaps equally important. On the intellectual level, a general shift in the theory of pathology conduced to specialization: When humoral theory was discredited in the late eighteenth century (although it lingered on among practitioners for more than a generation),[65] diseases ceased to be humo-

---

[62] *Mémoires sur les hôpitaux*, p. 15.

[63] A. de Beauchamp, ed., *Enquêtes et documents relatifs à l'enseignement supérieur*, Vol. 28 (Paris: Impr. nationale, 1888), p. 192.

[64] Gilibert, *Anarchie médicinale*, Vol. 3, p. 237. On the state's initiatives in the 1760s with respect to veterinary medicine, see Charles C. Gillispie, *Science and Polity in France at the End of the Old Regime* (Princeton, N.J.: Princeton University Press, 1981), pp. 25–26.

[65] See the retrospective account of this very gradual shift by a physician who lived through it. I. Bricheteau, *Discours sur Philippe Pinel, son école et l'influence qu'elle a exercée en médecine* (Paris: Impr. de C.L.F. Panckoucke, 1828), pp. 8–9.

ral events infusing the entire body. The new, early nineteenth-century conception of disease as a localized organic lesion, systematically corre-lated with a group of reported symptoms and observable signs, made the concentration of different doctors on different organs and organ systems a logical turn of events. "Every organ has its priest," as a German physician described the situation of medical specialization in Paris in the 1840s.[66] (It is a reflection of the humoral concept of pathol-ogy that eighteenth-century advocates of medical specialization spoke of dividing up diseases rather than organ systems.)

A second, even less direct force was the demographic and economic one: Only fairly large urban centers can support specialized medicine – as both the Abbé de Saint Pierre and Gilibert realized. (Gilibert, how-ever, included among the explanations of this phenomenon the then-accepted fact that peasants had little need of specialized care because their diseases, reflecting the simplicity of their lifestyle, were far less numerous and varied, indeed amounted to only "one-twentieth" of those afflicting city-dwellers.)[67] Hence it is hardly surprising that Paris became the chief locus of medical specialization, a process that seems to have begun there before the Revolution. One bureaucratic official, the subdelegate of Saumur, replying in 1786 to a questionnaire circu-lated by the Royal Society of Medicine about local medical personnel, said of one of the town's five physicians: "There is no disease that he treats especially; the same is true of his four colleagues; in this respect things in the provinces are not the way they are in Paris."[68] And Tenon's calculations about the four hospitals that would replace the Hôtel-Dieu indicate how the sheer size of the Paris population prompted institutional specialization as a rational response to practical problems: "This formation was decided upon in order to avoid having to build four hospitals with facilities for pregnant women, four with facilities for lunatics, four with facilities for fetid diseases, and four with facilities for contagious diseases."[69]

Some notion of the attitude of official medicine toward specialization at the very end of the eighteenth century can be gleaned from the case of Dr. Forlenze, *médecin oculiste*.[70] Forlenze was not an empiric, but a licensed medical practitioner who specialized in diseases of the eye; he had, as he described it, "given all his time to the study and practice of

---

[66] Quoted in Erwin H. Acknerknecht, *Medicine at the Paris Hospital, 1794–1848* (Balti-more: Johns Hopkins University Press, 1967), p. 163.

[67] Gilibert, *Anarchie médicinale*, Vol. 3, p. 236; Sainte Pierre, "Mémoire pour perfection-ner la médecine," pp. 860–61.

[68] Quoted in François Lebrun, *Les hommes et la mort en Anjou aux 17e et 18e siècles* (Paris and The Hague: Mouton, 1971), p. 224 n104.

[69] *Mémoires sur les hôpitaux*, p. xl.

[70] See AN: F¹⁵ 230. The whole carton is devoted to what the archivist has called "Affaire du Dr Forlenze, médecin oculiste," and it carries the story of his relationship with the government to 1823.

that branch of the healing art." In the Year VII, no doubt encouraged by the general fluidity of laissez-faire Revolutionary medicine and hoping to institutionalize that "branch of the healing art" in which he was skilled, Forlenze submitted to the minister of the interior a proposal for the "establishment of a hospice which would be exclusively devoted to the diseases of the eye"; he also proposed that he be named director of the hospice. (Forlenze had already received a similar though considerably smaller favor from the government in recognition of his specialty: permission from the minister of war "to treat diseases of the eye exclusively" in the infirmary of the Hôtel des Invalides.) The minister of the interior forwarded the proposal to the Ecole de médecine de Paris for an expert opinion; and a commission deputized to consider the matter prepared a report, written and signed by Michel-Augustin Thouret, the director of the school.[71]

The Thouret report reveals that official Paris medicine had at this date no principled hostility to specialization; but neither did it have an automatic predisposition in its favor. Rather, the burden of proof seems to have fallen upon each would-be specialty to satisfy the triple criterion of "utility . . . for the treatment of patients, for the instruction of students, and for the progress of the art." Applying this criterion, the Thouret commission found Forlenze's projected hospice lacking in all respects. Indigents suffering from eye disease, they said, were already adequately treated in existing hospices; and eye operations of the most advanced sort were already regularly performed in the presence of students in the teaching hospitals of Paris. Most important, nothing about a facility devoted exclusively to eye diseases seemed conducive to medical progress. In the first place, it was "generally recognized that most of the diseases which affect the organ of sight do not proceed only from local causes, or those residing in that organ; they are often the result of prior, internal diseases which must first be methodically treated if one wishes to obtain more than a superficial cure." In voicing this objection, which parallels so closely Tenon's ruminations on oculists more than a decade earlier, Thouret and his commission seem to have shared the traditional medical prejudice against specialists-as-empirics; for they noted that care of the diseases of the eye was to be entrusted by preference to "those who have studied the healing art in its plenitude rather than those who have voluntarily confined themselves to the exercise of the occupation of oculist." They even went on, uncharacteristically, to invoke Old Regime precedent on this point. The 1768 statutes of the College of Surgery had made no mention of the

---

[71] Under the Old Regime, Thouret had been a founding member of the Royal Society of Medicine and one of the doctors appointed to help Jean Colombier carry out his mission as inspector-general of the hospitals of the realm. This clear continuity of the personnel of Old Regime statist medicine into the Revolution will be discussed further in Chapter 3.

admission of oculists because "it was recognized that it is rather by the reasoned application of the true principles of the art to particular cases than by a local treatment that one can cure the diseases of the eye."

But other objections to Forlenze's project were articulated as well, and they indicate the factors that the Thouret commission would have regarded as justifying a specialized medical institution and a delineated specialty. "Note that there is no proposal here for a new method to follow, or for procedures, until now unknown, to put into effect," chides the report. And it concludes by observing that a special institution of the type that Forlenze has suggested might have had "real utility" if it were "intended for the observation of some diseases less well known than those of the eye." By inference, then, institutionalized specialization was warranted by a new method of treatment or by a relatively unexplored subject area, by the supposition that, through either of these novelties, it would bring about "progress that the [medical] art is susceptible of making and has not yet made at all."[72] The first of these implicit criteria suggests that Thouret had an intuitive notion of what Thomas Kuhn calls a "paradigm." Thouret's "new method" is like Kuhn's paradigmatic "puzzle solution . . . sufficiently unprecedented to attract an enduring group of adherents away from competing modes of scientific activity" and thus to found a new scientific community and, in some cases, a new scientific specialty.[73] Taken together, these two implicit criteria help to explain the more positive and facilitating attitude of official Paris medicine toward the beginnings of psychiatric specialization, which occurred at about the same date. For not only was that subject area still virtually unknown, but as we will see, a "new method" – a paradigm – would most definitely be put forth.

And what of Forlenze, *médecin oculiste*? His proposed hospice was quashed under the Consulate after Thouret's negative report, but he tirelessly continued his campaign for the recognition of his specialty. As he put it in the Year X, he was "submitting new proofs that the science of the oculist requires a full-time commitment from anyone who would ply it fruitfully." The minister of the interior continued to be the object of his solicitations, and he appealed both to the minister's

---

[72] AN: F^{15} 150. All of this paragraph as well as the information about Forlenze in the preceding paragraph have been drawn from Thouret, "Rapport sur l'établissment d'un hospice pour les maladies des yeux," 29 fructidor Year VII. The types of surgical procedures that Forlenze performed are indicated in his *Considérations sur l'opération de la pupille artificielle suivies de plusieurs observations relatives à quelques maladies graves de l'oeil* (Strasbourg: Levrault, Year XII/1805). That effective procedures of this sort had already been introduced in France before Forlenze is attested to in "Séance publique de l'école de médecine de Paris, 24 vendémiaire an X, Discours du Citoyen Sabatier . . . sur le perfectionnement de la médecine opératoire pendant le XVIIIe siècle," AN: AJ^{16} 6308, esp. pp. 2–3, 9, 14, 20–23.

[73] *The Structure of Scientific Revolutions*, 2d ed. (Chicago: University of Chicago Press, 1970), pp. 10, 175.

"generous sentiments" by conjuring up the plight of the indigent sick and to his calculative and prudential side with arguments drawn from health police: Blindness, Forlenze noted, was "onerous to the state," because having lost their sight, "the poor can no longer provide for themselves [and they] necessarily remain a burden to society."[74] After his defeat at the hands of the Thouret commission, Forlenze scaled down his request. He now desired only a place in the hospitals or "close to the government" where he could devote his practice full-time to the care of diseases of the eye. He petitioned with deed as well as word, taking circuit rides (*tournées*) into the provincial regions of France and performing free eye operations on the poor and on veterans. This philanthropic variation on the work pattern of the ambulant charlatan-specialist won him the tributes of many prefects and occasionally the title of departmental oculist.[75] By 1808, Forlenze had finally won his post. The Emperor Napoleon decreed him "*chirurgien oculiste* of the *lycées*, the civil hospices and all the charitable institutions of the departments of the Empire,"[76] and he continued his provincial *tournées*, now in his new official capacity. If this was hardly a decisive victory for a medical specialty, it was at least a step in that direction – and a reminder once again of the role of the state in medical developments in France. Perhaps equally significant was the degree to which Forlenze was able to convert what had once been an indisputably charlatanistic specialty into a legitimate one. Some decade and a half after the passage of the Law of 19 ventôse Year XI, he was responsible for initiating a government circular to the prefects urging a vigilant repression of empirics who, noted Forlenze, "seem to gravitate by preference to the diseases of the eye."[77]

The Forlenze of psychiatry was Philippe Pinel. Equipped with a "new method" to apply to an almost uncharted medical space, and well connected to the Revolutionary medical establishment, he would expend far less self-promotional effort, and meet with much greater success, than the stalwart oculist.

[74] AN: F^{15} 150, Letter of Forlenze to the minister of the interior, 9 fructidor Year X.
[75] Ibid., reports of the chief of the third division of the Ministry of the Interior, to the minister (28 vendémiaire Year X) and to the emperor (n.d.).
[76] Ibid., draft of imperial decree (n.d.).
[77] Archival sources cited in Matthew Ramsey, "Sous le régime de la législation de 1803: Trois enquêtes sur les charlatans au XIXe siècle," *Revue d'histoire moderne et contemporaine* 27 (1980): 494–95.

3

The transformation of charlatanism, or the moral treatment

A request to the office of the minister of the interior in 1810 reveals the importance, in Napoleonic bureaucratic circles, of a particular book. The prefect of the department of the Meurthe wrote:

> There exists in my Department, about three kilometers from the departmental capital, an institution called Maréville devoted exclusively to the reception of the insane (*les insensés*). I have already had occasion to communicate with your Ministry about its administration and the condition of its buildings. . . . The regimen of this interesting establishment has attracted my special concern, and I have recognized that, while the inmates would be considered very well treated if Maréville were only a simple hospice, the establishment leaves something to be desired with respect to its special aim – which is to succeed, while it is still possible, in restoring the mental faculties of the insane. . . . I thought, Sir, that . . . the book which indicates the method for the treatment of the insane followed by Doctor *Pinel* would provide me with trustworthy information. . . . I beg you to be so kind as to have the book sent to me. I will hasten to give an account of the arrangements that my reading of it leads me to adopt.[1]

At about the same time, a former cavalry officer in the Napoleonic army, enrolled at the state veterinary school at Alfort for a course in "rural economy" to help him prepare for an administrative career, decided to "instruct myself on the administration of public institutions" by visiting those in the vicinity. Among them was an establishment for the insane about which he prepared an extensive memoir, evaluating it in terms of the criteria set forth in "the treatise on insanity of Monsieur Pinel."[2] Nor was the appeal of the book confined to those with medical-bureaucratic interests. The young novelist-in-the-making Stendhal, always eager for a theoretical framework to guide his native insights into the human psyche, presented himself at the Paris Medical School one morning in 1805 "in order to read the *Aliénation mentale* of Pinel"; a year later, trying

---

[1] AN: F^{15} 2603, letter of October 18, 1810; *Pinel* underlined in the original.

[2] Archives de Paris et de l'ancien département de la Seine: D3AZ 212, "Notice sur l'établissement consacré au traitement de l'aliénation mentale établi à Charenton, près Paris," by H. de Colins, dated June 16, 1812, ms. pp. 1–5.

to acquire the book for his personal library, he was informed that the first and only printing was "entirely sold out."[3]

The book in question was Dr. Philippe Pinel's *Traité médico-philosophique sur l'aliénation mentale, ou la manie*, first published in 1801 and with a second, expanded edition appearing in 1809. It represented the most up-to-date and complete account of its subject to appear in France; and unlike the only text with which it can be meaningfully compared, the 1785 *Instruction* of Colombier and Doublet, it did not merely collect and codify accepted medical wisdom on the treatment of insanity but recommended a fundamental innovation: the "moral treatment" (*traitement moral*). Cursorily defined – the definition will be fleshed out in the course of this chapter – the moral treatment meant the use for the cure of insanity of methods that engaged or operated directly upon the intellect and emotions, as opposed to the traditional methods of bleedings and purgings applied directly to the lunatic's body. While it did not entail a total abandonment of the old repertory of physical remedies, it did entail an acknowledgment of their grave insufficiency.

Pinel, it must be stressed, never claimed to be the absolute creator of the moral treatment. From his earliest published references to it, which predate the Revolution, he acknowledged the derivative nature of the concept. He routinely assigned its distant origins to the ancients, citing the precepts of Celsus and Caelius Aurelanius; and he invariably noted its use among English practitioners of his own day, advising that they be emulated on that account. Particularly conspicuous among Pinel's Englishmen was Francis Willis, who during the period 1788–89 assumed the weighty responsibility of treating King George III's madness and who thus brought *moyens moraux* to widespread public attention.[4] One of Pinel's disciples added to this genealogy Samuel Richardson's novel *Sir Charles Grandison* (1753–54; French translation 1755–56), arguing that it had done much to propagate the idea of the moral treatment among "all classes of society."[5] When Richardson's fictional Ital-

---

[3] The quotes are from Stendhal's journal of 1805, cited in Jules C. Alciatore, "Stendhal et Pinel," *Modern Philology* 45 (1947): 118; and from a letter he received in 1806, cited in V. Del Litto, *La vie intellectuelle de Stendhal* (Paris: Presses universitaires de France, 1959), p. 289 n76.

[4] Pinel, "Observations sur le régime moral qui est le plus propre à rétablir dans certains cas la raison égarée des maniaques," *Gazette de santé*, 1789, no. 4: 13–15. The article mentions Willis. English parliamentary committees summoned Willis and others who treated George III during his bout with insanity to testify on "the state of His Majesty's health"; these parliamentary depositions were often reprinted in cheap popular editions – hence the particularly widespread knowledge of Willis's methods. See Richard Hunter and Ida Macalpine, eds., *Three Hundred Years of Psychiatry, 1535–1860* (London: Oxford University Press, 1963), p. 509.

[5] Moreau de la Sarthe, "Médecine mentale," *Encyclopédie méthodique*, Series: Medicine, Vol. 9 (1816), p. 138.

ian aristocrat Clementina succumbs to madness and is bled with leeches to no avail by local medical men, two English physicians "eminent for their knowledge of disorders of the head" are summoned, with the rationale that "the English physicians [are] more skillful than those of any other country in the management of persons afflicted with such maladies"; and "partly in pursuance of [their] advice," a new and ultimately successful course of "sooth[ing] and humour[ing] the Lady Clementina" is embarked upon.[6] In short, the proposition that insanity might require "moral" rather than physical treatment had begun to gain currency in the second half of the eighteenth century, and Pinel's *lack* of priority in the matter was never disputed. What Pinel did claim for himself was that he was the first to explicate the moral treatment fully: One combed the English literature in vain, he said, for a detailed description of the technique sufficient to guide the novice; the English "rivals" perversely touted it while keeping it, for all practical purposes, "impenetrably veiled."[7] He also claimed that he was the first to place the technique on a scientific footing.

Pinel's rendition of the moral treatment functioned as the originative psychiatric paradigm[8] – that is, as the puzzle-solution around which a community of like-minded medical men specializing in insanity first formed in France. It was the crucial additional element enabling the foundations of psychiatry discussed in the previous chapter to be built upon, focusing and energizing the whole venture. At least as early as 1806, Pinel began to recognize this development, then still in its infancy; he alluded to the existence of a new specialty, calling it "the medicine which has for its object the lesions of the functions of the understanding."[9] And in 1805 one of his students, in a dissertation on the causes and cure of insanity, also acknowledged the emergent spe-

---

6   Samuel Richardson, *The History of Sir Charles Grandison,* ed. Jocelyn Harris (London: Oxford University Press, 1972), Vol. 2, pp. 189–91, 193–94, 313, 480. Richardson was familiar with the English medical literature of his day concerning madness; see the editor's note to *Grandison,* Vol. 2, p. 673.

7   Pinel, "Observations sur le régime moral," p. 13; "Recherches et observations sur le traitement moral," (henceforth R & O), *M.S.M.E.* 2 (Year VII): 215–55, esp. 216.

8   A word about the loose and selective nature of my borrowing from Kuhn is in order. While I use the term "paradigm" throughout this book to refer to the moral treatment and its key role in the formation of the French psychiatric specialty, I have set aside the full Kuhnian model of scientific change in which that term figures. The ambiguities lodged in the term, as Kuhn employed it, are well suited to my purposes. A paradigm is both theory and technique; and even more important here, its meaning emphasizes the interpenetration of text and context. As a cognitive text, a paradigm offers a worked-out solution to a particular scientific problem; as a social-normative context, it provides a basis for the common loyalty and activity of the professional community that organizes around it. I could find no satisfactory synonym for the multilevel and evocative "paradigm."

9   See his letter of 11 nivôse Year XIV in E. Szapiro, "Pinel et Esquirol: Quelques commentaires sur les débuts d'une amitié" *Ann. m.-p.* 134 (June 1976): 61.

cialty, making more explicit its connection to its paradigm. Many men, he said, recoiled from the extensive contact with lunatics required by Pinel's moral treatment; and thus they revealed themselves as temperamentally unsuited to pursue the medical study of madness, "to cultivate this branch of the healing art."[10] In light of the founding role played by the moral treatment and the shaping influence it continued to exert, it is essential to understand the precise content of the paradigm, how it was derived, and how it was legitimated. A selective narrative of the career of the founder himself will open the way.

Philippe Pinel: a medical career in political context

Born in a small town in Languedoc in 1745, the son and nephew of physicians, Philippe Pinel received a degree from the faculty of medicine in Toulouse. But he was disappointed with the quality of his medical education – the "knowledge required for promotion to the doctorate was scant," he later recalled – and to satisfy his intellectual appetite spent an additional four years studying at the Faculty of Medicine of Montpellier. As he became increasingly absorbed in such avantgarde lines of inquiry as the applications of mathematics and the physical sciences to medicine and the methodological standards that those more advanced sciences set for his chosen field, he felt himself called to Paris; for, he remembered musing, "could one follow the progress [of medicine] anywhere but in the capital, where instruction in it is so superior?"[11]

The intellectually ambitious but personally shy provincial arrived in Paris in 1778, equipped only with a Toulouse medical degree which had no validity in his new place of residence. He soon met with distressing rebuffs at the hands of the Paris Faculty of Medicine: He twice failed in the competition for the prix de Diest, a scholarship for poor students which would have enabled him to complete free of charge the requisite training at the Paris faculty for medical certification in the capital and admission into the Regency. In the second of these competitions, held in 1784, the jury's verdict stressed Pinel's "painful" mediocrity in all areas of medical knowledge – an assessment so incompatible with everything that is known about Pinel's intellectual accomplishments that it is impossible not to suspect an ulterior motive. The men of the faculty may well have been punishing Pinel for his friendship with two prominent members of the Royal Society of Medicine – Thouret and the persona

[10] E. Esquirol, *Des passions considerées comme causes, symptômes et moyens curatifs de l'aliénation mentale* (Paris: Thèse de médecine, Year XIV/1805), p. 7.

[11] See Pinel's autobiographical reminiscences in "Analyse appliquée à la médecine," *Dict. des sci. med.*, Vol. 2, pp. 26–27.

non grata Fourcroy. In any case, Pinel found his experience with the faculty so profoundly depressing that he contemplated emigration to America.[12] His earliest first-hand impressions of the Paris medical community – "I see in those who exercise this respectable profession [in Paris] only baseness and intrigues," he wrote home to his brother[13] – had been amply confirmed.

Pinel's disillusionment with official medicine in the capital city where he had expected so much from it – a disillusionment which focused on its elitist and exclusive professional structure – is comparable to the experience of other members of his generational cohort. The aspiring young philosophes who came to the capital from the provinces in the 1770s and 1780s, for example, found that the much-vaunted "republic of letters" was a closed shop; and they responded to this discovery by becoming bitter Grub Street writers whose pre-Revolutionary productions were radically populist in outlook.[14] For his part, Pinel embraced a kind of medical populism, although as will be discussed later, he prudently gave expression to it only after the outbreak of the Revolution.

Employment as a medical journalist – in 1784 he was made editor of the *Gazette de santé*, a four-page weekly not quite of Grub Street calibre but many notches below the prestigious *Journal de médecine* – enabled Pinel to earn a satisfactory living and ended his ruminations about quitting his native country.[15] At about the same time, he began to develop an intense interest in the study of mental illness. The incentive was a personal one: A friend had developed a "nervous melancholy" that had "degenerated into mania." Pinel must have strongly identified with this young man, fourteen years his junior, whom he described as a provincial "of a gentle and timid character" who had "settled in Paris in order to devote himself to science." The friend easily completed the usual course of legal study and was admitted to the bar, but like Pinel, he could not rest with ordinary professional achievement: "The desire to distinguish himself and to acquire knowledge prompted him to seek out . . . the most efficacious means of making rapid progress." Under the sway of this ambition, he became eccentric, withdrawing into solitude and adopting a vegetarian diet in the belief that meat eating dulled the brain. Pinel stood by helplessly – "I was reduced to the role of spectator" – as his friend's adherence to this austere regimen became

[12] P. Chabbert, "Philippe Pinel à Paris (jusqu'à sa nomination à Bicêtre)," *Comptes rendus du XIXe Congrès international de l'histoire de la médecine* (Basel and New York: S. Karger, 1966), pp. 590–92.

[13] Letter of December 8, 1778, in Casimir Pinel, "Lettres de Pinel précédées d'une notice plus étendue sur sa vie," *Gaz. hebd. de med.* (June 17, 1859): 374.

[14] On this group, see Robert Darnton, "The High Enlightenment and the Low-Life of Literature in Pre-Revolutionary France," *Past and Present* (May 1971): 81–115.

[15] Chabbert, "Pinel à Paris," p. 592.

unshakable, his initial enthusiasm about his brilliant professional prospects turned into despair, and his agitation increased. Eventually there was nothing for Pinel to do but bring him to the lunatic ward of the Hôtel-Dieu, where a treatment consisting of baths and restorative nourishment seemed to calm him. But before the treatment was completed, the lawyer's anxious parents insisted that he return home to his village, where, immediately falling into despondency, he fled his surveillants and wandered into the woods. Some days later he was found dead, Plato's dialogue on the immortality of the soul poignantly clutched in his hands.[16]

The tragedy – and the gross mismanagement of the ailment, which suggested that the tragedy was unnecessary – seems to have haunted Pinel. It led him to seek employment at one of the best-known private sanatoria in Paris for the treatment of insanity, the *maison de santé* on the rue de Charonne, owned by Belhomme, a former cabinetmaker. Pinel became the physician of the establishment, a technically irregular status because he had no Parisian medical credentials. Despite his contempt for the mercenary Belhomme (whom he described as having a "marked indifference . . . to the cure of rich patients, or rather an unequivocal desire to see the remedies [employed on them] fail"),[17] he remained there for the five years preceding the Revolution, gathering observations on insanity and beginning to formulate his views on its nature and treatment.[18]

When the Revolution broke out, Pinel was eminently well situated to reap professional benefit from it. In addition to his ties with members of the Royal Society of Medicine, he was a friend of Cabanis, under whose sponsorship he had become a habitué of the "enlightened" salon of Madame Helvétius at Auteuil and hence a member of the circle of intellectuals later known as the Idéologues. His pro-Revolutionary sentiments were patent: In 1790 he became an *officier municipal* of Paris; in 1795 he hailed the birth of his first son in a personal letter by calling him "a little republican."[19] With the coming of the Revolution and the insistence that the "medical constitution" of France be overhauled, the Paris Faculty of Medicine, always unreceptive to Pinel, declined in

---

[16] The case is recounted in "Observation sur une melancolie nerveuse dégénerée en manie," *Gazette de santé*, 1786, no. 9: 34–35.

[17] R & O, pp. 218–19.

[18] Chabbert, "Pinel à Paris," p. 594. Pinel was invited to present a preliminary paper on this subject before the Royal Society of Medicine in 1788, and it was, he recalled, "very well received," though never published. R & O, p. 218 n1.

[19] Chabbert, "Pinel à Paris," p. 590. Pinel's letter to his brother dated November 7, 1792, in *Gaz. hebd. de med.* (September 24, 1858): 669, recounts his political activity of 1789, also noting that he was temperamentally ill-suited to the *tourbillon* of political life and withdrew after a year. The birth announcement is in a letter to his brother dated 26 messidor Year III quoted in René Semelaigne, *Aliénistes et philanthropes: Les Pinel et les Tuke* (Paris: Steinheil, 1912), p. 218.

influence, and decision-making power in medical affairs passed to "new men," often affiliated with the Royal Society of Medicine – and often Pinel's friends. Thouret became an advisor to the legislative Comité de mendicité appointed in 1790 to make recommendations about public institutions for the indigent and infirm; a new commission to administer the Paris hospitals, appointed by the municipality in 1791 after the resignation of the directors of the old Hôtel-Dieu and *hôpital-général*, included Thouret and Cabanis; and when the opening of the Ecole de médecine de Paris to replace the defunct faculty was decreed in 1794, Fourcroy headed the committee in charge of finding personnel, and Thouret emerged as the permanent dean.[20]

Some of these "new men" had already served as physician–bureaucrats under the Old Regime. Furthermore, the Maison du Roi, active in health affairs under the Old Regime, survived the Revolution, being rechristened the Ministry of the Interior in 1790 and still numbering hospitals and public assistance among its responsibilities.[21] Thus it is hardly surprising that the bureaucratic concern of the 1780s about rehabilitative institutions for the insane was carried directly into the revolutionary period. The very first of the many visits to public institutions made by the Comité de mendicité was to Bicêtre (Thouret was present); and when the Comité came to draw up its recommendations, they included, in the specializing spirit of Tenon, the "installation of two hospitals devoted to the cure of madness, until now treated only at the Hôtel-Dieu." In one of these projected hospitals, the committee advised additional treatment for those who had previously been labeled "incurable" and consigned to the *hôpital-général*.[22] The Paris municipality, surveying its public institutions at the same time as the national government was doing so, recorded testimony from the administrators of Bicêtre that also suggested the desirability of taking therapeutic initiatives with the allegedly incurable insane. No, the mayor's lieutenant for hospitals was told, there was no "curative method adopted for madness." "All the madmen sent to Bicêtre remain there *in statu quo* until it pleases nature to favor them." Still, about one-fifth of these inmates "annually recover their good sense and are returned to their families," and about three-fourths of these spontaneous cures came from the group which had undergone prior, unsuccessful treatment at the Hôtel-Dieu.[23]

[20] D. B. Weiner, "Le droit de l'homme à la santé – une belle idée devant l'Assemblée constituante, 1790–91," *Clio medica* 5 (1970): 211; Jean Imbert, *Le droit hospitalier de la Révolution et de l'Empire* (Paris: Sirey, 1954), p. 35 and p. 35 n111; and David M. Vess, *Medical Revolution in France, 1789–1796* (Gainesville: University Presses of Florida, 1975), pp. 169–72.

[21] See Clive H. Church, *Revolution and Red Tape: The French Ministerial Bureaucracy, 1770–1850* (Oxford: Clarendon Press, 1981), pp. 54–55, 157, 159.

[22] Alexandre Tuetey, ed., *L'assistance publique à Paris pendant la Révolution: Documents inédits*, Vol. 1 (Paris: Impr. nationale, 1895), pp. ii–iii, xv.

[23] Ibid., p. 237.

The outcome of these overlapping investigations was the decision by the new Paris hospital commission (which included Thouret and Cabanis) to "medicalize" the section for the insane at Bicêtre by appointing a physician-in-chief for the entire institution.[24] In 1793 the commission chose Pinel, who with his prior experience at the *maison* Belhomme (which he had recently brought to public notice in an article in the medical journal edited by Fourcroy),[25] his Idéologue views, and his ties to Thouret and Cabanis, was clearly the man for the job.[26] Shortly thereafter, a second professional plum fell into Pinel's lap – a chair in hygiene at the newly formed Ecole de médecine de Paris, an appointment in which Fourcroy was certainly instrumental.[27] In 1795 Pinel was transferred from Bicêtre to its counterpart for women, the Salpêtrière. In 1802 the Salpêtrière, still primarily a depot for the inveterately insane, received an infusion of curable *folles* from the Hôtel-Dieu, a redistribution of population designed in part to enable Pinel, as it was announced, "to give new breadth to [his] researches . . . on insanity."[28] Later that month the Conseil général des hospices de Paris – just formed by Minister of the Interior Chaptal (Pinel's old friend from his Montpellier days) and including among its members the ubiquitous Thouret – gave additional support to the researches of "citizen Pinel." It authorized him to select two medical students from among the *externes* at the Salpêtrière to aid him in "the new study, with which he has been charged, of the madwomen of that *maison*," and to reward these assistants with extra pay.[29] The

---

[24] Before the Revolution, the section was an entirely nonmedical operation, directed by a lay "governor" and staffed by attendants responsible for cleaning, distributing food, and maintaining security; ibid., pp. 236–37.

[25] "Observations sur une espèce particulière de mélancolie qui conduit au suicide," *La Médecine éclairée par les sciences physiques* 1 (1791): 154–59, 199–201. Pinel bluntly referred to *Médecine éclairée* as Fourcroy's medical journal in *Traité médico-philosophique sur l'aliénation mentale, ou la manie*, 1st ed. (Paris: Richard, Caille et Ravier, Year IX/1801), p. 187n.

[26] On the role of the commission in naming Pinel to Bicêtre by decree of August 25, 1793, see Semelaigne, *Aliénistes et philanthropes*, p. 43. The historical record is riddled with contradictions about the precise date of Pinel's arrival at Bicêtre; see, e.g., Casimir Pinel, "Deux lettres de Pinel," *Gaz. hebd. de med.* (September 24, 1858): 667–68.

[27] See Vess, *Medical Revolution*, pp. 170, 172. Within a year, Pinel was moved to the chair of internal medicine, vacated by the initial appointee – none other than François Doublet, coauthor of the 1785 *Instruction*.

[28] The announcement was made to the assembled Paris Medical School; see AN: AJ[16] 6308, "Séance publique de l'Ecole de médecine de Paris du 5 brumaire an XI, Discours du citoyen Hallé," p. 25.

[29] See decree of the Conseil général des hospices, 21 brumaire Year XI, quoted in Mireille Wiriot, *L'enseignement clinique dans les hôpitaux de Paris entre 1794 et 1848* (Paris: Thèse de médecine, 1970), p. 67. On Chaptal's friendship with Pinel and the founding and membership of the Conseil général des hospices, see J.-A. Chaptal, *Mes souvenirs sur Napoléon* (Paris: Plon Nourrit, 1892), pp. 18–20, 62–63.

Revolution had indeed, as Pinel once gracefully understated it, "opened for me a freer career."[30]

Pinel and the "concierges": the origins of the moral treatment

In the late eighteenth century, medical writers occasionally acknowledged – or perhaps let slip – the virtual indistinguishability of medical therapeutics and quackery in the area of insanity: Charlatans[31] could be as effective as fully accredited physicians, if not more so, in treating difficult cases of madness. According to the *Encyclopédie* article, "Mania is one of those diseases with which the most skillful physicians ordinarily fail, while the charlatans, the persons with secrets (*gens à secret*), very often succeed." And, the Encyclopedist continues, "Felix Plater recounts having seen a quack (*empyrique*) who cured all maniacs by bleeding them up to seventy times a week. A horde of celebrated physicians (*praticiens*) assure us that they know of no remedy for mania as efficacious as that." Similarly, arguing for the use of hellebore on maniacs whose condition had proved resistant to other purgatives, the *Instruction* of Colombier and Doublet noted, "Some happy examples of the application of this remedy in desperate cases by [the] learned physician [Lorry], several other equally favorable attempts by means of this medicament in the hands of charlatans, are authentic and powerful facts which ought to persuade us to have recourse to it."[32] With Pinel, recognition of the efficacy of charlatanistic treatments of insanity not only continued but was taken further: Selected aspects of charlatanism were to be deliberately appropriated by official medicine and transformed by it – transformed rather more in status than in content.

In the introduction to the first edition of his *Traité*, Pinel explained that his key concept, the moral treatment, derived from charlatanistic practice. "Men who [are] strangers to the principles of medicine, guided only by sound judgment or some obscure tradition, have devoted themselves to the treatment of the insane, and they have effected a great many cures." These men were "concierges," superintendents of the insane whose caretaking function was diffused over the

---

[30] R & O, p. 219.

[31] Here, as elsewhere in this book, I am using the term "charlatan" as it was used by contemporaries. Although many historians of medicine now make an analytic distinction between the charlatan, who deliberately dupes the public for personal gain, and the respectable lay healer, no such strict distinction was observed in eighteenth-century French usage. In the writings of that period, anyone who practiced medicine without the requisite university degree stood to be called a *charlatan* or *empirique* (quack), terms which were used interchangeably. See the *Encyclopédie* article "Charlatan" (Vol. 7, p. 326) for explicit comment on this point of usage.

[32] "Manie," *Encyclopédie*, Vol. 20, pp. 958–59; and [Jean Colombier and François Doublet], *Instruction sur la manière de gouverner les insensés* . . . (Paris: Impr. royale, 1785), p. 28.

entire day and night, who had "the habit of living constantly in the midst of lunatics." Pinel's roster of them, gleaned from the recent literature and his own personal experience, was international in scope and included some of the Englishmen whom he had long considered versed in the moral treatment.[33] The famous Francis Willis, caretaker to regal madness (he had treated the Queen of Portugal as well as King George III), was first among them. The proprietor of a private mad-house in Lincolnshire since 1776, Willis was a cleric who had perfunc-torily acquired a medical degree when harassed by the authorities to regularize his practice among his parishioners; his certification in both divinity and medicine earned him the nickname "the Duplicate Doc-tor." Pinel's source, however, described Willis only as "that respect-able ecclesiastic" and stressed his continued activity in a pastoral ca-pacity. Since Willis never in fact presented himself as a member of the medical community or as a possessor of scientific expertise, Pinel's labeling of him as a layman is essentially correct even if technically inaccurate.[34] Also listed by Pinel were John Haslam, "the apothecary of the Bethlehem Hospital ['Bedlam'] in London"; the "honest concierge" of the public establishment for the insane in Amsterdam, who had held the job for thirty years and had recently been written up in the Idéologue journal *Décade philosophique*; Père Poution, an old monk who tended the insane in an establishment in the French Alps; and most important, Pussin, the "governor" of the insane at Bicêtre, whom Pinel met and worked with after his appointment to that hospice in 1793. A tanner by trade, Pussin had as a young man in the 1770s been success-fully treated for scrofula at Bicêtre; and, following a familiar pattern – for large public institutions are worlds unto themselves – the former inmate was eventually recruited onto the staff of the hospice.[35] Else-where Pinel indicated that Madame Pussin, who aided her husband in his daily work, was also gifted in the moral treatment.[36]

Why should learned medicine look for guidance to such a motley crew? Pinel was quite clear about his reasons for advocating this unlikely strategy. The first was a matter of medical epistemology. During the course of the eighteenth century, as belief in deductive medical theoreti-cal systems was replaced by reliance upon clinical observation – a shift given an official imprimatur in 1794 when the Ecole de médecine was established with Fourcroy's pedagogical dictum "Read little, see and do

[33] Introduction to *Traité*, 1st ed., pp. xliii–xlv; p. xliv n1–5; p. xlv n1.

[34] Ida Macalpine and Richard Hunter, *George III and the Mad-Business* (New York: Pan-theon, 1969), pp. 269–70; "Détails sur l'établissement du docteur Willis pour la guérison des aliénés," *Bibliothèque britannique*, Series: Literature (1796): 760, 763–4, cited by Pinel in *Traité*, 1st ed., p. xliv n1.

[35] On Pussin's biography, see Semelaigne, *Aliénistes et philanthropes*, p. 501, which quotes the registers of Bicêtre on Pussin's 1771 admission.

[36] R & O, p. 247.

much"[37] – the "empiricism" that had become a synonym for quackery
no longer seemed an entirely bad thing. Rather, it could have great
redeeming scientific value; for as Pinel noted about the concierges,
"the continual spectacle of all the phenomena of insanity" necessarily
supplied them with a "multifarious and detailed knowledge that is
lacking in the physician," whose contact with insane patients was
"most often limited to . . . transitory visits."[38] By virtue of the structure
of their often humble jobs, the lay concierges had simply acquired
more information about insanity than bona fide medical men possessed. They were specialists in the old sense: lay healers who narrowed their focus to one ailment and treated it repetitively.

Pinel's second reason for gravitating to the concierges was a matter
of political ideology. Why had the skills of these men not been recognized earlier? The oversight was, of course, the result of the elitism of
the medical corporations. "An eternal struggle seems to have been set
up, from the very first centuries that medicine was in existence, between a blind quackery (*empirisme*) and the legal and regulated exercise
of medicine, between those who, through their limited knowledge or
their appetite for lucre, develop an exclusive favor for certain remedies,
and a class of men who submit themselves under the authority of the
laws to preliminary courses of study, to tests of ability and knowledge." Which side to take? Given his loaded description of the conflict,
Pinel seems to be leaning in the predictable direction ("the choice is
doubtless easy"), but in medias res he suddenly turns around, an
awkward textual maneuver that inadvertently discloses the disjunction
between his real emotions and what he knew to be the "correct" opinion on the matter. "Public opinion," he observes, does not always
choose the official practitioner; it vacillates, often favoring the quack
because of his manifest successes as a healer or because he is the
underdog in the corporate system, the "victim of a sort of tyrannical
oppression" with whom the public identifies and to whom it rallies by
a "natural interest." The public is not, Pinel now admits, wrong in its
preferences. "What intolerance! What insulting contempt has often
been lavished on men some of whom have talents, others the precious
results of a long experience . . ." Warming to his new theme, Pinel
declares that he would have medicine operate, like other sciences, as a
noncorporate career open to talent and as a free marketplace of ideas:

> I very much wish that in medicine a sound judgment, a natural wisdom,
> an inventive mind, *devoid of all other privilege*, counted for something – the
> way they do in physics, in chemistry, in botany; that people cared little if

[37] Fourcroy, "Rapport et projet de décret sur l'établissement d'une école centrale de
santé à Paris," 7 frimaire Year III, in A. de Beauchamp, ed., *Enquêtes et documents
relatifs à l'enseignement supérieur*, Vol. 28 (Paris: Impr. nationale, 1888), p. 204.

[38] Introduction to *Traité*, 1st ed., pp. xlv–xlvi.

a particular man had completed a certain course of study or fulfilled certain formalities, but only if he had examined thoroughly some aspect of medical science or if he had discovered some useful truth.

During his two years at Bicêtre, Pinel had, he said, become acutely aware that this kind of respect for the unaccredited was necessary if "some progress in the doctrine of insanity" was to be made. An invigorating new perspective was required; Pinel needed "to exit from a certain circumscribed circle" of traditional writings and hackneyed modes of seeing. And the obvious way to do this was to "enrich the medical doctrine of insanity with all the knowledge acquired by a sort of quackery (*empirisme*)" – that of the concierges.[39]

A defiant medical populism, then, accompanied Pinel's inauguration of the moral treatment. He sounded the note again in the closing paragraph of his introduction, thus greatly amplifying it:

> A work of Medicine published in France at the end of the eighteenth century ought to have a different character from one written in an earlier epoch: a certain soaring flight in the ideas, a wise freedom, and especially the spirit of order and research that reigns in all parts of natural history ought to distinguish it: no longer should egoistic (*particulier*) views or *the interest of a powerful corporation* dictate it.

In an article of 1798 that served as a trial run for one of the chapters of the *Traité,* Pinel had made the same point, holding up for opprobrium the physician "endowed with an exclusive confidence in his own knowledge and full of a doctoral pomposity (*bouffisure doctorale*)." French medicine, he told his readers, had just been "released from the fetters [i.e., its corporate structure] that gave it its spirit of routine . . . and its disfavor in public opinion."[40] Pinel's avowed populism was rooted, as a form of belated revenge, in his own pre-Revolutionary experience; and while it was particularly well-suited to the Revolutionary period of de jure medical deregulation in which he wrote, Pinel was even then rare among official medical men in espousing it.[41] That this populism was, on both sides of the Atlantic, the characteristic late eighteenth-century translation of republican political values into the medical idiom can be seen in the views of the eminent Philadelphia physician Benjamin Rush. In a lecture of 1789 on the practice of medicine as explicitly accommodated to "the history of the American revo-

[39] Ibid., pp. xlii–xliii, xlvi–xliv, my italics.

[40] Ibid., p. lvi, my italics; and Pinel, "Mémoire sur la manie périodique ou intermittente," *M.S.M.E.* 1 (1798): 94–119, esp. 118.

[41] Clearly, though, Pinel tailored the expression of his medical populism to the historical moment. When he reprinted the "Introduction to the First Edition" in the 2d edition of the *Traité* (Paris: Brosson, 1809) – at the height of the Imperial regime and after medical regulation had been reimposed – he carefully purged it of extreme populist comments, condensing the discussion of the concierges and changing the *corporation puissante* of the last paragraph to the innocuous *imagination ardente* (p. xxxii).

lution," Rush spoke with the accents of the ebullient Pinel of the period of the First French Republic. "A formal and pompous manner" – Pinel's *bouffisure doctorale* – "whether accompanied by a wig, a cane or a ring, should avoided" by the physician. "Improvement in medicine" would come not only from the requisite colleges and universities, where "men of genius and learning" produced "systems of physic," but also from ordinary people "in every walk of life." "Remember how many of our most useful remedies have been discovered by quacks. Do not be afraid, therefore, of conversing with them. . . . But further. In the pursuit of medical knowledge, let me advise you to converse with nurses and old women. . . . Even negroes and Indians have sometimes stumbled upon discoveries in medicine. Be not ashamed to inquire into them."[42]

Pinel's contemporaries took note of the immediately populist origins of the moral treatment and expressed neither surprise nor dismay. Cabanis observed that Pinel's ideas on the subject had come to him from "the ingenious and respectable Pussin, superintendent of madmen." The Idéologue economist Jean-Baptiste Say attributed the cure of a large number of lunatics at Bicêtre to the *moyens purement moraux* of Citizen Pussin. And, in keeping with his general outlook, Pinel remained open-minded toward other varieties of "charlatanism" as well. Although mesmerism, or animal magnetism, had been under official medical censure in France since 1784, Pinel is reported to have cordially received one of its chief exponents, the Marquis de Puységur, at the Salpêtrière in 1812. He told his visitor that he had read his works "with much interest"; he watched Puységur magnetize the young patient he had brought with him and, while prudently refusing to pronounce for or against "the new curative procedures you apply" for lack of sufficient evidence, he invited the layman to return that winter "in order to try out on some of [the madwomen of the Salpêtrière] the power of magnetic influence."[43]

Lest Pinel seem to be a thoroughgoing advocate of medical ecumenism or even of the laissez-faire model of a medical profession, it must be stressed that the founder of French psychiatry tempered these

[42] Benjamin Rush, "Observations on the Duties of a Physician and the Methods of Improving Medicine Accommodated to the Present State of Society and Manners in the United States" (1789), printed as a separately paginated appendix to his *Medical Inquiries and Observations* (Philadelphia: Prichard & Hall, 1789), pp. 21–39, esp. pp. 24–25, 36. I am grateful to Lamar Riley for calling this text to my attention.

[43] Cabanis, *Rapports du physique et du moral de l'homme, O.P.* Vol. 1, 587 n1 (Cabanis's own note); J.-B. Say, "Des hôpitaux et des hospices de Paris," *Décade philosophique* (20 floréal Year IX): 262; A.-M.-J. de Chastenet de Puységur, *Les fous, les insensés, les maniaques et les frénétiques ne seraient-ils que des somnambules désordonnés?* (Paris: J.-G. Dentu, 1812), pp. 81–83. On Puységur, see Henri F. Ellenberger, *The Discovery of the Unconscious: The History and Evolution of Dynamic Psychiatry* (New York: Basic Books, 1970), pp. 70–74.

democratic attitudes with a more conventional elitism. The wisdom of the concierges was, to his mind, radically incomplete. "Lacking the most rudimentary knowledge of the development of the human understanding, could [the concierges] put order and precision into their observations or even elevate themselves to a language appropriate for rendering their ideas?" In order that quackery be incorporated into medicine it had first to be "brought back to those general principles of which it is destitute."[44] It had, in other words, to be philosophized.

Like Cabanis, the Idéologue Pinel was insistent upon a philosophically grounded medicine. And he frequently noted the indispensable philosophical foundations of a medicine of insanity in particular: "Will one be able to delineate all the alterations and perversions of the functions of the human understanding if he has not deeply contemplated the writings of Locke and Condillac and familiarized himself with their principles?"[45] Thus the lay concierge, as diligent, perceptive, and talented as he might be, was inalterably the intellectual inferior of the *médecin-philosophe*. The latter would take the rough-hewn commonsensical knowledge of the former and transform it into something refined, scientific, and esoteric; the elite professional confraternity, at one moment threatened with dissolution by Pinel, was thus fundamentally – and quickly – restored by him. Pinel's ambivalent perch between populism and elitism was revealed in his candid account of his relationship with Pussin at Bicêtre in the years 1793–95:

> The dogmatic tone of the doctor was abandoned from that point on [i.e., from the moment that Pinel realized that Pussin had a great deal to teach him]. Frequent visits, sometimes during several hours of the day, helped me to familiarize myself with the deviations, vociferations and extravagances of the most violent maniacs. From that point on, I had repeated conversations with the man best acquainted with their anterior condition and delirious ideas: utmost attention to humor all the pretensions of his amour-propre, questions that were varied and went back over the same material when the answers were obscure, no objections on my part when what he advanced was doubtful or improbable, but a tacit return to further examination in order to illuminate or rectify it.[46]

In this way, Pinel used Pussin as a resource person, grateful to the layman for his wealth of information but always aware that this tanner-turned-healer was no equal; Pinel's manner, as he himself ingenuously reports it, is entirely condescending. Elsewhere – in the same text in which he criticized "doctoral pomposity" – Pinel summed up the via media between populism and elitism that characterized his attitude toward the practice of medicine. "Rousseau, in a fit of caustic humor,

---

[44] Introduction to *Traité*, 1st ed., pp. xlvi, xlix.
[45] *Traité*, 1st ed., p. 45 (also "Mémoire sur la manie périodique" p. 119); virtually the same sentence appears in *Traité*, 2d ed., Introduction, p. xi.
[46] *Traité*, 1st ed., Introduction, p. xlviii.

once called for Medicine and told her to come without the physician: he would have better served humanity by raising his eloquent voice against conceited ineptitude and by summoning talent and genius to the study of [this most necessary] science."[47]

Pinel's turn to charlatanism and to the wisdom of the laity to obtain material for medical-scientific theory must be seen in another context as well. It is analogous to the initiative taken by Cabanis in his *Rapports du physique et du moral* to incorporate into scientific medicine, on the theoretical grounds of psychophysiological reciprocity, the common-sensical concern for the emotional state of the sick individual, the precepts of soothing, reassuring, and of sustaining hope – the bedside manner, or what in the parlance of the day was frequently called a "medicine of the imagination." For Cabanis such a seemingly populist strategy had the thoroughly professional-imperialist aim of helping to constitute medicine as the omnibus science of man. Pinel shared the Idéologues' grand view of medicine, as an impromptu comment to his brother, written a few months after the republican revolution of 1792, indicates. "It must be admitted that, in the present disorganization of almost all the structures (*états*) of society, the profession of medicine will play one of the most glorious roles because it really exists *in* nature and it is from physicians that one can recover the greatest amount of accumulated knowledge."[48] For Pinel, as for Cabanis, the scope of medical knowledge was so uniquely vast because medicine embraced the domains of *le moral* and *le physique* and the relations that obtained between them, because it included a "medicine of the imagination."

Pinel's interest in a "medicine of the imagination" (to which he and Cabanis often referred under the more sober name of "moral hygiene")[49] is abundantly evident in his early writings. In one of his pre-Revolutionary *Gazette de santé* editorials, for example, he discoursed on the effects that an "exalted imagination" could wreak on the body. "The causes of [some people's] fears, often chimerical in the eyes of a man of sangfroid, can produce in them extreme upsets and real diseases." Thus a young ecclesiastic, who had playfully consulted a fortune teller and a reader of horoscopes, was told by both that he would die at the age of twenty-five. This double prediction provoked "the most violent alarm in his soul," and before too long "fever seized him, his body became withered and dessicated, and all the remedies lavished upon him during the course of a year were useless." A complete cure, however, was brought about by the uneventful passage of his

---

[47] Ibid., p. 45 (also "Mémoire sur la manie périodique," p. 119).

[48] "Lettres de Pinel," *Gaz. hebd. de med.* (September 23, 1859): 599, letter of November 16, 1792.

[49] Cabanis regarded the moral treatment as part of *hygiène morale; Rapports, O.P.*, Vol. 1, p. 587. See also his *Coup d'oeil sur les révolutions et sur la reforme de la médecine, O.P.*, Vol. 2, pp. 221–25.

twenty-fifth birthday. And commenting in the *Gazette* on a case of impotence in a young scholar, Pinel's prognosis was optimistic. It was "the diverse sentiments that besiege his soul" which had "suspended, as by enchantment, the functions of the organ of generation." Montaigne's "excellent essay on 'Imagination' " would, said Pinel, corroborate this view and confirm Pinel's own counsel: that time, patience, and the natural process of growing accustomed to the nuptial bed would clear up this apparently physical affliction. Similarly, in his entry in the 1793 prize essay contest held by the Society of Medicine on "the best manner of teaching practical medicine in a hospital setting," Pinel included a section on the *remèdes moraux* to be employed with patients of all types. During the hospital visits that were part of his own medical education, he said, he had become "convinced of the happy effects produced on patients by consoling and reassuring words" delivered at their bedside; and he proposed that this approach be stressed in the training of young physicians. Medical students in the wards were to be instructed to apply themselves to "reviving the patients' flagging courage and dispelling forebodings of doom from their imaginations."[50]

The moral treatment of the insane, then, was a subset of the *remèdes moraux* recommended by both Cabanis and Pinel to aid the recovery of patients suffering from any and all diseases. Both men were committed to taking these *remèdes moraux* from "charlatanistic" practice and assimilating them to official medicine by means of a theoretical or philosophical gloss. Odd as its provenance may seem, the moral treatment was really in the mainstream of the most advanced Idéologue medicine. Indeed, Pinel's work in helping to constitute medicine as the all-embracing "anthropology" through his championing of the moral treatment can be seen quite clearly if we examine for comparative purposes a text of 1787 which Pinel himself certainly read (for he cited it in the *Gazette de santé* two years later): a traveler's report about the treatment of the insane at "Bedlam" in London, followed by recommendations for their treatment at Bicêtre and the Salpêtrière. The author of the latter, the Abbé Robin, was the king's chaplain, and he came out strongly in favor of *moyens moraux* as the necessary accompaniment of baths and bleedings. "The art of healing madmen," he asserts, "is still in its infancy, and in order to possess it, it would be necessary to

---

[50] Pinel, "Hygiène: Les accès de mélancolie ne sont-ils pas toujours plus fréquens et plus à craindre durant les premiers mois de l'hiver?" *Gazette de santé* (1787): 201–2; "Extrait d'un mémoire à consulter sur une impuissance provenante d'une cause morale. Réponse des auteurs de la *Gazette de santé*," ibid. (1786): 18–80; and *Mémoire sur cette question proposée pour sujet d'un prix par la Société de médecine . . .* , in *The Clinical Training of Doctors: An Essay of 1793*, ed. Dora B. Weiner (Baltimore: Johns Hopkins University Press, 1980). I have translated from pp. 47–48 of the French text of this bilingual edition.

extend one's quests beyond the limits of medicine: it would be necessary to study *le moral* of patients sometimes even more than *le physique*."[51] While Pinel would have essentially concurred in this therapeutic prescription, he would have disagreed violently about the "limits" Robin placed on the proper domain of medicine. For at the core of Pinel's position was the insistence that medicine be defined so as to comprehend rather than exclude *le moral*.[52]

What was the moral treatment?

Pinel, it will be remembered, regarded as one of his two major contributions with respect to the moral treatment that he, unlike his secretive English predecessors, had specified the method fully. A review of the first edition of the *Traité* by the Idéologue physician Richerand took Pinel at his word and praised him precisely for supplying this much-needed explication. But not everyone, even among Pinel's most intimate and supportive circle of colleagues, proved so obliging. Cabanis, though willing to grant Pinel's claim that the moral treatment was genuinely curative, at least "for a rather large number of cases," expressed disappointment at the vagueness of his friend's use of the concept. Esquirol, the most important student and collaborator of Pinel, called Pinel's conceptualization the "fruit of observation and genius," but at the same time admitted that no thorough definition of the moral treatment had really been offered. The best approach both to understanding it and to demonstrating its efficacy was, he suggested, through an examination of cases.[53] This was, in fact, Pinel's own basic mode of presentation in the *Traité*. "Little stories (*historiettes*)," he once noted, when they were the "true results of observation," were serious scientific business.[54] Such remarks translate readily into Kuhnian terms. The paradigm of the moral treatment was not so much succinctly expressed in "shared rules" as embedded in an "arsenal of

---

51 Robin, *Du traitement des insensés dans l'hôpital de Bethléem de Londres, traduit de l'anglois, suivi d'observations sur les insensés de Bicêtre et de la Salpêtrière* (Amsterdam, 1787), pp. 46–51, 55. Pinel's reference to Robin in "Observations sur le régime moral" was solely for the purpose of corroborating his own point about the intolerable superiority of the "rival" English nation in the area of treatment of insanity.

52 See, for further confirmation of Pinel's views on this matter, *Traité*, 1st ed., Section 6, which, under the heading "Principles of the Medical Treatment of Lunatics," includes *both* traditional physical treatments and case histories of treatment by "moral" means.

53 A. Richerand, review of Pinel, *Traité*, in *Journal de médecine* 1 (nivôse an IX): 366; Cabanis, *Rapports, O.P.*, Vol. 1, p. 587; Esquirol, *Des passions*, pp. 7, 13, 78. On Richerand as Idéologue physician, see Martin S. Staum, *Cabanis: Enlightenment and Medical Philosophy in the French Revolution* (Princeton, N.J.: Princeton University Press, 1980), pp. 251–53.

54 *Traité*, 1st ed., pp. 228, 231–32.

exemplars," of "shared examples of successful practice."[55] Hence any attempt to clarify the nature of that therapy must begin with a look at these exemplars.

The exemplars are plentiful, even if we confine ourselves to the first edition of the *Traité*, which presents, scattered through the text and in varying degrees of detail, about a dozen cases.[56] From this group, I have selected four "full-length" cases and a pair of very condensed and elliptical ones. All are cases for which Pinel provided a certain amount of commentary and explication. All were singled out in an informed contemporary reading of the text – the combined review-abridgment of the first edition of the *Traité* prepared by Pinel's disciple Moreau de la Sarthe for the Idéologue journal *Décade philosophique.*[57] All the patients described in the cases are men: The sample comes from Pinel's years at Bicêtre; only after his transfer to the Salpêtrière did he systematically apply "moral methods" to women. I will recount the cases as narratives, adhering closely to Pinel's own choice of words, and will then gather and systematize his own middle-level generalizations about the therapeutic principles they illustrate. In the next section, I will examine the same material from another perspective by taking up the broader theoretical justifications of the moral treatment and higher-level generalizations about its fundamental principles.

Case 1: the furious soldier.[58] A soldier was brought to Bicêtre after the standard treatment for insanity at the Hôtel-Dieu failed to produce an improvement in his condition. He suddenly became dominated by the single idea of his imminent departure for the army. The "ways of gentleness" (*voies de la douceur*) were tried on him in vain, and force had to be applied to get him into his cell; since he tore everything to shreds during the night, he also had to be tied up. He spent a week in this condition, relentlessly violent, hurling invectives at Pinel. Then one morning during Pinel's rounds, his manner changed. In a submissive tone, humbly kissing the chief physician's hand, he said to Pinel, "You promised to let me at liberty inside the hospice if I were calm. Well, I am calling upon you to keep your word." Pinel smiled with pleasure and spoke to him kindly, at that same moment releasing him

---

[55] See "Postscript–1969" to Thomas S. Kuhn, *The Structure of Scientific Revolutions*, 2d ed. (Chicago: University of Chicago Press, 1970) and esp. "Second Thoughts on Paradigms" in Kuhn, *The Essential Tension: Selected Studies in Scientific Tradition and Change* (Chicago: University of Chicago Press, 1977), pp. 307, 318–19.

[56] Other major sources are Esquirol's *Des passions*, presenting cases in which Pinel and Pussin often figure, and his earlier article "Observations sur l'application du traitement moral à la manie," *Journal général de médecine* 1 (Year XI): 281–94.

[57] See Jacq. L. Moreau de la Sarthe, "Art de guérir: Traité médico-philosophique sur l'aliénation mentale par Ph. Pinel," *Décade philosophique* (20 prairial Year XI): 458–67.

[58] *Traité*, 1st ed., pp. 58–59 (also R & O, pp. 223–24).

from all physical constraints, for these were now, he believed, super-fluous or even harmful. Seven months later the soldier left the hospice, completely cured; he never experienced a relapse.

Case 2: the fasting Catholic.[59] A young man, dismayed by the reverses Catholicism had suffered in France during the Revolution, became a maniac and ended up in Bicêtre after an unsuccessful treatment at the Hôtel-Dieu. He was filled with a "dark misanthropy," spoke only of the torments of hell, and thought that he could avoid them by imitating the abstinence and mortifications of the ancient anchorites; hence he steadfastly refused to take any nourishment. After four days of this fast, Pussin suddenly appeared at his door with a group of hospital attendants, all armed and carrying chains which they rattled noisily. Pussin addressed the patient with fiery eyes and a thundering voice, saying that unless he ate during that night the soup they had brought him, he would incur the cruelest punishments. The patient did eventually eat the soup and, after this turning point in his conduct, submitted to a diet that restored his physical strength; gradually the use of his reason was restored as well.

Case 3: the clockmaker.[60] One of the most famous clockmakers in Paris succumbed to mania through a confluence of circumstances: his own obsession with building a perpetual motion machine, which kept him sleepless, working through the night; and "the recurrent terrors incited [in him] by the storms of the Revolution." His loss of reason took a singular form. He believed that he had been decapitated by the guillotine, that his head had been mixed in pell-mell with those of other victims, and that when the judges belatedly reversed their verdict, he had been given back a head other than his own – and a far less beautiful head at that. After a period of violent furor alternating with delirious gaiety, he calmed down somewhat. And because he remained obsessed with the perpetual motion machine, drawing sketches of it all over the walls of the hospice, Pussin allowed him to set up a sort of workshop in the antechamber of his cell furnished with clockmakers' tools supplied by his relatives. He worked with undivided attention for a month, and thought that he had succeeded; but just as he was hailing himself as the new Archimedes, the mechanism stopped. To save face before his fellow inmates and Pussin, the clockmaker declared that he could easily fix the machine but that he had grown tired of the whole enterprise and did not wish to bother. Thus the obsession with the perpetual motion machine was spontaneously laid to rest.

To "combat and destroy" the delirious idea about the alleged change

[59] Ibid., pp. 59–61 (also R & O, pp. 224–25).
[60] Ibid., pp. 66–70 (also R & O, pp. 229–31).

of heads, the complicity of a convalescent lunatic at Bicêtre was enlisted. This jovial man began to discuss with the clockmaker the miracle of Saint Denis, who carried his head in his hands and covered it with kisses as he walked. The clockmaker strongly defended the possibility of such an event, citing his own decapitation as confirmation. His partner now burst out laughing and said in a derisive tone: "Madman that you are, how do you think Saint Denis would have been able to kiss his head; was it with his posterior?"[61] This unexpected reply struck the clockmaker sharply and he retreated in confusion from the mocking laughter. He no longer spoke of his alleged mishap at the guillotine, and serious work at his clockmaker's occupation over the next several months fortified (*raffermir*) his reason. He was returned to his family and never had a relapse.

Case 4: the guilt-ridden tailor.[62] During the Jacobin phase of the Revolution, a tailor happened to muse in public on the sentence of Louis XVI. From that time on, his patriotism became suspect in his section. Exaggerating the significance of some menacing words that he overheard one day and believed directed at himself, he came home trembling, unable to eat or sleep, continually fearful. After treatment at the Hôtel-Dieu he was brought to Bicêtre; the idea that he had been condemned to death on the guillotine now absorbed him entirely. Pinel arranged for him to resume his occupation, to receive a small salary for repairing the clothing of the other inmates of the hospice. The tailor threw himself into this work; "nothing equaled his zeal for making himself useful," and after about two months he ceased to mention his alleged death sentence and seemed virtually cured. But several months later, his old melancholy returned. Pinel was at this time leaving his post at Bicêtre for one at the Salpêtrière, but he devised a treatment plan for the tailor and put Pussin in charge of executing it. Three young physicians dressed in the black suits of magistrates presented themselves at the hospice as a commission of the Corps législatif delegated to carry out the trial of the tailor. They interrogated him about his conduct, his favorite newspapers, his political opinions, and "the one with the most grave and imposing demeanor" then loudly proclaimed the verdict: acquittal. "We acknowledge having found in him only the sentiments of the purest patriotism." The "trial" relieved the tailor of his symptoms – although the cure, Pinel admitted, proved only temporary.

Case 5: some victims of stifled ambition.[63] A man in a high position falls into disgrace and shortly thereafter into a deep melancholy – that is

---

[61] R & O gives *derrière*; *Traité*, 1st ed. substitutes the more discreet *talon* or heel.
[62] *Traité*, 1st ed., pp. 233–37.
[63] Ibid., pp. 238–39.

what the physician Erasistratus once ingeniously called a "stifled ambition" (*ambition rentrée*). A comparable case is presented by the soldier
who led the successful assault on the Bastille and later became a lunatic
confined to Bicêtre. The expedient treatment for this man would not be
baths and showers but rather a captain's commission. Another such
case, recounted by the sixteenth-century physician Forestus, concerns
a rich German merchant who experienced a commercial setback.
Though minimal in itself, this reverse so deeply affected his imagination that he believed his resources totally depleted and himself condemned to die of hunger. In vain did people remind him that he still
had an immense fortune; even when they spread out before him all the
riches contained in his coffers, he dismissed this as a false appearance.
But the Reformation was able to accomplish what the medicaments and
adroit treatments of Forestus could not. The merchant became absorbed night and day in the zealous defense of popery and ended by
being entirely cured of his melancholy.

The most striking feature of the treatments employed in several of
these cases is their theatricality: Scenes and spectacles are staged. The
patient, however, is not aware of their fictive nature or, in the instance
of the joke told to the clockmaker, of their deliberate and planned
nature. These treatments are, to use a phrase of the period, "pious
frauds," deceptions that take advantage of the gullibility of an individual for his own benefit,[64] or, as Pinel sometimes described them, "innocent ruses."[65] The theatricality of the moral treatment is underscored
textually by Pinel's frequent use of the word *appareil* – that is, display,
show, pomp, appearance. The visitation to the fasting Catholic is an
"*appareil* suitable to induce fright"; the make-believe commission of the
Corps législatif presents itself to the melancholic tailor with the full
"*appareil* of authority."[66] This kind of therapeutic theater was not new
but had been traditionally used (by both medical men and charlatans)
much more in the treatment of melancholy than of mania – hence Pinel's insistence that "the moral treatment *of mania* is one of the most
important, and, until now, least advanced parts of the medicine of
observation."[67] The *Encyclopédie* article "Melancholy," a good typical
source, recommends a variety of curative "ruses," as they are called
there. If, for example, a melancholic believes that he has a live animal
in his belly, "one must pretend (*faire semblant*) to remove it" – to give

---

[64] See, e.g., the entry "Fraud: Should Pious Frauds be Practiced on the Common
   People?" in Voltaire, *Philosophical Dictionary*, trans. P. Gay (New York: Harcourt Brace
   & World, 1962), pp. 279–83, a dialogue on whether the common people need fables in
   order to be persuaded of the existence of God.
[65] *Traité*, 1st, ed., p. 95 (also R & O, p. 248).
[66] Ibid., pp. 60, 235 (also R & O, p. 225).
[67] Ibid., p. 103, my italics (also R & O, p. 254).

the patient a strong purgative and then "to throw this animal adroitly into the basin when the patient is not looking."[68] Theatricality is, however, an instrument of the moral treatment rather than one of its principles; its therapeutic significance will emerge when we enumerate the principles underlying the five cases.

The first is the overriding preference given to gentleness (*douceur*) and "the ways of gentleness" (*voies de douceur*), recurring terms in Pinel's vocabulary. This commitment to "philanthropy"[69] was not just an abstract ethical principle but also a practical therapeutic one, not just an end in itself but a means to an end. For the lunatic was not to be considered "absolutely deprived of reason," inert and "inaccessible to motives of fear and hope, to sentiments of honor."[70] He was, rather, feelingful and responsive; and hence *douceur* – in the form of "consoling words, the happy expedient (*artifice*) of reviving the hope of the lunatic and gaining his confidence" – produced therapeutic success, as "daily experience attests," while "maltreatment, or the ways of a too harsh repression, exacerbates the illness and can render it incurable."[71] The young Esquirol recounted in his dissertation a successful case in which this consoling *douceur*, and the doctor–patient rapport and camaraderie that it produced, was the central motif. A young man had suffered two brief bouts of insanity and consulted Pinel when he perceived in himself all the warning signs of a third. Entrusted with the case, Esquirol seems to have devoted most of his energy to cheering on the patient, who, "tormented by the fear of an imminent relapse," struggled to prevent its occurrence. On the brink of the patient's descent into madness, we find Esquirol "incessantly encouraging [him] with consoling words," using "forceful language in order to rouse his battered courage." The crisis passes, with a tranquil look coming over the patient's face and a light sweat spreading over his body. "You have saved me," he tells Esquirol, and that same evening the two play a game of billiards together.[72]

Unhappily, *douceur* is by itself often an inadequate principle: It can be ignored or exploited by the patient, as the case of the furious soldier

---

[68] "Mélancolie," *Encyclopédie*, Vol. 21, pp. 419–20. (It is unclear from the text whether or not the healer was obliged to produce a real animal.) There was, in other words, a more or less continuous tradition in the use of "moral means" for the treatment of melancholy, beginning with the counsels of the ancients and extending through the eighteenth century; but this medical tradition had lapsed with respect to mania. On ancient theatricality in the cure of mania, see Pinel, "Observations sur le régime moral," p. 13, on the *annonces spécieuses* of Celsus.

[69] *Traité*, 1st ed., pp. 52, 63, 86 (also R & O, pp. 219, 242).

[70] Ibid., p. 99 (also R & O, p. 251); Pinel is quoting approvingly the formulation of a Swiss-French Dr. Delarive in a 1798 article on the use of the moral treatment at the York Retreat.

[71] Ibid., p. 97 (also R & O, p. 250).

[72] Esquirol, *Des passions*, pp. 80–81.

exemplifies. Or, as Pinel wrote of a megalomaniacal patient who struck everyone he encountered and ordered them to prostrate themselves before him and do homage, "What good could come of the *voies de douceur* . . . with a lunatic who regarded other men as particles of dust?" In such cases, *douceur* must be momentarily abandoned and recourse had to the opposite principle – "an imposing *appareil* of repression." Pinel was quite explicit about the mentality that must accompany therapeutic acts of repression; they must be "exempt from feelings of animosity and anger."[73] They are to be construed as necessary evils, never to be sadistically relished but responsibly undertaken so that, as with the furious soldier, the desired mode of *douceur* can be fruitfully restored. Sometimes "it is necessary to subjugate [lunatics] first, and encourage them afterward."[74]

As regrettable as the task of repression might be, it was an integral part of the work of a healer of the insane, and his skill in this area was at a premium. The essential skill – if something so intangible can be called a skill – was to exude authority. Francis Willis was almost legendary in this regard, as the description of him cited by Pinel indicates. "On first meeting with a new patient, his usually gentle and friendly countenance changed its expression. He suddenly became a different figure, commanding the respect even of maniacs. His piercing gaze seemed to read their hearts and divine their thoughts at the very moment that they were being formed. In this way he gained control over them, which he used as a means of cure." Indeed, during parliamentary inquiries on George III's health, Edmund Burke questioned Willis's judgment in allowing the King to shave himself, doubting that Willis could have handled His Majesty had he suddenly become furious while brandishing the razor. Unruffled, Willis replied that he would have commanded him "by the EYE! I would have looked at him *thus*"; and Burke immediately averted his own eyes, graphically acknowledging Willis's rather astounding ocular ability to convey his authority.[75]

Pinel did not require that all practitioners of the moral treatment be possessed of such stunning powers, but he did stipulate that they be able somehow to communicate authority by their presence, their "physical and moral qualities."[76] What inhered naturally in their persons might, of course, be legitimately supplemented by theatrical devices – Pussin's fearsome chain-rattling band of men in the case of the fasting Catholic, for example. This theme of salutary coercive authority was a very old one in Pinel's thought on the treatment of the insane.

[73] *Traité*, 1st ed., pp. 61, 66, 101 (also R & O, pp. 225, 229, 252).

[74] Ibid., pp. 99–100, quoting Delarive (also R & O, pp. 251–52).

[75] Ibid., p. 48 (also R & O, pp. 216–17). Burke is cited in Macalpine and Hunter, *George III and the Mad-Business*, p. 272.

[76] *Traité*, 1st ed., p. 58 (also R & O, p. 223).

As early as 1786, in his analysis of the mania of his young lawyer friend, he had ascribed the futility of the situation to the fact that "no one had *enough authority over him*" to compel him to end his austere and unhealthy regimen; and in 1798 he repeated, almost obsessively, this same analysis of that personally crucial case: "In my treatment of mania [in the early 1780s], it was in my power to use a great number of remedies, but I lacked the most powerful . . . , that which consists in the art of subjugating and subduing the lunatic."[77]

The third principle of the moral treatment implicit in these cases is that of "combating and destroying the delirious idea" that characterized the insanity.[78] It was dependent on the first two principles – that is, on having previously made the patient minimally receptive to such intervention, either by securing his confidence through gentle means or by forcibly commanding his respect through repressive ones. Pinel and Pussin used two basic methods in this "idea-combat." One was distraction or diversion, turning the lunatic's attention away from the idea which, in his pathological condition, pervaded his entire being. Such distraction could be accomplished by engaging him in useful work, exemplified in the cases of the tailor and the clockmaker, or by having him listen to music.[79] The second method was to subject the lunatic to a startling or jolting experience, to "shake up the imagination" (*ébranler fortement l'imagination*), as Pinel usually expressed it,[80] in a manner calculated to discredit a particular idea. Sometimes a mild jolt sufficed, such as the joke told to the clockmaker, which caught him completely off guard and seems to have made him aware of the ludicrous illogic of his position regarding the aftermath of decapitation. Usually the jolt was more vigorous and sustained, such as the full-dress enactment of the trial of the tailor, with its official proclamation that the patient's dominant idea was erroneous and henceforth to be regarded as null and void. The theatricality of the moral treatment was particularly pronounced in the implementation of this method, for an appropriately jolting incident had to be staged, and staged dramatically.

The fourth and final principle concerns managing pathological passions as opposed to combating pathological ideas, and it reflects the distinction implicitly made by Pinel between the ideational and affective components of the moral treatment, a distinction parallel to Cabanis's definition of the two components of the domain of *le moral*. In

---

[77] Pinel, "Mélancolie nerveuse," p. 35, my italics; R & O, p. 223.

[78] *Traité*, 1st ed., p. 69 (also R & O, p. 231).

[79] On music, see Esquirol, *Des passions*, pp. 77–78. Some years later, at the Salpêtrière, Pinel made work a standard part of his treatment program, installing a "vast atelier of knitting and sewing" in which convalescent lunatics were employed for a small salary. *Traité*, 2d ed., pp. 372–73.

[80] See, e.g., R & O, p. 235, and *Traité*, 1st ed., pp. 76, 236.

his comments on the cases of "stifled ambition," Pinel said explicitly
that diseased passions should not be destroyed outright – although, as
we have seen, this was a completely suitable policy for delirious
ideas – but "counterbalanced by more powerful affections" or else simply "not thwarted."[81] Hence the proposal to cure the man who led the
assault on the Bastille in 1789 by giving him the formal recognition of
his prowess that he craved but had been denied – that is, by satisfying
his passion. The sixteenth-century German Reformation case illustrates
a fortuitous operation of the strategy of counterbalancing: Anxiety over
a commercial failure preoccupies the merchant entirely and cannot be
mitigated by realistic considerations, but it is pushed into the background by a suddenly incited religious passion.

One of the corollaries of the principle of therapeutic management of
the passions was the necessity of ascertaining just what the patient's
dominant passions were. Unlike delusional ideas, which Pinel believed
made their way repeatedly into the patient's conversation and tended
to be flaunted, the crucial pathological passions might be deliberately
concealed. This was one of the major obstacles to the study of insanity.
"The extreme distrust of everything around them that marks lunatics . . . often leads them to dissimulation or taciturnity. It would be
clumsy technique and a blunder (*maladresse*) to indicate to them an
overt intention to observe them and to penetrate their secret thoughts
with questions." Pinel instead recommended "a tone of candor, an
extreme simplicity and an affectionate manner" as a way of "triumph-
ing" over their self-protective reserve. The intuition and tactics of a
detective were useful as well. Recounting how Galen figured out that
the insomnia and continual agitation of a well-born lady (who evaded
all direct questions about the origins of her malady) had been provoked
by her amorous passion for an actor, Pinel commented that it was
regrettable that Galen "did not apply himself especially to the study of
insanity," for he possessed a necessary skill in that line of work, "a
rare sagacity for uncovering a hidden moral affection."[82] The young
Esquirol advised that the servants of wealthy insane patients be actively recruited into the treatment process and that they play the role of
trusted confidant and friend, never participating in any of the repressive measures that the physician might deem necessary. In this way
they could often furnish the physician with "the ideas, thoughts, projects of the lunatic . . . , a multitude of things useful for the restitution
of health." This seems to have been a time-honored therapeutic motif.
Galen got some of his most important information from the lady's
slave, and in Richardson's *Sir Charles Grandison*, Clementina's atten-
dant Camilla serves precisely the function that Esquirol later recom-

[81] *Traité*, 1st ed., p. 238.
[82] Ibid., Introduction, pp. xiii n1, lii, lv–lvi.

mended, of indulgence toward her melancholic mistress and communication of private information about her to family and physicians.[83]

"Scientizing" the treatment

In the account of the moral treatment given thus far, its non-esoteric,
lay origins – which Pinel so proudly and defiantly proclaimed – are
abundantly evident. We must turn now to Pinel's promise to add to
the moral treatment something that the concierges could not supply,
to upgrade it to a level suitable to a medicine with scientific pretensions, to "bring it back to the general principles of which it is destitute." There are several ways in which he attempted to make good
this promise.

Connecting treatment to etiology. For the concierges, the moral treatment
was a pragmatic method, devised by trial and error, applied because it
worked. These laymen had no inclination to extend it beyond the
bounds of its specific utility, to see what light its efficacy shed on other
problems concerning insanity. Thus a memoir prepared by the concierge Pussin – and sent by Pinel to the minister of the interior in 1798
as a supporting document in the request to transfer Pussin from Bicêtre
to the Salpêtrière so that he might continue his collaboration with
Pinel – delineated a variety of *remèdes moraux* that had proven reliable,
spoke out against the debilitating effects of bleeding on lunatics, but
went no further.[84] For Pinel, however, the success of the moral treatment in certain cases was a piece of data in a larger jigsaw puzzle; it
was seen as a function of the etiology of those cases – that is, the cases
in question were presumed to have a "moral" cause, a cause rooted in
ideas, or more especially in the passions.[85] This does not mean, of
course, that the body was not implicated, for the Idéologue Pinel took
as an article of faith the interrelation of *le moral* and *le physique:* Human
ideas and passions had a significant impact on the "animal economy."[86] But while an insanity susceptible to cure by the moral treat-

---

[83] Esquirol, *Des passions*, pp. 52–3; Pinel, Introduction to *Traité* 1st ed., p. xiii n1; and
Richardson, *Grandison*, Vol. 2, pp. 201–2, 297.

[84] The document, "Observations faites par le citoyen Pussin sur les fous," was discovered by Dora B. Weiner, who published the French text in "The Apprenticeship of
Philippe Pinel: A New Document," *Clio Medica* 13 (1978): 125–33. Samuel Tuke, the
lay director of the York Retreat, explicitly refused to theorize about the moral treatment, believing that the medical propensity for premature systematization impeded
the progress of therapeutic knowledge. See Andrew T. Scull, *Museums of Madness: The
Social Organization of Insanity in Nineteenth-Century England* (New York: St. Martin's
Press, 1979), p. 158.

[85] *Traité*, 1st ed., title of Section 3, para. 3, p. 110.

[86] Ibid., Introduction, p. xxi.

ment affected the body functionally, it could not be the result of a true organic lesion.

Contrary to the findings of eighteenth-century anatomists, whose dissections of the cadavers of lunatics had revealed almost universal abnormality and degeneration in the brain substance, Pinel cited the evidence of dissections conducted by himself and others to the effect that insanity could exist without discernible brain lesion or cranial malconformation.[87] "According to Pinel," wrote Cabanis, "this [latter] class of insanities is much more extensive than one would have thought"; and that is precisely why Pinel counseled such heavy reliance on the moral treatment.[88] In those cases where the anatomical substratum of the mental faculties had suffered a lesion, Pinel abandoned not only confidence in the moral treatment but all his therapeutic optimism, admitting the incurability of the condition. This was his pronouncement on the famous "wild boy of Aveyron," a child who had allegedly reared himself in the forests of southwestern France and who was brought to Paris in 1800 amid great expectations on the part of savants that he could not only be taught to speak but could have all his intellectual and moral faculties awakened. Pinel examined him and found "no sign of the capacity for improvement (*perfectibilité*)"; the boy was in his opinion afflicted with idiotism caused by a congenital deficit in his cerebral constitution or its defective development in early childhood. The one dissenting voice in the Parisian scientific community, Pinel was convinced that all therapeutic efforts with the boy would be futile.[89]

Sensationalist psychology and idéologie. Once having declared for the efficacy of the moral treatment in those cases of insanity with "moral" causes, Pinel was obliged, as part of his scientizing project, to specify the mechanisms of both cause and cure. For this purpose he enlisted the aid of philosophy – hence the adjective *médico-philosophique* in the title of the *Traité*. His brand of philosophy, as *médecin éclairé* and member of the salon of Madame Helvétius, was of course sensationalist psychology: We have already noted that it was in profound ruminations on Locke and Condillac that he located his own superiority as a healer over the unreflective practices of the lay concierges. Pinel embraced as well the emended version of Condillac given by his contemporaries and friends the Idéologues; and what he referred to as *idéologie* – literally, the science of ideas – was the whole strand of thought from Locke and Condillac through the post-Revolutionary Idéologues.

[87] Ibid., pp. 106–7, 111–12.
[88] Cabanis, *Rapports, O.P.*, Vol. 1, p. 587.
[89] See Pinel's 1800 "Rapport fait à la Société des observateurs de l'homme sur l'enfant connu sous le nom de sauvage de l'Aveyron," published for the first time in *Revue anthropologique* 21 (1911): 441–54.

In the introduction to the first edition of the *Traité*, he made his allegiances and his intentions clear. He specified the works of the *idéologistes*[90] as guiding the "science of facts" that he envisioned his emerging study of insanity to be. They provided the stationary point (*terme fixe*) from which one could begin to make sense of the ever-fluctuating chaos of insanity and to capture the distinctive features of the different classifications of lunatics.[90] *Idéologie* was an "accessory science"[91] to Pinel's study of insanity: He used the same term as Vicq d'Azyr had used for those bodies of knowledge outside medicine's own observational base with which medicine entered into a beneficial relationship. Pinel's fellow Idéologues were also fond of claiming Pinel's work on insanity as part of *idéologie*. Cabanis described Pinel as one "to whom *idéologie* will owe almost as much as will medicine." In his basic textbook for students, the *Eléments d'idéologie*, Destutt de Tracy "could not recommend Pinel's *Traité* too highly. By explaining how madmen reason falsely, he teaches wise men how they think. . . . It is physiologist–philosophers like Monsieur Pinel who will advance *idéologie*." And it was as a devotee, almost an addict of *idéologie* that the young Stendhal – admirer and personal friend of Destutt de Tracy, avid reader of Cabanis's *Rapports,* a man who regarded Condillac's *Logic* as a suitable gift for his mistress – heard about Pinel's *Traité* and turned up in the medical school library in quest of it.[92]

Within the *idéologiste* canon, the concept of imagination, given its fullest explication by Condillac, is most critical to Pinel's construction of the cause and cure of insanity. "Of all the faculties of the understanding," Pinel observed, "the imagination appears to be the one most liable to profound lesions."[93] This observation, which had the full backing of Condillac's psychology, has already been obliquely suggested by the tactic Pinel employed in the moral treatment of destroying a delirious idea by "strongly shaking the imagination." We must now further explore Pinel's philosophical rationale for this therapeutic procedure.

For Condillac, imagination was one of the earlier operations of mind to be generated from the first, simple act of perception. It was closely allied to memory, since both were powers of reviving past perceptions independently of the external objects which had initially given rise to them. Noting that Locke had confounded the two, Condillac went on

[90] *Traité*, 1st ed., Introduction, pp. xxxv, liv. *Idéologiste* was the original, self-referential name for a practitioner of *idéologie;* "Idéologue" was the coinage of a detractor, Chateaubriand, but it is the name that has survived. See Joanna Kitchin, *Un journal "philosophique": La Décade, 1794–1807* (Paris: Minard, 1965), p. 118 n6.

[91] *Traité*, 1st ed., Introduction, p. lii.

[92] Cabanis, *Rapports, O.P.,* Vol. 1, p. 587; Destutt de Tracy, *Eléments d'Idéologie,* 3d ed. (Paris: Courcier, 1817; facsimile reprint, Paris: J. Vrin, 1970), Vol. 1, pp. 299–300 n1; Del Litto, *Vie intellectuelle de Stendhal,* pp. 287–88.

[93] *Traité*, 1st ed., p. 70 (also R & O, p. 231).

to specify their differences. Memory required the use of "arbitrary" or "conventional signs" (*signes d'institution*) – that is, language – attached to old perceptions in order that they be retrieved. Imagination could use arbitrary signs, but it could also make do without them: Hence beasts have no memory, but they do have imagination. Imagination, in its capacity for nonverbal functioning, was the more "bestial" of the two operations. Its greater vividness and sensuous immediacy were attributable to the fact that it often "revives the perceptions themselves," while memory "only recalls the signs."[94]

Imagination had a second power, which Condillac added to his definition: It not only revived perceptions but, in so doing, made "new combinations of them at our pleasure." It was thus a potential danger to the sober working of the understanding, an obvious point of entry for error. It had the liberty to play, scramble, and embellish, to "transport the qualities of one subject to another," to "gather in one what for nature sufficed to adorn several" – in short, to dispose of our ideas in a manner "contrary to truth." Some of the linkages of the imagination were made voluntarily, some automatically under the influence of an external impression. (Condillac's example of the latter was the sight of a sharp precipice evoking the idea of violent death.) These automatic linkages were especially firmly cemented, and we were often powerless to separate them; we could, in effect, easily cease to be "masters" of imagination and instead become its "dupes," falling victim to "prejudices" based on merely circumstantial connections between ideas which appeared to be immutable principles. Imagination made us vulnerable to another source of error as well: We sometimes could not distinguish the imaginary objects in our minds from real objects. Condillac considered the example of daydreaming – building "castles in Spain," imagining ourselves fictional heroes or heroines. These were usually safe and innocent pastimes, but under the impact of chagrin and sadness, as we withdrew from ordinary social contact, such daydreams could become more firmly rooted, the power of our judgment to relegate them to the world of imaginary inventions could weaken. "Little by little, we will take all our chimeras for realities." Hence the danger of novel reading, especially for young women, who have little education and hence little capacity to distinguish the fictive from the real.[95]

It is from this discussion of imagination that Condillac derives his fundamental definition of insanity (*folie*): "an imagination which, without our being able to notice it, associates ideas in an entirely disorderly fashion and sometimes influences our judgments or our conduct." On

---

[94] *Essai sur l'origine des connoissances humaines*, in *Oeuvres de Condillac* (Paris: Ch. Houel, Year VI/1798), Vol. 1, pp. 57, 64, 75, 78–81, 88–9. There is concrete evidence that Pinel read this particular text of Condillac. He cites the *Essai* in his *Nosographie philosophique, ou la méthode d'analyse appliquée à la médecine*, 6th ed. (Paris: Brosson, 1818), Vol. 3, p. 20.

[95] Condillac, *Essai*, in *Oeuvres*, Vol. 1, pp. 119–20 n1, 119–29.

the basis of this broad definition, Condillac jovially acknowledges that "it is probable that no one will be exempt"; we are all a little bit mad. But the difference between the fundamentally sane and the mad individual is that in the former the eccentricities of imagination are marginal, rarely intruding into the ordinary course of life, while in the latter, they are central and put the victim "visibly in contradiction with the rest of mankind."[96]

Pinel's use of theatrical devices to "shake the imagination strongly" as an integral part of the moral treatment is now more fully comprehensible and theoretically grounded. An insanity viewed as an imagination gone awry can be countered by a procedure that "shakes up" the imagination in order to dislodge the erroneous idea that has taken hold or to rupture the "vicious chain of ideas."[97] Theatrical display – the *appareil* – is used for this purpose rather than logical argument because it can be assumed that a disordered imagination is operating on a primitive, nonverbal level and can be effectively addressed only on that level. Condillac stated explicitly that to the extent that imagination works by means of linguistic signs, the individual exercises control over it, and rationality prevails.[98] In this regard Pinel raised indirectly, but did not pursue, the issue of whether a jolt to the imagination could subsequently be translated into verbal terms and understood rationally by the patient, or whether the theatrical fiction had to be perpetuated in order that its salutary effect be retained. In the case of the guilt-ridden tailor, he ascribed the eventual therapeutic failure partly to "the imprudence of someone's having mentioned to [the patient] that the definitive sentence pronounced on him during his 'trial' was a mere practical joke."[99] Was the tailor's reason still insufficiently "fortified" at that moment to make the transition from the imagistic to the verbal, or could such a transition never be made? Pinel, the expositor of the moral treatment, does not say.

In its deliberate use of spectacle to address the imagination and alter its contents, the moral treatment bore a strong family resemblance to a contemporaneous phenomenon, the *fête révolutionnaire*. The organizers of these civic celebrations during the Revolutionary decade operated within the same sensationalist-psychological framework as Pinel. They believed in the power of sensory impressions, and of visual images in particular, to "imprint" the "soft wax" which was their characteristic metaphor for the mind. One of their goals was to create, through sensory bombardment, an imaginative connection between the idea of the Republic and that of a superabundant richness, a connection that they believed would produce unwavering political commitment and an

---

96 Ibid., pp. 130–31.
97 Phrase from *Traité*, 1st ed., p. 58 (also R & O, p. 223).
98 Condillac, *Essai*, in *Oeuvres*, Vol. 1, p. 86.
99 *Traité*, 1st ed., p. 237.

invincible heroism.[100] The *fête révolutionnaire*, then, sought to establish politically salutary linkages in the imagination, the moral treatment to sever medically pathological ones.

A school for the passions. But *idéologie* did not embrace the full scope of the moral treatment, for as has been noted, *le moral* had two distinct components – ideas and passions. "The analysis of the functions of the human understanding," wrote Pinel, "has no doubt been greatly advanced by the collected works of the *idéologistes*, but there is another analysis as yet hardly sketched out and for which the cooperation of medicine is needed" – that of the "moral affections" or passions.[101] Medicine was needed with particular urgency here because the passions were thought to belong to the organic life more intimately than did ideas. They arose from internal rather than external sensations, were "sensed" by bodily organs other than the senses. The epigastric region was supposed to be a kind of "home" (*foyer*) or congregating place for them, a visceral center where all passional impressions eventually impinged and where, according to their specific natures, they selectively and palpably altered digestion, respiration, circulation, excretion. From the epigastrium they were transmitted "by a kind of irradiation" or "sympathetic influence" along neural pathways until they reached the brain and, if they were violent enough, disrupted its functioning.[102]

Condillac, it should be said in his defense, was not entirely unmindful of the passions. He saw constitutionally rooted passions as involved in the operation of attention, determining the particular objects that attracted an individual and thus stimulating his or her capacity to attend selectively. Passions were likewise importantly involved in the operation of imagination, exciting it into action, sometimes coloring its products so that they acquired greater verisimilitude and, in extreme cases, became indistinguishable from reality. Condillac went so far as to observe that, for a full consideration of the workings of the mind, an analysis of the operations of the understanding was insufficient; the passions had also to be examined and notice given to "how all these things" – the ideational and the passional – "are combined and confounded." Nonetheless, he felt obliged to exclude a sustained study of the passions from his own work on the grounds that it would be unmanageable and premature.[103]

---

[100] On these points see Mona Ozouf, *La fête révolutionnaire, 1789–1799* (Paris: Gallimard, 1976), pp. 241–45.

[101] Introduction to *Traité*, 1st ed., p. xxxv.

[102] This depiction of the passions is a composite of scattered comments by Pinel – including Introduction to *Traité*, 1st ed., pp. xxxvii–xxxix; "Mémoire sur la manie périodique," p. 100; and *Nosographie philosophique*, 6th ed., Vol. 3, p. 53 – and the more focused discussion in Esquirol's *Des passions*, pp. 17–20.

[103] Condillac, *Essai*, in *Oeuvres*, Vol. 1, pp. 50, 67, 149, 154.

Destutt de Tracy was also aware that an *idéologie* without the passions was seriously flawed. In 1796, he drew a distinction between two ongoing Idéologue enterprises. "Physiological ideology," the project undertaken by Cabanis and other physicians, "required vast knowledge," empirical data about the human organism still in the process of being collected. "Rational ideology," to which Tracy had devoted himself, was by contrast a deductive-philosophical project and "demanded less knowledge."[104] Regarding the two projects as complementary, Tracy tried to incorporate Cabanis's findings into his own work, stating in the *Eléments* that "internal sensations" as well as external ones "set our sensitivity to work" and identifying "passions properly so-called" as "true internal sensations." Other "affections" could derive either from internal sensations (the joy caused by good wine) or from ideas (the joy caused by good news). Yet, however well-intentioned, this consideration of the passions and allied feeling-states remained cursory. As Tracy confessed at the very end of the volume: "This is, I believe, what constitutes *idéologie*. I only regret not having linked it more closely to physiology; but that would have been to go beyond the limits both of my plan and of my own expertise."[105]

Pinel was, in other words, quite correct in his assessment that *idéologie*, at the hands either of its precursor Condillac or its literal founder Tracy, was inadequate to guide his own examination of the passions as causes of insanity or as curative agents to be deployed in the moral treatment. Where then could he seek guidance? Most immediately in the work of an English physician, Alexander Crichton, to whose *Inquiry into the Nature and Origins of Mental Derangement* (1798) he frequently acknowledged his debt.[106] The *Inquiry* contained a long discussion of the passions, apparently tailor-made to Pinel's needs, for it was written from the joint viewpoint of sensationalist psychology – Crichton was familiar not only with "our British psychologists such as Lock [sic], Hartley, Reid, Priestley, Stewart," but also with the work of Condillac – and medicine. Indeed Crichton believed his own originality to lie in the fact that while "moralists and metaphysicians have written copiously on the subject [of the passions]" and their implications for good and evil, he was the first to consider them with the impartial "eye of a natural historian" as simply a "part of our constitution."[107] In

---

104 Cited in Staum, *Cabanis*, pp. 171–72.

105 Tracy, *Eléments*, Vol. 1, pp. 33–37, 424. Staum points out that Tracy oversimplified Cabanis's position on the nature of the passions; see *Cabanis*, p. 239.

106 See esp. the long section on Crichton (or Crighton, as Pinel usually misspells it) in *Traité*, 1st ed., pp. xxi–xxvii, xxxv–xl; and the reference to Chrigton [sic] in *Traité*, 2d ed., p. 12.

107 Alexander Crichton, *Inquiry into the Nature and Origins of Mental Derangement* (London: Cadell, Jr., & Davies, 1798; facsimile reprint, New York: AMS Press, 1976), Vol. 1, pp. xxvii–xxxviii; Vol. 2, pp. 98–99. Pinel explicitly praised him for taking this approach; see *Traité*, 1st ed., Introduction, p. xxii.

separate chapters on joy, melancholy, fear, anger, and love, Crichton discussed the bodily and ideational sources of each, their effects on the various faculties of the mind and on the body, and the continuum along which their more intense forms were converted into different types of mental pathology.

Crichton offered Pinel the most systematic discussion of the passions to be found anywhere in the scientific literature. But Pinel was quick to perceive a particular inadequacy in it; and he thereby revealed the identity of his other, more essential mentor on the subject of the passions. Crichton held that passions were secondary phenomena, arising when the primary phenomena, the desires (e.g., hunger, thirst, sex) – which had clear-cut biological causes and loci and which ministered to the indispensable goals of preservation of the organism and its perpetuation through reproduction – met with obstacles in their drive for satisfaction. It was these thwarted desires, the passions, which had definite pathogenic potential, not the desires themselves. Pinel accepted this primary–secondary distinction, but he questioned the alleged naturalness of all desires and insisted that a more nuanced taxonomy be supplied. The English author, he maintained, "should have added that social life . . . extends almost without limits the needs relative to existence, that it ushers in our concern to gain the esteem of other men, honors, dignities, wealth, fame – and these are artificial desires (*désires factices*) which, always in a state of excitement and rarely satisfied, often lead to the destruction of reason."[108]

Pinel supplied no source for these ideas, but their Rousseauean inspiration is clear. What Pinel has in fact presented here is a kind of capsule summary of the *Discourse on the Origin of Inequality*, with its emphasis on the malign *sentiment factice* of amour propre introduced into the human condition by the founding of society, and its passing comments, so consistent with the fundamental psychophysiological postulate of the Idéologue physicians, interpreting disease as largely a by-product of social life, fostered by "immoderate transports of all the passions."[109] Doubtless Pinel did not think, in this emendation of Crichton, to cite Rousseau by name. Explicit citation was superfluous, because Pinel was mentally saturated with Rousseau, a situation typical of the entire generation of Idéologues.[110] Indeed, Pinel's involvement with Rousseau was probably even greater than average. According to a legend current by the early nineteenth century, he had made a

---

[108] Crichton, *Inquiry*, Vol. 2, pp. 110–14; and Pinel, *Traité*, 1st ed., Introduction, pp. xxv, xxvi n1.

[109] J.-J. Rousseau, *Oeuvres complètes* (Paris: Gallimard-Pléiade, 1959–), Vol. 3, p. 138 and Rousseau's note 15, p. 219.

[110] See Marc Regaldo, "*La Décade* et les philosophes du XVIIIe siècle," *Dix-huitième siècle* 2 (1970): 113–30; and Jean Roussel, *Jean-Jacques Rousseau en France après la Révolution, 1795–1830* (Paris: Armand Colin, 1972), Part 1, Ch. 2.

pilgrimage to the tomb of Rousseau with his friend Chaptal in 1778; though he was unable to sleep for the entire five days and nights of the foot journey, his spiritual exhilaration was such that he returned to Paris fully alert and without a trace of fatigue.[111] To the Idéologues, Rousseau was primarily the great expert on the passions, so it is hardly surprising that Pinel should turn to him automatically when faced with an intellectual problem concerning the passional life. Pinel was, furthermore, well aware that Rousseau had intimate, introspective knowledge of this subject matter: He cited the Rousseau of the "last two parts of the *Confessions* and the *Reveries of a Solitary Walker"* as a case study in melancholia, illustrating the frequent connection of that malady with a fearful mistrust of other people and the abiding conviction that everyone is an enemy.[112] Fittingly, then, through the vehicle of Pinel's implicit and diffuse Rousseauism, Rousseau, so full of psychological suffering and insight himself, became a distantly presiding deity over the birth of French psychiatry.

Pinel gave, as we have seen, a shorthand version of the strategy of coping with diseased passions in the moral treatment – not to destroy them, but to counterbalance them with more powerful passions. This formula seems to have derived from both Enlightenment and ancient sources. At about the middle of the eighteenth century, a noticeable shift occurred in Enlightenment concepts of mind. In a substantial series of texts – including Rousseau's second *Discourse* – passion, once depicted primarily as the subverter of reason, came to be seen in a positive light as reason's indispensable partner.[113] This reevaluation of the passions lies behind Pinel's refusal to control disordered passions by destroying them, for to do so would be to strike at the core of the organism's vitality. As Diderot put it in 1746, the deliberate "ruination of the passions" was "the height of ridiculousness," since, if it succeeded, it would produce "a true monster" who "desired nothing, loved nothing, felt nothing."[114] At the same time, Pinel's proposal to use the device of "counterbalancing" to harness the vital energy of the passions while curtailing their pernicious effects seems to be Aristotelian in inspiration, derived from the definition of virtue in Aristotle's *Ethics* as the mean between an excess and a deficiency of a passion.[115]

---

[111] E. Pariset, "Eloge de Ph. Pinel," *Histoire des membres de l'Académie royale de medecine* (Paris: J.-B. Baillière, 1845), Vol. 1, p. 256.

[112] Pinel, *Nosographie philosophique*, 6th ed., Vol. 3, p. 95.

[113] Ernst Cassirer, *The Philosophy of the Enlightenment*, trans. F. C. A. Koelln and J. P. Pettegrove (Princeton, N.J.: Princeton University Press, 1951), pp. 107–8.

[114] Diderot, *Pensées philosophiques*, in *Oeuvres complètes*, J. Assézat, ed. (Paris: Garnier, 1875–77), Vol. 1, p. 128.

[115] Kathleen M. Grange, "Pinel and Eighteenth-Century Psychiatry," *Bull. Hist. Med.* 35 (1961): 442–53, makes this suggestion (p. 443), an entirely plausible one in light of Pinel's tendency to incorporate classical precepts into his medical science. An alternate source for Pinel's strategy might be inferred from Albert O. Hirschman, *The*

But while Pinel articulates this model of counterbalancing quite explicitly, he rarely applies it in his actual case studies of the moral
treatment.[116] The model widely if tacitly applied in Pinel's "exemplars"
is that of Rousseauean schooling – both the total pedagogy of the *Emile*
(the Idéologues' favorite text of Rousseau)[117] and the distinctive mode
of adult "reeducation" described in the popular epistolary novel *La
nouvelle Héloïse*.[118]

The ideal education described in detail in the *Emile* is centered on the
passions and on monitoring their development. Underlying it is Rousseau's assumption that man in society is alienated from his true, natural self and hence, in the words of one recent commentator, "requires
a healing education which returns him to himself."[119] Rousseau calls it
a "negative education" because its main goal is to prevent the emergence of the artificial social passions – especially amour propre – and as
a corollary to avoid the precocious stimulation of imagination, which as
the second *Discourse* had pointed out is the faculty that sabotages
man's moral progress, turning it into the source of his misery.[120] To
achieve this goal, the child must be withdrawn from society at large
and placed in a controlled environment which simulates the "natural"
situation. There he receives the constant ministrations of a full-time
tutor, who in order to be effective must have complete and absolute
authority over his charge. The tutor, paradoxically, works through
elaborate and even deceitful artifice to restore "naturalness." He carefully structures the environment, controls events, and prearranges experiences so that, while never overtly giving orders, he is omnipresent
and compels his pupil to learn. The noble estate owner Wolmar in the

Passions and the Interests: Political Arguments for Capitalism Before Its Triumph (Princeton,
N.J.: Princeton University Press, 1977), pp. 14–31, which contends that the search for
a secular method of controlling the passions was common to most European thinkers
of the seventeenth and eighteenth centuries. Hirschman discerns three proposed
methods: to repress the passions, to harness them for useful ends, and to "counter-
vail" a harmful passion with a less harmful one. The last is virtually identical to
Pinel's "counterbalancing."

116 Nor was Pinel absolutely consistent in his support of a nondestructive "balancing."
He urged, for example, that cured maniacs read Plato and the Stoics as a "moral
remedy" to guard against relapse by helping them "to vanquish [the] passions."
Traité, 1st ed., p. 36.

117 Roussel, *Rousseau après la Revolution*, p. 41. The Idéologues favored the *Emile* for
methodological reasons, regarding it as a work of "analysis."

118 The parallel between Emile's tutor and Wolmar in the *Nouvelle Héloïse* is made very
forcefully by Judith N. Shklar, *Men and Citizens: A Study of Rousseau's Social Theory*
(Cambridge University Press, 1969), Ch. 4, esp. pp. 146–50. As far as I know, Pinel
never cited the *Emile* by name, but he clearly alluded to that pedagogical text in
Nosographie philosophique, 6th ed., Vol. 3, p. 160.

119 Allan Bloom, Introduction to Jean-Jacques Rousseau, *Emile, or On Education*, trans. A
Bloom (New York: Basic Books, 1979), p. 3.

120 Ibid., pp. 7–9; on the "superfluity" of imagination, see also *Emile*, in *Oeuvres
complètes*, Vol. 4, pp. 304–5.

Nouvelle Héloïse uses artifice in an analogous fashion to cure Saint-Preux of his disordered and disabling passions – constant self-torment by regret and nostalgia. Wolmar and Emile's tutor are both images and embodiments of godlike paternal authority – figures typical in Rousseau's work – who serve as levers capable of rupturing and reversing the vicious trend of human history and raising man out of the corrupted social condition.[121]

The parallels with the moral treatment will be immediately apparent. Both Rousseauean schooling and Pinellian healing devolve upon an all-powerful, larger-than-life authority figure. (The lunatic would be cured, said Pinel, by putting him in a relationship of "strict dependence on a man who, by his physical and moral qualities, is able to exercise an irresistible authority over him.")[122] This authority tends to be vividly embodied. Much like the concierge Francis Willis, Wolmar has a penetrating eye, sometimes called his *oeil éclairé*, with extraordinary powers of looking into the hearts of others.[123] Both Rousseauean schooling and Pinellian healing require a controlled environment withdrawn from the larger society. ("The most powerful remedy . . . can only be found in a well-ordered hospice.")[124] And both call for astute management of the passions (Pinel proves, wrote Destutt de Tracy, that "the art of curing madmen is the same as that of governing the passions of . . . ordinary men"),[125] in both cases achieved through the use of contrived situations, artifice, and pious fraud.

Even the Rousseauean motif of alienation from and restoration to one's true nature is completely applicable to Pinel's therapy. For not only was insanity by its very name "mental alienation" (the formal term *aliénation mentale* had, in medical discourse at least, generally replaced the vulgar *folie*),[126] but Pinel's rhetoric typically depicted cure as an overcoming of alienation, a return to one's true self, a *retour sur lui-même*, and an act of being *ramené à lui-même*.[127] Such terminology is also used in the *Nouvelle Héloïse* to describe the effects of Wolmar's "therapy": "He return[ed] me to myself in spite of myself," his wife

---

121 Shklar, *Men and Citizens*, Ch. 4, pp. 127–50.
122 *Traité*, 1st ed., p. 58 (also R & O, p. 223).
123 Shklar, *Men and Citizens*, pp. 135, 143.
124 *Traité*, 1st ed., p. 58 (also R & O, p. 223).
125 *Eléments*, pp. 229–300 n1.
126 The terms *aliénation mentale*, *aliénation d'entendement*, *aliénation d'esprit* or simply *aliénation* entered French usage as synonyms for *folie* in the seventeenth century in both medical and literary writing; see Paul Robert, *Dictionnaire alphabétique et analogique de la langue française*. Pinel was strongly in favor of the adoption of *aliénation* and the abandonment of *folie* in medical discourse, seeing this linguistic purification as a necessary part of the effort to make medicine more like "the other sciences"; see *Traité*, 2d ed., pp. 128–29, and the discussion of language and psychiatric professionalization in Chapter 4 of this volume.
127 *Traité*, 1st ed., pp. 59, 65 (also R & O, pp. 224, 228).

gratefully testifies, recalling the earlier chaotic state of her passions, which had made her "experience myself as an 'other' outside of myself."[128] In the second edition of the *Traité*, Pinel even noted this parallel between the moral treatment and pedagogy: "What an analogy there is between the art of directing lunatics and that of raising young people! Both require great firmness, but not harsh and forbidding manners; rational and affectionate condescension, but not a soft complaisance that bends to all whims." It surely was not an accidental detail in Pinel's account of the case of the furious soldier that the patient, at the moment that he bows to medical authority, begins to *tutoyer* the chief physician of the hospice; his childish language is emblematic of the status of a child, to which he has, in the process of being cured, reverted.[129]

The Rousseauism that shaped the moral treatment spilled over into other areas of early psychiatric speculation, contributing most notably to the construction by Pinel, Cabanis, and Esquirol of a grand theory about the relationship of insanity to the stage of development of human civilization. The theory hinged upon the *passion factice*, which was a time-bound cultural product, summoned into existence by the birth of society and sensitive to historical change, growing in strength as society became more advanced, complicated, and "unnatural." The inherent insatiability of the *passion factice* made it prone to take on excessive and unruly forms, and these in turn readily conduced to insanity. Pinel's suggestive pronouncements on the pathogenic tendencies of the *passion factice* gave way, at the hands of his student Esquirol, to a series of environmental correlations. Among people who were *policés*, insanity of all types proliferated luxuriantly because of the preponderance of "vehement" and "impetuous" *passions factices;* hence cities more than countryside, capitals more than "cities of the second rank" were nurseries of insanity.[130]

Writing during the early years of the Revolution, Cabanis gave this theory a political – and messianic – dimension. He put his faith in the ability of a new republican political constitution "founded on human nature" to diminish the incidence of insanity and all other disorders of the mind. In the regenerated French polity, he predicted confidently, "society will no longer degrade man; . . . it will no longer stifle in him the passions of nature in order to substitute *passions factices* . . . suitable only for corrupting reason and habit." Citing Rousseau directly, Pinel expressed similar epidemiological views in a medico-political letter to

---

[128] "[Il] me rend à moi malgré moi-même," *La Nouvelle Héloïse*, Part 3, Letter 18, in *Oeuvres complètes*, Vol. 2, p. 356. "Je me sentis tout autre au dedans de moi," ibid., p. 351. The first passage is cited in Shklar, *Men and Citizens*, p. 143.

[129] *Traité*, 2d ed., p. 20; *Traité*, 1st ed., p. 59 (also R & O, p. 224).

[130] Esquirol, *Des passions*, pp. 14–15.

the editor of 1790. The nervous and chronic diseases rampant in France in the twenty or thirty years before the Revolution were, he said, characteristic of a "social order ready to expire," one in which people were mired in "softness and luxury," social bonds had slackened, and "self-interest had frozen all hearts." But the Revolutionary rejuvenation of society – the progress of liberty, "the development of what is called public spirit" – had literally "salutary effects" that were unmistakable to the physician. Within each Frenchman, the expansion of "the soul" produced by political events had redounded to the benefit of the "animal economy," lending it a "surplus of vigor and energy." "People can be heard to say, 'I feel better since the Revolution.' "[131]

When the period of revolutionary zeal was past, Pinel and Esquirol turned their Rousseauism to more conservative ends. Now they tended to view political upheaval as *increasing* the incidence of insanity precisely because it massively stimulated all the passions, and "gave wings" to the artificial ones related to interpersonal rivalries and the loss or gain of wealth and position. A numerical increase in the lunatic population had, said Esquirol, been "observed in France since the beginning of our revolutionary torment." And Pinel noted in 1805 that since the data in his *Traité* had been gathered during "the most stormy epochs of the Revolution," when passions were most inflamed, his assertions about the causes and treatment of insanity remained to be verified in normal times – one of the purposes of his then-current research at the Salpêtrière.[132]

Statistics. The final way in which Pinel sought to elevate the moral treatment to fully scientific status was through the application of statistical methods. The efficacy of the treatment, explained by reference to philosophy, was now to be measured and confirmed quantitatively. Clinical observation was for him (as for Vicq d'Azyr) the basis of medical scientific knowledge; but while he thought such observation entirely adequate for the relatively advanced task of classifying diseases, he felt it left much to be desired in the area of therapeutics. The foundations of this latter part of medicine were "shaky" and its contents only "vague precepts"; "everyone vaunts his own results and more or less cites facts in his own favor." Therapeutic experiments could not continue to be performed in an ad hoc, impressionistic manner, but in order "to be authentic and conclusive . . . must be made on a large number of patients." Cases in which the treatment had failed could not simply be omitted – to preserve an illusion of the physician's extraordinary powers or to avoid wounding his pride – but had to be frankly included in the

---

[131] Cabanis, "Vues sur les secours publics," *O.P.*, Vol. 1, p. 59; Pinel, "Aux auteurs du journal," *Journal de Paris*, January 18, 1790, p. 71.

[132] Esquirol, *Des passions*, p. 15; Pinel, "Recherches sur le traitement général des femmes aliénées," *Moniteur universel*, June 30, 1805, p. 1158.

report and preferably even analyzed at length, for by ascertaining what had gone awry, progress in the application of the treatment could often be made.[133] There had to be a recognized court of last resort in therapeutics lest "contrary opinions" be pitted against each other in an "eternal struggle."[134] In short, the compilation of statistics had to supplement clinical observation; the therapeutic enterprise of medicine "can take on the character of true science only by the application of the calculus of probabilities."[135]

Pinel embarked upon his statistical project around 1800, as soon as he received at the Salpêtrière the patient population of curable insane transferred from the Hôtel-Dieu. This much is apparent because in 1802 at a public session of the Ecole de médecine de Paris, the presiding officer, surveying the recent achievements of members of the faculty, revealed Pinel's interim statistics on the success of his treatment during the Year X.[136] But only in 1807, in an address before the Institut, did Pinel finally report fully on the four-year statistical "experiment" he had conducted. Its purpose was to decide which of the two competing methods then used to treat insanity was preferable: the traditional one, which "consists in hastening the malady on its course through repeated bleedings, strong showers, cold baths or even surprise baths"; or "the other . . . adopted at the Salpêtrière," which was essentially a combination of the moral treatment with what Pinel elsewhere called the "method of expectation" – allowing the malady simply to run its course on the assumption that a spontaneous recovery would ensue, but at the same time watching the patient assiduously so that the healing powers of nature could be supported and furthered by medical intervention of a "moral" or physical sort.[137] Pinel emphasized that he had spared no pains in rigorously carrying out his experiment. He had systematically collected data about each of his Salpêtrière subjects. He had delimited the timespan of the experiment and specified as clearly as possible the "elements" of the "Salpêtrière method" (the aspect of expectation remained constant, but the active remedies varied according to the specific case of insanity and could not be prescribed a priori). And he had made careful tabulations and scrupulously identi-

---

[133] Pinel, *Résultats d'observations et construction des tables pour servir à déterminer le degré de probabilité de la guérison des aliénés* (Paris: Baudouin, 1808), pp. 1, 1–2 n1. Pinel was adamant much earlier in his career about honest reporting of the failed case; see *Traité*, 1st ed., p. 47 and pp. 53–54, where he criticizes Willis on this account (also R & O, pp. 216, 220–21).

[134] Pinel, "Recherches sur le traitement des femmes aliénées," p. 1160.

[135] *Probabilité de la guérison*, p. 2 n1.

[136] Hallé, "Discours," p. 26. Another brief interim statistical report was offered by Pinel himself in 1805 in "Recherches sur le traitement des femmes aliénées," p. 1160.

[137] *Probabilité de la guérison*, pp. 5, 17–19. On the "méthode d'expectation," see *Traité*, 1st ed., p. 84 (also R & O, p. 241); and Pinel, "Expectation," *Dict. des sci. med.*, Vol. 14 esp. p. 252.

fied the "doubtful" cases (those whose prior history was unknown and those who had not been unequivocally cured).

The result of Pinel's study (in which there was no control group) was a 93 percent rate of cure for maniacs and melancholics treated by the "Salpêtrière method" whose illness was "of recent date and not treated elsewhere." Idiots, demented patients, and madwomen of long standing had been excluded from the sample as generally not susceptible to cure; so had those whose illness had been subject to a prior treatment, since they introduced unknown and imponderable factors into the experiment. This excluded population was of significant size: The 93 percent cure rate referred to less than half of the patients admitted to the Salpêtrière during the four years under consideration; and Pinel openly acknowledged that his cure rate for the Salpêtrière population as a whole was only 47 percent. But this was not, to his mind, a damaging concession because he regarded determining the population on which a therapeutic method is efficacious as part of the scientific task of the physician. He was confident that his excellent results with the delimited group could be replicated in any hospital that followed the same principles of treatment.[138]

Why was Pinel so wedded to statistics in his effort to render the moral treatment, as an instance of medical therapeutics, scientific? His own rhetoric provides us with part of the answer. By referring to the method he employed as the "calculus of probabilities," he placed himself, his statistical commitment, and his conception of science squarely in the camp of the mathematician–philosopher and progenitor of the Idéologues, Condorcet. As a recent study of Condorcet has shown, the thinkers of the late Enlightenment had come to regard probability theory as the essential building block of a science of man. An eighteenth-century philosophical commonplace held that, by contrast to the absolute certainty of mathematical knowledge, "knowledge" of the human world was defective, uncertain, merely probable. Apart from and initially unrelated to this epistemological lament, eighteenth-century mathematicians from Bernoulli to Laplace were developing, by reference to dice throwing and games of heads-and-tails, a sophisticated theory of probability. Condorcet's position was based upon the merger of the philosophical and the mathematical notions of probability. He was confident that skepticism could be overcome and that the "moral sciences" could achieve the same degree of certainty as their physical counterparts (though never the perfection of mathematical science) as soon as the calculus of probabilities became their language. The calculus would then measure on a sliding scale the accuracy of propositions about the human world; it would provide a

---

[138] *Probabilité de la guérison*, pp. 3, 23–24, 36–37.

sound basis for opinion and a "sure means of arriving at very great probability in some cases."[139]

Condorcet put these ideas into practice in his *Essai sur l'application de l'analyse à la probabilité des décisions rendues à la pluralité des voix* of 1785. His political science took the form of a mathematical rationale for representative government, a demonstration of the probability that, in an assembly, the vote of the majority would arrive at the truth and the laws so enacted would be "correct."[140] Analogously, Pinel attempted to construct a mathematical and therefore epistemologically sound science of medical therapeutics. His 1807 address to the Institute cited Bernoulli as one of his mentors in the application of the calculus of probabilities. In fact, Pinel's quantification, despite the impressive label he affixed to it, was quite simple – infinitely simpler than Bernoulli's or Condorcet's – and consisted merely in the arithmetical operation of finding the ratio between the number of lunatics cured and the total number of lunatics included in the experiment. But this in no way deterred him from presenting (or perceiving) himself as a disciple of Bernoulli, for as he pointed out, his approach relied upon "one of the elementary principles" of probability theory – "that the probability of an event is measured by a fraction whose numerator is the number of favorable cases and whose denominator is the number of all possible cases."[141]

If the direct intellectual influence prompting Pinel's turn toward statistics was Condorcet's conception of a human science, a more diffuse political influence moved him in the same direction. The period from the Directory to the Consulate, from the Year IV to 1804, was a "golden age" of bureaucratically inspired statistics-gathering, with circulars emanating from the Ministry of the Interior calling on the departments to inventory almost every aspect of local social and economic life, including the medical condition of the population. Since state administrative personnel were lacking for a project of this magnitude, the prefects were to enlist the collaboration of local savant societies and physicians, teachers, and engineers. This initiative, part of the effort to consolidate political control – as had been the statistical proclivity of the enlightened absolutists and, indeed, all French statistical inquiries since the time of Charlemagne's capitularies – was most intense during the periods (the summer of 1797 and June 1798–June 1799) when the philo-

---

[139] Keith Michael Baker, *Condorcet: From Natural Philosophy to Social Mathematics* (Chicago: University of Chicago Press, 1975), Ch. 3 passim, and esp. p. 183 for quote from Condorcet.

[140] Ibid., pp. 228–31.

[141] Pinel, *Probabilité de la guérison*, p. 4; Pinel explicitly mentions Bernoulli's *Ars conjectandi*. A discussion of Pinel as one of the founders of French medical statistics can be found in Terence D. Murphy, "Medical Knowledge and Statistical Methods in Early Nineteenth-Century France," *Medical History* 25 (1981): 301–19.

sophically inclined François de Neufchâteau held the post of minister of the interior.[142] He was the same minister to whom Pinel had sent Pussin's memoir on the moral treatment, together with his own request that Pussin be transferred to the Salpêtrière; and since these documents were found among François de Neufchâteau's personal papers,[143] it seems likely that there was some degree of personal contact between the minister and Pinel. In 1801, when Pinel had just embarked upon the statistical "experiment" at the Salpêtrière, his close friend Chaptal became minister of the interior and made a great contribution to statistics by sponsoring the publication and diffusion of the statistical labors commissioned by François de Neufchâteau.[144] To collect and deploy statistics, then, was manifestly to be in tune with and potentially useful to the government; and Pinel, who owed to the government the brilliant upswing in his career since the Revolution, could not have been oblivious to the political connotations of statistical method – or to the promise it held of continued political rewards.

A therapy for the Revolution

The odyssey of the moral treatment – its origins in "charlatanistic" practice; the salvaging operation by which Pinel converted it into a respectable tenet of official medicine, assimilating it to the models of sensationalist psychology and Rousseauean pedagogy and confirming it statistically – does not in itself explain its success as an originative paradigm. Kuhn offers some guidance here by providing two "internal" criteria for a paradigm. The moral treatment, it is not difficult to see, meets both of them. It was in the first place "sufficiently unprecedented to attract an enduring group of adherents"[145] – unprecedented, that is, in the context of official medicine, where the remedies traditionally sanctioned were of a physical nature. This fundamental novelty of the moral treatment was often remarked upon. Reviewing the first edition of the *Traité*, Moreau de la Sarthe described as "limited" the mentality of the traditional physician "for whom all the resources of the art are contained in the pharmacist's boutique. . . . The true physician will study the work of Citizen Pinel and will see the sphere of activity of the medical art enlarged." The young Esquirol described the moral treatment similarly as "pushing back (*reculer*) the limits of a science." Even in the mid-nineteenth century the moral treatment, as

---

142 See Jean-Claude Perrot, *L'age d'or de la statistique régionale française (an IV–1804)* (Paris: Société des Etudes Robespierristes, 1977), pp. 5, 24–28, 61; and Pierre Marot, *Recherches sur la vie de François de Neufchâteau* (Nancy: Berger-Levrault, 1966), pp. 279–329.

143 Weiner, "Apprenticeship of Pinel," p. 125.

144 Perrot, *Age d'or*, p. 33.

145 Kuhn, *Structure*, p. 10.

opposed to the usual practice of physicians who "exhaust the entire pharmaceutical arsenal," was being depicted by some as "this *new* way open to science."[146]

The second of Kuhn's criteria was also easily met: The moral treatment not only created a new scientific community bound by fundamental consensus but was "sufficiently open-ended to leave all sorts of problems for the . . . group of practitioners to resolve" and hence could usher in a period of "normal science."[147] Pinel had adumbrated the new approach, provided case studies and some implicit theoretical scaffolding, but many details of the new therapy remained to be worked out. He himself began this process by exempting dementia and idiocy – two of the four genres of insanity in his classificatory scheme – from the putative scope of efficacy of the moral treatment; he also exempted certain subspecies of mania.[148] But his scattered yet crucial suggestions that the tactics of the moral treatment had in every instance to be tailored a posteriori to the causes and precise ideational content of the delirium[149] were never systematically developed. Pinel left no shortage of "problems . . . to resolve"; his disciples report that he even underscored the "open-ended," capacious nature of his work. "Although," one wrote in 1818, "the *Traité* of Monsieur Pinel has been translated into every language [and] is the manual of every physician who treats lunatics, the celebrated professor, with that candor that belongs only to genius, never ceases to invite his students to improve upon what he has begun."[150]

But Kuhn's internal criteria do not exhaust the subject of why the moral treatment was so roundly hailed. They ignore the "fit" of this prospective paradigm with the external and in particular the political environment. As we have seen, Pinel's favor with the Revolutionary government and his resultant prominence in the newly created medical establishment enabled the moral treatment to pass readily into orthodoxy and to be institutionalized as the approved therapy for the insane at Bicêtre and the Salpêtrière. But the connection between the Revolution and the moral treatment went deeper than these circumstances, penetrating into the very nature of the therapy itself.

The politics of douceur. At the very opening of the Revolution, the lunatic acquired a peculiar importance – both real and symbolic – because

---

146 Moreau de la Sarthe, "Art de guérir," p. 464; Esquirol, *Des passions*, p. 13; E. L., "De la musique dans le traitement de la folie," *Gazette médicale de Paris*, 2d ser., 10 (February 12, 1842), my italics.
147 Kuhn, *Structure*, p. 10.
148 *Traité*, 1st ed., pp. 81–83 (also R & O, pp. 239–40).
149 See, e.g., "Recherches sur le traitement des femmes aliénées," p. 1160; *Probabilité de la guérison*, p. 18.
150 Unsigned "Avertissement" to "Série de fragmens sur l'aliénation mentale," *Journal générale de médecine* 62 (1818): 145.

his status happened to be enmeshed in a salient political issue. The royal lettre de cachet was to the revolutionaries a singularly blatant example of the exercise of arbitrary power that marked the Old Regime. The special prisons for victims of the lettres de cachet were thus suppressed at once, and the National Assembly appointed a committee to draft a law on the disposition of the illegally detained prisoners. The committee's report, presented in February 1790, divided the prisoners into four groups: those who had never been accused of a crime; those condemned without appeal; those against whom an arrest warrant had been issued but who had never been brought to trial; and finally, those locked up for madness. The last group was further subdivided into those who were truly insane and those about whom the allegation of madness was a deliberate subterfuge. (It was standard Old Regime practice for one party who wanted another removed from the scene for whatever nefarious reason to obtain a lettre de cachet from the Crown authorizing incarceration on grounds of lunacy; by this device, parents punished disobedient children and greedy relatives tampered with the laws of inheritance.) Because of this admixture of real and alleged *fous*, the committee recommended that each member of the fourth group be visited several times by a medical doctor in order that the state of his reason might be accurately determined – a significant provision in itself, indicating as it does the Revolutionary scientism that fostered the medicalization of insanity. Most striking, however, were the remarks of the committee's *rapporteur* concerning the way the bona fide insane were to be handled:

> You will still, gentlemen, have to take actions to ameliorate the condition of the unfortunates who, needing daily surveillance, cannot enjoy liberty. Until the present, they have almost always been treated in the different *maisons de force* of the realm with an inhumanity which, far from curing their illness (*mal*), was suitable only to aggravate it. Persuaded that it is by *douceur* and not by the ferocity of a barbarous regimen (*régime*) that it is possible to cure these unfortunates, you will probably resolve to assign – either from the already existing funds of the *maisons de force* or from the [nationalized] ecclesiastical properties – a portion of revenues sufficient to assure to the insane the help that their condition requires of the public charity (*bienfaisance*).

He went on to say that this *douceur*, while necessary in all eras, was a "still more sacred obligation for us." For in opening the special prisons, it had become apparent that some of the prisoners whose reason had been completely sound when they were locked away, had become insane "by their long captivity and by the torments they suffered when the laws were mute and the king's ministers all-powerful."[151]

This passage, simple on the surface, is upon examination extraordinarily rich in its conflation of levels of meaning: The medical and the

[151] *Arch. parl.*, 1st ser., Vol. 9, p. 661.

political become almost indistinguishable. *Douceur* is held up both as a medical treatment and as a political desideratum. It is contrasted to the "ferocity of a barbarous regime" – where *régime* is equally a part of the medical and political vocabularies, and the "barbarous" regimen/regime rejected is simultaneously the micro-regimen of chains and other corporal punishments applied to the mad inmates of the *hôpital-général*, and the old political macro-regime with its willful disrespect for law and its "ministerial despotism."[152] *Douceur* in the medical treatment of the insane, as in politics, is thus the inevitable choice of the Revolution, and it becomes appropriate to espouse this form of medical treatment in a national legislative forum by dint of the analogies, almost equivalencies, posited: The care of the insane has become a thoroughly political issue. Having seen that *douceur* is a recurring word in Pinel's description of the moral treatment, we can now appreciate the political resonance which the word had for him and his readers.

A second and related aspect of the conjoint medical-political nature of insanity is touched upon here: insanity as a civil status entailing the deprivation of liberty ("the unfortunates who, needing daily surveillance, cannot enjoy liberty"). Such a status raises new and serious problems in a revolutionary setting where the foremost commitment is to liberty as the right of the individual citizen. The lunatic must be protected insofar as possible from the morally degrading consequences of unfreedom; the double "captivity" of an incarcerative institution and a despotic polity can, says the report, even cause insanity. Where deprivation of liberty is unavoidable, the committee offers *douceur* as compensation – as recognition of the right to liberty which, though abrogated, still resides potentially in the individual who has "lost the use of reason." The argument here about the political necessity for *douceur* is replicated (though relativized) in Pinel's 1798 reasoning about the kind of political consciousness that necessitates the moral treatment:

> It would perhaps be to fall into intellectual vagueness to treat in a manner that is general and uniform for all peoples the question of the institution of corporal punishment for lunatics. For how can we be sure that Negroes who live in servitude on Jamaica or Russian slaves, shaped by an oppressive system for the whole of their lives, ought not, in the case of insanity, be subjected to the same harsh and despotic yoke. But (leaving aside some favorable effects that can be expected from the use of fear in the cure of mania) does not the lively sensibility of the Frenchman and his violent reaction – as long as he conserves a glimmer of his reason – against every shocking abuse of power determine on his behalf the forms of repression that are the most gentle (*douce*) and the most in conformity with his character?[153]

---

[152] Ibid. for this phrase.
[153] R & O, p. 227 (also *Traité*, 1st ed., pp. 63–64).

And of all the forms of *douceur* possible in treating the insane, this line of analysis might continue, the Pinellian moral treatment is, in terms of the ideology of the liberal Revolution, the most politically "correct." A diffuse, nonspecific kindness would, to be sure, go some distance toward satisfying the criteria of political liberalism by recognizing the essential humanness of the lunatic and hence his capacity for freedom. This point was made in a bureaucratic admonition of the Year VI, under the politically liberal regime of the Directory, that *douceur* be employed in institutions for the insane: "How culpable, then, are those who, in familiarizing themselves with this malady, cease to see their fellow-creatures (*semblables*) in its poignant victims and treat them with harshness!"[154] But the specific strategies of the Pinellian moral treatment go beyond this; by striving to make contact with the vestiges of reason remaining in the lunatic, they ratify most forcefully his status as *semblable* and his consequent capacity for freedom. The developmental theories of Condillac and Rousseau that underlie Pinel's rendition of the moral treatment allow a bridging of the gap between the sane and the insane. They lay bare how reason went awry – by the assaults of an overstimulated imagination and the insatiable demands of artificial passions – and thus make possible the charting of a hypothetical path back to reason. The lunatic is not consigned to total "otherness" but is located on a continuum with the sane person, sharing the same mental structures. The moral treatment thus postulates the same attitude as Condillac's pedagogy, that of the feasibility of building, with the tools of sensationalist psychology, a bridge to a qualitatively different mind. "To execute my plan," wrote Condillac in his prefatory remarks to the course of study he outlined for the prince of Parma, "I must approximate (*s'approcher de*) my pupil, put myself entirely in his place; I must be a child rather than a tutor."[155] So too could the Pinellian practitioner believe himself able to reconstruct rationally the mental world of the lunatic, to "put [himself] in [the lunatic's] place," and, through this momentary act of identification, to lead him back to sanity.

---

[154] AN: AJ² 60, "Circulaire du Ministre de l'Intérieur notifiant la réouverture de l'Hospice de Charenton," 1 nivôse Year VI. The "preliberal" conception of the lunatic as a being who had forfeited his humanness and reverted to animality was no liberal straw man. It survived residually even in the municipal police ordinances enacted by the National Assembly (the Laws of 16–24 août 1790 and 22 juillet 1791), and later in the Napoleonic civil code (Articles 475, 479), in provisions concerning penalties for those who had negligently "allowed madmen [*fous* or *furieux*] or wicked and ferocious animals in their keep to wander," either frightening or actually harming passersby or inflicting property damage. The insane individual and the wild beast were thus placed in a single category.

[155] Condillac, "Discours préliminaire" to *Cours d'études pour l'instruction du prince de Parme*, in *Oeuvres de Condillac*, Vol. 5, p. lxi.

The clamor for the moral treatment: non-Pinellian initiatives during the Revolution. Nothing makes clearer the incorporation of the moral treatment into revolutionary ideology and practice than the numerous attempts during the course of the Revolution to inaugurate the moral treatment – attempts that were wholly independent of the man who would eventually be credited with that accomplishment, Pinel. The first of these, which Pinel later cited in the introduction to the first edition of the *Traité*, was a 1791 pamphlet by an obscure civil servant in the department of the Var. Its message hinged upon the author's visit two years before to Père Poution, a monk and *guérisseur des fous* employing moral methods in the village of Manosque in the neighboring department of the Basses-Alpes. Mourre, the civil servant, described Père Poution in recognizably Rousseauean terms as a larger-than-life tutor – "a beneficent being who joins knowledge with *sensibilité*, [who] becomes the repository of [the lunatics'] pain and of their thoughts . . . , who goes back with them to the source of their ills . . . [and] breaks the spell of the illusions that surround them." Meeting some of the lunatics whom Père Poution has cured and moved by the depth of the gratitude they show for the monk, Mourre makes his resolve. "I said to myself: here a single man spreads so much benefit! and this man is ignored while the author of an epigram is known throughout France!" Addressing "my compatriots," he went on to present a scheme whereby *secours moraux* could be integrated into the treatment of lunatics throughout France without the expense of building a special hospital in each department. ("I aspire to reconcile . . . the calculations of economy with the duties of humanity.") The existing foundations – the hôtels-Dieu and the *hôpitaux-généraux* – were to remain, but their directors would work individually, in the fashion of Père Poution, with the lunatics dispersed among their inmate populations. Mourre explicitly assigned the moral treatment to lay personnel and gave to the accredited physician the function of attentively observing the course of the insanity and prescribing drugs. This projected new treatment program for the insane was an end to "barbarism" consonant with the Revolution, or as Mourre referred to it elliptically, the "history of the French nation . . . for almost the past three years."[156]

A similar proposal, also written in 1791, can be found in the archives of the revolutionary commune of Paris. It emanated from a certain Escourbiac, a surgeon and the proprietor of a Paris *maison de santé* – or as he called it, using the virtually synonymous term, a *pension bourgeoise* – which catered to patients of all types. Escourbiac's was one of the better known private facilities for lunatics in the capital, quite on a par in this regard with the *maison* Belhomme, which had once em-

---

[156] Mourre, *Observations sur les insensés* (Toulon: Impr. de Surre, 1791), pp. 5–6, 14, 19, 21–22.

ployed Pinel. In his manuscript memoir to the mayor of Paris, Escourbiac noted that he had always been especially interested in the treatment of *aliénés d'esprit* and had in his sanatorium made a study of the
various modes of therapy that could be applied to them. He had
achieved his most impressive results largely through "moral means
rather than physical means." In light of the expertise he had acquired,
which contrasted so sharply with prevailing techniques, he urged the
formation of a new "therapeutic national and patriotic" establishment
for the treatment of the insane where his principles would be followed.
He would generously lend his services to such an establishment – by
implication, he would also direct it – asking no salary but only government subsidies for food and equipment. At the end of his proposal.
Escourbiac gave Thouret as a reference; thus it seems that he traveled
in the same circles as Pinel. The surgeon, however, seems to have
traveled very much on the periphery, for he was unable to secure the
backing of those in power. While the reply of the mayor's office could
"only applaud" the humanity of the suggestions Escourbiac had submitted, it indicated that the municipality would have to wait until the
national legislature made good its promises to organize a broad system
of public assistance before undertaking any such projects on its own.[157]

Yet a third plan for the incorporation of the moral treatment into a
system of government-sponsored institutions was the subject of a
memoir by a Monsieur Broutet, the director of a hospice for lunatics
in Avignon. Unlike Escourbiac's, which ended up in the dim recesses
of a bureaucratic dossier, Broutet's memoir acquired a certain celebrity
when it received a medal from the Lycée des Arts in the Year V (1797)
and was subsequently published and discussed in the *Décade philosophique*.[158] The Lycée des Arts, founded in Paris in 1793 by an engi-
neer, was an expression of the antielitist, antiacademic ideology that
preponderated during the Jacobin phase of the Revolution. Its primary aim was to raise the dignity of the artisan by freeing him from
the clutches of the Academy of Sciences – giving him his own institutional center for the communication of his inventions and a series of
prizes that would spur him on to achievement.[159] That the moral

---

[157] See AN: F^{15} 242, no. 578. The memoir is undated, but textual evidence points to 1791
as its year of composition. On the prominence of the *maison* Escourbiac, see Tuetey,
Assistance publique, Vol. 1, p. xvii and p. xvii n1.

[158] See *Mémoire qui a obtenu une médaille au Lycée des arts le 30 Messidor an 5 . . . contenant
un exposé précis et succinct de la situation de l'Hospice des Insensés de la ville d'Avignon et du
mode de traitment qui a operé des cures . . .* (Paris: Impr. du Lycée des Arts, n.d.), BN:
Te^{66} 91. This four-page booklet contains Broutet's memoir and the appreciation of it
by the president of the Lycée des Arts. The *Décade philosophique* article, largely an
abridgment of the above, is "Extrait d'une mémoire sur la situation de l'hospice des
insensés de la ville d'Avignon" (20 thermidor Year V): 270–73.

[159] See Roger Hahn, *The Anatomy of a Scientific Institution: The Paris Academy of Sciences, 1666–
1803* (Berkeley and Los Angeles: University of California Press, 1971), pp. 217–18.

treatment was honored in this forum thus underscores its popular origins.

According to Broutet, a combination of *remèdes moraux* and *remèdes physiques* had been used at Avignon for almost twenty years[160] under the inspiration of English practitioners, especially Willis. Broutet gave a laudably precise account of the "moral" aspect, which he said consisted of "particular" and "general" strategies. The former, which were preferable, could be used when the exact cause of the insanity had been discerned, usually from information supplied by relatives. The "particular" strategies then aimed at "destroying" this cause by persuading the patient of its "imminent cessation." The example offered by Broutet was of a twenty-three-year-old woman whose father had volunteered that the cause of her madness was her jealousy of her brother; pressed by Broutet, the father acknowledged that this jealousy had an entirely real basis, for he had confiscated all of his daughter's earnings and used them to buy gifts for her male sibling. At Broutet's urging, the brother was now sent to another town for advanced training in his craft, and the father demonstrated his affection for the young woman by caresses and gifts. This constituted the *remède moral particulier*, which combined with physical means (baths, showers, purgatives, etc.) and general moral means produced a complete cure in something more than a month. The general moral means were "the most gentle (again, *douce*) consolations and a variety of distractions" – promenades, communal meals, games, pleasurable reading, music – skillfully combined and "lavished upon the patients."

Like Mourre, Broutet specified that the moral treatment be administered by laymen. Dr. Gastaldy (who will figure later in our story) had been employed at the Avignon hospice before the Revolution, but Broutet noted that his function – and that of the other accredited medical men who succeeded him – was to visit patients regularly and follow the course of each malady "in order to prescribe the most appropriate *physical* remedies." Elsewhere in the memoir Broutet was even more explicit and emphatic: "The administrators . . . to whom the lunatics would be entrusted [in his proposed scheme] would not have to take the trouble of becoming health officers (*officiers de santé*) as far as moral remedies are concerned." Broutet's proposal was that the pattern of the Avignon hospice be generalized, that the French government form comparable establishments, exclusively for lunatics and numbering one for every three departments. Broutet expressed suspicion of privately owned *pensions* for lunatics whose proprietors might be motivated by cupidity to skimp on the care of their patients. In keeping with this

---

[160] The medal elicited some debate over Avignon's priority and uniqueness in the implementation of the moral treatment in France. See the comments of the president of the Lycée des Arts in *Mémoire qui a obtenu une médaille*, p. 3 and p. 3 n9, and Pussin's testy complaint in his 1798 memoir, in Weiner, "Apprenticeship of Pinel," p. 132.

attitude, he even required that the administrators, who were to give the moral treatment in the public hospices he envisioned, be unsalaried, that they be chosen from among "affluent and charitable citizens," and that they dispense care "every day to this portion of suffering human-ity . . . in an entirely disinterested manner," finding recompense only in the gratitude of their patients and their own "utility to the Republic." To be a provider of the moral treatment was, then, to have a self-abne-gating secular calling, a republican vocation.

The final and most successful example of a non-Pinellian initiative to put the moral treatment into effect was the Revolutionary establishment of the Maison nationale de Charenton. Under the Old Regime the same buildings had housed the *pensionnat* of the Brothers of Saint-Jean-de-Dieu, which received lunatics on a charitable basis or for a fee and was also regularly used by the King as a prison for those seized by lettre de cachet. Tainted by this latter function, and on shaky financial grounds anyway after the state confiscation of monastic lands, the institution was closed by the Jacobins in the Year III.[161] Some two years later, however, the Executive of the Directory reopened it in fully secularized form, decreeing that "the hospice of the commune of Charenton, near Paris, known as a refuge for madmen, shall be restored to its initial purpose," and furthermore that it be turned into a model institution of its kind, a national showcase. "All necessary arrangements shall be made there to establish a *complete treatment* for the cure of insanity," for "there exists in France no establishment where madness is treated methodically by the medical art and in such a way as to arrive at a more verified cure." The new Charenton was intended to replace the lunatic wards of the Hôtel-Dieu, whose therapeutic techniques, once touted by Tenon, were now implicitly being labeled old-fashioned and inadequate. As soon as the "complete treatment" was put into effect at Charenton, the treat-ment of madness was to cease at the "Grand Hospice d'Humanité," as the Hôtel-Dieu was then called.[162]

Left vague in the original decree, the "complete treatment" was spelled out in the Year VI in a circular of the minister of the interior notifying the administrators of the departments of the reopening of Charenton. "Citizens, physical remedies are not the only ones to which we should resort for the cure of this malady; *moyens moraux* can also procure great successes. The doctor must call philosophy and the most tender humaneness to his aid." Hence the circular announced the appointment to Charenton of a *médecin philosophe*, one "who appears to have the greatest claim to this post." The man so honored had figured

---

[161] Imbert, *Le droit hospitalier*, p. 119; and the unsigned ms. "Notice historique et statis-tique sur la maison royale de Charenton" in AN: AJ² 87, dated (on AN dossier) 6 août 1818. The *maison* was founded in 1641 and was taken over by the Order of Saint-Jean-de-Dieu in 1644.

[162] AN: AJ² 60, decree of 27 prairial Year V, Preamble, Articles 1–2, my italics.

peripherally in the memoir for which Broutet had just received the medal of the Lycée des Arts. He was "Citizen Gastaldy, chief doctor at the hospice for the insane at Avignon since 1762," where he had contributed to the great fame of that hospice as a place where successful results were obtained by the "union of *secours moraux* and *remédes physiques*" and where the French had thus demonstrated that they were in no way inferior to the haughty English in such techniques.[163] A description of Gastaldy at Charenton written by one of his colleagues endows him with all the "classic" attributes of the practitioner of the moral treatment. "His gentleness (*douceur*), amiability, and general good nature in his relationships with the patients endeared him to these unfortunates, who considered him their father and comforter. Giving voice to his philanthropic musings, he used to say to me, 'A quarter of an hour of gaiety that we procure for the patients will, in effect, double our salaries and will be our sweetest recompense.' "[164]

"The success of the establishment," the ministerial circular read, "depends especially on the physician." But this statement did not anticipate the balance of power that would in fact evolve at Charenton, a balance of power far more consonant with the lay origins of the moral treatment and the never-implemented proposals of Mourre and Broutet. The story of the early years of Charenton thus reveals not only the affinity between the Revolution and the moral treatment but also the deep tensions produced by the ambiguous nature of the latter. The story deserves to be told here, at least briefly, because it clarifies the meaning of Pinel's historical role in laying claim to the moral treatment for official medicine and launching the specialty of psychiatry by effecting the transformation of charlatanism.

The dominant figure at the newly refounded Charenton was not the physician Gastaldy but the director, François-Simonnet de Coulmiers. This latter, also appointed by the government, had (as he put it with characteristic self-assertiveness) "taken possession" of his post in the Year VI.[165] Formerly a cleric, a member of the regular order of canons, the Prémontrés, de Coulmiers had gone under the name of the Abbé d'Abbécourt during the Old Regime and the early days of the Revolution. He was elected to the Estates-General in 1789 as a deputy of the first estate from Paris and soon emerged as a highly vocal member of the liberal clergy, speaking out in favor of the meeting together of the three estates in a national assembly and of the unerring rectitude of majority rule, and later urging his fellow clerics to swear the civic oath

---

[163] Ibid., circular of 1 nivôse Year VI.
[164] AN: AJ² 100, "Précis sur la maison de santé du gouvernement à Charenton," dated September 1812, ms. pp. 8–9. Unsigned, but from textual evidence clearly by de Coulmiers.
[165] Ibid., ms. p. 3.

in ratification of the Civil Constitution of the Clergy.[166] Unlike the Abbé Sieyès, another and more famous liberal cleric, the Abbé d'Abbécourt did not abandon his clerical identity in 1789 but championed the Revolution precisely from that vantage point, taking upon himself the role of shaping clerical opinion in a revolutionary direction. In February 1790 he was appointed to the Comité de mendicité as one of its four original members. There he met Thouret,[167] a circumstance which no doubts explains how he became part of that medical-bureaucratic nexus from which his appointment at Charenton eventually issued.

At Charenton, the moral treatment became as much the province of the lay concierge de Coulmiers as of the medical man Gastaldy. De Coulmiers described Gastaldy as "my counsel and my friend"; "we sought *together*," he wrote, "the means of dispelling [delirious ideas] by innocent games, concerts, dance, comedies in which the roles were played by the patients" – and this set of jointly devised therapeutic techniques, having distraction as their unifying principle, de Coulmiers called "this moral treatment."[168] Nor was Gastaldy a constant presence at the institution. Already of an advanced age when appointed, he made his medical visits there only every other day, and during the winter, "given the rigor of the season and the condition of the roads," often only once every four days.[169]

When Gastaldy died in 1805, it was de Coulmiers's firm intention to continue the quasi-lay regimen that had developed at Charenton since its refounding. His candidate for Gastaldy's successor was, logically enough, an insider – the surgeon at the institution, who "had accompanied Gastaldy on his visits for eight years" and had acquired "the habit of treating insanity" from this unpresumptuous man.[170] But de Coulmiers's preference was ignored in favor of a protégé of a divisional chief of the Ministry of the Interior. Suspicious from the outset of this candidate, de Coulmiers claimed that he had sought the opinion of his old colleague Thouret, who was reportedly "a little equivocal; he said nothing too affirmative about the talents of the subject."[171] But it is clear that Thouret and the other representatives of established medi-

---

[166] See "Motion de M. de Coulmier, abbé d'Abbécourt, député du clergé de Paris, extra muros," n.d., BN: Le^{29} 2142, esp. p. 1 n1; and "Opinion sur le serment civique par M. l'abbé d'Abbécourt, député à l'Assemblée nationale," 1791, BN: Ld^4 3229.

[167] C. Bloch and A. Tuetey, eds., *Procès-verbaux et rapports du Comité de mendicité de la Constituante, 1790–91* (Paris: Impr. nationale, 1911), pp. 1, 22.

[168] "Précis sur la maison de santé," ms. pp. 9–10, my italics. This therapeutic tenet was also de Coulmiers's justification for granting permission to a famous inmate, the Marquis de Sade, to stage plays at the asylum, the act for which de Coulmiers is best remembered today.

[169] AN: AJ^2 100, Draft of "Rapport au Ministre de l'Intérieur sur la nomination d'un médecin," n.d., from textual evidence written by de Coulmiers.

[170] Ibid.

[171] "Précis sur la maison de santé," ms. p. 11.

cine in the capital in fact intervened on behalf of this candidate in order to prevent virtually complete lay control of Charenton.[172] The new chief physician of Charenton was Antoine-Athanase Royer-Collard, who had received his medical degree in Paris three years before and who had a vastly different conception of medical power and its exclusivity than had the relaxed and latitudinarian provincial Gastaldy. Royer-Collard's insistence upon the superior authority of the physician in an institution for the insane provoked years of bitter quarrels with the equally strong-willed de Coulmiers.[173]

But while this lay–medical battle continued to smolder inconclusively at Charenton, its ultimate outcome had in a sense already been decided within the upper reaches of the bureaucracy. For as we have seen, the insane of the Hôtel-Dieu were to have been transferred to Charenton (as soon as the "complete treatment" had been installed there) in recognition of Charenton's status as the successor to the Hôtel-Dieu, the new-style "model institution" of its type in France. Not only were the lunatic wards of the Hôtel-Dieu to have been emptied "from that day forward" but, the 1797 decree of the minister of the interior continued, "the disease of madness shall no longer be treated *in any other Paris hospice.*"[174] In 1802, however, the Ministry of the Interior substantially reneged on this promise, sending only a portion of the Hôtel-Dieu population to Charenton and a large number to the Salpêtrière, the institution under Pinel's medical aegis.[175] The official, statist choice for the medicalized moral treatment of Pinel over the lay moral treatment of de Coulmiers had been made.

---

[172] This is the opinion of Esquirol in his highly polemical comments in "Mémoire historique et statistique sur la maison royale de Charenton," *Ann. d'hyg. pub.*, 1st ser., 13 (1835): 45. His opinion is confirmed by a much less biased source; see AN: AJ[16] 6308, "Séance publique de l'Ecole de médecine de Paris du 10 novembre 1806, Discours de M. le Professeur Jussieu," p. 22.

[173] See AN: AJ[2] 100, dossier labeled by the archivist "Démêlés de Royer-Collard et de Coulmiers." A typical reprimand of the overweening de Coulmiers by the irate Royer-Collard: "It is to me and not to you that the patients are entrusted for everything concerning their malady and its treatment. . . . As for you, you are charged with furnishing [them] with food, bedding, laundry and blankets, with keeping them clean, with insuring that all the measures . . . prescribed by the chief physician are executed." (Draft of a letter dated July 9 1813.) De Coulmiers's warfare included informing the minister of the interior, in the wake of the Mallet du Pan conspiracy, of Royer-Collard's lack of Bonapartist sentiment; see his letter dated November 22, 1812. The attitude of official medicine toward de Coulmiers's role at Charenton is also expressed, retrospectively and acerbically, by Esquirol in "Mémoire historique et statistique," pp. 44–45. I have analyzed another aspect of the quarrels between de Coulmiers and Royer-Collard in "Foucault among the Sociologists: The 'Disciplines' and the History of the Professions," *History and Theory* 23 (1984): esp. 188–91.

[174] Decree of 27 prairial Year V, Article 2, my italics.

[175] Marcel Gauchet and Gladys Swain give the details of the 1802 transfer in *La pratique de l'esprit: L'institution asilaire et la révolution démocratique* (Paris: Gallimard, 1980), pp. 53–54.

Healthy sentimentality

If the political resonance of the moral treatment helped it to achieve paradigmatic status, so too did its cultural resonance. Advocates of the moral treatment can be seen as proto-Romantics, declaring that the intellectual life did not embrace the whole human being, that the affective life had also to be considered. This was Pinel's essential point when he first noted the insufficiency of Condillac's philosophy and the corresponding impropriety of defining insanity solely in terms of intellectual errors, without regard to passional aberrations. Pinel's anti-intellectualist bias became more pronounced with time. For example, the brief discussion of the passions in the introduction to the first edition of the *Traité* – largely a precis of Crichton – gave way, by the second edition, to a new, full-blown typology of the passions as causes of insanity.[176]

As a result of this passional emphasis, descriptions of the moral treatment could take on a tone of effusive sentimentality that even verged on mawkishness. Thus, in the case of the guilt-ridden tailor, Pinel observed that, after the patient was set to work repairing garments and had emerged from the blackest depths of his melancholy, "he even spoke with a tender concern of his six-year-old child, whom he earlier appeared to have forgotten, and evinced an intense desire to have the boy near. This revival of his *sensibilité* appeared to me to be a most happy augury." The cycle was repeated: When melancholy again engulfed the tailor, he resumed his "indifference or rather aversion to his child, whom he seemed to push aside with disdain"; but after the use of the mock trial restored his mental equilibrium, "he solicited with all the expression of *sensibilité* the return of his child." The young Esquirol generalized this point about the annihilation of the natural *sensibilité* and its revivification through the moral treatment. "A symptom which accompanies all insanities – and which has not escaped Professor Pinel, who has given notice of it numerous times – is the alteration of the moral affections. Sometimes the attack is ushered in by coldness and aversion towards close relatives and intimate friends; sometimes the dominant idea of the insanity is that being in the bosom of one's family is intolerable. . . . This moral perversion is so striking, so constant, that is appears to me to be an essential characteristic of insanity . . . and [conversely] the desire to see relatives and friends, the joy, the tears of *sensibilité* in seeing them . . . offers an infallible sign of an imminent cure."[177] In Moreau de la Sarthe's case histories, where moral means are used to alleviate the emotional disorders of

---

[176] *Traité*, 2d ed., pp. 25–39. See also Moreau de la Sarthe's review of Pinel, *Traité*, 2d ed., in *Moniteur universel*, August 17, 1811, p. 877.

[177] Pinel, *Traité*, 1st ed., pp. 234–37; Esquirol, *Des passions*, p. 29.

soldiers wounded in the Napoleonic wars, healing power is imputed to a full, cathartic expression of painful feelings. An amputee "abandons himself without reserve and confides all his fears, his harrowing anxieties" about the future of his family to the *homme sensible* who has questioned him; the latter "cannot hold back his tears and lets them fall on the sickbed." Another soldier, filled with nostalgia for his home department, is encouraged to talk about that beloved place. "Several conversations, some moving scenes, [and finally] abundant tears that, until then, a spasm of repressed (*concentrée*) sadness had hardly allowed to flow."[178]

Thus certain stereotypic marks – tenderness for little children, the blissful harmony ascribed to the family circle, tears flowing freely and copiously in response to familial joys or sorrows – connect the moral treatment and its proponents' concept of human nature to the eighteenth-century cult of sentimentality, or, as it is sometimes called, the preromantic mode. It is no wonder then that Moreau de la Sarthe named Samuel Richardson's *Sir Charles Grandison* as a novelistic source for the dissemination of the idea of the moral treatment: Richardson was one of the chief representatives of the cult of sentimentality and was hailed in France for his ability "to make the passions speak."[179] Similarly, Pinel's Rousseauism takes on an added dimension when seen from this vantage point. The author whose *Nouvelle Héloïse* had called forth floods of "delicious" tears from his grateful readers[180] would have special significance for the physician who regarded an appropriately tearful sentimentality as a definitive sign of mental health.

Pinel was concerned to present the moral treatment as a lay-inspired and nonetheless thoroughly scientific approach to the cure of madness. But without in any way abandoning the framework of his scientific

---

[178] Moreau de la Sarthe, "Encore des réflexions et des observations relatives à l'influence du moral sur le physique, et à l'emploi médical des passions, des affections et des émotions," *Décade philosophique* (20 nivôse, 30 nivôse Year IX): esp. 74–75, 134–37. Moreau's use of the expression of pent-up feelings as a mode of moral therapeutics is quite different from Pinel's mode of "schooling" the passions; it also anticipates Freud's psychoanalytic technique of catharsis or abreaction.

[179] Diderot, "Eloge de Richardson" (1761), in *Oeuvres complètes*, Vol. 5, p. 215. Clementina in *Grandison*, on whom some variant of the moral treatment was used, was a particularly "sentimental" character and gained a wide following on the Continent for this reason; see Margaret Anne Doody, *A Natural Passion: A Study of the Novels of Samuel Richardson* (Oxford: Clarendon Press, 1974), pp. 326–27; and Diderot, "Eloge de Richardson," p. 226.

[180] See Robert Darnton, "Readers Respond to Rousseau: The Fabrication of Romantic Sensitivity," in *The Great Cat Massacre and Other Episodes in French Cultural History* (New York: Basic Books, 1984), esp. pp. 242–48, describing and quoting from the "fan mail" that Rousseau received in the 1760s.

rationalism, he wished to recognize the claims of sentiment as well. His was an *âme sensible* conjoined with an *esprit éclairé*,[181] and his moral treatment was entirely suited to the general cultural trend of his day, to Romanticism emerging out of Enlightenment.

[181] See Georges Gusdorf, *Naissance de la conscience romantique au siècle des lumières* (Paris: Payot, 1976), title of Ch. 2 of Part 1.

4

The politics of patronage

THE articulation of the moral treatment, as concept and as practice, took place at a crossroads in the history of medical organization in France. The Law of 19 ventôse Year XI was putting the final seal on the destruction of the medical corporations at just the moment when Pinel was growing in celebrity, gaining adherents as the author of the *Traité*, and beginning to quantify his therapeutic experiments at the Salpêtrière. The convergence of these two trends poses the question of early psychiatric organization: What sort of community of specialist practitioners originally grew up around the paradigm of the moral treatment? Clearly the absence of the corporation would powerfully affect the shape of any such community. And while other, nontraditional modes of "sociability"[1] might develop in place of the corporate one, helping to create a sense of solidarity and collective identity among the new specialists, the psychiatric community would probably be to some degree constituted by the state. Like French medicine as a whole after 1803, it would probably have a highly significant point of attachment to the bureaucracy.

The organizational structure of a "patron" and a "circle" fits these specifications. It has been suggested that this informal structure – in which the so-called patron holds an important post or academic chair, and a small group of his students and associates (the "circle") share and develop his intellectual beliefs and receive his support in the advancement of their careers – is the key to the sociology of modern French intellectual life within the system of higher education.[2] Accord-

---

[1] Maurice Agulhon has made this term a fundamental category of the historical analysis of associational life. See his *La sociabilité méridionale: Confréries et associations dans la vie collective en Provence orientale à la fin du 18e siècle*, 2 vols. (Aix-en-Provence: Travaux et mémoires de la Faculté des lettres, 1966), esp. Vol. 1, pp. 7–15; and, more relevant in this context, *Le cercle dans la France bourgeoise, 1810–1848: Etude d'une mutation de sociabilité* (Paris: A. Colin, 1977).

[2] Terry N. Clark and Priscilla P. Clark, "Le patron et son cercle: Clef de l'université française," *Revue française de sociologie* 12 (1971): 19–39: and Terry N. Clark, *Prophets and Patrons: The French University and the Emergence of the Social Sciences* (Cambridge, Mass.: Harvard University Press, 1973), Ch. 2. The latter (pp. 67 and 67 n3) opts in English for the social scientific term "cluster" but indicates that a variety of other terms,

ing to this view, the patron derives his authority – and, more tangibly, his patronage – from his place in the bureaucratized state university. The state presence, though usually only hovering in the background of the circle, is nonetheless essential to its operation. At the same time, the patron possesses a large area of personal freedom and discretion; and this unmonitored aspect of the system helps account for the fact that both greatly gifted aspirants and those of decided mediocrity have typically succeeded in moving up the ranks of French higher education.[3] This structure is applicable to the proto-organization of French psychiatry as well. Like an academic discipline, the new psychiatric specialty developed within the matrix of the system of higher education – in its case, at the Ecole de médecine de Paris (called once again, after 1808, the faculty) and especially in the Paris hospice system, crucially linked to the faculty through the post-Revolutionary commitment to clinical instruction. It also attached itself firmly to a second part of the state bureaucracy, that of the Ministry of the Interior. By the proto-organization of psychiatry, I mean that purely informal and officially unrecognized organization that began to take shape in the opening decade of the nineteenth century and sufficed until the founding of the first formal organization of French psychiatrists, the Société médico-psychologique, in 1852. Since, however, the formal Société did not even pretend to assume all the functions of the informal patron-and-circle structure, the latter persisted after 1852 in tandem with its formal counterpart.

During the period under consideration in this chapter, French psychiatry was organized in rudimentary fashion in two circles that were sequentially, indeed genealogically related – the circle of Pinel, and the larger and more self-consciously specialist circle of his student Esquirol. The careers of these two men overlapped significantly. Although Esquirol was almost thirty years younger than his mentor, the latter, due to his period of self-assigned additional study at Montpellier and his long moratorium on the fringes of the medical world in pre-Revolutionary Paris, had been a notably late starter. He was almost fifty years old when he obtained his Bicêtre post in 1793 and embarked upon his most creative and important work. Thus it behooved Esquirol, whose filiopiety was intense,[4] to wait patiently in the wings. Not until 1817, when his mentor was in his seventies and he himself was forty-five, did he seem to have felt it permissible to take the kinds of initiative

---

including "circle," are actually used by the participants. Contemporaries usually referred to what I have here called the "circles" of Pinel and Esquirol as their "schools" (*écoles*).

[3] Clark and Clark stress this point as the fundamental explanatory value of their model; see "Patron et son cercle," pp. 19–20.

[4] See the testimony in Camille Bouchet, *Quelques mots sur Esquirol* (Nantes: Impr. de C. Mellinet, 1841), p. 2.

that would upstage Pinel. In that year, Esquirol began a course of clinical instruction in *maladies mentales* at the Salpêtrière, not part of the official curriculum at the faculty but still the first course in France to be devoted solely to that subject. Only then did he begin deliberately to acquire students of his own and to bring his own circle into existence.

The Pinel circle and the Esquirol circle were quite different organizational entities, a result both of changing historical circumstances and of the different personalities and goals of their patrons. Of the two men, Esquirol exploited the potential of the patron-and-circle structure much more fully. At his hands, the structure's statist base was accentuated, while at the same time the sense of community within the circle was intensively cultivated. The combination of these two strategies eventually enabled the Esquirol circle to go some distance toward the professionalization of the new medicine of the insane, a process in which – given the peculiarly French nineteenth-century concept of "profession" – collaboration with and legitimation by the state would prove paramount. In this chapter, I will describe the origins and the modes of sociability of the two circles. Woven into the account will be an analysis of some of the professionalizing efforts of the Esquirol circle; but this latter subject, too large to exhaust here, will continue to figure in subsequent chapters.

The Pinel circle

Pinel's circle was not made up exclusively of psychiatric students, for Pinel himself wore two hats as a physician. He was as much a nosographer, attempting to reconstruct the whole classificatory system of disease in line with Idéologue principles of "analysis" and clinical observation, as he was a healer of the insane. Pinel's position as patron derived indirectly from two official posts: the chair in medical pathology he had held at the Ecole de médecine in Paris since 1795, and dating from the same year, his appointment as chief physician of the Salpêtrière. On the basis of these two posts, he devised a third function for himself. Recognizing that the Ecole's abstract commitment to clinical instruction far exceeded the actual provision that had been made for it, Pinel, on his own initiative, opened a private clinical course at the Salpêtrière, receiving extra tuition from the students who chose to attend.[5] Based in the infirmary of the hospice, where the full panoply of diseases could be observed, the *cours particulier* had a simple format. The medical history of a newly arrived patient was taken "by one of my more advanced and experienced students and . . .

---

[5] Mireille Wiriot, *L'enseignement clinique dans les hôpitaux de Paris entre 1794 et 1848* (Paris: Thèse de médecine, 1970), pp. 51–52. It was eighteenth-century custom for professors at the medical faculty to supplement their official lectures with private courses, for which students paid them special fees.

read aloud at the bedside. During this reading, I fix the attention of the [other] students on the features that can be regarded as specific to the disease under consideration, and then I assign the disease to the place it occupies within my nosographic framework. In certain doubtful cases, I discuss the greater or lesser value or the equivocal character of certain signs, and sometimes I suspend my judgment until the disease is further along in its course."[6] These clinical lessons in what was called medical semiotics or "the science of signs" – that is, in "reading" the sick body for purposes of diagnosis and prognosis – were extraordinarily popular among Parisian medical students during the era of the Consulate and Empire. Entailing much closer professor–student contact than official lectures from the podium at the Ecole, they were responsible for the formation of a circle of students around Pinel.

In the area of clinical instruction, still so relatively novel and so attractive to the student body, Pinel had only one rival at this time: Jean-Nicolas Corvisart, an expert in heart disease who occupied the sole official clinical chair established by the Ecole de médecine in 1794, that at the Charité hospital.[7] The popularity of Corvisart always seemed self-explanatory to his contemporaries – he had a forceful personality and a brilliant oratorical style – while that of Pinel always seemed to require explanation. For Pinel was timid and retiring, his teaching marred by a speech impediment. "He could not say two words without hiccuping," recalled one student, who nonetheless found himself in the Year X rushing "to bring my three louis to Monsieur Pinel for the privilege of attending his visit to the old women of the Salpêtrière." Devoid of the external trappings of pedagogical charisma, Pinel came to be highly valued and sought after by students for the pure content of his teaching. They cited his "great penetration as a clinician" and "great clarity as a professor." "It was he," said one, "who made me a physician."[8]

The cohesiveness of the Pinel circle was of a particular and limited sort. Although it is possible that the members were invited to gatherings in Pinel's rustic country home in Torfou, not far from Paris,[9]

---

[6] Pinel, *La médicine clinique rendue plus précise et plus exacte par l'application de l'analyse*, 3d ed. (Paris: Brosson, 1815), p. ii.

[7] See Wiriot, *Enseignement clinique*, pp. 47, 51. Clavareau, *Mémoires sur les hôpitaux civils de Paris* (Paris: Impr. de Prault, Year XIII/1805), pp. 103–4, indicates that Corvisart began clinical instruction at the Charité before the Revolution, in 1787. The gentlemanly Pinel–Corvisart "rivalry" is discussed by Leuret, "M. Esquirol," *Gazette médicale de Paris*, 2d ser., 9 (January 2, 1841): 1; and by E. Pariset, "Eloge de Ph. Pinel," *Histoire des membres de l'Académie royale de médecine* (Paris: J.-B. Baillière, 1845), Vol. 1, pp. 246–49.

[8] P.-B. Bailly, quoted in Wiriot, *Enseignement clinique*, p. 52 (for the first and last quotes); and Leuret, "M. Esquirol," p. 1.

[9] See I. Bricheteau, *Discours sur Philippe Pinel, son école et l'influence qu'elle a exercée en médecine* (Paris: Impr. de C. L. F. Panckoucke, 1828), pp. 17–18; and René Semelaigne, *Les grands aliénistes français* (Paris: G. Steinheil, 1894), p. 219.

gathering was not a central motif. The circle was constituted primarily through each member's tie with Pinel rather than through members' face-to-face relationships with one another. Pinel forged the ties, definitively claimed the students as his own, by his help in fostering their careers; and the kind of help he offered bore the strong imprint of his personal style.

The most favored students among those who came to the clinical course were treated in the usual patronal manner: Gainful employment was obtained for them. Thus, at Pinel's express request to the Paris hospice administration, Landré-Beauvais was made his assistant (*premier adjoint*) at the Salpêtrière in 1801 and was later promoted to the salaried position of "*médecin ordinaire* specially charged with indigent inmates." Esquirol was made "*médecin ordinaire* of the section for the insane" at the same institution in 1811 when, following the death of Pussin, Pinel requested a replacement for his trusted concierge in the form of a specialist – or, as he put it, "a physician . . . devoted exclusively to the study of insanity" – and argued that Esquirol, with his many years of *maison de santé* experience, was the only man around suited for the job.[10] Pinel dispensed to his students the other, unofficial patronage at his disposal. Thus Landré-Beauvais took over Pinel's private clinical course at the Salpêtrière in 1810, when handling both that assignment and his pathology lectures at the faculty become too arduous for the aging *maître*.[11] On Isidore Bricheteau, a former Salpêtrière intern who would later write a shrewd account of the modus operandi of the Pinel circle, Pinel bestowed the commission to prepare "in collaboration with him or, if you will, under his patronage" numerous articles for the sixty-volume *Dictionaire des sciences médicales*.[12] A full decade in the making, the *Dictionaire* was the project of the adventurously capitalistic publishing firm of Panckoucke, which had earlier masterminded the scheme for the *Encyclopédie méthodique*.[13] Pinel was part of the regular stable of authors for both these compendia.

On at least one occasion Pinel also used his own modest fortune to aid the career of a student. To enable Esquirol to undertake the intensive study of insanity in an appropriate milieu, he reportedly put up the security for the house and garden that Esquirol rented on the rue de Buffon in 1801 or 1802, and which he converted into a private *maison*

---

[10] Monique Dumas, *Etienne Esquirol: Sa famille, ses origines, ses années de formation* (Toulouse: Thèse de médecine, 1971), p. 108.

[11] Wiriot, *Enseignement clinique*, p. 53.

[12] Bricheteau's account of the circle is in his *Discours sur Pinel*; on Bricheteau himself, and for the phrase quoted here, see C. Sachaile de la Barre, *Les médecins de Paris jugés par leurs oeuvres* (Paris: Chez l'auteur, 1845), p. 147.

[13] On Panckoucke, see Robert Darnton, *The Business of Enlightenment: A Publishing History of the Encyclopédie, 1775–1800* (Cambridge, Mass.: Harvard University Press, 1979). It is Panckoucke *fils* who published the *Dictionaire*; Panckoucke *père* is the protagonist of Darnton's story.

de santé for lunatics.[14] Pinel then proceeded not only to refer patients to Esquirol's new *maison* but also to support the venture through discreet "advertisements" within his own widely-circulated texts. Already in 1803 the second edition of the *Nosographie philosophique* was touting "the commendable establishment . . . directed by Citizen Esquirol, one of my students especially concerned with the treatment of mania and with putting into practice the principles I developed in my *Traité de l'aliénation mentale.*"[15] The opening pages of the second edition of the *Traité* announced that, in addition to detailing the author's own treatment procedures at the Salpêtrière, "I have also set forth the happy results that have been obtained for the past several years in an analogous establishment (that of Dr. Esquirol) founded upon the same principles – that is, observation and experience." Later in that book, Pinel described Esquirol's *maison* in some detail – its lush vegetation, pleasant accommodations for patients and their domestic servants, and the attractively humane and efficacious use of such aspects of the moral treatment as musical soirées in "a vast salon" for convalescent patients.[16] By 1810, Esquirol's *maison* was well on the road to success. The *Annuaire médical de Paris* ranked it as one of the three best *maisons de santé* for lunatics in the capital, noting that it was well-known throughout France, visited by savants from abroad, and (no doubt a causal factor in all this) that it had been "justly esteemed by Professor Pinel in his new work on insanity."[17]

But, it must be stressed, these most-favored students were exceptional. In general Pinel did not make such concerted efforts to find suitable employment for the members of his circle. This failing was particularly evident by contrast to the very efficient placement system Corvisart had developed for his students. Recalling this fundamental difference between the two "rival" clinical professors, Bricheteau attributed Pinel's characteristic posture of "not worrying about [his students'] material advancement" to his deep-rooted disdain for questing after social status and esteem, his kind of otherworldly devotion to science. Drawing his pedagogical prescriptions from his autobiography, Pinel "wanted his students to devote a great number of years to study before undertaking the practice of medicine; he constantly distanced his private pupils from this latter goal. Thus several of them with merit and reputation lived in a condition of extreme poverty bordering on distress." Even later in life, Pinel denied himself many of the material rewards of his successful scientific career, choosing to live with his wife and children in the very modest apartment provided for him at the

14 Bouchet, *Quelques mots*, p. 3.
15 Cited in Dumas, *Esquirol*, p. 89.
16 Pinel, *Traité médico-philosophique sur l'aliénation, ou la manie*, 2d ed. (Paris: Brosson, 1809), pp. ii, 369–70 n1, 373.
17 Cited in Dumas, *Esquirol*, p. 92.

Salpêtrière, having "no equipage other than a hackney-cab," indulging
only in the purchase of the quite unpretentious Torfou property.[18] Corvisart, on the other hand, apparently experienced no conflict between
science and worldly success, and he went about skillfully furnishing
his students with "the means of reaping [from their talent and learn-
ing] a just profit for science and for themselves by obtaining for them,
on the strength of his credit, *positions* and places." Corvisart's whole-
hearted assumption of this aspect of the patronal role, Pinel's reluctant
and half-hearted one, seemed to Bricheteau to contain the seeds of the
future: It explained the longevity of Corvisart's influence in French
medicine while that of Pinel, since it had not generated a network of
students in institutional strongholds, "began to dwindle from the moment that the *maître* ceased to be able to exert himself personally (*payer
de sa personne*)."[19] Pinel's timidity, so often remarked upon by contemporaries, no doubt also helped to determine his choice of patronage
style. He must have preferred to avoid the bureaucratic politics of place
hunting just as he preferred to avoid, even when attacked, polemical
disputes over medical doctrine. In both cases he rationalized his avoidance by construing such activities as motivated by worldly ambition
rather than disinterested scientific curiosity and therefore as unworthy
of his attention.[20]

The patronage that Pinel did typically offer the members of his circle
took the form of highly visible printed praise. Just as he commended
Esquirol's *maison* in the pages of his *Nosographie* and *Traité*, so would he
"encourage those setting out on a career by generously citing their
works" in his own – "a sort of honor after which everyone [in the
circle] strove and which was almost always a happy augury" for a
debutant.[21] Thus a remark in the *Traité* about the importance of identifying diseases by unequivocal manifest signs is accompanied by the
following footnote: "I have always put great store by the semiology of
disease, and I have observed with pleasure that Monsieur Landré-

---

[18] Bricheteau, *Discours sur Pinel*, pp. 13, 13 n1, 17. Cf. the lifestyle of Etienne Pariset,
who while a physician at Bicêtre and later the Salpêtrière maintained two apartments,
one at the hospice and another in the center of Paris. George D. Sussman, "Etienne
Pariset: A Medical Career in Government under the Restoration," *Journal of the History
of Medicine* 26 (1971): 60–61.

[19] Bricheteau, *Discours sur Pinel*, pp. 13–14, italics in the original. Personal experience
underlay Bricheteau's comments. As Sachaile de la Barre noted, "Monsieur Bricheteau remained without a hospital appointment for a very long time," but apparently
modeling himself on Pinel, he also remained unembittered, caring only for "science"
and "smiling with pity" at those physicians who sought "fame and fortune." *Médicins
de Paris*, p. 148.

[20] With respect to polemics, Pinel also forbade his students to reply for him, even after
the particularly violent attack on his classificatory scheme by Broussais in 1816.
Bricheteau, *Discours sur Pinel*, pp. 15 and 15 n1.

[21] Ibid., p. 13.

Beauvais made it a special object of his researches. I have no doubt that his *Traité des signes des maladies* (one volume in-octavo, Paris, 1809, at Brosson, bookseller) will have all the success that it has the right to expect." To a discussion in the *Médecine clinique* of a chemical analysis of the Salpêtrière water supply conducted by a certain Schwilgué, Pinel appends a footnote informing the reader that "Since my first edition, a premature death has carried off, in the midst of his labors, Monsieur Schwilgué, whom I number among my most distinguished pupils. He published an excellent treatise on materia medica." A passing comment in the *Nosographie philosophique* informs the reader that Schwilgué's treatise was based upon years of careful study "at the Salpêtrière hospice of the action of pharmacological preparations on the living body" and adds that Pinel consulted the treatise "incessantly" for the treatment of disease.[22] Less effusive but nonetheless patently supportive references to the books, articles, and dissertations of his students lard Pinel's *Nosographie*.[23]

The system had its pros and cons. "All the works published by the pupils of Pinel lent one another a mutual support," observed Bricheteau, "and the assent of the *maître* covered all of them with the protection of eminence." But Bricheteau was also aware that Pinel's broad discretionary powers as patron – even in this clearly limited sense of patronage – did not always foster scientific excellence. The affectionate kindness which Pinel felt indiscriminately for most of his students and which motivated his laudatory citations of their efforts "sometimes had the disadvantage of exalting mediocrity"; within the Pinel circle's collective corpus, "the strong works sustained and propped up the weak ones."[24] Furthermore, through his strategy of citation Pinel created his circle in a reified fashion, as a corpus of scientific texts whose authors shared a common identity element rather than as a lively association of interacting physicians.

All of Pinel's students, whether or not their main interest was in the treatment of the insane, were kept abreast of the latest advances in that area. Pinel's *Nosographie philosophique*, the breviary of the post-1803 generation of French medical students,[25] contained discussions of mania and melancholia that summarized its author's specialized researches and presented his considered opinions. But only two of Pinel's students devoted themselves single-mindedly to the new medicine of the insane – Esquirol and Guillaume Ferrus. Already the holder of a Paris

---

[22] Pinel, *Traité*, 2d ed., p. iii n1; *Médecine clinique*, 3d ed., p. viii n1; *Nosographie philosophique, ou la méthode de l'analyse appliquée à la médecine*, 6th ed. (Paris: Brosson, 1816), Vol. 1, p. lxxxviii.
[23] See, e.g., *Nosographie philosophique*, 6th ed., Vol. 3, pp. 55 n1, 59, 75, 117 n1.
[24] Bricheteau, *Discours sur Pinel*, p. 13; Pinel's sympathetic relationship with his students is also described in Dupuytren, "Pinel," *Journal des débats*, November 7, 1826.
[25] Bricheteau, *Discours sur Pinel*, pp. 8–9.

medical degree by 1804, Ferrus entered Pinel's orbit only in 1814, upon reentering civilian life after serving for a decade as a military surgeon in the Napoleonic army. Pinel immediately brought him into the Salpêtrière as a humble *adjoint;* not until 1819 was Ferrus put on the payroll of that institution with the title and low salary of a *médecin suppléant.*[26] Indeed, Pinel's repeated requests to the Paris hospice administration failed to obtain a full-fledged post for him until 1826, when shortly before Pinel's death, Ferrus was made chief physician of the insane at Bicêtre.[27] Esquirol thus had a good fifteen years' head start on Ferrus, both in the study of insanity and as Pinel's protégé. There could be no doubt that, in things psychiatric, Pinel's mantle would fall to him.

The Esquirol circle

Almost as soon as Esquirol appeared at Pinel's private clinical course at the Salpêtrière around 1799 (he had already been enrolled in Pinel's official course at the Ecole de médecine for two years),[28] a deep bond formed between these two men of the Midi – "paternal attachment on the part of Pinel, truly filial love on the part of Esquirol," according to one source close to Esquirol.[29] But whatever fundamental emotional affinity they shared, they had significantly different social-class backgrounds, and these were reflected in the different styles of patronage they adopted.

While Pinel's father had been a small-town physician in the region of Toulouse, Esquirol's was a wealthy wholesale cloth-merchant in Toulouse itself, belonging, like his father before him, to the most prosperous and highly esteemed *corps* in that provincial capital. Commercial prominence in eighteenth-century Toulouse went hand in hand with prominence in public life: Esquirol *père* had been elected to the Bourse des marchands, a law court that decided commercial disputes and whose judgments, if appealed, went directly to the Parlement. On the eve of the Revolution, he was elected to the *capitoulat,* the traditional governing corporation of the municipality only recently opened to wholesale merchants, membership on which carried the automatic privilege of ennoblement. Esquirol hailed, then, from the uppermost stratum of the bourgeoisie, from that place in the social hierarchy where the bourgeoisie was on the verge of transformation into the robe nobility.

---

[26] AAP: Procès-verbaux du Conseil général des hospices civils de Paris (henceforth CGH), Liasse 58, f. 251. Ferrus received 1200 francs per year as opposed to Esquirol's 2000 francs as *médecin ordinaire;* see AAP: Salpêtrière 2K6.

[27] Sachaile de la Barre, *Médecins de Paris,* pp. 288–89; Semelaigne, *Grands aliénistes,* p. 219.

[28] See Dumas, *Esquirol,* pp. 73–74.

[29] Leuret, "M. Esquirol," p. 2.

Like any good Old Regime bourgeois with aspirations to *vivre noble-ment*, Esquirol *père* owned land outside the city. But his personality seems to have been marked not by the insouciant elegance of a would-be noble but by an austerity and strong sense of civic responsibility proba-bly typical of the Toulouse merchant corps. He served for at least a decade, without remuneration, as one of the directors of the Grave, the *hôpital-général* in Toulouse; this post, which involved time-consuming visits of inspection, was usually filled by members of the affluent com-mercial bourgeoisie of the city. He is reported to have used his own fortune to buy grain for the populace of Toulouse during a period of scarcity in 1789 when popular riots threatened. The two-story residence in a central square of Toulouse in which Esquirol grew up was a typical Toulousain merchant dwelling: the commercial establishment on the first floor and the family apartments above it, "the whole decor giving an impression of severity."[30] This portrait of Esquirol *père* is important here because, as a patron, his son replicated its central features: a sense of high social standing, which would put Esquirol at ease in his crucial dealings with men in power, coupled with a deeply ingrained serious-ness and a sense of obligation to those – be they lunatics or unemployed students – who could not fend for themselves.

The emergence of Esquirol as patron, 1817–1819. Esquirol launched him-self as a patron from a less secure official base than had Pinel: He was not a professor at the Paris faculty (nor was he ever to become one); he was not, at the outset, the chief physician of a Paris hospice but only a *médecin ordinaire*. What he did have was a clearer vision than his men-tor of what he wished to accomplish through the medium of organiza-tion. Hence, while Pinel's role as patron was generally characterized by influence unused and opportunities unrealized, Esquirol's was marked by an active but always tasteful creation of opportunities. In particular, the aspiring patron was able to ingratiate himself to great effect with the state bureaucracy.

For several years beginning in 1817, Esquirol laid the foundation for his new patronal role. In the first place, the clinical course in *maladies mentales* he initiated in the makeshift quarters of the Salpêtrière dining hall[31] proved a great success. Clinical instruction had proliferated at the Paris faculty since the days when Pinel and Corvisart had monopolized the field; noting that "the capital is very rich in *écoles de clinique*," a medical student handbook of 1818 advised that "the student ought not accord an exclusive preference to one rather than another [but] fre-quent them by turns." Nonetheless Esquirol was, a medical gossip columnist reported, one of the clinical instructors to whose hospital

---

[30] Dumas, *Esquirol*, pp. 21–43.
[31] Bouchet, *Quelques mots*, p. 4.

visits "students flock with a kind of frenzy."[32] But Esquirol did not stop there: Providing instruction in *maladies mentales* was only one element in a larger design. In 1810, 1814, and again in 1817 he had embarked, on his own initiative and at his own expense, on a series of systematic tours of the facilities for lunatics throughout France.[33] These fact-finding missions eventuated in two publications: a memoir presented to the minister of the interior in September 1818 and published six months later, and a much more extensive and detailed version of it, the 1818 article "Maison d'aliénés" in the *Dictionaire des sciences médicales*.[34] Together these texts comprised the basic program or manifesto of the new medical specialty which Esquirol envisioned and which he would gear his circle toward implementing.

That program, directed both to the medical community, by means of the *Dictionaire* article, and to the lay political world, by means of the often sentimental *Mémoire* ("It is impossible not to be moved almost to tears while traversing the country where Monsieur Esquirol paints for us the miseries of the insane," said a contemporary reviewer),[35] consisted of four interrelated main points. The first and overarching one was that the medicine of the insane was a specialty. Esquirol did not say this in so many words, but he said as much: Insanity should be treated in *hôpitaux spéciaux* by physicians with special training, those who had "fruitfully cultivated this branch of the healing art" and had renounced all other clientele.[36] A careful argument was mounted in support of these propositions. If lunatics continued to be housed in *hôpitaux-généraux* and *dépôts de mendicité*, as Esquirol had discovered the vast majority of them presently were, they would invariably continue to suffer neglect; for the entire staff in such institutions – physicians,

---

[32] J.-P. Maygrier, *Guide de l'étudiant en médecine*, 2d ed. (Paris: Gabon, 1818), p. 101; Véridique Alleyes-Allears, "Lettres médicales sur Paris," *Revue médicale historique et philosophique* 2 (1820): 194.

[33] The dates of the first two tours are given in the nearly contemporaneous article, "Esquirol," *Dictionaire des sciences médicales: Biographie médicale*, Vol. 4 (Paris: C. L. F. Panckoucke, 1821) p. 58. Esquirol requested and received permission for a three-week leave of absence from the Salpêtrière in August 1817 "to visit the hospices of the North, having seen those of the Midi and the West of France." AAP: CGH 48, ff. 384–85. Both Leuret, "Esquirol," p. 4, and Dr. Gérard Marchant, *Esquirol: Discours prononcé à la séance solennelle de la Société impériale de médecine . . . de Toulouse* (Toulouse: Douladoure, 1868), p. 13, testify that the tours were self-financed.

[34] Esquirol, *Des établissements des aliénés en France et des moyens d'améliorer le sort de ces infortunés. Mémoire présenté à son excellence le Ministre de l'Intérieur en septembre 1818* (Paris: Impr. de Mme Huzard, 1819); and Esquirol, "Maisons d'aliénés," *Dict. des sci. med.*, Vol. 30 (1818): 47–95. When he reprinted the *Mémoire* twenty years later, Esquirol prefaced it with the remark that it had been "written at the request of the Minister of the Interior," but this may well have been retrospective embroidery; see his *Des maladies mentales considérées sous les rapports médical, hygiénique et médico-légal* (Paris: Baillière, 1838), Vol. 2, p. 398.

[35] Unsigned, *Gazette de santé*, April 21, 1819, p. 375.

[36] Esquirol, *Mémoire*, pp. 23, 27; "Maisons," p. 62.

directors, nurses, orderlies – gave their attention by natural preference
to the other inmates in the heterogeneous population, finding all other
inmates easier and more pleasant to deal with than lunatics. The physicians had an additional reason for avoiding rather than succoring the
lunatics in their charge. Their utter ignorance of any cure for insanity
had left them profoundly "discouraged" – hence the need for a *médecin
spécial* with special expertise.[37] Esquirol's subsequent success should
not blind us to the fact that his tactics here were humble, suppliant,
and even contained a touch of "charlatanistic" showmanship. In financing a tour of France which furnished supporting evidence for a
proposal to the Ministry of the Interior that a specialized medical facility be established, Esquirol was operating much like the oculist Forlenze a decade or so before.

The second point might be characterized as the primacy of Paris.
Esquirol took as axiomatic that all expertise in France about the treatment of lunatics was to be found in Paris and that any improvement in
treatment procedures must necessarily take the form of an exportation
of that expertise from the Parisian center to the benighted periphery. In
his memoir and again in the very first sentence of his dictionary article,
he described the motivation of his tours as "wanting to assess the
influence in the rest of France of the ameliorations introduced in the
lunatic institutions of Paris."[38] He found that influence quite weak
indeed. Only in provincial capitals had "Paris furnished the example";
elsewhere "the most revolting barbarism" still prevailed. Lunatics, Esquirol believed, were best removed from "local influences," from those
"prejudices which, in many provinces, make [them] regarded as incurables."[39] So deep was Esquirol's Paris-centrism that he even felt com-
pelled to cast belated aspersions on the medal presented to the administrator of the Avignon lunatic hospice by the Lycée des Arts in 1797.
"That was a little comedy performed to gladden the hearts of the
patriots of the Midi," he said cuttingly. "That hospice never enjoyed . . . a reputation that would justify such a distinction. [Further-
more] when I visited [it], everything appeared to me contrary to the
success of the treatment of the insane."[40] There was, then, a perfect
congruence between Esquirol's belief that any reform of the care of the
insane had, for scientific reasons, to emanate from Paris, and his choice
of the central state bureaucracy as the agency of that reform.

The third point in Esquirol's program was that institution building
was urgently necessary for the development of the new medicine of
insanity. "A lunatic hospital is an instrument of cure," he asserted
laconically, thus fully integrating the internal therapeutic aspect of this

---

[37] Esquirol, *Mémoire*, pp. 12, 20, 22–23.
[38] *Mémoire*, p. 7; "Maisons," p. 47.
[39] *Mémoire*, pp. 7, 26.
[40] "Maisons," pp. 51–52.

new medicine with its external institutional aspect. Architectural features such as courtyards for promenades, separate wards for different varieties of madness, and ground floor lodgings for furious lunatics, where security could be achieved with a minimum of lugubrious bars and padlocks, would make specially constructed hospitals devoted exclusively to the insane markedly more therapeutic than the existent quarters within *hôpitaux-généraux* and *dépôts de mendicité*. Esquirol therefore proposed to the minister of the interior the construction of a network of twenty such "special public establishments" dispersed in a uniform manner throughout France and superimposed upon the network of royal law courts so that each lunatic hospital would be affiliated with a neighboring *cour royale*. The minister of the interior would appoint the directors and doctors of each such hospital and oversee and coordinate the whole network; each hospital would serve the population of several departments and the relevant prefects would participate in its administration.[41]

Esquirol's fourth point was the definitive medicalization of the care of the insane, a point already evident in the writings of Pinel but now made by his disciple much more forcefully and with much more overt preoccupation with issues of professional status. The lunatic hospital was to be, as Esquirol stipulated in a revealing passage, the domain of a grandiose and specifically medical authority:

> The physician must be, in some manner, the vital principle of a lunatic hospital. It is he who should set everything in motion; he should regularize all actions, just as he has been called upon to be the regulator of all thoughts. . . . The action of the administration, which governs the material aspect of the establishment and supervises all the employees, ought to be hidden. Never should the administration appeal a decision made by the physician, never should it interpose itself between the physician and the lunatics or between the physician and the non-medical staff (*les serviteurs*). The physician should be invested with an authority from which no one is exempt.

Continuing in much the same vein, Esquirol sought "to justify the necessity of this influence" by reference to its curative efficacy. He cited autobiographical example. He exercised, he had found, more influence over the lower-class madwomen of the Salpêtrière than over the wealthy patients in his private sanatorium: "The inmates of [the former] establishment regard me as being of a station much superior to their own; thus it has several times happened that I have returned a lunatic to reason, as if by enchantment, simply by granting her an interview in my office; some of these have given signs of cure that very instant." Esquirol is alluding here to the somewhat magical, authoritar-

---

[41] *Mémoire*, pp. 30, 38–41. The one "voluntaristic" aspect of the scheme is that money for building be raised by a public subscription, undertaken by the state bureaucracy.

ian component which had always been part of the Pinellian moral treatment.[42] But he now drew significant practical inferences from the indispensability of that component. The healing power residing in the person of the physician – the so-called enchantment of medical authority – might either be maximized or left to languish; and recognition of that fact entailed an obligation on the part of the "local authorities." They could not afford to be neutral bystanders but must treat the physician of lunatics "with distinction"; "thus will be prepared the influence that [the physician] should exercise over the individuals admitted to his hospice."[43] Esquirol's demand, in other words, was that lunatics be entrusted to physicians and that the physician of lunatics be accorded, with the aid of local notables and bureaucrats, a high and honorable place in the larger community.

Like Pinel before him, but again more insistently, Esquirol looked to linguistic change as an additional vehicle of medicalization, as a way to demarcate a specifically medical domain and to indicate the placement of insanity within it. Pinel had spoken of the desirability of purging medicine of everyday language, of the "jargon circulating in the commerce of civil life"; he had urged the substitution of the word *aliénation* for the vulgar *folie*.[44] Now, to signify a rite of passage – the formal transfer of insanity from the lay to the medical purview and the concomitant discarding of the traditional lay prejudices about its incurability – Esquirol suggested that a new name be affixed to the institution housing lunatics: "I would like these establishments to be given a specific name which presents no painful idea to the mind; I would like them to be called asylums." And he added, "Those who know how much influence words have over men will not be at all astonished at the importance I attach to these little details."[45] Conversely, he was during his tours of the provinces always alert to linguistic localisms that suggested the backward, premedical mentality it was his self-appointed mission to eradicate. "Angers is the first city where I heard the name *exilés* given to insane people (*aliénés*)."[46]

---

[42] The magical curative authority of the gifted *aliéniste* continued to be part of Parisian psychiatric rhetoric well into the nineteenth century. While an intern at Bicêtre, Paul Broca (who would later found French physical anthropology) wrote home to his mother regarding the chief physician Leuret: "I, like everyone else, admired the power of fascination (*pouvoir fascinateur*) he exercises over our madmen." Paul Broca, *Correspondance*, Vol. 1 (Paris: Typographie Paul Schmidt, 1886), April 4, 1845, p. 281.

[43] "Maisons," p. 84.

[44] *Nosographie philosophique*, 1st ed., Vol. 1 (Paris: Crapelet, Year VI), p. 1; and *Traité*, 2d ed., pp. iii, 128–29.

[45] *Mémoire*, p. 26.

[46] Quoted in Jacques G. Petit, "Folie, langage, pouvoirs en Maine-et-Loire (1800–1840)," *Revue d'histoire moderne et contemporaine* 27 (1980): 557.

The institutional direction in which Esquirol had pointed the new specialty in 1818 was confirmed in an affair at the Paris Faculty of Medicine that same year. By a decree of December 4, the Commission de l'Instruction publique, the five-man board that governed the Université de France under the Restoration, created at the Paris medical faculty a chair in "special pathology relating to mental diseases," giving as its rationale that it wanted to carry out the "original plan" of 1794 by "filling all the chairs which ought to compose" such an institution of higher learning and carefully "earmarking" the chairs so that they covered all "the branches of learning most appropriate to the current needs of medical science." The decree specified that the new and unprecedented chair of mental diseases would be created through the transformation of one of the two existent chairs of legal medicine – at that moment vacant – and that it would be filled either by a transfer from within the professoriate or by a new appointment.[47] When, four days later, this decree was read as a fait accompli before an extraordinary session of the faculty, Pinel and his colleague Duméril, "believ[ing] themselves duty-bound to protest against this act," immediately deposited their written objections on the table. To cope with "the difficult questions raised by this incident," the faculty decided to appoint an ad hoc committee to study it. Chosen on the spot by secret ballot, the committee included the clearly partisan Pinel.[48]

Reporting back to the assembled faculty two months later, the committee recommended that both chairs of legal medicine be retained but that one of the two professors be charged with "giving a course in mental medicine considered principally in relation to the public institutions devoted to the treatment of insanity." There was precedent for this sort of piggyback curricular strategy: A course in the history of medicine was at that time attached to the chair of legal medicine. A few days later, the Commission de l'Instruction publique declared itself amenable to these "somewhat tardy observations" of the faculty, which they conceded "tend to prove that a chair of pathology will ill attain the goal of the Commission and that it would be more fitting to attach this new instruction to legal medicine than to pathology." A new decree of February 23, 1819 modified the decree of December 4, 1818 accordingly.[49]

What can be made of this curious story in which Pinel, who had spent the previous two decades laying the groundwork for a cogent medicine of insanity, rushes forward to block the creation of a chair in that very subject? Since the supporting documents mentioned in the

[47] AN: F^{17*} 1764, Procès-verbaux de la Commission de l'Instruction publique, December 4, 1818, f. 556.
[48] AN: AJ^{16} 6232, Procès-verbaux . . . de la Faculté de médecine de Paris, December 8, 1818, f. 721.
[49] Ibid., February 13, 1819, f. 90; February 18, 1819, ff. 91–92.

faculty minutes are missing, we can only speculate about Pinel's motives. The president of the Commission de l'Instruction publique and
the signatory of the original December 4 decree was Pierre-Paul Royer-
Collard, the Doctrinaire political philosopher and cohort of Guizot.[50]
His brother was Antoine-Athanase Royer-Collard, the chief physician
of Charenton since 1806 and since 1816 the incumbent of a chair in
legal medicine. Indeed, A.-A. Royer-Collard had been the very first
appointment to the Paris medical faculty made by the newly created
commission under P.-P. Royer-Collard after the more democratic practice, devised by the Revolution, of selection by *concours* had been abandoned by the Restoration government.[51] Did Pinel believe that he saw
the handwriting on the wall – that A.-A. Royer-Collard would be transferred to the new chair in mental pathology – and did he seek to prevent such an outcome, if only by demoting the chair to a course?

Such a hypothesis is entirely plausible, for all the evidence points to
a discreetly conducted but bitter rivalry between the Pinel circle and
A.-A. Royer-Collard. The latter was, after all, an ambitious man who
headed one of the few special facilities for lunatics in France and who
had, through family connections, an independent "power base" in
medical politics. He had never studied with Pinel and had no affective
ties to him.[52] He had published virtually nothing about *aliénation mentale,* so that his high place in the nascent medical specialty could hardly
have seemed warranted by his scientific contributions. And he remained aloof, collaborating with Pinel in their area of supposed common scientific interest only when such collaboration was mandated, for
limited purposes, by a court of law or by the police.[53] The rivalry was
no doubt fueled when Pinel made an attempt to have Esquirol ap-

---

[50] P.-P. Royer-Collard had also been the chief advocate of the formation of the Commission de l'Instruction publique, a Restoration divergence from the bureaucratic structure of the Napoleonic Université. See Louis Liard, *L'enseignement supérieur en France,
1789–1893* (Paris: A. Colin, 1894), Vol. 2, pp. 125–47.

[51] That the abandonment of the *concours* had smoothed the way for the aid of the
medical Royer-Collard brother by the political one did not escape contemporary critics; see Rouzet, "Pétition addressée aux deux Chambres sur la nécessité de rétablir le
concours pour l'obtention des chaires vacantes dans la Faculté de Médecine," *Revue
médicale historique et philosophique* 2 (March 1820): 59–73.

[52] See his *Essai sur l'aménorrhée, ou suppression du flux menstruel* (Paris: Gabon, Year
X/1802), p. 66 n1, where he identifies Hallé as "mon illustre maître."

[53] One such collaboration is described at length by Royer-Collard in *Observations sur un
écrit ayant pour titre Mémoire pour Mme de Chambon, appelante du jugement qui nomme M.
Fréteau administrateur provisoire de la personne de Mlle d'Arbouville* (Paris: Impr. de Vincard, 1806), AN: AJ² 100, and it could not have endeared Royer-Collard to Pinel. The
two physicians had been named by a Paris tribunal as jointly responsible for treating
a certain Mlle d'Arbouville for insanity. The situation became an imbroglio; and after
Royer-Collard complained repeatedly about the conduct of Pinel's trusted coworker
Pussin, Pinel washed his hands of the whole business and resigned. For another
collaboration, see Maxime Laignel-Lavastine and Jean Vinchon, "Pinel médico-
legiste," *Ann. m.-p.,* 12th ser., 2 (1927): 67.

pointed to Charenton in 1806 after the death of Gastaldy,[54] and the post was captured instead by Royer-Collard. Later Royer-Collard became the butt of jokes in the pages of a new medical journal which Esquirol had helped to found, depicted as a beneficiary of nepotism, a man whose rewards were incommensurate with either his efforts or his achievements. It was said that a petition for meritocratic selection of professors at the medical faculty had been quashed for his sake; that his lectures on legal medicine were shamelessly cribbed from Fodéré's treatise on the subject; that he shirked his responsibilities at Charenton by visiting patients only three days a week.[55]

Esquirol, who was not a member of the faculty, did apply for the vacant chair of legal medicine, no doubt hoping to teach the new course in mental medicine; but his candidacy was unsuccessful.[56] And when the chair was won by the toxicologist Orfila, the assignment for the mental medicine course devolved, logically enough, upon the other professor of legal medicine, A.-A. Royer-Collard.[57] If Pinel's tactics were intended to keep official instruction in *maladies mentales* as the prerogative of his own circle, they had only minimal efficiency. But on another level, the tactics also aimed to assert a fundamental social and institutional orientation in the new medical specialty: Mental medicine, the emended decree implied, should not be taught narrowly in a pathology course, but in a broadly contextual manner as a part of legal medicine, and with particular emphasis on the public facilities for the care of the insane. Through his protest, Pinel was thus supporting and extending the message of Esquirol's memoir and dictionary article. Indeed, Esquirol had in the former alluded to the connection between mental medicine and legal medicine, suggesting that his proposed asylum network be superimposed on the network of royal courts in part because of the legal problems surrounding the civil status and institutionalization of lunatics.[58] In the long run, the creation of this course in *médecine mentale* was of little practical significance, for the punitive closing of the Paris Faculty of Medicine by the Restoration government in 1822 eradicated the new instruction entirely. But for our purposes, the episode is additional evidence of the efforts made by Esquirol – acting here largely through his cooperative mentor Pinel – to enforce a particu-

---

[54] See E. Szapiro, "Pinel et Esquirol: Quelques commentaires sur les débuts d'une amitié," *Ann. m.-p.*, 134 (June 1976): 59–61.

[55] Alleyes-Allears, "Lettres médicales," pp. 178–79, 195. On Esquirol's role in founding the *Revue médicale historique et philosophique*, see Semelaigne, *Pionniers*, Vol. 1, p. 194.

[56] See the details of the balloting in AN: AJ[16] 6232, February 23, 1819, ff. 94–95.

[57] The standard secondary sources usually state, erroneously, that A.-A. Royer-Collard received a "chair" in mental medicine; see, e.g., Semelaigne, *Pionniers*, Vol. 1, p. 109. The *Revue médicale* later discussed the forthcoming course with predictable sarcasm: "In the past year, Dr. Royer-Collard . . . has already, he says, prepared *six lessons* of this course, so all hope is not lost." Alleyes-Allears, "Lettres médicales," p. 201.

[58] Esquirol, *Mémoire*, p. 38.

lar definition of the emergent specialty of mental medicine as he prepared to assume the role of psychiatric patron.

Esquirol's tours of the lunatic institutions of France had the effect, which
he had no doubt hoped for, of providing him with an entrée into the
upper echelons of the bureaucracy. He presented his memoir to the
minister of the interior in September 1818; barely a month later he had
been "discovered" by Edouard Laffon de Ladébat, chief of the ministry's
bureau of assistance and hospitals and a career functionary whose interest in wresting lunatic institutions from local jurisdiction and welding
them into a new and uniform state system dated back at least to 1813.[59]
Laffon de Ladébat had found something of a soul mate in Esquirol. After
hearing about the physician, he hastened to establish personal contact
with him and was soon making copious use of Esquirol's data and
recommendations in support of his own. In a long memorandum to the
minister of the interior in October 1818, he observed that the Conseils
généraux of the departments had lately been voting funds for the enlargement of existing facilities for lunatics in *hôpitaux-généraux* and *dépôts
de mendicité;* he believed that this wrong-headed trend must be halted
and financial investment made instead in new "special establishments."
To this end he proposed the formation of a commission composed of an
architect, a physician and an administrator to design a model lunatic
institution that could be reproduced throughout provincial France. Four
months later this proposal was again addressed to the minister of the
interior, this time by Guizot, the newly appointed director-general of
departmental and communal administration. Guizot's version of the
proposal, which was ultimately accepted, expanded the size of the commission to include three physicians and two administrators; thus it was
that Esquirol and A.-A. Royer-Collard served on it side by side.[60]
The commission did get as far as drawing up the preliminary blueprint for the model institution; it printed a limited edition of its descriptive brochure, distributing the copies to those administrators and physicians deemed most qualified to suggest revisions.[61] And in July 1819,

[59] See G. Bollotte, "Les projets d'assistance aux malades mentaux sous la Restauration,"
Ann. m.-p. 124 (1966): 388–402, esp. 386 for Laffon de Ladébat's letter of September 9,
1813 to the minister of the interior arguing for "a certain number of central establishments" for lunatics; for the full text of that letter, see AN: F^{15} 444.

[60] See Bollotte, "Projets d'assistance," pp. 390–93, 396 for the texts of Laffon de
Ladébat's memorandum, with its numerous direct quotations from and paraphrases
of Esquirol, and Guizot's memorandum.

[61] AN: F^{15} 1892, letter from the vice president of the Conseil général des hôpitaux et
hospices de Paris to the minister of the interior, April 23, 1822. The brochure is
*Programme d'un hôpital consacré au traitement de l'aliénation mentale pour cinq cents malades
des deux sexes* (Paris: Impr. de Mme Huzard, 1821); a copy can be found in AN: F^{15}
1892. It was reprinted in 1824 in slightly altered form, with B. Desportes given as
author; see BN: Te^{66} 183.

Minister of the Interior Decazes issued a circular to the prefects calling for a suspension of all current projects for the enlargement of lunatic quarters in mixed facilities and the diversion of funds voted for this purpose to the construction (through the collaboration of several departments) of special *maisons centrales*. The circular bore the mark of Esquirol's influence and rhetoric, for it stipulated a daily medical visit at all lunatic establishments and observed, "It would be good to invest [the physician] with great authority."[62] Over the next few years, Laffon de Ladébat pressed for implementation of the circular and haggled with the prefects over the details.[63]

But these efforts gradually petered out, the result of the demise, in 1820, of the liberal Decazes ministry which had nurtured them. The commission, for example, "ceased meeting in 1821."[64] Just as Laffon de Ladébat's ideas had met with a relatively cool reception under the previous right-centrist ministry – Minister of the Interior Lainé had thought them important enough to mention in his 1818 report to the King, but he had counseled against using government monies to build special *maisons centrales* for lunatics and recommended passively waiting for private benefactors to endow them[65] – so they failed utterly to elicit ministerial favor during the period of almost uninterrupted right-wing ascendancy from 1820 until the end of the Restoration.[66] From Esquirol's own perspective, however, the gains of the short-lived *maison centrale* experiment had been substantial. He had made solid bureaucratic contacts – witness his appointment by the Ministry of the Interior to the lucrative post of inspector of the university in 1823[67] – and these would stand him in good stead during the next two decades.

---

[62] Circular of July 16, 1819 in *Circulaires, instructions et autres actes émanés du Ministère de l'Intérieure*, Vol. 3 (Paris: Impr. royale, 1821), pp. 487–91. In the *Mémoire* (pp. 27–28), Esquirol had stated his preference for medical visits several times a day and had made clear the unacceptability of any frequency less than once a day.

[63] See, e.g., AN: F^{15} 143, letter of the prefect of the Charente to the Bureau des secours et hôpitaux of the minister of the interior, July 24, 1822.

[64] This is Esquirol's testimony in the revised and expanded version of "Maisons d'aliénés" in *Maladies mentales*, Vol. 2 (henceforth "Maisons d'aliénés," 1838 ed.), p. 448.

[65] See Lainé, *Rapport au Roi sur la situation des hospices, des enfans trouvés, des aliénés, de la mendicité et des prisons* (Paris: Impr. royale, 1818), pp. 18–19.

[66] See Bollotte, "Projets d'assistance," p. 397 on Laffon de Ladébat's fruitless efforts to revive the *maison centrale* project in 1822 and 1828.

[67] Semelaigne, *Grands aliénistes*, p. 138. A.-A. Royer-Collard had held this post for many years and received an annual salary of 6000 francs for it, twice as much as his professorial salary; for the latter, see AN: F^{17} 2381. All aspects of public instruction were under the authority of the Ministry of the Interior from 1792 until 1824; see Jean Vial, "L'administration centrale de l'instruction publique en France de 1792 à 1855," *Paedagogica Historica* 9 (1969): esp. pp. 120–25.

The workings of the circle. Esquirol acquired a student following during the years 1817–25, when he taught his clinical course at the Salpêtrière. In 1825, A.-A. Royer-Collard died, thus removing from the scene the one man who might have become a rival psychiatric patron and leaving vacant the post of chief physician at Charenton, which was this time promptly offered to Esquirol. At Charenton, where he remained until his death in 1840, Esquirol did not continue his clinical course; probably the distance of that "suburban" institution from the medical faculty on the Left Bank seemed a decisive deterrent to student attendance. But since the regulations of Charenton provided for four *élèves internes* and an indeterminant number of *élèves externes*, he had not fully renounced his pedagogical role.[68] The membership of any informal group is difficult to determine with precision; but if three criteria are posited for membership in the Esquirol circle – training under Esquirol by a person either pursuing a medical degree (the usual case) or already in possession of one; a subsequent career in *médecine mentale*; and public self-identification or identification by others as an Esquirol pupil – a core circle of some nineteen members can be readily named. The vast majority among this group were born in the period 1794–1801 and encountered Esquirol in their twenties at the Salpêtrière; only two were products of Esquirol's later Charenton phase. The circle was thus a virtually complete and functioning entity before Esquirol left his Salpêtrière post. Almost all of its members were provincials who had migrated to Paris for medical training; with time they would be transformed into the bearers of a quintessentially "Parisian" medicine. Almost all were sons of the bourgeoisie, representing the full spectrum of the early nineteenth-century middle class – from coupon-clipping landowners, wholesale merchants, and wealthy lawyers, at the one end, to urban craftsmen and bakers at the other. A few diverged from this typical social background: Three came from peasant milieus; one, surely the most colorful of the lot, was born illegitimate and without officially known paternity into the old Norman sword nobility. (See Appendix.)

The core members have left vivid descriptions of the customs of the circle. Trélat and Brierre de Boismont remembered

> The Sunday luncheons where the disciples, mingled with other, already distinguished men, were invited, by the cordial affability of the *maître*, to take part in the most elevated discussions of the physiological and morbid phenomena of the mental realm.[69]

At these luncheons, Esquirol would typically "indicate the areas of the science which had [hitherto] been only superficially touched" and

---

[68] Semelaigne, *Grands aliénistes*, p. 132; Esquirol, "Mémoire historique et statistique sur la maison royale de Charenton," *Ann. d'hyg. pub.* 13 (1835): 111–12.

[69] Ulysse Trélat, "Notice sur François Leuret," *Ann. d'hyg. pub.* 45 (1851): 247.

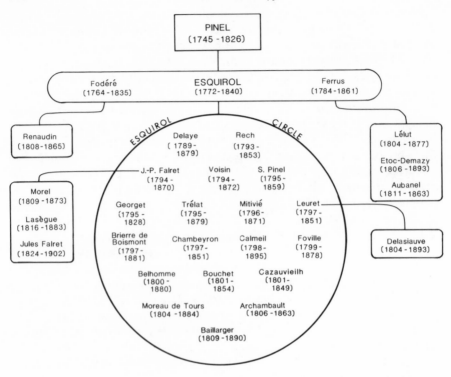

Figure 1. The "genealogy" of French psychiatry in the early nineteenth century: teachers and students

would thus put his students on the track of new and fruitful research.[70] The paternal ambiance that suffused these gatherings was uppermost in Bouchet's recollection of them. Esquirol, who was married but had no children, "loved to be surrounded by [his pupils], to unite them into a single family; . . . each Sunday saw seated at his table ten or twelve young physicians . . . , all joined by an equal tenderness for their *maître* and all regarded by him with the same paternal affection."[71] The students whose talents most impressed Esquirol he urged to compete for the annual prize – 300 francs and a copy of Pinel's *Traité* – which he had founded in the pivotal year 1818 to honor the best study of any aspect of insanity.[72] By means of this prize, he sought

---

[70] A. Brierre de Boismont, "Notice biographique sur M. F. Leuret," *Ann. m.-p.*, 2d ser., 3 (1851): 514.

[71] Bouchet, *Quelques mots*, p. 12. Some of Moreau de Tour's memories of this formative experience were, appropriate to a "familial" milieu, gustatorial; as an aging *aliéniste* at the Salpêtrière in the early 1880s, he used to say, "On déjeunait fort bien chez M. Esquirol." Semelaigne, *Pionniers*, Vol. 1, pp. 299–300.

[72] See Trélat, "Notice sur Leuret," p. 247; Bouchet, *Quelques mots*, pp. 5–6; and Semelaigne, *Grands aliénistes*, pp. 131–32.

"to excite [in his students] that spirit of competition (*émulation*) which elicits labor by supplying it with an immediate goal"; and, according to one student, the lure of the prize succeeded both in prompting individuals to undertake the study of insanity and in leading them to embark upon those significant projects that later made their reputations.[73] The prize contributed as well to the sense of cohesiveness and collective endeavor of the circle, since Esquirol, creating a kind of small-scale academy, chose the panel of judges from among the auditors of his course.[74]

Unlike Pinel, who usually shrank from the patronal function of finding positions and places for his students, Esquirol emphasized that function. Much more committed than Pinel to founding a specialty, he could not afford his circle to be evanescent and knew that to insure its continuity, he must give it institutional roots. The patronage most readily at Esquirol's disposal was within his own *maison de santé*. In the late 1820s he had moved the *maison* from the rue de Buffon to a more spacious property in the village of Ivry outside Paris, building a brand new facility there in accordance with his own therapeutic-cum-architectural precepts. In both locations, the *maison* was a flourishing enterprise, catering to a highly affluent clientele; and it was another source of Esquirol's celebrity, turning him into something of a household word. As a Paris newspaper wrote of his *maison* in 1827:

> Who has not heard about the excellent treatment that the doctor gives to lunatics, the care and attention of which they are the object? But who does not also know that it is impossible to be admitted on the rue de Buffon for less than 10 or 15 francs a day? . . . To see madhouses (*maisons d'aliénés*) risen to such extraordinary prices, one would be tempted to believe that insanity is a privilege and that, without being a bureaucrat or a capitalist, it is inadvisable to rave. However, the janitor, the bricklayer, and the errand-boy are allowed to go crazy just like the others for, if equality is anywhere, it is assuredly in human misery. Ah well, what I wish for then is a low-cost asylum, an inexpensive Esquirol.[75]

Professional positions at the *maison* were not numerous, and they were reserved for the students with whom Esquirol was most intimate: his own nephew Mitivié; the brilliant Georget; and, after Georget's premature death, Leuret, the last two virtually surrogate sons. (Was it only a coincidence that the social origins of these two specially favored students were among the humblest of any members of the circle? Georget's father was a peasant farmer and miller of grain, Leuret's a baker. Esquirol's self-conception as patron may have had a tinge of noblesse oblige, making him particularly responsive to talented young men who

---

[73] Bouchet, *Quelques mots*, pp. 5–6.
[74] Semelaigne, *Grands aliénistes*, p. 132.
[75] "Des maisons de santé," *Journal de Paris*, August 6, 1827.

were his inferiors not only in age and medical experience but also in social standing.)

Within Paris and the surrounding area, there was not much else available for the circle. The Salpêtrière slot vacated by Esquirol went to Etienne Pariset, a physician without psychiatric training who had earned the gratitude of the government by participating in a mission to Spain to study the yellow fever epidemic. Pariset's old slot at Bicêtre went to Guillaume Ferrus, for whom Pinel had long solicited a senior appointment. The resourceful Esquirol did inveigle the administration to reestablish a position which had fallen into desuetude at Charenton – that of *médecin-inspecteur du service de santé* – and, since the position was within his purview as chief physician, he placed his student Calmeil in it.[76]

But Esquirol's most significant achievement as a patron was his placement of students in provincial lunatic institutions, thus actualizing one of the circle's central tenets – the dissemination of the new Parisian expertise in *maladies mentales*. The bureaucratic contacts that Esquirol had acquired in the Ministry of the Interior, especially during the interval 1819–1821, together with those he had acquired in local administration through repeated provincial visits both before and after 1819,[77] were decisive here; for, lacking an official position legitimating his actions, he nonetheless, as Trélat put it proudly and approvingly, "endowed the principal *maisons de traitement* of our country with his former students, the most capable to honor science and to serve humanity well."[78] There was nothing covert about Esquirol's exercise of unofficial influence. As one member of the Esquirol circle, Chambeyron, stated it baldly in a letter to the minister of the interior: "In 1835, Esquirol made me chief physician of the hospital for the insane at Rennes."[79] In a public speech, another member of the circle, Bouchet, described (though without mentioning his own name) how he had happened to become physician at the new lunatic institution of Nantes in 1834:

> During one of [Esquirol's] voyages, in the year 1819, he went to Nantes and was received by the Commission administrative des hospices in a distinguished manner which touched him deeply . . . and which he always remembered with gratitude. Thus when in 1825 [that Commission] submitted to him the initial plans for the Saint-Jacques lunatic asylum, he

---

76 See Sussman, "Etienne Pariset," pp. 52–55; Esquirol, "Mémoire historique et statistique sur Charenton," pp. 109–10.

77 In 1821 Esquirol received permission for a two-month holiday from the Salpêtrière, both to mend his health and to visit "all the lunatic houses of France once more" in order to assess recent improvements. AAP: CGH 72, ff. 153–54.

78 Trélat, "Notice sur Leuret," pp. 247–48.

79 AN: F^{15} 3915, letter dated May 18, 1848.

considered his careful examination of them as an acquittal of a debt. Later he himself proposed the physician for [the asylum] . . .[80]

Esquirol made comparable unabashed avowals. Of the new Saint-Yon lunatic institution at Rouen: "Much admired are the order and discipline introduced there from the beginning by Dr. Foville, a Salpêtrière student who was appointed chief physician of the asylum when, on the invitation of the prefect, I put his name forward."[81] Of the renovated lunatic facility of the Grave in Toulouse, where Esquirol's father had long ago been an overseer: "Dr. Delaye, who had been my student at the Salpêtrière and whom I pointed out to the administration, was named physician of the division of the insane."[82]

To these various posts the Esquirol students – missionaries in their own way – brought the enlightened methods vindicated in Paris. Bouchet stressed the "moral treatment" in Nantes, construing it to mean primarily the patient's resumption of work in his former occupation. Only work (as he reasoned in Pinellian vocabulary) could provide a sustained "distraction from delirious impressions and thoughts" while avoiding any dangerous bombardment of "the imagination with sensations which cause it to stray from real life."[83] Chambeyron testified that, at the Saint-Méen hospice in Rennes, he had done everything possible "to transform into a *maison de santé* what had really been merely a lunatic depot." At a meeting of the local society of savants, he displayed with a dramatic flourish the instruments used "to contain madmen" at Saint-Méen before his arrival and which he had promptly banned – "iron shackles, thumbscrews, a type of large bag in which was enclosed the head of a lunatic whose screams were troublesome and which was then attached to a wall or some other stable point." In their stead Chambeyron had introduced "the new method" of "hygienic and moral care" whose "better effects are incontestably demonstrated by the higher rate of cure."[84] And irritated that the local hospital administration had publicly reversed one of his decisions, he sternly lectured its members about the "lessons that I received" – obviously from Esquirol – "on the governance of lunatic houses." "Permit me to tell you, gentlemen, that if you desire the reform and prosperity of

[80] Bouchet, *Quelques mots*, p. 7.
[81] Esquirol, "Maisons d'aliénés," 1838 ed., p. 453. Esquirol's Rouennais connection was of long standing; in 1821 the Ministry of the Interior had sent him to Rouen to confer with local administrators about their institution for the insane, then in the planning stage; AAP: CGH 68, f. 495.
[82] Esquirol, "Maisons d'aliénés," 1838 ed., p. 479.
[83] Bouchet, "Compte moral du quartier des aliénés de l'hospice général de Nantes," *Ann. m.-p.*, 1st ser., 8 (1846): 405, 407.
[84] ADIV: 18Td 1, Société des sciences et arts de Rennes, Session of June 15, 1840. I learned of this document in Jacques Léonard, *Les médicins de l'Ouest au XIXème siècle* (Lille: Atelier reproduction des thèses, 1978).

Saint-Méen, material amelioration will not suffice. You must also give to the medical chief whom you have appointed *an authority that, in the eyes of his subordinates, is entirely autocratic* and subject only to the direct but hidden control of the administration."[85]

In Montpellier at a newly constructed special quarter for the insane at the Saint-Esprit hospice, Dr. Rech, a native of the city who had trained under Esquirol during a three-year stay in Paris – and who had been chosen for the post in 1821 by a supervisory board of local notables committed to what Rech called "modern principles" – disseminated the influence of the *maître* by touting "the moral treatment," insisting upon the superiority of medical authority in the institution, and offering clinical lessions in *maladies mentales*. "Should that happy innovation be confined to the capital?" he mused about this new instruction.[86] (Rech identified himself and was identified by others as an Esquirol student, but Esquirol did not claim him as such. No doubt the young provincial's sojourn at the Salpêtrière made more of an impression on him than on his pedagogue.)[87]

In at least one instance local doctors balked at the imposition – so integral to Esquirol's plan – of "Parisian" medicine and medical personnel. The appointment of Chambeyron to the Saint-Méen hospice in Rennes brought forth a written protest signed by twenty-eight of the town's physicians. A "revolting injustice," they charged, had been perpetrated against their "honorable colleague" Dr. Macé, who had held the then part-time post of physician at the lunatic hospice for twelve years but had been summarily dismissed to make way for Chambeyron – not named but called here, significantly, "a stranger" – on the "ridiculous pretext" that the latter possessed "special knowledge." "The administration" had even had the gall to solicit applications for Macé's vacant post, a procedure later revealed to be a sham – and an "insult" to the two physicians of Rennes who did apply – because the "stranger" had already been appointed. The outrage of these physicians was at root a response to their entirely accurate perception that "the

---

[85] ADIV: Fonds de l'Asile Saint-Méen (as yet uncatalogued during my September 1982 visit to Rennes), letter of Chambeyron dated May 7, 1836, my italics.

[86] Rech, "Clinique de la maison des aliénés," *Ephémérides médicales de Montpellier* (June 1826): 120, and "Quelques considérations sur l'étude des aliénations mentales," *Nouvelles annales cliniques de la Société de médecine pratique de Montpellier* 1 (1822): 354. See also Colin Jones, "Treatment of the Insane in Eighteenth- and Early Nineteenth-Century Montpellier," *Medical History* 24 (1980): 385–87.

[87] Rech described himself as "the pupil and friend" of Esquirol in "Quelques considérations," p. 358 n1. Cf. Esquirol, "Maisons d'aliénés," 1838 ed., p. 455, which describes Rech only as "professor at the faculty of Montpellier," as opposed to descriptions of other young alienists as Salpêtrière pupils. But Marchant, once a Charenton intern under Esquirol, regarded Rech as a member of Esquirol's "school"; see his *Esquirol*, p. 12. So did the editorial in the first number of *Esculape: Journal des spécialités médico-chirurgicales* (June 1, 1839): 2.

administration," itself an emanation from Paris, disparaged local medical talent, preferred its Parisian equivalent, and was able to enforce that preference.[88]

When Esquirol was unable to place a student in a full-time position, he often resorted to a temporary palliative. One variety of the moral treatment he prescribed for some of his private patients was travel, a distracting "change of milieu"; and at such times he characteristically selected one of his students to accompany and care for the troubled voyager. Moreau de Tours, for example, began his career in this manner and even traveled to the Orient, where he undertook research on the psychological effects of hashish. Indeed, one of Esquirol's elegists compiled a list of some fourteen students for whom the *maître* had found temporary employment as glorified travel companions.[89] Penurious students were sometimes given lodging in Esquirol's own home: Georget stayed there for a full eight years.[90] Bouchet summed up matters by saying that Esquirol "never ceased helping his students . . . , facilitating their debuts in *le monde* with all his influence." When all else failed, the help came, with "unostentatious generosity" from their mentor's own purse.[91]

There was a significant difference between the way Esquirol conducted the circle internally and the face that it turned to the outside world. Internally, the intellectual independence of the students was respected, never sacrificed as the price that had to be paid for patronal support. Esquirol may have "reigned uncontested in the field of insanity" after 1826 (by which time death had removed both Pinel and A.-A. Royer-Collard), but he apparently did not reign autocratically over his students or strive to turn them into epigones; he was not one of "those princes of science who can tolerate only mediocrities around him."[92] "I will never forget," said one member of the circle, "that he gave me his first testimony of affection after a discussion in which we held conflicting views."[93] In its external relations, however, the circle presented a united front. "That medical phalanx," one of the members dubbed it retrospectively, referring to its solidarity in combat.[94] Its capabilities as a "phalanx" were most apparent in its defense of the diagnostic cate-

---

[88] ADIV: 20 Md 3, Petition dated August 5, 1835. A note in Léonard, *Médicins de l'Ouest,* brought this document to my attention.

[89] Semelaigne, *Pionniers,* Vol. 1, p. 295; Pariset, "Eloge de J.-E.-D. Esquirol," *Histoire des membres de l'Académie de médecine,* Vol. 2, Note A, p. 476.

[90] Raige-Delorme, "Nécrologie: Georget," *Arch. gen. de med.* 17 (1828): 328; Leuret and Baillarger also lived with Esquirol; see Pariset, "Eloge," Note A, p. 476.

[91] Bouchet, *Quelques mots,* p. 11.

[92] Brierre de Boismont, "Notice sur Leuret," p. 514.

[93] Bouchet, *Quelques mots,* p. 11.

[94] Brierre de Boismont, "Notice biographique sur C. Bouchet," *Ann. m.-p.,* 2d ser., 6 (1854): 312. Clark, *Prophets and Patrons* (p. 67 n3) indicates that military names – "regiment," "militia" – are typically used for clusters by their members.

gory monomania, which became the subject of a long, heated controversy beginning in the mid-1820s. In this endeavor, the geographical dispersal of the circle through provincial appointments did not vitiate its force but enhanced it; for since cohesiveness had been maintained despite physical separation, the circle had acquired a national presence.[95] The monomania controversy and its larger significance, as well as the circle's role in it, will be explored in the next chapter. I will confine myself here to a discussion of another of the circle's "combat maneuvers," one which at the same time illustrates the way in which the organizational form of patron-and-circle might work to discourage excellence: the case of Antoine-Laurent Bayle.

Bayle is now recognized as a major theoretical innovator in French psychiatry. In the early 1820s he identified general paralysis as a discrete disease entity characterized by speech impairment, progressive weakening of motility in the arms and legs, and a delirium degenerating into dementia. General paralysis quickly caught on as a diagnostic category (or as Bayle put it with fine wit, "assumed the rank of bourgeoisie among disease families").[96] Less than two decades after it was identified, between one-ninth and one-sixth of the patients in Paris lunatic institutions were being diagnosed as its victims.[97] Yet Bayle was never able to obtain a position as a physician in a lunatic institution. The precise reasons for this professional failure are obscure, but by all accounts Esquirol was the crucial factor.[98] While a medical student in Paris, Bayle had attached himself to A.-A. Royer-Collard at Charenton, and it was there, in what he described as "one of the finest and most beneficial establishments devoted to the treatment of the insane" and with "bounties" constantly heaped upon him by Royer-Collard, that he had carried out his original researches on general paralysis on almost 200 patients.[99] When Royer-Collard died in 1825, Bayle was without a

---

[95] Not only had the identity "Esquirol student" been deeply impressed upon those placed in the provinces, but these emissaries seem also to have stayed in close touch with the Paris psychiatric scene. In 1839, for example, Delaye came back to Paris with Gérard Marchant, a former Esquirol intern who now assisted Delaye at the Grave lunatic hospice in Toulouse, and the two visited Bicêtre to observe Leuret's new therapeutic experiments. See Marchant, "Quelques mots sur l'influence thérapeutique de la musique exécutée par les aliénés," *Esculape*, October 15, 1840, pp. 85–86.

[96] Bayle, "De la cause organique de l'aliénation mentale accompagnée de paralysie générale," *Ann. m.-p.*, 3d ser., 1 (1855): 411.

[97] Baillarger, "Nouvelles considérations sur la paralysie générale incomplète," *Ann. m.-p.*, 1st ser., 8 (1846): 425.

[98] See Erwin H. Ackerknecht, *A Short History of Psychiatry*, trans. S. Wolff, 2d ed. (New York and London: Hafner, 1968), p. 51; Semelaigne, *Pionniers*, Vol. 1, pp. 244–49; Stefan Müller, *Antoine Laurent Bayle: sein grundlegender Beitrag zur Erforschung der progressive Paralyse* (Zurich: Juris, 1965), p. 19.

[99] A. L. J. Bayle, *Nouvelle doctrine des maladies mentales* (Paris: Gabon, 1825), p. 15. For lavish praise of Royer-Collard's intellect and a subtly competitive remark about the

protector, and Esquirol showed no inclination to take the talented young man, the protégé of his rival, under his wing. Instead Bayle found himself ousted from his adjunct position at Charenton as soon as Esquirol took charge of that institution, and he retreated to the assistant librarianship of the Paris medical faculty. Decades later, the Esquirol circle showed its mettle as a "phalanx": It banded together to vindicate the master's ostracism of Bayle by insisting that Bayle had no claim to the discovery of general paralysis, that the real priority belonged to one of their own number, Delaye.[100]

The dynamics of recruitment: specialization and the "doctor glut"

In 1824 Esquirol was pondering aloud the new popularity among young physicians of the study and treatment of insanity, a popularity manifested in the large enrollment of his Salpêtrière clinical course and the ease with which he had formed his circle. He had always recognized that tending lunatics was an intrinsically unattractive occupation requiring "a sort of self-abnegation."[101] Thus Esquirol opined in 1824 that the "happy efforts of medicine and the daily successes it obtains" since the Pinellian breakthrough had led "a greater number of physicians to turn to the study of *maladies mentales*, however painful that study may be."[102] This roughly Kuhnian analysis is surely accurate, but it is also incomplete: Not only internal factors – advances in medical theory and therapy – but also external ones involving professional demography must be taken into account to explain how psychiatry attracted its recruits in the crucial period of its formation.

The Restoration and July Monarchy were a period of medical overcrowding (or *encombrement*, as contemporaries called it), a surplus in the supply of doctors over the effective demand for their services – at least in the major cities, where doctors congregated by preference. The phenomenon was probably part of a broader one, extending to the liberal professions generally and touching all the countries of Western

scientific superiority of Charenton over Bicêtre and the Salpêtrière, see Bayle, *Traité des maladies du cerveau et de ses membranes* (Paris: Gabon, 1826), "Avant-Propos."

[100] See the assertions in Baillarger, "Nouvelles considérations sur paralysie générale," p. 424, and Trélat, "De la paralysie générale," *Ann. m.-p.*, 3d ser., 1 (1855): 233. In 1855 Bayle defended his own claims to priority before the Académie de médecine; see his "De la cause organique," p. 410.

[101] Esquirol, *Mémoire*, p. 27.

[102] Esquirol, "Existe-t-il de nos jours un plus grand nombre de fous qu'ils n'en existait il y a quarante ans?" (1824), as reprinted in *Maladies mentales*, Vol. 2, p. 734. The Paris administrator Desportes offered a similar analysis in *Compte rendu au Conseil général des hospices et hôpitaux civils de Paris sur le service des aliénés . . . pendant les années 1822, 1823, et 1824* (Paris: Impr. de Mme Huzard, 1826), p. 25.

Europe.[103] It was described and bemoaned in the medical literature,[104] and acknowledged as a fact of social life in the fiction of the day. The narrator of Balzac's *Z. Marcas*, a law student living in a Left Bank garret in the 1830s with his medical student friend, offered a typically somber and ironic description of the situation:

> We thought only of amusing ourselves. . . . We could see no future in the two professions our parents had forced us to embrace. There are a hundred lawyers, a hundred doctors for every place. The crowd obstructs these two avenues . . . , which are really two arenas: one kills oneself there, one enters into combat not with steel or firearms but by intrigue and calumny, by horrible labors, by campaigns in the realm of the intellect as murderous as those in Italy were for the republican soldiers.[105]

The causes of *encombrement* in France were manifold: the high birth rate under the Empire; the end of corporate control over entrance into the medical faculties; the deeply ingrained bourgeois prejudice against mercantile activity and the post-Napoleonic decline of the army, both of which narrowed career options and operated forcefully to channel young men into what began to be called the liberal professions.

It was in the midst of this *encombrement* that a second phenomenon, medical specialization, emerged in Paris in a highly conspicuous way. Symptomatically, the year 1839 saw the founding of two new medical journals devoted to specialization, the *Revue des spécialités et des innovations médicales et chirurgicales* and *Esculape: Journal des spécialités médico-chirurgicales*. Each included the medicine of the insane within its purview and carried articles by full-fledged or peripheral members of the Esquirol circle.[106] At about the same time physicians who

---

[103] See George D. Sussman, "The Glut of Doctors in Mid-Nineteenth-Century France," *Comparative Studies in Society and History* 19 (1977): 287–304; and Lenore O'Boyle, "The Problem of an Excess of Educated Men in Western Europe, 1800–1850," *Journal of Modern History* 42 (1970): 471–95.

[104] See, e.g., Munaret, *Du médecin de campagne et de ses malades* (Paris: Librairie anatomique de Baillet, 1837), p. 4; and Delasiauve, *De l'organisation médicale en France sous le triple rapport de la pratique, des établissements de bienfaisance et de l'enseignement* (Paris: Masson, 1843), pp. 53–4.

[105] *La comédie humaine* (Paris: Gallimard-Pléiade, 1976–81), Vol. 8, pp. 831–32. For another contemporary fictional account of medical *encombrement*, see the popular novel by Louis Reybaud, *Jérôme Paturot à la recherche d'une position sociale* (Paris: Dubochet, Le Chevalier, 1846), p. 100.

[106] During its first year, the *Revue des spécialités* serialized a long article by Charles Londe, "De la folie: De ses causes, de ses symptômes et de son traitement." Londe, a hygienist, had "often observed *maladies mentales* with Georget and under Esquirol"; see Sachaile de la Barre, *Médecins de Paris*, p. 437. *Esculape* listed "maladies du système nerveux" as the eighth (of fifteen) specialties on its masthead. Its introductory editorial (June 1, 1839, p. 2) gave Esquirol credit for having "made a special study of mental maladies"; subsequent issues carried articles by Brierre de Boismont, Belhomme, and Moreau de Tours.

worked in lunatic institutions began, in accordance with the linguistic currents of the day, to speak of their area of medical expertise as a "specialty." (Somewhat earlier it had been referred to as a "branch" of medicine.)[107] Writing a letter of recommendation in 1845, Leuret praised a young doctor for the success with which he had plied "the study of *maladies mentale* under the direction of Monsieur Esquirol" and ended by pronouncing him "très instruit dans la spécialité."[108] Renaudin, a temporarily unemployed young physician whose only post since his graduation from the Paris faculty had been in a lunatic institution in Strasbourg, commented in 1840 on the separate identity which that medical occupation had acquired: "After having been exclusively devoted to *a specialty*, after having spent several years in an establishment for lunatics, it is difficult to give oneself over to general practice, which presents all the less chance of success because the public usually regards the doctor of lunatics as less familiar with the other branches of the healing art."[109]

Medical *encombrement* was certainly one of the factors conducing to medical specialization – that is, the latter can be regarded from one perspective as an economically rational response to the former, a subdivision of the "product" so as to increase consumer demand. This view of occupational specialization would be propounded at the end of the century by Emile Durkheim, whose *Division of Labor in Society* (1893) saw specialization as a benign solution – a "mellowed denouement" – to the Darwinian struggle for social survival. Through diversification of function, peaceful coexistence among competitors for scarce resources became possible in human society: "The oculist does not struggle with the psychiatrist (*le médecin . . . qui soigne les maladies mentales*), nor the shoemaker with the hatter."[110] Interestingly enough, ordinary observers in the first half of the nineteenth century also routinely came to the conclusion that medical specialization was a function of a competitive marketplace, of an oversupply of medical services. As early as 1828, a Paris physician suggested that, with "the number of doctors increased tenfold," only three courses of action were open to a medical man: to renounce medical practice altogether, to adopt an unscrupu-

---

[107] For this usage, see, e.g., Amédée Dupau in a book review in *Revue médicale historique et philosophique* 8 (1822): 347; and Rech, "Quelques considérations sur l'étude des aliénations," p. 352.

[108] AN: F^{15} 3914, letter to the minister of the interior dated September 22, 1845.

[109] Ibid., letter to the minister of the interior dated August 15, 1840, ms. p. 3, my italics. See also ADIV: X359, letter of Chambeyron to the prefect of Ille-et-Vilaine, September 26, 1840.

[110] Emile Durkheim, *The Division of Labor in Society*, trans. G. Simpson (New York: Free Press, 1933), pp. 267, 270 for "mellowed denouement"; for Durkheim's French phrase for "psychiatrist," see *De la division du travail social*, 6th ed. (Paris: F. Alcan, 1932), p. 250.

lous form of it, or to find "a specialty" and "mine it with success."[111] A German visitor to Paris, initially puzzled by the new phenomenon of medical specialization he encountered there, ascribed it to the large number of doctors in the French capital and the resultant competition among them: "The wish and the need to distinguish oneself from one's colleagues in the most remunerative way possible occasions the widespread custom of choosing one particular form, species or class of illness as one's favorite subject-matter."[112] A Paris newspaper decried "an unseemly industrialism" among doctors as revealed by the "launching of specialties."[113]

The implicit assertion here is that medical specialties had arisen in response to market conditions, that their ethos was essentially an "industrial" one. It was an assertion – and accusation – frequently made; the medical specialties, the editor of *Esculape* lamented, were "today more ill-appreciated than ever, now that they are considered as veritable *industries*."[114] Indeed, the etymology of the word *"spécialité"* bore witness to the pervasive economic interpretation of the phenomenon. The term initially arose "in our Parisian patois" in the context of mercantile competition: The shopkeeper was said to endeavor to lure the client into his shop by stocking *spécialités*, or items that could not be found elsewhere.[115] In this view – so common during the July Monarchy – that medical specialization was part and parcel of a (now-rejected) pure laissez-faire model of the medical profession, that it entailed the assimilation of the healing art to any craft or trade that had but to prove itself at the marketplace, medical specialization was once again presented as a species of charlatanism. Hence the defensive posture adopted by both of the new medical journals of the specialties; hence the warning in a popular career guide of the 1840s that if a young doctor elects to follow one of the specialties, he must be prepared to live with the "opprobrium or at least low esteem" of his colleagues.[116]

The economic roots of medical specialization, so apparent to contemporaries, cannot be discounted here. Indeed, as the correspondence of

---

[111] Eusèbe de Salle, as cited in a review of his *Lettre d'un médecin à un avocat, Journal de Paris*, April 23, 1828.

[112] Dr. Emil Kratzmann, *Die neuere Medizin in Frankreich, nach Theorie und Praxis* (Leipzig: F. A. Brockhaus, 1846), p. 191.

[113] *Correspondant*, March 24, 1847, as cited in Louis Trénard, *Salvandy en son temps, 1795–1856* (Lille: R. Giard, 1968), p. 795.

[114] June 1, 1839, p. 1, italics in original.

[115] See Georges Matoré, *Le vocabulaire et la société sous Louis-Philippe* (Geneva: Droz, 1951), p. 32; and Marc Fournier, "Les spécialités parisiennes," in *La grande ville: Nouveau tableau de Paris comique, critique et philosophique*, ed. Paul de Kock et al. (Paris: Maresq, 1844), Vol. 2, esp. pp. 57, 59: *"Spécialité*, si je ne me trompe, est née industriel" (p. 59).

[116] See editorials to the inaugural numbers of the *Revue des spécialités* and *Esculape*; the career guide is Edouard Charton, *Guide pour le choix d'un état* (Paris: Lenormant, 1842), p. 398.

Dr. Chambeyron attests, the drive to psychiatric specialization was much attenuated in areas outside Paris where the professional population was less dense and its membership less ambitious. Chambeyron had perennial trouble recruiting an intern for the Saint-Méen lunatic institution in Rennes: Sometimes he had no applicants at all; he begged the professors in the local medical school to counter the "repugnance of the students"; he lost one intern to a military hospital in the vicinity, and another was content to become an *officier de santé*, a second-class citizen of the medical professional world.[117]

Against this background, the decision of a young Parisian medical student to become a disciple of Esquirol and join the new *spécialité* becomes a complicated one. The student was probably responding, on different levels and in different degrees, to the intellectual excitement of a new paradigm; to the sentimental appeal of an ideology of humanitarianism; to Esquirol's personal magnetism as a teacher; and finally, to the economic pressures experienced by an entrant into the already overcrowded profession of medicine. But however these factors might be weighed in individual cases, serious initiation into the new specialty, and ultimately the ability to earn a living in a psychiatric career, would come via the institutional form of the circle.

[117] ADIV: Fonds Saint-Méen, letters of Chambeyron dated May 19, 1838; May 26, 1838; April 7, 1840; October 11, 1836.

5

Monomania

IN a letter to J. S. Mill in 1836, Tocqueville apologized for his failure to deliver an article he had promised to the *London and Westminster Review*. He had, instead of producing it, compulsively returned to his work on democracy in America: "I have at this moment *la monomanie de la Démocratie*."[1] In 1834, Balzac described his protagonist Balthazar Claës, the seeker after the alchemical quintessence: "At that age [59 years], the idea which dominated him had acquired the crabbed fixity with which monomanias begin"; and, as Balthazar grew older, his almost perpetual disquietude was occasionally relieved by "a hope which gave [him] the expression of a monomaniac."[2] A Balzac disciple, Charles de Bernard, wrote in a serialized novel of 1836 of a man "too much reformed by marriage" who vehemently discarded the philandering habits of his youth and embarked upon a course of pious wife-worship: "Since that time, a fixed preoccupation, like the idea of a monomaniac, had dictated his conduct."[3] Daumier's biting depiction of the Guizot cabinet, the government which had already imprisoned him for his audacity, appeared in *Caricature* in 1832 under the title of "The Ministerial Charenton: Monomaniacal Varieties of Political Lunatics."[4] In this multicolored lithograph replete with captions, each of the sixteen celebrities of the Juste-Milieu could be seen engaged in his characteristic obsession. A barefoot, barelegged Guizot, for example, is "preaching his system of quasi-perfidious legitimacy in the desert"; while d'Argout, "playing at censorship," rides a giant pair of scissors

---

[1] Letter dated April 10, 1836 in Alexis de Tocqueville, *Oeuvres complètes* (Paris: Gallimard, 1951–), Vol. 6, p. 309. Tocqueville seems to have had a predilection for the term; see his description of philanthropists who focused exclusively on prison conditions: "Ils ont la monomanie du système pénitentiaire." Gustave de Beuamont and Alexis de Tocqueville, *Système pénitentiaire aux Etats-Unis et de son application en France*, 3d ed. (Paris: Gosselin, 1845), p. 139.

[2] Honoré de Balzac, *La recherche de l'absolu* in *La comédie humaine* (Paris: Gallimard-Pléiade, 1976–81), Vol. 10, pp. 770, 814.

[3] Charles de Bernard, *Un acte de vertu* in *Le noeud gordien* (Paris: Michel Lévy, 1854), p. 207.

[4] Loys Delteil, *Le peintre-graveur illustré (XIXe et XXe siècles)*, Vol. 20 (Paris: Chez l'auteur, 1925), Plate 44.

like a hobbyhorse and waves a white banner emblazoned with gold fleurs-de-lys. In a Paris daily in 1829, a spokesman for the new liberal generation just entering politics complained of the cold welcome he and his cohorts had received from the elderly incumbents: "We are reproached . . . with having boasted of our age; we are believed to be afflicted with a youth-monomania."[5]

These examples claim our attention as evidence of the remarkable success of one of Esquirol's theoretical contributions to the new *médecine des aliénés* – the disease entity monomania. Named by Esquirol around the year 1810,[6] "monomania" had already percolated down to the nonmedical French intelligentsia and been incorporated into their language by the late 1820s.[7] Some linguistic purists might complain of it: "The words of the people are abandoned today to make way for words invented or introduced by scholars. . . . Pedantry is especially fashionable in the newspapers, and the foolish bourgeoisie, who get their opinions from their newspapers, accept these foul words. . . . One no longer says, it is his hobbyhorse (*dada*), his fancy (*marotte*). One says, like a grave physician: it is a monomania."[8] But even the Académie française succumbed and officially admitted the neologism "monomania" into the French lexicon in 1835, after it had been in circulation for a mere three decades[9] – an achievement all the more noteworthy when it is compared to the linguistic fate of "nostalgia," a late seventeenth-century medical coinage that required almost a century and a half to win this same approval.[10]

Monomania captured the lay imagination and acquired the status of a general cultural category during the period of the constitutional monarchy only because it had first captured the medical imagination. During this period, the teaching of *médecine mentale* in the French capital seems to have given it pride of place. As one psychiatrist who began his professional training at the Salpêtrière in the 1830s attested, monomania had been introduced to him and became "the subject of my scientific preoccupations from the very first moments of my initia-

---

[5] "Aide-toi le ciel t'aidera," *Journal de Paris,* August 8, 1829.

[6] The only indication of the date of origin is given in Esquirol, "Note sur la mono-manie-homicide," in J.-C. Hoffbauer, *Médecine légale relative aux aliénés et aux sourds-muets,* trans. A. Chambeyron (Paris: J.-B. Baillière, 1827), p. 311: "Il y a plus de quinze ans que j'ai proposé d'imposer à la folie partielle le nom de monomanie."

[7] In the case of Balzac, "percolated down" is inaccurate since the omnivorous novelist actively sought medical knowledge; for his familiarity with the technical writings of Georget, a leading exponent of the monomania concept, see Madeline Fargeaud, *Balzac et "La recherche de l'absolu"* (Paris: Hachette, 1968), pp. 138–45.

[8] "Le grammairien et le causeur," *Journal de la langue française,* 3d ser., 2 (1839): 522.

[9] Hatzfeld and Darmesteter, *Dictionnaire général de la langue française.*

[10] Jean Starobinski, "La nostalgie: Théories médicales et expression littéraire," *Studies in Voltaire and the Eighteenth Century* 27 (1963): 1507.

tion into the study of insanity."[11] At a time when medical men regarded physiognomy as an important diagnostic indicator of mental
illness – Esquirol had a large collection of plaster casts of the faces of
insane persons[12] – Georget, a member of the Esquirol circle, commissioned the painter Géricault to paint ten studies of lunatics, arranging
for him to make extensive institutional visits in order to sketch his
subjects from life. The canvases from this group which survive, executed between 1821 and 1824, reflect their patron's scientific concerns:
They are all portraits of monomaniacs.[13] (Plate 3.)

At the same time, cases of monomania were being readily discovered
in certain clinical contexts. In the years 1826–33, years for which statistics were carefully gathered by Esquirol himself or under his supervision, it was the single most frequent diagnosis made of patients entering Charenton and accounted, on average, for a staggering 45 percent
of the inmate population.[14] Esquirol's student Rech reported that at the
Montpellier lunatic institution in the years 1826–29, some 23 percent of
the entering patients were monomaniacs.[15] According to my own com-
putations from the admissions registers of the Salpêtrière and Bicêtre
for 1841 and 1842, monomania diagnoses accounted for about 10 percent of the total, making monomania alternately the most or second
most common diagnosis, being narrowly surpassed on occasion only
by general paralysis.[16] Indeed, the fact that general paralysis was honored as a diagnosis in the two Paris hospices – by contrast, Esquirol
regarded it as "a complication" of insanity but not as a disease entity in
its own right,[17] and it likewise failed to figure in Rech's tabulations –

---

11 B.-A. Morel, *Etudes cliniques: Traité théorique et pratique des maladies mentales* (Nancy:
   Grimblot; Paris: J.-B. Baillière, 1852), Vol. 1, p. 411.

12 Ms. diary of Sir Alexander Morison, entry for March 22, 1818 reporting a visit to the
   Salpêtrière, in Richard Hunter and Ida Macalpine, eds., *Three Hundred Years of Psychiatry, 1535–1860* (London: Oxford University Press, 1963), p. 738.

13 See Margaret Miller, "Géricault's Paintings of the Insane," *Journal of the Warburg and
   Courtauld Institutes* 4 (1941): 151–63, and Lorenz E. A. Eitner, *Géricault, His Life and His
   Work* (Ithaca, N.Y.: Cornell University Press, 1983), pp. 241–49. Esquirol had earlier
   set the example for Georget by sending the artist G.-F.-M. Gabriel into the Paris
   asylums to record the facial expressions of the patients. See Jean Adhémar, "Un
   dessinateur passioné pour le visage humain: Georges François Marie Gabriel (1775–v.
   1835)," extract from *Omagiu lui George Oprescu* (Bucharest, 1961), BN: Estampes, Yb³
   2721(28); Eitner, *Géricault*, p. 244; and Plate 2 in this book.

14 See Esquirol, "Rapport statistique sur la maison royale de Charenton pendant les
   années 1826, 1827 et 1828," *Ann. d'hyg. pub.*, 1st ser., 1 (1829): 124; and "Mémoire
   historique et statistique sur la maison royale de Charenton," ibid., 13 (1835): 147.

15 Rech, *Clinique de la maison des aliénés de Montpellier* (Montpellier: J. Martel, 1829), p. 4.

16 See AAP: Salpêtrière 6Q2-4, 6Q2-5; Bicêtre 6Q2-2, 6Q2-3, 6Q2-4. The exact figures for
   monomania are: Salpêtrière, 7.7% in 1841, 13% in 1842; Bicêtre, 9.4% in 1841, 9.3% in
   1842. Those for general paralysis are: Salpêtrière, 9.4% in 1841, 9% in 1842; Bicêtre,
   13.9% in 1841, 14.9% in 1842.

17 See, e.g., Esquirol, "Rapport statistique," p. 129.

helps to explain the lower percentage of monomaniacs in those institutions. The "delirium" following or accompanying the speech and motility impairments that characterized general paralysis often took the
form of a so-called monomania.[18] To such cases Esquirol would likely
affix the label "monomania" and a Salpêtrière or Bicêtre physician the
label "general paralysis."[19]

The vogue of monomania proved time-bound. As curious as the flourishing of that disease soon after its entrance into the nosological scheme
was the obverse phenomenon: its virtual disappearance several decades
later. At the Salpêtrière, through whose admissions registers I have
traced the process, newly diagnosed monomaniacs had all but vanished
by 1870.[20] What confronts us, then, is the rise and fall of a disease – and a
disease significant not only in the usual medical context but also in a lay
context, where, construed more figuratively than literally, it became
contemporary shorthand for a particular state of mind. The purpose of
this chapter is to explore this disease entity – Esquirol's theoretical construct – from the multitude of perspectives that shaped, indeed overde-
termined, its singular career: the medical, the cultural, the professional,
and the political. In other words, monomania will be viewed here as a
scientific contribution in its own right; but it must also be viewed as the
scientific core of a particular stage in the professional development of
the psychiatric specialty, and as carrying with it in that role distinctive
political and cultural baggage.

The initial definition of the disease

The meaning of *monomania*, in the technical medical sense in which it
was first used, was very close to the popular meaning it would soon
acquire. It denoted an idée fixe,[21] a single pathological preoccupation in

---

[18] See Bayle, *Traité des maladies du cerveau et de ses membranes* (Paris: Gabon, 1826; facsimile reprint, New York: Arno Press, 1976), which divides the disease family
"aliénation mentale avec paralysie incomplète par suite de méningite chronique" into
six varieties; in all but the second variety, *monomanie ambitieuse* is a typical part of the
clinical picture; see pp. 2, 18, 144, 250, 311, 352.

[19] See, e.g., Esquirol, "Rapport statistique," pp. 126–27, which opts for the diagnosis
monomania for a patient who also displays "the first symptoms of that paralysis so
deadly to lunatics." Cf. Salpêtrière 6Q2-4 (1841), entry 12032, where Mitivié, ordinarily a liberal dispenser of monomania diagnoses, steadfastly avoids one for an elderly
day laborer whose obsessions with money he has detailed; the diagnosis of her
condition is "general paralysis with predominance of ideas of grandeur and wealth."

[20] AAP: Salpêtrière 6Q2-55; the registers were sampled at five-year intervals.

[21] *Idée fixe* was also originally a medical term, probably coined by the phrenologists Gall
and Spurzheim in connection with Esquirol's delineation of monomania; see their
Anatomie et physiologie du système nerveux en général et du cerveau en particulier, Vol. 2
(Paris: F. Schoell, 1812), p. 192. It too was readily transferred to nonmedical culture,
most notably by the composer Hector Berlioz, who used it to signify a recurrent,

an otherwise sound mind. Yet in this technical sense, the monomania-cal idée fixe was not the benign quirk that it was, for example, for Tocqueville, when he spoke jokingly of his monomania for his book on democracy in America: It was a true, full-fledged insanity.

Esquirol's articulation and naming of monomania occurred as part of his renovation of the classificatory system of mental diseases, a project that would continue to occupy French psychiatry throughout the nineteenth century. Pinel had taken over unchanged two of the traditional classifications: Where Doublet and Colombier had spoken of mania, melancholy, frenzy, and imbecility, Pinel spoke of mania, melancholy, dementia, and idiotism.[22] But Esquirol was a less relaxed borrower from the past. Highly attentive to the role of a pristine and specialized vocabulary in establishing scientific authority, he regarded one of the traditional classifications as fundamentally acceptable in content but unacceptable in name. This was melancholy. As its Greek etymology implies, melancholy had since ancient times been viewed as a humoral imbalance, a superabundance of black bile emanating from the liver and overwhelming the brain. But the sensationalist psychology of the Enlightenment (to which Esquirol, like his teacher Pinel, subscribed), by lodging mental life solely in the nervous system and in its property of sensitivity, had obviated the necessity of invoking the mediation of fluids ("humors") from other bodily organs. Within this framework, melancholy could be redefined as a disorder of the nervous system causing the mind to be dominated by a single idea, a sad idea representing a false or at least exaggerated judgment of the real situation; these ideational characteristics were now recognized as the very essence of the disease and not, as the humoral theory had held, incidental effects of changes in black bile. Esquirol insisted that linguistic usage reflect this shift in conceptualization, that the word "melancholy" be jettisoned. Centuries of association with humoral theory had lent the word a morass of poetic, popular, and otherwise extraneous and unscientific connotations. He proposed in its stead "lypemania," a word that never really caught on, even in technical writing.[23]

The concept of monomania—and here Esquirol's neologizing was to prove much more successful—followed logically from that of lypemania. Writing an article entitled "Monomania" in 1819 in the *Dictionaire des sciences médicales*, Esquirol announced the need for delineating a new and separate disease entity. "All that relates to monomania," he

insistent melodic motif in a symphony. See the program for the *Symphonie fantastique* (1830) in Berlioz, *Complete Works*, Vol. 1 (New York: Kalmus, n.d.), n.p.

[22] See Pinel, *Traité médico-philosophique sur l'aliénation mentale, ou la manie*, 1st ed. (Paris: Richard, Caille et Ravier, Year IX/1801), Section 4.

[23] Esquirol, "Mélancolie," *Dict. des sci. med.*, Vol. 32 (1819), pp. 147–48, 150; and Jean Starobinski, *Histoire du traitement de la mélancolie des origines à 1900* (Basel: Geigy, 1960), p. 49.

asserted, "is [presently] confounded in the literature." He went on to provide the desired clarification: "Monomania is the type intermediate between mania and lypemania; it shares with lypemania the fixity and concentration of ideas and with mania the exaltation of ideas and the physical and mental activity."[24] By way of explicating this highly compressed formulation, it should be noted that mania, one of the oldest identified forms of insanity and the standard form in this period, signified for Esquirol "a general delirium," a global and all-inclusive "disorder of the understanding."[25] As he put it elsewhere, "The maniac presents the very picture of chaos, whose moving elements collide with and contradict one another incessantly. . . . He lives isolated from the world . . . as if locked in a dark room; sensations, ideas, images offer themselves to his mind without order, without connection, and without leaving a trace."[26] This chaotic, rapidly fluctuating mental life "exalted" the maniac, whose mien was typically active or hyperactive. Now both lypemania and monomania were circumscribed versions of mania; both were *"partial deliria"* in which the understanding was diseased in some aspects and healthy and well-ordered in others. The diseased aspects were referred to as the "ideas on which the delirium turns"; such ideas were "exciting, expansive" in monomania and "debilitating, oppressive" in lypemania. While this meant that the preoccupation of the lypemaniac was necessarily sad, it did *not* mean that the preoccupation of the monomaniac was necessarily pleasant or gay. Rather, the distinguishing feature of monomania was for Esquirol the propensity to garrulousness and energetic activity centered around the preoccupation: In this monomania was akin to manic "exaltation" and antithetical to lypemaniacal sluggishness.

Esquirol thus posited a perfect formal symmetry in his triad of mania, monomania, and lypemania, the new disease sharing one trait with and having one essential difference from each of the others. Whether he had initially derived monomania by such "geometric" methods or had only presented the disease in that manner for didactic purposes is unclear. But as a devotee of *la clinique,* he naturally felt called upon to bolster his formal definition with clinical observations. The dictionary article contained a half dozen case studies, the most detailed of which were drawn from patients at Esquirol's private *maison de santé:* a man who developed the unshakable belief that he was dauphin of France; a second who clung to the idea that he was "Apollo-Caesar," the ultimate world ruler; and a third who became wholly obsessed with an idea for uniting the world's people. In these case studies Esquirol illustrated and underscored the defining marks of

[24] "Monomanie," *Dict. des sci. med.*, Vol. 34, p. 115.
[25] Ibid.
[26] "Manie," *Dict. des sci. med.*, Vol. 30 (1818), p. 447.

monomania: the discreteness of the delusion ("he reasons properly on all other subjects") and the high level of excitation and even audacity that the delusion generated in the patient.[27]

Professional ramifications (I): charting "mental tendencies"

Esquirol's interest in monomania did not long remain purely nosological, confined to the accurate identification of a clinical syndrome. From the loosely Rousseauean intellectual tradition that viewed disease as an index of the progress of civilization–a tradition in which he had been steeped at least as early as his 1805 dissertation–Esquirol sought to derive an ancillary function for the new *médecin des aliénés*, a characteristically French professional function predicated upon an integration of the "expert" into the apparatus of the state. At the annual inaugural lesson of his Salpêtrière clinical course in 1822, he told his students: "He who is called upon to give care to the insane has more than one function to fulfill. . . . This malady associates the physician in some manner with the public administration. The physician enlightens the government about mental tendencies (*la tendance des esprits*); his familiarity with the causes and character of regnant madnesses furnishes [the government] with the most certain (*positifs*) elements of a moral statistics of the population."[28]

The monomania concept was central to this governmental advisory capacity that Esquirol envisioned for psychiatrists, for from the outset Esquirol had emphasized the peculiar porousness of monomania to cultural values and cultural changes. A certain grandiosity even touched his claims about the revelations that the disease could be expected to provide. "Monomania is, of all diseases, the one whose study offers the broadest and most profound subjects for meditation: the study of it embraces . . . that of civilization." According to Esquirol, the familiar proposition that "madness is the disease of civilization" could be more correctly stated by substituting "monomania" for "madness"; for it was the monomaniacal form of madness, and not madness *tout court*, whose incidence increased as civilization advanced. And monomania changed qualitatively as well as quantitatively over time, borrowing its objects from the dominant passions of the era. Thus it was "superstitious and erotic in the earlier epochs of our society."[29] "The person of Don Quixote affords an admirable description of the monomania that reigned throughout almost all of Europe following the Crusades: a mixture of

[27] "Monomanie," *Dict. des sci. med.*, Vol. 34, pp. 117–22.
[28] M. Esquirol, "Introduction à l'étude des aliénations mentales (Fragmens de la première leçon du cours clinique fait à la Salpêtrière sur ces maladies)," *Revue médicale française et étrangère* 8 (1822): 36.
[29] "Mélancolie," *Dict. des sci. med.*, Vol. 32, pp. 148–49.

amorous extravagance and gallant courage which, in certain individuals, was a veritable madness."[30] On the other hand, the "religious
disputes provoked by Luther" in the sixteenth century produced a
pan-European *monomanie superstitieuse.*[31]

Hence the crucial importance of monomania to the hypothetical psychiatric bureau of mentalities which Esquirol proposed as one of the
statistics-gathering units of the central administration. Such a bureau
would chart monomaniacal epidemiology and thus be in a position to
inform the government with precision about the place of what Esquirol
called "our political convulsions" in the general mental and passional
configuration of the French population. For Esquirol believed that the
revolutionary upset of traditional structures of order and authority, the
appearance of "new kings," was responsible for the burgeoning of that
variety of monomania in which individuals "believe themselves emper-
ors or kings, empresses or queens."[32] Put in more general terms, the
special monomania of the early nineteenth century was overweening
ambition of all sorts, stimulated by the more fluid society that was a
legacy of the Revolution. Esquirol assumed that any prudent government would want to know how long and in what forms immoderate and
pathological ambition – a vestige of unsettled times and a perpetual
threat to order – would continue to dominate the outlook of the French
nation.

There is no indication that the French government was attracted to the
possibility of employing the new physicians of the insane in any formal
capacity as its "moral statisticians," although Esquirol's conception may
have directly influenced a circular sent to the prefects by the minister of
the interior in 1833 eliciting information not only about facilities for
lunatics but also about the "causes of insanity" prevalent in the
localities.[33] Yet even if Esquirol's rather fanciful project failed to make
real headway, the use of the monomania concept that he
recommended – as a kind of "moral" or social commentary – did become
widespread. Thus in the pages of the satiric journal *Caricature*, Philipon
expressed the idea that Esquirol had earlier advanced in a technical
medical forum – that the prevalent variety of insanity should be read as
an index of the *Zeitgeist*. Glossing his friend Daumier's cartoon of the
monomaniacal inmates of the "Ministerial Charenton," Philipon wrote:
"It is at Charenton that you will, at a glance, sum up the spirit, the
tastes, the manners, the beliefs, the eccentricity of your epoch. I have

---

[30] "Monomanie," *Dict. des sci. med.*, Vol. 34, pp. 122–23.
[31] "Mélancolie," *Dict. des sci. med.*, Vol. 32, p. 149.
[32] Ibid.
[33] See question 9 in "Résumés synoptiques des réponses faites par MM les Préfets aux
15 questions présentées par la circulaire du 14 septembre 1833 concernant les
aliénés," a multipage foldout table appended to Guillaume Ferrus, *Des aliénés* (Paris:
Huzard, 1834).

seen Charenton only once . . . , but I would bet my life that the Republic, the Empire, and the Restoration have populated it with men as different as those epochs were themselves different."[34] An asylum doctor in the Sarthe (a student of Pinel's student Ferrus who had obtained his provincial post through the predictable interventions of Esquirol) expounded much the same synecdoche before the learned society of Le Mans:

> Other illnesses . . . reveal themselves to us by constant signs, as invariable as their causes. . . . Only madness (*folie*), a kind of morbid Proteus, is the transitory and changing image of the interests that govern men, of the emotions that agitate them; and, like the world, a lunatic asylum is a mosaic of the passions.[35]

Thus too the perception of many lay and medical observers that individuals in post-Revolutionary society were likely to fall prey to the "torments of ambition"[36] was translated into assertions about the prevalence of a subspecies of monomania called *monomanie ambitieuse:* Social commentary and medical diagnosis were here conflated.

In Esquirol's pioneering dictionary article, the three long case studies had described men whose monomanias, exaggeratedly self-aggrandizing in nature (dauphin of France, "Apollo-Caesar," unifier of the world), had been rooted in earlier quotidian ambitions and in a high degree of sensitivity to the nuances of social status. The would-be dauphin had, while a young adult, "traveled a great deal in the hope of retrieving the remains of a considerable fortune"; eagerly contracting a marriage with a very rich young woman, he then "gave himself over with fervor to all the transports of his ambition" and succumbed to monomania when his financial speculations in state bonds collapsed in 1815. The would-be Apollo-Caesar was described by Esquirol as "very sensitive to not receiving the deference that is owed one in society and always wanting to pass for an important personage." The would-be unifier of the world was a veteran of Napoleon's campaigns and had "filled an important function" in them; although he received a respectable post upon his return to civilian life, the experience of the Napoleonic army had whetted his ambition

---

[34] *Caricature,* May 31, 1832.

[35] G.-F. Etoc-Demazy, "Statistique médicale de l'asile de la Sarthe," *Bulletin de la Société d'agriculture, sciences et arts du Mans* 2 (1837): 166. On Etoc-Demazy, see Semelaigne, *Pionniers,* Vol. 1, pp. 319–21.

[36] The phrase comes from Georget, "Folie," *Dict. des sci. med.,* Vol. 9, p. 217. For other examples of the currency of this perception among psychiatrically oriented physicians, see C. Lachaise, *Topographie médicale de Paris* (Paris: J.-B. Baillière, 1822), pp. 240–42; Cerise, *Des fonctions et des maladies nerveuses dans leurs rapports avec l'éducation sociale et privée, morale et physique* (Paris: Germer-Baillière, 1842), pp. 378–80, 382–83; and P. Buchez and U. Trélat, *Précis élémentaire d'hygiène* (Paris: Raymond, 1825), pp. 275, 279–80.

in ways that could find no ordinary satisfaction and thus led to his monomaniacal affliction.[37]

The recurring motif in these initial case studies persisted. For example, the admissions registers for the years 1841–42 reveal that *monomanie ambitieuse* accounted for over 25 percent of the monomania diagnoses at Bicêtre and over 10 percent of those at the Salpêtrière – the difference in frequency reflecting either the behavioral fact or the physicians' perception that ambition was a more salient trait in men than in women.[38] At just about the same time, Dr. J.-B.-F. Descuret, a Paris general practitioner not associated with the Esquirol circle but thoroughly conversant with its printed writings, produced a handbook on the *Médecine des passions* in which he declared that "the passion of ambition usually terminates in *monomanie ambitieuse*" and that among the affluent patients in the private sanatoria of Esquirol, Belhomme, and Falret and Voisin, the number of these "lunatics by ambition" was proportionately greater than in public institutions.[39] What is being asserted here through the "neutral" language of medical statistics is that the middle classes were more likely to be seized and devoured by ambition than were their social inferiors. A careful look at the "ambitious monomaniacs" at Bicêtre during 1841–42 tends to confirm that this was the prevailing assumption, for the patients so diagnosed often had relatively high-prestige or aspiring occupations – paper manufacturer, printer, medical student, law student, jeweler, a worker in gold and one in munitions, businessman (*agent d'affaires*)[40] – making them stand out among an inmate population that is typically more socially humble.

That Esquirol conceived of monomania as an indicator of the *tendance des esprits* may help to explain the ease with which lay intellectuals adopted the monomania concept: The way from technical-medical to ordinary discourse had been conveniently paved by the physician himself. It is arguable as well that monomania was so quickly assimilated into the early nineteenth-century vocabulary because of its special relevance at that historical moment. It corresponded to – indeed, it magnified and even caricatured – a salient mind-set and behavioral pattern of early bourgeois society, with its new possibilities for "self-

---

[37] Esquirol, "Monomanie," *Dict. des sci. med.*, Vol. 34, pp. 117–21. The compound label *monomanie ambitieuse* was not used by Esquirol in these case studies.

[38] This seems to have been the opinion of the psychiatrist J.-P. Falret; see his personal communication to the journalist Alphonse Esquiros cited in the latter's *Paris, ou les sciences, les institutions et les moeurs au XIXe siècle* (Paris: Imprimeurs-Unis, 1847), Vol. 2, pp. 110–11.

[39] J.-B.-F. Descuret, *La médecine des passions, ou les passions considérées dans leurs rapports avec les maladies, les lois et la religion* (Paris: Béchet jeune & Labé, 1841), pp. 579–80. On Descuret, see C. Sachaile de la Barre, *Les Médecins de Paris jugés par leurs oeuvres* (Paris: Chez l'auteur, 1845), pp. 236–37.

[40] See AAP: Bicêtre, 6Q2-2, 6Q2-3, 6Q2-4, entries 8453, 8810, 8455, 9566, 9536, 8816, 8652.

making": a single-mindedness and goal directedness, an intense and exclusive fixation on particular ends and rigidly defined patterns of striving, as opposed to a dedication to the spontaneous, diverse, and well-rounded "good life." As a kind of obsessive narrowing, monomania may have seemed to contemporaries an apt name for what they intuitively sensed was the characteristic *mal du demi-siècle.*[41]

Professional ramifications (II): the emergence of forensic psychiatry

Since Esquirol's vision of an official psychiatric corps of "moral statisticians" and tabulators of monomania failed to materialize, monomania might have been relegated to a primarily medical setting and its conceptual validity judged solely by reference to the internal medical criteria of clinical prognosis and treatment. As to the kind of vogue (medical or lay) it would then have enjoyed, we can only speculate; for such a circumscribed existence was not to be its lot. In 1825 a new extra-medical role was assigned to monomania, this time not by Esquirol but by his favorite student, Etienne-Jean Georget. At Georget's hands, monomania became the subject of a long and raucous nationwide controversy that spilled over into the medical setting and powerfully affected the fate of the monomania concept and the epidemiology of that disease.

Georget proposed, in brief, that monomania form the basis of a broadened insanity defense in criminal cases, and concomitantly that the new *médecin des aliénés* be given a central place in the deliberations of the courtroom. On the surface, this would not seem a controversial proposal. The Napoleonic penal code (Article 64), following traditional practice, had already exempted from responsibility all those who committed crimes and misdemeanors while in a state of insanity (*démence*). Furthermore, the Napoleonic code of criminal procedure (Articles 43 and 44) bade the state's prosecutor to invite medical experts into court routinely, to call upon the services of persons "presumed by their art or profession capable of appreciating the nature and circumstances of a crime or misdemeanor." While this applied most directly to examination of cadavers in cases of violent death, less tangible matters, such as the mental condition of the accused, were apparently subsumed. The penal code (Article 160) prescribed penalties for these medical experts if they falsified testimony or accepted bribes. The court empowered them to write "reports" for the edification of the magistracy; and when two or

---

[41] On the controversial relationship between a "fashionable" psychiatric diagnostic category and the general sociocultural environment in our own day, see Christopher Lasch, *The Culture of Narcissism: American Life in an Age of Diminishing Expectations* (New York: Norton, 1978), pp. 35 and 35n.

more of these reports conflicted, a group of physicians could be summoned to address themselves collectively to the problem, this constituting a "medico-legal consultation."[42] Thus all the formalities of the law
would seem to have conduced automatically and effortlessly to active
forensic intervention on the part of the new *médecins des aliénés*. But in
the mid-1820s, when Georget began his campaign, the facts of the matter were quite the opposite.

In the first place, the judicial understanding of the nature of insanity
was a commonsensical and consensual one – that is, insanity was regarded as a propensity to make "false or erroneous judgments about
the relations of things most frequently encountered in life and about
which all men agree," a lack of that "aptitude to judge things in the
way of the generality of mankind."[43] Hence the judicial belief that
laymen could readily identify insanity in their fellows and could provide the court with entirely adequate testimony concerning the mental
status of an accused person. Technical discussions about determining
insanity for legal purposes – the expertise that is now called forensic
psychiatry – scarcely existed in France at this time. In fact, the first
full-length treatise on the subject to appear in France was an 1827
translation from the German.[44] Insofar as French medical men of the
opening decades of the nineteenth century did consider the matter,
they tended to concur with current judicial practice or to oppose it only
in a timid, guarded fashion. Thus in a text that had gone through three
editions by 1819, J.-J. Belloc, a surgeon in southwestern France, advised the medical profession to disown the function of making medico-
legal evaluations concerning insanity. A much more reliable source of
information, said Belloc, would be "the testimony of several neighbors
or people who lived daily with this person or who saw and conversed
with him frequently" and who could thus accurately assess changes in
his behavior. A physician making a special evaluative visit could not
hope to compete with the in-depth knowledge of the local folk, especially given the possibility that he might arrive just when the insane
person was temporarily lucid or in a state of partial remission.[45]

Even the far more sophisticated physician François-Emmanuel
Fodéré, who was familiar with the work of Pinel and had once had
first-hand experience treating the insane, found distinct merit in the
position of Belloc. But in the final analysis he had to admit that he
distrusted "the testimony of the multitude," of that "great number of,
if one will, ignorant persons judging according to their manner of

---

[42] Orfila, *Leçons de médecine légale*, 2d ed. (Paris: Béchet jeune, 1828), Vol. 1, pp. 22, 40.

[43] This standard legal formula for insanity is given in Fodéré, *Traité de médecine légale et
d'hygiène publique* (Paris: Mame, 1813), Vol. 1, pp. 183–84.

[44] Hoffbauer, *Médecine légale relative aux aliénés* (see n.6).

[45] J.-J. Belloc, *Cours de médecine légale, théorique et pratique*, 3d ed. (Paris: Méquignon,
1819), pp. 255–56. Earlier editions were published in the Year IX and 1811.

being, scarcely concerned with the matter, and easily seduced." It could be dangerous to allow retrograde popular prejudices to define insanity. "I have several times seen men devoted to the study of natural science considered as mad (*insensé*) by their fellow citizens," he recounted darkly. Thus Fodéré opted for medical evaluation of legal allegations of insanity not so much because of any technical expertise that physicians possessed – although their medical experience gave them an advantage in deciding "if a certain state of madness is permanent or temporary" – as because of their general attitude of enlightenment and their moral probity, the latter having "as a guarantee their reputation and the dignity of their position."[46] Even Pinel himself, who wrote in 1816 a preliminary sketch for a longer work (which he never produced) on "judicial reports in cases of insanity," expressed little eagerness and less self-confidence about this venture. He described it as "a painful and delicate task" which physicians were presumably obliged to undertake but about which he was glad to postpone "to a more or less distant time" the formulation of any precise rules. For, he wondered scrupulously, "can the most enlightened experience and the most invariable rectitude always save the physician from involuntary error?"[47]

On the eve of Georget's provocative initiation of the monomania controversy, then, it is hardly surprising to find that lay evaluations of mental condition were given considerable weight in French courts and were put at least on a par with those of medical men. In February 1825, for example, in the Paris trial of the notorious Papavoine – an apparently impeccable fellow who had suddenly stabbed two young children to death in the Bois de Vincennes in the presence of their mother – the prosecution witnesses who testified to Papavoine's sanity (while admitting to his moroseness and other temperamental oddities, which they confidently distinguished from insanity) included a naval administration clerk, a high-ranking navy official, and a Parisian banker. An attorney from the vicinity of Papavoine's hometown made what was thought to be a significant contribution when he testified that he "had never heard it said in the countryside that Papavoine was a lunatic." Although two medical men – a navy surgeon and a country doctor – were among the prosecution witnesses, their opinions were not given any special prominence or presented as ultimately authoritative.[48]

46 Fodéré, *Traité de médecine légale*, Vol. 1, pp. 192–93, 199–201. On Fodéré's career, see Semelaigne, *Pionniers*, Vol. 1, p. 100.

47 Pinel, "Résultats d'observations pour servir de base aux rapports juridiques dans les cas d'aliénation mentale," *M.S.M.E.* 8 (1817): esp. 683–84. Belloc, Fodéré, and Pinel are all primarily concerned here with evaluations of insanity for purposes of civil rather than criminal law – i.e., proceedings of interdiction against individuals who, if found insane, would be reduced to the legal status of minors. At this time, a lay perspective on insanity obtained equally in the civil and criminal realms.

48 "Cour d'assises de Paris: Affaire d'Auguste Papavoine," *Journal de Paris*, February 25, 1825.

The tenor of medical discussion of insanity and the law changed completely in the two brochures by Georget which appeared in 1825 and 1826. The young *médecin des aliénés*–he was then about thirty years old–boldly reviewed a series of *causes célèbres* which had recently been tried in and around Paris. Addressing his findings not only to his medical colleagues but also to "magistrates, lawyers, jurors" and a general audience, he faulted, in the first brochure, three out of five of the court's decisions. Léger, the winegrower who withdrew from all social intercourse into a secluded grotto where, overcome by cannibalistic urges, he murdered a young girl and drank her blood, was, said Georget, not "a great criminal" or "a monster" but "an unhappy imbecile . . . who ought to have been shut up in Bicêtre among the lunatics, not sent to the scaffold." Lecouffe, who murdered an old woman and robbed her of a negligible sum of money, believing himself to have been commanded by his mother and pardoned in advance by God, was, according to Georget, a congenital epileptic suffering from symptoms of the insanity which characteristically accompanies the advanced stages of that disease. About the aforementioned Papavoine, Georget declined to make a definitive pronouncement, but he believed that the indications of insanity were sufficiently plentiful to warrant sending this child-murderer to a *maison des aliénés* for extended medical observation.[49]

Clearly the judges had made far too great a proportion of errors in these cases. Diplomatically, Georget refrained from accusing them of carelessness or intentional malevolence ("far from us the thought of wanting to blame their conduct"). Rather, he surmised, they had acted out of "fear and alarm"; ignorant of the nuances of insanity, they were apprehensive lest real criminals feigning the symptoms of madness escape punishment. The solution was obvious: The judges must "proceed with the greatest circumspection" and, above all, must rely upon the counsels of doctors. This reliance was most critical in "obscure cases"–and here Georget singled out cases of monomania for special notice and extended discussion. There existed, he asserted, a variety of monomania called *monomanie homicide* which propelled its victims to commit murder. Closely allied varieties of this disease produced other crimes, notably theft.[50]

Georget's 1825 brochure had an almost immediate practical impact. The very next year, Henriette Cornier, a servant girl who had suddenly and inexplicably murdered her employers' small child, was tried in Paris. A host of physicians were enlisted to provide opinions; and a

---

[49] Georget, *Examen médicale des procès criminels des nommés Léger, Feldtmann, Lecouffe, Jean-Pierre et Papavoine, dans lesquels l'aliénation mentale a été alléguée comme moyen de défense, suivi de quelques considérations médico-légales sur la liberté morale* (Paris: Migneret, 1825), "Avis" (n.p.) and pp. 15, 32, 64.

[50] Ibid., pp. 16, 65–66, 71.

prominent physician evaluating the accused for the defense at the time of her arrest pronounced Mlle Cornier a victim of *monomanie homicide*[51] – thus marking the first use of that new diagnostic category in connection with a criminal case. Because the sensationalism of the Cornier trial from the outset excited enormous public interest ("An immense crowd of curious people so obstructed the avenue du Palais-de-Justice this morning that it was necessary to evacuate them," reported a Paris newspaper on the opening day),[52] the monomania concept received wide publicity and immediately became the focus of public debate. Fueled by other criminal trials and, in 1828, by an eloquent book-length polemic by one Elias Regnault, the controversy continued into the 1850s, though its furious intensity abated after the first five years.

In considering Georget's novel and aggressive insistence upon a medical presence in criminal court to pronounce upon matters of insanity, a series of questions come to mind. Why did Georget embark upon this course of action? And why was monomania the emblem and chief instrument of his campaign – that is, what internal conceptual characteristics made it so suitable for this purpose?

A boundary dispute with the legal profession

With respect to Georget's reasons for embarking upon a campaign to "medicalize" the insanity defense, I will pass over personal psychological motivations, although Georget's precocious brilliance and his tempestuous "Romantic" temperament – his contemporaries described his radical mood swings and the herculean, almost demonic, energy with which he could approach his work[53] – do suggest a man likely to conceive and carry out a bold and controversial project. More germane here is the collective motivation, the place of the campaign in the development of French psychiatry as a recognized professional entity.

Like Esquirol with his less plausible-sounding scheme for psychiatric "moral statisticians," Georget was aiming, through the specific agency of the monomania concept, to enhance the standing of the *médecin des aliénés* by integrating his functions into those of the state. The essential difference between the strategies of master and pupil was that Esquirol sought to accomplish the goal by creating an entirely new work-function, while Georget sought to carve one out of territory traditionally occupied by an older and established profession, that of law. Georget's approach is typical of many emerging professions: As one American sociologist has noted, emerging professions and emerging academic

---

[51] The physician was C.-C.-H. Marc; see the account in *Gazette des tribunaux*, June 23, 1826, p. 3.

[52] Ibid., June 25, 1826.

[53] René Semelaigne, *Les grands aliénistes français* (Paris: G. Steinheil, 1894), pp. 357–58.

disciplines frequently seek to define themselves through competitive clashes with their already established counterparts over the determination of their respective boundaries.[54] Indeed, Pinel seems to have recognized the boundary dispute lurking in his tentative plan to formalize the medical role in legal evaluations of insanity, for, using the cartographic metaphor, he wrote quite explicitly of that role in 1816 that it "opens such a vast field to research that I am still far from wanting to offer an outline of it. One cannot hide the fact that its fundamental bases are little known and that the *reciprocal limits between the domain of jurisprudence and that of medicine* are still far from having been established."[55] That Pinel should be finely attuned to such competition and describe it in this language is, from a historical standpoint, hardly surprising. For as part of the Anglo-American sociological canon, the concept of the "boundary dispute" can be viewed as preserving within the category "profession" an aspect of what I have called the corporate model. That is, the boundary dispute is a variant on those fierce squabbles over monopolistic jurisdictions – over which functions, for example, belonged to the grocer and which to the apothecary – that were ubiquitous among the corporations of the Old Regime.

A boundary dispute with the profession of law exercised an especially powerful appeal to an emergent psychiatric profession in early nineteenth-century France. To be conceded a share in the workings of the legal system would mean not only to establish firm and intimate connections with the state but also to partake of the prestige associated with the legal profession at this date. The hybrid field of legal medicine (*médecine légale*), which epitomized the claim of physicians for a portion of the law's terrain (lawyers made much less effort, it should be noted, to develop this same hybrid field by staking out a portion of medical terrain),[56] was a direct descendant of the late eighteenth-century model of a statist medicine. What was called in the terminology of the early nineteenth century "political medicine" – the sum total of the government-related functions assumed by medical

---

[54] Terry N. Clark, "Institutionalization of Innovations in Higher Education: Four Models," *Administrative Science Quarterly* 13 (1968): 6. While Clark's model is specifically geared to academic disciplines, he observes (p. 3) that "certain stages of the model parallel those followed by emerging professions."

[55] "Résultats d'observations pour servir de base aux rapports judiciaires," p. 682, my italics.

[56] During the Revolution the ad hoc law schools created after the abolition of the legal corporations did institute the first legal courses on legal medicine; see Michael P. Fitzsimmons, "Dissolution and Disillusionment: The Parisian Order of Barristers, 1789–1815," Ph.D. dissertation, University of North Carolina at Chapel Hill, 1981, Ch. 6., p. 274. In the early nineteenth century medico-legal lawyers (e.g., C. P. Collard de Martigny and Adolphe Trebuchet) do occasionally appear on the scene, but they are much outnumbered by medico-legal doctors.

men – had two branches: medical police (or, as we have seen, administrative programs to promote public health) and legal medicine.[57] In the early nineteenth century, then, the pursuit of legal medicine conjured up the whole constellation of images of "professionalism" and professional legitimation associated with the statist model. In addition, early nineteenth-century medical men looked upon the legal profession with undisguised envy: It possessed a dignity and high status which they believed were unfairly denied to them. Lawyers, they complained, were exempt from the patent, the tax on all income derived from mercantile pursuits, while physicians suffered the ignominy of being *patentables;* lawyers were more likely to be accepted into aristocratic social circles than were physicians; lawyers had ready access to public office, whereas physicians were generally excluded; the proud legal corporation had been essentially reconstituted by Napoleon in 1810, while physicians presented to the public an indecorous spectacle of disorganization and indiscipline. The medical jeremiad went on and on.[58] And it seems to have had a realistic basis. Charton's *Guide* advised the career-minded young man that the profession of lawyer was "the most alluring today" while that of physician was the most "subjugating, painful" in terms of the expected monetary rewards and especially in terms of the degree of public esteem in which it was held.[59]

Cultivating the field of legal medicine was one obvious way to redress the balance, to deflect some of the prestige enjoyed by the legal profession onto its poor medical cousin. Hence it is not surprising that medical arguments on the importance of legal medicine, while couched primarily in the rhetoric of humanitarianism and science, often disclose a preoccupation with status, a yearning that the French judiciary publicly recognize the worth of medical expertise. The "esteem" traditionally accorded to medico-legal reports in Germany was held up for emulation. "In Germany, a reciprocal deference reigns between physi-

---

57 For this definition see, e.g., Prunelle, *De la médecine politique en général et de son objet* . . . (Montpellier: J. Martel, 1814), p. 3; and the editors' "Introduction" to the inaugural issue of the *Revue médicale historique et philosophique* (January 1820): viii. Esquirol was a founding editor of this journal.

58 This subject is discussed at length in my Ph.D. dissertation, "French Psychiatry in Social and Political Context: The Formation of a New Profession, 1820–1860," Columbia University, 1978, pp. 46–60.

59 Charton, *Guide pour le choix d'un état*, pp. 47–48, 389, 393. This dimension of the doctors' professional situation casts doubt upon the adequacy of Michel Foucault's formulation when, in a round table discussion of 1977, he asserted that the "constitution of a medico-legal apparatus" should not be attributed to the intentionality of a subject. Focusing on forensic psychiatry, he asks, "Can one talk of interests here? In the case of the doctors, why should they have wanted to intervene so directly in the penal domain . . .?" Foucault, *Power/Knowledge: Selected Interviews and Other Writings, 1972–77*, ed. Colin Gordon (New York: Pantheon, 1980), p. 204.

cians and jurisconsults. That supremacy which in France the latter tend to exercise over the former is unknown."[60]

The branch of legal medicine dealing with insanity was an intellectually treacherous one, as Pinel acknowledged with characteristic caution; and there were sound reasons to avoid it or, as Pinel proposed, to postpone until some indeterminate future date full-scale involvement in it. But the attractions were also compelling, and once Georget – encouraged no doubt by the proto-organization of psychiatry which had taken shape between 1817 and 1825 – had the temerity to engage the legal profession in a boundary dispute, the Esquirol circle joined him.

It must be stressed that this particular boundary dispute was fated to be a highly visible public affair. For during the 1820s the criminal courts had taken on a new significance for the French public; there was, at least in Paris, a preoccupation and fascination with crime as an ever-present danger to the city-dweller.[61] In 1825 the royal government began the annual statistical compilation of the crimes committed in France (already a practice of the prefect of the department of the Seine for some years), and one journal regretted that this official publication was available only to peers and deputies, especially in light of "the taste of enlightened men" for such documents and the "eagerness with which they go about buying and pondering them."[62] Readily available to this latter group was a daily newspaper, the *Gazette des tribunaux*, which began its long and successful career in 1825 offering detailed, often verbatim accounts of court proceedings. And the criminal court itself drew great crowds, whose legal right of admission as spectators to the debates had been secured by the Charter of 1814. In short, the experts in *médecine mentale* would make their appeal and display their wares to a broad general audience as well as to the relevant agencies of the state.

The elusive insanity: its partisans and its varieties

The monomania concept was an ideal instrument for this boundary dispute, because its internal logic defied the working assumption of the legal system – that laymen were competent to identify insanity. "To

---

[60] Marc, "Considérations médico-légales sur la monomanie et particulièrement sur la monomanie incendiaire," *Ann. d'hyg. pub.* 10 (1833): 372–73. Similar Franco-German comparisons can be found in Prunelle, *Médecine politique*, pp. 22–23, and Marc, "Introduction," *Ann. d'hyg. pub.* 1 (1829): xxxii–xxxiii.

[61] See Louis Chevalier, *Laboring Classes and Dangerous Classes in Paris during the First Half of the Nineteenth Century*, trans. F. Jellinek (New York: Fertig, 1973), esp. General Introduction.

[62] A. Taillandier, Review of *Compte général de l'administration de la justice criminelle pendant l'année 1825* in *Revue encyclopédique* 34 (1827): 361.

speak of a madman," wrote Esquirol, "is for the common herd (*le vulgaire*) to speak of a sick person whose intellectual and moral faculties are entirely denatured, perverted or abolished."[63] Thus defined, a madman was of course unmistakable to a layman. But the essence of monomania was that it was not a total but a partial insanity and hence elusive, readily concealable, and to be discerned, needful of the trained medical eye.

This elusiveness characterized both of Georget's main subcategories of monomania – the intellectual (or ideational) and the volitional. Intellectual monomania was the disease that Esquirol had described in his 1819 dictionary article. When delirium was confined to a single idea and all other ideas remained unaffected, it was easy for an untrained, unsuspecting observer to be misled. Under the rubric of *manie partielle* (the older diagnostic label, upon which Esquirol based his neologism *monomania*), Fodéré had described the syndrome in 1813: "These lunatics are peaceful, dutiful, obliging, reasonable in conversation until the moment that they encounter in speech or in the world some analogy to the thing which produces the error in their judgment." For example, a twenty-year-old laundress whom Fodéré had treated at the hospital of Martigues, "a well-behaved girl of irreproachable manners," had become convinced that her lover (who had in fact been conscripted) had been taken from her by the machinations of his mother; the girl appeared quite sane – except when reminded of this hated older woman.[64] One of Esquirol's administrative officials at Charenton enumerated in 1826 the types of ideational monomania, arranging them in order of ascending elusiveness and difficulty of diagnosis:

> There are those cases (and they are the most common) in which the monomaniac reasons perfectly about all sorts of things, except for the object of his delirium. . . . There are others in which even about the object of delirium the propositions are so well-knit, the narratives so probable and the reasoning so superficially convincing that the most skilled observer can be taken in. . . . There are others still in which the monomaniac purposely hides his condition and, led back to the object of his delirium repeatedly [by the interviewer], obstinately dodges it because he knows that a trap is being laid for him and that everything he says on that point will be regarded as madness: such a monomaniac generally has a strong head and conserves most of his intellectual faculties.[65]

The Salpêtrière admissions registers confirm the elusiveness of ideational monomania. Some monomania diagnoses could be made only

---

[63] Esquirol, "Note sur la monomanie-homicide," p. 309.

[64] Fodéré, *Traité de médecine légale*, Vol. 1, pp. 197–98.

[65] Letter of Gandois, chief secretary of Charenton, to the lawyer Dupin (1826), in Leuret, "Monomanie érotique méconnue par des personnes étrangères à l'observation des aliénés," *Ann. d'hyg. pub.* 3 (1830): 216.

after the patient had been under observation for a full two weeks. After his initial interview with a middle-aged seamstress, Mitivié wrote: "Replies with precision. She recounts that, while going from St. Denis to Vertus (a town in her native department) to care for a young man bitten by a dog reputed to be rabid, she had been arrested and brought to the prefecture and to the Salpêtrière. Since her arrival has been calm, compliant, and laborious and presents no signs of delirium." But two weeks later he was able to report with confidence on the diagnostic certificate, "state of monomania with hallucinations." Of another inmate, Mitivié wrote at the end of her first two weeks in the hospice: "This punctual and laborious woman who responds with precision seemed at first not to be at all insane, but by examining her at close range one sees that she is dominated by certain illusions that she does not wish to discuss but that influence her conduct and feelings in such a way as to transform her totally and turn her into a true monomaniac."[66]

Even farther from the layman's notion of insanity – and even more critical in the forensic setting – was the second subcategory, volitional monomania. It was this subcategory that Georget had in effect inaugurated when in his 1825 brochure he announced the existence of a *monomanie homicide* and of analogous monomanias driving afflicted individuals to the enactment of other specific crimes. Esquirol had always recognized specific forms of monomania – for example, theomania, erotomania, demonomania[67] – but these had referred to particular ideational preoccupations or idées fixes. *Monomanie homicide*, by contrast, denoted an impulsion to translate into action a preoccupation with the idea of murder, and Georget's problem was to create a theoretical framework capable of dealing with this added dimension of action. To solve it, he postulated that insanity was of two main types: "lesions of the intelligence," the traditional type, long known under the name of "delirium" and meaning "aberrations of ideas, disturbances in intellectual combinations, manifestations of bizarre ideas and erroneous judgments"; and "lesions of the will," meaning "perversions of the natural penchants, affections, passions, sentiments."[68] Since *monomanie homicide* entailed a lesion of the will, an irresistible impulsion to brutal action was the hallmark of the malady.

But could it entail only a lesion of the will? Georget made a very controversial strategic decision when he answered in the affirmative.[69] For this meant that not all homicidal monomaniacs were, on the basis of their cognitive processes, identifiable as abnormal. A person suffer-

---

[66] AAP: Salpêtrière 6Q2-4 (1841), entries 12526, 12256; for other diagnoses adhering to this same pattern see, e.g., Salpêtrière 6Q2-5 (1842), entry 13156.

[67] "Monomanie," *Dict. des sci. med.*, Vol. 34, p. 125.

[68] Georget, *Examen médical des procès*, p. 69.

[69] Ibid.

ing from an isolated lesion of the will could have "fits of furious and
murderous mania without alteration of judgment"[70] and could easily
masquerade as a sane person. This was the most elusive of all aspects
of monomania and the one that argued most forcefully against lay
testimony on insanity in the criminal courts.

In asserting the validity of an isolated lesion of the will, Georget was
reviving (and placing under the monomania rubric) Pinel's category of
manie sans délire, a category that Esquirol, Pinel's student and Georget's
teacher, had already rejected. Pinel formally introduced *manie sans
délire* in the 1798 memoir that was to form the opening chapter of the
first edition of his *Traité*. Quite contrary to his expectations, he had
stumbled upon three inmates in Bicêtre (out of a total of some 200)
"who present no trouble or disorder in their ideas, no extravagant
deviation of the imagination; these madmen (*insensés*) respond in the
most correct and precise manner to questions put to them, but they are
dominated by the most impetuous furor and by a sanguinary instinct
of which they themselves sense all the horror but which they cannot
master." This clinical finding, Pinel immediately pointed out, was irre-
concilable "with the notions of Locke and Condillac," who presented
an intellectualist construction of madness as "consisting exclusively in
a disposition to link incompatible ideas and to take ideas thus linked
for truth."[71] But the anomalous status of this "mania without delirium"
in the canon of Locke and Condillac must have increased its credibility
and appeal to Pinel, who as we have seen consistently faulted his
philosophical mentors for overlooking the importance of the nonintel-
lectual aspects of the mind.

Pinel's most striking case history of *manie sans délire*, set against the
background of the September Massacres of 1792, clearly indicates his
conception of that disease. After the massacre in the jails, the "brig-
ands" broke into Bicêtre to liberate the political prisoners of the Old
Regime detained there. Faced with the practical necessity of making
distinctions between the political prisoners and the lunatics, they
foundered upon encountering a man who "made the most bitter complaints" about his confinement and spoke with "apparent rationality."
Pussin assured them that this inmate was insane, explaining that maniacs could be "free from delirium but at the same time extremely dangerous from their outrageous passions"; but they did not believe him,
"answered him only with abuse," and liberated the man in question
from his chains with shouts of "Vive la République!" This shouting
"roused the madman's fury" and he seized one of their sabers and
turned upon his liberators – thus convincing the "savage mob" that

[70] Ibid., p. 72.
[71] Pinel, "Mémoire sur la manie périodique ou intermittente," *M.S.M.E.* 1 (1798): 98
       (also *Traité*, 1st ed., pp. 13–14).

Pussin, "the voice of reason and experience," had spoken truly.[72] What Georget would later emphasize in a polemical context with respect to monomania is already present here as the moral of Pinel's story of *manie sans délire:* that it is an elusive illness, recognizable only to those with special expertise and clinical experience.

Manie sans délire entrenched itself firmly in Pinel's nosological schema. His article on insanity published in 1808 in the *Encyclopédie méthodique* shows that Pinel not only continued to adhere to the category but was actively developing his understanding of it. He now asserted that *manie sans délire* might be traceable to "a nonexistent or badly directed education" – that is, to an upbringing which indulged all of the child's caprices, so that impetuous "penchants grow and are fortified." He again stressed that victims of *manie sans délire* were often aware of "the full horror of [their] situation" and struggled in vain against their impulses. They experienced intrapsychic conflict – what Pinel now called "interior combat" – because their still "sane reason" found itself "in opposition to a sanguinary cruelty."[73]

Despite Pinel's own timidity in forensic matters, the utility of his pronouncements on *manie sans délire* was not lost on certain members of the legal profession. An opportunistic, ad hoc forensic psychiatry which cited Pinel, but which never received his sanction, thus grew up in France in the decade and a half preceding Georget's offensive. "It is to *manie sans délire*," noted Fodéré in 1817, "that defense attorneys most often impute the atrocious crimes of their clients."[74] Indeed, in the Papavoine murder trial of 1825, reviewed by Georget in his first brochure, the defense attorney's brief drew upon this same textual arsenal and featured Pinel's remarks on *manie sans délire.*[75]

In psychiatric circles, however, the career of *manie sans délire* had been called to a halt by Esquirol, who was highly skeptical of the validity of that putative disease entity. Expressing his opinion in a dictionary article in 1818, he insisted that what seemed to Pinel to be a mad furor divorced from any impairment of the understanding was actually always ushered in by some "premonitory" delirium – a distorted chain of logic, bizarre ideas, or perhaps a hallucination; all of its victims, when pressed, "avowed that they experienced trouble, albeit subtle and hard to articulate, in the exercise of their reason."[76] With respect to creating a practical forensic psychiatry, Esquirol's viewpoint posed a serious inconvenience:

---

[72] *Traité,* 1st ed., pp. 153–55.

[73] Pinel, "Manie, vésanies, aliénation mentale," *Encyclopédie méthodique,* Series: Medicine, Vol. 8 (1808), pp. 484–85.

[74] Fodéré, *Traité du délire appliqué à la médecine, à la morale et à la législation* (Paris: Crouillebois, 1817), Vol. 2, p. 501.

[75] Paillet, "Plaidoyer pour Louis-Auguste Papavoine," *Annales du barreau français, ou choix des plaidoyers et mémoires les plus remarquables: Barreau moderne,* Vol. 10 (Paris: B. Warée, 1837), pp. 629–34.

[76] "Manie," *Dict. des. sci. med.,* Vol. 30, pp. 452–54.

It confirmed popular prejudice and thus narrowed the scope of the insanity defense, making it inapplicable to those criminals lacking demonstrable intellectual aberration. This had been, in fact, precisely the difficulty in mounting an insanity defense for Papavoine in 1825. Though his lawyer had argued eloquently that nis client had been in the throes of a *manie sans délire* during the homicidal episode – and though there were "few people who, after having read [the lawyer's brief], were not of this opinion"[77] – Papavoine's own replies under examination were so closely reasoned, such "masterpieces of dialectic," that the prosecution successfully convinced the jury that a man of such obvious intellectual acuity could not possibly be insane.[78]

In his 1825 brochure, then, Georget had boldly ignored the strictures of his *maître,* and he was therefore visibly delighted when, some two years later, Esquirol came around to his own way of thinking. The "Note on Homicidal Monomania" (1827), written for inclusion in the French translation of Hoffbauer's manual of forensic psychiatry, was Esquirol's first sustained statement on the subject of monomania in nearly a decade. In it, Esquirol admitted the possibility of a lesion of the will accompanied by "no appreciable alteration of the intelligence."[79] Georget hastened to publicize the "Note," announcing that it had reversed Esquirol's initial opinion on *manie sans délire* and would thus, on the strength of Esquirol's reputation, "powerfully serve the cause of the unfortunate [that is, the criminally insane] before the tribunals" and "contribute not a little to the destruction of those false notions of the character of madness which are still so generally held."[80]

Esquirol's "capitulation" to the theoretical exigencies of the boundary dispute initiated by Georget heralded two important features of the monomania controversy. The first, already alluded to, was the solidarity of the Esquirol circle in the venture. Almost without exception, the members of the circle agreed on the existence of monomania and on the desirability of a strong medical presence in the courtroom; indeed, a public statement of these positions appears to have become virtually de rigueur for them, a badge of their membership in the circle. Thus, for example, even before Esquirol's public conversion, Brierre de Boismont made his literary debut as an *aliéniste* with a series of articles supporting and embellishing Georget's concept of *monomanie homicide.*[81]

---

[77] Georget, *Examen médical des procès,* p. 53.

[78] L. H. Moulin, "Notice sur Paillet," *Annales du barreau français: Barreau moderne,* Vol. 10, pp. 599–600.

[79] Esquirol, "Note sur la monomanie-homicide," p. 311.

[80] Georget, "Discussion médico-légale sur la folie, ou aliénation mentale," *Arch. gen. de med.* 13 (1827): 482–83.

[81] A. Brierre de Boismont, *Observations médico-légales sur la monomanie homicide* (Paris: Méquignon, 1827), originally published in 1826 in the *Revue médicale française et étrangère.*

Chambeyron translated Hoffbauer's manual, revising it substantially to include the monomania classification of his *savant maître*. He later served as an emissary of the monomania concept in the provinces, emphasizing in a medico-legal report commissioned in 1836 by the Royal Court of Rennes (where he was chief physician of the town asylum) the special expertise required to make a monomania diagnosis, for "monomaniacs know how to elude with a remarkable shrewdness those questions which touch on the ideas upon which their delirium turns."[82] Leuret repeatedly used the *Annales d'hygiène publique et de médecine légale,* on whose editorial board he served, as a forum for the exposition and defense of the monomania concept[83] – and an ideal forum it was, having been founded by Esquirol and Marc in 1829 upon the proposition that "the function of medicine is not only to study and cure disease; medicine has an intimate relationship with social organization, sometimes aiding the legislator in the drafting of laws, often enlightening the magistrate about their application."[84] Belhomme and Calmeil, Esquirol circle members situated in Paris, read papers and wrote journal articles on the monomania concept; so too, from the provincial outposts where they manned public asylums, did Cazauvieilh and Bouchet.[85] Moreau de Tours wrote his doctoral thesis on monomania.[86]

The Esquirol circle's partisan stance toward monomania, its collective championing of the concept for forensic purposes, was replicated in its diagnoses of patients in purely clinical settings; and thus the professional solidarity of that "medical phalanx" must certainly have shaped the epidemiology of monomania. In the first trimester of 1840, for example, Esquirol's nephew Mitivié and Pariset, a physician from outside the Esquirol circle, jointly admitted patients to the Salpêtrière. A sample of one hundred admissions from that period shows that *all* the diagnoses of monomania were made by Mitivié. In two instances,

---

[82] Chambeyron, translator's preface in Hoffbauer, *Médecine légale relative aux aliénés,* p. x; also pp. xii–xvi. Chambeyron indicates (p. xviii) that Esquirol "reread [the translation] several times" and supplied many of the explanatory notes. On the Rennes court case, see Chambeyron, "Affaire Péchot," *Ann. d'hyg. pub.* 18 (1837): 224.

[83] See, e.g., his review of Regnault, *Degré de compétence,* in *Ann. d'hyg. pub.* 1 (1829): 281–92, and his "Monomanie érotique méconnue," pp. 198–224.

[84] "Prospectus," *Ann. d'hyg. pub.* 1 (1829): v.

[85] See Belhomme, "Rapport sur le mémoire de M. Bonnet (de Bordeaux) intitulé 'Considérations médico-légales sur la monomanie homicide,' " *Bulletin des travaux de la Société médico-pratique de Paris,* July 1840, pp. 49–56; Calmeil, "Monomanie," *Dictionnaire de médecine,* 2d ed., Vol. 20 (Paris: Béchet jeune et Labé, 1839); Cazauvieilh, "De la monomanie homicide," *Ann. d'hyg. pub.* 16 (1836) and *Du suicide . . .* (Paris: J.-B. Baillière, 1840), pp. v–vi; and Bouchet, "Meurtre commis dans un état d'ivresse ou un accès de monomanie," *Ann. m.-p.,* 1st ser., 3 (1844).

[86] "De l'influence du physique relativement au désordre des facultés intellectuels et en particulier dans cette variété de délire désignée par M. Esquirol sous le nom de monomanie" (Paris: Thèse de médecine, 1830).

the hospice register even records disagreement between the two medical men over this precise point. Pariset once altered Mitivié's diagnosis of "monomania" to "disorder in ideas and actions"; and Mitivié once replaced Pariset's diagnosis of "a state of stupor which appears to be the consequence of a dream in which she saw herself dead" with "monomania – believes herself dead."[87]

The second feature of the monomania controversy indicated in Esquirol's 1827 "Note" is the pressure that professional needs exerted on the formulation of psychiatric theory. It is in the nature of a boundary dispute that an emergent discipline or profession address outsiders and attempt to make impressive self-legitimating claims on the basis of its expertise. Extrascientific goals are paramount, and disinterested discussion *within* the specialized scientific community of the theoretical points at issue is curtailed or even ceases altogether. Hence such boundary disputes may actively foster what might be called conceptual deformation. By this I mean a falling away from those qualities of definitional clarity and internal consistency that the concept, whatever its other scientific merits, possessed in its original form – here, Esquirol's 1819 articulation of an exclusively ideational monomania.

In the case of Esquirol himself, a careful reading of the "Note" reveals that the *maître* engaged in some terminological sleight of hand. While he wanted to lend his support to Georget's effort, he was still not really willing to accept the notion of *manie sans délire*. What he therefore did was to acknowledge two distinct types of homicidal monomania – one in which "the monomaniac is moved by an acknowledged and unreasonable motive, and . . . always offers sufficient signs of partial delirium of the intelligence or the affections"; and the other in which the monomaniac presents "no appreciable alteration of the intelligence or the affections" but is under the sway of "a blind instinct," of "something indefinable which pushes him to kill" and which conquers his "diseased will," so that he is "in the clutches of a partial delirium."[88] Thus, strictly speaking, Esquirol never admitted the validity of a mania "without delirium." He specified that the intelligence and the will could be diseased independently of one another – and this was, of course, the crucial point for courtroom strategy – but in the one case he predicated a selective delirium of the intelligence and in the other a selective delirium of the will. However, in the medical parlance of the day, the term "delirium" was strictly reserved for an *intellectual* aberration; Esquirol had even joked a decade earlier about the careless and inaccurate meanings attached to the term in "vulgar language."[89] Esquirol's own 1827 usage of "delirium" thus introduced

---

[87] AAP: Salpêtrière 6Q2-3, entries 11173, 12236.
[88] Esquirol, "Note sur la monomanie-homicide," pp. 311–32.
[89] Esquirol, "Manie," *Dict. des sci. med.*, Vol. 30, p. 454.

a fundamental semantic ambiguity that neither he nor Georget bothered to discuss. Indeed, the same confusing usage would be adopted by others – a book of 1834 by Leuret, for example, was divided into sections called "Délire de l'intelligence" and "Délire des passions"[90] – but the ambiguity lurking in it would go unacknowledged in the French psychiatric community for almost twenty-five years.

Nor was that the only ambiguity introduced into the conceptual model of monomania by Georget's marshaling of it for forensic purposes. The status of the "passions" or "affections" was notably unclear and also went undiscussed. Passion was a crucial category in a nineteenth-century forensic context. Its crime-producing power was beginning to be widely acknowledged, and one strand of French judicial opinion held that when inflamed and violent passions propelled a person to commit a crime, he could not be held responsible for his act.[91] Well aware of this opinion, Georget asserted as early as 1825 that the insanity that led to crime, though it might involve the passions, was fundamentally different from the ordinary inflamed passions that had the same outcome.[92] He was obliged to make such an assertion if he was to demarcate a special forensic domain for *médecine mentale*. But he could not, it appears, go beyond mere assertion: He did not even attempt to specify the difference between normal and pathological manifestations of passion.[93] Challenged on this point in 1828 by a lawyer trained in legal medicine, who argued that volitional monomania, far from being a newly identified form of insanity, was merely a new and fancy name for ordinary inflamed passions – that "we are 'monomanizing' (*monomaniser*) all the passions"[94] – neither Georget nor anyone else in the Esquirol circle replied or bothered to clarify their doctrine of the passions.

Instead, chaos reigned among them even over the much simpler issue of where the passions (or "affections," or "sentiments") fit into the typological scheme of monomania. Georget allied them with the will, making aberrant emotions part of the disease he called a "lesion of the will."[95] In the "Note," Esquirol, as we have just seen, paired the emotions with the intellect, making "diseased" emotions part of his

---

[90] Leuret, *Fragmens psychologiques sur la folie* (Paris: Crochard, 1834).

[91] See the famous brief by the lawyer Bellart, "Plaidoyer pour Joseph Gras" (1791), *Annales du barreau français: Barreau moderne*, Vol. 3, pp. 18–51, which was repeatedly cited in arguments over this issue.

[92] Georget, *Examen médical des procès*, pp. 22–25, 117–18.

[93] See, e.g., ibid., pp. 19, 27, for a confusing discussion of the murderer Feldtmann, whom Georget adjudged to be not insane but to have an obsessive incestuous passion which became "a veritable malady."

[94] C. P. Collard de Martigny, "Examen médico-légal de l'opinion émise par divers médecins sur la monomanie homicide," *Questions de jurisprudence médico-légale* (Paris: Auger-Méquignon, 1828), p. 15.

[95] Georget, *Examen médical des procès*, p. 69.

category of monomania with intellectual delirium. Marc presented a classification scheme of *monomanie raisonnante* affecting the intelligence and *monomanie instinctive* affecting the will and neglected all mention of the passions, sentiments, or affections.[96] In 1838, Esquirol offered his final word on the subject, a tripartite classification of *monomanie intellectuelle, monomanie instinctive,* and *monomanie affective*.[97] Accentuation and perversion of a single emotion was thus erected into a separate disease entity, lending apparent credence to the charge that the doctors were simply "monomanizing all the passions."

The conceptual deformation of monomania took yet another twist. Sometimes the doctors tailored their classifications of the disease so perfectly to the current state of judicial opinion that the disinterested scientific nature of their theorizing stood almost self-impugned. In the Henriette Cornier case of 1826, the prosecution made much of the absence of any evidence that Mlle Cornier had suffered from mental derangement *prior* to her murder of a small child; this lack of "anterior insanity" was held up as a reliable indication that the murder itself was not an insane act. It was, it would seem, precisely to silence this line of argument that, after the partisans of monomania had lost the Cornier case, Brierre de Boismont introduced his particular classificatory scheme: In one type of *monomanie homicide,* an overt "incubation period" marked by "exaggerated passions, idées fixes, false judgments, [and] strange conduct" directly preceded the criminal act; in another, equally valid type, the disease appeared suddenly and without warning "in individuals who before the event enjoy[ed] the full integrity of their intellectual faculties."[98]

In the context of a boundary dispute, the external efficacy of a concept may become more highly prized than its coherence or internal consistency. Thus it is not surprising that, at least before midcentury, experts in *médecine mentale* evinced no discomfort about the weaknesses of the monomania concept but instead confidently extended the range of the concept's applicability. From the late 1820s on, special subcategories of monomania were offered as explanations for such phenomena as alcoholism, arson, and suicide.[99] Indeed, this last subcategory became so entrenched in French scientific culture that, writing his great work *Suicide* in 1897, Emile Durkheim felt obliged to clear the ground for his sociological speculation on the subject by asserting the nonexistence of monomania.[100]

---

[96] Marc, "Considérations médico-légales sur la monomanie," pp. 383–87.
[97] Esquirol, "De la monomanie," in *Des maladies mentales considérées sous les rapports médical, hygiénique et médico-légal* (Paris: J.-B. Baillière, 1838), Vol. 2, p. 1.
[98] Brierre de Boismont, *Observations médico-légales sur la monomanie homicide,* pp. 32–35.
[99] See Calmeil's dictionary article "Monomanie" (n.85) for a good catalogue of the phenomena subsumed under particular variants of the monomania label.
[100] Emile Durkheim, *Suicide: A Study in Sociology,* trans. J. A. Spaulding and G. Simpson (New York: Free Press, 1951), pp. 57–62.

The politicization of the monomania doctrine

How erroneous, exclaimed Hippolyte Royer-Collard, professor at the Paris Faculty of Medicine (and son of Antoine-Athanase Royer-Collard), to depict monomania as "a new contrivance of liberalism" and to hold that "the current vogue of medical opinion on homicidal monomania is inspired and promulgated by the spirit of the opposition!"[101] That Royer-Collard felt moved to make such a disclaimer in 1829 reveals an important fact: The disease of monomania had become deeply enmeshed in the politics of the Restoration monarchy, and its proponents were invariably seen as arrayed on the side of militant liberalism.

It is difficult to assess the extent to which Georget intended this. At certain points in his writing, a sympathy with the liberal cause surfaces; but the issues of national politics seem for him to have been overshadowed by those of professional politics. In this instance, however, the two types of issues came in the same package; and whatever Georget's intent, the effort to broaden the insanity defense in the 1820s inevitably had a national political dimension deriving from the contemporary debate over the Napoleonic penal code.

Based upon the principle that deterrence was the most reliable means of protecting society against crime, the Napoleonic penal code of 1810 was unapologetically draconian. Its penalties were designed to inspire dread in potential offenders, and ample use was made of the death penalty. In contrast stood the Enlightenment tradition of humanitarian jurisprudence, expressed in the works of Voltaire, Montesquieu, and Beccaria and having come to short-lived fruition during the Revolution in the penal code promulgated in 1791 by the Constituent Assembly. With the return of some measure of constitutional government in 1814, this latter tradition was revived in some quarters: Liberal jurisconsults forming the so-called "neoclassical" school of jurisprudence began to press for mitigation of the Napoleonic penal code. But the Restoration government, regarding severe penalties as a bulwark of social order and a necessary preventive against renewed political revolution, viewed the academic reform movement with alarm and, in 1819, even removed one of its most outspoken members, François-Nicolas Bavoux, from his professorship at the Paris law faculty.[102]

The juries became another, ad hoc locus of pressure for reform. In the 1820s they regularly adopted a subversive strategy – dubbed "the omnipotence of the jury" – of delivering verdicts contrary to evidence in order to prevent the application of stipulated penalties that they regarded as overly harsh. Liberals applauded this strategy as an ex-

---

[101] H. Royer-Collard, review of Regnault, *Degré de compétence*, in *Journal hebdomadaire de médecine* 2 (1829): 188.

[102] See Bavoux's preface to his offending lectures, which he eventually published himself as *Leçons préliminaires sur le code pénal* (Paris: Antoine Bavoux, 1821), p. iv.

pression of popular sovereignty, "an arm of the same nature as the rejection of the budget in the hands of the chambers,"[103] while royalists attacked it as "perjury" and a violation of "the order established by law in the distribution of punishment," a topsy-turvy "handing over of everything to the caprice" of inexperienced and sometimes "unlettered" men.[104] The government responded to the juries' obstructionism with the deliberate placation of the Law of June 24, 1824, empowering judges to reduce the penalties for certain crimes when "extenuating circumstances" existed. The measure was inadequate; because of its short list of relevant crimes and its placement of the power of mercy in the hands of a purged and hence uniformly royalist judiciary that was unlikely to use it, it failed to end the extralegal maneuvers of the juries. But Georget was well aware of its passage and mentioned it in his 1825 brochure as "a most wise amelioration of our penal code."[105] And, as Georget must have recognized, a situation of intense political polarization had developed around the issue of the relaxation of criminal penalties, so that the monomania doctrine (that is, the use of the monomania diagnosis as a legal defense) would necessarily be assimilated into the political categories of the preexistent debate.

The magistrates of the *monarchie censitaire*, carefully selected by the government to serve as "emanations of . . . the principle of authority,"[106] became the chief spokesmen for the royalist position on the monomania doctrine. In fact they turned Georget into a kind of political persona non grata (with the result that Esquirol was never able to obtain a post in a public lunatic institution for him) because of their outrage over the very *form* of his initial advocacy of his position. Without mentioning him or his 1825 brochure by name, the chief prosecutor Bayeux subjected the young physician to public castigation during the Henriette Cornier trial. He "especially disapproved of a publication whose author dared to attack one of the things most sacred to mankind – the case that has been decided (*la chose jugée*) – by applying himself to examination of several recently judged cases, by criticizing the judgments rendered and by permitting himself to rehabilitate the memory of condemned persons."[107] But the content of the monomania doctrine and what they perceived as its clear implications for social order concerned the magistrates far more than the trespasses of an impudent young man. With

---

[103] "De l'omnipotence du jury," *Revue française* 11 (1829): 236.
[104] See "Du jury et de *La Quotidienne*" and "Pourquoi *La Quotidienne* attaque le jury," *Journal de Paris*, October 6, 1828, and August 17, 1829; and the speech of the judge Duplessis de Grénédan, session of the Chamber of Deputies of June 15, 1824, *Arch. parl.*, 2d ser., Vol. 41, p. 465.
[105] Georget, *Examen médical des procès*, p. 119.
[106] Marcel Rousselet, *La magistrature sous la Monarchie de Juillet* (Paris: Sirey, 1937), pp. 9–10.
[107] *Journal des débats*, June 25, 1826.

respect to these larger issues, the tone of judicial response was set by the Comte de Peyronnet, the chief prosecutor of the Papavoine case. Peyronnet's comments carried particular weight because he was also minister of justice at the time, a member of the ultraroyalist Villèle cabinet.

Because the trial of Papavoine preceded Georget's 1825 brochure by some months, it presented Peyronnet not with the monomania doctrine per se but with a primitive though quite analogous version of it based on Pinel's descriptions of *manie sans délire*. Peyronnet spoke as a strict constructionist of Article 64. The Napoleonic codifiers had, he said, intended that exemption from criminal responsibility be granted only on the grounds of total insanity, not partial insanity. But he departed from this purely technical argument when he added that the inclusion of partial insanity would be "injurious to morality and alarming for society"; it would

> transform into acts of insanity crimes which strike us dumb with horror and would by a false pity tend at nothing less than leaving . . . society disarmed in the presence of great criminals: their impunity would in fact be all the more assured by the enormity of their transgression.[108]

The accusation of "false pity," or "misguided philanthropy," or of "disruptive . . . new systems which claim to be protectors of humanity,"[109] was made repeatedly in debates over monomania. Since the forensic physicians typically stressed, in the liberal mode, the praiseworthy humanitarianism of their stance on monomania, their rightwing opponents in the magistracy typically responded by seeking to expose the hypocrisy, or at least wrong-headedness, of this pretension and to lay bare the threat to society which the monomania doctrine contained.

Even the presiding judges, though theoretically neutral participants in the proceedings of the criminal court, spoke out energetically against monomania. Georget, who studiously followed the Pannetier trial in Versailles in 1827, reported that in the summation the presiding judge admonished the jurors that they "must be forewarned against modern systems, that to acquit the guilty was to embolden them." So agitated about monomania was this same magistrate that he even tried behind the scenes to influence expert testimony in the case. One Dr. Courties, who had been Madame Pannetier's physician before the murder, was

---

[108] Transcript of the Papavoine trial quoted in Georget, *Discussion médico-légale sur la folie ou l'aliénation mentale, suivie de l'examen du procès d'Henriette Cornier, et de plusieurs autres procès* . . . (Paris: Migneret, 1826), pp. 3, 17.

[109] The second phrase is the depiction of the magistrates' charge against the monomania doctrine given in A. Chauveau and F. Hélie, *Théorie du code pénal* (Paris: Gobelet, n.d. [1836]), Vol. 2, p. 218. The third phrase was used by the *avocat-général* in the Cornier case; see "Cour d'assises: Procès d'Henriette Cornier," *Journal des débats*, June 25, 1826.

called as a witness; as he confided to Georget, he had before the session casually "informed the magistrate whom he was accompanying of his opinion on the mental state of Pannetier." The magistrate cautioned: "Mind that you do not speak of monomania; that is a system suited to promote crime." "I will speak according to my conscience," Courties replied.[110]

So familiar a figure had the monomania-debunking magistrate become by the early years of the July Monarchy that he was even brought to the stage. The main character of Charles Duveyrier's play *Le Monomane*, performed in Paris at the popular boulevard theater of the Porte-Saint-Martin in 1835, was the provincial Restoration chief prosecutor Balthazar. Deeply bound up in his professional identity as keeper of law and preserver of the fabric of society, spokesman for an anxiety-laden political conservatism, he explains himself to the audience in a long monologue:

> We live in a century of strange contradictions in which society, disjointed and tottering, has no fulcrum or anchor but the law and in which, however, everyone fails to appreciate the law, insults and blasphemes it. . . . In the midst of this unmanned and worn-out world, I have sworn that there would be one man at least in whom old-fashioned firmness and virtue would be revived! . . . a man who would devote himself entirely to the law and, in order to defend it, would make himself as impassive and unshakable as it! . . . And I have kept my oath, I tell you. . . . And if everywhere my researches are crowned with success, if the prisons overflow with wrongdoers, then I gaze on the tranquility of the town and the countryside, I see the order and the calm, and I glory in my work; I am proud.

Two of Balthazar's friends – both, significantly, doctors – try to persuade him to show more leniency in the exercise of his judicial functions; and one of them tries to convince him that a poor and hardworking Italian refugee who has voluntarily confessed to theft and murder is in fact a monomaniac, obsessed with an erroneous and self-invented idée fixe that he is a criminal. But the concept of monomania is anathema to Balthazar, who describes it as

> indefensible, dangerous, subversive of all principles of order and morality. . . . Thanks to this new system of nerve ailments and brain lesions, the most atrocious crimes could be committed in perfect innocence! There would be neither crimes nor criminals. . . . [The monomania doctrine] is fine for amusing students on the schoolbenches; but that it should be imposed on the law, that serious men should adopt it – never, never!

Like other magistrates of his era, Balthazar places the monomania doctrine under the rubric of "tearful philanthropy"; it is part of "a fever,

[110] Georget, "Discussion médico-légale sur la folie," *Arch. gen. de med.* 15 (1827): 517 n1, 521.

an intoxication of mercy and pity" which assaults him from all sides.[111]
The fictional Balthazar thus stands as an epitome of the early nineteenth-century magistrate, implacably hostile to those liberalizing tendencies, including monomania, which in his eyes threaten to vitiate the
efficacy of the law. And, the creation of a playwright active in the
Saint-Simonian movement and in the agitation for penal code reform,[112]
Balthazar also stands as an epitome of the politicization of monomania.

That politicization emerges again with utmost clarity in contemporary newspaper reports of the monomania controversy. Like the royalist magistracy, the royalist press decried the doctrine as perilous to
society. In the *Gazette de France* (which received a direct financial sub-
sidy from the Villèle ministry) the tender humanitarian sentiment of
Georget's 1825 brochure was deftly satirized. Of the blood-drinking
Léger, whose death sentence Georget had deplored, the journalist
wrote:

> It must be agreed that in the bosom of a civilized nation accustomed to
> more decorous banquets, anthropophagi endowed with reason offer a
> phenomenon difficult to explain; but those insane ones – since they are
> supposed to be such – are the most perplexing of all. I do not know of
> anything from which it is more important to deliver society, which ought
> not, after all, be the victim of the singularity of their tastes.

To this journalist's mind, capital punishment was entirely appropriate
for such criminals; to keep them under close watch in a *maison des fous*,
as Georget suggested, was to afford inadequate protection to society,
for even the most active surveillance was often faulty. "Woe, then,
woe to those whom the innocent cannibals would encounter on their
path!" And what of the surveillants themselves?

> I believe Monsieur Georget very brave, but would he want to care for
> such lunatics, to take their pulse in the morning and in the evening? I
> would not advise him to do so: patients of this type probably make no
> exceptions, and when the appetite comes to them, they are ready to eat
> their own physician, should they find him in the vicinity of their teeth.[113]

With earnestness rather than wit, newspapers and periodicals of
liberal persuasion such as the *Globe,* the *Figaro,* and the *Mercure de
France au XIXe siècle* adduced characteristically liberal arguments to en-
dorse the monomania doctrine. They put their trust in the findings of
science: Georget had made "a special study . . . [of] the different varieties of insanity," and his scientific method and that of his colleagues

---

[111] See Charles Duveyrier, *Le monomane, drame en cinq actes* (Brussels: J.-A. Lelong, 1835),
pp. 28–29, 31, 34–36.

[112] On Duveyrier, see Pierre Larousse, *Grand dictionnaire universel du XIXe siècle.*

[113] Colnet in *Gazette de France,* December 19, 1825, quoted in Georget, *Discussion suivie de
l'examen du procès d'Henriette Cornier,* pp. 106–7.

was rigorous. "We repeat, when one speaks of homicidal monomania it is not on the basis of a few rare or poorly observed cases; one can cite examples by the hundreds."[114] Furthermore, they welcomed the diagnosis of homicidal monomania because it enabled them to maintain their optimistic liberal belief that radical evil was not a component of human nature but rather a pathological denaturation.[115] And finally, viewing their own epoch as a progressive one in which "all ideas are turned toward philanthropy," they opposed the death penalty as cruel, vengeful, and pointless – and especially so for sick individuals who, "similar to inert bodies, kill like tile that falls from a roof."[116]

Rounding out this picture of thoroughgoing politicization, the nascent socialist wing of Restoration politics offered its own particular slant on monomania. Writing in the Saint-Simonian journal *Producteur*, Philippe Buchez, a medical doctor by training, gave his full assent to the diagnosis and its use in a forensic context. But he stressed the conceptual incompleteness of monomania. It was currently defined superficially, "empirically," as a cluster of symptoms, but the nature and locus of the organic lesion giving rise to these symptoms remained unknown. At its present stage, monomania was an individualistic doctrine: It benefited the sick individuals whom it (justly) rescued from punishment. But only when medical science had progressed to the next stage through the discovery of the specific organic lesion would it be possible to predict monomaniacal behavior, to treat incipient monomaniacs preventively, and thus to spare society from their mad violence. With this increase in scientific knowledge, then, the individualist monomania doctrine of the liberals would be superseded by the truly social monomania doctrine of the Saint-Simonians.[117]

The medical defense of monomania and the self-defense of psychiatric specialization

Insofar as its terms were set by royalist opponents, the monomania controversy was primarily political. Concerned with issues of suitable punishment and maintenance of social order, it tended to neglect discussion of the internal scientific validity of the monomania concept itself. In fact, the chief prosecutor in the Cornier case could reject the concept out of hand for its social implications while explicitly refusing even to entertain the possibility that the concept might be scientifically

---

[114] *Globe*, December 22, 1825, p. 1044; for similar testimonials, see *Figaro*, November 3, 1828, and *Mercure de France au XIXe siècle* 23 (1828): 117–18.

[115] *Globe*, December 22, 1825.

[116] *Figaro*, November 3, 1828; see also *Globe*, September 24, 1825, pp. 837–39, and June 24, 1826, p. 421.

[117] Buchez, "Monomanie homicide," *Producteur* 5 (1826): 106–108.

accurate. "A supposed insanity is invoked," he told the jury, "and we are transported to a terrain which is not our own and involved in questions foreign to our usual studies. The law does not ask so much of us: it would have put a metaphysician in our place and twelve medical men in yours."[118]

But another aspect of the controversy, given its most dramatic impetus by the publication in 1828 of Elias Regnault's *Du degré de compétence des médecins dans les questions judiciaires relatives aux aliénations mentales*, did focus attention on scientific issues. Regnault, a young lawyer at the royal court of Paris (who dedicated the book to his colleagues there), had apparently been moved by professional motives and a sense of professional territoriality to attack the monomania doctrine. The testimony of experts on *médecine mentale*, he observed, added a new and incalculable element to the balance of power in the courtroom, complicating the lawyer's task and vitiating his influence over the jury. But if his motives were lawyerly – if he was, in other words, a self-conscious participant in a professional boundary dispute – Regnault's chief line of attack was scientific and philosophical. He produced a broad historical survey of medical opinion on insanity, beginning with Boerhaave and running through Pinel and Esquirol, which revealed that the literature contained nothing but a mass of contradictions about the nature and bodily locus of mental disease. Commendably possessed with "the zeal for arriving at . . . the truth," the doctors had simply failed to arrive there. Their entire classificatory enterprise, based on a Linnaean model, was intrinsically futile, for unlike the tangible objects studied by naturalists, "the nuances of madness [are] . . . no more amenable to being classified than are clouds." Hence the total medical contribution was nil. "In order to be at the level of current knowledge in this branch of human science," stated Regnault flatly, "plain common sense suffices."[119]

The medical community took Regnault's attack very seriously. His book was reviewed in virtually every Parisian medical journal, and the reviews, all expressions of a wounded professional amour propre, usually contained attempts at reasoned rebuttal and refutation. While the strategies employed varied – one Comtean physician, for example, held that the contradictions in medical conceptions of insanity over time were entirely normal and expectable because medicine was progressing by stages to its ultimate positive form[120] – the most characteristic medical defense of the monomania concept rested upon the assertion of the clinical principle then ascendant in Paris medicine. That is, medical

---

[118] *Journal des débats*, June 25, 1826.

[119] Elias Regnault, *Du degré de compétence des médecins dans les questions judiciaires relatives aux aliénations mentales* (Paris: B. Warée, 1828).

[120] Auguste Boulland, review of Regnault, *Degré de compétence* in *Journal des progrès des sciences et institutions médicales* 11 (1828): esp. 41–43.

respondents alleged that Regnault's criticisms, especially those concerning the classification of mental diseases, were not as damning as they might seem, nor did they even need to be answered in their own terms, because they were abstract and bookish; they had been framed in ignorance of the privileged knowledge accruing to the physician through clinical experience.

Leuret used this line of argument in the inaugural issue of the *Annales d'hygiène publique et de médecine légale* to counter Regnault's incredulity about *monomanie sans délire.* "Let us go into a mental hospital (*maison d'aliénés*)," he suggested, "and let us try to appraise the value of Monsieur Regnault's ideas about madness. . . . Will we find them consonant with observation?" In his hypothetical mental hospital, Leuret comes upon a straitjacketed woman whose extremities, lips, and tongue bear the marks of self-inflicted wounds and who continues to try to bite herself:

> Let us question her. "What are you doing there?" "Little that interests you. I am mad. Don't you see that I am mad?" "Why do you torment yourself that way?" "Could I prevent myself? It is stronger than I am."

"Where is the thought disorder here?" asks Leuret rhetorically. "The patient is mad, knows it, says it; but she cannot control it. Her will is perverted." And he adds, affirming the absolute validity of the clinical datum even in the absence of theoretical explanation: "How to understand that one can do ill when one condemns [one's actions] oneself? . . . I do not know. I explain nothing; I say to those who doubt: come and see."[121] Similarly, Hippolyte Royer-Collard attempted to disarm Regnault by describing metaphorically the peculiar intuitive knowledge, often unsystematized or even unarticulated, that accumulated clinical experience brings to the medical practitioner:

> We are ignorant of many facts, it is true; but is this to say that the layman is not ignorant of a hundred times as many facts? Our knowledge of the habits of patients is alone already an enormous difference. Place several people in the midst of darkness, they will see nothing around them; but let them sojourn there for some time and they will end up very nearly distinguishing the objects which surround them. It is the same with medical science. . . . We who by force of living there and exercising our senses to get our bearings there, we have developed, so to speak, a sort of visual faculty, a faculty that is entirely artificial and entirely personal, to see something where others can discover nothing; and except for the false steps which are inevitable in spots where it is too dark, we know very well how to get along.[122]

---

[121] Leuret, review of Regnault, *Degré de compétence* in *Ann. d'hyg. pub.* 1 (1829): 282–84.
[122] H. Royer-Collard, review of Regnault, *Degré de compétence,* pp. 185–86.

Reiterating the same theme, another medical reviewer said simply, "Monsieur Regnault proves . . . that he has never observed lunatics, or that he has observed them very badly."[123]

The emphasis on *la clinique* in the defense of the monomania concept against its detractors was closely connected to another aspect of the monomania controversy: its function as a forum for the public announcement of a discrete psychiatric specialty. When Georget wrote his initial brochure, he spoke, perhaps with deliberate ambiguity, in the name of the medical profession as a whole, urging that "physicians" be consulted in judicial matters concerning insanity. But such medical unity lasted only briefly. Physicians were soon not only battling anti-monomania judges and lawyers but also quarreling among themselves, with specialists in *maladies mentales* in one camp and nonspecialized medical practitioners in the other. In this regard the monomania controversy reflected a much wider phenomenon. The mass of the medical profession greeted the trend toward specialization with open hostility, or at least suspicion. Whether due to economic or status rivalry or to the longstanding association of specialization with charlatanism, such antagonism remained strong in Europe until 1850 and in America well after that date.[124]

The intraprofessional conflict within the monomania controversy was set off by a little-known military doctor, Urbain Coste, who denounced outright the very procedural innovation that Georget was attempting to promote. "Nothing," wrote Coste, "would be more gratuitous than the presumption of a special capacity of physicians" to make evaluations of mental condition in criminal cases. In these matters any sane layman was "as competent as Monsieur Pinel or Monsieur Esquirol"–perhaps even more so, since the layman had "the advantage of being foreign to all scientific prejudices."[125] Thus Coste did not launch an explicit attack on the pretensions of a psychiatric specialty–like Georget he referred to the group of "physicians" as a whole–but the allusion to Pinel and Esquirol left little doubt as to his meaning. And it was to this latent meaning that Leuret responded vigorously, indicating in no uncertain terms in the *Annales d'hygiène publique et de médecine légale* that medical specialization was a principle fundamental to the monomania doctrine:

---

[123] F. B., review of Regnault, *Degré de compétence* in *Annales de la médecine physiologique* 14 (1828): 660.

[124] George Rosen, *The Specialization of Medicine with Particular Reference to Ophthalmology* (New York: Froben, 1944), Ch. 5, esp. pp. 49, 58–59, 68. See also the protest of the general surgeons of the Paris hospitals against the creation of a new position in surgery of the urinary tract, "De l'admission des spécialités dans les hôpitaux de Paris," *Arch. gen. de med.*, 3d ser., 7 (1840): 373–77.

[125] U. Coste, review of *Dictionnaire abrégé des sciences médicales* in *Journal universel des sciences médicales* 43 (1826): 53.

It would result from the opinion of Monsieur Urbain Coste that one would be all the more capable of judging a fact if one were less occupied with the science to which it is attached. I leave this opinion to those whom it may beguile, and *I establish a distinction among doctors*. Besides the degree of intelligence apportioned to each of them, one can never fail to consider the type of studies to which they have devoted themselves. Thus, the patient who has a wound, a fracture, places his confidence in a doctor who has most occupied himself with external pathology; the one who has a fever or an inflammation of the respiratory or digestive organs places his confidence in the doctor who has most occupied himself with internal pathology. *Specialties, then, are admitted in theory and in practice. . . . Let us prove . . . that a special study is indispensable in order to pass correct judgments on insane persons.*[126]

This endorsement of medical specialization – and of the study of insanity as one of the legitimate specialties – was made in the context of Leuret's review of Regnault and came but a few pages after his argument for the clinical verification of the monomania classification. It was a logical enough progression, for the clinical epistemology served as a primary justification for specialization. The doctor in daily contact with a sizable number of insane patients would necessarily possess the most thorough and reliable knowledge of mental illness; and the ordinary practitioner, who could not hope to offset with book learning the relative infrequency of his encounters with lunatics, would suffer a diminution of authority in this area. This intimate connection between *la clinique* and psychiatric specialization was contained in a popular locution for the *médecin des aliénés* – the physician who "lives with the insane and observes them."[127] Chambeyron, reflecting on a murder trial in Rennes, made precisely the same connection, underscoring what he called the "dissidence" between his specialist evaluation of the mental state of the accused and the evaluation of a general practitioner:

> One of the two physicians charged with examining Péchot, struck by the man's repeated assertion that he had been an imbecile for forty years and by his obstinacy in responding to certain situations only with the words "I want some cider," was inclined to think that the madness was feigned. But the other [i.e., Chambeyron himself] *who regularly lives in the midst of madmen*, was persuaded by the peculiar configuration of details and occurrences to believe in the reality of the disease.[128]

Within the context of the monomania controversy, the nonspecialist protesters generally wanted assurance that the prestigious function of courtroom expert would be shared in an egalitarian manner among all physicians; they resisted the suggestion that advantage ought to accrue

---

[126] Leuret, review of Regnault, *Degré de compétence*, p. 286, my italics.
[127] See, e.g., Dr. Munaret enumerating the "great family of specialties" in *Du médecin de campagne et de ses malades* (Paris: Librairie anatomique de Baillet, 1837), p. 25.
[128] Chambeyron, "Affaire Péchot," p. 239, my italics.

only to the mental specialists. And their arguments also turned on *la clinique* – on what, in their view, constituted adequate clinical facility and expertise for forensic purposes. Thus a certain Dr. Boisseau could

> hardly believe that by the fact that a doctor has been an intern in a public hospice for the insane or has been attached to a private sanatorium for lunatics, he alone should be competent, not only among people in general but also *among all his colleagues* to speak wisely about madness. It is claims of this sort which cover our profession with ridicule.

He went on to say that an intangible gift for medical observation, not the formal criterion of service in a specialized institution, qualified a doctor for forensic psychiatric testimony.[129] One Dr. Worbe called "the supreme prerogative" of doctors at lunatic hospices to pronounce on these cases a "ridiculous privilege destructive of all judicial truth and all medical liberty." He dismissed the claim that "this so-called continual care and attention" to insane patients could alone supply the expertise required by the courts; and he cited some monomaniacs he had encountered in his own practice to show that nonspecialists had ample clinical experience with the varieties of insanity.[130]

Thus the monomania controversy functioned not only as an appeal for psychiatric legitimacy through a negotiation of interprofessional boundaries; it served as well to sharpen the intraprofessional line of demarcation between psychiatric specialists and other medical practitioners.

The decline of monomania

From its privileged position in the 1830s and 1840s – a much-used diagnostic category, the shibboleth of the growing contingent of *médecins aliénistes*[131] – monomania fell rather abruptly. The turning point came in 1852, when a student of the Esquirol circle member Jean-Pierre Falret wrote a *thèse de médecine* on the "non-existence" of the "instinctive monomanias." In that same year, Benedict-Augustin Morel, a more advanced Falret student with a post in a provincial lunatic asylum, published a totalistic criticism of the monomania classification, which

---

[129] F. G. Boisseau, review of Regnault, *Degré de compétence* in *Journal complémentaire du dictionnaire des sciences médicales* 31 (1828): 272, my italics.

[130] Worbe, review of Regnault, *Degré de compétence*, Part 1, in *Journal universel des sciences médicales* 52 (1828): 315–16.

[131] On the universal acceptance of the monomania doctrine by the *"hommes spéciaux* who spend their lives amidst the insane" and by "all the *médecins-aliénistes* of our era," see, respectively, Alexandre Bottex, *De la médecine légale des aliénés dans ses rapports avec la législation criminelle* (Paris: J.-B. Baillière, 1838), p. 100; and H. Aubanel, "Mémoire médico-légal sur un cas de folie homicide méconnue par les assises du Var," *Ann. m.-p.*, 2d ser., 1 (1849): 81.

was followed two years later by Falret's own essay on the "non-existence of monomania."[132] By May 1853, the issue had become such a
pressing one in the French psychiatric community that the recently
formed Société médico-psychologique began a formal discussion of it, a
discussion that lasted until May of the following year.

The triumvirate of Falret, Morel, and the thesis-writer Bariod attacked monomania on clinical grounds. (Their armamentarium also
contained a related attack, based on philosophical psychology, which
will be considered in Chapter 7.) They held that the multitude of earlier
clinical observations which had been adduced in support of the monomania concept were all fundamentally flawed – that is, incomplete or of
insufficient duration. Skillful and thorough questioning of a supposed
monomaniac, or daily contact over a long period of time, would inevitably reveal that the delirium was not confined to a single subject:

> Let us take, for example, a lunatic preoccupied with religious ideas who
> would be classified among the religious monomaniacs. . . . Interrogate
> him more carefully and you will not be long in discovering other patho-
> logical ideas: you will find parallel to the religious ideas a tendency to
> arrogance. He will believe himself called not only to reform religion but
> also to reform society; perhaps he also imagines himself . . . a prince or
> monarch. There, then, is a delirium which appears religious at first glance
> and is at the same time prideful or political.

Furthermore, the reasoning processes of this supposed monomaniac
were not, as the exponents of monomania alleged, normal apart from
the single delusional idea. The patient did not logically deduce all the
consequences of a single false premise. Rather, his thought was rife with
"lacunae, inconsistencies, contradictions that would revolt a man of
sound mind."[133] Elsewhere, in a sophisticated discussion of styles of
clinical observation in psychiatry, Falret offered a somewhat different
view of the source of the medical error that had spawned the monomania diagnosis. He noted that a common but highly distortive style was
for the physician in a lunatic hospital to imitate the novelist (*romancier*)
unwittingly. Seeking to replace the chaos of nature with the order of art,
the physician perceived and represented each patient he encountered as
a "character" in La Bruyère's sense, a person governed by a single

---

[132] J.-A. Bariod, "Etudes critiques sur les monomanies instinctives: Non-existence de
cette forme de maladie mentale" (Paris: Thèse de médecine, 1852); B.-A. Morel, "De
la monomanie," *Etudes cliniques*, Vol. 1, Ch. 8; J.-P. Falret, "De la non-existence de la
monomanie," *Arch. gen de med.* (August 1854): 147–64, reprinted in *Des maladies
mentales et des asiles d'aliénés* (Paris; J.-B. Baillière, 1864), the text cited here. In the
manner of Pinel, Falret called attention in his footnotes to these works of his students
Morel and Bariod. Bariod's thesis even received notice from psychiatrists in Germany; see E. Renaudin, review of "Journaux allemands," *Ann. m.-p.*, 3d ser., 1
(1855): 301.

[133] Falret, "De la non-existence de la monomanie," pp. 437–38.

passion or idea. He remained unaware of the disconfirming clinical evidence screened out for the sake of his artistry. Obviously, monomania had received much support from this observational style, which belonged, said Falret disparagingly, to the "infancy" of the specialty.[134]

The speakers at the Société médico-psychologique meetings on monomania occupied almost every conceivable position with respect to that disease classification. Brierre de Boismont, one of the earliest champions of monomania, defected entirely from the position of the old Esquirol circle, seconding the argument from extended clinical experience. The concept, he said now, "loses all of its prestige when patients can be subjected to daily examination." Belhomme, another early supporter of monomania hailing from the Esquirol circle, remained steadfast. Casimir Pinel, the nephew of the founding father and the director of a Paris *maison de santé* for lunatics, appealed to the tradition, albeit short, of the profession. He saw "not the slightest defect" in the monomania concept and was "astonished that a doctrine established by such great *maîtres* . . . had been attacked."[135]

The protracted debate at the Société ended inconclusively on the theoretical level.[136] But, on the practical level, it effectively dispelled the aura that had for several decades surrounded the monomania concept. The confidence of *médecins-aliénistes* in the validity of the classification was shaken. The number of patients diagnosed as monomaniacs began to decline steadily – from 14 percent of the newly admitted inmate population of the Salpêtrière in 1850, to 10 percent in 1858, 8 percent in 1860, 2 percent in 1865, and if one subsequently altered diagnosis is discounted, none at all in 1870.[137] The word "monomania," so alluring from the outset, demonstrated stubborn powers of survival, but by the latter third of the century psychiatrists were making deliberate attempts to purge it from the technical vocabulary. Some psychiatrists, who found themselves using it out of habit rather than intellectual conviction, cautioned that the term was outmoded and ought not be construed "in its narrow etymological sense."[138] One prominent Pari-

---

[134] Falret, "Leçons faites à l'hospice de la Salpêtrière, 1850–51," in *Maladies mentales*, pp. 109–10, 139–40.

[135] Minutes of the Société médico-psychologique in *Ann. m.-p.*, 2d ser., 6 (1854): 104, 106, 111.

[136] In fact, the Société returned to the subject of partial, encapsulated impairments of mental functioning in 1866–67, though now, significantly, under the rubric of *folie raisonnante* rather than monomania; this debate was as inconclusive as was its predecessor, but its tone was much less polemical. *Ann. m.-p.*, 4th ser., 7 (1866) and 8 (1867).

[137] AAP: Salpêtrière 6Q2-15, 6Q2-22, 6Q2-34, 6Q2-46, 6Q2-55; the figures are based on samples of 100 admissions for each year indicated.

[138] See Ambroise Tardieu, *Etude médico-légale sur la folie* (Paris: J.-B. Baillière, 1872), p. 199; and, for a similar comment, Henri Legrand du Saulle, *Etude médico-légale sur les testaments contestés pour cause de folie* (Paris: A. Delahaye, 1879), p. 265.

sian psychiatrist of the early Third Republic lectured his students sternly about those who persisted in employing the old nomenclature, calling them "incapable of shaking off the sin (*péché*) of monomania in which they have so long been mired. The first lesson that must be well-learned is that there is no such thing as monomania!"[139]

How can the demise of monomania, dating from the sudden and discrete crisis of 1852–54, be explained? A whiggish view would point simply to a progressive accumulation of clinical data that eventually exposed scientific error and falsified the category. But such a view assumes that the *médecins-aliénistes* were entirely neutral truth-seekers with no stake in the validity of the monomania concept; it ignores the pivotal role of the concept in a professional boundary dispute – a particular social context which, for a time, could render monomania immune from the criticism of the very scientific community which had produced it. In fact, the timing of events strongly suggests that the scientific fortunes of monomania were tied to tactical considerations.

Thus Falret, who together with his students opened fire on the concept in the 1850s, had *never* given credence to it. He had expressed his doubts in his own doctoral dissertation of 1819, and these "fruits of my very first studies" had been subsequently "fortified by repeated observation under the most favorable conditions."[140] Yet prior to 1854, Falret had remained on the whole publicly silent about his doubts. He did incorporate them into the clinical teaching at the Salpêtrière which he began in 1843;[141] but this did not constitute publicizing them in any meaningful sense. In accordance with new regulations of the Paris hospice administration designed to protect the "secret" of insane inmates, Falret's course was closed to all but enrolled students and a handful of authorized medical auditors.[142] Printed reports of his lessons began to appear in a medical journal only in 1848, and not until 1850 did they touch upon the monomania question.[143] One can only surmise that the situation of interprofessional conflict and the demands of loyalty to the Esquirol circle made him regard scientific debate over mono-

---

[139] V. Magnan, "Leçon d'ouverture (Asile Sainte-Anne)," *Progrès médical* 11 (1883): 87.

[140] J.-P. Falret, *Observations et propositions médico-chirurgicales* (Paris: Thèse de médecine, 1819), pp. 10–15; and "De la non-existence," p. 425.

[141] This is Falret's own testimony in "De la non-existence," p. 425.

[142] De Lasiauve [sic], "Deux visites à la Salpêtrière (section de M. Falret)," *Expérience* 7 (April 20, 1843): 258. For the precise regulations and the events which provoked them, see AAP: CGH 173, no. 92564 (November 2, 1842) and 175, no. 94360 (April 5, 1843).

[143] See *Gazette des hôpitaux*, 2d ser., 10 (1848), August 5, 15, and 22; these lessons concern psychiatric therapeutics. During the 1850–51 series Falret briefly outlined his objections to the "theory of monomania"; ibid., 3d ser., 2 (1850), July 2, p. 311. There is a passing allusion to his skepticism about monomania in his *Observations sur le projet de loi relatif aux aliénés* (Paris: Everat, 1837), pp. 38–39; but he is here careful to show deference to reigning psychiatric opinion on the subject.

mania as temporarily inappropriate and counterproductive, and that he deliberately refrained from it.

A roughly obverse case is Esquirol's public "conversion" to *monomanie homicide;* very likely he was not merely indulging his favorite student. In 1825, when Georget initiated the monomania controversy, the Restoration monarchy had, with the accession of the ultraroyalist Charles X, moved farther to the right. Esquirol must have despaired of realizing the plans for nationwide adoption of a model lunatic asylum, plans already tabled in 1821 after another and less dire liberal setback, the fall of the Decazes ministry. Esquirol's program for the legitimation of *médecine mentale* had always devolved upon the proliferation of public asylums; but pessimism about that program, at least for the immediate future, must have made him amenable to endorsing Georget's strategy for recognition of the new specialty in a forensic setting – even if that alternative strategy entailed revision of one of Esquirol's own scientific beliefs.

In putting forth an external argument of this kind, and one imputing "opportunistic" motives to scientists, it is unusual to be able to cite first-hand confirmatory evidence. But in this case some of the protagonists do provide such testimony. A particularly rich source is the 1852 published review of Morel's *Etudes cliniques* (the collection of essays that contained his anti-monomania views) by Brierre de Boismont. The latter speaks with surprising directness and freedom about the profound impact of the professional environment and of calculations of professional success upon theoretical developments within psychiatric science. Strikingly, Brierre does not even seem to entertain the idea that he is involved in a purely scientific enterprise. He writes:

> My opinions on monomania are, then, basically similar to those of Monsieur Morel. Only I believe the moment inopportune for upholding this [anti-monomania] thesis. The true ideas to whose propagation the doctrine of Esquirol conduces are far from having made their way in the world, and it is to be feared that the numerous opponents they have met with would hurry to take advantage of this medical dissension in order to stage a new protest. In the sciences as in ordinary affairs, one should never lose sight of this aphorism: "All things come to him who waits."

Brierre and Morel had exchanged personal letters on this very point; and Brierre cites Morel's letter as indicating that the latter "does not share our fears about the benefit that the jurisconsults could reap from this disunion," believing instead that a sounder classificatory scheme, without "absurdity" and logical inconsistency, could only strengthen the position of the *médecin aliéniste* in the courtroom.[144] Morel reiterated

---

[144] Brierre de Boismont, review of Morel, *Etudes cliniques* in *Ann. m.-p.*, 2d ser., 4 (1852): 621.

this idea a year later before the assembled Société médico-psychologique, "happy that my visit to Paris coincides with your meeting" so that "I may exculpate myself of an accusation that weighs on my medical conscience" – "that I have furnished magistrates with another weapon for diminishing the role that *médecins aliénistes* are called upon to play as experts on medico-legal questions." In fact, he declared, the abandonment of the monomania concept could only enhance their forensic credibility. "Called one day before a tribunal in Nancy as an expert, I heard the presiding judge say that whenever an accused individual was presented to the jurors as having a theft monomania or a swindling monomania, one must have a monomania of convicting him."[145] Falret was of the same mind: A "special science" from which the inaccurate category of monomania had been removed, he wrote, would make the *médecin aliéniste* all the more "the natural and necessary auxiliary of the tribunals."[146]

In fact, this kind of explicit recognition of the "fit" between the scientific theory of the new specialty and the efficacy of that theory in the outside nonmedical world surfaced frequently in the psychiatrists' debate over monomania. Bariod's doctoral thesis asserted that "the legal importance" of monomania had "shaped the thinking of all the physicians" who accepted and elaborated the concept; foreign influences had thus "slipped into science."[147] He was no doubt echoing his teacher's similar comments about conceptual deformation. "The exigencies of legal medicine," Falret had written with respect to the invention of certain subspecies of monomania, "have led alienists to accord more importance to the penchants for theft and murder than to any other penchants."[148] At the Société médico-psychologique, Casimir Pinel also acknowledged the extrascientific factors which had shaped the career of monomania, but like Brierre and unlike Falret and Bariod, he was entirely tolerant of them. "Innovations in science," he declared, must be judged by their "utility," which meant in this case forensic and humanitarian utility, their capacity to "save the lives of a great number of sick people who would otherwise have perished on the scaffold." Monomania had already accomplished that very end, and – here his reading of the trend was antithetical to Morel's – it showed signs of gaining greater acceptance by the magistrates. On these pragmatic grounds alone the diagnostic category should not be questioned by members of the psychiatric community, who would thus "provide the distressing spectacle of anarchy in a science which has many adversaries."[149]

---

[145] Minutes of the Société médico-psychologique, *Ann. m.-p.*, 2d ser., 6 (1854): 284, 286.
[146] Falret, "De la non-existence de la monomanie," pp. 447–48.
[147] Bariod, "Etudes critiques," p. 6.
[148] Falret, "Leçons faites à l'hospice de la Salpêtrière, 1850–51," in *Maladies mentales*, p. 142.
[149] Minutes of the Société médico-psychologique, *Ann. m.-p.*, 2d ser., 6 (1854): 110.

In short, by the early 1850s some psychiatric defenders of monomania as well as some of its psychiatric detractors openly acknowledged that a boundary dispute had both influenced the internal development of the monomania concept and bolstered that concept "artificially" by preventing disinterested scrutiny of it by *médecins aliénistes*. Once Falret and his students had violated the tacit taboo and made that scrutiny unavoidable, most *médecins aliénistes* were willing to consider seriously the internal weaknesses of the monomania doctrine, weaknesses they had overlooked decades earlier, or had denied or studiously ignored when outsiders called them to their attention. Thus, for example, when the philosophy professor Adolphe Garnier spoke at the Société médico-psychologique of the "uncertainty of knowing the precise limits between passion and madness," and especially the limit between inflamed passion and the intensely powerful "inclinations" attributed to monomania, the psychiatrists listened respectfully and even praised him[150] – although they had turned a collective deaf ear to virtually the same argument when it was made in 1828 by the lawyer Collard de Martigny. The Société debates also revealed the confusion surrounding the term "delirium," a term critical to all discussions of volitional monomania. Archambault announced that he had reread Esquirol's 1827 dictum and had noticed that the *maître* had never, strictly speaking, admitted a monomania without delirium into the nosological canon.[151] Ferrus stated that "there is a true delirium only in the intelligence," implying that Esquirol's depiction of one type of monomania as a partial delirium of the sentiments or inclinations was an equivocation and a semantic impossibility.[152]

Why did Falret decide to end his decades of silence concerning monomania? Taking Brierre's position as a model, that silence was probably prudential, concerned to protect the public image of a fragile nascent specialty. Falret's shift to outspokenness must then have been prompted by an assessment that the specialty had become hardier, more resilient. And this new hardiness was clearly in evidence. By the 1850s the *médecins-aliénistes* had succeeded in winning, not the monomania controversy, but a more significant professional victory. The Law of 1838 had, in realization of Esquirol's dream, mandated the establishment of a nationwide asylum system – an event of which Falret was of course well aware, having served as one of the government's consultants in the framing of the Law. With the security and official recognition provided them by the Law, the *médecins-aliénistes* could afford to evaluate the monomania doctrine from a more disinterested standpoint; their professional future no longer seemed to hinge on it.

---

[150] Ibid., p. 278.
[151] Ibid., p. 106.
[152] Ibid., p. 279.

The monomania doctrine qualifies as a professional "utopian" ideology, an aggressively hyperbolic claim made for the emergent specialty of psychiatry by its practitioners and addressed primarily to the outside world.[153] As such, it belonged to a particular moment in the development of the psychiatric profession, a moment at which it was beginning to have some confidence in itself but was not yet fully secure; and a moment at which a setback in the plans for a national asylum system made an alternative mode of recognition – in this case, in the forensic sphere – appear especially urgent. A profession with too little self-confidence could not have enunciated the monomania doctrine. American physicians of this same period, like their French counterparts at the beginning of the century, withdrew from the forensic psychiatry role. They found it "embarrassing and irksome" to be summoned into court on questions of insanity. The "liability to be called on to elucidate or substantiate theories [of mental pathology]," commented one American medical man, "creates a strong disinclination in most members of the profession to discharge this important part of their duties toward society."[154] On the other hand, a profession with more self-confidence could have been more self-critical. When French psychiatry became more secure, and when it was prodded by Falret, it ceased its obdurate defense of the overblown and inherently problematic monomania doctrine before nonspecialists and the public at large. That is not to say that it abandoned its forensic aspirations. Indeed, with other diagnoses entering the breach to defend the criminal lunatic after the passing of monomania, court testimony remained one of the more prestigious and sought-after functions of the psychiatrist.[155] But the psychiatric community had turned inward; and conferring among themselves, *médecins-aliénistes* finally subjected monomania to the critical scrutiny it required.

[153] For this concept, see Clark, "Institutionalization of Innovations," pp. 4–5.

[154] R. E. G., review of Regnault, *Degré de compétence* in *American Journal of the Medical Sciences* 4 (1829): 190.

[155] On the successors to monomania, see Paul Dubuisson, "De l'evolution des opinions en matière de responsabilité," *Archives de l'anthropologie criminelle et des sciences pénales* 2 (1887): esp. 118–33. On the continued prestige of court testimony, see the touching bit of evidence in a letter of the Paris psychiatrist and *maison de santé* proprietor Antoine-Emile Blanche to his little son Jacques. Blanche, who rarely mentioned anything about his work in his correspondence with the boy, one day stated proudly: "I have a great deal to do right now, important criminals to examine. Today there is a story about me in the newspaper *Le Droit*." Institut de France, Ms. 4828, f. 80, letter dated August 18, 1874.

6

Religious roots and rivals

THE monomania controversy arose out of the attempt by psychiatric practitioners to define their professional domain in relation to the neighboring domain of law. If, pursuing this metaphor, we seek to complete the "map" of psychiatry and its environs in the first half of the nineteenth century, we must consider at least two other domains contiguous to it – those of religion and philosophy – which, through processes both of amicable borrowing and acrimonious territorial dispute, helped determine its shape. This chapter will consider the relationship, often troubled and always intensely complicated, between *aliénistes* and clerics. In the next chapter, the philosophical parameters of the new science of insanity will be explored.

A religious mission to the insane

Long before a handful of Parisian physicians decided to specialize in the care of the insane, certain religious congregations had already embarked upon that course, or at least something closely approximating it. Foremost among them were the Brothers of Saint-Jean-de-Dieu, also called the Brothers of Charity or the Charitains. Established in France in 1601, they were operating twenty-three hospitals by 1789, and seven of these – the most famous being Charenton – were reserved primarily for lunatics.[1] The Franciscan monks, or Bon-Fils, the Cordeliers, and the Brothers of the Christian Schools each maintained several *maisons d'aliénés* during the Old Regime.[2] A less imposing eighteenth-century enterprise, but one which would later achieve national prominence, was that of the Sisters of the Bon-Sauveur of Caen. Founded in 1723 by two young women of the artisan class, this local charitable order came

---

[1] Jean Caradec Cousson, *Un promoteur de la renaissance hospitalière et religieuse au XIXe siècle: Paul de Magallon d'Argens* (Paris & Lyon: E. Citte, 1959), p. 142.

[2] Paul Sérieux, "Le traitement des maladies mentales dans les maisons d'aliénés du XVIIIe siècle (d'après des documents en grande partie inédits)," *Archives internationales de neurologie*, 17th ser., 2 (1924): 113. This article appeared in seven installments from October 1924 to April 1925, as follows: 17th ser., 2 (1924): 97–119, 145–54, 191–204; 18th ser., 1 (1925): 21–31, 50–64, 90–105, 121–33.

through a series of accidental events to devote itself to prostitutes and female lunatics.[3] As the mixed clientele at the Bon-Sauveur of Caen hints, the "specialization" of these congregations during the Old Regime was of an imperfect sort. Thus in the relevant houses of the Charitains the lunatics shared the premises and the ministrations of the monks with the so-called *correctionnaires,* individuals whose "wicked," antisocial, or libertine lifestyles had been adjudged, usually by their own families, as needful of reform. But the populations of these religious houses were still far less heterogeneous than those of the secular *hôpitaux-généraux* of the period; the lunatics clearly formed the numerically preponderant group.[4]

The Revolutionary suppression of the regular clergy interrupted this religiously organized mission to the insane. But the nursing orders, admitted back into France somewhat grudgingly under Napoleon, experienced a veritable renaissance after 1815 in the proclerical atmosphere of the Restoration.[5] Thus a massive early nineteenth-century expansion of religious facilities for the insane coincided with the emergence of a scientific *médecine mentale*–a pattern which must cast doubt on any theory postulating a uniformly rising curve of professionalization, modernization, or secularization.

In the 1820s the Brothers of Saint-Jean-de-Dieu vigorously resumed their efforts, founding in diverse regions of France eight new hospitals exclusively for the insane.[6] Their work dovetailed with and received indirect encouragement from the ministerial pressures being brought to bear upon the prefects to remove lunatics in the public charge from makeshift quarters (usually prisons) and to place them in separate institutions especially designed for them. This ministerial policy seems to have grown out of the implementation of an imperial decree of 1810. By laying down homogeneity as a principle for the central prisons– that is, insisting that their casually mixed populations of undesirables now be rigorously restricted to a single type of inmate, the criminal offender–the decree necessitated the relocation of a sizable number of

---

[3] Marcel Jaeger, "Naissance d'un hôpital psychiatrique," *Pensée,* no. 158 (July-August 1971): 69–77.

[4] See the detailed study of one of the Charitains' eighteenth-century *maisons d'aliénés et de correctionnaires* by Hélène Bonnafous-Sérieux, *La Charité de Senlis d'après des documents en grande partie inédits* (Paris: Presses universitaires de France, 1936), esp. Ch. 3. The recent research of Claude Quétel indicates that all of the religious orders mentioned above accepted *correctionnaires* as inmates during the eighteenth century; see *De par le Roy: Essai sur les lettres de cachet* (Toulouse: Privat, 1981), pp. 174–75.

[5] See Jacques Léonard, "Femmes, religion et médecine: Les religieuses qui soignent en France au XIXe siècle," *Annales E.S.C.* 32 (1977): esp. 888–89; and Guillaume Bertier de Sauvigny, *The Bourbon Restoration,* trans. L. M. Case (Philadelphia: University of Pennsylvania Press, 1966), p. 116.

[6] Cousson, *Magallon,* p. 143.

lunatics.[7] Put on the spot by the prison reorganization and, later, by the 1819 circular of the liberal Minister of the Interior Decazes,[8] many prefects turned gladly to the local clerical asylums as a way to discharge their obligations. Thus the prefect of the Loire responded defensively in 1825 to a pointed query from the Ministry of the Interior about the lunatics of that department still detained in prisons, mentioning "an institution newly created in the department of the Lozère by the Brothers of Charity and solely devoted to the treatment of madmen. This institution, about which my colleague [presumably the prefect of the Lozère] has told me the most favorable things, receives the moderate sum of 300 francs for each lunatic sent there by the neighboring departments. I have already approached the head of the *maison* about admitting those of my department."[9]

The story of the Sisters of the Bon-Sauveur unfolded in similar fashion, with bureaucrats among the key dramatis personae. Gathering at Caen after their dispersion during the Revolution and finding their old property sold, the sisters bought a much larger one to replace it. But the Bonapartist government was slow to formalize their legal status, and their fortunes were markedly reversed only with the return of the Bourbons. At the urging of the Restoration prefect, the Conseil général of the Calvados voted funds to the sisters for the construction of new buildings, and in 1818 the same prefect decided that all lunatics maintained at the expense of the department (and at that moment housed in a central prison) would be entrusted to the order of the Bon-Sauveur. With this influx of public patients the institution grew prodigiously, from a population of sixteen lunatics as the time of its closing in 1790 to well over three hundred by 1835. Nor did its operations remain permanently confined to Normandy. A branch of the order was established in Alby in the south of France in 1832 for the express purpose of setting up and running a lunatic hospital modeled on the mother institution in Caen. Significantly, the initiative for this project came not from within the order but from the prefect of the Tarn, who, having heard of the special skills of the Bon-Sauveur from the bishop of Alby, now hoped to deal with the problem of the

---

[7] On the decree of September 22, 1810, on the central prisons, see Patricia O'Brien, *The Promise of Punishment: Prisons in Nineteenth-Century France* (Princeton, N.J.: Princeton University Press, 1982), p. 22. The rationalization of incarceration by the sorting out of inmate populations is a theme in Michel Foucault, *Folie et déraison: Histoire de la folie à l'âge classique* (Paris: Plon, 1961), Part 3, Ch. 2.

[8] Circular of July 16, 1819, in *Circulaires, instructions et autres actes émanés du Ministère de l'Intérieur*, Vol. 3 (Paris; Impr. royale, 1821), pp. 487–91. This circular called both for the establishment of large *maisons centrales* for lunatics (see Chapter 4 of this book), and in the interim, for the removal of lunatics from all facilities not reserved for them exclusively.

[9] AN: F^{15} 143, letter of October 15, 1823.

lunatics in the charge of his department by emulating the solution devised in the Calvados.[10]

In the closing years of the Restoration, comparable proposals were made to the Bon-Sauveur by the prefects of Maine-et-Loire and Pas-de-Calais, but in both instances the order drove a hard bargain and protracted negotiations ultimately failed.[11] Indeed, a perusal of the relevant Ministry of the Interior archives conveys the impression that the Bon-Sauveur (and other congregations which provided care of various sorts for the insane) had during the 1820s and 1830s more business from the bureaucracy than they could readily handle. The prefect of the Ariège, for example, wrote to the ministry in 1836 of his efforts to put the new *maison départementale* for lunatics at Saint Lizier into working order: "I have not ceased to concern myself with its organization, but I have not yet succeeded in entrusting [its internal] administration to a religious congregation. . . . I have just opened discussions with the Abbé Jamet, superior of the congregation of the Bon-Sauveur at Caen, with the *mères générales* of the Sisters of Saint-Vincent-de-Paul and the Sisters of Nevers, and I must hope that these new attempts will lead to a satisfactory solution."[12]

The moral treatment as religious consolation

Certainly the *médecins-aliénistes* were vulnerable to competition from this traditional and newly resurgent group of religious caretakers of the insane whose services were so much in demand in provincial France. Their vulnerability was intensified by the peculiar nature of the *aliénistes'* own curative expertise – that is, the moral treatment. As a paradigm underpinning an explicitly medical claim to the treatment of insanity, the moral treatment was hardly ideal; and Pinel's various attempts to give a scientific patina to the techniques he had openly – and, at first, proudly – adopted from uncertified practitioners had not eradicated the problem. Even as French physicians trained in the Pinellian mold championed "moral medicine," they expressed discomfort and defensiveness about its dubious pedigree and about the rivals it therefore seemed to invite rather than to exclude. The Esquirol circle member Félix Voisin noted in his 1819 doctoral dissertation that when the physician properly seeks to "sustain the moral energy" of a patient by encouraging his hopes and even his illusions, he does *not*

---

[10] Jaeger, "Naissance," pp. 75–76; Esquirol, "Des maisons des aliénés," *Des maladies mentales considérées sous les rapports médical, hygiénique et médico-légal*, Vol. 2 (Paris: J.-B. Baillière, 1838), pp. 473–74, 480; and G.-A. Simon, *Une belle figure de prêtre et d'homme d'oeuvres à la fin du XVIIIe siècle: L'abbé Pierre-François Jamet* (Caen: Jouan et Bigot, 1935), pp. 135–37, 144–45, 149, 183–85.

[11] Simon, *Abbé Jamet*, pp. 304–15.

[12] AN: F^{15} 3910, letter of December 29, 1836.

thereby "walk in the tracks of the charlatan." The charlatan's reckless and "gigantic promises" of cure were to be carefully distinguished from the physician's sober efforts to promote confidence and a positive outlook; the former have "influence only on the vulgar rabble (*tourbe populaire*) who do not know how to separate truth from falsity."[13] And a comparison with the contemporary English situation reveals just how audacious and precarious, just how imprinted with the antielitism of its Revolutionary origins, the stance of the French *aliénistes* was. Across the channel, the moral treatment – wielded primarily by outsiders to the medical profession – functioned in the early nineteenth-century as an alternative approach to the insane, threatening the growing dominance of medicine in that field.[14]

Among the various charlatanistic roots of the moral treatment (and of moral medicine generally) was religious healing. Père Poution may have been the only *religieux* on Pinel's list of pioneers in the use of moral means on the insane, but Poution, actually the superior of a *maison d'aliénés* at Manosque founded by the order of the Cordeliers,[15] was not an isolated figure. The eighteenth-century regulations, ordinances, and archives of the Brothers of Saint-Jean-de-Dieu make this abundantly clear. The brothers treated a condition which they variously denominated mental alienation (*aliénation d'esprit*), mental disorder (*dérangement d'esprit*), or a "cracked head" (*tête fêlée* or *timbrée*); but they did not attribute any diabolical causal agency to the condition, did not call it "demonic possession," and did not have recourse to exorcism to combat it.[16] Thus they appear to have belonged to the most naturalistic and "enlightened" wing of eighteenth-century French Catholic opinion.[17] And while they provided formal religious offices for

---

[13] Félix Voisin, *De l'utilité du courage et de la réaction morale dans les maladies* (Paris: Thèse de médecine, 1819), pp. 17–19. Falret's pupil Charles Lasègue took similar pains to dissociate the moral treatment from charlatanistic ruse; see "Questions de thérapeutique mentale," *Ann. m.-p.*, 1st ser., 7 (1846): 393.

[14] See Andrew Scull, "From Madness to Mental Illness: Medical Men as Moral Entrepreneurs," *Archives européennes de sociologie* 16 (1975): esp. 225–28. One English midcentury alienist stated that English physicians had expressly rejected the moral treatment and insisted upon the purely organic causes of insanity in order to avoid the suggestion that "the clergyman rather than the physician is the logical person to treat insanity." Quoted in Scull, *Museums of Madness: The Social Organization of Insanity in Nineteenth-Century England* (New York: St. Martin's Press, 1979), p. 167.

[15] Sérieux, "Traitement des maladies mentales" (1924): 113; (1925): 101.

[16] Bonnafous-Sérieux, *Charité de Senlis*, pp. 39, 169.

[17] Among Catholic clerics in the late seventeenth and eighteenth centuries, the concept of demonic possession and the practice of exorcism were in a state of flux. The validity of both had been challenged by physicians and naturalists claiming that the conditions that went under the name of possession should be attributed to natural causes ("black bile, excessive heat in the brain, or a disorder of the imagination") and treated with natural remedies. But it was still officially heretical to disbelieve in the validity of either possession or exorcism. See "Démoniaque" in N. S. Bergier, *Diction-*

their patients – edifying readings of Christian doctrine, daily prayers[18] –
this was hardly the sum total of their intervention.

Rather, the provincial of the order admonished the monks to be
"courteous and gentle" toward the insane residents of their houses, to
"console them," to "speak to them with gentleness and have for them
all the courtesy, tenderness and compassion that befits their condition," even to cater to those (presumably the melancholics suffering
from loss of appetite) who find themselves "disgusted" with the food
served and "wish something special." Regular visits by the religious
personnel were scheduled. The director, who lodged in the same
building as the insane, was to come four times a day, the assistant
prior daily, and the prior weekly; it was specified that the prior see the
lunatics *one after another and separately,* in order to console them, to
guide them to better conduct and to assure himself that they are being
treated as they ought to be."[19] Elsewhere the purpose of these visits
was depicted as *"to recall [the lunatics] to themselves,* to inspire in them a
horror of their disorderliness and the desire to repair it."[20] Repeated
"consolations" were especially recommended for the melancholics,
whose despair aroused apprehension about possible suicidal intent.[21]
The director was also to provide entertaining diversions and "sweeten-
ing appeasements" (*adoucissements*) for the lunatics, including promenades in the garden and games of billiards (for which equipment was
specially purchased at the Charité of Senlis in 1780), lotto, and
tric-trac.[22] Group activities among the lunatics were usually recommended, but only after a new arrival had been screened – kept in a
private room long enough for the monks "to study his character."[23] In
its individual attention and its emphasis on persuasive *douceur,* diver-

naire de théologie (Liège: Société Typographique, 1789–92), Vol. 2, pp. 590–97, esp. p.
594; and "Exorcisme" in ibid., Vol. 3, pp. 362–67. Presumably the Brothers of Saint-
Jean-de-Dieu could avoid the use of exorcism and still remain orthodox by holding
that possession was a rare occurrence rather than an outright impossibility. They
would then form part of a strand of eighteenth-century Catholic opinion which took
the "enlightened" position that the frequent use of exorcism pandered to the super-
stitions of the people. See "Exorcisme," p. 366. It should be added that from at least
the sixteenth century on, possession had been potentially medicalized. Its manifestations were believed to be so similar to those of certain natural diseases (epilepsy,
melancholia, hysteria) that a physician was usually consulted to determine whether a
given condition were possession or a disease, or a combination of both. See D. P.
Walker, *Unclean Spirits: Possession and Exorcism in France and England in the Late Sixteenth and Early Seventeenth Centuries* (Philadelphia: University of Pennsylvania Press,
1981), pp. 10–11.
18 Bonnafous-Sérieux, *Charité de Senlis,* p. 175.
19 Quoted in Sérieux, "Traitement des maladies mentales" (1924): 151–52, my italics.
20 Ibid. (1925): 101, my italics.
21 Quoted in Bonnafoux-Sérieux, *Charité de Senlis,* p. 174.
22 Sérieux, "Traitement des maladies mentales" (1925): 123–24.
23 Ibid., p. 61.

sion, and overcoming self-alienation – and despite a tendency to ignore the distinction between lunatics and *correctionnaires* – the regimen laid down by the eighteenth-century Brothers of Charity thus bears a distinct resemblance to the moral treatment. And not merely warm-hearted custodians of the insane, the Charitains had modest therapeutic ambitions, speaking of their practices as *remèdes* and, in the most favorable circumstances, saying that "after all the remedies appropriate to his cure were administered to him, he returned to his good sense."[24]

Even apart from the care of the insane, religious sick-nurses were fundamentally reliant upon what physicians had come to call "moral medicine" and saw it as their special genius, an expression of their spirituality. On the eve of the Revolution, the Augustinian nursing sisters of the Paris Hôtel-Dieu, protesting administrative reforms which would subordinate them to secular medical men, justified their traditional sovereign position in the hospital wards by citing the curative efficacy of their verbal interventions. As in the moral treatment, the ability to console was crucial:

> It is to women and especially to those who by their vocation are devoted to the continual care of the sick to whom is reserved that empire so sweet that nature and religion give them over the sick, that Providence confers on them. Who better than they know how to console despair, to temper chagrin, to calm anxiety . . . constantly at bedside talking, consoling, does she not more often influence healing than the application of medicines that almost never aid nature?[25]

The art, or science, of consolation, alluded to here and in the documents of the Charitains, was one that Catholicism had cultivated assiduously. To console one's neighbor in times of adversity had always been a duty imposed by Christian charity; and from the patristic period on, Christian ecclesiastics – initially borrowing and transforming the genre of the *consolatio* found in the Greco-Roman philosophical literature – had systematized the rhetorical forms through which human beings might bring this soothing psychological aid to one another. Christian consolation was defined as the presentation of true and solid reasons for accepting suffering; it did not aim at suppressing pain but rather at helping the spirit to bear pain by renewing or expanding hope and fortifying courage. For Catholics, the most effective consolations derived from faith, from the recognition of the terrestrial and therefore limited nature of suffering and of the better life awaiting the individual

---

[24] Ibid., p. 93, which also quotes the Cordeliers to this effect.

[25] Quoted in English translation in Louis S. Greenbaum, "Nurses and Doctors in Conflict: Piety and medicine in the Paris Hôtel-Dieu on the eve of the Revolution," *Clio Medica* 13 (1978): 248, from a manuscript by Joly de Fleury, the champion of the sisters. Much the same idea was expressed by a nineteenth-century handbook on sick-nursing written by a monk; see Frère Hilarion, *Le manuel de l'hospitalier et de l'infirmier* (Paris: L'Editeur, 1829), p. iii.

after death.[26] Some of the abundant Christian consolation literature was directed especially toward the sick and thus had particular resonance and utility for the religious nursing orders.[27] In short, the Idéologues had placed consolation among the moral means available to the physician ("It doubtless behooves the physician to bring the sweetest and wisest consolations to the patient lying on the bed of pain," wrote Cabanis), and Pinel had placed consolation first among the "ways of gentleness" available to the physician employing the moral treatment on the insane;[28] but in matters of consolation, the medical man was the amateur and the cleric the expert and past master.

What happened to these techniques of religious healing once Pinel had subsumed them under the rubrics of "moral treatment" and "moral medicine," formally articulating them as a part of medical-scientific discourse? Certainly it was Pinel's intention that their religious character be effaced. But since religious practitioners continued to be active in the care of the insane – a turn of events that Pinel could not have anticipated from the vantage point of the Revolution – this was no foregone conclusion. The possibility remained that the *aliénistes* would be, in a sense, hoisted by their own petard – that religious healers would not merely survive but would make use of the imprimatur newly placed on moral means by medical-scientific discourse to legitimate their own activities all the more emphatically.

Charenton in the opening years of the nineteenth century, though officially secularized, provided a foretaste of this ironic outcome. Under the administration of the aggressive ex-cleric de Coulmiers, the moral treatment was always touted but, given de Coulmiers's preoccupation with the maintenance of his authority in that institution, it was never represented as an exclusively medical cure. Not only did de Coulmiers insist upon his own equal partnership with the physician Gastaldy in treating lunatics by moral means, but he cultivated, and apparently encouraged his staff to cultivate, specifically religious elements of the treatment. In 1803 he proposed to the Councillor of State

---

[26] Most of these points are discussed in "Consolation chrétienne," in *Dictionnaire de spiritualité ascétique et mystique*, Vol. 3 (Paris: Beauchesne, 1937), esp. columns 1611, 1613. On the classical *consolatio*, see Robert C. Gregg, *Consolation Philosophy: Greek and Christian Paideia in Basil and the Two Gregories* (Philadelphia: Philadelphia Patristic Foundation, 1975), Ch. 1; on the difference between Christian consolation and its classical models, see Charles Favez, *La consolation latine chrétienne* (Paris: J. Vrin, 1937), esp. pp. 169–76.

[27] "Consolation chrétienne" mentions such titles as Etienne Binet, *Consolation et réjoissance pour les malades et les personnes affligées* (1616); Pierre de Besse, *La practique chrestienne pour consoler les malades et assister les criminels qui sont condamnés au supplice* (1624); and Martin de Noirlieu, *Le consolateur des affligés et des malades* (1836).

[28] Cabanis, *Coup d'oeil sur les révolutions et sur la reforme de la médecine*, *O.P.*, Vol. 2, p. 247; Pinel, "Recherches et observations sur le traitement moral des aliénés," *M.S.M.E.* 2 (Year VII): 215.

and Minister of Religion Portalis the appointment of a priest to aid in the moral treatment at Charenton and in the "consolation" that it entailed:

> Charged with the management of a hospice reserved for the treatment of insanity (*démence*), I have noticed that the unfortunates attacked by this cruel malady can find, during the lucid intervals which the malady may allow them, much consolation in spiritual aid dispensed with wisdom. I thought that this moral means could even contribute to reestablishing equilibrium in heads disordered by unforeseen calamities or by revolutionary principles. Consequently I undertook a search for a virtuous and prudent ecclesiastic who had enough courage not to fear communicating with madmen. I believe I have found all the qualities I was seeking in Citizen Godeffroid [*sic*], former curé, my colleague at the Constituent Assembly. . . . He has devoted a part of his time to visiting the poor at the Hôtel-Dieu, and it is there that I went to find someone I could engage in helping me to console the insane at Charenton.[29]

In this patronage effort, de Coulmiers was clearly motivated by bonds of friendship – Godefroy was experiencing "interminable difficulties in obtaining his pension"[30] – but he was no doubt concerned as well with the balance of power at Charenton and, to this end, wished to increase the size and influence of the nonmedical staff.

The climate of opinion de Coulmiers successfully fostered at Charenton – before the arrival of the "medicalizing" Dr. Royer-Collard – is also revealed in a brochure published in 1804 by a certain Dr. Giraudy, the adjunct physician of the establishment and a disciple of de Coulmiers's collaborator Dr. Gastaldy. The brochure, entitled "Should not religious morality be employed in certain cases as a means of curing insanity?" and intended as a sketch for a larger work on the subject, is suffused with Catholic piety. Taking as his starting point the Pinellian position that the "passions play a great role" in the etiology of insanity, Giraudy sought to determine which "moral means" were most forceful for "combating, curbing and weakening" pathological passions, or alternatively for "directing" them. His conclusion, albeit still tentative and based on only four case studies, was that the "application of religious morality" – "always gentle (*douce*), consoling" – was decidedly superior. Significantly, two of the treatments described in the brochure were not even performed by Giraudy himself but by a "sensitive, spiritual, virtuous and learned ecclesiastic." One reclusive melancholic who had suffered a reverse of fortune was made more cheerful and sociable when Giraudy "fixed his attention on a comparison between the good things of this short life and the eternal felicity which an

---

[29] AN: AJ² 81, Dossier: Culte, letter dated 21 frimaire Year XI.

[30] Ibid., undated petition to the director-général de la dette publique; and a doleful letter of Godefroy to de Coulmiers dated 2 fructidor Year XI, stating "Je me repose sur la continuation de vos bontés."

irreproachable conscience assures us." Another melancholic, following
the example of the priestly counselor assigned to him, became a regular worshiper; this new turning was said to have caused his reason
gradually to "resume its dominion." Pervasive fears of persecution
were overcome in yet a third melancholic by "frequentation of the
tribunal of penitence." In the final case, that of a peasant afflicted with
mania, reasonableness and an "ineffable calm" were produced when
the patient was brought back to the Catholic faith of his childhood and
was "made to feel the impossibility of penetrating the mysteries of
religion and the necessity of believing in them without reservation."[31]
Thus, placing himself in the Pinellian tradition at the outset of his
investigations, Giraudy ended by suggesting implicitly that the moral
treatment might be metamorphosed into a form of pastoral care for
which ecclesiastical personnel were especially well equipped. It is likely
that the antimedical de Coulmiers applauded this conclusion.

The culmination of the tendency seen in germ at de Coulmiers's
Charenton came several decades later with the offensives of one of the
leading members of the order of Saint-Jean-de-Dieu, the personally
eccentric Xavier Tissot, who took the name of Frère Hilarion. A mental
patient at Charenton himself between 1810 and 1814 (his "delirium," as
Esquirol later reported, had alternated between mania and long intervals of melancholy), Tissot enrolled briefly at the Paris medical faculty
and ultimately decided, under the joint influence of a book on insanity
by the phrenologist Spurzheim and a biography of Saint-Jean-de-Dieu,
to devote his life to the care of the insane. In the 1820s and 1830s he
was instrumental in creating a half dozen new lunatic institutions. One
of these was in the Lozère, an autarkic backwater of nineteenth-century France, where the ever colorful Hilarion rode on horseback
flanked by a bodyguard of mounted monks, causing the madmen in
his care to take him for the returned emperor Napoleon and the peasants of the region to "pronounce his name with a veneration tinged
with superstitious terror."[32] Well versed in the basic writings of the
Parisian psychiatric school, Tissot/Hilarion undertook a militant campaign against the psychiatric doctors and in favor of a thoroughgoing
religious appropriation of the moral treatment.

---

[31] Giraudy, *La morale religieuse ne doit-elle pas être employée dans certain cas, comme moyen curatif de l'aliénation mentale?"* (Paris: Impr. de Laurens, n.d.), esp. pp. 5, 7–8, 7 n1, 9–11. No title page; the BN catalogue gives the publication date as the Year XII. On Giraudy's position at Charenton and his relation to Dr. Gastaldy, see Ch. Fr. S. Giraudy, *Mémoire sur la maison nationale de Charenton exclusivement destinée au traitement des aliénés* (Paris: Impr. de la Société de Médecine, Year XII/1804).

[32] On these biographical details, see G. Bollotte, "Les châteaux de frère Hilarion," *Information psychiatrique* (October 1966): esp. 723–25; and André Chagny, *L'ordre hos-pitalier de Saint Jean de Dieu*, Vol. 2 (Lyon: Impr. de M. Lescuyer, 1953), pp. 5–7. Robert Castel touches briefly on Hilarion in *L'ordre psychiatrique: L'âge d'or d'aliénisme* (Paris: Minuit, 1976), pp. 216–17.

Like Giraudy, Tissot began with the Pinellian premise: Insanity is frequently produced by *causes morales* and, as such, can be cured by *remèdes moraux*. This basic fact determined the division – and the hierarchy – of labor in the treatment of the insane. The primary caretaker was the "director of the moral treatment"; subordinate to him was the physician, who attended to physical matters, prescribing the usual array of baths, purgatives, laxatives, and infusions for the bodily ailments which were supposed routinely to accompany and complicate insanity. As to the content of the moral treatment, Tissot distinguished rigorously between the "religious-moral treatment" ("my method") and the "moral-philosophical treatment" advocated by physicians who had studied insanity and who were almost universally "blemished with atheism." "In the twenty years that I have successfully treated lunatics," he wrote in 1837, "I have always employed religious means as the foundation of the moral treatment." "Supernatural effects," drawing their source from the Divinity, were undoubtedly the most potent healing agents available. "What a difference between the morality of the Gospel and the maxims of the philosophers! between divine consolations and human consolations!" Thus, for example, "religious monomania" – note that Tissot had assimilated the most up-to-date psychiatric nomenclature – could be expeditiously cured through "prayer, religious consolation, religious music" and sometimes "confession to an enlightened and charitable priest."[33]

As might be expected of someone of his religious calling, Tissot had an in-depth knowledge of the techniques of consolation. A chapter of the general manual of sick-nursing he published in 1829 set forth an entire repertory of consolations to be offered to the afflicted under various circumstances and noted that inventiveness at consolation, a therapeutic gift called the "thousand ingenuities for mitigating chagrin," was an inspiration of the Holy Spirit. "Nothing," he reminded his readers, "will better prove your charity toward your fellows than vigilance and constant application in consoling the sick." A sympathetic sharing of pain was sometimes recommended: "If you see a patient who is troubled and anxious, tell him how much you are touched by what he is suffering." With those patients whose illness had removed their "good sense" and who stubbornly refused their medicine or even all nourishment – a perennial problem in any hospital setting – Tissot's strategy of consolation entailed tender cajolery and religious example. "Take care not to irritate them. Try to persuade them by words such as these: 'If you love life, my dear brother, you ought to consider that you are rejecting what is given you to prolong it and for your cure. This

---

[33] Tissot, *Mémoire en faveur des aliénés* (Lyon: Impr. de Pelagaud, Lesne et Crozet, 1837), pp. 6–9, 11, 13, 18–19, 22, 35.

food (or medicine) is not as bitter as the gall which was presented to Jesus Christ on the Cross; he, however, tasted it out of love for you and to carry out the will of your Celestial Father. For love of him and in honor of his passion, then, do not refuse what is offered you for your relief and to carry out in you the will of God.' "[34]

Tissot's characterization of the moral treatment of the physicians as "moral-philosophical" derived from a passage in Pinel's *Traité* which advised that the pathological passions of certain mental patients be "vanquished" and their minds "fortified" by the "moral maxims of the ancients, the writings of Plato, Plutarch, Seneca, the *Tusculan Disputations* of Cicero."[35] In addition to harboring a pious distrust of the putative wisdom of the pagans of antiquity, Tissot advanced an astute, practical objection to Pinel's erudite therapeutic strategy:

> Since the majority of lunatics belong to the working classes, how can one speak to them of Plato, Seneca, Plutarch and Cicero? What sort of impression will that produce on them . . . ? But the words of the Gospel! These are at the elevated level of the greatest geniuses and equally within the grasp of the most humble peasant.[36]

A final justification for Tissot's choice of "religious means" was provided by his historical understanding of the specific nature of the moral cause of most insanity. The number of lunatics was, he believed, growing continually, and the trend was attributable to increasing "forgetfulness of religious principles." The case of England had long since demonstrated this verity: The abandonment of Catholicism at the time of Henry VIII had produced a "prodigious multitude of lunatics," turning that island country into the "classic land of madness."[37] Religious therapy, then, could be safely assumed to supply precisely the ballast that was lacking in a lunatic.

From all of these considerations combined issued Tissot's concrete recommendations for selecting the personnel of an institution for the insane. The accredited medical doctor, as already noted, was relegated to a peripheral role. The central figure, the so-called director of the moral treatment (a neologism with overtones of the familiar term *directeur de conscience*, a priest who served as a personal confessor), was not defined by a set of formal professional credentials. Rather, he was described as a "man of lofty charity and observant religiosity who inspires in the insane a well-deserved trust and attachment." Similarly,

---

[34] Tissot, *Manuel de l'hospitalier*, pp. 5–7. Cf. Pinel's moral treatment for a lunatic refusing to eat, described in Chapter 3 of this book.

[35] See Pinel, *Traité médico-philosophique sur l'aliénation mentale, ou la manie*, 1st ed. (Paris: Richard, Caille et Ravier, Year IX/1801), p. 36; and Tissot, *Mémoire*, p. 8.

[36] *Mémoire*, p. 9.

[37] Tissot, prospectus for the sanitorium at Leyme, Article 1, reprinted in Bollotte, "Châteaux," pp. 725–26; *Mémoire*, p. 11.

the attendants (*infirmiers*) were to be "men of a tested virtue and piety; for how can lunatics, most of whom are addicted to vicious and erotic habits, be cured if those who surround them do not bear a religious stamp?" Tissot's prospectus for the sanatorium at Leyme identified these attendants and nurses simply as "monks and nuns" trained by religious communities especially founded for that purpose.[38] In a somewhat later and more strident phase of his career, Tissot appropriated medical values but reversed the standard medical labels by asserting that his own treatment program followed the "rules of science," while the physicians' attempt to cure insanity "without spiritual means" was a brand of "ignorance and charlatanism." He also began to model himself more literally on the saintly exorcist Hilarion whose name he had assumed.[39]

The potential challenge to the medicalization of insanity represented by Tissot's program is obvious, especially in light of the palpable success of his own and other religious congregations in establishing and operating lunatic hospitals throughout provincial France during the period of the constitutional monarchy. The degree to which the nursing orders had become serious rivals of the *médecins aliénistes* will be further discussed in Chapter 8 in the context of the debate over the Law of 1838. The crucial point here is that the monks and nuns did not so much advance an alternative mode of treatment as interpret the *aliénistes'* mode to their own advantage – reclaiming and accentuating the religious elements that had originally helped to inspire the moral treatment, using the medical-scientific authority that validated moral means in order to subvert that same authority. For both the Parisian *aliénistes* and the Charitain healers of the insane, the moral treatment was the founding paradigm; for both, gentleness and consolation led the way to cure.

Indeed, at the very same time that the *aliénistes* began to mythologize Pinel's introduction of the moral treatment as the literal act of unchaining the lunatics at Bicêtre,[40] the Brothers of Charity gave iconographic representation to their own variant on that same dramatic gesture. In a

---

[38] Tissot, *Mémoire*, p. 13; Leyme prospectus, Article 6, in Bollotte, "Châteaux," p. 726.

[39] According to Walker, *Unclean Spirits*, p. 9, Jerome's *Life of St. Hilarion* was "one of the most authoritative and frequently cited Patristic sources for exorcism." In his later phase, Tissot construed insanity as possession and stipulated that a "holy exorcist" participate in its treatment. See, for this and the phrases quoted above, his *Le discernement des esprits, ou relation d'une possession du démon à St-Laurent-du-Pape (Ardèche)* (Montélimar: Impr. de Bourron, n.d. [1842]), pp. 11–14.

[40] The mythologization began in 1823 and was given canonical form in a paper presented to the Academy of Medicine by Pinel *fils* in 1836; see Gladys Swain, *Le sujet de la folie: Naissance de la psychiatrie* (Toulouse: Privat, 1977), pp. 41–47. On paintings depicting the mythic event, see Dora B. Weiner, "The Apprenticeship of Philippe Pinel: A New Document, 'Observations of Citizen Pussin on the Insane,' " *American Journal of Psychiatry* 136 (1979): esp. 1128.

lithograph dating from about 1830, a large and sparsely clad man (identified in the caption as a "poor lunatic") is leaning on the shoulder of a Charitain, who is removing heavy chains from him. Another monk is adorning him with new robes, indicative of the fundamental transformation in his nature that has just occurred. The lunatic's eyes are haggard yet filled with gratitude. A jailer, carrying his ring of keys, looks on astonished.[41] Nor were the Charitains alone in appropriating this symbolism. The Sisters of the Bon-Sauveur of Caen made use of the same symbolic motif to suggest that *they* had spontaneously invented the basic principle of the moral treatment. In a paper read before the local savant society of Caen in 1835, the abbé Jamet recounted a memorable incident from the annals of the order. The mother superior, proclaiming that a lunatic was not a slave, had ordered the iron shackles removed from a furious madwoman and had found her thereby rendered wondrously calm and tractable.[42]

The anticlerical current in early médecine mentale

A residual religious sensibility may have initially shaped the secular moral treatment, with its emphasis on consolation. After all, both Pinel and Esquirol had trained for careers in the church before choosing medicine and, at least in Pinel's case, a life devoid of Catholic observance.[43] But nonetheless – indeed perhaps because of its close and ambivalent ties to religion – early *médecine mentale* was marked by a persistent strain of anticlericalism, of hostility toward organized religion and distrust of religion generally. These sentiments clustered around three practical and closely related issues: the role of religion in the etiology of mental illness (or what might be called the "hygienic" value of piety); the role of religion in the treatment of mental illness; and finally the optimal composition of the nursing staff of a *maison d'aliénés*.

The tone was set in the writings of Pinel, which address the first two

---

41 See the lithograph by Langlumé, reproduced in Cousson, *Magallon,* plate following p. 144, and described in ibid., p. 158.

42 Abbé Jamet, "Congrégation du Bon-Sauveur," *Mémoires de l'Académie royale des sciences, arts et belles-lettres de Caen* (1836): 391–92. The event took place in 1820 during the transfer of the lunatics from the departmental prison.

43 See Semelaigne, *Les grands aliénistes français* (Paris: Steinheil, 1894), pp. 16–17, 120–21. Pinel received minor orders from the Pères de la Doctrine. He seems not to have undergone a religious crisis, but just to have drifted away from these religious mentors and toward the medical calling traditional in his family. Esquirol was enrolled in the seminary of Saint-Sulpice at Issy, near Paris, when the Revolution disrupted his clerical training. On Pinel's adult religious beliefs and practices, see the testimony of his nephew Casimir Pinel, "Lettres de Pinel précédées d'une notice plus étendue sur sa vie," *Gaz. hebd. de med.* 6 (1859): 340–41. I have found no comparable source for Esquirol.

of these issues. In 1790, following the decrees of the Constituent Assembly that abolished the religious communities and released monks and nuns from their vows, Pinel published an occasional piece. The decrees did not make departure from the monasteries and convents mandatory. Rather, the eventual withering away of these institutions was insured by provisions forbidding the taking of vows by new recruits and the future foundation of comparable communities.[44] Hence many who had chosen the cloister now found themselves paralyzed by uncertainty and subjected to intense pressure from the church, which reminded them of the irrevocable nature of their promises and of the disgrace attached to a return to the world. It was to these "pusillanimous and irresolute" monks and nuns that Pinel addressed his "Medical Reflections on the Monastic Condition," believing that it was "perhaps reserved to Medicine" to counsel and reassure them – to transform, in other words, a problem of religious conscience into a clearcut medical and hygienic matter concerning the "immutable laws which [our] mental faculties and physical organization prescribe for us." While not wanting to "alarm the piety of devout persons," he could not evade his obligation to point out the unhealthy aspects of the cloistered life. "Man is made for society," he stated, giving assent to the credo of forthright gregariousness of the eighteenth-century philosophe; and he who "breaks his ties with society can only denature his being." For most people, days spent in silent and sedentary contemplation without external stimuli produced a numb enervation in whose wake came ill humor, attacks of the deepest melancholy, or even madness. In addition, the cloistral requirement of "shackl[ing] all the penchants of the heart," including the sexual impulses, engaged the regular clergy in "recurring self-combat."[45]

A brief case history of a "young monk whom I have directed by my counsels" illustrated these points and indicated the novel professional role Pinel had already carved out for himself. Over the course of several years, he dispensed to the young man not medical help strictly construed – the "resources of pharmacy" had already been exhausted when this young man sought him out – but a kind of secular pastoral care reliant on moral means. The young man's problem was his unsuccessful struggle with his sexuality. Despite his elevated piety, he had been unable to banish from his mind "enticing images of voluptuousness," which filled him with remorse and made him almost wish for death. Marriage, which Pinel regarded as the obvious natural remedy, had already been ruled out. And so, diagnosing as nervous illness (*maux*

---

[44] On the decrees of February 13–19, 1790, see Jean Imbert, *Le droit hospitalier de la Révolution et de l'Empire* (Paris: Sirey, 1954), pp. 137–38; and Marcel Garaud, *La Révolution et l'égalité civile* (Paris: Sirey, 1953), pp. 122–27.

[45] "Reflections médicales sur l'état monastique," *Journal gratuit*, 9th Class: Health (1790): 81–93, esp. 81–83, 85–86, 91–92.

nerveux) what the young man experienced as spiritual imperfection, "I assumed a consoling tone to reestablish calm in the timorous spirit of this unfortunate cenobite." (Was the physician deliberately playing on stock religious language here? A sixteenth-century religious manual had, for example, the title *La consolation des âmes timorées;* and helping the perplexed and anxious to make confident choices between alternatives had always been one of the standard functions of pastoral care.)[46] In addition, Pinel prescribed a special diet, long walks, and strenuous agricultural labor for the patient, and thus succeeded in diverting him from his melancholy preoccupations. But as proud as he was of this therapeutic success – a quotation from the monk's most recent letter was even offered as a testimonial – the point of the case history, and of the entire article, was to underscore the unsalutary nature of extreme religious devotion. Having had clinical experience with the illnesses such practices brought in their train, Pinel could only commend the legislative measures of the Constituent Assembly against the religious congregations.[47]

In the *Traité,* Pinel expanded the scope of this theme through a discussion of "religious insanity," the manias and melancholias with religious motifs that afflicted the ordinary layman as well as the cleric. He repeatedly stressed the tenacity of this form of insanity and its virtual imperviousness to cure. For how could one find a countervailing "moral means" that carried more authority and was more striking to the imagination than religion itself – the very religion that was here nourishing the pathological obsessions, delusions, and fears? The symbolic practices and the rhetoric of religion were, from the Pinellian perspective, the ultimate moral means.[48] Thus Pinel believed that insofar as cure was possible in these cases, its precondition was a thoroughgoing secularization or moral sanitization of the environment, a radical scheme for which permission was apparently never granted him at Bicêtre.[49] One actual approximation of this "ideal type" of therapy met with resounding failure: Pinel reported trying to cure a lunatic at Bicêtre who believed himself the omnipotent fourth person of the Trinity by having a convalescent patient recite in his presence verses by Voltaire expounding the principles of natural religion. But the "fanatic" only called Voltaire a godless blasphemer and, far from improving, entered into a state of furor.[50] By the time of the second edition of the

---

[46] See "Consolation chrétienne," column 1616; the treatise, by Louis de Blos, is the French translation of his *Consolatio pusillanimorum* (1555). On the traditional functions of pastoral care, see William A. Clebsch and Charles R. Jaekle, *Pastoral Care in Historical Perspective* (New York: Harper & Row, 1967), pp. 8–10.

[47] Pinel, "Etat monastique," pp. 91–93.

[48] See Pinel, *Traité,* 1st ed., pp. 70–71; and *Traité,* 2d ed. (Paris: Brosson, 1809), p. 266.

[49] *Traité,* 1st ed., pp. 75–76, describes the scheme in detail.

[50] Ibid., pp. 73, 73–74 n1.

Traité, Pinel seems to have given up active doctrinal intervention as a mode of therapy and to have settled instead upon a strategy of omission – routinely withholding, despite repeated requests from the patient, books of devotion and visits from the confessor. He had learned from experience that continued access to the paraphernalia of religion was the "surest way of perpetuating the insanity or even of rendering it incurable."[51]

Exploring the etiology of religious insanity, Pinel observed that special historical circumstances might play an influential role. Thus the Revolution, creating strife between those priests who did and those who did not accept the Civil Constitution of the Clergy, had proven a "fecund source of insanity for fretful consciences." But in general the crucial causal factor was the quality of the religious experience itself. Pinel believed that religious insanity stemmed from a febrile and fanatical religion, and hence the great pathogenic potential of certain forms of religious belief and practice did not, in his canon, impugn all forms. He cited the contemporary English psychiatric literature on the demonstrably "baneful effects" of the "rigid intolerance of the Methodist sect and . . . its desolate doctrine, always filled with threats of celestial vengeance and of the torments of hell." Methodism, he said, had its analogue in France in that variety of Catholicism whose sermons, confessionals, and works of piety were "suffused with a tinge of black melancholy and with . . . a fiery morality, suitable to reduce human weakness to despair." So strong was this connection between "desolate" religion and insanity that Pinel had even been able to draw up an ecclesiastical topography of Paris on the basis of clinical data provided by his large patient population of urban lunatics. "My daily notes, taken at the time of admission of insane women into the hospice [of the Salpêtrière], can serve to indicate the neighborhoods of Paris where this morose and splenetic devotion predominates" and those where, by contrast, the prevalence of "a compassionate and enlightened piety" could temporarily "suspend the development of a [religious] insanity ready to declare itself."[52] (Pinel left the two types of Catholicism unnamed, but he was probably referring to the rigorism of the Jansenists as opposed to the more lenient attitude toward sin adopted by the Jesuits.)[53]

Religious counsel of the second type was, Pinel acknowledged with his customary frankness, much akin to the moral treatment of the physician; so professional boundaries could be genuinely blurred. Here

---

[51] *Traité,* 2d ed., p. 268.
[52] Ibid., pp. 268, 270.
[53] See the discussion of nineteenth-century Jansenism and Jesuitism in Theodore Zeldin, "The Conflict of Moralities: Confession, Sin and Pleasure in the Nineteenth Century," in T. Zeldin, ed., *Conflicts in French Society: Anticlericalism, Education and Morals in the Nineteenth Century* (London: Allen & Unwin, 1970), esp. pp. 22–30.

Pinel's illustrative case study concerned a female counterpart to the monk of his 1790 article – a domestic servant whose strict piety conflicted wth the "effervescence of [her] ardent temperament" and drove her to a state of bad conscience bordering on suicidal despair. Just as the history of the monk had shown that the physician dispensing moral medicine took on a pastoral role, so, conversely, the history of the servant girl showed that religious pastoral care could be medically beneficial:

> In her extreme perplexity, she turned to a compassionate and enlightened confessor who sought to rouse her courage and who often repeated to her gently (*avec douceur*) that she ought to cleave to God in order to recover her inner peace. The good priest persevered, holding out consoling words to her and inviting her to wait with resignation for the triumph of grace. . . . Thus, far from inspiring fear for the future, he sought to restore calm in that agitated soul and to oppose great passion with the best remedy – patience and time. But the [girl's] anxieties and prolonged sleeplessness eventually produced an insanity which was treated at the Salpêtrière *following the same moral principles.*[54]

Thus Pinel's *médecine mentale* entailed a highly selective anticlericalism. As a physician, he approached religion with entirely human and pragmatic criteria, noting, almost like a functionalist anthropologist of a later era, the reality of its natural effects but giving no credence to its putative supernatural powers or significance. Hence he vigorously opposed all those religious practices with negative natural consequences, just as he was forthcoming in his praise for those with positive and healing ones.[55] Applying this general and even-handed principle, he came out against religious ministrations to gravely ill hospital patients – including presumably even the sacrament of extreme unction – on the grounds that they lowered patient morale and hence compounded physical disability. Again disclaiming any intent to deprive "pious souls" of the "consolations of religion" that they craved, he wrote in 1793, "I have sometimes applied myself to comparing the condition of patients before and after these religious ceremonies, and how many times have I not seen the most striking [physical] differences. . . . Let us refrain from aggravating the dark despondency of a

---

[54] *Traité*, 2d ed., pp. 270–71, my italics.

[55] Elsewhere in his writings Pinel acknowledged the healing power religious ceremonies exercised on the insane but insisted that this efficacy derived, not from the supernatural causes the priests alleged, but from the natural, "moral means" that these ceremonies actually mobilized – especially the calming, diverting, or persuasive effect of the ceremonial pomp itself. He applied this interpretation to the techniques used by ancient Egyptian priests on "crowds of melancholics" gathered on Nile riverboats (*Traité*, 2d ed., pp. 259–60) as well as to the Christian exorcism of maniacs (*Traité*, 1st ed., pp. 247–48).

fainthearted patient who sees in the approach of the priest only a preliminary to the approach of a sepulchre."[56]

This suspicion of religious intervention in the treatment process quickly became a stereotypical feature in the popular conception of the new science of insanity. A satire of 1826 took the form of letters written home by an Englishman traveling in France who feigns madness in order to enter, explore, and ultimately to expose Esquirol's sanatorium. It included an episode in which the protagonist, suddenly seized by fever, asks Esquirol's nephew Dr. Mitivié to send for a confessor. His request is met with stony, categorical refusal. Abandoning his arch tone, the author ended the piece with an earnest plea that, instead of driving away the ministers of religion, the Parisian *maisons d'aliénés* allow their most despairing inmates to participate in religious observances. "For wouldn't that only be to offer up to the All-Powerful these cruel ailments, the sole ailments whose cure the Supreme Intelligence seems to have reserved entirely to Himself?"[57]

The satirist, of course, exaggerated the situation, but his depiction was far from wholly inaccurate. "Several important physicians wish never to hear a chapel or priests mentioned in a lunatic hospice," attested Scipion Pinel, the son of the founding father, in 1836. Yet most early nineteenth-century *médecins aliénistes*, including Pinel *fils* himself, adopted a more nuanced and less obdurate anticlerical position. Ferrus, who like his teacher Philippe Pinel was fond of quoting ancient pagan authors on the "remedies for the maladies of the soul," achieved a certain centrality in the new profession when he was appointed to the state bureaucracy in 1835 as inspector-general of lunatic houses. Although he took the position that religious services and images ought to be forbidden in the asylum lest they "exacerbate the delirium of religious maniacs," he softened his dogmatism by adding that it was permissible for certain mental patients to be brought to a "separate chapel" for purposes of worship. Scipion Pinel's opinion was similar. Given the etiology of certain forms of insanity, no physician could afford to adopt a laissez-faire policy toward religion in a lunatic asylum. "In those countries still profoundly subjected to Catholic authority and in which, for this reason, religious monomanias proliferate in a thousand bizarre and mystical varieties, the influence of a house of worship and the presence of those who officiate at it can often be very injurious." But as long as religion was rigorously excluded from the lunatic hospital itself and confined to a chapel where carefully selected patients could attend services, it could be quite useful to certain convalescents who, recovering

---

[56] Pinel, *The Clinical Training of Doctors: An Essay of 1793*, ed. Dora B. Weiner (Baltimore: Johns Hopkins University Press, 1980), p. 48 (of French text), my translation. The same opinion was expressed in Voisin, "Utilité du courage," pp. 26–27.

[57] *Supplément au voyage en France de M. Leigh* (Montpellier: Impr. Tournel, 1826), pp. 21–22, 36, BN: Te[66] 3.

along with their reason a need for their former religious customs, might "draw from these observances incentives both for hope and for resignation." Salutary results depended, however, upon strict rationing:

> [Priestly] exhortations should be rare. . . . Too often repeated they lose their effect or even become dangerous, as can be observed in the asylums for madmen which the Quakers founded in Pennsylvania. The patients are brought to the chapel twice a week and are almost always more agitated when they exit: religious monomanias become incurable there.[58]

The issue of religion in the asylum was not simply one of therapeutic strategy. It was also one of establishing definitively the locus of authority within that institution; and this latter aspect of the problem evoked the most visceral expressions of anticlericalism from the *aliénistes*. The nature of the moral treatment endowed the *aliéniste* with something of the persona of a secular priest. As Scipion Pinel described him, "Such a man is more than a physician, he is a consoler and a father, and it is not easy to find him in our era of egoism and greed for gain." To have both ecclesiastic and physician in a lunatic hospital was thus to have two father figures, two bringers of consolation, two healers of the spirit who employed moral means. The redundancy might well undermine the authority of the nontraditional figure, the *aliéniste*. Members of the Esquirol circle were acutely aware of this potential conflict. Scipion Pinel stated as axiomatic that ministers of religion should be permitted to enter the asylum only if the chief physician retained "complete authority."[59] Jean-Pierre Falret noted the "objections" which this "delicate and complex" issue characteristically raised in his colleagues: "What ought to be the relation of the priest to the physician and to the lunatics? Is it not to be feared that the priest will usurp, even destroy the authority of the physician?" Or, reduced to its simplest terms, "Will the priest submit to medical authority?"[60]

The *aliénistes* said little of a specific nature about their conflicts with priests, probably regarding the subject as a highly sensitive one best left undiscussed. But about another strained relationship, that with the nursing sisters, they were less reticent – perhaps because the skirmishes occurred with greater frequency, perhaps because the sisters, being lower than the priests in the hierarchies of both church and gender, were perceived as more acceptable objects of overt hostility. In

---

58 G. Ferrus, *Des aliénés* (Paris: Huzard, 1834), pp. 257, 265; Scipion Pinel, *Traité complet du régime sanitaire des aliénés, ou manuel complet des éstablissements qui leur sont consacrés* (Paris: Mauprivez, 1836), pp. 14–15.

59 S. Pinel, *Traité complet*, pp. v, 14.

60 Falret, *De l'utilité de la religion dans le traitement des maladies mentales et dans les asiles d'aliénés* (Paris: Impr. de Bourgogne et Martinet, 1845), pp. 14–15. This brochure is identical to pp. 93–106 of part 2 of Falret's article "Visite à l'établissement d'aliénés d'Illenau"; the entire article can be found in *Ann. m.-p.*, 1st ser., 5 (1845): 419–44 and 6 (1845): 69–106.

any case, an examination of this latter relationship is necessary to complete our discussion of early psychiatric anticlericalism.

As noted above, the nursing orders, reinstated during the Napoleonic regime, proliferated during the Restoration. They continued to hold their own under the July Monarchy, and they experienced a euphoric expansion after the Falloux Law of 1850. The reasons for their post-Revolutionary success were not only ideological (a reason more relevant in some regions of France than in others) but practical. In the absence of any concept of lay "professional" nursing, it was difficult to conjure up a substitute corps of sick-nurses. Those recruited with great difficulty during the Revolution had been untrained and lacking in the dedication of their religious predecessors; they demanded much higher wages, and they readily quit to get married or to accept better paying jobs elsewhere.[61]

But if the reinstatement of the nursing sisters solved certain practical problems, it created others. The prerogatives of these grey-clad women wearing the cornettes of their order frequently collided with the prerogatives of an increasingly self-conscious medical profession. The historian Jacques Léonard has enumerated the kinds of quarrels to which the two groups were prone in an urban hospital setting. They had rival material interests, the sisters giving priority to the maintenance of their chapel and convent, the doctors wanting to repair or enlarge dilapidated or cramped hospital facilities. They disagreed about the administration of the hospital pharmacy, the nuns wanting to run it themselves, although they were technically required to be supervised by a certified pharmacist. They clashed over the internal regimen of the hospital, the nuns asserting their moral authority, in defiance of hospital rules, by refusing admission to pregnant girls, prostitutes, and women afflicted with venereal disease. Far from winning easy victories, physicians, Léonard notes, generally "suffered in the nineteenth century from their rather subordinate position in matters of . . . hospital management." They were inexperienced interlopers on terrain long occupied, controlled, and tenaciously held by nuns.[62]

How did this situation affect the *médecin aliéniste* in particular? Three basic arrangements, or combinations of lay and religious elements, offered themselves as options in post-Revolutionary lunatic institutions: (1) A public institution could be staffed by wage-earning lay *filles* (or *femmes*) *de service* or their male counterparts, *serviteurs*; (2) a public institution could, by means of a formal agreement called a *traité*, engage a religious congregation to furnish the requisite nursing personnel for a specified fee; or (3) a private institution accepting patients from

---

[61] Léonard, "Femmes, religion et médecine," pp. 889–91; Dora B. Weiner, "The French Revolution, Napoleon, and the Nursing Profession," *Bull. Hist. Med.* 46 (1972): esp. 290.

[62] Léonard, "Femmes, religion et médecine," pp. 894–95.

the public authorities could be established and run by a religious congregation so that a virtual religious homogeneity in the personnel
obtained.[63] The Paris hospices of Bicêtre and the Salpêtrière fit the first,
atypical model. Staffed by the sisters of charity before the Revolution,
they remained in lay hands even after *religieuses* of various orders had,
under the Consulate and Empire, resumed charge of the nursing in
most Paris public hospitals.[64] Thus in 1807, several years before Pussin's death, Pinel pressed for the appointment of a second superintendent to aid him at the Salpêtrière; and, in sharp contrast to the clerical
appointment de Coulmiers lobbied for at Charenton at about the same
time, the candidate Pinel advanced – Mme Dufresne, a "benevolent"
widow possessed of "a sound judgment" – was devoid of "any religiosity or religious affiliation worth mentioning.[65]

If instead a public institution turned over the nursing function to a
religious congregation, it automatically turned over a large and not
clearly bounded area of managerial authority as well. "In all the hospices of Angers [of which there were four, all receiving lunatics, at the
beginning of the nineteenth century], the police and the general super-
intendence are entirely in the hands of the mother superior," wrote the
local administrative commission to the prefect of the Maine-et-Loire in
1819. And when, a decade later, the prefect of that same department
was negotiating with the Sisters of the Bon-Sauveur of Caen about the
possibility of their staffing a projected departmental asylum, the nuns
insisted that they, rather than the prefect, would choose the physician
of the establishment and that the physician would be responsible to
them alone.[66]

No wonder, then, that the nursing sisters got a bad name in certain
circles. When the Conseil général of the Eure decided that the department would establish its own lunatic asylum, it appointed a commission to research the best way of carrying out the project. Seeking advice on the issue of a nursing staff, the commissioners interviewed the

---

[63] In this last case, nursing was done by the members of the congregation, though if the
latter were nuns and the institution catered to lunatics of both sexes, lay *gardiens* were
hired as surveillants in the male wards. Heavy manual labor was also assigned to lay
male employees, but nuns attended to secretarial work and lighter menial chores such
as cooking and laundering. On these points see Claude Quétel, "Garder les fous dans
un asile de province au XIXe siècle: Le Bon-Sauveur de Caen," *Annales de Normandie*
(1979): 79, 97–98.

[64] Weiner, "Nursing Profession," pp. 277–78; and Imbert, *Droit hospitalier*, pp. 251–52,
which notes, however, that a resident priest was provided for both Bicêtre and the
Salpêtrière by a decree of the Conseil général des hospices in the Year X.

[65] AN: AJ[16] 6308, "Séance publique de l'Ecole de médecine de Paris du 11 novembre
1807, Discours de M. le Professeur Sue," pp. 7–8.

[66] Cited in Jacques Petit, "Folie, langage, pouvoirs en Maine-et-Loire (1800–1841)," *Revue d'histoire moderne et contemporaine* 27 (1980): 538–39. The Sisters of the Bon-Sauveur
adhered to the same principle in Caen; see Quétel, "Garder les fous," p. 101.

Salpêtrière *aliénistes* Mitivié and Falret, who pronounced strongly in favor of hired lay help. " 'With *serviteurs à gages,'* they told us, 'you will be masters in your own house.' " They readily acknowledged that a lay staff brought problems of its own, usually in the form of its members' distracted preoccupation with their personal lives. But, compared with the problems entailed by a religious community, it was, in their view, doubtless the lesser evil. Most of the provincial physicians whom the commissioners consulted made similar pronouncements, citing the refusal of the nursing sisters to submit to administrative supervision even in such technical matters as bookkeeping; their tendency to ne-glect the prescriptions of medical men in matters of treatment; and their frequent absence from service due to their numerous pious and devotional commitments.[67]

The experience of Dr. Antoine Chambeyron with the nursing sisters of Saint-Vincent-de-Paul at the public asylum in Rennes in the 1830s and 1840s happens to be richly documented; and the physician's writ-ten testimony conveys the quality of that daily friction between medical and clerical personnel that could inspire and sustain psychiatric anti-clericalism. Chambeyron, a member of the Esquirol circle, was a highly literate man of generous liberal-democratic political sentiments. He had translated Hoffbauer's manual of forensic psychiatry from the German and in 1834 had prepared a volume for the Bibliothèque Populaire entitled *Constitutions and Charters: Elementary Notions of Political Right* intended to aid the lower classes in their self-education for participa-tory government.[68] Predictably enough, Chambeyron arrived in Brit-tany in 1835 full of plans for the reform of Saint-Méen, the institution to which he had been appointed. When he found himself thwarted, as was often the case, he wrote copious letters to the local hospice admin-istration (his employer) voicing his complaints, defending himself against allegations, sometimes scolding the commission itself for its insufficiently enlightened attitudes.[69] Founded in 1627 as a shelter for pilgrims visiting a nearby sanctuary, which was said to have miracu-lous powers for curing leprosy and other diseases of the skin, Saint-

[67] See Lefebvre-Duruflé, *Rapport présenté au Conseil général du département de l'Eure dans sa session de 1839 au nom de la commission des aliénés* (Evreux: J.-J. Ancelle, 1839), pp. 33, 39, 43. Not all Parisian psychiatrists held this view, however; for a very positive evaluation of nursing sisters in lunatic asylums, see Brierre de Boismont, "Mémoire pour l'établissement d'un hospice d'aliénés," *Ann. d'hyg. pub.* 16 (1836): esp. 74–75.

[68] *Constitutions et chartes: Notions élémentaires de droit politique* (Paris: 30, rue et place St-André-des-arts, 1834). In a letter to the Ministry of the Interior on May 18, 1848, Chambeyron said of this volume, "I stigmatized the abuses of power in energetic satires"; see AN: F[15] 3915.

[69] See ADIV: Fonds de l'Asile Saint-Méen (a collection of documents which had not yet been assigned a catalogue number at the time of my visit to Rennes in September 1982), esp. Dossier 40: Letters and reports of the physician, and Dossier 30: Letters of the bursar and mother superior.

Méen had always been a municipal institution, constructed with and maintained by the funds of the commune of Rennes. The first lunatic had been placed there in 1724, and in 1735 the nuns of Saint-Thomas-de-Villeneuve had been installed to tend what was by then a heterogeneous agglomeration of pilgrims, old people, orphans, the skin-diseased, and the insane. By the early nineteenth century, Saint-Méen housed only these last two categories of inmates, and the sisters of Saint-Vincent-de-Paul had been engaged to provide the nursing staff.[70]

Though alert to some of the potential difficulties of working with such a staff, Chambeyron seems in the final analysis to have been ill-prepared for the nexus of entrenched "matriarchal" and religious power into which he was entering, where his own presence, male and medical-scientific, was bound to be experienced as deeply offensive and disruptive. Nor does he seem to have anticipated the sorts of retaliatory measures that the charitable sisters would devise. In the first months of his tenure at Saint-Méen, Chambeyron had taken, or so he thought, adequate pains to win over the sisters through accommodating gestures. He arranged his own workload so as to leave them free on Sundays. He adopted a latitudinarian attitude toward ordinary religious observance by patients. "Some physicians censure all religious practices in a lunatic hospital; I by contrast allow them, regarding them as a duty for those who are able and as a means of treatment in certain cases." He even permitted several patients to leave the hospital to attend mass in the city of Rennes during the week. True, he had removed the devotional paintings hanging in the wards – an action that caused the sisters to draw hasty and unfavorable conclusions about him – but he had done so, he said, only out of a concern for cleanliness and the condition of the walls. And he had compensated for this seeming desecration by recommending that a crucifix and a holy water basin be placed in wards where the lunatics were tranquil.[71] But the nuns were not so easily coopted, and severe and tangled problems arose almost immediately.

One protracted quarrel concerned the intern, a position of apprenticeship which did not exist at Saint-Méen before Chambeyron's arrival. Chosen from among the advanced medical students at the local

---

[70] See Dr. Sizaret, "Notice sur l'asile d'aliénés dit de Saint-Méen de Rennes," *Bulletin de la Société scientifique et médicale de l'Ouest* 15 (1906): esp. 183–85; *Mémoire adressé à Monsieur le Ministre de l'Intérieur par la commission administrative des hospices civils de Rennes*, ADIV: X 359, printed brochure from the 1840s, pp. 4, 10; and ADIV: Fonds Saint-Méen, letter of Chambeyron of February 7, 1840. Sizaret does not indicate at what date the sisters of Saint-Thomas-de-Villeneuve were replaced by those of Saint-Vincent-de-Paul, but textual evidence in the Fonds Saint-Méen indicates that the latter were in residence during Chambeyron's tenure; see letter of the mother superior to the Commission administrative dated January 29, 1838.

[71] ADIV: Fonds Saint-Méen, letter of Chambeyron to the Commission administrative, April 25, 1836.

medical school, the intern was perceived by the nuns, quite correctly, as a symbol of encroaching medicalization. Indeed, Chambeyron's request to the Administrative Commission of Hospices for an intern had justified the new post explicitly on the grounds of the nuns' inadequacies and the allegedly fixed boundaries between religious and medical functions. "And, it will be said, why not hand over these matters to the sisters of charity? Because even the simplest dressing of wounds requires knowledge which these pious women do not possess; because their sex and their vocation impose on them a timidity and caution (perhaps exaggerated) with the opposite sex; and finally because it is a principle on which there is universal agreement that the sisters ought to remain completely foreign to the practice of medicine."[72] When Chambeyron's request was granted and the intern materialized, the sisters attempted to even the score by making the young man's life miserable. They "groaned" about his "conduct": The chambermaids and the doorkeeper, "who are witnesses to the comings and goings of people," were reportedly "scandalized' by the "habits" (*moeurs*) of the intern. For his part, the intern refused to be ruffled by the mother superior's chastisements and coolly told her to address any complaints about him to the chief physician. The sisters now felt sufficiently anxious about the intern's alleged moral turpitude that they knowingly overstepped the bounds of their authority and violated the rules of the institution by contriving to "prevent him from changing the bandages in the women's ward while we are at Mass."[73] When Sister Victoire began regularly to lock the intern out of the section over which she presided as head nurse, Chambeyron removed her from her post and proclaimed the "filthy story" (*sale histoire*) the nuns were telling about the young man an "abominable lie."[74]

Soon Chambeyron perceived that the sisters' suspicions had spilled over to him. Noticing the strange "obstinacy" with which the mother superior followed him each time he visited the women's division of the hospital, he speculated cynically about her motives. Either "she fears undergoing [my] inspection or . . . she is mistrustful of the morality of [my] intentions and is preparing an accusation [against me] as well-founded as those she has brought against the intern."[75] In calling nineteenth-century incarcerative institutions "panoptic," Michel Foucault was referring only to the constant visibility of the inmates to the experts. Inattentive to the continuing lively presence of religious person-

---

[72] Ibid., report of Chambeyron to the Commission administrative, February 27, 1836, ms. pp. 2–3.

[73] Ibid., letter of the mother superior to the Commission administrative dated only 1838.

[74] Ibid., letters of Chambeyron to the mother superior, one dated November 30, 1837 and another, not dated, referring to the same incident.

[75] Ibid., letter of Chambeyron to the Commission administrative, July 14, 1838.

nel in most of these institutions, Foucault failed to point out that the public space of hospitals and asylums was regularly the site of another penetrating gaze: that directed toward medical men by angry and suspicious nuns.[76]

An even more complicated imbroglio at Saint-Méen – and one in which the nuns again raised the hue and cry of scandal – concerned two mental patients, Messieurs Héteau and Nicolas. During his first year at the asylum, Chambeyron encountered Héteau, the victim of a religious insanity or, as the physician phrased it, a man "given over to the practices of an exaggerated devotion." Since he was a paying patient, Héteau had a private room, and he habitually remained inside it, isolated from all social intercourse. Chambeyron described his behavior graphically:

> I never entered his room without finding him prostrate, leaning on his knees and elbows, his forehead a few inches from the floor, his eyes fixed on a prayer book. The time that he does not spend in this tiring position is devoted to the analysis of sermons, the copying of works of piety and the minute description of ceremonies of worship; often he made use even of a part of the night for occupations of this sort.

All of Chambeyron's attempts to persuade Héteau (who believed himself "possessed by Satan") to alter his ways failed. But the *aliéniste* achieved an accidental "demi-success," as he put it, when an eye infection necessitated placing Héteau in the infirmary. There a "continual surveillance, the influence of society and the distractions that it provided him despite himself, as well as the example of other people's submission to my authority, led to a marked improvement in the patient." Freed to some degree from his old obsessions, Héteau even began to study Italian. The delighted Chambeyron kept him in the infirmary even after his eyes were completely healed, fearing that renewed solitude would precipitate a relapse.[77]

Two problems arose. First, Héteau had not given up writing his descriptions of religious ceremonies; and although Chambeyron regarded this as pathological behavior, he "dared not suppress it," lest this prohibition be misinterpreted by the nuns as a gesture hostile to religion. He found himself constrained in his capacity as a healer by what he wryly referred to as the "Trinitarian organization" of the hospice – that is, the division of authority among a Trinity composed of the physician, the religious congregation, and the municipal ad-

---

[76] On "panopticism," see Michel Foucault, *Discipline and Punish: The Birth of the Prison*, trans. A. Sheridan (New York: Pantheon, 1977), Part 3, Ch. 3. Jacques Léonard has also noted Foucault's failure to recognize the nineteenth-century battle between "medical power" and "clerical power." See "L'historien et le philosophe," *Annales historiques de la Révolution française* 49 (1977): esp. 167.

[77] ADIV: Fonds Saint-Méen, letter of Chambeyron to the Commission administrative, October 15, 1836.

ministrative commission. Second, Héteau began to insist that he be returned to his own room. Finding Chambeyron unbending on this point, he appealed to the mother superior, thus playing one authority against the other and making an overt clash almost inevitable. "My conscience does not permit me knowingly to place a patient in unfavorable circumstances," Chambeyron wrote to the administrative commission about his opposition to the move. A few weeks later his pangs of conscience gave way to anger and wounded pride; he observed to them that Héteau had always regarded the nuns as the "principal authority in the establishment."[78]

All this would have put strain enough upon medical-clerical relations at Saint-Méen, but the plot soon thickened. Another patient, Monsieur Nicolas, prone to fits of violent furor and attempts at escape, happened to be a priest.[79] Sometime during October 1836 he armed himself with a knife and brandished it in the asylum. According to Chambeyron, the standard techniques for handling a "menacing" lunatic were applied to him – "to hurl oneself against him with sufficient force so as to stun him and deprive him of the time needed to collect himself; to clasp his arms and press them against his chest" – and the physician and his assistants thus succeeded in retrieving the dangerous weapon. Now Héteau was among the bystanders present at this impromptu scene. Construing it as an antireligious gesture, he began to speak out against the "vile manner in which he had seen a priest treated." He even penned a letter to this effect to the bishop of Rennes, and like the rest of his correspondence (for he had developed a close relationship with the sympathetic nursing sisters), it was transmitted via the convent.[80]

When Nicolas died a short time later, the mother superior told Chambeyron that a "rumor was circulating in the city of Rennes to the effect that Monsieur Nicolas had been seriously," apparently mortally, "wounded by the orderlies" on the day of the knife episode. Getting ever deeper into clerical affairs, Chambeyron now paid a visit to the

---

[78] Ibid., letters of October 15, 1836, and November 3, 1836.

[79] There was nothing inherently unusual about this fact: Ecclesiastics regularly entered lunatic hospitals as patients in the early nineteenth century, a testament to the acceptance by the church of a naturalistic concept of mental illness. The bishop of Rennes arranged and paid for the placement of priests from his diocese in Saint-Méen, referring to their condition by such phrases as "attacked by a fit of madness (*folie*)," "has lost his head," "attacked by a mental alienation," "the aberration of his mind." ADIV: Fonds Saint-Méen, Dossier 29: letters of May 3, 1828; May 24, 1829; August 31, 1836. The superior of the seminary of Nancy, writing on behalf of a "young tonsured cleric," went even further along this naturalistic axis by attributing the "mental alienation" to the young man's excessive studiousness, which had "unsettled his weakened organs." AN: F^{15} 1946, letter to the minister of the interior dated September 18, 1818.

[80] ADIV: Fonds Saint-Méen, letter of Chambeyron to the Commission administrative, November 3, 1836.

bishop, who "received me with kindness, appeared convinced by the frankness of my explanations" and told him that the original source of the rumor about the maltreatment of Nicolas was a nursing sister at Saint-Méen, who wished to keep her identity shielded. The bishop decided that the most effective way to quell the rumor would be to have an autopsy performed on the priest's body, and he gave his written order to the chaplain of Saint-Méen to postpone the burial for this purpose. The mother superior then tried to prevent the autopsy, telling Chambeyron that the bishop had asked her to convey by word of mouth his withdrawal of permission.[81]

At the time that Chambeyron described the situation to the administrative commission, he was being assured by the mother superior that no nursing sister had started the rumor (it must, she said, have been a patient masquerading as a nun). But she conceded that in private conversations Sister Victoire was reporting that she had witnessed the physical abuse of Nicolas by the asylum staff. Chambeyron wanted to assure the administrative commission that his records of medical examinations of Nicolas indicated that a fall the priest had taken in church three weeks before his death "had left very distinct marks," but that subsequent instances of forcible restraint by the orderlies had left no traces. By recounting yet another episode, in which Sister Victoire had reported that a patient had cut an artery, while his own examination revealed wounds only to the skin and the small subcutaneous blood vessels, he sought to undermine the sister's credibility by emphasizing her medical ignorance and its connection with her malicious rumor-mongering. "Now gentlemen, a person who carries out bleedings ought to know at what depth the arteries in the arm are situated. If I had arrived less quickly [in order to alter the diagnosis], the town idlers would have had another little story to circulate."[82]

In these minutely detailed epistolary narratives, Chambeyron's tone is factual and dispassionate. Yet, from their cumulative effect, the reader cannot help but infer the fatigue bordering on exhaustion which the religious politics of asylum life, the atmosphere of accusation and counter-accusation, must have produced in this young, idealistic doctor. By 1840, when Chambeyron was being put forward for promotion to the new combined post of chief physician and director at Saint-Méen, the prefect of the Ille-et-Vilaine could write to the minister of the interior that the *aliéniste* had been "at first vexed by the opposition of the sisters of charity who were accustomed to having full control of the establishment before his arrival," but that the eventual engagement of a different congregation to fill the nursing function had much improved his position and his efficacy. Chambeyron did receive the pro-

[81] Ibid.
[82] Ibid.

motion, but subsequent quarrels with the administrative commission – the third point in the triangulated power structure at Saint-Méen – ended his tenure in 1845, prompting his removal to the asylum at Orléans. During the Second Republic, the scenario was repeated when Chambeyron's successor, Dr. Belloc, was removed from Saint-Méen after being denounced by the nursing sisters at the hospice.[83] Especially in this region, where the power of the clergy was traditionally strong, the pitched battle between nuns and asylum-doctors continued.

Not every locality was the scene of such dramatic confrontations, which required the simultaneous presence of a reformist Paris-trained *aliéniste* and a staff of zealous nursing sisters. But to more tranquil institutions psychiatric-clerical tensions were spread by Dr. Ferrus in his capacity as peripatetic inspector-general of lunatic houses. Well-known for his published views on banning both religious practices and religious nurses from the asylum proper,[84] Ferrus lived up to the reputation that preceded him. When he arrived in 1843 at the lunatic quarters of the hospice of Evreux in the department of Eure, for example, he hastened to make known his "astonishment" at the condition of the inmates and the state of the matriculation register. The local hospice administrative commission felt not only that the expectations of "this Inspector General" had been unrealistically high but also that he had tactlessly and unfairly taken out his wrath on the head nursing sister. Had he bothered to call upon one or more members of the commission, "their presence would have avoided the bitterness of Monsieur Ferrus's reproaches of Sister Félicité, who for the past ten years, at the peril of her own life, has given the most assiduous care to the lunatics. Everyone knows that she has several times been the victim of their furor and that, despite the gravity of the injuries she has sustained, nothing has been able to make her abandon her charitable enterprise."[85] But Ferrus did not know – nor, more important, was he predisposed to have a positive regard for the religious personnel he encountered in the medical domain.

The collaborative possibility

"In this important question," wrote Jean-Pierre Falret in 1845, "my deep convictions separate me completely from Pinel and Esquirol."[86] Interviewed at about the same date by the young Dr. Delasiauve (later to be a prominent Parisian *aliéniste*), he said, "For a long time they

---

[83] ADIV: X 359, letters of the prefect of Ille-et-Vilaine to the minister of the interior dated August 21, 1840, May 7, 1845; and Sizaret, "Notice sur Saint-Méen," pp. 188–89.

[84] Ferrus, *Des aliénés*, pp. 34n, 230–31.

[85] AN: F^{15} 3913, Commission de l'hospice d'Evreux, report by the president, September 11, 1843.

[86] Falret, *Utilité de la religion*, p. 6.

frightened us away from religious intervention in the treatment of lunatics and, I must admit that, despite my convictions, it was not without hesitation that I deviated from the doctrine of my *maîtres* in this regard."[87] Within early nineteenth-century Parisian psychiatry, then, Falret self-consciously represented the dissenting minority position – that the treatment of insanity by physicians required a substantial religious component and that, for maximal efficacy, the latter was to be provided by a member of the clergy. "The physician can doubtless speak of religion to his patients with dignity and at opportune moments, but he will rarely exert influence on their minds because he is not invested with a sacred character and it is not his mission to call men back to divine laws."[88]

It was in the context of a laudatory report on the new lunatic establishment of Illenau across the Rhine in Baden – where the physician-director was supported by a harmonious team of two medical colleagues and two pastors[89] – that Falret first publicly described the organization of the section for lunatics at the Salpêtrière of which he had assumed charge in 1841. His chief "auxiliary" (the term is Falret's) was a certain Abbé Christophe, the resident chaplain of the hospice, a man of engaging manners and athletic build.[90] Like Falret himself, Abbé Christophe visited all the inmates daily; in addition he gave group religious instruction twice weekly to about fifty lunatics; and he held private conversations with patients designated by Falret, using the physician's own office for this purpose. In this last capacity, the abbé was expected to become the repository of those intimate confidences which illuminated the etiology of insanity and which women were reputedly prone to share most readily with priests.[91] Another facet of the program was the religious tenor that Falret gave to the large inmate assemblies he favored as a means of reviving the "sentiments of sociability so often altered in madness." Delasiauve reported:

> They began by a prayer and some canticles; then came two hours of recitations and various songs, closed by a sacred hymn. It was really a surprise to observe the calm bearing and brightening faces of these lunatics, whose extravagant language and gestures we had sadly noted just a moment before.[92]

It is unclear whether or to what extent Falret was a believer. His psychiatric writing gave some vague, implicit credence to the tenets of

---

[87] De Lasiauve [*sic*], "Deux visites à la Salpêtrière (section de M. Falret)," *Expérience* 7 (April 20, 1843): 260.
[88] Falret, *Utilité de la religion*, p. 13.
[89] Falret, "Visite à Illenau," Part 1, pp. 430–31.
[90] On Christophe, see Semelaigne, *Grands aliénistes*, pp. 289–90.
[91] Falret, *Utilité de la religion*, pp. 19, 22–23.
[92] De Lasiauve, "Deux visites," p. 258.

Catholicism. (Religion "steadies the present and prepares for the future," he wrote.) But ultimately he justified his use of "religious intervention" in treatment with an argument which, while not exactly opportunistic in its use of religion, hinged more on its natural than on its supernatural efficacy. "Religious sentiment is inherent in our nature"; and hence those "eternal principles" which regulate both human relations and the relations of man to the divinity are propagated wherever men gather together to form societies. Despite their mental confusion, most lunatics conserved at least glimmerings of this vital sentiment; by cultivating it, the healer aided their reentry into the human community. Furthermore, insanity was a disturbance of the "equilibrium of the powers of our soul (*âme*)" which the moral treatment aimed at rectifying; in this enterprise the energies of the religious sentiment ought to be enlisted, for they were the ones "most capable of effecting a strong and durable reaction." To self-hating melancholics, religion held out "consolations" which had all the more chance of success because they elicited the most "worthy" elements of our nature. On those melancholics absorbed in "silence and immobility," religion impressed the divinely ordained duty of activity and work. Where mental chaos reigned and needed to be overcome, as most urgently in cases of mania, "religion, better than all human contrivances, suspends . . . extreme disorder by the majesty of its words, by the stately ceremony of its worship."[93]

Finally, religious ministrations could be readily integrated into the medical treatment program because they relied upon the same "ways of gentleness," "persuasion," and "insinuation" that formed the "basis of the physician's conduct toward lunatics." This compatibility implied, of course, the choice of a certain style of religiosity, one in which "the omnipresence of God is invoked rather as a source of mercy than of punishment."[94] As Falret told Delasiauve, expressing clearly Pinellian preferences, in matters of psychiatric therapy "one must take for a guide the evangelical gentleness of Fénelon rather than the militant energy of Bossuet."[95] And he made the same point in more homely language to a journalistic interviewer: "Not being able to give them [his female patients at the Salpêtrière] a lover to comfort (*consoler*) the solitude of their hearts, I seek to give them God."[96]

Thus the structure of Falret's argument on religion in psychiatric treatment is quite similar to Pinel's – and remarkably so, in that Falret, identifying himself as a deviant, took the argument to a resoundingly positive conclusion rather than to Pinel's negative one. That opposite

[93] Falret, *Utilité de la religion*, pp. 4–9.
[94] Ibid., pp. 4, 11.
[95] De Lasiauve, "Deux visites," p. 260.
[96] Alphonse Esquiros, *Paris, ou les sciences, les institutions et les moeurs au XIXe siècle*, (Paris: Imprimeurs Unis, 1847), Vol. 2, p. 258.

conclusions on this issue could be derived from similar premises underscores the essential likeness between religious guidance and the moral treatment – the medical tendency to interpret the former naturalistically as a "moral means" and thus to subsume it under, or at least to ally it closely with, the latter. Once that strategy had been adopted, as it was by both Pinel and Falret, the choice to accentuate the divergence or convergence of religion and *médecine mentale* was one of "taste," shaped by professional or ideological considerations, rather than the working out of an internal logic.

Falret believed that the use of religion not only accelerated the cure of mental illness but warded off relapse, strengthening vulnerable individuals discharged from the asylum and subjected to the stresses of ordinary life. As an extension of this belief, he organized in the early 1840s a society for the protection of indigent convalescent lunatics and sought to involve the Paris ecclesiastical community in the project. With Abbé Christophe, he made the rounds of all the parish priests in the capital and even succeeded in persuading the archbishop of Paris to assume the title of honorary president.[97] To encourage donations to the society, an annual sermon was preached at Notre-Dame; one year the preacher was the fiery liberal Catholic Lacordaire, whose theme was the causal connection between the godless philosophy of the Enlightenment and insanity.[98]

Thus Falret had, qua psychiatrist, involved himself rather deeply in the organized church. He seems to have had no qualms about this involvement. Some years earlier he had even paid a collegial visit to Xavier Tissot/Frère Hilarion in the Lot, Falret's native department, where he owned an extensive landed property[99] and where Hilarion had founded a lunatic establishment. According to the Charitain's report of the meeting, the two men discussed suicide among the insane; Falret admitted to high rates of suicide in the Paris hospices and was very impressed by Hilarion's claim to have prevented suicide entirely among his patients by construing it "as the result of a temptation to despair" and thus combating it by the employment of "religious consolations and the properly understood practice of religion."[100]

Falret's "clericizing" of psychiatric treatment, his avowed departure from the tenets of the founders in this regard, influenced some of his students, whom he had organized into a small circle of his own after

[97] De Lasiauve, "Deux visites," p. 260; Semelaigne, *Grands aliénistes*, pp. 290–91.

[98] See Esquiros, *Paris*, Vol. 2, p. 259. The sermon appears to be number 29 in Henri-Dominique Lacordaire, *Conférences de Notre Dame de Paris*, Vol. 2 (Paris: Sagnier & Bray, 1845), pp. 203–29.

[99] Semelaigne, *Grands aliénistes*, p. 297.

[100] Tissot, *Mémoire*, note 1, pp. 38–39; Hilarion dates the visit as late 1836.

Esquirol's death.[101] In 1844, for example, Benedict-Augustin Morel and Charles Lasègue wrote a long and sympathetic précis of J. C. A. Heinroth's *Lehrbuch der Störungen des Seelenlebens* (1818), a text which one modern commentator has called the "embodiment of theological psychiatry."[102] Their reading of Heinroth, a German divinity student turned physician who saw an affinity between madness and "sin," inspired them to use religious analogies to conceptualize the healing powers of the *médecin aliéniste*. A line from the *Imitation of Christ*, which admonished the reader to find consolation in the inner life, now struck them as having great relevance to their own professional calling: "Begin by establishing peace within yourself and you will later obtain it for others."[103] And there is evidence that as a physician at Maréville, a lunatic institution near Nancy, Morel like his teacher Falret formed a close tie with the clergy. When in 1852 he published the clinical lessons he had given at Maréville, he did so, he wrote, on the "advice offered me alike by physicians, teachers and priests."[104]

His students apart, Falret's position seems to have inspired little emulation from his fellow *aliénistes*. Yet despite some earlier French psychiatric condemnations of Heinroth,[105] neither did it evoke overt controversy or criticism. Recognizing the explosive nature of religious questions – especially in the medical world, with its unsavory reputation for irreligiosity – most medical journals, including the *Annales médico-psychologiques*, made a deliberate policy of avoiding them.[106] Furthermore, Falret had doubtless fended off criticism in advance by his unequivocal and oft-repeated commitment to medical supremacy

---

[101] Charles Lasègue noted that the group originated in the clinical instruction which Falret began (in 1843) at the Salpêtrière. But "the lessons held only a secondary place; alongside the audience in the amphitheater was the smaller circle (*cercle*) of diligent students. [Falret's] service [at the Salpêtrière] was accessible to all of them, and no doctrines were imposed. Each studied according to his own bent and reported his observations, which were then discussed . . . in common, with the indulgent participation of the *maître*. Thus we lived immersed in an amicable activity of the mind." "Nécrologie: Falret," *Arch. gen. de med.*, 6th ser., 17 (1871): 587.

[102] Klaus Dörner, *Madmen and the Bourgeoisie: A Social History of Insanity* (1969) trans. J. Neugroschel and J. Steinberg (Oxford: Blackwell, 1981), p. 238.

[103] Lasègue and Morel, "Etudes historiques sur l'aliénation mentale," *Ann. m.-p.*, 1st ser., 4 (1844): 1–10, 157–72; esp. 172.

[104] Morel, *Etudes cliniques*, Vol. 1 (Nancy: Grimblot; Paris: J.-B. Baillière, 1852), p. xiii.

[105] Lasègue and Morel, "Etudes historiques," p. 4, mentioned the "hardly favorable welcome" accorded Heinroth's work in France. On a number of occasions the Esquirol circle member Leuret had spoken out against Heinroth's association of insanity with sin; see his *Fragmens psychologiques sur la folie* (Paris: Crochard, 1834), pp. 21–22; and *Du traitement moral de la folie* (Paris: J.-B. Baillière, 1840), pp. 146–48.

[106] See Cerise, "Quelques mots sur la liberté de discussion dans les *Annales medico-psychologiques*," *Ann. m.-p.*, 1st ser., 7 (1846): 160 n1; and the editorial statement of Cayol, *Revue médicale française et étrangère* (September 1845): 136n.

in the medico-clerical alliance he postulated. "The more powerful this lever [the cultivation of religious sentiment] is upon the soul, the more careful must the physician be to oversee its employment . . . in the light of his special science."[107] Or, more bluntly, the priest "subordinates the exercise of his ministry to science and obeys medical directives humbly, punctually and exactly."[108]

The collaborative possibility articulated by Falret reveals two of the most important aspects of the psychiatrists' relationship to the clerics. First, Falret's notable lack of success in marshaling significant psychiatric support for his position – despite the existence in the 1830s and 1840s of a liberal Catholic movement, with which Falret seems to have been associated and which could only have made a clerical alliance more appealing to his colleagues – reveals the deeply entrenched nature of psychiatric anticlericalism. Second, it is striking that anticlericalism or collaboration were the only possibilities that the *aliénistes* entertained. None of them, it appears, could be indifferent to the clerics; the available options were to beat them or to join them. That the clerical presence imposed itself upon the new specialty as an inescapable fact of life was, in part, a function of the specialty's own choice of paradigm. The religious roots of the moral treatment could not, in the nineteenth century, be ignored. And unless one used the pastoral resonances of that treatment as the basis for collaboration, the only remaining stance toward the clerics was rivalry.

[107] Falret, *Utilité de la religion,* pp. 12–13, 19.
[108] Delasiauve's quote or paraphrase of Falret, "Deux visites," p. 260.

Le médecin,

*Pourquoi, diable, mes malades s'en vont ils donc tous?.... j'ai beau les saign-
les purger, les droguer.......... je n'y comprends rien !*

Plate 1. Portrait of a nineteenth-century psychiatrist?

Labeled by Daumier only "The Physician," this 1833 lithograph
was executed while the artist was serving a jail sentence for violation of the censorship laws. He served most of that sentence,
however, in the private *maison de santé* of Dr. Casimir Pinel, who
routinely expressed his liberal sympathies by having the political
prisoners of the July Monarchy remanded to his care. Art historians therefore believe that Daumier's physician is Pinel *neveu* himself. Unlike many of Daumier's depictions of doctors and lawyers,
this portrait has no satiric intent. Its subject appears as a tired and
pensive man, dressed in the austere garb of the bourgeois, clutch-
ing a handkerchief tensely in his fist. The caption has him musing
sadly on the limits of his medical knowledge: "Why the devil do I
lose all my patients? In vain do I bleed them, purge them, drug
them. I understand nothing!" (The Armand Hammer Daumier
Collection)

231

(a)   *(b)*

(c)   *(d)*

Plate 2. Esquirol investigates the physiognomy of insanity

Firmly convinced that the "study of the physiognomy of lunatics is no object of idle curiosity" but could materially aid the psychiatrist's diagnostic task, Esquirol began, as early as 1813, sending artists into the Paris asylums to record the facial characteristics of the inmates. These four sketches come from a group of about thirty executed for Esquirol by an obscure draftsman, G.-F.-M. Gabriel (1775–1836). The first was done in 1813, the other three around 1825. The patients represented are: (a) a "fanatical priest," (b) a "melancholy banker," (c) a "military man calling himself king of Sweden" and (d) a "commercial lawyer turned maniac." (Paris, Bibliothèque Nationale, Cabinet des Estampes; Phot. Bibl. Nat., Paris)

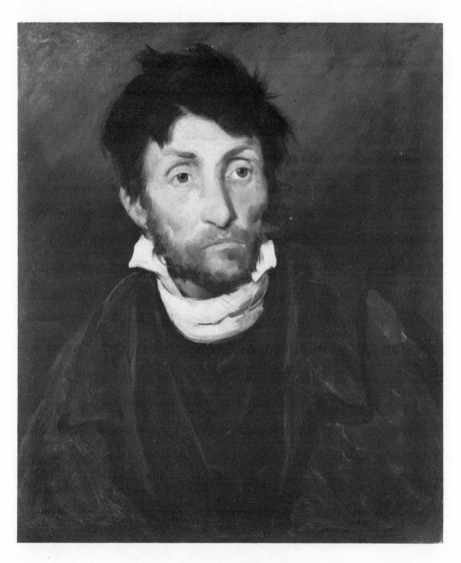

Plate 3. The physiognomy of monomania

Géricault's portrait of a theft-monomaniac is one of a series of canvases on the theme of monomania that he painted around 1822 for the Paris psychiatrist Dr. Etienne-Jean Georget. The assignment Géricault carried out for Georget seems to have paralleled the one Gabriel carried out for Esquirol – to document, through painstaking observation from life, the physiognomy of insanity or, in Géricault's case, one species of insanity. But what Gabriel performed skillfully, Géricault infused with genius. His monomaniacs appear deeply absorbed in their private thoughts; the tension in their faces betrays a powerful inner agitation held back, momentarily, from active expression. (Ghent, Museum voor Schone Kunsten)

_ Ce qui m'chiffonne c'est que j'suis accusé de douze vols!..
_ Il y en a douze... tant mieux... je plaiderai la monomanie!..

Plate 4. The emergence of forensic psychiatry

Daumier's cartoon, which appeared in *Charivari* in 1846, plays on the public's familiarity with the use of the monomania defense in criminal trials. The arrested man says despondently, "What really bothers me is that I've been accused of twelve robberies." "Twelve of them," replies the lawyer. "So much the better. I will plead monomania." (Benjamin A. and Julia M. Trustman Collection, Brandeis University Library)

Plate 5. The nursing sisters unembattled

Amand Gautier's painting *The Sisters of Charity*, exhibited at the Paris Salon of 1859, conveys the esteem in which this group—so maligned by psychiatrists—was generally held by nineteenth-century Frenchmen. Reviewing the painting at the time, Charles Baudelaire spoke of the "tender poetry contained in those long, uniform garments, in those rigid headdresses and those attitudes as modest and serious as the religious life itself." (Lille, Musée des Beaux-Arts)

SCRUTIN DE BALLOTTAGE DU 4 FEVRIER 1883

BIBLIOTHÈQUE DIABOLIQUE

ECOLE CHRETIE

BOURNEVILLE

Candidat Républicain Radical Socialiste

Plate 6. Psychiatric anticlericalism in action

This newspaper cartoon from the early Third Republic comments on the candidacy of Dr. D.-M. Bourneville for the Chamber of Deputies from the fifth arrondissement of Paris. For the cartoonist, Bourneville's whole identity as a politician is bound up with anticlericalism. The candidate champions the laicization of the Paris public hospitals (note the fleeing nursing sisters in the lower left-hand corner). He edits the Bibliothèque Diabolique (in whose doorway he stands), the series of books reinterpreting famous episodes of demonic possession as instances of hysterical pathology. Bourneville's bid for election in 1883 proved successful. (Paris, C.M.T. Assistance Publique)

ATTAQUE DEMONIAQUE

Plate 7. The hysteric as the modern demoniac

The demoniacal variety of hysteria – part of the second period of the four-part attack of "grand hysteria" outlined by Charcot – was the linchpin in the medical-scientific appropriation of the phenomenon of demonic possession. An engraving from an 1881 text by a member of the Salpêtrière school unabashedly emphasizes the grotesqueness of a woman in the throes of this pathology. (Paul Richer, *Etudes cliniques sur la grande hystérie* [Paris: Delahaye & Lecrosnier, 1881])

Plate 8. The iconography of the hysterical body

The lawful regularity of the hysterical attack, asserted by Charcot, was minutely analyzed by him and his school. This synoptic table displays the full range of bodily postures involved. (Paul Richer, *Etudes cliniques sur la grande hystérie*, 2d ed. [Paris: Delahaye & Lecrosnier, 1885]; Phot. Bibl. Nat., Paris)

F   G   H   I   J   K   L

239

7

Choosing philosophical sides

ALL Enlightenment-inspired physicians liked to think of themselves as *médecins-philosophes*. But the psychiatrists were, and throughout the nineteenth century would remain, the most relentlessly philosophical of the breed. Their interest in philosophy derived in part from the fact that their own subject matter, the human mind, was also the philosopher's subject matter par excellence. It derived as well from the conviction that, in nature, abnormal forms were so intimately connected to their normal counterparts that their examination could illuminate, and might even provide a privileged mode of access to, the principles of normal functioning. Direct testimony on this latter point abounds. The Idéologue progenitor Condorcet explained in his famous *Sketch* (1794) his intention to trace not only the triumphal progress of human reason but also the "history of [those] general errors" which had served as impediments to progress: "The operations of the understanding which lead us into error or detain us there, from the artful paralogism which can trip up the most intelligent man to the dreams of madness (*démence*), belong no less to the theory of the development of our intellectual faculties than does the method of correct reasoning or of discovering the truth."[1] Similarly, the Idéologue physician Moreau de la Sarthe explained in the Year VIII why he had paid a visit to the Salpêtrière and why he urged others to do likewise:

> If aberrations, deviations and monsters make the constant and general ways of Nature better known, if a profound examination of disease discloses the laws and conditions of health, man in the state of madness ought to be an important subject for observation; and to extend more rapidly the still so narrow limits of a sound metaphysics, the savants of the Second Class of the Institute ought to send commissioners or at least travel occasionally themselves to the establishments devoted to the shelter and treatment of the insane.[2]

[1] Condorcet, *Esquisse d'un tableau historique des progrès de l'esprit humain*, ed. Yvon Belaval (Paris: J. Vrin), 1970, p. 10.
[2] J.-L. Moreau, "Voyage à la Salpêtrière," *Décade philosophique* (20 thermidor Year VIII): 268.

In the nineteenth century, the psychiatrists picked up this theme. At first they invited philosophers to share the data so plentifully at the disposal of the asylum-doctor. What riches, exclaimed Esquirol in 1816, await "the philosopher who, stealing away from the tumult of the world, surveys a lunatic establishment." There he would find "the same world," but modified in such a way as to facilitate his task: "The features are stronger, the nuances more marked, the colors more vivid, the effects harsher because man exists in all his nakedness."[3] Later the psychiatrists depicted philosophical speculation as one of their own functions. The Paris-trained *aliéniste* Michéa, employed in a sanatorium in the capital, explained at midcentury that the treatment of patients was only one aspect of mental medicine. The new specialty also had "for its goal . . . to aid in dissipating the so thick clouds which still surround the mechanism of sound and orderly intelligences."[4] And Brierre de Boismont declared the well-trained *médecin aliéniste* "perhaps the man most suited to elucidate the questions of philosophy."[5]

The connection between mental pathology and philosophy, insisted upon by Enlightenment spokesmen and by the psychiatrists themselves, became part of the nineteenth-century image of the new medical specialty. During a parliamentary debate of the 1830s over state provision for the care of the insane, one deputy called for the creation of institutions where treatment would be directed by psychiatrists whom he depicted, lacking that word, as "physicians who are in some manner special and who have joined philosophical studies to their medical studies."[6] At the fin de siècle, Gabriel Tarde, constructing the science of sociology as an intermental psychology, noted the importance of hypnotism in his conceptual scheme. For his own understanding of this "supremely mysterious phenomenon," he had leaned upon the research of the asylum-doctors, whom he called "our *aliénistes philosophes.*"[7]

But to point out the affinity between psychiatry and philosophy in the nineteenth century is only to scratch the surface. A deeper exploration of the relationship poses serious methodological difficulties for the historian. The psychiatrists' zeal for philosophy was rarely, if ever, matched by their rigor in pursuing or applying that form of intellectual inquiry. Their central tasks of clinical observation, diagnosis, and treatment left them little time for such a pursuit. Nor, in general, did the welter of empirical data to which their daily rounds exposed them fit

[3] Esquirol, "Folie" (1816), *Dict. des sci. med.*, Vol. 16, pp. 151–52.

[4] Michéa, "Lettre au citoyen Thierry," *Ann. m.-p.*, 1st ser., 11 (1848): 451.

[5] Quoted in Motet, "Discours aux obsèques de Brierre de Boismont," *Ann. m.-p.*, 6th ser., 7 (1882): 348–49.

[6] Calemard de Lafayette, session of the Chamber of Deputies of April 3, 1837, *Arch. parl.*, 2d ser., Vol. 109, p. 342.

[7] Gabriel Tarde, *Les lois de l'imitation*, 2d ed. (Paris: F. Alcan, 1895), p. 82.

neatly into available philosophic categories. Hence psychiatric philoso-
phizing was perforce a secondary activity, summoned when it seemed
especially useful or pertinent, turned to on occasion for general orientation; but neither a sustained nor a systematic project, it was most
often expressed in vague, allusive language. Reinforcing this tendency
toward allusiveness was the fact that nineteenth-century psychiatrists
often had, as we will see, political reasons for avoiding a precise statement of their philosophical commitments. Yet, as fragmented and incomplete as the evidence is, it repays investigation, for it makes possible a historical reconstruction of a key element in the intellectual world
of nineteenth-century psychiatry, as well as a view of psychiatry's negotiation of its boundaries with a neighboring disciplinary domain.

The philosophical choice

No discussion of the relationship between *médecine mentale* and philosophy of mind in the first half of the nineteenth century can speak of
philosophy in the singular. Rather, it is the two great competing philosophical currents of the day – and the way *médecine mentale* situated
itself with respect to them – that become the focus of the story.

Contemporaries called these two currents by a variety of names and
tended to represent them as dichotomies: materialism versus spiritualism, in one rendition; positive philosophy versus metaphysics, in the
special vocabulary of Auguste Comte and his followers; and, the formulation which sounds strangest to our ears but which was probably
the one used most widely at the time, "physiology" versus "psychology." A remark from the 1820s that "one studies the nature of man
either as a psychologist or as a physiologist" is nearly opaque to us but
was perfectly lucid to educated Frenchmen of the period.[8] The basic
program of the first, "physiological" current was to treat mental life as
a property or manifestation of the intricately organized physical stuff
composing the human body (hence "organization" was another of its
contemporary code words), to confine the study of it to externally
observable phenomena, and to build a science of mind inductively on
Baconian principles. This current thus appeared to be monistic but was
actually somewhat ambiguous. Its proponents limited what was scientifically knowable about mind to mind's material embodiments; but
they declined to say, as would self-proclaimed monists or materialists,
that they therefore regarded matter as the sole and ultimate reality.

---

[8] The remark was made by a Dr. Worbe, review of Georget, *Examen médical des procès
criminels* . . . in *Journal universel des sciences médicales* 41 (1826): 316. For the same usage
in a journal for educated laymen, see the articles by L. Peisse, "De la physiologie dans
ses rapports avec la philosophie de l'entendement," *Mercure du dix-neuvième siècle* 14
(1826): esp. 497; and "M. Bérard," ibid. 15 (1826): esp. 581.

The basic program of the second, "psychological" current was to treat mind as a reality distinct from body, as a radically free entity not subject to the laws prevailing in the physical world and properly investigated only from the inside, through introspection or the so-called *sens intime*. This second current was thus explicitly and unproblematically dualistic.

The first current was identified with medicine. Its chief proponents, Cabanis, Gall (the founder of phrenology), and Broussais – a triumvirate almost invariably mentioned in the same breath – were all physicians.[9] This current might even be viewed as leading imminently to the full-scale collapse of traditional philosophy of mind into the medical science of physiology – to the end of abstract discussions of mental states and processes and their replacement by concrete, experimentally derived descriptions of the intellectual and affective functions of the nervous system and, especially, of the brain. Certainly this was the view of Auguste Comte. In the 1820s he was enthusiastically cheering on the trend which began with Cabanis, hailing the work of Gall and Broussais as the arrival of the "positive philosophy" and as "this revolution which . . . has not yet become popularized [but] has been definitively consummated in all the intellects which are truly at the level of their century."[10]

Not surprisingly, then, the second current, which arose in reaction against the first, was primarily the work of professional philosophers, of the men of Victor Cousin's "regiment" who taught philosophy as an autonomous discipline in the state educational system and who would presumably be rendered obsolete if Comte's apocalyptic prediction were to come true.[11] In a Sorbonne lecture of 1830, Cousin's pupil Théodore Jouffroy argued for the indispensability of that metaphysical examination of pure mind which he called "psychology." "Disputes about the divisions of the sciences," he warned, had serious consequences for the state of knowledge. "A false science" – and such was his verdict on a science of mind in bodily context – "erases real distinctions [and] creates artificial relationships."[12] The opposing camps met

---

[9] For this grouping together of Cabanis, Gall, and Broussais, see, e.g., Hippolyte Royer-Collard, "Examen critique des travaux anatomiques et physiologiques de M. le docteur Gall," *Journal hebdomadaire de médecine* 1 (1828): 139; and Auguste Comte, "Examen du traité de Broussais sur l'irritation" (1828) in *Opuscules de philosophie sociale* (Paris: Leroux, 1883), p. 291.

[10] Comte, "Examen du traité de Broussais," pp. 291–92.

[11] On the role of Cousin in transforming philosophy in France from an amateur to a professional vocation, see R. R. Bolgar, "Victor Cousin and Nineteenth-Century Education," *Cambridge Journal* 2 (1949): 357–68.

[12] Théodore Jouffroy, "De la légitimité de la distinction de la psychologie et de la physiologie," in *Nouveaux mélanges philosophiques*, 3d ed. (Paris: Hachette, 1872), esp. pp. 165–67. On the dating and provenance of this piece, see the editor's preface, pp. vii–viii.

in face-to-face combat at the Academy of Sciences in 1838, with Dr. Broussais attempting to "prove that philosophy ought to be allied with physiology and that phrenology was the most positive philosophy that exists" and Professor Jouffroy replying that "psychology was a separate science having its own peculiar language" and (as one clearly biased reporter of the event put it disparagingly) "studying man denuded of his organs." It is a fitting symbol of the uncompromising, die-hard stance of both sides that Broussais succumbed to intestinal cancer in the midst of preparing his rejoinder to Jouffroy.[13]

Here I will generally call the two philosophical currents at issue "physiology" and "psychology," putting those words in quotation marks when I wish to indicate the idiosyncratic, secondary meaning they took on in early nineteenth-century France – as philosophical positions and not merely as branches of knowledge. I have adopted this terminology for two reasons. In the first place, I want to avoid a routinized use of the term "materialism," which had a highly pejorative sound to contemporaries and was never used by the proponents of the first current to depict themselves. "Physiology" was not such an outright slur: It connoted a movement toward the materialist end of the philosophical spectrum, but not necessarily an arrival there. By being more nuanced, it is probably more faithful to the views actually held by most proponents of the first current and certainly more faithful to the way they preferred to represent themselves.

In the second place, precisely because the term "physiology" subsequently lost its idiosyncratic early nineteenth-century meaning, it is able to convey to us something of the specific mentality of the period in which it flourished. It underscores the looming importance to contemporaries of advances in the new science of physiology,[14] the perceived potential of that scientific endeavor, perhaps above all others, to shape in fundamental ways the accepted view of human nature. Still it must be stressed that "physiology" is not identical with literal physiology – the use of surgical procedures to explore animal organisms for the purpose of ascertaining the functions of their constitutive parts. Certain literal, experimental physiologists of the period, notably those of the Montpellier school, took great pains to dissociate themselves from imputations of "physiology"; and by the same token it was possible to

---

[13] The report of the Academy of Sciences debate was given by J.-E. Belhomme as part of his homage to the recently departed Broussais; see "Compte rendu des travaux de la Société phrénologique pendant le cours de l'année 1839," *Esculape* 1 (September 1, 1839): 78.

[14] Although its subject matter had been studied much earlier (e.g., under the name "animal economy"), physiology achieved self-definition and public recognition as a science in France in the years 1790–1821. See John E. Lesch, *Science and Medicine in France: The Emergence of Experimental Physiology, 1790–1855* (Cambridge, Mass.: Harvard University Press, 1984), pp. 13, 15.

qualify as a "physiologist" on the basis of purely philosophical endeavors which made no use of scalpels or cadavers.

The dispute between "physiology" and "psychology" was anything but a narrowly technical one. Rather, its wide resonance touched beliefs about almost every aspect of culture. By removing the philosophical grounding from such theological tenets as the immortality of the soul and the freedom of the will, the "physiological" program became linked with or even equated to hostility to religion. Responding to this threat, the "psychological" program was explicitly committed to the defense and shoring up of religion. The "physiological" program had its roots in the Enlightenment and had flourished during the Revolution, prompting its indelible association with radical politics, social upheaval, and disrespect for tradition. Here again the "psychological" program conceived of its mission as restorative. Its exponents wanted to discourage revolutionary impulses, and they had at the outset tied their epistemology to the so-called Doctrinaire political theory, that peculiar brand of intensely conservative liberalism epitomized in the dictum, "Establish authority first, then create liberties as counterweights."[15]

Thus a whole set of interlocking partis pris were presumed to flow inexorably from one or the other philosophical position, and early nineteenth-century public language gave credence to this regular clustering of attitudes and to the stereotypes it produced. The atheistic "physiologist," heedless of social disorder, and the thoroughly retrograde "psychologist," attempting to pump life into a dead metaphysics, became familiar figures in the rhetoric of the day. The former caricature, however, was by far the more familiar. For in the officially cautious and conservative atmosphere of both the Restoration and the July monarchies, "physiology" was generally regarded as a leftist peril while, for all but dogmatic Catholics and confirmed ultraroyalists, "psychology" was in the benign mainstream. As one contemporary observer, Karl Marx, put it with characteristic acerbity, "In the . . . Cousins, Royer-Collards, . . . bourgeois society had, in its sober reality, begotten its true interpreters and mouthpieces."[16]

Médecine mentale *and "physiology"*

Where did *médecine mentale* stand in this highly charged and polarized philosophical debate? By dint of its historical origins in the Revolution and in the work of Pinel, as well as its geographical location in Paris –

---

[15] Pierre-Paul Royer-Collard, quoted in Dominique Bagge, *Le conflit des idées politiques en France sous la Restauration* (Paris: Presses universitaires de France, 1952), p. 100.

[16] Karl Marx, *The Eighteenth Brumaire of Louis Bonaparte* (New York: International Publishers, 1963), p. 16.

the medical heartland of "physiology"[17] – it had acquired an unmistakably "physiological" stamp.

Pinel had set the pattern when he appealed to the sensationalist psychology of Condillac for a conceptualization of the normal mind and its functioning which could help him interpret his clinical data about the lunatics of Bicêtre and the Salpêtrière. Now sensationalist psychology was, from the vantage point of the early nineteenth century, a rudimentary form of "physiology" (and the diametric opposite of the metaphysical "psychology" promoted by Cousin and his circle). It was, to be sure, a nonexperimental discipline, silent on the technical details of neural and cerebral anatomy and physiology; but by showing how the development of mind from a tabula rasa depended wholly upon the sensory organs, it stressed the mind's "animality" – a point brought home by Destutt de Tracy's pithy phrase, "*Idéologie* is a branch of zoology."[18] As an adherent of sensationalism, Pinel won a reputation for subversiveness that his early nineteenth-century supporters, tailoring their hero to the antirevolutionary tenor of a new day, attempted to counter. According to one anecdote they told, Pinel once met the astronomer Lalande, who mentioned that he was preparing a new edition of his notorious *Dictionary of Atheists* and had included an entry on Pinel. The latter replied that he himself was preparing a new edition of his treatise on insanity and was reserving a place in it for Lalande.[19]

Esquirol perpetuated this pattern of reliance upon sensationalism, but he favored a different sensationalist. During the Napoleonic Empire, the philosophy of Pierre Laromiguière, a somewhat wayward discipline of the Idéologue Destutt de Tracy, was in the ascendant. Believing that the Idéologue construction of mind relied too exclusively on the passive reception of sensations, Laromiguière had, as a corrective, imputed an additional, explicitly active power to the mind, lodging it in the attention – which had already figured in Condillac's epistemology as an "operation" but which was now given new prominence and raised to the

---

[17] As Balzac has his self-consciously atypical Parisian doctor Horace Bianchon say, "Contrary to the opinion of my colleagues, I am entirely convinced of the power of the will." *L'interdiction* (1836), in *La comédie humaine* (Paris: Gallimard-Pléiade, 1976–81), Vol. 3, p. 445. In Montpellier, by contrast, the vitalist tradition continued into the nineteenth century, provoking Comte's scornful epithet, "the metaphysician-pathologists of the school of Montpellier"; "Examen du traité de Broussais," p. 304.

[18] Destutt de Tracy, *Eléments d'idéologie* (Paris: J. Vrin, 1970), preface to the 1801 edition, p. xiii. For this interpretation of Condillac, see, e.g., Peisse, "M. Bérard,," pp. 582, 587. The phrase "animality of the human mind" is used to describe the Idéologue view in George Boas, *French Philosophies of the Romantic Period* (New York: Russell & Russell, 1964), p. 26.

[19] See Dupuytren, obituary for Pinel, *Journal des débats*, November 7, 1826; and Casimir Pinel, "Lettres de Pinel précédées d'une notice plus étendue sur sa vie," *Gaz. hebd. de med.* 6 (June 1, 1859): 341.

status of a faculty.[20] Under the aegis of Laromiguière, Esquirol moved away from Pinel's focus on imagination and recast the definition of insanity in terms of a malfunction of the attention. The lunatic, he wrote in 1816, "no longer enjoys the ability to fix, to direct his attention; that privation is the original cause of all his errors." Esquirol then went on to translate the standard nosology of insanity into terms compatible with this general proposition. In mania, he asserted, the "impressions are so fleeting and so numerous, the ideas so abundant" that the maniac cannot fasten his attention upon any of these mental contents long enough to separate them, assess their mutual relationships, and discard the incongruous ones. Monomania was the reverse condition, in which "attention is exercised with so much energy" that it becomes strongly attached to a single object and cannot be pried loose. In dementia, the sensory organs become so weak that they cannot transmit impressions lively enough to attract and sustain attention, so the understanding simply ceases to be. Similarly, Esquirol construed the moral treatment as a manipulation of attention: "Its principles rest on the direction to be given to [this faculty], whether one fixes, diverts or excites it."[21]

But what is particularly important for our purposes is the general gloss that Esquirol gave to the system of Laromiguière. While modern commentators have seen in Laromiguière's discontent with his Idéologue mentors and his emphasis on mental activity the seeds of the "psychology" that would shortly emerge,[22] and while at least one contemporary even classed him among the spiritualists,[23] these subtleties were apparently lost on Esquirol. The Laromiguière whom Esquirol took as his guide was straightforwardly "physiological" in his approach. "Does the study of the pathology of the powers of mind lead to the same results as those set forth by Monsieur Laromiguière in his eloquent lessons on philosophy?" asked Esquirol, proceeding to answer his own question in the affirmative. For man was not an effortlessly rational creature: "Our ideas conform to external objects" and are joined together coherently "only by dint of efforts of attention," and such efforts "presuppose in their turn an active state in the organ of thought, just as a muscular effort is necessary to produce move-

[20] See Boas, *French Philosophies*, pp. 33–42; Pierre Laromiguière, *Leçons de philosophie sur les principes de l'intelligence, ou sur les causes et les origines des idées*, 4th ed., Vol. 1 (Paris: Brunot-Labbe, 1826), lessons, 4, 6, 7; and, on status of attention in Condillac, his *Essai sur l'origine des connaissances humaines* in *Oeuvres de Condillac*, Vol. 1 (Paris: Impr. de Ch. Houel, Year VI/1798), p. 42.

[21] "Folie," (1816), *Dict. des sci. med.*, Vol. 16, pp. 162–63, 229.

[22] See, e.g., Boas, *French Philosophies*, pp. 33–42; and Emile Bréhier, *The History of Philosophy*, trans. Wade Baskin, Vol. 6, *The Nineteenth Century, Period of Systems, 1800–1850* (Chicago: University of Chicago Press, 1968), pp. 74–75.

[23] Ph. Damiron, *Essai sur l'histoire de la philosophie en France au XIXe siècle*, 3d ed., Vol. 2 (Paris: L. Hachette, 1834), pp. 102–17.

ment."[24] Esquirol's choice of analogy here is in the great tradition of "physiology"; it recalls Cabanis's more flagrant remark that the "brain in some fashion digests impressions [and] organically performs the secretion of thought."[25] Formulations of this sort, found throughout Esquirol's work ("a very great effort of attention fixed on a single object" was once described as "a sort of lockjaw of the brain")[26] gave cues to contemporaries about a philosophical allegiance that Esquirol was generally loath to specify. They prompted one observer of the psychiatric scene to depict Esquirol's conception of insanity in obviously "physiological" terms as a "lesion of the forces of the brain."[27]

More explicitly "physiological" than this adherence to sensationalism were the pronouncements occasionally made by leading psychiatrists in the relatively private context of the classroom. The opening lesson of Esquirol's Salpêtrière clinical course in 1822 must surely qualify as the most programmatic statement about the relationship between *médecine mentale* and philosophy ever to emanate from the psychiatric *maître*. What inspired this extraordinary departure from Esquirol's usual cautious reticence about things philosophical, we can only guess. Certainly the date is crucial: Esquirol seems to have been alarmed by the growing popularity of the new spiritualism and its aggressive bid for adherents and to have wanted to make his own philosophical loyalties unusually clear in order to prevent his students from being seduced by the latest philosophical fashions. He began by painting metaphysics as the major historical enemy of *médecine mentale*. Its long hegemony over the sciences had thwarted the development of a clinical study of lunatics, had made such a study virtually unthinkable or, in Esquirol's phrase, "not yet dreamed of":

> The metaphysicians claimed that this malady belonged exclusively to the domain of their discussions and that they alone had the right to discourse upon it. They lost from view the true point of departure: they disdained familiarity with the physical man, threw themselves into empty theories and obscured [the subject matter] with metaphysical abstractions.

Thus the very existence of a *médecine mentale*, which Esquirol dated from the late eighteenth century, had entailed the repudiation and vanquishment of metaphysics. These extreme measures had been necessary to establish that empirical data-gathering was a valid means of

---

[24] Esquirol, "Folie," *Dict. des sci. med.*, Vol. 16, p. 162. Esquirol does add the qualification, "although the movement is no more in the muscle than the thought is in the brain." This is a version of the standard "physiological" strategy for avoiding allegations of materialism; see p. 271 of this book.

[25] Cabanis, *Rapports du physique et du moral de l'homme, O.P.*, Vol. 1, p. 196.

[26] "Hallucination" (1817), *Dict. des sci. med.*, Vol. 20, p. 67.

[27] Frédéric Dubois (d'Amiens), "Quelques considérations sur l'aliénation mentale au point de vue de la psychologie," *Ann. m.-p.*, 1st ser., 6 (1845): esp. 123.

obtaining knowledge about mental disorder and that considerations of the "physical man" formed an integral part of such knowledge. Later in his lecture Esquirol returned to this theme, as if to a perpetual irritant; he now addressed the problem not of pre-Enlightenment metaphysics but of that newly resurgent metaphysics called "psychology." He stated unequivocally, "Psychology can serve as the basis neither for the study nor for the classification of mental maladies." It was itself too vague and internally unstable, its categories too "mobile" for such a task. More important, it was fundamentally inappropriate. "Why abstractions," Esquirol put it with uncharacteristic bluntness, "when one is dealing only with physical elements?" Rather than psychology serving as the scaffolding for *médecine mentale*, the dependence ought to go in the opposite direction; Esquirol urged that psychology "prop itself up on the observations which medicine furnishes" about the brain, the sensory receptors, and other bodily organs and how they serve to process impressions and to determine the ultimate form and content of our ideas. In his concluding remarks, Esquirol reiterated his antimetaphysical bias. "Thus gentlemen," he admonished his students, "you should not expect of me that I will condense the study of mental maladies into abstractions."[28] In light of the opinions expressed in this lecture, it is not surprising to learn that Esquirol attended the 1829 private course on positive philosophy conducted by his ex-patient Auguste Comte.[29]

In the late 1830s, Ferrus, the feisty inspector-general of lunatic houses, espoused in his clinical course at Bicêtre much the same positivist view of the historical antagonism between *médecine mentale* and metaphysics. He hailed Cabanis, who by "attaching the intellectual faculties to the material conditions indispensable to their manifestation" had "laid down the true foundation outside of which the science we pursue is nothing but a vain chimera." For Ferrus, as for Esquirol, this late eighteenth-century reconstruction of the study of mental maladies had required the retreat of the old philosophy, of that "spiritualism" which persisted in viewing the "mind as a finespun (*subtile*), imperceptible thing independent of matter." The new scientific approach to insanity, he argued, had been made possible in part because "philosophy" in traditional guise had accepted the fact of its own decline and become "less bellicose."[30]

[28] Esquirol, "Introduction à l'étude des aliénations mentales," *Revue médicale française et étrangère* 8 (1822): 31–32, 36–38.

[29] See C. Bouglé and E. Halévy, eds., *Doctrine de Saint-Simon: Exposition, première année, 1829* (Paris: Marcel Rivière, 1924), p. 443 n308. Esquirol probably met Comte in 1826 when the latter was a patient at his *maison de santé* for eight months and left "not cured"; see Henri Gouhier, *La jeunesse d'Auguste Comte et la formation du positivisme*, Vol. 3 (Paris: J. Vrin, 1941), p. 319.

[30] See the account of the last lecture of Ferrus's 1839 course, *Esculape* 1 (1839): 81.

A third identifying mark of the "physiological" orientation of early *médecine mentale* was the consistent practice by *aliénistes* of investigative autopsies – or, as they were typically called, "openings (*ouvertures*) of corpses." Autopsy occupied a salient place in the early nineteenth-century "physiological" canon because both Gall and Broussais had made it the cornerstone of their work. Gall and his collaborator Spurzheim had performed masterful and technically innovative brain dissections, on the basis of which they claimed to have demonstrated definitively the brain's anatomical and functional diversification – that is, the localization of different mental operations in different portions or "seats" (*sièges*) of that organ.[31] Brain dissection thus helped provide them with those "exact and scientific (*positif*) facts" which, they asserted, would enable them finally to clear up the confusion about the nature of the mental faculties that marked the doctrines of all purely "philosophical writers."[32] Broussais's system, which he named "physiological medicine," was likewise predicated upon localization. To define diseases on the basis of symptoms was, for Broussais, to construct them arbitrarily and "ontologically." Such definitions, he believed, rested on a concealed idealist assumption that diseases were real "entities" (*êtres*) in the manner of Platonic forms and that symptoms were their palpable appearances. Instead, diseases were to be defined by and simply equated with specific organ lesions, all of which were held by Broussais to result from a single process – overstimulation or "irritation" of the tissue followed by inflammation at the site.[33] Thus in the business of nosology, "a judicious mind is constantly drawn toward a search for sick organs," a search that was necessarily reliant upon – and would ultimately be vindicated by – the autopsy. "If cadavers sometimes appear mute to us," wrote Broussais, "it is because we are ignorant of the art of interrogating them."[34] Somewhat later in his career, in 1828, Broussais explicitly assimilated mental pathology into his general schema, predictably (and parsimoniously) explaining insanity as brain irritation.[35]

---

[31] See François Laplassotte, "Quelques étapes de la physiologie du cerveau du XVIIe au XIXe siècle," *Annales E.S.C.* 25 (1970): esp. 600; and, for a nuanced view of the relationship between brain dissection and phrenological doctrine, Robert M. Young, *Mind, Brain and Adaptation in the Nineteenth Century: Cerebral Localization and Its Biological Context from Gall to Ferrier* (Oxford: Clarendon, 1970), pp. 23–27.

[32] F. J. Gall and G. Spurzheim, *Anatomie et physiologie du système nerveux en général et du cerveau en particulier*, Vol. 2 (Paris: F. Schoell, 1812), p. 6.

[33] Erwin H. Ackerknecht, "Broussais, or the Forgotten Medical Revolution," *Bull. Hist. Med.* 27 (1953): esp. 323; Michel Foucault, *Naissance de la clinique*, 2d ed. (Paris: Presses universitaires de France, 1972), pp. 188–96.

[34] Quoted from Broussais, *Examen de la doctrine médicale généralement adopté*, and *Histoire des phlegmasies*, in Foucault, *Naissance*, pp. 194, 192.

[35] F.-V.-J. Broussais, *De l'irritation et de la folie* (Brussels: Librairie Polymathique, 1828), Part 2, Chs. 1, 7.

The use of the autopsy in *médecine mentale* predated the work of Gall and Broussais, though the tendency to reach for the scalpel was certainly reinforced by the influence of both. Already in the first edition of the *Traité* (1801), Pinel referred to "my observations upon the particular condition of the brain, meninges and other parts of the bodies of persons who have died insane," promising to report his results in detail at some future date; in the subsequent three years, he supervised over 250 *ouvertures* of deceased lunatics. His purpose in this endeavor was largely negative. He wanted to refute the contention of earlier eighteenth-century investigators, such as the Swiss naturalist Charles Bonnet and especially the pioneering Italian pathological anatomist Giovanni Battista Morgagni, that insanity was always found in persons whose cerebral substance displayed some fundamental abnormality: its surface too hard and calloused or too soft, its fibers too taut or too slack. Pinel was committed to opposing this proposition because he believed it equivalent to the proposition, or "popular prejudice," that insanity was generally incurable.[36] Yet Pinel's refusal to localize insanity in the brain was by no means a move to disembody that malady. Cabanis had acknowledged that the bodily seat of insanity might be *either* the cerebral "pulp" or the intestinal viscera; and Pinel's preference for a moral or "passional" etiology of insanity involved "original" (*primitif*) visceral lesions, usually in the abdominal region, which were then communicated "sympathetically" to the brain. (He did not specify whether these visceral lesions were the cause or the effect of the disordered passions.)[37] Over half of the numerous lunatics Pinel "opened" during the period 1802–1804 presented lesions of this visceral sort only, thus tending to confirm his hypothesis.[38]

With Esquirol, the interest in the physical correlates of insanity continued. Like his *maître*, Esquirol was prone to favor visceral lesions over cerebral ones, a point he had developed at length in his 1805 dissertation on the passions. In 1818 he announced what he regarded as a significant finding of his autopsies: that in lunatics, and especially in melancholics, the transverse colon was often displaced into a perpendicular or oblique position.[39] However, the brain–viscera issue had lost

---

[36] See Pinel, *Traité médico-philosophique sur l'aliénation mentale, ou la manie*, 1st ed. (Paris: Richard, Caille et Ravier, Year IX/1801), pp. 106–7; and, for the statistics, the report of his son, Scipion Pinel, *Recherches sur les causes physiques de l'aliénation mentale* (Paris: Impr. de David, 1826), p. 9.

[37] Cabanis, *Rapports*, *O.P.*, Vol. 1, pp. 154–55, 585; and Pinel, *Traité*, 1st ed., p. 16.

[38] S. Pinel, *Recherches sur les causes physiques*, p. 9. About one-fourth presented cerebral lesions, and the remaining one-fourth yielded indeterminate results.

[39] Esquirol, "Remarques sur le déplacement du colon transverse dans l'aliénation mentale," *Gazette de santé* (1818): 212–13. Sir Alexander Morison reports this discovery in his diary entry on his 1818 visit to Esquirol; see Richard Hunter and Ida Macalpine, eds., *Three Hundred Years of Psychiatry, 1535–1860* (London: Oxford University Press, 1963), p. 738.

much of the polemical edge it had for Pinel since the curability of certain types of insanity by the moral treatment had begun to be widely conceded; and hence Esquirol was more eclectic, more willing to admit without defensiveness the possibility of psychopathogenic brain lesions. The key issue for Esquirol became whether the precise sites of the organic lesions correlated with insanity would ever be revealed through the agencies of the scalpel and microscope. He was struck by the fact that research results had thus far been "contradictory" and inconclusive; he insisted that until "all the varieties of the cranium and brain compatible with the integrity of the faculties of the understanding" had been specified, no meaningful inferences about the "material conditions" of insanity could be drawn, and pathological anatomy was doomed to "remain mute" on this subject. It was possible, he reiterated, that *recherches cadavériques* might one day become more "fruitful," but they had first to be given a "new and better direction."[40]

Thus, while Esquirol continued to link *médecine mentale* and autopsy, his dominant attitude toward the venture was one of ambivalence and lack of true zeal and urgency. He may have believed healing to be the primary task of the *aliéniste* and determination of the organic lesions correlated with insanity to be by comparison decidedly secondary, not worth the effort expended. "And besides," he once observed, "this knowledge [of organic lesions] is not necessary for the cure of lunatics."[41] Gall and Spurzheim interpreted Esquirol's ambivalence as resulting from a conflict between fidelity "to the principles of his *maître*" concerning the abdominal site of insanity and his own findings, under the influence of their work, of more "organic defects in the brains of lunatics" than the Pinellian canon would allow.[42] Some of Esquirol's students regarded his attitude as a "fear" of pathological anatomy stemming from the potential "audacity of its deductions" – that is, presumably, from the socially delicate issue of materialism which it might raise in stark and unavoidable form.[43] Whatever the reasons for Esquirol's personal ambivalence, it is clear that he did not transmit that ambivalence to his students; on the contrary, as one member of his circle attested, "he pushed his students down that path [of pathological anatomy]; he never stopped encouraging them in this type of research."[44]

---

[40] Esquirol, "Folie," *Dict. des sci. med.*, Vol. 16, p. 214; "Introduction à l'étude des aliénations," pp. 34–35.

[41] Esquirol, "Folie," *Dict. des sci. med.*, Vol. 16, p. 216.

[42] *Anatomie et physiologie du système nerveux*, Vol. 2, pp. 289–90.

[43] See Camille Bouchet, *Quelques mots sur Esquirol* (Nantes: Impr. de C. Melinet, 1841), p. 5; and E. Georget, *De la folie* (Paris: Crevot, 1820), p. vii.

[44] Bouchet, *Quelques mots*, p. 5. Esquirol retained his own interest in the subject through the last decade of his life. In the only piece of his personal correspondence that I have

During the second decade of the nineteenth century, when the dissections of Gall and Spurzheim gave new impetus to the enterprise of charting the territory of the brain,[45] the young psychiatrists of the Esquirol circle responded with an unalloyed enthusiasm, which was in turn rewarded by their *maître*. The first two of the newly instituted Esquirol prizes were given to research projects of this nature – the 1819 prize to Georget's memoir on "autopsies of the corpses of lunatics" and the 1820 prize to Delaye and Foville's investigation of the "delirium produced by the irritation of the cortical substance of the brain."[46] Georget explicitly integrated the autopsy into his philosophical credo as a scientist. Speaking harshly of the vitalists, whose "spiritualism" was a "powerful cause of the retardation of progress in physiology," he noted their refusal to invoke "organization as the sole cause of the operations of living beings" and their "habit of considering a multitude of pathological phenomena . . . as having no organic seat." Whence their typical expressions and turns of phrase, which deserved to be "banished from the domain of science":

> . . . life forces, the principle of life, . . . vital maladies; the organs are not sick, it is their functions, their vital properties which are sick, and nothing will therefore be found in an autopsy (*ouverture du corps*).[47]

Echoing the metaphor popularized by Broussais, Scipion Pinel expressed before the Academy of Sciences in 1826 the new self-confidence of the seekers after the "sick organs" responsible for insanity. "The autopsied cadavers of lunatics have perhaps been mute until now," he said, "only because no one knew how to interrogate them."[48]

The results of the autopsies failed to meet such high expectations, and by the third decade of the century *aliénistes* were forced to cope with that fact. One basic strategy for salvaging a "physiological" commitment was a willing suspension of disbelief in the lesions that could not be seen. This was the strategy that Gall and Spurzheim had recommended as early as 1812: "If, in some mental maladies, one finds no evident defect in the brain, it is not thereby proven that no such alteration actually exists."[49] Leuret adopted this position in the mid-1830s,[50]

---

been able to locate, he writes from Italy, describing the medical school at Padua: "Its specimen collections in pathological anatomy, its facilities for physiology, are magnificent." Letter to Dr. Bloiguer in Saint-Maurice dated May 8, 1834. Bibliothèque historique de la Ville de Paris, Ms. CP 6356.

45 Laplassotte, "Etapes de la physiologie du cerveau," p. 600.
46 See Semelaigne, *Pionniers*, Vol. 1, pp. 127, 168, 172, 189.
47 Georget, *De la physiologie du système nerveux et spécialement du cerveau*, Vol. 1 (Paris: J.-B. Baillière, 1821), pp. 48–49.
48 S. Pinel, *Recherches sur les causes physiques*, p. 10.
49 Gall and Spurzheim, *Anatomie et physiologie du système nerveux*, Vol. 2, pp. 272–73.
50 François Leuret, *Fragmens psychologiques sur la folie* (Paris: Crochard, 1834), pp. 125–26 ("Does an organic modification occasion the derangement of our ideas? I believe so. What is the modification? I do not know.").

but by 1840 he was finding it more difficult to maintain, and he compared himself in this regard to the more dogmatically steadfast Ferrus:

> I willingly acknowledge, with Monsieur Ferrus, that our means of investigation are often inadequate and that our anatomical knowledge is imperfect on many points. But if, when I see no alteration in the brain [of a lunatic], I abstain from concluding that there is, in fact, no alteration in that organ, by the same token I carefully guard against concluding that there is one. When the brain of a lunatic appears healthy to me, I do not affirm with Monsieur Ferrus that this brain is diseased. I remain in doubt.[51]

On the other hand, Scipion Pinel's confidence in the revelatory efficacy of the autopsy, so strong in 1826, remained, like that of Ferrus, fundamentally unshaken. In the 1840s he gently chided those of his colleagues who had become discouraged with the venture, while offering them methodological guidelines for greater success. "We can boldly say that in the brain and throughout the nervous system, material lesions are less difficult to perceive than is commonly thought." The correct approach was to study these lesions in themselves, without comparing them to their counterparts in other organs. "Since Bichat, it has been constantly repeated that each organ and each tissue becomes sick in its own fashion"; yet this scientific verity was rarely applied in daily practice. A skillful, experienced, and above all specialized dissector of the nervous system would come to recognize even slight histological alterations, which would surely elude the eye of a generalist. Moreover, a "multitude of exact observations" was required, for in a large sample of data the seemingly contradictory evidence, so troubling to the researcher with a small number of cases, "grows weaker and ends up by disappearing altogether." Once again revealing the strong influence of Broussais upon him, Scipion Pinel deemed·a study of insanity which proceeded by cataloging symptoms, instead of discovering correlative cerebral alterations, as nonsensical as a study of respiratory disease which proceeded by cataloging the varieties of the cough.[52]

Yet another indication of the "physiological" orientation of *médecine mentale* was the strong public presence of Parisian psychiatrists in the phrenological movement. Phrenology was an archetypal variety of "physiology": It was on the experimental evidence furnished by their brain dissections that Gall and Spurzheim professed to have erected their twin phrenological doctrines of "organology" and "cranioscopy." The first doctrine held that all human mental characteristics, including both "intellectual faculties" and "feelings," were innate and determined by the size of the relevant controlling organs in the brain, some 28 or 30 of which had been located. The second doctrine held that the

---

[51] Leuret, *Du traitement moral de la folie* (Paris: J.-B. Baillière, 1840), p. 44.

[52] Scipion Pinel, *Traité de pathologie cérébrale, ou des maladies du cerveau* (Paris: Just Rouvier, 1844), pp. 11, 14–15.

size of these brain organs was discoverable by noting the shape of the skull and especially any protuberances, since the cranium was supposed to correspond closely to the contours of the brain it housed. Furthermore, phrenology had acquired that reputation for sociopolitical subversiveness that was typically the lot of "physiology." Gall had established himself in Paris in 1807 and made the French capital his permanent base of operations only after he had been effectively hounded out of Vienna, ordered by the Hapsburg authorities to suspend his private teaching "due to the peril it represented for religion and good morals."[53] This alleged peril was not lost on the French, though the more radical among them regarded it as one of the distinct advantages of phrenology. "Everyone supposed that Dr. Gall was a materialist," observed the philosopher Damiron in 1828, the year of Gall's death; and, he continued, many of Gall's supporters had a "hidden political agenda" (*arrière-pensée politique*) which led them to "construe this system as antimystical, antitheological and antisacerdotal" and then to "raise it and defend it like a flag."[54]

Thus phrenology became a symbol of liberal opposition under the Restoration; and soon after the Restoration government closed and purged the Paris medical faculty in the years 1822–23, it also forbade all private medical courses which had not received special authorization, intending through this measure to suppress phrenological instruction.[55] Conversely, the advent of the July Monarchy was seen as a go-ahead signal for phrenology; a Société phrénologique was founded in Paris in 1831.[56] Yet even under the new liberalized regime, phrenology retained some of its stigma. When Broussais's 1836 course at the Paris medical faculty – the first official institutionalization of Gall's doctrine in France – drew such an overflow of rowdy students that a larger auditorium had to be found for it, a nervous administrative official began to have second thoughts about the whole venture. He told Broussais, as the latter reported (probably with some embellishment), that phrenological doctrines were "inflammatory and dangerous for a youth that is ardent, materialist, atheist, anabaptist, anarchist."[57]

Phrenology had great potential interest to the new group of *médecins aliénistes* because its doctrine of organology included a doctrine of in-

---

53 Georges Lanteri-Laura, *Histoire de la phrénologie: L'homme et son cerveau selon F. J. Gall* (Paris: Presses universitaires de France, 1970), pp. 126–27.
54 Damiron, *Essai*, Vol. 1, p. 190 n1.
55 Paul Delaunay, "Un médecin broussaisien: Le docteur Beunaiche la Corbière," *Bulletin de la Société d'histoire de la médecine* 20 (1926): 412.
56 Lanteri-Laura, *Histoire de la phrénologie*, pp. 146–47.
57 Letter of May 22, 1836 to H. de Montègre, in H. de Montègre, *Notice historique sur la vie, les travaux, les opinions médicales et philosophiques de F.-J.-V. Broussais* (Paris: Baillière, 1839), p. 66. Broussais had converted to phrenology late in his career; see Owsei Temkin, "Gall and the Phrenological Movement," *Bull. Hist. Med.* 21 (1947): 294–97.

sanity. When, said Gall, a given brain organ was excessively developed in size or momentarily affected by an inflammation or other powerful irritant, a predisposition to insanity existed.[58] One of the first *aliénistes* to take a serious interest in phrenology was Georget, who had frequented Gall's private courses before 1820 and reported himself to have been transformed by them. When he began to study the "intellectual functions of the nervous system," he was very dissatisfied – "disgusted" (*je me dégoûtai*) is his own word – with what his physiology professors and "the most vaunted books on the subject" had to teach him. Then he encountered Gall:

> I will say it proudly. It was through the lessons and the writings of Dr. Gall that I reconciled myself to the [medical] study of the most noble attributes of man. . . . Those who see, or rather who suppose to find in the works of this savant only a hypothetical structure, only a doctrine of bumps, only the division of the cranium into compartments, will perhaps be astonished by this eulogy. Let them read and meditate upon the works of Monsieur Gall; that is my only reply.[59]

In his *De la physiologie du système nerveux et spécialement du cerveau* (1821), Georget "openly professed materialism" (as he was to put it in a testament of recantation written before his premature death in 1828) by attempting to translate the a priori categories of Kant's transcendental metaphysic into Gall's innate brain organ functions.[60]

Leuret was another precocious devotee of phrenology, going on foot to Paris while an intern at Charenton in the early 1820s to attend (though ultimately not to be persuaded by) Spurzheim's course.[61] Thus, while endorsement of phrenology was hardly universal among Parisian *aliénistes*, the influence of Gall was pervasive, and the Esquirol circle was notably well-represented in the newly founded Société phrénologique. Falret, Voisin, and Brierre de Boismont were all founding members, as was an adjunct member of the circle, Ferrus. Foville, employed in Rouen, affiliated himself as a corresponding member. And when, in 1839, Voisin was president of the Société and Belhomme its secretary

---

58 See the discussions of individual brain organs in Gall and Spurzheim, *Anatomie et physiologie du système nerveux*, Vol. 3 (1818), passim; and, for examples of this formulation about the etiology of insanity, pp. 157, 174.

59 Georget, *Physiologie du système nerveux*, Vol. 1, pp. 77–78.

60 The text of the testament is given in Raige-Delorme, "Nécrologie: Georget," *Arch. gen. de med.* 17 (1828): 155; the capsule description of the central philosophic point of Georget's 1821 text is given in Amédée Dupau's obituary for Georget, *Revue encyclopédique* 39 (1828): 533; Georget discusses the Kant-Gall "rapprochement" in *Physiologie du système nerveux*, Vol. 1, pp. 104–11, 132–34.

61 Semelaigne, *Pionniers*, Vol. 1, pp. 215, 217–18. After his youthful flirtation with phrenology, Leuret took pleasure in lambasting the system; see his "Histoire d'une tête phrénologique," *Gazette médicale de Paris*, 2d ser., 4 (1836): 335, and his review of George Combe, *Nouveau manuel de phrénologie*, in ibid., pp. 15–16.

general, the intertwining of *médecine mentale* and phrenology could hardly escape public notice.[62]

The inroads of spiritualism

The challenge to "physiology" – both in its rudimentary form as sensationalism and in its mature form as epitomized in the work of Broussais and Gall – came from a philosophical doctrine variously known as "spiritualism," "psychology," and "eclecticism" and promulgated by a close-knit cluster of philosophers that included Pierre-Paul Royer-Collard, Victor Cousin, and Théodore Jouffroy. For strategies, they drew their inspiration from foreigners – from the eighteenth-century Edinburgh "common sense" philosopher Thomas Reid and from Immanuel Kant. "The Scottish philosophy will prepare you for the German," Cousin told his students at the Sorbonne in 1829. And Taine would later recount with malicious wit how Royer-Collard, appointed to the Sorbonne as a philosophy professor in 1811 and knowing only that he did not want to be a purveyor of Condillac, stumbled upon a forlorn volume of Reid in a bookseller's stall on the Seine and purchased it for thirty sous: "He had just bought and founded the new French philosophy."[63]

The spiritualists devised their position with at least as much political as philosophical intent. Their very choice of terminology was heavily freighted with polemical meaning: By reinstating the enterprise of "psychology," they wanted to undo the work of the republican Destutt de Tracy, who during the Revolution had coined the neologism "ideology" as a substitute for "psychology" with its distasteful etymological overtones of an immaterial soul.[64] Belligerently, Cousin described his own "tormenting efforts" during the period 1816–17, "entirely occupied with the method of psychology" in order to "discover all that is contained in consciousness"; he had considered it a major breakthrough when, "from psychology which is the vestibule and, if we may so express ourselves, the antechamber of science" – and which had already offered up "the *moi*, or voluntary and free activity" – "we

---

[62] See Lanteri-Laura, *Histoire de phrénologie*, pp. 145, 147–48; "Liste des membres," *Journal de la Société phrénologique de Paris* 1 (1832): 21–28; and *Discours prononcé à la Société phrénologique de Paris par M. le Dr Félix Voisin, président, dans la séance du 9 janvier 1839* (Versailles: Impr. de Flefer, n.d.), BN: T⁷ 559.

[63] Victor Cousin, *Cours de l'histoire de la philosophie*, Vol. 2 (Paris: Pichon & Didier, 1829), p. 556; Hippolyte Taine, *Les philosophes classiques du XIXe siècle en France*, 6th ed. (Paris: Hachette, 1888), pp. 21–22.

[64] The neologizing was explained in this way in Tracy's *Mémoire sur la faculté de penser;* see Emmet Kennedy, " 'Ideology' from Destutt de Tracy to Marx," *Journal of the History of Ideas* 40 (1979): esp. 354–55.

reached the sanctuary itself, that is, metaphysics."[65] From its minority status under the First Empire, spiritualism gained in strength. By the 1840s, as a result of Cousin's key position in the national education administration and his responsibility for determining the philosophy curriculum, it had become what was generally conceded to be the "official" philosophy in France. As the editor of the *Annales méd-ico-psychologiques* observed in 1843, "*psychologism* (if we may be par-doned that expression) forms the basis of the doctrine officially taught in the University."[66]

The emergence of spiritualism could not fail to have an impact on the philosophically attuned Parisian psychiatric community. But sig-nificantly, the first *aliéniste* to become a convert to, and a would-be disseminator of, the antisensationalist philosophy was not a member of the Esquirol circle but rather that circle's foremost outsider and sometime rival, Antoine-Athanase Royer-Collard. As the brother of Pierre-Paul Royer-Collard, he had likely known about the new spiritu-alism since its inception. As a Jansenist, steeped in that tradition during his youth in Sompuis and, in adulthood, "openly religious," "always faithful to the religion of his forefathers,"[67] he doubtless felt a need for a philosophy that would harmonize his medical endeavors with his religiosity. Royer-Collard's short-lived appointment in 1819 to teach a course on *médecine mentale* at the Paris faculty provided the occasion for the first concerted effort to erect that science on explicitly spiritualist principles.

In this endeavor, Royer-Collard turned not to his brother (who had by this time already given up philosophy for politics) or to any of the self-identified spiritualists, but to a more isolated figure on the French philosophic scene, François-Pierre Maine de Biran. Unlike the spiritual-ists, who became philosophers with the refutation of sensationalism as their express mission, Maine de Biran began as a staunch Idéologue and found himself inadvertently and progressively eroding that tradi-tion from within. Most of his work remained unpublished until after his death. Royer-Collard was thus obliged to seek him out personally and, receiving a promise of help, visited him at his home in the sum-

---

[65] See Victor Cousin, *Introduction to the History of Philosophy* (1828), trans. H. G. Linberg (Boston: Hilliard, Gray, Little & Wilkins, 1832), pp. 414–15, 417. I have modified the translation slightly.

[66] L. C. [Cerise], footnote to [A.-A.] Royer-Collard, "Examen de la doctrine de Maine de Biran sur les rapports du physique et du moral de l'homme," *Ann. m.-p.*, 1st ser., 2 (1843): 4; and Doris S. Goldstein, " 'Official Philosophies' in Modern France: The Example of Victor Cousin," *Journal of Social History* 1 (Spring 1968): 259–79.

[67] This is the testimony of M. Jolly, "Eloge historique de M. le Professeur Royer-Collard, lu à la séance du 15 avril 1826" of the Academy of Medicine, pp. 11–12; Bibliothèque de l'Académie nationale de médecine, Paris: 55 025 (45).

mer of 1820.[68] Maine de Biran, who was becoming more religious at this time (his later work is usually characterized as verging on Christian mysticism) apparently found a kindred spirit in the Charenton physician, whose pedagogical aim in these lectures was "to substitute the rudiments of a sound philosophy for a false (*mensongère*) philosophy and to attack materialism down to its very foundations."[69] He would later describe Royer-Collard as a "profound observer" of man, a "friend of science and morality," noting parenthetically, "and I make this judgment on the basis of a single conversation which sufficed to reveal to me a soul with which my own resonates with all its forces."[70] He generously volunteered to revise for the physician's benefit his prize-winning 1811 memoir to the Academy of Copenhagen, and after spending more than a month (as he recorded in his diary) totally and happily absorbed in this project, he consigned the manuscript to Royer-Collard.[71]

The latter struggled with it for almost a year, remarking apologetically to its author "how difficult the study of these subjects is, especially for someone not yet familiar with them." But by June of 1821 he had composed a summary of the treatise signaling the points he found obscure or debatable. This he sent along to Maine de Biran with self-deprecating comments about its haste and poor composition and with hopes that the philosopher would "be able to tolerate reading it."[72] In fact, Royer-Collard's *abrégé* is an entirely creditable performance for a novice. Certainly Maine de Biran took it seriously, returning it with marginalia that clarified or defended his arguments.[73] This, then, is one of those rare historical episodes in which intellectual influence does not have to be speculated about, but has left behind traces of the most tangible sort.

Maine de Biran's Copenhagen memoir and his revised version of it concern the relation between *le physique* and *le moral*. The once loyal Idéologue disciple drew his theme and some of the key terms of his discussion from Cabanis, but his intent was to reformulate both the

---

[68] See letter of Royer-Collard to Maine de Biran dated June 27, 1820 in "Lettres de divers à Maine de Biran," ed. abbé Mayjonade, *Revue de Lille*, 2d ser., 4 (1896): 611.

[69] This is Jolly's paraphrase of Royer-Collard's remarks at his inaugural lecture, "Eloge historique," p. 9.

[70] Maine de Biran, *Nouvelles considérations sur les rapports du physique et du moral de l'homme*, author's preface, *Oeuvres*, ed. Pierre Tisserand, Vol. 13 (Paris: Presses universitaires de France, 1949), pp. 4–5.

[71] See the entry for "fin d'août" 1820 in *Journal intime de Maine de Biran*, ed. A. de la Vallette-Monbrun, Vol. 2 (Paris: Plon, 1931), p. 226.

[72] Letter of Royer-Collard to Maine de Biran dated June 9, 1821, "Lettres de divers," pp. 612–13.

[73] The manuscript of the *abrégé*, complete with Maine de Biran's notes, was published by Hippolyte Royer-Collard as "Examen de la doctrine de Maine de Biran," in *Ann. m.-p.*, 1st ser., 2 (1843): 1–45.

premises and the conclusions of Cabanis's famous text. Maine de Biran started from a radical dualism: on one side of the dividing line, the active and free volitional force of the self (*moi*), the "person" with a conscious awareness of "self-possession" whose phenomena must be perceived by a *sens intime* because their "interiority" makes them inaccessible to the "method of Bacon"; on the other side of the divide, the "organized" matter of the living sensory being passively obeying necessary laws.[74] Although the fundamental differences between these two aspects of human nature might have seemed to seal them off one from another, Maine de Biran, reflecting the truly "eclectic" nature of this spiritualist current, insisted upon a reciprocal though not fully symmetrical influence.

For him, as for Cabanis, the imagination was the "point of contact," the "link." Deriving from a persistent "vibrating property" common to the brain and the organs of sight, the imagination was "passive" by nature. It was situated in the domain of *le physique* called the *sensibilité*, joined there by the appetitive movements of organs (that is, the passions), which were communicated to other organs by "sympathy." According to Maine de Biran, the total state of *sensibilité* at any given moment has important consequences for mentation; it "associates its hidden or unnoticed products with the exercise of the senses and of thought," imparting the tonal colors to the objects of our experience, making them "cheerful" or "covered with a funereal veil." Now while the imagination, as part of the *sensibilité*, itself lacked freedom, it nonetheless participated in both aspects of our nature. It had two masters, which influenced it in different ways and to differing degrees. The *moi* directed it, both by "braking" it and by selectively exciting it; it usually performed this role with some efficacy, though under certain circumstances it could fail and thereby become "consumed" in animal feeling. The mastership exercised by *le physique* was confined to exciting the imagination, and in the absence of effective surveillance by the *moi*, it did so in an inherently limitless and unregulated fashion.[75]

Thus, to translate this relational system into slightly different terms, through the intermediary of the imagination, *le moral*, in the form of the self, ordinarily acted upon *le physique*. But, through this same intermediary, *le physique* did not, in a technical sense, "act" upon *le moral*. While its unfree, spontaneous movements colored *le moral* in undeniably significant ways, its influence was blind and automatic; the capacity to initiate or suspend that influence did not reside within it; and the influence obtained only insofar as the *moi* allowed – or, in cases of pathology, was unable to resist. Maine de Biran tried to explicate this

---

[74] Ibid., pp. 9–11, 25; see also F. C. T. Moore, *The Psychology of Maine de Biran* (Oxford: Clarendon, 1970), esp. Part 2, Section 2.

[75] "Examen de la doctrine de Maine de Biran," pp. 32, 34–36, 40, 44.

point in a marginal note to Royer-Collard's précis: "As light acts upon our eyes, so the soul (*âme*) acts upon the organization. This organization can be predisposed in such a way as not to receive the action of the soul, or to predominate over it, but it does not follow from this that the organization acts upon the soul." Thus Biran was able to embed the mind in a physical setting, salvaging the aspect of Cabanis so appealing to medical men, without either compromising the radical freedom of the self or negating the epistemological value of introspection. Within this framework, he defined insanity primarily in terms of the psychological domain, as the literal alienation of the normally "self-possessed" self, the loss of its free activity and its consciousness of itself.[76]

The most extensive report on Royer-Collard's course on *médecine mentale* has been provided us by Maine de Biran himself. According to this account, the "professor" began by taking "his young listeners" through a summary review of the state of anatomical and physiological knowledge. Then came the crucial Biranian, or spiritualist, turning:

> Having arrived at the end [of this summary], he asked them if they could really believe that this was man in his entirety, man not only as he is seen from the outside – as other objects are seen or represented – but man as he is for himself or as he is inwardly manifested to the eye of consciousness. Thus was the point where psychology begins and physiology leaves off distinctly marked – namely, at the fact of consciousness, at the first exercise of a free activity, at the first willing.

The professor then put forth his central claim as an *aliéniste* – that the study of insanity "rises higher" than that of physiology, which "has the living body as its object"; for insanity was an affliction of the very principle and source of the "moral life" and could "kill the person while letting the animal live."[77]

Maine de Biran concluded his description of the course with a condemnation of its suspension less than a year after it was inaugurated: "a veritable calamity for the genuine friends of morality, of religion, of the true philosophy – the foundations of which we must hasten to lay in the minds of youth so they may learn better than the preceding generation to live the life of the spirit." Indeed the full-scale closing of the medical faculty by a Restoration government intent on stamping out the subversive currents rife in the world of medical science does seem to be ironically self-defeating with respect to Royer-Collard's course. However unintentionally, the physician of Charenton was taking the government's work upon himself in his crusade against materialism, and his lectures drew a large student audience.[78] But the failure

---

[76] Ibid., pp. 17–18, 39, 39 n1.
[77] See Maine de Biran, *Nouvelles considérations*, *Oeuvres*, Vol. 13, pp. 128–29.
[78] Ibid., pp. 129–30; Jolly, "Eloge historique," p. 9.

to spare or, later, to reinstate Royer-Collard's psychiatric teaching was, we can surmise, no administrative oversight. The connection between the generic philosophic position of spiritualism and a brand of conservative liberalism considerably to the left of the political doctrine of the Restoration monarchy was likely the decisive factor, forcing the royalists to forgo the occasional benefits of that philosophy to their own cause. The Restoration government had gotten into a similarly ironic situation when its ousting of the spiritualists from the university between 1820 and 1828 invested by default the quasi-sensationalist Laromiguière with a monopoly over philosophic instruction for that entire period.[79]

What inroads did spiritualism make in the psychiatric community following the abortive lectures and, a few years later, the death of its initial sponsor Royer-Collard? Of the nineteen *aliénistes* who have been designated here as core members of the Esquirol circle, only three – Falret, Brierre de Boismont, and Baillarger – had clearly articulated a spiritualist position by the early 1850s. Falret, a founding member of the Société phrénologique, described his own intellectual sea change:

> After having for a long time sought the basis of mental pathology in the alteration of the brain, I gradually [during the 1830s] arrived at the realization that these lesions, as important as they are, could not suffice to explain scientifically the great diversity and the delicate nuances of the mental phenomena of insanity. I then began to look to psychology for the means to supply the deficiencies of pathological anatomy. I studied with perseverence the abundant writings of the psychologists, especially those of the Scottish school.[80]

Eventually he came to regard "psychology" as the "principal source of progress in *médecine mentale*."[81] Brierre de Boismont's odyssey followed a similar pattern, for like Falret he was a member of the Société phrénologique in the early 1830s. By 1851, he had published a succinct profession of faith on "human duality," citing introspective experience of the activity of the *moi* as proof of the "legitimacy and power of the psychological method" and as assuring an "indestructible success" to the "great doctrine of spiritualism."[82]

Baillarger, who was some fifteen years younger than the other two and who appears to have skipped the stage of great expectations regarding "physiology" common in the previous generation, enunciated

[79] See Prosper Alfaric, *Laromiguière et son école: étude biographique* (Paris: Belles Lettres, 1929), pp. 97–98. For another interpretation of this irony, see Alan B. Spitzer, *The French Generation of 1820* (Princeton, N.J.: Princeton University Press, in press), Ch. 3.
[80] Quoted in Semelaigne, *Les grands aliénistes français* (Paris: G. Steinheil, 1894), p. 285.
[81] Falret, "Visite à Illenau," *Ann. m.-p.*, 1st ser., 5 (1845): 436.
[82] A. Brierre de Boismont, "De la dualité humaine," *Union médicale* 5 (February 1, 1851): 53–54.

in 1845 a doctrine rich in Biranian overtones which he called "automatism." He postulated a split between the voluntary and directed use of the faculties of memory and imagination and their involuntary and unregulated use. The latter was the "point of departure for all deliria"; and since it entailed an inertness or abdication of the *moi* or personality, it accounted for the tendency of the insane to experience the ideas which preoccupied them as belonging not to themselves but to an alien being. The hallucination, the memory or fantasy perceived as an external object, was the prime example of this pathological type of involuntary mentation. Baillarger used Jouffroy's charming metaphor to describe the second stage, which depending upon its degree of intensity could be either an innocent reverie or a true delirium: "We feel . . . our understanding let loose in the country while we ourselves are not on holiday; it runs hither and thither like a schoolchild at recess and brings back to us ideas, images, memories that were found without our aid and without our ever having requested them." On the basis of his spiritualism, Baillarger sought to revise the position of "my renowned *maître*" Esquirol on the fundamental nature of insanity. According to Baillarger, Esquirol's definition (derived from Laromiguière), which had identified insanity simply as a "lesion of the attention," failed to penetrate to the heart of the matter. "The attention," Baillarger stated, "is only the applied will." It was far more accurate, then, to see insanity as a failure of the voluntary direction of all the faculties of the understanding, a failure due to a "cerebral overexcitation" that enormously increased the task before the will and rendered it ineffectual.[83]

Practical implications of philosophical positions

In a psychiatric community thus divided, however unequally, between positivist and spiritualist philosophical commitments, had the basis for fundamental consensus been lost? This issue will be explored with respect to two areas of professional psychiatric knowledge: the treatment of insanity (most important in this regard because of the nature of the specialty's originative paradigm) and the classification of its varieties.

Therapeutics. Jean-Pierre Falret and Félix Voisin were partners in the ownership and direction of a psychiatric *maison de santé* which they had

---

[83] Baillarger, "Théorie de l'automatisme" (1845) in *Recherches sur les maladies mentales*, Vol. 1 (Paris: G. Masson, 1890), pp. 494–500. Although he does not supply the precise citation, Baillarger is quoting Jouffroy's "Des facultés de l'âme humaine" (1828), reprinted in *Mélanges philosophiques*, 4th ed. (Paris: Hachette, 1866), esp. pp. 250–52. The Biran–Baillarger comparison is drawn by Henri Baruk, *La psychiatrie française de Pinel à nos jours* (Paris: Presses universitaires de France, 1967), p. 95 n1.

founded at Vanves, a suburb of Paris, in 1822.[84] Initially the two men, Esquirol circle members of exactly the same age, had similar approaches to *médecine mentale:* Both were devoted to pathological anatomy and attracted to phrenology. Later they diverged philosophically, Falret turning to spiritualism and Voisin remaining a lifelong partisan of Gall; yet apparently neither their close friendship nor their collaboration at Vanves suffered any adverse effect. Could their philosophical differences really have engendered no major quarrels about the treatment of the patients entrusted to their care?

The fact of the matter is that the moral treatment, the originative paradigm of *médecine mentale,* did not hinge upon one or another of the two basic philosophical positions; it was compatible with both, provided that reciprocal influence between *le moral* and *le physique* was admitted. This criterion was met in France. Cabanis had made psychosomatic reciprocity the hallmark of "physiology"; and, as illustrated by Maine de Biran's Copenhagen memoir – and by the arguments of Cerise, the spiritualist founding editor of the *Annales médico-psychologiques*[85] – a somewhat altered version of psychosomatic reciprocity could be accommodated to "psychological" dualism as well.

Thus the most dedicated "physiologists" recommended the moral treatment. Georget embraced it as "exert[ing] its action on the brain," which, he added, no "physical agent" was able to do without provoking "disturbances more severe than those one wishes to destroy." Indeed his only reservation about the moral treatment was its name, which he regarded as misleading to the uninitiated because it seemed "to exclude the idea of any action on the organization."[86] Broussais, whose physiological medicine recommended bleeding, and especially leeching, as the universal remedy for the "irritation" which supposedly constituted all disease, was consistent in his prescription for "brain irritation." The school of Pinel, he noted in another of his memorable phrases, "has shown itself too stingy with the blood of lunatics." But Broussais's therapeutic regimen for insanity also included the Pinellian moral treatment, a measure which he justified on grounds analogous to those of Georget. Powerful emotional states, such as rage or imperious grandiosity, "can only exacerbate cerebral irritation"; and by mitigating these, by establishing calm, the moral treatment promoted the health of the brain itself and facilitated cure.[87] Similarly, Scipion Pinel endorsed the moral treatment not only out of

[84] Semelaigne, *Grands aliénistes,* p. 326.
[85] See Cerise's introduction to his new edition of Cabanis, *Rapports du physique et du moral de l'homme* (Paris: Fortin, Masson & Cie, 1843), p. xiv; and his "Que faut-il entendre, en physiologie et pathologie, par ces mots: influence du moral sur le physique, influence du physique sur le moral," *Ann. m.-p.,* 1st ser., 1 (1843): esp. 4–8, 10–21.
[86] Georget, *De la folie,* p. 260.
[87] Broussais, *Irritation et folie,* pp. 369, 375.

filiopiety but because his "physiological" presuppositions convinced him of the utter continuity between *le moral* and *le physique*. The passions, often the primary cause of insanity, were to be considered "as nothing more than simple phenomena of the organism," as the "exaggeration of certain functions of the brain," and hence as capable of "bringing about in that organ the disturbances which congest it and later disorganize it." Logically enough, then, the moral treatment could, by targeting the passions, intervene in insanity at its point of origin – the point from which "all the physical alterations which [moral causes] imprint upon the organism" followed ineluctably.[88]

From the opposite philosophical camp, Falret's young student Morel addressed a Paris medical society in 1842 on the subject of postpartum insanity. He began by identifying himself as a spiritualist and by imploring his audience "not to be astonished" at his "too psychological" approach to a disorder so obviously rooted in the bodily changes accompanying pregnancy, childbirth, and lactation. He gave the moral treatment pride of place in the therapy for this disorder, arguing that the doctrine of the "spontaneity of the soul" meant that psychological forces could act efficaciously upon organic ailments, especially when those forces had been bolstered by the "counsels and authority of a friend, or of a physician in whom the patient has confidence." Thus in this as in other mental maladies, moral means were to reestablish equilibrium among the patient's penchants, and if need be recourse was to be had to a "transfusion of the will of the physician into that of the patient" – a therapeutic strategy, or metaphor, consonant with the spiritualist emphasis on volition and the spiritualist definition of insanity.[89]

The postulate of psychosomatic reciprocity, attached to both materialist and spiritualist philosophies, had a second implication for therapy. Not only was the moral treatment for insanity impervious to philosophic preferences, but the standard treatment for insanity across philosophical lines contained both moral and physical elements. Esquirol, working within the framework supplied by Cabanis, had laid down the dictum for this "mixed" treatment at the very beginning of the nineteenth century,[90] and *aliénistes* of all stripes echoed it. Describing two monamaniacal patients brought to his private sanatorium in the wake of the 1830 Revolution, the enthusiast of phrenology Belhomme said, "The treatment was simple: bloodletting (*déplétions sanguines*) at the beginning, baths with cold affusions on the head, purgatives and counter-irritants; as for the moral treatment, here is the one I

---

[88] S. Pinel, *Traité de pathologie cérébrale*, pp. 552, 525.

[89] B.-A. Morel, *Mémoire sur la manie des femmes en couches* (Paris: Impr. de Cosse et Gaultier-Laguionie, 1842), pp. 8–10, 54–55, 57. The "transfusion" metaphor is a favorite of Morel's and is used in various forms three times in the pages cited.

[90] See "Observations pour servir à l'histoire du traitement de la manie," *Journal général de médecine, de chirurgie et de pharmacie* 19 (Year XII/1804): esp. 130–33.

followed."[91] The very structure of his prose indicates the routinization of his thinking about treatment under these dual rubrics. Chambeyron's correspondence with the local administrative commission of the Saint-Méen asylum in Rennes clearly indicates that he too considered the treatment of insanity to have a double character: "medicaments" on the one hand, and "moral action" on the other.[92]

Moreau de Tours, branded "an exclusive partisan of organization" by his fellow Esquirol circle member Brierre de Boismont after the latter's conversion to spiritualism, was indeed a sarcastic critic of spiritualism, which he believed ought rightly to be contained on the German side of the Rhine.[93] This "physiological" bent had, in the 1830s and 1840s, led Moreau to make innovative use of pharmacology both in simulating insanity experimentally and in treating it, and he proclaimed unabashedly that these researches met the criteria established by "the men called positivists." Among the drugs Moreau used (after traveling to Egypt as the companion of a mental patient) was hashish – taking it himself, urging it on his friends, prescribing it to patients at Bicêtre. He more than once invited Balzac to a hashish-smoking party so that the novelist might partake of the imagination-liberating experiences touted by his fellow writer Théophile Gautier, who had also been supplied with the drug by Moreau. Yet for all his pharmacological emphasis, which had become an integral part of his public persona, Moreau plied the "moral" side of the treatment as well – for example, by continuing Esquirol's earlier work with music therapy.[94]

The twofold treatment program was found among *aliénistes* of spiritualist persuasion as well. The manuscript which Maine de Biran prepared for Royer-Collard indicates that "a well-directed physical regimen" can "change, up to a point, the character and cast [of our ideas] by modifying . . . the organs which are the seat of our sensitive dispositions," just as a "well-conceived regimen of the mental faculties" can "regulate . . . our sensitive dispositions and . . . usually influence the state of our organs."[95] Similarly, after expounding on the moral treatment for women in the throes of postpartum insanity, Morel went on to discuss the "physical treatment" assuming as a matter of

---

[91] Belhomme, "Influence des évenemens politiques sur le développement de l'aliénation mentale," *Bulletin des travaux de la Société médico-pratique* (1832): 29.

[92] ADIV: Fonds Saint-Méen, letter of Chambeyron dated October 25, 1836.

[93] Brierre de Boismont, "Dualité humaine," p. 54; Moreau de Tours, "Mémoire sur les prodromes de la folie," *Ann. m.-p.*, 2d ser., 4 (1852): 176.

[94] See Baruk, *Psychiatrie française*, p. 117; H. de Balzac, *Correspondance*, Vol. 5 (Paris: Garnier, 1959), letter of Moreau to Balzac, April 22, 1846, p. 113; and for Moreau's self-proclaimed adherence to positivist criteria and his relationship to Gautier, J. Moreau (de Tours), *Du haschish et de l'aliénation mentale* (Paris: Fortin, Masson et Cie., 1845), pp. 20, 30.

[95] "Examen de la doctrine de Maine de Biran," p. 45.

course that there would be one and considering only whether it ought to precede the moral treatment or be applied simultaneously.[96]

Thus neither a monist nor a dualist inclination in philosophy, but rather a belief in reciprocal psychosomatic influence, guided the therapies of early nineteenth-century French *aliénistes* and created a fundamental uniformity, despite some deliberate differences in emphasis, among treatment practices. By an apparent but readily clarified paradox, the psychotherapy called the moral treatment had been initially nurtured and established in France in an overwhelmingly "physiological" milieu.

Diagnostics: the case of monomania. In stark contrast to the philosophical neutrality of treatment practices, the diagnostic category monomania was routinely perceived to be a "physiological" parti pris. To Hippolyte Royer-Collard, professor at the Paris Faculty of Medicine, the supporters of monomania, "those missionaries of themselves," formed a "great medical league" devoted to "physiology." A certain Dr. Michu referred to the acceptance, which he ardently desired, of the monomania doctrine by the courts as "the application . . . of physiological principles to morals and legislation." And the *Gazette des tribunaux* described the Henriette Cornier trial, in which monomania was pleaded by the defense, as "that case which excites such a high degree of curiosity in the public and prompts the meditations of physicians (*gens de l'art*) and physiologists."[97]

What accounted for this philosophical labeling of monomania? In the first place, the use to which monomania was put in criminal court lent that disease a materialist cast. While it was traditional to exempt raving lunatics from responsibility for criminal acts on the ground that they had acted without free will, the monomania diagnosis attempted to extend this immunity – and this absence of free will – to people who appeared quite normal and could mingle in society without attracting undue attention. The diagnosis thus seemed to be tending in the direction of a blanket denial of free will, to be materialist in its essence. Furthermore, the peculiarly compartmentalized nature of monomaniacal insanity was readily explained by the most conspicuously "physiological" systems of the period, those of Gall and Broussais, and the disease figured prominently in the nosological canons of both.

Since the phrenologists believed in independent brain organs, each controlling a single aspect of mental life, it was easy for them to postu-

---

[96] Morel, *Mémoire sur la manie des femmes en couches*, p. 60.
[97] H. Royer-Collard, review of Regnault, *Du degré de compétence* in *Journal hebdomadaire de médecine* 2 (1829): 182–83; Worbe, review of Georget, *Examen des procès criminels* in *Journal universel des sciences médicales* 41 (1826): 315; J.-L. Michu, *Discussion médico-légale sur la monomanie homicide, à propos du meurtre commis par Henriette Cornier* (Paris: Chez l'auteur, 1826), p. 8; *Gazette des tribunaux*, June 18, 1826.

late the existence of a limited and discrete insanity, affecting a single such organ and leaving the rest of the brain intact. And since they classified brain organs as governing either "intellectual faculties" or "feelings" (the latter class including "penchants" as well as "sentiments"), it was logical for them to argue that the springs of action could be diseased without intellectual impairment. Hence their schema accommodated both homicidal monomanias and purely intellectual idées fixes. In fact, as early as 1812 Gall and Spurzheim had given credence to "partial insanity" (*aliénation partielle*) and "reasoning insanity" (*aliénation raisonnante*), the diagnostic forerunners of monomania. They had even indicated the equivalence of these conditions to something called monomania, a term which they italicized and which they must have picked up from the oral usage of Esquirol, who claims to have coined it at about this date. Gall and Spurzheim were more heavily invested in monomania still, for they offered its clinically confirmed existence as one of several proofs of their central doctrine of the plurality of mental organs: "If the brain were only a single organ, if the entirety of its homogeneous mass acted in the manifestation of each of the moral qualities or each of the intellectual faculties, I do not see why in such cases the individual would not fall into a general mania rather than a partial mania."[98] Phrenology and the diagnostic category monomania were thus caught up in a mutually supportive, even circular relationship.

Finally, it should be noted that the phrenologists pioneered and almost certainly inspired the campaign later taken up by Georget and the rest of the Esquirol circle to promote judicial leniency in cases of crime committed in the throes of partial insanity. A long section of their 1812 text was devoted to the "application of our principles to man considered as the object . . . of correction and punishment." They argued that, on the basis of the "sentiments drawn from their organization," all human beings did not have "equally numerous and strong impulsions to good and to evil"; and hence, for their actions to be judged equitably, these different physiological "interior circumstances" had to be taken into account. Insanity formed one such class of "interior circumstances." In this regard, Gall and Spurzheim found no fault with contemporary judicial practice toward "general insanity," since those individuals afflicted with it were seldom if ever mistaken for sane, and their lack of "moral freedom" was universally conceded. But cases of intermittent and especially partial insanity were apt to pass unnoticed, and the attenuation of moral freedom and of criminal responsibility which they produced when "noxious penchants acquir[ed] a very decided energy" was likely to be ignored by the courts.[99] The precocious articulation of this viewpoint by the phrenologists could

---

[98] Gall and Spurzheim, *Anatomie et physiologie du système nerveux*, Vol. 2, pp. 194–95, 417–18.

[99] Ibid., pp. 141–212, esp. pp. 142, 191, 196, 209–10.

only help to strengthen the public perception that the monomania doctrine of the psychiatrists was in the phrenological mold and hence "physiological."

Broussais's commitment to physiological localization likewise provided grounding for monomania. Bringing the whole body into play, Broussais classified the different genres of monomania according to their original organic seats and the other, intermediary organs to which the "irritation" spread. Suicidal monomania, for example, was caused by a "bad condition of the stomach" with subsidiary irritation of the heart and lungs; demonomania resulted from a "strong and tenacious irritation" in the entire digestive tract. In these and all other monomanias, the organic irritations eventually affected the "innervation of the brain tissues" and thus produced the characteristic subjective psychological state and often a corresponding "imperious" compulsion to action. Broussais was aware of the fundamental similarity between his approach to monomania and that of Gall – the partial nature of the insanity being mirrored in the discrete organic locus or loci which gave rise to it – yet he raised a "grave objection" to Gall's approach. Phrenology limited the number of possible monomanias to the number (some 28 or 30) of brain organs. To Broussais, who wanted to account for an almost infinite spectrum of "intellectual and affective nuances" in monomania, some two dozen organs were inadequate, and a whole new arsenal of physiological variables had to be added. Not only were the viscera variously involved in the etiology of monomania, but the brute "mass" of the brain organ and especially the "mode of action" of this mass also played a role: Depending upon its "greater or lesser irritability and contractility, its greater or lesser permanence in the state of condensation, the suppleness or rigidity of the nervous fiber," the monomaniacal pathology was subtly altered.[100] The name of Broussais became popularly associated with the monomania diagnosis. In the medical consultation scene of Balzac's *Peau de chagrin* (1831), the thinly disguised Dr. Brisset, identified as the "successor to Cabanis," has been called in to examine the mysteriously shrinking wild ass's skin. He announces that the shrinkage is a false monomaniacal perception resulting from the physiological condition of its owner:

> The progressive deterioration wrought in the epigastric region, the seat of vitality, has vitiated the whole system. Thence, by continuous fevered vibrations, the disorder has reached the brain by means of the nervous plexus, hence the excessive irritation in that organ. *There is monomania.* The patient is burdened by a fixed idea. That piece of skin really contracts, to his way of thinking; very likely it has always been as we have seen it.[101]

[100] Broussais, *Irritation et folie*, pp. 258, 267, 337–44.
[101] The English translation quoted here is Balzac, *The Wild Ass's Skin* (London: J.M. Dent, 1954), p. 202, my italics.

The ascription of a philosophical allegiance to monomania, the wide-spread tendency to view it as a "physiological" doctrine, added another element to the politics of the monomania controversy. Not only did the royalists depict the monomania doctrine as subversive of social order because of its refusal to mete out appropriate punishments to criminal offenders; it was subversive on a deeper level as well, because it attacked, through its "materialist" assumptions, the very foundations of religion and morality. The controversy thus provided an occasion for the stereotypic combination of "atheistic physiology" to make frequent appearances in public rhetoric. Bayeux, the chief prosecutor in the Cornier case, contended that the "system which tends to attribute the most atrocious crimes to a supposed monomania" subscribed to "that fatalism [which is] the only god of the materialists."[102] The magistrate in a provincial murder trial in 1826 "forcefully combated the system of monomania which is, he said, nothing other than fatalism."[103]

However, not all of the assailants of monomania on religious grounds had political roles or clear political purposes. One obscure French physician, well-equipped with all the standard clichés on the subject, entered the pamphlet warfare as an orthodox Catholic, "ashamed" that medical science seemed to be authorizing "by the false reasonings of physiology – which lead to a materialism and a fatalism undermining of religion, morality and good order – a perverse doctrine." There was nothing "irresistible," said Dr. Grand, about the murderous impulse which constituted the putative monomania of Henriette Cornier. True piety could have supplied an effective counterpoise:

> If instead of abandoning herself to her homicidal idea, Mlle Cornier had had recourse to divine grace by appealing to a priest (to whom she would have confessed the idea which preoccupied her), the counsels of religion would have deterred her.[104]

The religious argument against monomania, spelled out in greater detail here than in the magistrates' capsule denunciations, was that the very notion of a "diseased" will, the substitution of pathological categories for moral ones, attributed necessity to an individual's actions and implicitly negated not only the freedom of the will but also the efficacy of prayer, confession, and divine intervention. Furthermore, for persons experiencing difficulty in the management of their wills, the appropriate "professional man" to whom to turn was the priest, not the physician.

The leaders of the Parisian psychiatric community, distressed at the

---

[102] *Journal des débats*, June 25, 1826.

[103] "Cour d'Assises de l'Ain (Bourg)," *Gazette des tribunaux*, September 9, 1827.

[104] Grand, *Réfutation de la discussion médico-légale du docteur Michu sur la monomanie homicide à propos du meurtre commis par Henriette Cornier* (Paris: Chez l'auteur/Gabon, 1826), p. 18.

scurrilous publicity that monomania had attracted to itself, attempted to deny that the disease was a materialistic construct. "There prevails in France among many people and especially among the older magistrates," wrote an obviously piqued Marc, "a spirit of misplaced religiosity which has singularly militated against [acceptance of] the reality of monomania and the irresistible urges which ordinarily accompany it." But surely, he exclaimed, even the "most religious of men" had to agree that the soul "acts only through the physical organization" and that a blow on the head that obliterates the capacity for thinking does not constitute evidence of the nonexistence of the soul. The monomaniac was like a musician possessing a discordant lyre who, despite his good intentions and his God-given endowments, could not produce melodious sounds.[105] Marc's argument here is a variant on the one which the diligent casuists Gall and Spurzheim had put forth some two decades earlier to extricate phrenology from the charge of materialism: An organ, the "material condition which makes possible the manifestation of a faculty," had to be carefully distinguished from the faculty itself; the latter was called a "property of the soul" (*âme*), and its precise nature left tactfully unspecified. "If to be a materialist," they had added in exasperation, "it suffices to declare that the exercise of the intellectual faculties depends on the organization, what writer, ancient or modern, could not be justly accused of materialism?"[106] Esquirol would not go as far as Marc in publicly representing monomania as a flaw in the "organization." In 1827 he affirmed the existence of the disease and at the same time tried to dissociate it from all philosophical issues by taking refuge in *la clinique:*

> God forbid that, fomentors of materialism and fatalism, we wanted to create or defend theories subversive of morality, society and religion. . . . That word "monomania," we have already said, is neither a system nor a theory; it is the expression of a reality observed by doctors.[107]

Thus the psychiatric proponents of monomania attempted to protect their concept from social criticism by declaring its philosophical neutrality. The psychiatric opponents of monomania, however, took the other tack with respect to philosophy. In contrast to Esquirol's assertion that *la clinique* was a pure Baconian inductive method generating classificatory categories from the sheer accumulation of empirical data (monomania was "neither a system nor a theory"), J.-P. Falret held that such pure Baconianism was an impossibility. The clinical observer,

---

[105] Marc, "Considérations médico-légales sur la monomanie et particulièrement sur la monomanie incendiaire," *Ann. d'hyg. pub.* 10 (1833): 376–77.

[106] Gall and Spurzheim, *Anatomie et physiologie du système nerveux,* Vol. 2, pp. 81–82.

[107] Esquirol, "Note sur la monomanie-homicide" in J.-C. Hoffbauer, *Médecine légale relative aux aliénés et aux sourds-muets,* trans. A. Chambeyron (Paris: J.-B. Baillière, 1827), p. 358.

he said, inevitably came to the lunatic ward equipped with latent or
explicit principles of selecting from and making sense of the jumble of
data presented to his gaze.[108] Hence Falret and his students did not rest
with their clinical refutation of monomania: They supplemented it by
reference to the spiritualist philosophy they had embraced; they revealed, in effect, the "bias" they had brought to their work as clini-
cians. They could avail themselves of this kind of explicit philosophical
argument because, unlike the proponents of monomania, their philosophy was entirely socially acceptable.

The spiritualists had always contended that the sensationalists, the
first "physiologists," were unable to introduce an adequate concept of
the self, or personal identity, because their system constructed mind
atomistically from the raw material of sensation and provided no
means for it to overcome its fragmentary origins. By contrast, the spiritualists' *moi* was a unified, holistic, integrated entity – and, added the
spiritualist *aliénistes*, it consequently afforded no theoretical grounding
for a disease affecting a single idea or a single faculty.[109] Morel even
went so far as to blame the creation of monomania on the long "official" ascendancy of the philosophy of Condillac.[110]

The debates on monomania at the Société médico-psychologique self-
consciously addressed these issues. The opening paper by the *aliéniste*
Delasiauve took a position intermediate between those of Georget and
the Falret camp by asserting the "solidarity" of the intellectual faculties
(thus ruling out the monomania of a single idea) but postulating a "fundamental boundary" dividing the intellectual faculties from those of the
"moral and instinctive order," as well as a lack of "solidarity" among the
latter. Hence the isolated lesion of the will which had for three decades
been the focus of intense controversy had, in his view, theoretical
plausibility.[111] Brierre de Boismont, already an avowed convert to spiritualism, came out in favor of the solidarity of all mental faculties and the
concomitant nonexistence of all varieties of monomania, while Belhomme upheld the diagnosis in all its aspects by arguing against solidarity on phrenological grounds.[112]

Philosophical disagreement within the psychiatric community contributed to the erosion of the earlier psychiatric consensus about monoma-

---

[108] Falret, "De la direction à imprimer à l'observation des aliénés" (1850), in *Des maladies mentales et des asiles d'aliénés* (Paris: J.-B. Baillière, 1864), pp. 105ff. As far as I know, Falret was the first French psychiatrist to articulate an anti-Baconian view of the revered clinical principle.

[109] Falret, "De la non-existence de monomanie," *Maladies mentales*, p. 431; Morel, "De la monomanie," *Etudes cliniques* (Nancy: Grimblot; Paris: J.-B. Baillière, 1852), Vol. 1, p. 428.

[110] Morel, "De la monomanie," pp. 415, 419.

[111] Delasiauve, "De la monomanie au point de vue psychologique et légale," *Ann. m.-p.*, 2nd ser., 5 (1853): 358, 361.

[112] Minutes of the Société médico-psychologique, *Ann. m.-p.*, 2d ser., 6 (1854): 104, 111.

nia, and hence to the gradual decline and eventual abandonment of that contested diagnostic category. For the time being, however, the debates at the Société médico-psychologique could only have reinforced the impression, articulated decades before in the public rhetoric of royalist judges and orthodox Catholics, that monomania was a "physiological" concept. Indeed the decades of championing monomania had stamped upon the emergent profession of *médecine mentale* a popular identity as a continuator of the extremist wing of Enlightenment philosophy and as a bearer of antireligious values.

Some comparative remarks

Having looked at the relationship between early nineteenth-century *médecine mentale* and each of two "neighboring domains" – religion and philosophy – some comparative remarks are in order. Psychiatrists both borrowed from and competed with clerics. They borrowed certain key techniques of psychological healing, and they perforce competed with clerics who continued, after the Revolution, to be active in the care of the insane. Their relationship to philosophy was different – not with respect to borrowing, for psychiatrists frequently and overtly took their general conceptualizations of the mind from philosophers, but with respect to rivalry. Here, obviously, patients were never a bone of contention; and what serious rivalry there was for control of discourse about the malfunctions of the understanding was mainly historic – that is, psychiatrists charged that the hegemonic power of metaphysics before the Enlightenment had delayed the emergence of their own inductive, observational science of insanity. The new metaphysics of the nineteenth-century spiritualists did not really compete with *médecine mentale*. Threatened by the growth of positive science, reconciled to the demotion of philosophy from its once queenly status, the spiritualist "psychologists" were content to have the legitimacy of their intellectual and pedagogical enterprise recognized and their coexistence with medical men assured. Their main concern in the adjudication of disciplinary boundaries was, in other words, that they not be pushed off the map entirely. Hence hostile rivalry colored the relationship of philosophers to *aliénistes* only when the latter adopted a "physiological" stance of an extreme and intolerant sort.

One easily overlooked aspect of the relationship between philosophy and psychiatry during this period is that both parties were newly professionalizing disciplines. Despite the very traditional nature of philosophy, it had, during the first third of the nineteenth century and until the creation of Cousin's "regiment," no firm or official institutional base. The creaky universities of the Old Regime had been destroyed during the Revolution. The Enlightenment philosophes, for all their putative influence, had been free-lance intellectuals, operating in salons rather than university lecture halls or the classrooms of *lycées*. This fragile institutional condition may help to explain why philosophy did not put up a more vigorous fight against the encroachments of an upstart *médecine mentale*. Here a comparison between the emergence of forensic psychiatry in Germany and in France is instructive. In Germany, the philosophers, proud holders of state university chairs represented in this instance by Immanuel Kant, disputed with the physicians over which group should be entrusted to make determinations of insanity for legal purposes.[113] In France, as we have seen, the comparable contest took place between judges, who upheld the ability of the ordinary layman to make such determinations, and physicians: Philosophy, less institutionally powerful and self-assured than in Germany, played no part.

The relative weakness of philosophy in France, which fostered its unaggressive behavior, emerges again when its international stature as a discipline in the early nineteenth century is compared with that of medicine. This was the period when the fame of French medicine reached an apogee, when the clinical lessons at the Paris faculty drew students from all over Europe and America; and *médecine mentale* naturally partook of the prestige of its parent discipline. But the French philosophical school was hardly an international magnet. Widely regarded abroad as derivative and shallow, it inspired instead Heine's satiric assessment of Cousin: "Your great eclectic, who . . . was desirous of giving you instruction in German philosophy, had not the slightest comprehension of the subject."[114] That some early nineteenth-century American philosophers gave Cousin a serious reading only proved the rule: They were interested in the French thinker not for his own sake but as an aid to understanding German idealism.[115]

Thus the boundary dispute of which we came in quest was a decidedly muted one. But the lack of full-blown conflict does not diminish the importance of philosophy to the development of French psychiatry. The religious and philosophical themes, though treated here in separate chapters, were in fact intertwined. The very small minority of Parisian *aliénistes* who wanted to give a religious cast to the medical treatment of insanity – that is, J.-P. Falret and possibly his student Mo-

---

[113] Kant put forth his views in a discussion of mental disorders in Part 1, Sections 35–43 of his *Anthropologie in pragmatischer Hinsicht abgefast* (1798). Among his medical opponents was a Dr. Metzger; see Dr. J.-J. Ballard, "Discourse préliminaire du traducteur," in J. Dan. Metzger, *Principes du médecine légale ou judiciaire* (Paris: Gabon, 1813), p. xviii.

[114] Heinrich Heine, *Religion and Philosophy in Germany*, trans. J. Snodgrass (Boston: Beacon Press, 1959), p. 157.

[115] See Bruce Kuklick, *Churchmen and Philosophers: From Jonathan Edwards to John Dewey* (New Haven: Yale University Press, 1985), pp. 130, 135, 162.

rel – were also the bulwark of philosophic spiritualism within the psychiatric community. The far greater number of psychiatric "physiologists" adopted an anticlerical attitude toward the etiology of insanity and the management of lunatic hospitals. Hence the philosophical and religious views held by the typical *aliéniste* combined to create a powerfully unambiguous public image of psychiatry which, in turn, had clear practical consequences. It helped to determine, as the next two chapters will show, which nineteenth-century political regimes would prove most hospitable to psychiatry's professional growth.

8

The Law of 1838 and the asylum system

THE historian, always on the lookout for pivotal moments, cannot help but find gratification in the passage of the Law of June 30, 1838. Building on a variety of developments from the late eighteenth century on, the Law marked the decisive step in the emergence of a psychiatric "profession" in France – a profession, that is, construed in terms of the statist model. The Law integrated the new medical specialty into the apparatus of the state.[1] It mandated the creation of a nation-wide network of asylums staffed by full-time medical doctors and brought into existence a race of psychiatric functionaries appointed by the minister of the interior, removable by him, and paid salaries in accordance with a scale determined by him. It also made provision for "students attached to these lunatic establishments," thus formalizing the status of the asylum not merely as a hospital for patients but also as a training institute that would insure the transmission of the new medical knowledge.[2] The Law can be seen as a belated (though imperfect) realization of the professional project articulated by Esquirol during the period 1818–19. And its crucial role in solidifying a sense of collective identity among French *aliénistes* is shown by the fact that it supplied the impetus for the founding of the first psychiatric journal in France. When the inaugural issue of the *Annales médico-psychologiques* appeared in 1843, its editor noted that this was the journal envisioned by Pinel decades earlier but which had only recently become feasible. "The science of insanity indisputably exists today," he said with confidence, for it had received the endorsement not only of "physicians" but of "legislators" and "statesmen" as well.[3]

The Esquirol circle member Archambault pronounced the Law an outstanding example of "political medicine," meaning by this phrase that it represented a joint effort by political authorities and medical

---

[1] This last formulation agrees with that of Robert Castel, *L'ordre psychiatrique: L'âge d'or de l'aliénisme* (Paris: Minuit, 1976), p. 191.

[2] See Loi sur les aliénés, June 30, 1838, Title 1, Article 1; and its implementing Ordonnance relative aux établissements publics et privés consacrés aux aliénés, December 18, 1839, Title 1, Articles 3, 10, 14.

[3] "Introduction," *Ann. m.-p.*, 1st ser., 1 (1843): i–iii.

men, the latter having "enlightened" the former on the "grave ques-tion" of insanity.[4] Archambault was correct. In preparing the legisla-tion and guiding it through the chambers, the government and the psychiatrists had worked together in close and conspicuous partner-ship. This chapter examines the 1838 Law from a number of perspec-tives relevant to our main themes: the overlapping aims of psychiatrists and the state, which made possible the collaborative effort necessary to establish the profession on statist lines; the effect of the forthcoming legislative campaign on psychiatric theoretical formulations – in this case, the doctrine of "isolation"; and the two boundary disputes en-tailed by the legislation, one with the judiciary and the other with the clergy, which continued the gradual process of the delineation of a psychiatric domain.

Lunacy legislation and the constitutional monarchy

Ever since Esquirol had called for a state-organized asylum system in 1819, the statist orientation of the *aliénistes* – their wish to have their expertise both validated and concretely institutionalized by the state – had been unwavering. What fluctuated in the twenty years between the articulation and the realization of this goal was the receptivity of the government.

As soon as the 1838 Law was proposed, it was universally recog-nized by political observers as a "Doctrinaire" measure.[5] This label is important for our purposes, for it points to the fact that, during the two decades under consideration here, the "professional" fate of psy-chiatry in France was tied to the vicissitudes of liberalism, and more precisely to that peculiarly conservative form of liberalism espoused by the so-called Doctrinaires. François Guizot and Pierre-Paul Royer-Col-lard, the most prominent of these Doctrinaires, earned the group its austere name by trying to construct a political philosophy to guide their political practice. But because they constructed this philosophy largely to exclude unacceptable alternatives – the nostalgia of the coun-terrevolutionaries, the revolutionary theories of equality and majority rule – the product of their philosophical speculations has been justly called "a counter-system rather than a system."[6] Why should the Doc-trinaires have been interested in institutions for the insane? A sche-matic representation of their political mentality, consisting of three principal and interlocking components, will help to explain why such institutions naturally became one focus of their political attention.

---

[4] Archambault, review of Cazauvieilh, *Du suicide,* in ibid., pp. 170–71.
[5] See, e.g., *Siècle,* April 6 and April 9, 1837; *Echo française,* January 7, 1837.
[6] Douglas Johnson, *Guizot: Aspects of French History, 1787–1874* (London: Routledge & Kegan Paul, 1963), pp. 36–37.

The Doctrinaires were, first of all, anxiously concerned to maintain social order. Hence, for example, their political-philosophical maneuver of lodging sovereignty in the abstract concept of "reason" rather than in the vagaries of any representative assembly or group of mere human beings.[7] The distrust of the political process which this philosophical strategy disclosed had its practical ramifications in the Doctrinaires' commitment to a severely restricted suffrage and their partiality for bureaucratic solutions to the problems of social order. In this tendency to see the requirements of "reason" fulfilled by the actions of a state bureaucracy, the Doctrinaires bore a strong family resemblance to the enlightened absolutists of the late eighteenth century.

Second, the Doctrinaires wanted to insure the vitality of religion, which they regarded pragmatically as a brake on human action and therefore as indispensable to the stability of society. They were, as we have already seen, appalled by the atheistic implications of the sensationalist epistemology, and their own rational spiritualist epistemology declared the concepts of God and an immortal soul to be a priori truths. Their religion of choice was not, however, orthodox Catholicism (which they associated with the pre-1789 corporate order), but rather a more general, minimally dogmatic Christian creed; after all, Guizot was a Protestant and Royer-Collard a Jansenist. A third component was humanitarianism, dedication to the cause of the weak and the downtrodden. For Guizot at least, this attitude had positive roots in the strong social conscience instilled by a Protestant education.[8] But it also had deep negative roots – that is, it belonged to the Doctrinaire "counter-system" – in that it was informed by political anticlericalism, by a distaste for traditional Catholic charity and its assumption of social functions that could be discharged instead by secular agencies or, ideally, by the secular state. In short the Doctrinaires did not prize all "humane" endeavors equally; and if their politics emphasized *bienfaisance*, it was partly because *bienfaisance* had the virtue of replacing that religious charity which had figured in the political dispensation of the Old Regime and which they regarded as inimical to the integrity of a constitutional state. The first and third components of this Doctrinaire program were mutually reinforcing, for as will be discussed below, public welfare institutions were unabashedly portrayed by their Doctrinaire advocates as instruments of social order.

It was no accident, then, that the high-water marks of psychiatric professional success under the *monarchie censitaire* coincided with the apogees of Doctrinaire influence. It was in 1819 and under the most

[7] Ibid., pp. 37–40; and François Guizot, *History of the Origin of Representative Government in Europe*, in *Historical Essays and Lectures*, ed. Stanley Mellon (Chicago: University of Chicago Press, 1972), pp. 43–49.

[8] Charles Pouthas, *Guizot pendant la Restauration: Préparation de l'homme d'état (1814–1830)* (Paris: Plon, 1923), p. 221.

liberal ministry of the Restoration, that of Decazes (an ally of the then newly formed group of Doctrinaires),[9] that the bureaucracy initiated the project to draw up a blueprint for a model asylum to be built throughout provincial France – a project Esquirol had helped to inspire and in which he participated actively. At the very same time, Guizot was serving in the Ministry of the Interior as director-general of departmental and communal administration, pouring forth a steady stream of circulars on such topics as hospitals, abandoned children, and lunatics.[10] From the vantage point of 1819, it looked as if Esquirol's hopes for the new specialty of *médecine mentale* were about to come to fruition. But with the assassination of the Duc de Berry and the fall of Decazes a year later, the Restoration regime turned away from its brief liberal experiment and from the secular statist *bienfaisance* that was its corollary. The government suspended the model asylum project in medias res. Nor would *médecine mentale*, tainted with "physiology" and anticlericalism, have been a suitable (or even thinkable) partner for the Restoration regime of the 1820s, which was tilted toward the ultraroyalists and generally committed to the verities of throne and altar.[11] The same set of events had blocked the Esquirol circle's professional ambitions and the Doctrinaires' political ambitions.

The centrality of *bienfaisance* to the Doctrinaire program can be seen in one of the activities that occupied the group during its decade out of power: the Société de morale chrétienne, founded in the autumn of 1821. Dedicated to a nondoctrinal Christian humanitarianism – and adhering to that typically Enlightenment distinction between a rational, methodical, and far-reaching "philanthropy" and a more personally fervent but less effective "charity"[12] – the Société became involved in a variety of causes, including the abolition of slavery and aid to the refugees of the liberal revolution in Greece. But it addressed most of its energies to those social problems already the subjects of Guizot's 1819 bureaucratic circulars: prisons, lunatic asylums, orphaned children, public hygiene. It thus removed into the sphere of voluntary associational activity what was conceived of as "interrupted government work." The Société helped to keep the Doctrinaires together as a collectivity, and retrospectively it can be seen to have served as a hatchery for liberal politicians. "Almost all the future personnel of the July Monarchy made their debuts there under the auspices of philanthropy."

---

[9] Johnson, *Guizot*, p. 32.

[10] Pouthas, *Guizot pendant la Restauration*, pp. 219–23.

[11] On the hostility of the Restoration regime to the progress of medicalization and its attempts to bolster clerical power in the hospitals, see Jacques Léonard, "La Restauration et la profession médicale," *Historical Reflections/Réflexions historiques* 9 (1982): esp. 81.

[12] Quoted in Ferdinand Dreyfus, *Un philanthrope d'autrefois: La Rochefoucauld-Liancourt, 1747–1827* (Paris: Plon, 1903), p. 496, from an 1824 speech before the Société.

Guizot was prominently affiliated with the Société from the start; other members, whose names would be linked with the framing and passage of the 1838 Law, included Gasparin, Vivien, d'Argout, and Montalivet.[13]

The 1830 Revolution, accompanied by an explosion of popular anti-clericalism, brought the Doctrinaire liberals back into the government, now as a mainstay rather than as the marginal and tenuously accepted group they had been during even their brightest moments under the Restoration. Guizot even served as minister of the interior during the first year of the new regime. Thus bureaucratic concern with the insane quite naturally resumed in the 1830s – not picked up precisely where the Decazes ministry had left off a decade before, but picked up just the same. Though cabinets shifted with notorious rapidity, the policy had a consistent drift. In September 1833, Minister of the Interior d'Argout, a veteran of the Société de morale chrétienne, sent a circular to the prefects requesting detailed information about the kinds of facilities available for the insane in each department and the sizes of their inmate populations. Not satisfied with the quality of the data returned, his successor created the new post of inspector-general of lunatic houses and in October 1835 appointed to it Guillaume Ferrus, the chief physician at Bicêtre, whose frank anticlericalism in matters of asylum management coincided nicely with the government's own view that public assistance should be secular in nature.[14] Ferrus soon distributed another questionnaire to the departments he visited, one which generally reiterated the questions posed in 1833 but which also sounded a new note: overt concern with the status of the psychiatric professional project in the localities. Ferrus inquired about the existence of a "physician specially attached to the establishment," the frequency of his visits to the lunatics, whether he kept a daily "notebook of observations," the extent of his authority within the institution, his salary – in short, matters which had not piqued the curiosity of the minister and which evidenced the merger of governmental and professional-psychiatric aims now taking place.[15] By the beginning of 1837, a draft bill on the insane was ready for presentation to the chambers.

In all of this busy and carefully orchestrated activity, was the govern-

[13] Pouthas, *Guizot pendant la Restauration*, pp. 348–48; Guizot's disciples and "all of the old Doctrinaire group, except Royer-Collard" joined; so did Edouard Laffon de Ladébat, the bureaucrat who had made common cause with Esquirol in 1818–19. On Montalivet's membership, see his *Fragments et souvenirs*, Vol. 1 (Paris: Calmann Lévy, 1899), pp. 32–34.

[14] See the carefully worded support given by the minister of the interior to Ferrus's position on state administrative supervision of charitable institutions. A.-E. de Gasparin, *Rapport au Roi sur les hôpitaux, les hospices et les services de bienfaisance* (Paris: Impr. royale, 1837), p. 98.

[15] A copy of Ferrus's questionnaire, which was dated June 25, 1836, can be found in AN: F^{15} 3905, Dossier: Charente, in the context of that department's reply to it.

ment motivated by humanitarian zeal? The issue was a live and pressing one by 1837, with newspapers of the political opposition voicing
cynical suspicions that the generous humanitarianism of the government's bill concealed "some underlying political design" – that the government intended to create, through its proposed legislation on the
incarceration of the insane, new bastilles for its political enemies, or a
new device for managing elections which consisted of putting "under
lock and key" those individuals "afflicted only with the madness of an
inconvenient opposition."[16] That there was any factual basis for these
particular allegations (part of an inflated political rhetoric of conspiracy
current at the time)[17] is highly improbable. But the allegations pointed
to a more general truth. The government did seek more than humanitarian ends in the insanity legislation; it sought – as the interlocking
parts of the Doctrinaire program would suggest – a kind of control, a
technique for the maintenance of social order.

In fact, it admitted this quite openly. In his *Report to the King on
Hospitals, Hospices and Benevolent Services,* written while the lunacy bill
was in preparation and published in 1837, Minister of the Interior
Adrien-Etienne de Gasparin offered two reasons for his assertion that
insanity was one of the problems that "demand most imperiously the
solicitude and the intervention of the Government." One reason was
humanitarian: "to come to the aid of misfortune, to assuage the most
distressing of human infirmities." The second was concern for social
order: "to preserve society from the disorders which these sick persons
can perpetrate."[18] The progovernment *Journal des débats* reiterated this
dual justification when it praised the proposed law on the insane as
"simultaneously a law of philanthropy and general police"[19] – a formula
which became the usual characterization of the Law, invoked even decades later as a guide to its proper enforcement.[20] There was nothing
automatically invidious about the sound of *police générale* at this date

---

[16] *Siècle,* April 6, 1837 and April 9, 1837; see also *Courrier français,* February 12, 1838.
Both of these newspapers supported the Orleanist regime but sided with a left-liberal
faction led by Thiers against the Doctrinaire liberal faction led by Guizot. See Eugène
Hatin, *Histoire politique et littéraire de la presse en France,* Vol. 8 (Paris: Poulet-Malassis &
de Boise, 1861), pp. 582, 590.

[17] See, e.g., the comparable accusation made a decade later that the state-salaried cantonal physicians included in the Salvandy project on medical reorganization would
serve as "electoral courtiers" for the government; Prince de la Moskowa in the Chamber of Peers, *Moniteur universel,* June 5, 1847, p. 1437.

[18] Gasparin, *Rapport au Roi,* p. 93.

[19] *Journal des débats,* April 8, 1837; see the nearly identical phrase in ibid., April 4, 1837.

[20] See, e.g., the prefect's remarks ("not only a law of police but also a law of
bienfaisance") in AN: F^{15} 3904, Dossier: Hérault, excerpt from the minutes of the
Conseil général, 1839; and AN: F^{15} 3912, Dossier: Landes, circular of the prefect to the
mayors of the department dated February 12, 1855 ("less a law of *bienfaisance* than a
law of police").

(though the term had lost some of its eighteenth-century innocence during the Napoleonic regime),[21] nothing self-incriminating about a government's announcing it as a goal. Indeed the dual justification for the bill of 1837 was virtually identical to that of the 1785 administrative *Instruction* of Colombier and Doublet. But however much the tradition of enlightened absolutist "health police" persisted, the content of *police*, what that term most denoted to a government, had undergone a shift of emphasis during the intervening, revolutionary half-century. For the Doctrinaire liberals of the 1830s, the single most salient meaning of the term was not the positive, optimistic one of promoting the welfare of the population but the negative, anxious one of preventing lower-class disorder. As Gasparin said on the opening page of his *Report to the King*, the issue of public assistance was inseparable from an awareness of the disruptive, law-breaking potential of the lower echelons of society: "It is hardly possible, while one is seeking to ameliorate the regimen of prisons, not to inquire into the influence exercised on the morality of the poor classes by the modes of assistance offered them."[22]

Gasparin's own biography made him a highly qualified spokesman for the conjoint philanthropy and police of the lunacy legislation. He was, it would seem, the very prototype of the Doctrinaire. A veteran of the Société de morale chrétienne, a Protestant, the author of a treatise on epizootics written in the mode of statist health police,[23] he had also been prefect of the Rhône during the Lyon silkworkers' uprising of 1834, the largest civil disturbance in France between 1830 and 1848. Called to that post immediately after the Lyonnais rebellion of 1831 and expressly charged with preventing a recurrence of that event, Gasparin had spent a tense and wary three years, sensing even when the city was quiet that it was, as he put it, "filled with the elements of disorder."[24] Gasparin failed, of course, to accomplish his assigned mission, but he was not thereby disgraced. The military preparations he had begun in and around Lyon from the moment of his arrival enabled him to be swift and brutally effective in his repression of the workers, and his reestablishment of "order" won him an

---

[21] It even had begun to acquire a primarily pejorative meaning in certain quarters. See, e.g., the opposition newspaper *Siècle* of April 9, 1837 on the lunacy bill: "It is a great measure of *philanthropy* and of *general police*, the *Journal des débats* says naively. Now those, certainly, are two words rather astonished to be keeping company."

[22] Gasparin, *Rapport au Roi*, p. 1.

[23] Gasparin stressed that the loss of valuable farm animals through contagious disease "often necessitates the intervention of [state] authority for the execution of severe measures, which cannot be expected from the softness of private resolves." *Des maladies contagieuses des bêtes à laine* (Paris: Huzard, 1821), pp. 1–2. On the Protestantism of the Gasparin family of Nîmes, see Johnson, *Guizot*, p. 16n.

[24] Robert J. Bezucha, *The Lyon Uprising of 1834: Social and Political Conflict in the Early July Monarchy* (Cambridge, Mass.: Harvard University Press, 1974), pp. 67, 79, 93.

elevation to the peerage. A year after the uprising, he was summoned to Paris to serve as an undersecretary in the Ministry of the Interior, and in September 1836 he became minister of the interior himself in the short-lived Molé–Guizot cabinet.[25]

In Gasparin and his Doctrinaire colleagues, humanitarian concerns fused with a keen appreciation of the fragility of order in an industrializing society with a revolutionary tradition. Together they produced a faith in institutions of incarceration, institutions which had the presumed virtue of benefiting their inmates while they "tidied up" a society thus relieved of their menacing presence. In its marvelous ability to synthesize the kindly and the stern faces of government, the lunacy bill was of a piece with the other projects which Gasparin sponsored during his short tenure in the ministry: a cellular system for the departmental prisons (such a regimen qualified, he said, as "enlightened philanthropy," for it could "change the hearts" of unhardened criminals and "at least preserve from the contagion of example those who were not entirely corrupted"); the abolition of the chain gang (*chaîne des forçats*) as a mode of transporting prisoners (punishments, Gasparin observed, "ought never to be surrounded by circumstances which excite in the public either a corrupting curiosity which leads to callousness or an imprudent compassion which leads to effeminacy"); and a reorganization of the hospices for the aged and the infirm and for abandoned children.[26] It was a typical array of projects in this "era of the triumphant prison," as one historian has called the entire period from 1815 to 1848 in France.[27]

Michel Foucault's *Discipline and Punish* has put this thesis about the natural early nineteenth-century affinity between "philanthropy" and "police" in its strongest form. Including schools together with asylums, hospitals, and prisons under the rubric of "normalizing" incarcerative institutions – and Guizot's own 1833 law on primary education openly avowed its intention to moralize the still malleable children of the lower classes – Foucault regarded these institutions as the necessary and inconspicuous underpinnings of bourgeois liberalism, the "micro-powers" which keep people in check when the "macro-power" of government, having exchanged brute coercion for gentle constitutionalism,

---

[25] Ibid., p. 70; "Gasparin" in Adolphe Robert et al., *Dictionnaire des parlementaires français*, Vol. 3; on the Molé–Guizot cabinet (September 6, 1836–April 15, 1837), see Maurice Deslandres, *Histoire constitutionnelle de la France de 1789 à 1870*, Vol. 2 (Paris: Colin, 1932), pp. 178–79.

[26] See "Gasparin," in Robert et al., *Dictionnaire des parlementaires;* and Gasparin's reports and circulars as undersecretary and as minister of the interior, printed as an appendix to his *Rapport au Roi sur les prisons départementales* (Paris: Impr. royale, 1837), esp. pp. 57–58, 63.

[27] Michelle Perrot, "Délinquance et système pénitentiaire en France au XIXe siècle," *Annales E.S.C.* 30 (1975): 81.

ceases to play that role.[28] While Foucault was most concerned with the systemic features of an entire social order, and for methodological reasons uninterested in the consciousness of specific historical actors, he has nonetheless accurately depicted the intentions of the Doctrinaire liberals of the constitutional monarchy: They wanted to make a gentle humanitarianism do double service, to make it control and contain as well as to heal and improve. Indeed, insofar as historians have criticized Foucault's rendition of the early nineteenth century, they have stressed that the "normalization" was in fact far less successful than he implied, that the incarcerative institutions could not always enforce their own regulations and that they even bred new varieties of disorder within their walls.[29] But no historian has disputed that a "normalization" through supposedly humanitarian means was what the men in bourgeois government typically strove to achieve.

An alliance with the *aliénistes* of the Esquirol circle thus suited the aims of the Doctrinaire liberals. It is true that the Doctrinaires were, philosophically, "psychologists," while most of the *aliénistes* were and would remain "physiologists"; but this philosophical difference was an insufficient deterrent. Besides, the psychiatrists' mild anticlericalism was attractive to these men of the July Monarchy, for they wanted the incarcerative system for the insane to be run with the rigor of medical science and under vigilant bureaucratic surveillance – and most emphatically not with the autonomous and unregimented spirit of private religious charity. They perceived bureaucracy and science as naturally compatible, bureaucracy and piety as naturally at odds.

The psychiatrists, for their part, seem to have understood implicitly the political dimension of the government's charge to them – the charge that they will be, in Foucauldian terms, "micro-powers" while being at the same time healers and scientists. For just as Esquirol had suggested in 1822 that *aliénistes* serve as the "moral statisticians" of the government, informing it of the dominant passions of the population at large and thus monitoring the national mood, so in 1840 Dr. Emile Renaudin, a student of Fodéré, petitioned the minister of the interior for an asylum appointment by performing a similar service on a smaller scale: He prepared and enclosed a memoir on the "working class" (*classe ouvrière*) of the Haut-Rhin, where he was then practicing as a country doctor. Pointing out his capacity for careful observation of all the details of his patients' lives, he provided (among other things) an assessment of the

---

[28] Michel Foucault, *Discipline and Punish: The Birth of the Prison*, trans. A. Sheridan (New York: Pantheon, 1977), Part 3, esp. p. 222.

[29] See, e.g., Jacques Léonard, "L'historien et le philosophe," *Annales historiques de la Révolution française* 49 (1977): 166–67; Olivier Faure, *Genèse de l'hôpital moderne: Les hospices civils de Lyon de 1802 à 1845* (Lyon: Presses universitaires de Lyon, 1982), p. 219; and Patricia O'Brien, *The Promise of Punishment: Prisons in Nineteenth-Century France* (Princeton, N.J.: Princeton University Press, 1982), pp. 8–10, 304.

revolutionary potential of the area. In the towns with which Renaudin was most familiar, he reassured the minister, "one does not have to fear those tumultuous coalitions which trouble some cities." In the Haut-Rhin, the working class was too "physically debilitated" to participate in a "revolt" (*levée des boucliers*); it was their bodily weakness and not their "morality" that was responsible for "the calm."[30] Renaudin's attempt to ingratiate himself succeeded. His self-representation as a potential psychiatric *fonctionnaire* apparently pleased the minister, for within two years the politically astute Renaudin was made director of the departmental asylum of the Meuse.[31] It is of course impossible to know what factors influenced the minister's favorable decision.[32] But the ease with which Renaudin expressed himself in the idiom of "political medicine" – and geared that idiom especially to the fear of revolution prevalent among the governing class of the July Monarchy – provides striking evidence of the tacit mutual understanding between the specialists in insanity and the bureaucrats.

The obstacle of interdiction and the theory of isolation

Against this general background, we can situate the immediate origins of the 1838 Law, the specific means by which the *aliénistes* and the government forged their alliance in the 1830s. The initial common cause was not, as in 1819, a utopian model asylum project but a more modest attempt to surmount a judicial obstacle to the professional progress of the one partner and the political goals of the other. Due to an ambiguity in French law, it was unclear whether interdiction, or the legal certification of an individual as insane and incapable of managing his or her own affairs, was a necessary prerequisite for internment in a lunatic institution. Practice was diverse in this regard: In Paris, very few of the mad inmates of Bicêtre and the Salpêtrière had obtained a prior interdiction (a mere 19 out of 613 for Bicêtre in the year 1835), while in most provincial areas "the public establishments refuse to accept [the lunatics], the judges are opposed to their admission, unless an interdiction is pronounced."[33] It was the judges themselves who

---

[30] AN: F¹⁵ 3914, letter of Renaudin to the minister of the interior dated September 13, 1840, ms. pp. 1, 3–5.

[31] Semelaigne, *Pionniers*, Vol. 1, p. 328.

[32] Renaudin was not a new appointment to the asylum system, having been forced to resign a post at the Stéphansfeld asylum because of squabbles with its administrative personnel; see AN: F¹⁵ 3914, letter of Renaudin to the minister of the interior dated August 15, 1840. The dossier contains numerous supplications from Renaudin, and its cover bears a secretarial notation that he had the backing of the prefect of the Bas-Rhin.

[33] Gasparin, *Arch. parl.*, 2d ser., Vol. 106, pp. 267, 271; and Gasparin, *Rapport au Roi*, p. 97.

pronounced these interdictions; they had done so since the fifteenth century, when the parlements, in an effort to extend their influence into family affairs, had first claimed the right.[34] Interdiction was a long, tedious, complex, and costly procedure. Most commonly undertaken by affluent families to protect their fortunes from the irresponsible antics of insane heirs, the litigation had to be initiated and financed by the government in order to confine dangerous, indigent lunatics who could not otherwise be incarcerated.[35] From the viewpoint of the Doctrinaire liberals of the July Monarchy, such a procedure was incompatible with the efficient system of incarceration of the insane which social order seemed to require. From the viewpoint of the psychiatrists, it meant an irritating – if not intolerable – dependence of *médecine mentale* upon the prerogatives of the judiciary. Only judges could make insane persons eligible, so to speak, for hospitalization in the care of medical doctors; the judge stood between the *aliéniste* and his patient.

The Esquirol circle began its criticism of interdiction shortly before the July Revolution. At the end of 1829, Brierre de Boismont presented a memoir on the subject before the Institut de France. He said nothing at all about the role of the interdicting judge as gatekeeper to the asylum; that highly charged issue (which scarcely affected Parisian psychiatry in any case) would be raised later. He focused instead on the internal dynamics of the interdiction proceedings, and his complaints were parallel, in the domain of civil law, to the complaints that Georget had lodged against trial proceedings in the domain of criminal law – that is, that these legal proceedings needed to be made *medico*-legal. Traditional in form, they had failed to keep pace with the progress of science and had now to integrate the specialized knowledge and the counsels of the *médecin aliéniste*.[36] Balzac's novella *L'Interdiction* (1836), set in 1828, provides a good illustration of the situation to which Brierre was referring. Popinot, the wise and benevolent magistrate, interviews both the Marquise d'Espard, who filed the demand for interdiction with a Paris tribunal, and her allegedly monomaniacal husband (among his "symptoms" is an absorption in the study of Chinese history) and decides that the latter is quite sane. Although Popinot brings along his nephew, Dr. Horace Bianchon, on one of these investigatory visits, he never seeks medical advice from the young man and confidently makes his determi-

---

[34] Brierre de Boismont, "Considérations médico-légales sur l'interdiction des aliénés," *Journal hebdomadaire de médecine* 6 (1830): 364.

[35] For the interdiction of an indigent agricultural day-laborer, Yves Robert, in the court of Saint-Brieuc (Côtes-du-Nord) in the Year XI, see AN: F^{15} 2604. Although Robert had been repeatedly violent toward his wife and children, he could not be sent to the *hôpital de fous* of Saint-Méen in Rennes without a formal interdiction, which had to be obtained by government suit.

[36] Brierre, "Considérations sur l'interdiction." The original memoir was presented on September 14, 1829; see the report in *Ann. d'hyg. pub.* 3 (1830): 192–98.

nation unaided.[37] Brierre wanted to have such determinations made by medical doctors "under oath" and "chosen exclusively from among those who devote themselves to the study of mental maladies." Well aware that he was embarking upon a border dispute, he tried to reassure the judges that their total displacement was not his intent. "To propose this change is not to submit law to medicine but only to join the latter as an adviser. The sciences embrace and never suffocate one another."[38]

As it turned out, the Esquirol circle never pursued the claims that Brierre articulated for them here. They were diverted from this course by the 1830 Revolution and the rise to power of the Doctrinaire liberals. Although there was no public sign before 1833 that the bureaucrats of the July Monarchy were actively interested in developing a policy regarding lunacy, it is hard to imagine, given the prior ties, that Esquirol was not meeting with officials in the Ministry of the Interior of the new regime well before that date. For in October 1832, Esquirol suddenly announced with great panache, also before the Institut de France, the theory of isolation (*isolement*), a theory which would play a crucial part in the internal logic of the government's 1837 lunacy bill and which represented a more elegant tactical solution to the problem of interdiction than the solution Brierre had proposed.

Isolement is an excellent example of the way external factors shaped psychiatric theory, or at least shaped the way psychiatrists chose to represent that theory at different historical moments. The basic idea – that the therapy for insanity required the removal of afflicted individuals from their habitual milieus – was not new, even in the short history of *médecine mentale*. It was implicit in Pinel's case histories of cure by the moral treatment that the controlled and often artificial environment upon which the treatment depended could be created only in a special setting insulated from ordinary society. It was implicit as well in the pronouncements of Pinel and Esquirol about the "enchanting" curative power contained in the person of the *aliéniste* that this power derived, in part, from that doctor's total supremacy in the small, self-contained world of an institution. The word *isolement* appears occasionally in psychiatric writings before 1832, including the second edition of Pinel's *Traité* (though not, to my knowledge, in the work of Esquirol).[39] What

---

[37] See also the interdiction of Yves Robert (n. 35), who was legally pronounced *fou et furieux* on the sole testimony of the cantonal justice of the peace.

[38] Brierre, "Considérations sur l'interdiction," pp. 367, 373.

[39] See, e.g., A.-A. Royer-Collard's early reference to the therapeutic "système d'isolement," which he attributed to Pinel, in *Observations sur un écrit ayant pour titre: Mémoire pour Mme de Chambon . . .* , (Paris: Impr. de Vincard, 1806), p. 8; AN: AJ² 100. A similar usage is found in the opening sentence of the promotional brochure of J.-P. Falret and F. Voisin, *Etablissement pour le traitement des aliénés des deux sexes fondé en juillet 1822 à Vanves, près Paris* (Paris: Impr. A. Belin, 1828). In the 2d edition of Pinel's *Traité médico-philosophique de l'aliénation mentale, ou la manie* (Paris: Brosson, 1809), by contrast, *isolement* (pp. 193–94) means the segregation of furious patients from tranquil

Esquirol did in his 1832 memoir, then, was to recast already existing ideas about the therapy for insanity, to make absolutely explicit and prominent what had previously been only a shadowy background element. Whereas *aliénistes* had once proclaimed the *douceur* of the moral treatment as their special curative expertise – and while a psychiatric controversy over the nature of the moral treatment would erupt almost immediately after the passage of the Law, indicating that the concept had lost none of its paradigmatic status[40] – in the context of lobbying for the lunacy legislation they said almost nothing about the moral treatment per se and trumpeted instead the doctrine of isolation. This shift of theoretical emphasis was a deliberate response to professional exigencies, as we will see in detail after examining the doctrine itself.

Isolation was, Esquirol told the membership of the Institut, "the most energetic and ordinarily the most useful means of combating the mental maladies." Simple in its outlines, it "consists in removing the lunatic from all his habitual pastimes, distancing him from his place of residence, separating him from his family, his friends, his servants, surrounding him with strangers, changing his whole way of life." An analogy with ordinary experience helped to explain how the procedure worked:

> Everyone has felt that indefinable shock that grips our being when we are suddenly taken away from our habitual activities and the objects of our affections. Withdrawn from the influence of the things and persons in whose midst he has been living, the lunatic [similarly] feels, in the first moments of his isolation, a sudden astonishment which upsets his delirium and delivers over his intellect to the guidance that is going to give him new impressions.

ones in an asylum, though *isoler* (p. 6) is used in the sense of Esquirol's 1832 memoir. The only sustained discussion of *isolement* I have found prior to 1832 is Georget, *De la folie* (Paris: Crevot, 1820), pp. 263–69. On the other hand, Esquirol's "Maisons d'aliénés" (1818), *Dict. des sci. med.*, Vol. 30, pp. 80, 83, mentions only *reclusion* and uses the term to refer to a more extreme degree of confinement within an asylum, a forced exclusion from the communal life of the institution.

[40] The controversy was started by Leuret, who departed from the Pinellian canon by declaring that harshness and repression producing "strong emotions" in the patient were the real mainstay of the moral treatment and *douceur* was dispensable. See his memoir in *Bulletin de l'Académie royale de médecine* 2 (1838): 1051–53; and his books *Du traitement moral et de la folie* (Paris: J.-B. Baillière, 1840); and *Mémoire sur la révulsion morale dans le traitement de la folie* (Paris: J.-B. Baillière, 1841). Leuret was rebutted by Dr. Espirit Blanche, owner and director of a well-known Parisian sanitorium for lunatics, in *Du danger des rigueurs corporelles dans le traitement de la folie* (Paris: A. Gardembas, 1839) and *De l'état actuel du traitement de la folie en France* (Paris: A. Gardembas, 1840). Discussion of the issue continued into the 1840s in the Academy of Medicine and the medical press; see, e.g., J.-P. Falret's reaffirmation of the centrality of *douceur* in "Du traitement moral des aliénés," *Gazette des hôpitaux*, 2d ser., 10 (1848): 373.

Isolation was thus a large-scale and long-term version of the "distraction" that he and Pinel had recommended as one of the forms of the moral treatment; and it was grounded, like most of the strategies of the moral treatment, in eighteenth-century sensationalist psychology. The radical change in environment was supposed to alter the stimuli impinging upon the mind and thus to "shake up" and dislodge the pathological configuration of ideas entrenched there. With this demolition accomplished, the psychiatrist was in a position to provide new stimuli, which would result in new and sane ideas for the patient. Conversely, a premature termination of the isolation would undo the psychiatrist's salutary labor of mental reconstruction. If the patient were returned to his old milieu before the sanguine set of ideas had settled in, "before the nervous system is made entirely firm once again," the "power of the association of ideas with external objects" might well induce a relapse, a reinstatement of the old delirium. Esquirol noted that travel, the "change of scene," was a type of isolation, especially therapeutic when the patient was accompanied by a stranger instead of by friends or relatives; he himself frequently used it to "prolong the isolation of convalescents" and to smooth the transition "between the privation of social contacts and the reentry into the world." But the basic form of isolation was a stay of some duration in an asylum.[41]

Esquirol adduced some twenty case histories to demonstrate the efficacy of this approach. Subjected to the regimen of isolation, most patients improved gradually, others with dramatic suddenness. A middle-aged provincial merchant, for example, plunged into melancholy and a succession of suicide attempts after sustaining a minor business loss, appeared to be "restored to reason" almost as soon as he was brought to Esquirol's sanatorium on the outskirts of Paris. " 'The impression I received,' he told me, 'upon seeing myself transported into a strange house has cured me.' " And, Esquirol added, "in fact, the sleep, the appetite, the very coherent and sometimes gay conversation [of this patient] make this cure credible."[42]

A method of healing will not always be adopted simply because it works; it must also be consonant with the mores and values of the community.[43] Esquirol apparently recognized this truth because he did not assume that his rational scientific argument, the abundance of

---

[41] Esquirol, *Question médico-légale sur l'isolement des aliénés* (Paris: Crochard, 1832), pp. 31, 54, 74–75.

[42] Ibid., pp. 36–37; the scrupulous Esquirol acknowledged that, overestimating the durability of the cure, he had discharged the merchant too soon.

[43] For comments on this point in another historical context, see Henri F. Ellenberger, *The Discovery of the Unconscious: The History and Evolution of Dynamic Psychiatry* (New York: Basic Books, 1970), p. 57.

clinical data he had cited attesting to the success of isolation, would automatically persuade his audience. Given the centrality of bonds of family in nineteenth-century French life, he anticipated that the deliberate rupture of those bonds by the method of isolation would seem offensive and provoke strong objections. Taking on the persona of a hostile member of his own audience, he asked rhetorically: "Is there not some barbarity in depriving a sick person of the care which family tenderness lavishes upon him? How can one separate from the objects of his affections an unfortunate being who is consumed with chagrin?" But, Esquirol continued, answering himself, "experience has replied, it has proven that lunatics are rarely cured in the bosom of their family."[44] A strange and potentially iconoclastic fact – yet Esquirol's interpretation of it soothed his audience, for it in no way impugned the family. It in no way implied, as would twentieth-century theorists of mental illness such as Freud, that the family milieu could itself be pathogenic, that there were treacherous antagonisms, overt or covert, between parents and children, husbands and wives. Esquirol insisted that the continued presence of the family would perpetuate or even aggravate a case of madness, but in his canon the reasons for this were largely fortuitous.

Lunatics, because their "sensibility is perverted" and their "relations with the outside world abnormal," were by nature mistrustful. Such was the lot of all "weak minds" and "undeveloped intellects": Peasants were more mistrustful than city-dwellers; men of letters and savants were the least mistrustful of all groups. Having once succumbed to madness, a person would necessarily become suspicious of those around him; he would spurn the members of his household, believing himself to have been betrayed by them. This delusion, which had no basis in reality and which reassurances were powerless to correct, exacerbated the torment of the lunatics who remained at home. For how much worse it was to feel oneself deceived and betrayed by relatives than by the anonymous personnel of an institution! In addition, lunatics had impeccable memories. They "rarely forget their actions; they remember all the incidents which signaled the beginning of their malady – the deviations of conduct, the fits, the acts of violence. . . ." When lucid, they were stricken by "regrets, remorse," painful emotions which retarded the curative process and which were *"continually irritated* by the presence of those persons" – usually family members – "who were the victims of their [initial] furor."[45] These intrinsic characteristics of insanity dragged the family, by the accident of its proximity, into the dynamics of insanity; and

---

[44] Esquirol, *Question sur l'isolement,* p. 68. Pinel also recognized the distressing character of isolation from the perspective of French familial norms; see *Traité,* 2d ed., p. 6.
[45] Esquirol, *Question sur l'isolement,* pp. 38–40, 49, my italics.

they alone and not any impurity of familial love, made the lunatic's removal from his family desirable.[46]

Having thus addressed to his own satisfaction what he perceived to be a crucial cultural bias against isolation, Esquirol turned to specific therapeutic recommendations. Isolation was not good for every lunatic. It had to be prescribed selectively by an "experienced physician." In cases of mania, monomania, and lypemania (especially a lypemania tending to suicidal preoccupations), it was almost certainly indicated. Peacefully demented persons could, on the other hand, stay at home; they were incurable and had nothing to gain from isolation. Lower-class lunatics formed a separate category to which these subtleties did not apply. "They ought in general to be isolated," said Esquirol, "their relatives being deprived of all means of surveillance and treatment."[47] In this detail, Esquirol's doctrine of isolation gave ringing medical-scientific support to the government's concern with police, its desire to end the threat to social order posed by all forms of unmonitored deviance among the lower classes.[48]

How then was the doctrine of isolation relevant to the border dispute between the judges and the psychiatrists over interdiction? Unlike Brierre de Boismont, who wanted to "medicalize" interdiction, Esquirol suggested that this impediment simply be bypassed. He stressed that isolation was a purely medical maneuver; it was concerned not with the management of the lunatic's finances, which was the sole and the entirely legitimate province of interdiction, but with the health and well-being of the lunatic himself. "Indispensable to cure, . . . [it] ought," he argued, "to be sanctioned by law." And functionally separate from interdiction, it ought also to be legally separate – that is, placed under the control of the physician and outside the authority of the judge.[49] The doctrine of isolation was thus, from its "official" inception in 1832, presented not only or even primarily as a claim for psychi-

---

[46] Throughout the nineteenth century, French psychiatrists remained generally silent about family relations as a cause of insanity. The first forthright statement that I have found on the subject comes from Brierre de Boismont's daughter, not a psychiatrist but the lay *directrice* of her father's private sanatorium, who observed that the "absence of harmony between mothers and daughters is incontestable in some families," often took the form of jealousy, and was an important cause of mental disturbance; see Mme M. Rivet, *Les aliénés dans la famille et dans la maison de santé* (Paris: G. Masson, 1875), esp. pp. 45–46.

[47] Esquirol, *Question sur l'isolement*, pp. 70–71.

[48] The class consciousness which informed the framing of the Law of 1838 was also evident in its implementation. See, e.g., a prefect's letter to the minister of the interior justifying the discharge from Rech's private sanatorium in Toulouse of a young woman who, after four years there, was still in the grip of a furious mania: "This lunatic belongs to a rich family" whose "position of fortune . . . guarantees [its] ability to take the precautions that public order and the safety of persons demand." AN: F[15] 3904, Dossier: Hérault, letter dated June 23, 1842.

[49] Esquirol, *Question sur l'isolement*, pp. 75–79.

atric efficacy but as a way to shake off, through a kind of logical distinction, the judicial interference that threatened the expansion of *médecine mentale*. Some years later, Falret forcefully reiterated Esquirol's position on this matter. "In order," he wrote, "that there cannot remain the slightest doubt in any mind, let us show by a comparison of the circumstances surrounding isolation and interdiction that these two measures are of an entirely different order and that isolation excludes all idea of prior interdiction. . . . [I]nterdiction is a judicial measure. . . . Isolation, on the contrary, is a medical measure."[50]

The government's bill: an exercise in "political medicine"

Gasparin's original lunacy bill – which would eventually be substantially accepted and find its way into the Law of 1838, though it would not constitute the sum total of that much broader legislation – was simply an effort to clarify and streamline the procedure for admission into a special institution for the insane. Gasparin wanted that procedure in the hands of administrators who were firmly under government control, who could be counted on to implement uniformly and with alacrity the government's policy of philanthropy-cum-police. Accordingly, the bill he presented to the Chamber of Deputies in January 1837 stated that lunatics should be confined to institutions (and kept there until medical doctors deemed them cured, or at least fit to leave) without having been interdicted and by order of the prefect.[51] The bill thus decided twice against the judiciary: It proposed to end the ambiguity which had enabled judges to assert that the route to the *maison d'aliénés* had to include a stop in the courtroom to obtain an interdiction; and it did not propose judges as the officials to oversee and authorize the internment of noninterdicted lunatics.

The basic program of the government was, in other words, virtually identical to the one Esquirol had outlined in his 1832 memoir on isolation. It is possible that this was prearranged, that the two programs had been developed in tandem. In any case, Gasparin hastened to capitalize upon the striking congruity. He justified the bill by reference to the latest medical-scientific knowledge. His long preamble included a discussion of the psychiatric theory of isolation and announced his intention to employ that technical term throughout the proposed legislation: "The shutting away (*séquestration*) of lunatics as it is conceived in medical language does not correspond to the idea of detention (*séquestration*) as it is found in the language of our laws and especially in that of the penal code." He emphasized that firm support for his stance against prior interdiction could be found in the medical commu-

---

[50] Falret, *Observations sur le projet de loi relatif aux aliénés* (Paris: Everat, 1837), p. 9.
[51] See Projet de loi, Articles 1, 4, in *Arch. parl.*, 2d ser., Vol. 106, p. 275.

nity: "Here the fundamental question which comprises almost the whole substance of the law presents itself. The isolation of the lunatic . . . ought it, can it be subordinated to civil interdiction? The medical doctors (*hommes de l'art*) respond in a unanimous voice: no."[52] Thus it was the doctrine of isolation, not that of the moral treatment, which the government highlighted from the outset and repeatedly invoked in the legislative context as the epitome of the new specialized medical knowledge about insanity.

The reasons Gasparin adduced for his position on interdiction were manifold, and nearly all had been borrowed from Esquirol's 1832 memoir or from other psychiatric sources. In its early stages, he maintained, mental illness was frequently impossible to diagnose as either "febrile or chronic," curable or incurable, and so the need for isolation became known before the need for interdiction could be ascertained. Furthermore, the former need tended to be urgent, whereas the legal procedures leading to interdiction were cumbersome and usually involved long delays; those same legal procedures, with their searching interrogations of the lunatic in the fearsome presence of a judge in full regalia, were likely to aggravate madness and to become a permanent obstacle to cure.[53]

When Gasparin turned to the second half of his proposal – that the "administrative authority" rather than the "judicial authority" be empowered to consign lunatics to special institutions – his arguments were less wholly reliant upon medical opinion. First, he cited statutory precedent. He next cited the nature and scope of the administrative function (or as he called it, the *police administrative*) which "embrace[d] in its concern . . . catastrophes of all kinds" having implications for "public safety [and] public order." In this regard, free-roaming lunatics could be considered "analogous" to floods and fires. But in his final argument, on the style of the administration function, he returned to medical considerations: "The measures . . . relating to isolation ordinarily demand an extreme rapidity, a prudence, a discretion which are not easily reconciled with the slowness and solemnity of judicial forms [but] are easy and natural to administrative operations." And a pamphlet by Dr. Jean-Pierre Falret, distributed to every deputy when discussion of the bill began a few months later, reiterated and reinforced the government's third argument, sometimes adding special psychiatric touches – for example, that the administration, whose "essence is to be paternal," had an appropriately reassuring and salutary effect on the mental state of the insane individual whose admission to an institution was pending.[54]

---

[52] *Arch. parl.*, 2d ser., Vol. 106, pp. 94–95, 270.

[53] Ibid., p. 270; cf. Esquirol, *Question sur l'isolement*, pp. 75–78, and Brierre de Boismont, "Considérations sur l'interdiction," pp. 377–78.

[54] *Arch. parl.*, 2d ser., Vol. 106, p. 272; and Falret, *Observations sur le projet de loi*, pp. 17–18; on the distribution of this pamphlet to the deputies, see *Arch. parl.*, 2d ser., Vol. 109, p. 346.

Indeed not only the government's original bill but all subsequent discussion of it and its amended versions in the chambers was larded with arguments drawn from medicine.[55] The relevance and sometimes even the compelling nature of such arguments seem to have been tacitly assumed by almost all the participants to the legislative discussion, and this prevailing assumption became explicit only on the few occasions when it was publicly challenged. In a heated debate in the Chamber of Peers in February 1838, when one detail of the bill was in dispute and medical opinion was again being invoked to settle it, the Comte de Montalembert and the Duc de Broglie suddenly cast doubt upon this whole mode of reasoning. The argument of the previous speaker, said Montalembert, was inappropriate, derived much more from medical theory than from legislative considerations. "We are not," he observed caustically, "an academy of medicine." And besides, the relativism of medical knowledge had to be taken into account:

> It is not a question here, for us, of such and such a system of medical science, which varies according to the country, the time and the individuals who are at the head of the medical profession. We ought to examine only the facts and the interests of society.

De Broglie seconded him, also stressing the fluidity of medical knowledge, which made it unwise "to admit it into [the] perpetuity" of law. The quotidian business of administration might justly apply such knowledge and make it binding, but the legislative authority could not. De Broglie mentioned the roughly analogous situation of the cordon sanitaire during the yellow fever epidemic of 1822. The doctors were divided on the issue of whether this disease was contagious; and the legislature had, said de Broglie, clearly overstepped its bounds in accepting the contagionist opinion as the basis for a law mandating the death penalty for all violators of the cordon. He had argued this position sixteen years ago, he recalled, with "as lively a repugnance" as he felt now.[56]

In their principled refusal to be guided as lawmakers by the dicta of medicine, Montalembert and de Broglie were clearly exceptional among their parliamentary colleagues. That such dicta were, in general, respectfully heard in the chambers and often treated as representing a neutral scientific authority above the political fray no doubt explains the eagerness with which the government marshaled the psy-

[55] Nor was Falret's pamphlet the only instance of direct psychiatric input into the lawmaking process. A commission of deputies charged to study the bill heard the testimony of Esquirol, Ferrus, Falret, and Pinel's son Scipion; *Arch. parl.*, 2d ser., Vol. 108, p. 482. When the debates carried over into 1838, a new Chamber of Deputies received a pamphlet from the pen of Esquirol himself, *Examen du projet de loi sur les aliénés* (Paris: J.-B. Baillière, 1838); on its distribution to the deputies, see *Arch. parl.*, 2d ser., Vol. 118, p. 7.

[56] *Arch. parl.*, 2d ser., Vol. 115, pp. 294, 297–98, 329.

chiatric theory of isolation to its own cause. For Gasparin's bill proved to be, as he fully expected, controversial; and a medical justification helped to defuse its political connotations and thus to make the measure more widely acceptable. It was, in other words, wiser in this instance for Gasparin to engage in "political medicine" than to engage in politics *tout court*.

The controversial aspect of the bill was its transformation of judicial functions into administrative ones, a transformation that fueled the longstanding French debate over bureaucratic centralization and, correlatively, seemed to critics of the government to violate the constitutional principle of separation of powers. When the legitimists came to power in 1814, after the fall of the highly centralized Napoleonic regime, they professed a desire to decentralize France and a theoretical preference, articulated by Bonald and Chateaubriand, for the corporate liberties and rich pluralism that had supposedly characterized the pre-Revolutionary Bourbon monarchy. Once the Napoleonic bureaucracy was in their hands, however, they found it too useful an instrument to relinquish.[57] The Doctrinaire liberals of the Restoration were, by contrast, theoretically enamored of centralization, which they considered the sine qua non of the modern regime; and when the Revolution of 1830 raised them to positions of power, they began unapologetically to put these views into effect. Municipal laws of 1831 and 1837 gave the localities little autonomy and brought forth angry cries of "centralization" on the floor of the chamber. Similarly, Guizot's 1833 law on primary education vested the minister of public instruction and the prefects with broad powers of surveillance over the local schools and over the certification and appointment of schoolteachers.

These centralizing provisions of the Guizot law – and not financially onerous provisions about the obligation of each commune to create a school, or the minimum wage for teachers, or free instruction for those too poor to pay – provoked strong opposition in the chambers; and the government, much to its embarrassment, secured their passage only with difficulty. A voluminous pamphlet literature pressing for administrative decentralization appeared in the 1830s, accusing the government of annihilating the vitality and individuality of local communities, of creating a society that resembled a pyramid resting on its point.[58] In addition, the trend toward strong central administration had a demonstrated potential for encroachment upon the judiciary. Already, under the Restoration, the Ministry of the Interior had endowed the prefect's office with ample powers of *police générale*; and this administrative police, charged with keeping the public order,

---

[57] Alan B. Spitzer, "The Bureaucrat as Proconsul: The Restoration Prefect and the *Police Générale*," *Comparative Studies in Society and History* 7 (1965): 371–72.

[58] See Félix Ponteil, *Les institutions de la France de 1814 à 1870* (Paris: Presses universitaires de France, 1966), pp. 156–60, 163–64; and Johnson, *Guizot*, pp. 131–32.

overlapped in function with the judicial police emanating from the office of the state prosecutor, which was likewise assigned broad responsibility for the maintenance of public order.[59] Gasparin's lunacy bill could be viewed as one instance in which this overlap of function had been converted into the complete exclusion of the judiciary from the function.

It is no surprise, then, that one of the most vehement opponents of Gasparin's bill in the Chamber of Deputies was a judge and that he lodged his protest against "centralization." François-André Isambert, *conseiller de la cour de cassation* and deputy from the Vendée, was implicitly defending the prerogatives of his own professional group – as well as articulating his political principles as a left-liberal opponent of the Doctrinaires – when he attributed the bill to "that centralizing fanaticism, so often repulsed by the Chambers, and most recently during the discussion of the municipal law." A general lunacy law was needed in France, Isambert admitted, but the one before the chamber courted danger by violating the principle of separation of powers:

> The great principle of the separation of powers, the limits marked out until now between the administrative police and the judicial police, the immense security that citizens derive from the conviction that no agent of the government has direct or indirect power over their persons, that their liberty and their honor are placed exclusively under the protection of irremovable magistrates to whom the promptings of politics are foreign . . . does not all this forbid even the thought of making prefectorial power intervene in such a matter?[60]

Isambert's argument provoked a lively and, apparently, not inconsequential argument in the chamber: A vote on April 7, 1837 gave Gasparin's bill a comfortable majority; but, reported the *Courrier français*, the 47 negative ballots (out of a total of 230 ballots cast) were due "solely" to the fact that "the prefects have been invested, in the place of judges, with the right of pronouncing on the liberty of citizens."[61] And looking back on the event several years later, the social democrat Louis Blanc could still summon up passion for Isambert's position. The law on the lunatics, he wrote in his history of the first decade of Orleanist rule, "was almost odious, for it put at the mercy of the administrative power the liberty of all individuals suspected of insanity."[62]

Thus the controversial issue was not whether the lunatic should be confined but whether that confinement should be accomplished through further administrative centralization and with dubious respect

---

[59] Spitzer, "Bureaucrat as Proconsul," pp. 384–87.
[60] *Arch. parl.*, 2d ser., Vol. 109, p. 334.
[61] *Courrier français*, April 9, 1837.
[62] Louis Blanc, *Histoire de dix ans, 1830–1840*, Vol. 5 (Paris: Pagnerre, 1844), p. 303.

for the separation of powers. To aid passage of the bill, Gasparin and his successor in the Ministry of the Interior, Montalivet, resorted to cajoling rhetoric about the trustworthy nature of the central bureaucracy under the constitutional regime of the Orleanists, the irrelevance of lessons drawn from the prerevolutionary past. "That time is no longer, gentlemen, when administrative activity is held in permanent suspicion. . . . Today its responsibility is real, its conduct legal, its intervention protective." "Who will seriously believe that under the present regime individual liberty could be truly threatened? To speak today of bastilles is to commit a willful anachronism."[63] It was because the government was treading on this sensitive ground and had such a strong stake in the principle of bureaucratic centralization that an alliance with the doctors and the use of medical-scientific argumentation – in short, the depiction of the legislation as a value-neutral exercise in "political medicine" – had been so attractive. The government, observed Isambert wryly, accurately sizing up the strategy, "congratulates itself on the fact that politics is foreign to this law."[64]

The establishment of a nationwide asylum system

As originally drafted by Gasparin and amended by the commission of deputies headed by the Doctrinaire Vivien, the lunacy bill did not provide for the establishment of an asylum system. It merely changed the procedures for the confinement of lunatics and, by way of justifying this change, expressed an abstract commitment to the new medical treatment of them. In April 1837, Calemard de Lafayette, an obscure deputy from the Auvergne and a physician, rose in the chamber to point out the internal contradiction that riddled the bill. Most of France – 48 out of 86 departments, to be exact – lacked the facilities to give the insane the potentially curative treatment the government had just endorsed; and yet, in the name of maximizing the possibilities for cure, all the prefects were being bidden to intern lunatics without delay. "Isn't it one of those anomalies which would be inexplicable," he asked, "if one did not remember that the laws elaborated in the bureaus [of the ministries] are prompted by the needs and resources of the capital and that, too often, cut to the measure of the capital, they apply only with great difficulty to our provinces?"[65]

Had Calemard been a less kindly interpreter of this "anomaly," and had he wanted to join the political opposition to the bill, he might have suggested that the government was primarily interested in the speedy detention of disruptive individuals and had invoked humane medical

---

[63] Gasparin, *Arch. parl.*, 2d ser., Vol. 106, p. 272; Montalivet, ibid., Vol. 110, p. 321.
[64] Ibid., Vol. 109, p. 350.
[65] Ibid., pp. 340–41.

care only as a rationale. But Calemard chose instead to take the government at its word about its medical intentions, and on that ground he insisted that the proposed law be expanded to include explicit requirements for the availability of specialized lunatic institutions "directed by well-informed and, in some sense, special physicians." In making this recommendation he may have been inspired or at least encouraged by Falret's pamphlet on the bill: Falret had applauded the government's stance against prior interdiction and in favor of prefectorial internment, but had concluded with a polite "appeal to the wisdom of the government," urging it to carry further its concern "to improve the lot of unhappy lunatics" by inaugurating a "general system" of asylums in France.[66] But whatever its source, Calemard's unimpeachable argument was heeded by the chamber, and his intervention resulted in a swift reorientation of the legislation at hand – a reorientation that subsumed the procedural provisions already advanced by the government but went far beyond them.

Almost immediately, discussion in the chamber turned to the form that a mandatory system of lunatic asylums ought to take. Calemard had pronounced himself a partisan of centralization: He wanted the asylums to be created and run by the state in order that the care of the insane "escape from the whims, the uncertain or parsimonious notions of the local authorities" and receive a "powerful and uniform impetus." To his mind, the precedent of state financing of railroads and canals argued for such an arrangement, as did the many aspects of French life routinely organized by the central bureaucracy:

> France is divided into 26 judicial divisions, 21 military divisions, 13 ecclesiastical divisions, 20 forestry wards; you already have central prisons; well, following these same principles, create public mental institutions![67]

Calemard was not alone in appreciating the "geometric" virtues of centralization. When the bill was turned over to the peers, the Comte d'Alton-Shée, a reliable supporter of the Doctrinaires, declared that only a system of state asylums would provide "a perfect equality of good treatment in all of France."[68]

The Parisian psychiatric community also favored the highly centralized solution. Calemard had rightly asserted that his own position had a certain classic status, since it revived the one "set forth for the first time by Monsieur Esquirol in 1819."[69] The Comte d'Alton-Shée re-

---

[66] Ibid., p. 340; Falret, *Observations sur le projet de loi,* pp. 81–82.

[67] *Arch. parl.,* 2d ser., Vol. 109, pp. 342–43.

[68] Ibid., Vol. 115, p. 244. Alton-Shée's remark fits neatly with Tocqueville's thesis that the craving for "equality" was partly responsible for the French zeal for bureaucratic centralization; see *The Old Regime and the French Revolution,* trans. S. Gilbert (New York: Doubleday, 1955), esp. pp. 163, 165.

[69] *Arch. parl.,* 2d ser., Vol. 109, p. 342.

ported to the Chamber of Peers that he had consulted four eminent psychiatrists ("men most engaged with this sad subject") and that all had concurred that an asylum ought to house from 300 to 500 inmates. Since most departmental asylums would perforce be much smaller (the average number of lunatics per department in France being only 141), it would be wise to place the whole asylum system in the hands of the state, which could then cross over departmental lines and create institutions of the appropriate size.[70] The psychiatrists had a thoroughly scientific justification for the desirability of these large asylums: They made possible the most sophisticated psychiatric research. As Ferrus had written some years before, an asylum had to be large enough to contain simultaneously all known genres of insanity; it could then be the site of "the comparative study of the different degrees of this ailment, a study which is so necessary to the progress of science."[71] Still, it is likely that the psychiatrists also endorsed the highly centralized system because of its greater susceptibility to their influence. French psychiatry had, after all, been based in Paris since its inception, and it would be much easier for its leaders to maintain their hegemony if the appointment of asylum-doctors and the management of asylums were under the control of the Ministry of the Interior in Paris.[72]

But centralization also had its vocal opponents. In the Chamber of Peers, the Comte de Montalembert made his case by vividly depicting the excess of paperwork that already cluttered and clogged the offices of the Ministry of the Interior:

> There is no one among us who has not had some request of local interest to address to the offices of the ministry. When I am in that position, I see that the minister often does not reply at all, or, when he does, that it takes three or four months for his reply to traverse the immense distance from the rue de Grenelle [the location of the ministry] to the rue Saint-Dominique, where I reside. I explain this to myself by the great quantity of business which occupies him; but I am astonished that he wants to augment it still more. It seems to me . . . that a minister of the interior already has a sufficiently abundant harvest of great affairs . . . [and has] no need to absorb everything, even the sad domain of people who have lost their minds.[73]

[70] Ibid., Vol. 115, pp. 243–44; those consulted were Esquirol, Ferrus, Lélut (Ferrus's student and his colleague at Bicêtre), and Londe (the physician who wrote on psychiatric subjects for the *Revue des spécialités*).

[71] G. Ferrus, *Des aliénés* (Paris: Huzard, 1834), p. 203.

[72] Psychiatrists were bold enough to say as much – not in 1837–38, but in 1852. When a government decree of March 25, 1852 transferred the power of appointment of asylum-doctors from the minister of the interior to the prefects, Brierre de Boismont criticized this "decentralization," asserting that Paris was the only place in France to learn psychiatry properly and that the senior *aliénistes* who taught at Bicêtre, the Salpêtrière, and Charenton were the only true arbiters of a candidate's suitability for an asylum post. "Observations sur le nouveau mode de nomination des médecins d'asiles d'aliénés," *Union médicale*, April 27, 1852.

[73] *Arch. parl.*, 2d ser., Vol. 115, p. 225.

As Montalembert's sardonic remarks suggest, two different aspects of centralization were at stake in the lunacy bill. The opponents of a centralized asylum system were not, like the opponents of prefectorial internment of lunatics, worried about the arbitrary use of political power in violation of civil rights; they were worried about the hypertrophy of the central state and the consequent engulfment of the private sector by the public sector. With respect to the care of the insane, the "private sector" meant both the *maisons de santé* owned and operated by profit-oriented lay entrepreneurs and the lunatic institutions owned and operated by the religious congregations. These two types of private institutions must be considered separately.

Whether or not "private establishments founded by speculators" would be incorporated into the asylum system did not, to most legislators, seem a question of great moment. The asylum system under discussion in the chambers was designed to cater primarily to the poor and indigent; the *maisons de santé*, with their comfortable and even lavish accommodations, catered explicitly to a middle- and upper-class clientele, and hence their exclusion from such a system would not adversely affect their fortunes.[74] Where the issue of laissez-faire economics – of the freedom of the trade in lunacy – did arise pointedly was in discussion of a relatively peripheral provision of the bill concerning regulation of the *maisons de santé*. On the unanimous recommendation of the psychiatrists it consulted, the commission of deputies reviewing Gasparin's original bill had added a new stipulation: Only those *maisons de santé* that treated lunatics exclusively should be authorized to treat them at all; so-called "mixed establishments" (which accepted patients with physical ailments as well as lunatics) should be prohibited on the ground that the serious treatment of the insane required a uniquely strict regimen and the undivided attention of a large staff of surveillants.[75] Coupled with this medical-scientific rationale was an unspoken pragmatic rationale. The "mixed establishments" were typically the enterprises of commercial speculators or general medical practitioners; abolishing them would thus remove most of the nonspecialist competition from the field of private care for the insane and give the *aliénistes* a virtual monopoly over a lucrative market.

Certain deputies, quick to discern this latter implication, rallied to the

---

[74] See Barthélémy summarizing the opinion of the commission of peers charged to examine the bill; *Arch. parl.*, 2d ser., Vol. 113, p. 543. The *maisons de santé* defined and advertised themselves in precise social-class terms. Falret described the establishment he and Voisin ran at Vanves as "devoted to the rich class of society"; *Observations sur le projet de loi*, p. 11n. Brierre de Boismont described his *maison* as "specially intended for persons belonging to the middle classes" in his leaflet *Maison de santé du docteur Brierre de Boismont, rue Neuve-Sainte-Geneviève no. 21, près du Pantheon*, n.d., p. 3.

[75] *Arch. parl.*, 2d ser., Vol. 108, pp. 483–84; ibid., Vol. 115, p. 293.

defense of economic freedom. As Minister of the Interior Montalivet later summarized their argument: "It was said in the Chamber of Deputies, 'You are attacking private industry. There are [mixed] *maisons de santé* already formed which have lunatics. You will deprive them of their means of existence; the madman is an object of speculation like any other commodity.' "[76] In fact, the provision was eventually defeated – not by the deputies but by the peers, and not on laissez-faire economic grounds but as violating the so-called "liberty of families." A family, it was contended, had the right to safeguard its reputation and to conceal the shameful secret of the insanity of one of its members; and this could be accomplished only by placing that person in an institution of ambiguous definition rather than in an institution universally recognized as a madhouse.[77] (Note that the family's objection to the intrusion of psychiatry into its affairs, which Esquirol had anticipated when first presenting the doctrine of isolation, now unexpectedly appeared in a different guise, blocking the full attainment of one of the psychiatrists' professional goals.) The legislators thus evinced some concern to protect the private, profit-making sector from excessive state regulation. And in this regard, the peers successfully resisted the pressure exerted by the alliance of the government and the psychiatrists. But protection of the entrepreneur's trade in lunacy can hardly be called one of the salient issues raised by the bill.

Far more salient and far more explosive in the chambers was the issue of government encroachment upon the other portion of the private sector – the clerical asylums. Here a boundary dispute, comparable to the one with the judiciary over interdiction, was joined in earnest. For in the first place, decisions about how the mandatory asylum system would be constituted stood to undermine the religious asylums: Those asylums, unlike the private lay *maisons de santé,* did cater to poor and indigent lunatics. In the second place, the role of religion in the care of the insane tended to arouse passionate emotion in certain legislators, for healing and religion were traditionally linked categories, healing being an integral part of the Catholic mission and self-conception. Parliamentary discussion turned on the specific issue of whether the law should allow a religious asylum to serve as the "official" asylum of a department. Should the law require, in other words, that every department have at its disposal a government-operated public asylum, or was a clerical asylum an acceptable alternative?

The legislators revealed a remarkably detailed knowledge of the reli-

[76] Ibid., Vol. 115, p. 327; the arguments to which Montalivet is referring can be found in ibid., Vol. 109, pp. 365, 402.

[77] See, e.g., Montalivet's summary of this argument, ibid., Vol. 115, p. 325. The peers ultimately accepted a modified form of the article, which was written into the Law (Article 5): private "mixed" establishments were to be allowed only if they had entirely separate quarters for lunatics.

gious asylums in France. The specificity of the data cited – as well as the affective charge, whether positive or negative, that such data carried – surpassed anything to be found in comparable discussions of the *maisons de santé*. Yet the rhetoric and the tone of the discussion differed in the two chambers. Among the deputies, defenders of the religious asylums were low-key and their defenses tended to be hedged round with qualifications. A politically conservative deputy from the Calvados brought up the matter of the Bon-Sauveur of Caen, the perfectly "admirable" asylum in his department run with "benevolence" by a religious congregation and serving all the needs of the indigent lunatics in the locality. How redundant, then, to impose upon the Calvados the "onerous" burden of founding a public departmental asylum – especially since public asylums, with their hired staff, "cost ten times more" than their religious counterparts! The deputy did not, he added cautiously, want to be misconstrued. He favored maintaining and giving legal sanction to religious asylums only where they already existed; he was not enunciating a general principle that the religious congregations rather than the agencies of the state assume responsibility for the care of lunatics. "God forbid that I draw [that] conclusion."[78] This viewpoint was seconded by the left liberal Destutt de Tracy, the son of the famous Idéologue, who also regarded the economic argument for the clerical asylums as compelling but gave it a different twist. He noted that straining the resources of the departments for the construction of new, "grandly imposing edifices" to house the insane would entail increasing the tax burden upon the poor as well as upon the rich.

Yet Tracy trusted the religious caretakers of the insane far less than did his colleague from the Calvados, and he wished to combine the economy of using their services with the wary precaution of submitting them to strict administrative surveillance. On the floor of the chamber, he engaged in some allusive badinage with Minister of the Interior Gasparin concerning an asylum founded by Frère Hilarion and the Brothers of Saint-Jean-de-Dieu at Clermont in the department of the Puy-de-Dôme, near Tracy's own department of the Allier. Since the brothers had also constructed a large lunatic institution at La Guillotière on the outskirts of Lyon, they were in the early 1830s in contact with Gasparin as prefect of the Rhône.[79] "I can cite," Tracy told the deputies,

> the experience that I acquired while serving on the Conseil général of my department. All of us on the Conseil had, without exception, been seduced by the offers made by the director of a very respectable religious

---

[78] Goupil de Préfeln, *Arch. parl.*, 2d ser., Vol. 109, p. 354.

[79] See André Chagny, *L'ordre hospitalier de Saint Jean de Dieu en France*, Vol. 2 (Lyon: Impr. de M. Lescuyer, 1953), pp. 17–18. Gasparin gave prefectorial endorsement to the Charitains' institution at La Guillotière in 1831.

congregation in Lyon. The Minister of the Interior ought to know what I am speaking of. (Gasparin: "Perfectly.") Near Clermont this congregation had established a hospital on a beneficial plan, where work, agricultural labor and good air offered sound means of curing lunatics. We seized eagerly upon this favorable and economical means of attending to the lunatics [in the charge of the department]. . . . Ah well, the next year we had legitimate qualms because we heard that this establishment, no longer directed by the person who had conceived and founded it, had fallen into deplorable condition.[80]

The theme of the necessary administrative surveillance of religious asylums was articulated more firmly and given a snide anticlerical edge by the Doctrinaire Vivien, the spokesman for the commission of deputies charged with examining the government's bill. Vivien, too, illustrated his theme with an allusive anecdote:

An establishment of this sort (I do not wish to name it . . . but this fact has been attested to us by very serious persons, by physicians who visited it in a public capacity), an establishment of this sort is directed by an individual who truly ought rather to find a place among the persons kept within the establishment than among their keepers. This individual does not have the command of his faculties. He thinks that with the aid of supernatural means, of superstitious procedures which have no relationship to those recommended by science, he will be able to cure insanity. Do you want such an individual to be kept on at the head of his establishment?[81]

The anonymous individual thus lambasted was Frère Hilarion: Lest there be any uncertainty on this point in the minds of the public, Hilarion identified himself in a pamphlet of 1837, announcing that he would, in the cheek-turning manner of the true, peaceable Christian, "accept the insult and the gross injury inflicted by Monsieur Vivien." Of course, the pamphlet continued, Vivien's allegations were false; Hilarion was a "benefactor of humanity" who had always counseled the use of "medical treatment and hygiene" in conjunction with "prayer and religious consolations."[82] In Vivien's speech, then, the rivalry between physicians (allied with bureaucrats) and clerics for control of the treatment of the insane was dramatized and briefly occupied the attention of the national legislative forum.

That rivalry would soon occupy the Chamber of Peers at greater length, for the noblemen in the upper chamber included a significant number of outspokenly devout Catholics. The commission of peers charged with examining the bill was split unevenly on the issue of religious asylums. The minority clung to the secular ideal of a network

---

[80] *Arch. parl.*, 2d ser., Vol. 109, pp. 354–55.
[81] Ibid., p. 404.
[82] Tissot, *Mémoire en faveur des aliénés* (Lyon: Impr. de Pelagaud, Lesne & Crozet, 1837), p. 11 and p. 11n.

of special public asylums and held that the right of the departments to make use of religious asylums in fulfillment of their legal obligations ought to be a temporary expedient, expiring after ten years. These peers believed, in a Voltairean manner, that priestly religion unsettled the rational faculties and hence that "in the establishments belonging to the congregations . . . an exclusively religious direction might be given to the minds of the patients and hinder their cure." The majority, however, was happy to accept the religious asylums as a fait accompli; it saw no need to create afresh a homogeneous national asylum system but preferred to construct that system as a permanent patchwork of public and private-religious elements. To do otherwise would be simply to "bring ruin to the charitable *maisons*," an outcome both unjust and undesirable. For it was sheer nonsense that the religious character of an asylum aggravated the condition of its inmates: Statistics drawn up by the Paris hospices showed that "religious exaltation" was an insignificant cause of madness, coming near the bottom of the list after "heredity, drunkenness, sexual promiscuity, reverses of fortune, thwarted passion," and the like.

Furthermore, the choice of the moral treatment as the medical-scientific paradigm for the treatment of the insane did not exclude religious healers from this vocation but instead validated them. The peers had thus located the same vulnerability in the professional program of the *aliénistes* as had Hilarion:

> In a malady for whose cure moral means are recognized as so efficacious, medicine (*les secours de l'art*) can only find a powerful auxiliary in the care that Christian charity inspires. Religious devotion discloses by turns the firmness and the gentleness (*douceur*) necessary for the direction of a house for madmen.[83]

This was not the only time in the debates when the psychiatric theory of the moral treatment was marshaled against the psychiatrists. Months later a deputy also noted the natural affinity between the "prudent and enlightened" priest and that "moral medicine" which science touted for the cure of the insane. In cases of suicidal melancholia, he asked, could mere "philosophy furnish the physician with effective consolations? Would not such consolations need to be drawn from consideration of another life?"[84]

The majority opinion of the commission received much support from the floor of the chamber – praise for the "fine establishments founded

---

[83] The account of the minority and majority opinions of the commission comes from its rapporteur, Barthélémy, *Arch. parl.*, 2d ser., Vol. 113, pp. 543–44.

[84] Calemard de Lafayette, ibid., Vol. 118, p. 9. Calemard's position enraged the republican newspaper *National* (whose editorial board included Ulysse Trélat, a former Esquirol circle member who would resume his career as an *aliéniste* after 1848); see unsigned article of April 14, 1838.

by piety," ardent injunctions "to multiply them, to encourage them to grow in scale."[85] But the most trenchant speech on behalf of religious healing of the insane was delivered by the liberal Catholic Comte de Montalembert. Committed – as a way of defending the institutional church against a statist anticlericalism – to a program of bureaucratic decentralization and to laissez-faire in all its aspects,[86] Montalembert questioned the proposed measure by which the departments could make use of private lunatic institutions only on condition that they receive authorization from the minister of the interior. What did such a measure mean in fact? The minister himself could not possibly handle such business directly but would be obliged to delegate it to the appropriate "agent in charge." Here Montalembert discerned the anticlerical bias of the government, a bias implicit in the choice of Ferrus for a key administrative post:

> I beg the pardon of the Chamber for entering into details which will perhaps appear only personal in nature, but these details are entirely germane to the bill before us. That agent, gentlemen, is the inspector general of lunatic houses; it is Monsieur Ferrus. Ah, well! Monsieur Ferrus, in a book on lunatics, expresses himself thusly: "In houses for the treatment of the insane, the presence of religious sisters entails, in my opinion, more disadvantages than advantages."

Continuing his argument, Montalembert noted the natural harmony between bureaucracy and science and the radical incongruity between the bureaucratic spirit and the spirit of charity. "Science," he said, "lends itself perfectly to unity, to regularity; charity does not lend itself to these at all." Montalembert's insight was one which the Doctrinaires shared entirely, one which had, in fact, prompted them to forge a working alliance with the *aliénistes*. But Montalembert carried an identical insight to the opposite conclusion. The religious caretakers of the insane must be allowed to survive, and this meant allowing them to function in their full spiritual plenitude, free of bureaucratic strictures, for, as he put it, "You cannot regulate or manage charity any more than you could invent it." Montalembert then summed up his classically liberal Catholic position: "However high my esteem for these [religious] institutions, I do not ask that they be given a monopoly. . . . I demand in their favor only the benefits of competition and liberty."[87]

The Doctrinaire Minister of the Interior Montalivet also called for a compromise solution, though one in which, contrary to Montalem-

---

[85] See the speeches of the Vicomtes de Villiers du Terrage and Dubouchage and the Marquis de la Moussaye, *Arch. parl.*, 2d ser., Vol. 115, pp. 246–47, 249, 252.

[86] On this typical strategy of the liberal Catholicism of the 1830s and 1840s, see Roger Henry Soltau, *French Political Thought in the Nineteenth Century* (New York: Russell & Russell, 1959), p. 82.

[87] *Arch. parl.*, 2d ser., Vol. 115, p. 255.

bert's views, statist criteria were to monitor charitable impulses. Literally invoking the juste-milieu which was the ethos of the middling regime he served, Montalivet was greeted with shouts of "Très bien!" when he upheld both the preponderant role of irreligion in causing insanity and the preponderant role of science in treating it, a position which admitted, conditionally, the legitimacy of clerical *guérisseurs:*

> We are all in agreement on this subject. It is certain that insanity derives especially from the habitude of vice which afflicts humanity. Thus everyone agrees that the first preservative against it ought to be . . . primary education . . . [which], with all its religious content, is doubtless the best means for keeping human reason intact. . . . Now . . . , does it follow that any preference ought to be accorded to lay or religious establishments? We do not think so. Where lay establishments exist in which science is practiced and order prevails, we think it good to support and protect them. If there exist, on the other hand, establishments directed by legally authorized religious congregations, if order prevails and *if science is well practiced there, if the door is not shut on it as a kind of worldly invention,* we will be eager to protect and maintain these establishments as well.[88]

Montalivet went even further in the direction of jettisoning, in the face of powerful opposition, the government's ideal of a secular asylum system. Provided that religious healers fulfilled the condition indicated, he believed that the much sought-after juste-milieu would be found only in a "mélange" of lay and clerical asylums; the latter would not, in other words, be merely suffered.[89]

It was Montalivet's compromise solution and not Montalembert's which ultimately won the day. The first article of the 1838 Law required that each department "have a public establishment especially designed to receive and care for lunatics or negotiate (*traiter*) to this effect with a public or private establishment either in the department or in another department." Such "treaties," it continued, "must be approved by the minister of the interior"; and one of the criteria for approval was that a clerical asylum employ a full-time resident physician.[90] Thus, although the Law did not provide for that absolutely unfettered competition between the medical and clerical spheres that Montalembert desired, although the necessity for state surveillance of

---

[88] Ibid., p. 253, my italics. Montalivet's formulation here provides striking confirmation of Foucault's thesis about the construction, from interdependent institutional elements, of a "carceral archipelago" (*Discipline and Punish*, p. 297). The primary schools, fostered by the Doctrinaires' Law of 1833, would provide, through a stabilizing moral and religious instruction, inoculation against insanity; the asylums, fostered by the Doctrinaires' Law of 1838, would in turn receive the failures of the primary school regimen.

[89] *Arch. parl.*, 2d ser., Vol. 115, p. 253, my italics.

[90] Loi sur les aliénés, June 30, 1838, Article 1; Ordonnance relative aux établissements publics et privés consacrés aux aliénés, December 18, 1839, Articles 19, 30.

charitable enterprises for the insane was laid down as a principle, neither did the Law end the rivalry between the new *médecins aliénistes* and the clerics. However substantial a victory for psychiatry the Law represented, it left that problematic boundary dispute unresolved – an item of unfinished professional business which could not be forgotten and which would be taken up by the psychiatrists at a more propitious historical moment.

Assessing the clerical "threat"

What was the balance of power between medical and clerical "forces" in the domain of the treatment of the insane in the years following the passage of the Law of 1838? What difference, if any, did the Law make?

Enforcement of the Law began almost immediately, revealing a seriousness of intent on the part of the central administration.[91] As early as September 1838, the minister of the interior had rebuked the prefect of the Morbihan for a reported "infraction of the law of this past June 30th." Apparently a small town in the department which had no acceptable facility, not even an inn with private rooms, was continuing to detain furious lunatics in the local jail.[92] A series of ministerial circulars to the prefects between 1839 and 1841 explicated the subtleties of the text of the Law and provided specific directives for its implementation.[93] And sharp-tongued reprimands continued to emanate from Paris. The prefect of the Vienne, for example, was found by the minister of the interior to harbor "a poorly disguised resistance . . . to the spirit of the recent legislation on the insane," as seen in his failure to appoint a special salaried official to head the lunatic quarters of the hospice of Poitiers. Nor, while he was writing, could the minister refrain from pointing out that the engineering and design of that same lunatic quarters had been a pathetic comedy of errors. The ambitious project by which an annex to the hospice had been constructed in a riverbed (necessitating a diversion of the river) had yielded only two noteworthy results: The rooms looked out on "barren rocks," and the foundation was so weak that the walls had everywhere begun to crack, facilitating the escape of the inmates.[94]

---

[91] Cf. the assertions of Robert Castel that the government took little interest in implementing the Law after having engineered its passage and that mere passage adequately served its purposes; *Ordre psychiatrique*, pp. 235, 241–43. Had Castel consulted the cartons of the F[15] series which document the government's efforts to implement the Law during the remaining ten years of the July Monarchy, the seeming paradox for which he supplied an explanation would have disappeared.

[92] AN: F[15] 3909, Dossier: Morbihan, letters dated August 30 and September 22, 1838.

[93] Circulars of April 10 and August 5, 1839; August 5, 14 and 16, 1840; and August 12, 1841.

[94] AN: F[15] 3908, Dossier: Vienne, letter of March 12, 1841.

The message from Paris was compliance. But before midcentury compliance rarely took the form of construction of new public asylums. According to a government survey of 1874, only three such asylums were actually built in France between 1838 and 1852.[95] The rash of asylum building came later, leading one modern commentator to observe that "it was the same for the asylums as for the railroads: the regime of Louis-Philippe devised the plans, but the Second Empire and early Third Republic actually laid the iron rails and erected the psychiatric institutions."[96] The early phase of implementation of the Law consisted instead in a variety of makeshift measures: transformations of existing public facilities such as hospices or *dépôts de mendicité*, which had traditionally housed heterogeneous populations, into institutions solely for the insane; and formal treaties with public and private asylums inside and outside the department. As deputies such as Tracy had predicted, financial considerations weighed heavily on the departments as they puzzled out how best to meet the new obligations imposed upon them by the Law.

The department of the Eure, which lacked a public asylum, provides a case in point. A commission appointed by its Conseil général to study the available options unabashedly declared its preoccupation with money. "In the midst of numerous sacrifices which the needs of civilization have simultaneously required of the departments for primary education, for highways and local roads, for the cadastral survey and soon, no doubt, for prisons," it could only view the new lunacy law with a jaundiced eye as "add[ing] to these other expenses, aggravating their burden." The commissioners' immediate impulse was to investigate the least costly strategies first. Would they be able to make an arrangement with one of the recognized asylums in the area, with the Bon-Sauveur at Caen or with Saint-Yon at Rouen (the public institution reformed by the Esquirol circle member Foville)? Unfortunately, the two asylums in question were too crowded to guarantee adequate space to the lunatics of the Eure; both would sign treaties covering only a limited number of patients. And so, with great reluctance and trepidation, the department conceived in 1839 a project for constructing a new asylum, "the best possible at the least possible cost" – a project not to be realized until August 1866.[97]

[95] Constans, Lunier, and Dumesnil, *Rapport général à M. le Ministre de l'Intérieur sur le service des aliénés en 1874* (Paris: Impr. nationale, 1878), p. 63.

[96] G. Lanteri-Laura, "La chronicité dans la psychiatrie française moderne," *Annales E.S.C.* 27 (1972): 562.

[97] See Lefebvre-Duruflé, *Rapport au Conseil général du département de l'Eure, dans sa session de 1839 au nom de la commission des aliénés* (Evreux: J.-J. Ancelle, 1839), pp. 9–10, 12. On the date of completion of the Evreux asylum, "of grandiose proportions in expectation of 600 lunatics," see P. Berthier, *Excursions scientifiques dans les asiles d'aliénés*, 4th ser., (Paris: Savy, 1866), p. 52. On the treaties with the Bon-Sauveur of Caen and Saint-Yon, see AN: F[15] 3906, Dossier: Eure.

The example of the Eure suggests that the 1838 Law might well have thrown the departments into the arms of the clerical asylums. After all, that long-term outcome was narrowly averted in the case of the Eure only by the nonreceptivity of the Sisters of the Bon-Sauveur. But other clerical asylum directors might be more ready and willing to accommodate the departments in their regions. The bureaucratic pressures exerted on the departments to provide suitable facilities for their indigent insane had already redounded to the benefit of the clerical asylums as early as the second decade of the nineteenth century. Wouldn't the 1838 Law, which intensified and systematized those same pressures, redound all the more to their benefit? Fortunately, we are in a position to test this supposition. The Ministry of the Interior conducted a complete department-by-department survey of the whereabouts of the indigent insane not only in 1833 but again in 1842.[98] The data furnished by the respondents to both surveys are often incomplete and imprecise, but they allow us to assess in rough terms the immediate consequences of the 1838 Law for the clerical asylums and, by extension, for the rivalry between clerics and *aliénistes*.

First a word about terminology. What exactly is a "clerical asylum"? While some cases are unambiguous (the Bon-Sauveur of Caen, for example), the admixture of lay and clerical elements in the ownership and management of many institutions produces real uncertainty about their "essential" nature, especially when self-representation and public image are considered along with technical legal status. One particularly important example of thorny classification – important because of its size and the number of neighboring departments it served – was the hospice of Maréville near Nancy. Routinely referred to during the parliamentary debates as an establishment founded by a religious congregation or by "public piety,"[99] Maréville was also in some sense a state facility – witness the 1810 letter of the prefect of the Meurthe to the minister of the interior (cited at the beginning of Chapter 3) in which he requested a copy of Pinel's *Traité* to help improve the treatment offered at the presumably departmental facility of Maréville. In fact, Maréville had a long tradition of overlapping state sponsorship and private religious managerial control. Founded by the Duke of Lorraine at the beginning of the eighteenth century as a house of correction, it was entrusted to the Brothers of the Christian Schools in 1749 when its inmate population was expanded to include lunatics. After the Revolution, the prefect of the Meurthe appropriated it as a departmental lunatic institution, turning over the care of its inmates to a freelance

---

[98] The results of the 1833 survey appear as eight pages of foldout tables (henceforth 1833 Tables) at the back of Ferrus, *Des aliénés*. The results of the second survey, which was mandated by a ministerial circular of August 31, 1842, were never tabulated or published, but the prefects' replies fill an entire carton; AN: F[15] 3906.

[99] See Barthélémy, *Arch. parl.*, 2d ser., Vol. 113, p. 541; Villiers du Terrage, ibid., Vol. 115, p. 246; Dubouchage, ibid., p. 255.

contractor, an "entrepreneur who was paid on a per diem basis for each lunatic"; but the proclerical Restoration regime had its predictable impact, and beginning in 1818 both "the attendance [on the patients] and the administration of the *maison* were entrusted to the Sisters of Saint-Charles."[100] The institution was thus a hybrid secular and clerical one, defying neat classification; and it was hardly unique in this regard. What, for example, are we to make of the Saint-Alban asylum founded in the Lozère by Frère Hilarion, which was according to all administrative accounts a public departmental facility?[101] Or of the newly opened wing for female lunatics at the public hospice of Morlaix (Finistère), whose self-representation in a prospectus of 1846 stressed that the patients were "cared for by the religious nursing sisters of the order of Saint-Thomas-de-Villeneuve" and mentioned only secondarily that these sisters were under the supervision of a resident physician?[102]

Recognizing this typical combination of public-secular and religious elements, I will, for purposes of this chapter, avoid addressing the almost infinite shadings of ambiguity. I will regard as a "clerical asylum" one which is owned, administered, and staffed by a religious congregation; I will depart from this strict definition only to include Maréville, a departure justified by the strong contemporary consensus about that institution's predominantly clerical character (despite its technically public status) and by the salient and conspicuous role in the care of the insane which it played in France in the first half of the nineteenth century. On the basis of these criteria, thirteen clerical asylums used in an official capacity by the departments in 1842 can be listed (see Table 8.1).

Comparison of the two government surveys makes it clear that intensified bureaucratic pressure on the prefects to "put their houses in order" with respect to the indigent insane had, by 1842, resulted in a modest gain for the clerical asylums. The gain was not so much in new foundations – all but two of the clerical asylums listed in Table 8.1 were already in existence in 1833[103] – as in increased official use of the private

---

100 The historical account is found in Esquirol, "Des établissements consacrés aux aliénés en France," in *Des maladies mentales considérées sous les rapports médical, hygiénique et médico-légal,* Vol. 2 (Paris: J.-B. Baillière, 1838), pp. 495–96. Ferrus described Maréville in 1834 as "directed by the sisters of the order of Saint Charles"; see *Des aliénés,* p. 179.

101 On its public status, see 1833 Tables, entry "Lozère," and AN: F^{15} 3906; Hilarion described himself as the founder of the "departmental hospice for female lunatics of Saint-Alban" in *Mémoire en faveur des aliénés,* p. 28.

102 Ms. prospectus, AN: F^{15} 3909, Dossier: Morbihan.

103 The post-1833 foundations were the Bon-Sauveur of Saint-Lô and La Cellette. While Lehon did not exist in 1833, it was the direct successor to the Charitains' pre-1833 foundation of Saint-Aubin, also in the Côtes-du-Nord, which closed due to the dilapidation of its buildings; see Chagny, *Ordre hospitalier,* Vol. 2, pp. 23–25. Lommelet, absent from the 1833 Tables because of prefectorial negligence in replying to the circular, was founded in 1825; ibid., p. 21.

Table 8.1 *Clerical asylums serving in a public capacity: 1842 (listed by department of location)*

1. Ain
    (a) Saint-Lazare (for men), at Bourg, directed by the Sisters of Saint-Joseph of Bourg
    (b) Sainte-Madeleine (for women), at Bourg, directed by the Sisters of Saint-Joseph of Bourg
    (serves the Ain, Saône-et-Loire)

2. Ardèche
    Sainte-Marie, at Privas, directed by the Brothers of Sainte-Marie-de-l'Assomption
    (serves the Ardèche)

3. Aude
    Limoux, at Limoux, directed by Sisters of Saint-Joseph-de-Cluny
    (serves the Aude, Pyrénées-Orientales)

4. Calvados
    Bon-Sauveur, at Caen, directed by the Sisters of the Bon-Sauveur of Caen
    (serves the Calvados, Eure)

5. Corrèze
    La Cellette, at Monestier-Merlines, directed by the Brothers of Sainte-Marie-de-l'Assomption
    (serves the Corrèze, Allier, Creuse, Indre, Lozère, Puy-de-Dôme)

6. Côtes-du-Nord
    Lehon (for men), at Dinan, directed by the Brothers of Saint-Jean-de-Dieu
    (serves Côtes-du-Nord, Morbihan)

7. Manche
    Bon-Sauveur, at Saint-Lô, directed by the Sisters of the Bon-Sauveur of Saint-Lô
    (serves the Manche, Ille-et-Vilaine)

8. Meurthe
    Maréville, directed by the Sisters of Saint-Charles
    (serves the Meurthe, Ardennes, Aube, Côte d'Or, Haute-Saône, Moselle, Vosges)

9. Nord
    Lommelet; at Marquette, directed by the Brothers of Saint-Jean-de-Dieu
    (serves the Pas-de-Calais)

10. Puy-de-Dôme
    Sainte-Marie, at Clermont, directed by the Brothers of Sainte-Marie-de-l'Assomption
    (serves the Ardèche, Indre)

Table 8.1 *(cont.)*

---

11. Rhône
     Saint-Pierre et Saint-Paul, at La Guillotière, near Lyon, directed by the
         Brothers of Saint-Jean-de-Dieu
     (serves the Drôme, Gard, Loire)

12. Tarn
     Bon-Sauveur, at Alby, directed by the Sisters of the Bon-Sauveur of Caen
     (serves the Tarn)

Source: AN: F^{15} 3906

religious facilities. By 1842, seven departments which had had no dealings with the clerical asylums in 1833 had entered into formal arrangements with them.[104] On the other hand, three other departments had by
1842 withdrawn their business from asylums founded by the Brothers of
Saint-Jean-de-Dieu in favor of secular establishments.[105] Maréville was
booming. With room for almost 600 patients, it had nonetheless become
overcrowded by 1840 and could no longer accommodate all the prefectorial requests it received. By 1842 it was in the process of enlarging its
already capacious buildings.[106]

The appeal of the clerical asylums to the departments which made
use of their services was partly financial, not only by obvious comparison with the enormous cost of creating a new public departmental
asylum but also by comparison with the other available makeshift
options. To be sure—and despite a pervasive belief that through a
combination of charitable donations, unsalaried nursing staffs, and
simple thrift, religious congregations could feed, clothe, and care for

---

[104] The Eure, as already mentioned, had made a treaty with the Bon-Sauveur de Caen;
       the Ille-et-Vilaine had supplemented its own facility of Saint-Méen by a treaty with
       the Bon-Sauveur of Saint-Lô; the Indre had made treaties with Sainte-Marie at Cler-
       mont (Puy-de-Dôme) and La Cellette; the Morbihan with Lehon; the Pas-de-Calais
       with Lommelet; the Pyrénées-Orientales with Limoux; and the Saône-et-Loire with
       Saint-Lazare and Saint-Madeleine.

[105] The Cantal had abandoned Clermont for its own civil hospice of Aurillac, built
       according to Esquirol's specifications and his actual "sketches" (AN: F^{15} 3906, Dos-
       sier: Cantal), which opened its doors in 1836. The Haute-Loire had transferred its
       male lunatics from La Guillotière to Aurillac; the Somme had abandoned Lommelet
       for public asylums in the Nord and a private lay *maison de santé* in the Oise. In
       addition to this loss of business by the Charitains, the 1835 completion of the asylum
       of Stéphansfeld in Strasbourg (Bas-Rhin) had resulted in the removal of the lunatics
       of the Bas-Rhin and Haut-Rhin from Maréville.

[106] See AN: F^{15} 3906, Dossier: Moselle, letter of the prefect dated September 28, 1842;
       Dossier: Meurthe, "Etat des établissements publics et privés d'aliénés," dated De-
       cember 29, 1842.

mad patients for as little as 0.60 francs per day[107] – the clerical asylums did not always "undersell" their competitors, the public and private-lay asylums that accepted indigent lunatics from outside departments. But in general their fees for such patients were at the lower end of the scale.[108] I have come across only one instance of a public asylum complaining of the competitive advantage achieved by a local clerical asylum because of its lower fees. The prefect of the Haute-Vienne, eager to populate the "vacant places" at the recently renovated departmental asylum of Limoges, was bitter about the conduct of the departments of the Dordogne, Creuze, Corrèze, Charente, and Indre. Because of geographical proximity, they had been expected to do business with Limoges; but by 1843, all had chosen instead to make treaties with private asylums. Especially popular was the clerical *maison* of La Cellette, which charged 300 francs per year as opposed to the 328 charged by Limoges but which, the prefect alleged angrily, "is far from offering the same guarantees [as Limoges]" and probably failed to satisfy the conditions imposed by the 1838 Law. The prefect of the Haute-Vienne was contemptuous of the way his fellow prefects had sought out the "slight economy" provided by La Cellette and accused them of being in their approach to the lunacy question "too preoccupied with the financial question." He implored the minister of the interior to use his

---

[107] See, e.g., Dubouchage in the Chamber of Peers, *Arch. parl.*, 2d ser., Vol. 115, p. 250.

[108] The fee scales of nineteenth-century French asylums present a dizzying variety. Most, both public and private, had a tripartite scale: fees charged for indigent lunatics from the home department; fees charged for indigents from outside departments; and fees, by far the highest, charged to private paying patients, the so-called *pensionnaires*. Hence fees did not simply vary among asylums but also varied within asylums along these three separate axes. In addition, different fees were sometimes charged for men and women (men, being larger, physically stronger and presumably more unruly, were regarded as more expensive to tend). For our purposes here, certain generalizations can be made. First, Maréville was one of the least expensive facilities available to the indigent insane, charging most departments what it charged the home department of the Meurthe: 225–55 francs per year (which at 0.625–0.7 francs per day came very close to the ideal figure). Secondly, most clerical asylums charged between 300 and 365 francs per year, and most charged about as much as the public asylums in the area. For example, in the department of the Rhône, the public asylum of the Antiquaille, which accepted only local indigent lunatics, charged the department 300 francs per year per lunatic; the Charitains' establishment at La Guillotière charged 0.85 francs per day, or about 310 francs per year for indigent lunatics of any departmental provenance. (AN: F^{15} 3906, Dossier: Rhône). In the Manche, the clerical asylum of the Bon-Sauveur at Saint-Lô asked in 1842 to be allowed to raise its fees to 98.6 centimes per day in order to match those of Pontorson, the public asylum in the same department. (Ibid., Dossier: Manche) On the other hand, in 1833 at least, the Charitains' Lommelet undersold the public asylum at Lille in the same department, charging the outside department of the Somme 0.80 francs per day while Lille charged the Somme 1.13 francs per day. (1833 Tables, entry "Somme") Further specifics about fees can be found in AN: F^{15} 3906, passim.

power of refusal of treaties to rectify the situation and to insure the success of the public asylum in his department.[109]

The financial advantages of the clerical asylums were supplemented by another factor critical to their success – cultural appropriateness. Most of the departments making official use of such asylums (see Figure 2) fell within those regions subsequently identified by French sociologists of religion as characterized by devout and regular practice of the Catholic faith: Brittany, Normandy, the East (Alsace, Lorraine and Franche-Comté) and the Massif Central.[110] In general, the clerical asylums had been strategically located by their founders; and the prefects who patronized them had apparently made deliberate decisions to tailor the form of public welfare in their departments to the religious temperament and needs of their *administrés*.

More important than the modest concrete gains the clerical asylums had achieved by 1842 was the fact that their directors read the post-1838 situation optimistically. Highly sensitive to shifting political currents, if not always accurate judges of their implications (the sisters of the Bon-Sauveur of Caen had mistakenly believed that the Revolution of 1830 would deprive them of all protectors in high places and lead to their imminent demise),[111] the religious orders that operated lunatic establishments saw in the passage of the 1838 Law a portent favorable to their enterprise. In 1842 many of them reported plans for expansion. The Bon-Sauveur of Alby was in the process of doubling the size of a facility already housing 200. The proprietors of the Asile de Sainte-Marie announced themselves "inclined to make . . . repairs" which in less than a year would allow the capacity of their institution to approach 400. The "devotion of the Brothers [of Saint-Jean-de-Dieu]" who ran the *maison* at Lehon "has been so highly esteemed by the public that numerous requests for admission are addressed daily to the director," inspiring him to order the construction of two new buildings and four adjoining courtyards ("we are already busy gathering building materials") which would expand the capacity of the asylum from 420 to 600. The Brothers of Saint-Jean-de-Dieu were, in fact, immersed in building projects. At La Guillotière, "they are right now [1842] erecting new edifices" which within two years were supposed to raise the capacity of the *maison* from 280 to 400. At Lommelet, Frère Simon Caussade was sizing up the needs of the surrounding departments and had conceived a flexible building

[109] AN: F^{15} 3906, Dossier: Haute-Vienne, letter of the prefect dated June 4, 1843.

[110] John McManners, *Church and State in France, 1870–1914* (New York: Harper & Row, 1973), pp. 5–6; and F. Boulard, *An Introduction to Religious Sociology: Pioneer Work in France*, trans. M. J. Jackson (London: Darton, Longman & Todd, 1960), Chs. 1, 3.

[111] See G.-A. Simon, *Une belle figure de prêtre et d'homme d'oeuvres à la fin du XVIIIe siècle: L'abbé Pierre-François Jamet* (Caen: Jouan & Bigot, 1935), p. 334.

Departments Using Clerical Asylums in an Official Capacity

• Departmental Capital

Figure 2. The geography of clerical caretaking of the insane, 1842 (AN: F^{15} 3906)

program which would respond, incrementally at three-month intervals, to the demands of the bureaucratically created market: "The vast terrain [that the institution encompasses] permits the construction of every type of building."[112]

[112] AN: F^{15} 3906, Dossiers: Tarn, Puy-de-Dôme, Côtes-du-Nord, Rhône, Nord. The ministerial circular had explicitly elicited information about current *constructions nouvelles* as part of its effort to assess the availability of places for lunatics in the different localities.

The flourishing of these clerical asylums in the 1840s was acknowledged by one blatantly unsympathetic observer, whom the historian is inclined to trust on this point because the rest of the
evidence points in the same direction. The observer was a certain
concerned citizen protesting to the new Minister of the Interior Ledru-
Rollin two months after the February 1848 Revolution that the
Brothers of Saint-Jean-de-Dieu had received authorization to take up a
collection or offertory (*quête*) in the city of Vannes, and that such
"monkish beggary" was not only outmoded ("certainly no longer of
our time") but also morally offensive because it siphoned resources
away from "the present needs of the country and especially of the
poor class." The Charitains, Citizen Gonidet added indignantly, were
affluent enough that their resort to such antiquated practices was all
the more unjustified:

> I must tell you, Citizen Minister, that these Brothers have a lunatic insti-
> tution in the Côtes-du-Nord which houses nearly 400 of these sick per-
> sons, who are supported either by their families or by the departments
> (with which the Brothers have treated for a fee of 300 francs for each
> indigent lunatic). I happen to know that these Brothers do a very good
> business indeed because last year they sold for the sum of 200,000 francs
> a fine property close to their lunatic establishment.[113]

The clerical asylum directors' reading of their long-term post-1838
situation differed, however, from the situation that the administration
hoped to create. The Law of 1838 was silent on the issue of how long
private asylums would be allowed to function in an official, departmental capacity – a silence that could be construed as a mandate for the
permanent inclusion of the clerical asylums in the national system. Yet,
belying Montalivet's earlier, conciliatory rhetoric in the Chamber of
Peers, the administration chose to construe the silence differently, as
meaning that the die had not yet been cast. It remained committed to
its ideal of a uniformly public and secular asylum system – not an immediate goal, it had by now tacitly conceded, but one nonetheless to
be worked toward and prepared for. Two circulars from the minister of
the interior to the prefects, one in 1839 and the other in 1840, pursued
this goal. "The circular of August 5, 1839," the minister reminded his
prefects when reiterating the point a year later, "enjoined you never to
put yourself under obligation [in a treaty with a private asylum or a
public asylum outside the department] for more than one year, or at
least always to reserve to yourself the right to annul your obligation"
with three to six months' notice. Recognizing that "the directors of
private [including clerical] asylums especially" would be prone to

[113] Ibid., Morbihan, letter dated April 6, 1848.

press for longer engagements in order to insure a steady flow of clientele, the minister nonetheless adhered to his position as the only one appropriate to an asylum system of such recent vintage, one whose outlines were still so incomplete.[114] In other words, the administration was wary of stabilizing any solution to the lunacy problem except the creation of special public asylums, and this attitude included a wariness about entrenching the clerical asylums in an officially endorsed system.

The administration's intention to monitor the specifically religious component of asylum (and other hospice) management was expressed in another ministerial circular to the prefects, that of September 25, 1838, which called for a regularization of all treaties between congregations of nursing sisters and the public institutions of *bienfaisance* they served. Some congregations, the minister observed, were presently engaged in such service without any formal treaties; others had formal contractual agreements which had never been submitted to the minister for approval. Both sorts of "irregular condition" were no longer to be tolerated.[115] One major ministerial criterion for approval of a treaty was that religious nursing be kept within a delimited sphere, that it be prevented from becoming clerical domination of a public institution. Of a treaty made with the hospice of Coutances (Manche), the prefect wrote the minister that it was not "in accord with the current rules":

> The nuns have all the keys to the interior [and] they alone can hand them over to such persons as possess their confidence; they close the granaries and the wine cellars at will. . . . They take their own vegetables and fruits from the gardens of the hospice; they not only care for the poor and sick; they run a boarding school for young girls, admit novices and train nuns for their order. . . . The hospice, as your predecessor remarked in a letter [four years ago], has been, in a sense, transformed into a convent.[116]

A similar though less thoroughgoing prefectorial critique was made of the treaties concluded by the Sisters of Saint Vincent de Paul with the hospices of Toulouse. The sisters had assumed so much responsibility for the financial affairs of the institution that they had encroached upon the legitimate territory of the secular office of the bursar (*économe*); they (like their counterparts at Coutances) were custodians

---

[114] See circular of August 16, 1840, p. 3; and for an example of its use as a guide to prefectorial action, AN: F^{15} 3899, Dossier: Aube, letter dated January 8, 1842.

[115] Circular of September 25, 1838, AN: AD XIX I; for the correspondence generated by this circular, see AN: F^{15} 193.

[116] AN: F^{15} 193, letter of the prefect of the Manche dated June 17, 1839.

of the "keys of the *maison*," a function with great symbolic as well as practical significance.[117] In general, the prefects complained of having difficulty amassing the information required and overcoming "the force of inertia" which militated against drawing up formal treaties and making clear-cut distinctions between the prerogatives of nuns and bursars.[118] Whether the bureaucratic campaign for the regularization of the treaties was successful these documents cannot tell us; but they do bear witness to the government's wish, under the July Monarchy, to circumscribe rigorously the function of the religious nursing sisters, to move, albeit by small steps, toward the secularization of public welfare institutions, including those for the insane.

Finally, on at least one occasion in the early 1840s the bureaucracy refused legal authorization outright to a clerical asylum. The nuns at Baugé (Maine-et-Loire) had been operating their "eminently charitable" institution since its endowment by a devout benefactress in 1804 and claimed not even to have heard, in the backwaters of western France, about the passage of the 1838 Law.[119] The bishop of Angers, who came to the defense of this "threatened congregation," alleged that the prefect's unfavorable opinion of the institution was based solely upon self-interest: With the opening of a public lunatic hospice in the department imminent, the prefect feared a damaging competition between the two.[120] But the prefect himself said nothing about intradepartmental competition between public and clerical institutions, arguing solely on the grounds that the Baugé establishment was contrary to "the spirit of the Law [of 1838]." It was, he wrote, "almost common knowledge" that the patients of these nuns "receive the attentions of physicians only in the case of maladies foreign to their mental infirmity and that they are submitted to no regular and special treatment to ameliorate their intellectual faculties"; that the nuns justified this policy of neglect by their patients' incurability, while in fact "it is difficult to judge whether a lunatic is incurable or not"; and finally and most damagingly, that the money paid by the lunatic *pensionnaires* was diverted to the support of the religious community itself, which was in dire financial straits.[121] Whether it was the bishop's or the pre-

---

[117] Ibid., letter of the prefect of the Haute Garonne dated April 4, 1839; and a copy of the *traité* itself, dated March 9, 1815. This treaty was presumably in effect at the hospice of the Grave when the Esquirol circle member Delaye was appointed *aliéniste* there.

[118] Ibid., letter of the prefect of the Aveyron dated January 28, 1839; letter of the prefect of the Indre-et-Loire dated January 5, 1839.

[119] AN: F[15] 3899, Dossier: Maine-et-Loire, letter of Soeur Goulard, superior of the order, to the bishop of Angers dated August 6, 1843, ms. pp. 1, 4, 8–9.

[120] Ibid., letter from bishop of Angers to the minister of the interior dated September 16, 1843.

[121] Ibid., prefect's decree on the Baugé establishment's request for authorization, untitled, dated June 17, 1843.

fect's understanding of the situation that was accurate, the "psychiatric" enterprise of the nuns at Baugé was in fact suppressed.[122]

The originally Rousseauean and subsequently Pinellian discourse about madness as a by-product of civilization was much in vogue during the period of the constitutional monarchy, both among psychiatrists and among the educated public.[123] One Paris newspaper, giving credence to the "appalling" psychopathogenic effect of France's revolutionary proclivities – the "alternation of fears and hopes . . . , the condition of fever and overstimulation (*surexcitation*) produced by an all-consuming politics" – expressed approval of the new law on the insane, which it described laconically as "our civilization repairing the damage it has itself inflicted."[124] But the concept "civilization" is amenable to different glosses; it embraces human achievements of different kinds. For the Doctrinaires, for whom it was a key word,[125] as well as for those to the left of them politically, the reparative "civilization" called into action by the 1838 Law was medical science. As the same Paris newspaper continued, the Law "charges science with a cure it has often been able to obtain, an admirable conquest of our civilization."[126] Similarly, a republican newspaper saw science and the French Revolution as the joint essence of the Law: The Law would spread from Paris to the provinces that new treatment which arose both from "medical science" and from that general *adoucissement des moeurs* and recoil from violence that were part and parcel of "our revolution of 1789."[127] But for others in nineteenth-century France, the Catholic religion was the mainstay of "civilization"; and neither the Law nor its subsequent im-

---

[122] Ibid., letter from the Ministry of Justice and Religion to the minister of the interior, dated January 12, 1846. In enforcing the 1838 Law, the administration showed severity to other clerical asylums as well; on the asylum of Limoux (Aude), forced to remain in a legal limbo until 1855, see Giordana Charuty, *Le couvent des fous: L'internement et ses usages en Languedoc aux XIXe et XXe siècles* (Paris: Flammarion, 1985), pp. 87–94, 98.

[123] From the abundant psychiatric literature on this subject, I will mention only a few key items: Esquirol's 1824 address to the Academy of Medicine, "Existe-t-il de nos jours un plus grand nombre de fous qu'il n'en existait il y a quarante ans?" reprinted in *Maladies mentales*, Vol. 2, pp. 723–42; and two articles by Brierre de Boismont (the most active psychiatric proponent of the thesis), one for a lay audience, "De la loi sur les aliénés; des principales causes de folie; de la folie dans ses rapports avec la civilisation . . . ," *Revue française* (April 1838): 104–121; and one for his professional colleagues, "De l'influence de la civilisation sur le développement de la folie," *Ann. d'hyg. pub.* 21 (1839): 241–95.

[124] *Presse*, April 7, 1837.

[125] See Lucien Febvre, "*Civilisation:* evolution of a word and a group of ideas," in *A New Kind of History*, ed. Peter Burke, trans. K. Folca (New York: Harper & Row, 1973), esp. pp. 240–48.

[126] *Presse*, April 7, 1837.

[127] *National*, February 11, 1838.

plementation had excluded this "civilizing" influence from the govern-
ment-endorsed cure of insanity.

While the Law had insisted that clerical asylums employ full-fledged
resident physicians,[128] it did not thereby necessarily "medicalize" those
institutions. The 1841 remarks of one such physician, who had since
the passage of the Law served the asylum of the Brothers of Saint-Jean-
de-Dieu near Lyon, indicate rather the merger of religious and medical
culture that was likely to result from this legal provision. "The *hospitaliers* of Saint-Jean-de-Dieu," wrote Dr. Carrier, "exercise day and night
an unceasing surveillance over their patients; the divisional chiefs, ordinarily chosen from among the most experienced, carefully direct the
moral and physical treatment prescribed by the physician and bring to
these functions that zeal and devotion that only an ardent charity can
inspire." Dr. Carrier regretted that his respect for "the modesty of
these pious *hospitaliers*" prevented him from lavishing even more
praise upon them; but he had no qualms about flatly asserting the
superiority in an asylum setting of religious personnel, of "persons
whose devotion derives from a principle more elevated than all human
calculations!" And he went on to describe a type of moral treatment in
which religion played a salient role.[129] As these remarks inadvertently
but eloquently attest, the parliamentary debates over the Law of 1838
may have articulated the border dispute between medical psychiatry
and clerical healing of souls with unprecedented clarity; but in the
aftermath of the Law, the outcome of that dispute was still fundamentally undecided.

On this point, the psychiatrists entertained no illusions. An 1844
article in the *Annales médico-psychologiques* by the Esquirol circle member
Bouchet typified their concern for the future. Cast innocuously enough
as a gloss on the royal ordinance implementing the 1838 Law, it concluded with a long tirade against the ill-founded pretensions of clerics
who directed lunatic asylums, with special attention to the outrages
perpetrated by Frère Hilarion.[130] How the psychiatrists eventually tri-

---

[128] On this enforced medicalization, see, e.g., AN: F^{15} 3907, letter of Père Magallon,
dated March 30, 1841. Complaining that the Charitains' *maisons* at Lyon, Lille, and
Dinan have still not received formal ministerial authorization, he notes their dutiful
compliance to the 1838 Law, including building special residential quarters for the
physicians ("who have their families with them") and "negotiating detailed and
costly contracts with these gentlemen."

[129] See J.-B. Carrier, *Etudes sur les aliénés traités dans l'asile de St-Jean-de-Dieu près Lyon
pendant les années 1838, 1839, and 1840* (Lyon: Savy; Paris: J.-B. Baillière, 1841), pp. 9–
10, 12; the statistical project addressed in this text shows that Carrier has also been
influenced by Parisian scientific psychiatry. Another area of incomplete medicalization of the clerical asylums is indicated in the fact that the Sisters of the Bon-Sauveur
of Caen, defying the 1838 Law, refused to include an intern on their staff until
midcentury; see Claude Quétel, "Garder les fous dans un asile de province au XIXe
siècle: Le Bon-Sauveur de Caen," *Annales de Normandie* (1979): 101.

[130] Bouchet, "Surveillant, infirmier et gardien," *Ann. m.-p.*, 1st ser., 3 (1844): esp. 56–61.

umphed – or, more accurately, nearly triumphed – over their religious rivals, and how they otherwise widened their professional field before 1900, is the subject of the next chapter. That chapter also provides a second installment in the story of classification, the act of scientific naming, as a technique for the enhancement of professional power. For just as the monomania diagnosis formed the core of a psychiatric pro-fessionalizing effort in the period before the passage of the 1838 Law, so the hysteria diagnosis played an analogous role afterward, in the last three decades of the nineteenth century.

9

Hysteria, anticlerical politics, and the view beyond the asylum

WHEN monomania, the regnant madness of the July Monarchy, was on the wane, another mental malady was waxing – as statistics culled from the admissions registers of the Salpêtrière and Bicêtre show clearly. During the two-year period 1841–42, the names of 648 women were entered as "official placements" into these leather-bound folio ledgers; and of this number, only seven, or about one percent, were diagnosed by the attending physicians as hysterical or as manifesting some hysterical symptoms. Some forty years later the picture had changed dramatically. Of the 500 women admitted during the two-year period 1882–83, eighty-nine, or 17.8 percent, were diagnosed as hysterical or as manifesting some hysterical symptoms; and if these admissions figures are corrected to exclude the senile, idiots, and imbeciles (who also typically found their way to this house of refuge), leaving only the bona fide mentally ill population, the proportion of hysterics rises to an even more imposing 20.5 percent. Among the men admitted to Bicêtre during 1841–42, there were none at all who displayed hysterical symptoms; but there were two in the year 1883.[1]

These statistics corroborate some impressionistic generalizations frequently made by historians of medicine and cultural historians alike. First, the fin de siècle was the "golden age" of hysteria, not only in France (where the disease seems to have proliferated so suddenly and conspicuously that, looking back in 1928, the Surrealists could designate 1878 as the official "birthdate" of hysteria and call for a semicentennial celebration!),[2] but throughout Europe and America as well. Perhaps most notable was its flourishing in the Hapsburg monarchy, where Viennese hysterics provided the material with which Sigmund Freud and Josef Breuer worked when they devised the rudiments of the psychoanalytic method. Second, while hysteria was above all a

---

[1]   AAP: Salpêtrière 6Q2-4, 6Q2-5, 6Q2-68, 6Q2-69; Bicêtre 6Q2-2, 6Q2-3, 6Q2-4, 6Q2-61, 6Q2-62.

[2]   Aragon and Breton, "Le cinquantenaire de l'hystérie (1878–1928)," *Révolution surréaliste* 4 (March 15, 1928): 20–22.

female affliction, by the later nineteenth century the existence of male hysteria was beginning to be recognized. But inherent in the statistics is also a puzzle. Why should the incidence of hysteria have attained so high a level in the 1880s when the disease was so uncommon among Parisian asylum inmates earlier in the century?[3]

This chapter will take the epidemiological problem posed by hysteria as its starting point and its continuing *point de repère*. It will be concerned only with the French case; but given French psychiatric prominence during this period, the importance of the category hysteria in other national medical communities very likely owed something to French influence. The scientific pilgrimages of the young, pre-psychoanalytic Sigmund Freud to medical centers in Paris (1885–86) and Nancy (1889), where hysteria was being intensively studied, are only the most famous and consequential instances of a typical "turning to France" on the part of late nineteenth-century physicians interested in mental aberration. Within the French context, the phenomenon of hysteria was in fundamental ways parallel to the earlier phenomenon of monomania. Just as monomania was intimately bound up with and hence almost the summation of a particular stage in the development of psychiatry, so too hysteria was the point of convergence for a similar multitude of strands: the internal development of psychiatry as a science; its professional trajectory; and its involvement with the politics of the French state.

The hysteria diagnosis and the epidemiology of hysteria

Unlike monomania in the 1820s, hysteria in the 1880s was hardly a novelty. Rather it was one of the oldest disease entities in the canon of Western medicine. The Hippocratic school had identified it in the fifth century B.C. and had given it its graphic name, derived from the Greek for "uterus" and denoting the belief that the condition was a pathological wandering of a restless womb from its normal position in the body; hence the longstanding axiom that hysteria was an exclusively female malady.[4] Its chief symptoms, from classical antiquity on, were convulsions, spasmodic seizures, and feelings of strangulation (a "hysterical ball," presumably the unmoored womb, was said to rise ominously in the throat). To these symptoms were added by the eighteenth and nineteenth centuries a plethora of others, including faintings and swoonings (the so-called vapors), paralyses of the limbs, anesthesias

---

[3] A sampling of the Salpêtrière registers at five-year intervals between 1841–42 and 1882–83 indicates that the sharp rise in hysteria diagnoses occurred in the mid-1870s. See AAP: Salpêtrière 6Q2-15, 6Q2-22, 6Q2-34, 6Q2-46, 6Q2-55, 6Q2-59.

[4] See, e.g., Ilza Veith, *Hysteria: The History of a Disease* (Chicago: University of Chicago Press, 1965), pp. 9–13.

(that is, losses of sensation in the skin), coughing, trancelike states – in short, a hodgepodge of disparate and usually temporary symptoms that sometimes even refused to stay put and migrated from one part of the body to another.

Thus the disease, unlike monomania, defied neat classification in an era when classification – the construction of universal taxonomies of disease based upon the presumption that each disease had fixed defining marks – was one of the overriding theoretical preoccupations of physicians; and it prompted many of them to express bewilderment and frustration. Some admitted to uncertainty about the fundamental nosological status of hysteria: Was it a "distinct" and "sui generis" entity, or was it the name traditionally and erroneously given to hypochondria in women?[5] All complained about the chaotic clinical picture hysteria presented. To say, observed Dr. Pomme in the mid-eighteenth century, that hysteria was "the Proteus in its metamorphoses and the chameleon in its change of colors is to express but weakly the variety and bizarreness of the symptoms."[6] In the mid-nineteenth century, Dr. Briquet announced his intellectual "repugnance" for hysteria, an ailment which "all authors agree in regarding as the very epitome of instability"; he had stoically undertaken the study of it only "as a matter of duty" (*pour l'acquit de ma conscience*).[7] The general mid-nineteenth century attitude was summed up pithily and with wry humor by Briquet's contemporary, the psychiatrist Charles Lasègue, who pronounced hysteria "the wastepaper basket of medicine where one throws otherwise unemployed symptoms."[8] Thus, while hysteria was among the most traditional and entrenched of disease entities, it was not for that reason a closed book. Instead, changes in medical assumptions and standards of rigor had rendered it increasingly problematic.

Why, then, should the incidence of hysteria have risen so markedly? In considering this question, it is useful to make explicit a principle that remained implicit in our discussion of monomania. It takes two to make a diagnosis – a patient with a set of symptoms, and a physician who gives them the label he deems appropriate – and hence it takes a multiplication of *both* parties to make an epidemiological trend. Insofar as explanations have been offered for the upsurge of hysteria at the fin de siècle (and that phenomenon has received far more attention than the comparable upsurge of monomania earlier in the century), they

[5] Louyer-Villermé, "Hystérie" (1818), *Dict. des sci. med.*, Vol. 23, p. 227.

[6] Pomme, *Traité des affections vaporeuses des deux sexes* (Paris: Impr. royale, 1782), pp. 1–2. The first edition appeared in Lyon in 1760.

[7] P. Briquet, *Traité clinique et thérapeutique de l'hystérie* (Paris: Baillière, 1859), p. v.

[8] Cited in Henri Cesbron, *Histoire critique de l'hystérie* (Paris: Thèse de médecine, 1909), p. 198. Cesbron was Lasègue's grandson (as the dedicatory page of the thesis indicates) and may have heard his grandfather make this remark; he gives no printed source for it.

have focused on the first of these two parties, the patient. The late nineteenth-century social and cultural milieu has been scanned for those characteristic attitudes and tensions which, impinging on the private lives of many individual women, seem capable of having provoked hysterical responses on a wide scale. Sigmund Freud offered one such explanation in 1908 as a corollary of his own psychoanalytic redefinition of hysteria. If, as Freud argued, hysteria was the somatization of repressed sexual wishes and fantasies, then the social and cultural factors that enforced the relegation to unconsciousness of these highly charged mental contents also encouraged the spread of the disease. Freud lumped these factors together under the heading of " 'civilized' sexual morality." By this he meant the ethic which placed work and "getting ahead in life" before pleasure, which prescribed sexual abstinence before marriage and countenanced only male deviation from this norm, and which held that a "proper" woman was effortlessly chaste, lacking in curiosity about sexual matters, and utterly unconcerned with her own sexual satisfaction.[9]

More recently, a historian studying nineteenth-century American middle-class women has proposed that the contradiction between the relentless stress of their domestic life and the prevailing feminine ideal of frailty, docility, and subordination to men made the "flight into illness" through hysteria an appealing form of indirect dissent, a way of entering covertly into a power struggle with the male world. The symptoms of hysteria – really parodies of femininity – enabled women to take to their beds, thus defeating both their husbands, whose households they left untended, and their male physicians, whose remedies they showed to be inefficacious.[10] These two explanations complement one another and, taken together, suggest that the flowering of hysteria in the late nineteenth century was coincident with and a pathological by-product of the flowering of the bourgeois value system of patriarchal authority and sexual asceticism. Fin-de-siècle hysteria, it appears, was a protest made in the flamboyant yet encoded language of the body by women who had so thoroughly accepted that value system that they could neither admit their discontent to themselves nor avow it publicly in the more readily comprehensible language of words.

As persuasive as this hypothesis is, it cannot account for the statistics cited earlier. For the numerous hysterics admitted to the Salpêtrière were virtually all working-class women – seamstresses, laundresses, flower-sellers[11] – who lived outside the framework of a

9 " 'Civilized' Sexual Morality and Modern Nervous Illness," in *Standard Edition of the Complete Psychological Works of Sigmund Freud,* Vol. 9, esp. pp. 182, 193–95, 197–99.
10 See Carroll Smith-Rosenberg, "The Hysterical Woman: Sex Roles and Role Conflict in 19th-Century America," *Social Research* 39 (Winter 1972): 652–78.
11 The registers record the occupation of each patient below her name. Very occasionally a petit bourgeois occupation, such as *institutrice* or *employée de commerce,* appears in

bourgeois value system. In seeking an explanation for the upsurge of hysteria among this group, as well as a fuller understanding of middle-class hysteria, one obvious strategy – which has already proved valuable with respect to monomania – is to consider the second and thus far ignored half of the epidemiological equation, the physician. He presented himself more readily as a candidate for scrutiny in the case of monomania, because we found him, as it were, caught in the act of inventing and elaborating the disease category at the same time that monomaniacs were becoming one of the largest components of his patient populations. By contrast, the long continuous history of something called hysteria has made that disease category appear a changeless, natural given – a "prediscursive referent" instead of a "discursive object," in Foucault's terms – and has thus deflected attention from the diagnosing physician as a factor in its epidemiology.[12] But might physicians have contributed to the trend documented here? Could they have concentrated more heavily on the disease of hysteria and made hysteria diagnoses with greater frequency and alacrity than before?

The evidence points unmistakably in that direction. Beginning in the 1870s, the work of Jean-Martin Charcot, chief physician at the Salpêtrière, revolutionized hysteria as a nosological category. Charcot took the old, amorphous "wastepaper basket" of symptoms and replaced it with a coherent and conceptually elegant array. In an era of self-conscious positivism in the natural sciences (as well as in sociology, history, and even literary criticism), Charcot's goal was to subsume the seemingly random symptoms under positive laws; and he succeeded, asserting on the grounds of "attentive and sufficiently repeated observations" that the symptoms unfolded with complete predictability. In the hysterical attack, he taught, "four periods follow one another with the regularity of a mechanism." These were: (1) tonic rigidity; (2) clonic spasms or *grands mouvements*, also called, with a whimsical pun, *clownisme* because of the circus-like acrobatics produced; (3) *attitudes passionnelles*, or vivid physical representations of one or more emotional states, such as terror, hatred, love; the patient, endowed with an acrobat's agility in the second period, was now said

the latter nineteenth-century registers, but for the most part the class composition of the Salpêtrière inmates emerges as remarkably homogeneous. For the period 1882–83 all of the hysterics for whom specific information was supplied were engaged in working-class occupations.

12 Michel Foucault, *The Archaeology of Knowledge*, trans. A. M. Sheridan Smith (New York: Pantheon, 1972), pp. 31–33, 47 and 47 n1. Foucault argues that when "statements different in form and dispersed in time" all seem to refer to a "single object, formed once and for all," we should not be misled into treating them as if they really do refer to the same "thing." The madman (or hysteric) of the seventeenth century is a different constructed category than the madman (or hysteric) of the nineteenth century.

to display the talents of a mime or dramatic actress; (4) a final delirium marked by sobs, tears, and laughter and heralding a return to the real world.[13] This full panoply, Charcot hastened to add, need not be present in every hysterical attack; rather the "grand" four-part attack was the "fundamental type" against which abbreviated or truncated attacks could be measured to determine whether they were truly hysterical. Definitive diagnosis would now be "easy for those who possess the formula"; the clinician could "learn to orient himself" in what hitherto had been an "inextricable maze."[14]

As these evocations of the circus and theater suggest, Charcot's approach emphasized the external and visual rather than the unseen and purely psychological. Thus, in order to prove the invariability of the hysterical sequence and to develop a full catalog of its component postures and gestures, he set one of his interns to work in the 1870s covering page after page with quick sketches of the hysterical patients at the Salpêtrière.[15] As the technology of the camera advanced, ink drawing was replaced by photographic records of the so-called iconography of hysteria; an annual publication entitled *Iconographie photographique de la Salpêtrière* was founded in 1876, a year after a photographic atelier had been installed at the asylum. The camera, an admirer of Charcot aptly remarked, was as crucial to the study of hysteria as the microscope was to histology.[16] Having gathered his iconographical evidence, Charcot concluded this phase of his research with the supremely confident claim of the positivist: The laws which he had discovered and which governed hysteria, he said, were "valid for all countries, all times, all races," and "consequently universal."[17]

The refurbished hysteria diagnosis, the placing of hysteria on a firm positivistic footing, was only the first phase of Charcot's work on that disease. By the end of the 1870s he had begun to investigate the applications of hypnotism to his hysterical patients, and this later work, which gradually opened the way to conceptions of the "splitting of the personality" and of the role of the unconscious in mental pathology, provides a fascinating and typically fin-de-siècle case study of a dialectical process by which the most committed and hardheaded positivism eventually led to a legitimation of the realm of unreason. This later work, however, is only tangentially relevant here. It is Charcot's initial

---

[13] Descriptions of the four periods can be found in many places in Charcot's writings; the account given here is a composite of J.-M. Charcot, "Leçon d'ouverture," *Progrès médical* 10 (1882): 336; and J.-M. Charcot and Paul Richer, *Les démoniaques dans l'art* (Paris: Delahaye & Lecrosnier, 1887), pp. 91–106.

[14] Charcot, "Leçon d'ouverture," p. 336.

[15] "Richer (Paul-Marie-Louis-Pierre)" in Maurice Genty, ed., *Biographies médicales* (Paris: Baillière, 1930–36), p. 68.

[16] See the review of Vol. 1 of the *Iconographie photographique de la Salpêtrière* in *Progrès médical* 7 (1879): 331.

[17] Charcot, "Leçon d'ouverture," p. 336.

"breakthrough" in hysteria studies – the positivistic foundation which he laid down and never called into question – that will remain our focus.

Charcot was not the only *aliéniste* of his generation to attempt to make sense of hysteria. In the 1860s the Esquirol circle member Moreau de Tours, also employed at the Salpêtrière, tackled the problem in a long series of journal articles. He suggested that the hereditary nature of the nervous diseases (of which hysteria was one) helped to explain their baffling "protean" quality. Since the nervous propensity "belongs . . . to the entire genealogical tree," the individual family member possessed the biological potential for a broad array of different symptomatic expressions of that propensity and could pass swiftly and easily from one to another. This ingenious hereditarian postulate, however, failed to aid Moreau when he turned to the familiar problem of defining the hysterical syndrome through clinical observation. In the end, he compiled a list of symptoms so long and rambling as to cast doubt on whether he had succeeded at all in removing the disease from the "wastepaper basket" of Lasègue's sardonic depiction.[18]

For his own part, Lasègue worked intermittently from the 1850s into the 1870s on a clinical study of hysteria. More methodical in his approach than Moreau de Tours, he confined himself to painstaking examination of single symptoms – the cough, the anesthesias, the loss of appetite – attempting to specify how the hysterical form of each differed from the form assumed in other pathological syndromes, and planning only "after this prior work of analysis, to gather up the fragments and recompose the whole malady."[19] But his project proceeded slowly and inconclusively. Charcot had, in effect, posed the problem differently. Focusing on the temporal development of the symptoms in the individual case – a dimension overlooked by both of his colleagues[20] – he had arrived at an utterly simple and compelling result. If these three doctors can be regarded as having offered competing scientific conceptions of hysteria, it is clear why Charcot won the competition handily.

The new hysteria concept made an already respected Charcot famous. The concept may have been strong on description and weak on

18 "De la folie hystérique et de quelques phénomènes nerveux propres à l'hystérie (convulsive), à l'hystéro-épilepsie et à l'épilepsie," *Union médicale*, June 10, 1865, pp. 499–500, 502–4. This is the first of ten articles.

19 For Lasègue's work in this vein, see "De la toux hystérique," *Arch. gen. de med.*, 5th ser., 3 (May 1854): 513–31; "De l'anathésie et de l'ataxie hystériques," ibid., 6th ser., 3 (April 1864): 385–402; and "De l'anorexie hystérique," ibid., 6th ser., 21 (April 1873): 385–403. The quotation comes from the last-named article, p. 385.

20 Gladys Swain points out that Charcot's four-period succession, though hailed at the time as a novelty, was really the application to hysteria of the "canonical form of the course of madness," as established in Bayle's 1822 thesis on general paralysis. *Le sujet de la folie: Naissance de la psychiatrie* (Toulouse: Privat, 1977), p. 91n.

etiology, as Sigmund Freud could not help but politely observe when he embarked upon his own researches into the subject.[21] But initially, at least, this mattered little. Hysteria was the major source of the national and international renown that Charcot and the close-knit group of some fifteen or twenty of his students who formed the "Salpêtrière school"[22] had acquired by 1880. At a banquet given for Charcot at the time of his election to the Institut de France, the first speaker made this point quite clearly: "And finally hysteria. That was the ticklish business. That study of hysteria could have brought you triumphant to Rome or dragged you into the mud. You were courageous, and Fortune has rewarded your audacity."[23] The fame of Charcot and his rendition of the hysteria diagnosis spread beyond scientific circles into the realm of the average literate layman. "To mention the name of Charcot," wrote a contemporary commentator, "is to conjure up in the same breath the image of hysteria . . . a subject discussed over and over, almost milked dry (*rebattue à satiété*) by all the organs of the press."[24] Charcot became something of a phenomenon, a mad-doctor lionized by the public at large and not merely by his medical colleagues. His death in 1893 made newspaper headlines, and in the following year a Paris street was named for him – a posthumous honor which had required a quarter-century in the case of Pinel, and one year short of that in the case of Esquirol.[25]

Certainly it is reasonable to suppose that in such a climate, given all the éclat surrounding Charcot's accomplishment, physicians would make more hysteria diagnoses and thus "create" instances of the disease by labeling them. Charcot purported to have supplied a rigorous set of diagnostic indicators – a "formula," he called it – but since the four-period "grand" attack was not required for a hysteria diagnosis, the new "formula" was in fact quite flexible. Many ambiguous convulsive conditions that in previous decades might have received other labels could now easily be seen as imperfect, truncated versions of Charcot's *grande hystérie* – and were likely to be seen in this way by physicians who had been impressed by Charcot, who were eager to

---

[21] "Charcot" (1893) in *Standard Edition*, Vol. 3, p. 21.

[22] For one version of the membership of the Salpêtrière school, see Levillain, "Charcot et l'école de la Salpêtrière," *Revue encyclopédique* 4 (1894): 113 (picture caption).

[23] Speech of Prof. Bouchard, "Banquet offert à M. le professeur Charcot," *Progrès médical* 11 (1883): 999.

[24] G. Hahn, "Charcot et son influence sur l'opinion publique," *Revue des questions scientifiques*, 2d ser., 6 (1894): 367. Charles Féré, "J.-M. Charcot et son oeuvre," *Revue des deux mondes* 122 (1894): 416, 418, names the research on hysteria as one of the main sources of Charcot's fame among "the public" as opposed to his "reputation in the medical world."

[25] Jacques Hillairet, *Dictionnaire historique des rues de Paris*, 7th ed. (Paris: Minuit, 1963). The rue Charcot was named in 1894, the rue Pinel in 1851, and the rue Esquirol in 1864.

keep abreast of the latest advances in medical knowledge, and whose clinical perceptions were, quite without guile, shaped accordingly. Indeed there is evidence that in the early 1880s Salpêtrière psychiatrists approached patients with the expectation of finding hysteria. Interviewing a 23-year-old cook from the Auvergne whose marriage plans had fallen through, who had fled from the house of an uncle whom she accused of mistreating her, and who displayed both "maniacal excitation" and "melancholy," Dr. Charpentier began his diagnostic comments: "Negative information furnished by the patient from the point of view of hysteria . . ."[26] This is, to be sure, not a hysteria diagnosis; but it is a tacit admission that hysteria was very much on the doctor's mind. And not surprisingly, Salpêtrière psychiatrists, who came under Charcot's influence most directly, did manage to "find" more hysterics than did their counterparts at other institutions. At Charenton, for example, hysterics accounted for only 7.7 percent of the women admitted during the period 1879–88.[27]

A diagnostic preference or preoccupation, if shared by a sufficiently large number of doctors, can thus contribute powerfully to an epidemiological trend because certain equivocal pathological phenomena come to be labeled in a uniform manner. In this regard, the epidemiology of hysteria was fundamentally analogous to, though in sheer numbers even more striking than, the epidemiology of monomania earlier in the century. Such diagnostic preferences and preoccupations among doctors may also elicit the "correct" symptomatology from patients. As the ethnopsychiatrist George Devereux has remarked, "cultural preconceptions of 'how to act when insane' " are one very important determinant of the prevalent psychopathologies in a given society.[28] The "iconography" of hysteria as defined by Charcot – with all its vividly theatrical contortions and grimaces – seems to have been so widely publicized at the fin de siècle, in both pictorial and verbal form, as to constitute for that historical moment a reigning "cultural preconception of 'how to act when insane.' " In fact, a very similar if more limited assertion was made by certain contemporaries in the form of a harsh criticism of Charcot's work. These skeptics contended that patients learned the four-part *grande attaque* within the confines of the Salpêtrière itself, by observing other patients and imitating them. They charged that Charcot's hysteria, far from existing spontaneously in

---

[26] AAP: Salpêtrière 6Q2-68, entry 38120.

[27] See Dr. Antoine Ritti, *Maison nationale de Charenton: Rapport sur le service médical de la division des dames pendant la période décennale 1879–88* (Paris: Typographie Gaston Née, 1889); Table 7, p. 14, gives the breakdown of admissions by diagnostic category. If idiots, imbeciles, and the demented are excluded from the female population, the proportion of hysterics rises to 9.1 percent.

[28] See *Basic Problems in Ethnopsychiatry*, trans. M. B. Gulati and G. Devereux (Chicago: University of Chicago Press, 1980), p. 37.

nature, was a "cultural hysteria" (*hystérie de culture*) – a phrase which Charcot snidely called "very picturesque," and a concept which was of course anathema to him as a positivist and which he did his best to counter at every opportunity.[29]

The appropriation of the demi-fou

Why should Charcot and other leading French psychiatrists of the latter nineteenth century have tackled the problem of hysteria almost simultaneously and with such earnest intensity? In the context of the earlier tradition of *médecine mentale*, their expenditure of so much effort on this particular problem seems quite anomalous. The pioneering psychiatric *maître* Esquirol, a good case in point, had evinced almost no sustained interest in hysteria during his long career. From the handful of remarks on the subject in his printed writings, it is clear that hysteria was a marginal phenomenon for him because it was not a full-fledged insanity (*folie* or *aliénation mentale*) but a generically related lesser ailment that might accompany insanity as a "complication" or eventually "degenerate into insanity." Less dangerous to the well-being of the individual and to the safety of society, it presumably could not in its own right command his attention or stimulate his scientific curiosity as insanity did.[30] The measure of Esquirol's relative indifference to hysteria can be found in the statistical reports on which he so much prided himself. As director of Charenton from 1825 to 1840, Esquirol did not even bother to tabulate and count his hysterical patients. Instead, for statistical purposes, he mixed them heedlessly with maniacs on the basis of certain common characteristics such as "persistent agitation, inexhaustible loquacity, incessant mobility."[31]

Charcot shared the view that hysteria was not a variety of full-fledged insanity[32] – indeed this was the generally accepted view among the psychiatrists of his day[33] – but for him its lesser severity did not

---

[29] Charcot, *Leçons du mardi à la Salpêtrière, Policlinique, 1887–88*, 2d ed., Vol. 1 (Paris: Bureaux du Progrès Médical/Babé, 1892), p. 105.

[30] Esquirol, *Des maladies mentales considérées sous les rapports médical, hygiénique et médico-légal* (Paris: Baillière, 1838), Vol. 1, pp. 38, 75, 81, 289–91; according to the "Table analytique," these are the only references to hysteria in this two-volume work, which contains virtually all of Esquirol's printed writings.

[31] See Ritti, *Charenton Report*, p. 15. Esquirol's statistical articles show that he tabulated only four types of insanity – monomania, mania, dementia, and idiocy; see "Rapport statistique sur la maison royale de Charenton pendant les années 1826, 1827 et 1828," *Ann. d'hyg. pub.* 1 (1829): 124; and "Mémoire historique et statistique sur la maison royale de Charenton," ibid. 13 (1835): 147.

[32] See, e.g., J.-M. Charcot, *Leçons sur les maladies du système nerveux faites à la Salpêtrière*, 3d ed., Vol. 1 (Paris: A. Delahaye, 1877), p. 321.

[33] Their terminology, because nonstandardized, is confusing in this regard, but the general trend of thought can be discerned. Moreau de Tours spoke of a *folie* (or *délire*)

constitute a detraction. By the later nineteenth century the specialty of psychiatry, more securely established than in the time of Esquirol, had begun to expand its medical domain, adding to the pathological phenomena over which it exercised jurisdiction. "One is either insane or one is not," Minister of the Interior Montalivet had declared during the parliamentary debate over the 1838 Law, responding to the criticism that the word *aliéné* was "too vague and uncertain" to be made the basis of a binding legal decision about the fate of an individual.[34] Certainly the absolute black-and-white clarity of the distinction between madness and sanity (at least to the discerning eye of the psychiatric specialist) had been a crucial element in the argument for the proposed law. But for the new professional situation facing *médecine mentale* after the victory of 1838, a correspondingly new position on the distinction between madness and sanity gradually came to seem both scientifically and professionally preferable.

At midcentury, hysteria and a bevy of other newly and loosely defined nervous conditions – *surexcitation nerveuse, nervosisme, névropathie* – which typically included some hysterical symptoms and which, like hysteria, "fell short" of insanity, had come to the fore in the medical community. Initially, they were the common property of all physicians, discussed as avidly by the general practitioner as by the psychiatric specialist.[35] But intraprofessional rivalries soon began to mar this state of scientific communism: As early as the 1860s, a psychiatrist addressing the Société médico-psychologique could speak invidiously of the errors in diagnosing hysteria frequently made by *médecins non aliénistes*.[36] By the 1880s, such observations had become the basis for programmatic statements. Psychiatrists now elaborated an argument in support of their contention that these various nervous conditions, although not tantamount to *aliénation*, should be removed from the purview of the generalist and fully integrated into their own, specialist domain. After all, the physiologist Claude Bernard, the hero of the late nineteenth-century positivists, had pointed out that there was a gradated continuum between bodily health and bodily illness.

hystérique which he regarded as fundamentally different from "ordinary madness" (*folie*); "De la folie hystérique," p. 500. By contrast, Jules Falret spoke of *hystérie* as synonymous with the *névrose hystérique*, which could not be "considered as constituting a true madness" (*folie*); but he also postulated, as a separate syndrome, a *folie hystérique proprement dite* and an equivalent *manie hystérique*, a composite of two disease entities in which the symptoms of hysteria and those of bona fide insanity were combined. See his remarks at the Société médico-psychologique, *Ann. m.-p.*, 4th ser., 7 (1866): 404, 407–8; and ibid., 9 (1867): 83.

[34] *Arch. parl.*, 2d ser., Vol. 115, pp. 325–26.

[35] See, e.g., the discussion of Bouchut's paper on *nervosisme* at the Academy of Medicine, *Bulletin de l'Académie impériale de médecine* 23 (1857–58): 980–83; and 24 (1858–59): 467–72, 501–39.

[36] Falret, "Discussion sur la folie raisonnante," p. 404.

The asylum-doctor Alexandre Cullerre now cited him, reasoning by analogy that there was no "definitive barrier between reason and madness" but rather a large gray area, an "intermediary zone" of *demi-fous,* and that these less grave manifestations of mental pathology were proper and necessary objects of psychiatric investigation.[37]

With an irony that was no doubt inadvertent, the psychiatrist Benjamin Ball made the same point by summoning up an episode from French colonial history to justify the professional imperialism of the psychiatrists. During the July Monarchy, he told his students, an official of Louis-Philippe had been charged to negotiate a treaty with Morocco delimiting the boundary between that nation and Algeria. The line of demarcation was made precise from the Mediterranean only as far as the interior; the French official accepted the word of the Moroccans that the boundary might just as well be left vague from that point onward because the territory in question was virtually uninhabited. Alas, the French had allowed themselves to be duped by the clever and wily natives, and they thus provided a useful lesson to psychiatrists. For, Ball stressed, just as "we know today that on that allegedly uninhabited [North African] territory there exists a population of some 600,000," so too "in that region also believed deserted and situated on the frontier between reason and madness . . . are housed (*renfermé*) not 600,000 but several million inhabitants."[38] The psychiatrists, Ball implied, must not through a similar lack of vigilance let this rich territory slip from their hands.

Adopting, then, the language of the psychiatrists themselves, Charcot's interest in hysteria can be seen as part of – and one of the most stunningly successful sallies in – an expansionist movement in French psychiatry to capture this "intermediary zone." Capture here entailed the assertion that insanity and the "intermediary" nervous pathologies shared an essential nature, making it only logical that the latter be entrusted to the already proven experts on insanity – hence the importance of the new label *demi-folie.* It also entailed the demonstration of cognitive mastery of the symptom patterns presented by these nervous conditions: Hysteria, as Charcot commented after delineating his four-period schema, had *earlier* "offered itself to us as a kind of sphinx."[39]

The effects of the capture proved lasting. The new pair, *demi-fou* and

[37] A. Cullerre, *Les frontières de la folie* (Paris: Baillière, 1888), pp. 5–8, 23–24. On Cullerre's career, see *Ann. m.-p.*, 5th ser., 20 (1878): 313; and 6th ser., 4 (1880): 329–30. The concept of a gradated continuum between health and illness was propounded earlier by the father of positivism; see "Cours de philosophie positive" (1832–40) in Gertrud Lenzer, ed., *Auguste Comte and Positivism: The Essential Writings* (New York: Harper & Row, 1975), p. 191.

[38] "Cours de M. Ball. Les frontières de la folie," *Revue scientifique de la France et de l'étranger*, January 6, 1883, p. 1.

[39] Charcot, "Leçon d'ouverture," p. 336.

aliéné, both now claimed as the legitimate objects of psychiatric knowledge and solicitude, foreshadowed an analogous pair that would become fundamental to the enterprise of twentieth-century psychiatry: the "neurotic," whose minimal maladaptations do not preclude getting on in ordinary society, and the "psychotic," whose contact with reality is severely ruptured. Indeed the "neurotic" would not only assume the classificatory space once occupied by the *demi-fou* but would also be descended from the latter linguistically. By the second half of the nineteenth century, hysteria and other forms of *demi-folie* were routinely called *névroses*, or nervous diseases – the French translation of the Latin and English "neurosis." The meaning of the term *névrose* had undergone many changes since its introduction into the French medical vocabulary by Pinel.[40] But by the time of Charcot the term, which once had a very broad range of referents, was approaching its narrower modern meaning. It had come to denote a physiological, or functional, abnormality of the nervous system not attended by any discernible anatomical lesion.[41] And most important for our purposes, it had also come to be reserved for the "intermediary" forms of mental aberration, as distinguished from the full-fledged insanities or *maladies mentales*.[42] With a certain amount of prescience, Charcot had had his eye on these *névroses* as early as 1858, when he wrote to the Ministry of Public Instruction expressing his particular interest in studying them.[43]

With hindsight, it appears that the way for the psychiatric capture of hysteria (the so-called *grande névrose*) had been paved some decades earlier by the revision of the accepted wisdom about the social-class basis of that disease. Throughout the eighteenth and early nineteenth centuries, hysteria was associated with delicacy of constitution and refinement of manners and was regarded as primarily an affliction of the leisured classes. "A too sedentary life . . ., a too succulent and varied diet" (spices, truffles, shrimp) "favors the invasion of this vesania."[44] Only in 1859 did Briquet's study of a large sample of hyster-

---

[40] Part of this complicated story, which begins with William Cullen's coinage of "neurosis" in 1769, has been told in José M. López Piñero, *Historical Origins of the Concept of Neurosis*, trans. D. Berrios (Cambridge University Press, 1983), esp. Ch. 3.

[41] Ibid., pp. 49–54. This was the contribution to the *névrose* concept made by the Esquirol circle member Foville in 1834.

[42] One benchmark in this development was the 1863 publication of A.-P. Requin's multiauthored *Elémens de pathologie médicale* (Paris: Germer Baillière, 1863), with separate sections on the *névroses* (by Alexandre Axenfeld) and the *maladies mentales* (by Brierre de Boismont). By the end of the century, the *névroses* so construed came to be called *psycho-névroses;* see the early usage of this term by Féré, "Charcot et son oeuvre," p. 122.

[43] See AN: F[17] 6672, Dossier: Charcot (1860). The letter, not dated by Charcot, is stamped as received on June 12, 1858.

[44] Louyer-Villermé, "Hystérie," p. 232.

ics (430 cases) dispel this belief that "women of the people" were insufficiently "impressionable" and of too coarse a sensibility to succumb to hysteria, that the muscular exertion of manual labor dulled their nerves and hence protected them against the disease. The figures adduced by Briquet showed, in fact, that the popular classes were somewhat more susceptible to hysteria than their betters.[45] Since the bulk of psychiatric practice in France at this date took place in public asylums (rather than in private *maisons de santé*),[46] a clientele of lower-class hysterics was necessary to place hysteria securely within the purview of the specialty.

The sort of expansionist maneuver represented by the hysteria diagnosis was soon reenacted by Charcot and his school with respect to an even milder nervous aberration called neurasthenia. A disease entity identified in 1869 by the New York physician George M. Beard, this *nouvelle névrose* (in certain respects similar to hysteria) received so much attention from Charcot that one of his disciples quipped, "If Beard was the father of neurasthenia, M. Charcot has almost been its French godfather."[47] Charcot regarded neurasthenia as having been "disentangled from the chaos of the old *nervosisme*" and, as a diagnostic category which truly "correspond[ed] to the reality of things," having replaced its shaky and questionable predecessor. "Henceforth," he wrote, gravitating instinctively to the metaphor of political imperialism favored by his colleagues, "it will occupy a legitimately conquered place" in the neuropathological "domain."[48] Just as hysterics were only *demi-fous* – they were, Jules Falret had written in 1866, "in some manner normal"[49] – so too did neurasthenia leaven fundamental normality with only a touch of abnormality. And its epidemiological reach went even further: Neurasthenia and its related conditions constituted a "universal neurosis," because "everyone submits more or less to the influence of this morbid nervous hyperexcitability."[50] Clearly, a "universal neurosis" would provide psychiatrists with a vast new patient population. Following the pattern set by Briquet with respect to hysteria, Charcot argued for this

---

[45] Briquet, *Traité*, pp. 104–9. Charcot endorsed the work of Briquet as a stepping-stone to his own; see, e.g., "Leçon d'ouverture," p. 336.

[46] In January 1865, e.g., patients in *maisons de santé* accounted for only 3.6 percent of all interned mental patients in France; ten years later they accounted for 3 percent. See Constans, Lunier, and Dumesnil, *Rapport général à M. le Ministre de l'Intérieur sur le service des aliénés en 1874* (Paris: Impr. nationale, 1878), pp. 510–11 (table). These figures do not cover all the interned middle- and upper-class mental patients (since many public asylums had wings for paying patients), but they convey an accurate sense of the predominantly lower-class population on which nineteenth-century psychiatry drew.

[47] Fernand Levillain, *La neurasthénie, maladie de Beard* (Paris: A. Maloine, 1891), p. 13.

[48] Charcot, preface to Levillain, *Neurasthénie*, p. vii.

[49] "Discussion sur la folie raisonnante," p. 408.

[50] Such is the dictum of Charcot's student and disciple Fernand Levillain, *Hygiène des gens nerveux* (Paris: Alcan, 1891), pp. vii–viii.

universality by stipulating that neurasthenia afflicted every stratum of society. By his own account, he even crusaded heroically to have this truth acknowledged:

> The neurasthenic neurosis is far from belonging exclusively to the man of the privileged classes, softened by culture, exhausted by the abuse of pleasures, by preoccupation with business affairs and by excessive intellectual labors. That is a prejudice which I have many times striven to combat but against which it will doubtless be necessary to struggle still, and for a long time, for it appears to be hardly uprooted.

Neurasthenia was, Charcot continued, found "on a grand scale among urban proletarians and artisans,"[51] and at times he was unabashedly frank about the implications of this epidemiological fact for the size of his clientele. Interviewing a railway brakeman as part of his clinical instruction at the Salpêtrière, Charcot noted the pathogenic impact of the man's almost sedentary and often nocturnal labor, which entailed serious responsibility and required constant attention to avoid collisions. He then observed with a certain amount of good cheer, "Neurasthenics are not rare among railway employees. Our neighbor, the Orléans railway company [then located near the Salpêtrière] furnishes us with numerous clients."[52]

Charcot's emphasis on the existence of proletarian neurasthenia in no way foreclosed his appreciation of its bourgeois counterpart. Indeed he seems to have viewed neurasthenia as constituting a form of cultural criticism, a commentary on the effects, felt primarily by the middle classes, of republican meritocracy. Beard, he noted, had called neurasthenia the "American disease," believing that it originated in the single-minded and unrelieved approach to work peculiar to the parvenus of the New World. Charcot, on the other hand, denied that Americans "have the exclusive privilege of this malady"; similar work habits could be found among upwardly mobile social types familiar in France. For example, "the young men who graduate from the Ecole Polytechnique, who intend to become heads of factories and rack their brains over mathematical calculations, often become victims of these afflictions."[53]

While the working-class origins of significant numbers of *demi-fous* enabled these pathological specimens to swell the ranks of the public asylums (and while their middle- and upper-class counterparts might seek cure at private *maisons de santé*), psychiatric ministrations to the group of *demi-fous* opened yet another possibility for psychiatric expan-

---

[51] Charcot, preface to Levillain, *Neurasthénie*, p. viii.
[52] *Leçons du mardi, 1887–88*, pp. 62, 64. Charcot believed that the only members of the working class unlikely to contract neurasthenia were those with physically strenuous occupations; see ibid., p. 35, and preface to Levillain, *Neurasthénie*, p. viii.
[53] *Leçons du mardi, 1887–88*, p. 33.

sion – outpatient care. Charcot was quick to recognize and seize upon this new opportunity. In 1879 he announced that a "public consultation" would "soon be established at the entrance of this hospice [the Salpêtrière]," thus providing him and his colleagues with numerous examples of the new type of patient and hence "the occasion to improve in singular fashion our clinical observations."[54] Middle-class patients even came from neighboring provinces to receive the advice of the Salpêtrière doctors at the new facility. "Pardon me if I take the liberty to write you," a man in the Loiret, whose ten-year-old son was afflicted with epileptoid convulsions, began his letter to Charcot, "but the condition of my dear child worries me. Tuesday morning I brought him to see you at the Salpêtrière."[55] Two years later the "public consultation" had grown significantly. Since the number of "patients who frequent the hospice in the capacity of *externes*" was quite large, and not all could be handled satisfactorily in that fashion, Charcot had persuaded the director of the Assistance Publique of Paris to create a new service of sixty beds at the Salpêtrière for the "temporary admission of some of these patients who come to us from outside." Also inaugurated was an electrotherapy section "where numerous patients" – truly outpatients – "come three times a week to receive the treatment suitable to their condition."[56]

The success of these outpatient consultations also bore fruit in Charcot's pedagogical practice. His formal Friday lessons were set pieces, presentations of patients from the Salpêtrière wards whom he had "previously studied with the greatest care and whose cases he had long pondered." But the impromptu Tuesday lessons, which achieved almost immediate fame for the spontaneous and original aperçus with which the *maître* spiced them (Sigmund Freud, for one, hurried to attend them as soon as he arrived in Paris), dated only from the 1880s. They consisted of diagnostic and prognostic interviews with people – usually hysterics and neurasthenics – who came, as it were, off the streets to the Salpêtrière *consultation externe* and whom Charcot had never before encountered.[57] As Charcot said of these cooperative outpatients newly

---

[54] Charcot, untitled speech at the Salpêtrière, *Progrès médical* 7 (1879): 913. Interestingly enough, this arrangement had been suggested as part of the utopian model asylum project under the Restoration, but like the rest of that project, it came to naught at the time; see AN: F[15] 1892, *Programme d'un hôpital consacré au traitement de l'aliénation mentale . . .* (Paris: Impr. de Mme Huzard, 1821), p. 33.

[55] See AAP: Salpêtrière 6R-90, Registre de diagnostics. This informal ledger, bearing the date 1880, concerns male outpatients; notations are filed alphabetically by the name of the patient; the letter quoted above, from a G. de Bassonière, is under "P" for "Pierre," the name of the boy.

[56] Charcot, "Leçon d'ouverture," p. 316.

[57] For the description and comparison of the Friday and Tuesday lessons, see J. Babinski, preface to Charcot, *Leçons du mardi, 1887–88*, pp. i–ii. Levillain, *Neurasthénie*, p. 13, notes that neurasthenics constituted about "one-fourth of the patients who ap-

invited to the hospice: They "do not refuse to participate in clinical demonstrations. They understand that the more they are minutely and curiously observed, the greater their chances of cure or, at least, relief."[58]

The asylum remained, in the closing decades of the nineteenth century, the symbol of psychiatric practice and power; but the new mode of outpatient care, made possible by the appropriation of the *demi-fou*, was pregnant with implications for the future of the specialty. It led the way to the twentieth-century practice of psychiatry in the doctor's own office, using a technique called, since the 1890s, "psychotherapy."[59] In the idiosyncratically French model of a medical "profession" outlined in the first chapter, there were, it will be remembered, two poles – the state, and the individual doctor in the market economy. For the *médecin aliéniste* the statist pole perforce predominated, almost to the exclusion of the other pole, throughout the nineteenth century because of the massive scale of the facilities required, both by the state and by the scientific canon, for the incarceration and treatment of lunatics. When only the asylum model was available, doctors who wanted to enter the private practice of *médecine mentale* were forced to make the high capital investment, impossible or unpalatable to many of them, required to found a *maison de santé*.[60] By the opening years of the new century, however, the appropriation of the *demi-fou* – an individual who could pass for an ordinary citizen, who certainly did not disturb the public peace, and who could live at home while making periodic visits to the psychiatric doctor – placed the second pole, setting up in private office practice, within the reach of the average *aliéniste*. "You will be cured," says a doctor to his neurasthenic female client, "you will be cured as soon as you resolve to abdicate all personal control. . . . Do not get discouraged, put yourself in the hands of your doctor, obey him blindly." This bit of professional didacticism is found in a one-act play written by a French psychiatrist in 1905 and tellingly titled *Dans un cabinet de médecin*.[61]

pear" at the Salpêtrière public consultations. On Freud and the Tuesday lessons, see *Letters of Sigmund Freud*, ed. Ernst L. Freud, trans. T. and J. Stern (New York: McGraw-Hill, 1964), pp. 171, 175, 177.

58 Charcot, "Leçon d'ouverture," p. 316.

59 See, e.g., Hippolyte Bernheim, *Hypnotisme, suggestion, psychothérapie* (Paris: Doin, 1891); and for a precocious nonmedical use of the term, Maurice Barrès, *Trois stations de psychothérapie* (Paris: Perrin, 1891).

60 For testimony on this point, see e.g., the psychiatrist Michéa, "Lettre au citoyen Thierry," *Ann. m.-p.*, 1st ser., 11 (1848): 452.

61 Gasters, pseudonym for Joseph Grasset, *Dans un cabinet de médecin: Pièce en un acte* (Paris: Société française d'imprimerie et de librairie, 1905), pp. 3–4. Grasset was a major proponent of the *demi-fou* diagnosis in a forensic context; see Robert A. Nye, *Crime, Madness, and Politics in Modern France: The Medical Concept of National Decline* (Princeton, N.J.: Princeton University Press, 1984), pp. 259–60.

A profession's progress, 1838–1876

Having broached, through a discussion of the integration into psychiatric practice of the hysteric and related *demi-fous*, the issue of the specialty's growth after the Law of 1838, it remains to explore this issue more systematically and to detail the increasingly self-conscious "expansionist" agenda which the specialty set for itself. Such an exploration will pave the way for an understanding of the multifaceted professional apotheosis psychiatry achieved under the early Third Republic, with Charcot as its acknowledged *maître* and hysteria as its watchword. Two main indices, among the several conventionally enumerated by sociologists of the professions, are especially relevant to gauging psychiatric professional development in the decades following 1838: organization, both formal and informal; and the institutionalization of instruction in psychiatry.

The obvious benchmark in psychiatric organization was the founding of the Société médico-psychologique in 1852, an event that gave the *aliénistes* a certain claim to precocity, since despite the efforts of the organizers of the 1845 Medical Congress, the general body of French physicians did not succeed in forming an association on a national scale until 1858.[62] As the virulence of anticorporate sentiment in the Revolutionary era might suggest, the formation of professional associations in nineteenth-century France was hardly a simple, straightforward affair but rather a delicate operation fraught with tension and hedged round with legal restrictions. The perceived need to protect the state from the disruptive influence of so-called intermediary bodies and to protect the individual from the envious tyranny of organized groups kept the Le Chapelier Law of 1791 (directed primarily against working-class cooperation but technically banning any nominally professional association) in force until 1848. Similarly, strict government surveillance of all associations of more than twenty members was stipulated by the Napoleonic penal code and maintained throughout the July Monarchy.[63] Some contemporaries, of whom Tocqueville is the most famous, bemoaned the snuffing out of the spirit of voluntary association in post-Revolutionary France – an exaggerated depiction of the situation that recent historiography has attempted to revise.[64] But nu-

---

62 George Weisz, "The Politics of Medical Professionalization in France, 1845–48," *Journal of Social History* 12 (1978): esp. 8.

63 Paul Bastid, *Les institutions politiques de la monarchie parlementaire française, 1815–1848* (Paris: Sirey, 1954), pp. 385–86, 385 n2.

64 One contemporary who shared Tocqueville's view is the lawyer Ferdinand Béchard, *Essai sur la centralisation administrative*, 2 vols. (Marseille: Olive; Paris: Hivert, 1836–37). For an instance of the revisionist historiography, see Maurice Agulhon, *Le cercle dans la France bourgeoise, 1810–1848* (Paris: Armand Colin, 1977).

ances apart, the evidence from the first half of the nineteenth century bespeaks a strong ambivalence, even at times a taboo, surrounding the formation of a medical professional organization. A typical performance is a feuilleton of 1837 in the *Gazette médicale de Paris*, which began with a confident assertion of the importance of medical association (without it "the profession has not ceased to decline, as does everything without a base and a fulcrum") but then went on to contest and vitiate its own argument. With an immediacy reminiscent of Fourcroy, it rehearsed all the dangers to which the individual physician had been exposed by the corporations of the Old Regime and which could presumably be revived – "an exclusive, touchy and egotistical esprit de corps," an "expunging despotism," and sometimes an "esprit de corps pushed beyond measure, small-minded, rapacious and niggardly."[65]

The checkered early history of the Société médico-psychologique can be understood only against this background. The idea for an association of asylum-doctors was first expressed in 1843 by Jules Baillarger, who pointed to an already existing association of this kind in England and to the Law of 1838, which had created numerous potential members for a French equivalent. Baillarger envisioned annual meetings of the association in Paris at which questions of asylum architecture, organization, and management, and most important questions of therapeutic technique would be discussed.[66] A few years later, after he had published another communication to this effect – adding to the functions of the proposed association the coordinated collection and analysis of statistical data about insanity[67] – two of his colleagues, Emile Renaudin of the public asylum of Fains in the department of the Meuse and Honoré Aubanel of the public asylum of Marseille, wrote letters of support published in the *Annales*.

But, complicating the situation immeasurably, Renaudin and Aubanel outlined plans more far-reaching than Baillarger's. They wanted the association to be not only a specialized scientific academy but also a kind of interest group. "Financial questions," said the recently unemployed Renaudin, presumably referring to asylum budgets, which included the salaries of psychiatrists as well as provision for patients, "are of a no less compelling interest [than theoretical matters], and the physician cannot neglect them. They are the material representation of

---

[65] R. P., "Les médecins d'autrefois, les médecins d'aujourd'hui," *Gazette médicale de Paris*, January 7, 1837, pp. 1–7. For a similar assessment of the French bar, a fear that healthy esprit de corps could turn into destructive *esprit de parti*, see Dupin, "IVe lettre sur la profession d'avocat," *Gazette des tribunaux*, February 3, 1826.

[66] J. B., "Association des médecins des hospices d'aliénés en Angleterre. De l'utilité que pourrait avoir une association semblable parmi les médecins français," *Ann. m.-p.*, 1st ser., 1 (1843): 181–83.

[67] Baillarger, "De la statistique appliquée à l'étude des maladies mentales," *Ann. m.-p.*, 1st ser., 7 (1846): 165.

his doctrines" and hence, rather than being left to the "common herd" (*profane vulgaire*), ought to be of foremost concern to a professional association.[68] For his part, Aubanel depicted the association in one of its aspects as a political lobby and liaison: "It would powerfully promote . . . the demands that we will subsequently have to address to the government in the interest of this unfortunate class of society entrusted to our care." In another of its aspects it would be a sort of trade union, regulating the conditions of psychiatric work, including hiring practices, the structure of authority within the asylum, and even such bread-and-butter issues as vacation time and retirement pensions. Now an association of asylum-doctors dedicated exclusively to the advancement of psychiatric science was, in France, a much more acceptable proposition than an association committed to the pursuit of its collective occupational interests. Aubanel must have realized how tinged with subversion his ideas were, for as if to legitimate the hypothetical association he had outlined, he went on to suggest that the government-appointed inspector-general of lunatic houses be its presiding officer and the minister of the interior its sponsor.[69]

A psychiatric association, the Société médico-psychologique, was founded in 1847 and refounded some five years later, the original charter never having been fully implemented due to the upheavals of the 1848 Revolution. The "New By-Laws of the Société médico-psychologique" of 1852 is a revealing text, both for the criticisms it levels against its short-lived predecessor and for the typically nineteenth-century French squeamishness it expresses about the concept of association. The 1847 Société had apparently been conceived along the lines sketched by Renaudin and Aubanel – that is, as a professional interest group as well as a scientific society. The authors of the "New By-Laws" recoiled from this arrangement:

> The preamble of the first [i.e., 1847] set of regulations seemed to us to contain views that were too narrow, too imprinted with esprit de corps. By their tendency to exclusivism, they would certainly have been unfavorable to the purpose that the Society proposes for itself: a rapprochement between the natural sciences and the moral sciences.

What were the marks of this undesirable esprit de corps? The 1847 regulations had been written with a distinctly medical bias: "Great care was taken to point out the services that medical science can render to religion, morality, jurisprudence, education, metaphysics, etc." But nowhere had the incompleteness of medicine itself been acknowledged. In particular, philosophical psychology had been slighted, its ability to illuminate the physiology and pathology of the nervous system overlooked.

---

[68] "Lettre de M. Renaudin . . . à M. Baillarger . . .," ibid., p. 469.
[69] "Lettre de M. Aubanel . . . à M. Baillarger . . .," ibid., pp. 470–71.

The refounders of the Société were intent upon defining the association so that its disinterested scientific purpose would be paramount and it would never be mistaken for a professional interest group of asylum-doctors. Insisting that the study of insanity was multidisciplinary by nature, they insisted that the Société be multidisciplinary in membership. "In order that there remain no doubt as to the purpose of the Society, it has appeared necessary to designate by name the different categories which will form its component elements: the Société méd-ico-psychologique will be composed, then, of physicians, philosophers, magistrates, lawyers, ministers of religion, historians, moralists, school-teachers, poets, etc."[70] So strong was the fear of displaying a militant and offensive brand of associationism that the various boundary disputes waged by psychiatry in its quest for disciplinary self-definition were, ironically, suspended in the context of this "association." Formal association should, in theory, have enhanced the process of psychiatric self-definition. But since the specialty was called upon to make a public show of amicably joining hands with everyone, its efficacy in this regard was minimized.

Because the Société médico-psychologique turned out to be primarily a scientific academy – although it did, with time, become somewhat responsive to the practical needs of the profession and established a fund for disabled asylum-doctors and for their widows and orphans[71] – this new, formal organizational mode could not begin to supplant the older, informal mode of the patron and his circle. Hence the prominence of Charcot and the Salpêtrière school (as his "circle" was usually called) from the 1870s until Charcot's death in 1893.

At that same 1883 banquet in honor of Charcot's election to the Institut, Dr. Bouchard enumerated the ties that bound him and his cohort to the eminent doctor. "We are here," he said,

> because you are the *Maître* and because we are your School; because your doctrine has guided us, because your method has served us; because you have pointed out to us the questions which needed elucidation and have traced the route to follow; because you have moderated our enthusiasms or restored our courage; because you have been associated with our research and have not disdained to associate us with yours. In difficult crossings, you have taken the rudder. You have steered our boat well. Today is a *fête* of the patron and also a *fête* of the crew.

Charcot replied in kind, using the typical language of the patron but shifting from Bouchard's nautical metaphor to the military one em-

---

[70] *Nouveau règlement de la Société médico-psychologique* (Paris: Impr. L. Martinet, 1852), pp. 3–5; BN: T[7] 505.

[71] The Caisse d'assistance mutuelle des médecins aliénistes, an offshoot of the main Sociéte, was founded in 1865; see the article of that name in *Ann. m.-p.*, 4th ser., 5 (1865): 531–35.

ployed by the Esquirol circle of the 1830s: He called those who identified themselves as his students "this phalanx of distinguished men." He, too, underscored the collaborative nature of their scientific enterprise, acknowledging the contributions to his research made by the long succession of interns "in this good hospice of the Salpêtrière."[72]

The banquet speeches did not dwell upon the "material basis" of the school – that is, the patron's ability to find places for the members – although Charcot did mention in passing that his students had in their turn "all become or were on the way to becoming *maîtres*."[73] The most explicit assertions about Charcot's genius at place-finding, as well as the richest documentation of the internal workings of his school, come to us not from a sympathetic member (comparable to Bricheteau on Pinel, or Bouchet on Esquirol) but from a hostile quasi-insider: Léon Daudet, who studied at the Paris medical faculty for seven years during the Charcot era, served as a hospital extern and intern, and then quit in disgruntlement before producing the short perfunctory thesis required for a diploma.[74] The son of the writer Alphonse Daudet (a friend of Charcot) and a man whose sympathies with the extreme right developed early (he joined Action française in 1904 and kept that group afloat financially), Daudet satirized Charcot in a novel of 1894 entitled *Les Morticoles* and returned to Charcot and the structure of French medicine repeatedly in his later writings.[75]

Daudet depicted Charcot's patronal power as the "Caesarism of the Faculty." Charcot, he contended, was an "omnipotent and uncontested *maître*" whose approval was required for all medical appointments and who could make or break the careers of all aspirants. If the dean of the medical faculty said, " 'Charcot is against him,' that simple little sentence was equivalent to the knife and guillotine," and the unfortunate individual was immediately relegated "to the second zone" and to a "stunted clientele." But if the dean murmured instead, " 'approved by Charcot,' then the election, the title, the diploma were carried off and assured."[76] Granting Daudet's jaundiced viewpoint, it nonetheless seems very likely that his depiction of Charcot was more exaggeration than pure fabrication. A contemporary observer who held Charcot in great esteem, the young Sigmund Freud, produced a re-

[72] "Banquet offert à M. le professeur Charcot," pp. 999–1000.

[73] Ibid., p. 1000.

[74] See Daudet's own account of his abortive medical career in *Devant la douleur: Souvenirs des milieux littéraires, politiques, artistiques et médicaux de 1880 à 1905*, reprinted in *Souvenirs littéraires* (Paris: Grasset, 1968), p. 100.

[75] On Daudet's political connections, see Eugen Weber, *Action Française: Royalism and Reaction in Twentieth-Century France* (Stanford, Calif.: Stanford University Press, 1962), pp. 44–48. On his early satire, see Toby Gelfand, "Medical Nemesis, Paris, 1894: Léon Daudet's *Les Morticoles*," *Bull. Hist. Med.* 60 (1986): 155–76.

[76] Léon Daudet, "Le professeur Charcot, ou le césarisme de Faculté," *Revue universelle* 4 (1921): 273.

markably similar description of Charcot's style in exercising patronal authority. One day in 1886, Charcot bade his assistant Joseph Babinski to collaborate with Freud in taking a case history. "The point of the incident," Freud wrote to his fiancée, "is that Charcot singled me out at all, and since then the assistant's behavior towards me changed." That very day Babinski invited Freud for the first time to lunch with him and the other Salpêtrière doctors, "as their guest, of course," in the Salle des Internes. "And all this in response to one nod from the Master!"[77]

Not surprisingly, Charcot seems to have kept firm supervisory control over the publications of the members of his school. As one of them wrote shortly after the master's death, "none of [Charcot's] pupils ever published a piece of work of any importance without his having read it more than once and corrected it with his own hand." This particular student regarded as generous and helpful what others might have found intrusive. "And how much," he exclaimed, "we gained from his annotations!"[78]

The analogue of Esquirol's homely Sunday luncheons were Charcot's elegant Tuesday soirées, held initially in his apartment on the quai Malaquais, and after 1884 in his magnificent townhouse on the traditionally aristocratic boulevard Saint-Germain, a residence he had decorated sumptuously with Indian and Chinese antiques and Gobelins tapestries.[79] The soirées were far from exclusively medical gatherings; the guest list included *le tout Paris*, all the significant literary, artistic, and political figures of the capital. But the soirées served a socializing function for the Salpêtrière school as well, since Charcot regularly invited his favorite pupils. According to Léon Daudet, he tried to proscribe medical shoptalk in this setting, subtly conveying that "he preferred that for once nobody speak to him of *concours* or theses," that everyone instead enjoy making music and witty conversation.[80] It is hard to know whether the Salpêtrière interns found these expectations of social grace as trying as did the foreigner Sigmund Freud, who as an occasional guest at the soirées in 1886 coped by taking cocaine in advance. But the ostentatious luxury of the weekly event struck at least one member of the school as an embarrassment, and after Charcot's death he tried to explain it away, attributing it to Charcot's family rather than to the tastes of the *maître* himself.[81] In any

---

[77] *Letters of Sigmund Freud*, p. 199. On Freud's idealization of Charcot, see J.-B. Pontalis, "Le séjour de Freud à Paris," *Nouvelle revue de psychanalyse*, no. 8 (1973), esp. pp. 236–37.

[78] Gilles de la Tourette, "Le professeur J.-M. Charcot," *Revue hebdomadaire* 15 (1893): 621.

[79] Most of the accounts of the Tuesday soirées mention only the second location, but cf. ibid., p. 611.

[80] Daudet, *Souvenirs*, p. 111.

[81] On Freud's attendance at the soirées, see *Letters of Sigmund Freud*, pp. 193–97, 203–4, 206–8. The apologist for conspicuous consumption at the Saint-Germain townhouse is Debove, "Eloge de J.-M. Charcot," *Presse médicale*, December 19, 1900, p. 204.

case, it is surely a telling indicator of the change in the social status of French psychiatry that outside the invariably grim workplace of the asylum, the Salpêtrière school mingled and forged its collective identity in such a luxurious milieu, amidst music, chocolates, liqueurs, and fine pâtés.

With respect to its second remaining professional goal, the specialty made, even on a superficial level, less rapid progress. Apart from the new requirement that each public asylum have an *élève interne*, a requirement that increased opportunities for practical psychiatric training in the provinces, the Law of 1838 had no impact on psychiatric education. Instruction continued to be given informally, in clinical courses authorized by the Paris hospital administration; and in the 1840s, this lack of progress was even compounded by the threat of regression. A sudden popular outcry against the invasion of privacy constituted by clinical instruction in the asylums was so roundly seconded by hospital administrators and (perhaps for reasons of intraprofessional rivalry) by "many physicians," that Jean-Pierre Falret was moved to write a long polemical essay attempting to refute the critics' position. His own argument rested on three points: the overriding necessity of perpetuating the specialty through education, of "mold[ing] young men to the treatment of medical illness"; the "entirely scientific curiosity" of the medical students who attended these courses, an attitude which was "full of professional seriousness [and] of respect and pity for the unfortunate" and hence could not be equated with the "raillery and inconsiderate curiosity" of casual visitors; and finally, the aid to the treatment process actually provided by the didactic setting – the flock of deferential medical students, hanging on their professor's every word, lent his utterances "a weight, a solemnity which they would not otherwise have" and thus enhanced that somewhat magical curative "authority" with which French psychiatry had been preoccupied since its inception. Falret's aim in this essay was not merely to defend old ground. He wanted clinical instruction in the asylums to be expanded, to be integrated into the curriculum of the faculty, and to be made available not only to those medical students intending to devote themselves to a psychiatric career but to all prospective physicians.[82]

The semi-crisis of the 1840s was successfully weathered; but the marginality of psychiatric instruction remained. In its curricular marginality, psychiatry was, however, in very good company. The conser-

---

[82] J. P. Falret, "De l'enseignement clinique des maladies mentales," *Ann. m.-p.*, 1st ser., 10 (1847): esp. 233–34; and 2d ser., 1 (1849): esp. 530–31, 576. In his reference to "inconsiderate curiosity," Falret was alluding to the popular eighteenth-century custom (unacceptable to the nineteenth-century sensibility) of paying an admission fee to visit madhouses such as Bicêtre for a Sunday afternoon's entertainment; see Michel Foucault, *Folie et déraison: Histoire de la folie à l'âge classique* (Paris: Plon, 1961), p. 180.

vatism of the nineteenth-century French medical faculties was almost legendary. Indeed the deep-seated unwillingness to change the official program of study would have rendered the whole system obsolete had not compensatory *enseignement libre*, or independent instruction (usually of a clinical character), been widely offered outside the faculties, keeping an elite of highly motivated students apprised of new developments in medical science. In Paris, this *enseignement libre* was of two sorts. Some, as we have already seen, took place in facilities provided by, and with the authorization of, the Paris hospital administration; some took place in facilities provided by, and with the authorization of, the Ecole pratique de médecine, a dependent institution of the Paris faculty. By the 1850s, psychiatry was making use of both kinds of instructional arrangements.[83]

By the middle of the Second Empire, the mushrooming of *enseignement libre*, obvious to everyone concerned, had produced antithetical responses. The conservative medical establishment, whose goals and rhetoric often savored of the Old Regime, feared that the faculty was in the institution of the Ecole pratique raising up its own "rival." To avoid such an outcome it promulgated an order that the courses at the Ecole clearly label themselves as such, so that their unofficial and presumably inferior character would be underscored.[84] Progressive reformist forces, on the other hand, expressed a zeal to integrate the specialized subject matter of the *enseignement libre* into the faculty curriculum. Clearly the psychiatrists stood to benefit from this second current of opinion, which met, however, with forceful resistance.

A good example of this resistance is a report of the "commission on chairs" prepared for the faculty, probably in the late 1850s, by the eminent Professor L.-D.-J. Gavarret. Siding with the "condemnation" long ago delivered by "Hippocrates, Galen and Celsus," as well as by all later "masters of the art," the Gavarret report repeated the familiar arguments against medical specialization. Specialization pandered to the tastes of the public ("a bad judge in such matters"). It had negative intellectual effects on the individual physician, "who becomes, in spite of himself, a specialist" and, "absorbed in the exclusive consideration of one corner of nosological space," loses that broad holistic perspective needed for the study of disease. It had negative consequences for the total medical scientific enterprise, "cutting it up into an infinitude

---

[83] AN: F^{17} 6672 contains petitions and authorizations to teach *médecine mentale* at the Ecole pratique in the 1850s and 1860s. On the critical role of *enseignement libre*, see George Weisz, "Reform and conflict in French medical education, 1870–1914," in R. J. Fox and G. Weisz, eds., *The Organization of Science and Technology in France, 1880–1914* (Cambridge University Press, 1980), esp. pp. 62–63.

[84] See AN: F^{17} 6672, "Note pour le Conseil impérial de l'Instruction publique," no. 470, n.d. and unsigned; a marginal note identifies the author as the vice-rector of the council and indicates that the council adopted his conclusions on June 28, 1858.

of pieces." The Gavarret report therefore found nothing wrong with the existing structure of medical education, which accurately reflected this verdict on specialization. The *enseignement officiel* of the faculty established the general principles, and the *enseignement libre* initiated students into the knowledge of innumerable – and peripheral – empirical details.

The report went on to address specifically the "often requested" inclusion of the study of mental maladies in the official sector of the curriculum. It energetically denied the utility or appropriateness of such a project. The average physician needed only to know how to diagnose insanity for purposes of transferring a mad patient from an ordinary hospital to a special asylum. Such diagnosis was easy, except for the early, ambiguous premonitory stages of insanity, its so-called prodrome. Now clinical instruction in the prodrome was virtually impossible by dint of the transience of the condition. Bringing medical students into an asylum for clinical instruction would not help because all institutionalized mental patients were well past the prodromic phase. Thus, the report concluded, relevant information about the prodrome "can be set forth only in theoretical instruction" and was already adequately handled as part of the faculty course in internal pathology. The *aliéniste*, whose "career is very different from that of the average physician," who "is almost cloaked with a public function," had no grounds to insinuate his specialized knowledge any further into the official teaching of the faculty. With a certain condescension, the report held up the founding father as a worthy example to present-day *aliénistes*. "The great progress in the treatment of lunatics" had been due to Pinel, and "no one would attempt to classify the immortal author of the *Nosographie philosophique* as a specialist."[85] In short, then, the bias against specialization had not much hampered the establishment of *médicine mentale* as a mode of practice in the nineteenth century because there had been little prior investment in the care of the insane on the part of general physicians. But the new specialty did encounter the full force of this traditional prejudice in the instructional context, where the professoriate of the medical faculty intended to guard its exclusive status against an influx of newcomers.

The reformist current in medical pedagogy was, however, given a boost in 1862 by Pierre Rayer, the newly appointed dean of the medical faculty. Recognizing the greater progress the English and Germans had made in modernizing the teaching of medicine, Rayer arrived at a half-way measure – introducing certain kinds of specialized clinical instruction into the technically official curriculum, but segregating them

[85] AN: AJ[16] 6310, "Rapport de la commission des chaires, Gavarret, Professeur, rapporteur," ms. pp. 5–8, 11–13. This is an undated draft with inserts and corrections; the first four pages are missing; the archivist's notation suggests 1859 as the date of composition.

and granting them a lesser status. This compromise solution, designed to overcome French prejudices against medical specialization through a gradualist approach, took the form of *cours cliniques complémentaires* to be taught by *agrégés*, rather than professors, of the faculty – that is, by the tier of "junior" (though not always youthful) faculty members who had previously performed such tasks as grading examinations and substituting for professors temporarily unable to teach.

One of the six new complementary courses was in "mental and nervous maladies" and was entrusted to Charles Lasègue, then forty-six years old.[86] It became apparent immediately after Rayer's "little medical coup d'état" (as one sympathetic observer called it) that Lasègue's complementary clinical course was a farce. The fault lay not with the instructor, whose lessons were "beautiful and brilliant," nor with the audience, which was large, eager, and applauding, but with the institutional arrangements. The Paris hospital administration, always wary of encroachment by the medical faculty and justifying this wariness by its responsibility to place patient care above instructional needs, had refused Lasègue access to a lunatic asylum for purposes of the course. Hence, like a "persecuted and ostracized missionary who cannot even find . . . a safe roof from which to preach the holy scripture," Lasègue was forced to conduct the course in the amphitheater of the faculty and at the general Necker hospital. For lack of more than a handful of lunatics to interview, the expressly "clinical" course remained almost entirely theoretical.[87] To the proponents of psychiatry, the only solution seemed the establishment of a "true chair" at the faculty.[88]

The French defeat in the Franco-Prussian War hastened the attainment of that end. Producing an almost universal conviction that France had declined militarily because she had ceded her scientific hegemony to the Germans during the nineteenth century, the war in effect bludgeoned the medical conservatives into treating the reform programs of the medical progressives with respect.[89] By 1875, at the initiative of the

[86] The details of the 1862 arrangement can be found in AN: F^{17} 4510, Chauffard, "Rapport sur la réorganisation des cours cliniques complémentaires à la Faculté de médecine de Paris," October 24, 1875, ms. pp. 1–2, 4–5. The other courses were in skin disease, venereal disease, pediatrics, ophthalmology, and diseases of the urinary tract.

[87] The quotations come from A. Linas, "Sur quelques publications récentes relatives à la pathologie mentale," *Gaz. hebd. de med.* 10 (June 12, 1863): 390. On the attitude of the Paris hospital administration, see AN: F^{17} 4510, Administration générale de l'Assistance publique à Paris, *Rapport fait au nom de la commission chargée d'étudier la question de la réorganisation des cours complémentaires de clinique dans les hôpitaux* (Paris: P. Dupont, 1876), pp. 5–9.

[88] See, e.g., Linas, "Sur quelques publications," p. 390.

[89] Sustained rumination on the relative merits of French and German science can be found in AN: AJ^{16} 6310, *Rapport sur la création des chaires cliniques spéciales à la Faculté de médecine*, Léon Lefort, rapporteur (Paris: A. Parent, [1878]), pp. 3–7.

minister of public instruction, two commissions had been appointed to study the question of clinical teaching. One, headed by the pioneering physical anthropologist Paul Broca, was composed entirely of professors at the medical faculty. The other, headed by Dr. Emile Chauffard, the inspector-general for medical affairs, was composed largely of bureaucrats and members of the Academy of Medicine, the Institut, and the Assistance Publique, a membership designed to settle the longstanding conflict, which had so sabotaged Rayer's reforms, between the Paris hospital administration and the Ministry of Public Instruction.[90] The conclusions of the two reports differed somewhat, but both came out in favor of a clinical chair in psychiatry, a regular full-fledged chair in the case of Broca (perhaps reflecting a bias rooted in his own early psychiatric training as Leuret's intern) and, in the case of Chauffard, a kind of second-class chair – a renaming of the old complementary clinical course and an upgrading of its instructor to professor, but *not* to the status of "titular professor" of the faculty.[91]

The assembly of the professors of the Paris medical faculty debated these conclusions in the winter of 1875–76. While a few participants wanted simply to maintain the status quo, such total antagonism to change was, in the shadow of Sedan, much muted; discussion turned on the precise details of implementing change. The Chauffard plan retained much of the traditional disdain for the specialties: As Chauffard expressed it orally (and far more bluntly than in his written report), "raising the holders of the special clinical chairs to the titulary professoriate" represented an "equality about which there is something shocking, something against nature." It was necessary to establish a line of "demarcation, as a scientific dignity, between this institution and the rest" and to "leave to the former its well-established superiority."[92] Professor Hardy attempted to rebut Chauffard's argument by pointing out that the holders of these chairs would not be "specialists in the narrow" – that is, invidious – "sense of the word." Furthermore, to attract the most talented men to the new chairs, the holders must be full members of the faculty, not consigned to a demeaning rank between professor and *agrégé*. Finally (and probably most persuasively), he argued that bold change was necessary if the

---

[90] The members of Chauffard's commission are listed on ms. p. 1 of his "Rapport sur la réorganisation." Chauffard explained the absence of faculty members from his commission at a meeting of the Paris Medical Faculty, December 30, 1875; see AN: AJ[16] 6256, ff. 400–401. I found references to or paraphrases of the Broca commission report in several archival documents, but could not locate a copy of the text.

[91] On the recommendations of the Broca report, see AN: AJ[16] 6257, January 27, 1876, f. 49; on those of the Chauffard report, see "Rapport sur la réorganisation," ms. pp. 8–9, 13.

[92] AN: AJ[16] 6256 (1875), ff. 401–2.

Paris faculty was to be "placed at the level of foreign universities and enabled to compete with equal weapons for foreign students, who now take the road to Germany, a country better favored than we in its system of higher education." The politically left-wing psychiatrist Trélat, firmly on the side of the Broca report, replied bitingly to Chauffard regarding the proposed group of quasi-professors: "Monsieur Rayer created a course, you will create a corporation." The vote on the matter was close, demonstrating that specialization had lost neither its stigma nor its ability to provoke intraprofessional jealousies. Sixteen members of the faculty voted in favor of new special clinical professors with full titles, ten voted against.[93]

A second debate among the faculty assembly took place over a fine but critical terminological point. The subject matter of the complementary clinical course had been denominated in 1862 as "mental and nervous maladies"; the Broca report now recommended a chair in "mental medicine." What, asked Professor Trélat, would be the purview of the new chair – simply "mental maladies" or the broader and, in his opinion, more intellectually defensible one of both nervous and mental maladies? Implicitly at stake here was psychiatry's professional imperialist ambitions, its desire to colonize the domain of the *demi-fous;* and hence it is hardly surprising that it was Trélat, a member of the old Esquirol circle and one of the few *aliénistes* on the faculty, who raised the issue. But on this subject debate was less protracted and consensus more readily obtained: The professors preferred a restrictive definition of the specialty by a margin of twenty-one to four. The term "nervous maladies," noted one participant, was "too vague"; the chair, it was announced, "will carry the title of mental maladies."[94] This was the same title that had been given to the only other official psychiatric instruction at the faculty – Royer-Collard's short-lived course over a half-century before.

By the beginning of 1876, then, the psychiatrists had gotten a pledge from the Paris faculty for the official institutionalization of their instruction – or, more precisely, the older mainstream portion of that instruction dealing with insanity. But the pledge existed only on paper, and it deliberately omitted the *névroses* – two reasons for only partial satisfaction.

---

[93] AN: AJ[16] 6257 (1876), ff. 4–6, 22, 43. The psychiatrist Lasègue sided with the Chauffard report, a move which is difficult to comprehend except by attributing rather mean-spirited motives to him. Having waited as an *agrégé* for a full fifteen years before finally being made a professor (of general pathology) at the faculty in 1867, at the age of fifty-one, he may have wished to preserve the exclusivity of the professoriate. He said (f. 33): "A specialty is attractive because it is lucrative. All specialists naturally give courses and there is no reason to solicit them to do so . . . or to assimilate them to other professors."

[94] Ibid., ff. 49–51.

Shifting political configurations, 1838–1876

The place in the sun that the psychiatric profession and the hysteria diagnosis acquired under the early Third Republic was hard won, but a discernible logic underlay the eventual victory. That historical logic can be understood only by tracing, in addition to psychiatry's professional progress, its political situation after 1838 – that is, its relationship to the various political regimes and ruling groups that came to power between the July Monarchy and the late 1870s.

After the passage of the 1838 Law, the vast majority of *aliénistes* doubled, by virtue of their posts in public asylums, as *fonctionnaires*, paid bureaucratic servants of the state – a status that entailed at least superficial conformity to whatever political ideology happened to be in the ascendant. As *fonctionnaires*, they were theoretically vulnerable to those administrative purges that might accompany the establishment of a new regime. Indeed, the old Esquirol circle member Foville, a scion of the Norman sword nobility (see Appendix), did apparently lose his post at Charenton after the 1848 Revolution because of his strong Orleanist connections.[95] But such politically motivated removals of psychiatrists were exceptional. Aubanel, a student of Ferrus employed at the Marseille asylum, believed in 1848 that his job was being "threatened" by the "machinations" of a rival physician who was casting doubt on his republican loyalties, and he preemptively defended himself in a letter to the minister of the interior. "You know that the revolution . . . calls forth a crowd of ambitious mediocrities who will stop at nothing in order to succeed," he warned, and went on to enumerate his achievements at the asylum, to attest his political purity ("I regard the Republic as the triumph of the fatherland") and even to trace the left-wing sentiments of his family back to his grandfather in 1792 and to his father, assiduous "reader of the newspaper *Le Constitutionnel* from 1815 to 1830, always known for his liberalism under the Restoration."[96] Aubanel's anxieties proved unfounded, however, and his meticulously argued brief on his own behalf was probably superfluous. His tenure at the Marseille asylum remained untroubled until his death some fifteen years later.

But if purges of individual *aliénistes* were rare, a political regime might still inflict a kind of collective discomfort upon the members of the specialty; and the Second Empire illustrates this perfectly.

The Empire was by no means univocally hostile to the psychiatrists. Its policy proved rather to be a peculiar mixture in which the negative elements preponderated – and were even, perversely, fueled by the positive ones. On the positive side was the work of Baron Haussmann,

---

[95] Semelaigne, *Pionniers*, Vol. 1, p. 255.
[96] AN: F^{15} 3915, letter dated May 9, 1848.

the prefect of the Seine, who undertook as part of his rebuilding of Paris a massive expansion of the overcrowded asylum system in the capital, an enterprise inspired at least as much by his concern to safeguard the Bonapartist government from disorder in the streets as by his humanitarian concern for the plight of the insane. The utility of lunatic asylums as instruments of social control, so apparent to the Doctrinaire liberals of the July Monarchy, was equally apparent to their more authoritarian Bonapartist successors; and Haussmann's deep investment in his asylum project is nowhere more evident than in the fact that he drew up the regulations for the new Sainte-Anne asylum himself.[97] The government gave another public testament of its esteem for the psychiatrists when it deployed them to quell an epidemic of nervous disease in the mountain province of Savoy, newly annexed from Italy. In this curious episode of the 1860s, the partnership of psychiatry and coercive state authority could hardly have been more apparent, for the asylum-doctors were aided by a small detachment of infantry and a brigade of *gendarmerie*.[98] But if psychiatrists were being further integrated into the apparatus of the state under the Imperial regime (it is a fitting token of historical continuity that in the late 1860s they still applied to some of their activities the eighteenth-century absolutist term "medical police"),[99] they now paid a high price for their statist professional success. That price was especially high because it was doubly exacted: The psychiatrists were penalized both by the Imperial regime which sponsored them and by their own traditional political allies, the liberals.

Let us turn first to the latter group. The psychiatrists, who typically stressed their enlightened humanitarian origins and whose fortunes, since 1789, had been tied to those of liberalism, were now the conspicuous beneficiaries of a regime which had forced the liberals into opposition. And their discomfort was manifest when liberal opposition to the Empire took the asylum system as a particular target. The suspicion that lunatic asylums endangered civil liberties, even doubling as political prisons – a suspicion voiced by liberals to the left of the Doctrinaires during the debate over the 1838 Law – now became the subject of a liberal press compaign of (if one accepts the perception of the psychiatrists) major and damaging proportions.

First came the Sandon affair. Under the Second Republic, the lawyer

---

[97] Gerard Bleandonu and Guy Le Gaufey, "Naissance des asiles (Auxerre-Paris)," *Annales E.S.C.* 30 (1975): 93–121; and G. E. Haussmann, "Règlement pour le service intérieur de l'Asile de Sainte-Anne," ms. dated June 6, 1868, AAP: 29f° D-142.

[98] I have discussed this episode and the psychiatric theorizing that warranted it in " 'Moral Contagion': A Professional Ideology of Medicine and Psychiatry in 18th- and 19th-Century France" in G. L. Geison, ed., *Professions and the French State, 1700–1900* (Philadelphia: University of Pennsylvania Press, 1984), esp. pp. 211–14.

[99] See the heading given to an article on the Paris asylum system, *Ann. m.-p.*, 4th ser., 9 (1867): 356.

Léon Sandon had attempted to aid a colleague, Adolphe Billault, in the latter's bid for reelection to the Legislative Assembly on the democratic socialist platform. Sandon had in his possession a series of letters from Billault detailing strategy and containing a political profession of faith, including expressions of deep contempt for Louis Napoleon. Shortly after failing to be reelected, and perceiving the way the wind was blowing, Billault became a Bonapartist, eventually rising to the position of cabinet minister to the Emperor Napoleon III. Sandon refused to return the incriminating letters. On the testimony of several Parisian *aliénistes*, he was confined to Charenton as a lunatic. Whatever the truth in this controversial and byzantine affair – whether Sandon was an innocent victim or a shrewd blackmailer[100] – the liberal press naturally chose to dramatize Sandon's victimization by an arbitrary government; and it included the complicitous psychiatric profession in its condemnation. In one detail, history repeated itself: The journalist most active in the attack on the psychiatrists was Elias Regnault, who in 1828 had authored the sensational book-length attack on the monomania doctrine. "In the past thirty-five years," Regnault now wrote on the front page of the *Avenir national*, "the science [of psychiatry] has not advanced one step; the same obscurities, the same uncertainties exist, the same arguments persist."[101] Adding to this sensationalism was Sandon's prosecution of his own case before a Paris tribunal in 1865. He was suing the *aliénistes* who, by certifying him afflicted with an "ambitious delirium," had presided over his incarceration in Charenton; and his impassioned rhetoric brought forth frequent uproar and indignant exclamations from spectators in the courtroom. He denounced the doctors, including former Esquirol circle members Foville, Baillarger, and Mitivié, as "miserable slaves of power, police assassins" who had "obeyed [the government] out of self-interest and servility." One of them, he alleged, had even openly acknowledged Sandon's sanity and offered him a bribe in return for the letters.[102]

The bad publicity kept increasing at the end of the 1860s; that it came from the liberal camp, with which the psychiatrists still wished to be identified, made it all the more painful. In 1864 the proclerical *Journal des villes et des campagnes* had led an attack on the Law of 1838, alleging that it provided insufficient protection for individual liberty, encour-

---

[100] The version given under "Sandon" in Pierre Larousse, *Grand dictionnaire universel du XIXe siècle*, Vol. 14 (1875) is entirely pro-Sandon. That in a recent biography of Billault tends to be sympathetic to the minister; see Noel Blayau, *Billault, ministre de Napoléon III d'après ses papiers personnels, 1805–1865* (Paris: Klincksieck, 1969), pp. 386–87.

[101] See Regnault, "Question des aliénés," Part 2, *Avenir national*, December 12, 1865.

[102] See *Plaidoyer de M. Léon Sandon . . . contre les médecins Tardieu, Blanche, Parchappe, Foville, Baillarger et Mitivié, prononcé à Paris devant la première chambre le 9 mai 1865* (Brussels: Impr. de A. Mertens, 1865), esp. pp. 3, 22–23. The doctor whom Sandon accused of attempted bribery was Tardieu.

aged "medical omnipotence" in the asylums, and was based upon the erroneous "morbid psychology of Esquirol," which deviated from the great tradition of "French philosophy – that is, good sense and Descartes."[103] The psychiatrists could handle an attack of this sort without too much loss of equanimity. Focusing on the still sensitive issue of the true nature of the originative psychiatric paradigm, Delasiauve suggested that religious concerns were at the root of this denunciation by a right-wing newspaper, that what was really being demanded "is that the chaplain inherit from the physician the direction of the moral treatment."[104] But by 1866, this interpretation of the attack on the 1838 Law was no longer tenable; for the attack had spread, becoming the darling of the liberal press.

Writing to the editor of the *Avenir national* and using, appropriately, the language of pathology, Delasiauve could scarcely contain his rage:

> Where, good God, are we going? What madness (*frénésie*) has taken hold of the liberal press in its opposition to the psychiatrists (*aliénistes*) and to the Law of 1838? After the *Opinion nationale*, the *Presse* and the *Siècle*, today is the turn of the *Avenir national* to echo the retrograde newspapers.

There had been, said Delasiauve with a touch of nostalgia, a period after the disturbances of the monomania controversy in the late 1820s and early 1830s "when mental medicine, justly honored, pursued its course of research in a fruitful and serious quietude. That time has fled." Speaking of the psychiatrists as "our laborious and devoted phalanx" – the military metaphor habitually invoked in times of professional crisis – he asserted that, far from endangering individual liberty, the 1838 Law had created an "insurmountable obstacle" to "arbitrary incarcerations." The liberal credentials of both the Law and the psychiatrists were, he insisted, impeccable. The Law had been framed carefully, in the "serene era of parliamentary deliberations"; those who criticized it would become its admirers if they could appreciate "the liberalism that characterizes it"; the Law had a "shining face" because, in the natural rights tradition of liberalism, it "proclaimed the RIGHT OF THE LUNATIC TO ASSISTANCE." And again, several pages later, "The most disinterested liberalism stands out in our concerns."[105]

---

[103] For the content of these articles, see the extensive quotations in C. Pinel, "Quelques mots sur les asiles d'aliénés et la loi de 1838 . . .," *J. de med. ment.* 4 (1864): 144, 146. On the ideological position of the *Journal des villes et des campagnes*, see Claude Bellanger et al., eds., *Histoire générale de la presse française*, Vol. 2 (Paris: Presses universitaires de France, 1969), p. 267.

[104] See Delasiauve, "Note du rédacteur en chef," in C. Pinel, "Sur la séquestration et le traitement des aliénés," *J. de med. ment.* 4 (1864): 260n; see also the interpretation of C. Pinel, "La loi du 30 juin 1838 et ses détracteurs," ibid. 5 (1865): 24.

[105] Delasiauve, "Les médecins et les asiles d'aliénés: Double lettre à M. Peyrat, rédacteur en chef de l'*Avenir national*," ibid. 6 (1866): 18–19, 51, 57 (capital letters in the origi-

Protesting their liberalism to a constituency on which they had always relied but which had turned against them, the psychiatrists were, at the same time, being punished for certain liberal tendencies that the Imperial regime had discerned in them. Theirs was a classic no-win situation.

Since the Bonapartists had strongly backed the asylum system and had thus indirectly entrusted to the *aliénistes* additional responsibility for the maintenance of social order, they seem to have felt obliged to demand an unusual measure of ideological purity of the psychiatric doctors. At issue was the familiar doctrine of "physiology," or in cruder terms philosophic materialism, which might be lurking beneath the medical-psychiatric quest for mental functions in brain functions and mental aberrations in localized cerebral lesions. Lacking the anticlerical streak of the leaders of the July Monarchy, the Bonapartists showed distinctly less tolerance for "physiology" than had their Orleanist predecessors. Sympathetic to the church and tending to use it "as a kind of police force,"[106] they ferreted out this subversive doctrine whenever it was condoned or, worse still, disseminated. Their attention turned to the state-run faculties of medicine, and especially to the most important and progressive of these, the one in Paris.

An early manifestation of this vigilance was the suspension of a series of informal evening lectures on the history of medicine given during the academic year 1865 at the Paris faculty on the initiative of its *agrégés*. These extracurricular lectures, part of the diffuse program of *enseignement libre*, were open to interested medical students and to physicians.[107] The arcane lore of medical history must have seemed entirely apolitical and nonthreatening to the administration when it authorized the series; but in fact the lectures could serve as the forum for the espousal of radical and dangerous opinions, as was shown by Alexandre Axenfeld's lectures on Jean Wier. Axenfeld, described in a medical-professional newspaper of the day as "well-known and well-loved" by his audience, was a Russian-born, French-educated doctor affiliated with no organized religion (obituaries in 1876 delicately declined to speculate on his religion of birth) and decidedly free-thinking in outlook. Though not an asylum-doctor, he had a special interest in the *névroses* and taught an independent course in the "morbid

---

nal). The *Avenir national* was founded in the 1860s as a republican and intensely anticlerical daily; see Bellanger et al., *Histoire générale de la presse française*, Vol. 2, p. 322.

[106] Adrien Dansette, *Religious History of Modern France*, trans. J. Dingle, Vol. 1 (Freiburg: Herder; Edinburgh-London: Nelson, 1961), p. 289.

[107] See Delasiauve, "Jean Wier et la sorcellerie," *J. de med. ment.* 6 (1866): 387; and editor's preface in Faculté de médecine de Paris, *Conférences historiques faites pendant l'année 1865* (Paris: Baillière, 1866), p. v.

physiology of the nervous system" at the Ecole pratique of the faculty.[108]

The lectures on Wier, delivered according to one journalist "in a language that was always elevated, often spiritual, sometimes eloquent," were a paean to that courageous sixteenth-century physician who, at the height of the European witch craze, had dared to declare that many of the women condemned to death on charges of witchcraft were not culpable at all, but simply ill. There were, Axenfeld noted, severe limitations to Wier's independence of mind: He was enough the product of his age to believe in the existence of the devil and in black magic. But nonetheless Wier's role as the "witches' advocate" exemplified for Axenfeld the fundamental clash of opposing value systems – the enlightened-humanitarian ethos of medicine pitted against the brutally punitive fanaticism of religion. At the close of the lectures, Axenfeld drew out, somewhat elliptically, the implications of the Wier story for current forensic medical practice. Progress had been made since Wier's time, following the model he had so precociously set. "People are no longer killed for a fantastic crime like magic," and the insanity plea was admitted. But the task of reform was as yet incomplete. "We continue to kill, with perfect tranquillity, criminals who are not insane because, apart from insanity, moral liberty seems indisputable. . . . The will is free, that is the dogma." It was, then, freedom of the will that Axenfeld was calling into question. The judiciary would, he said, have to relinquish that "dogma" and take into account "a universal extenuating circumstance – the infinitely unequal capability of individuals to do good and to do evil." And he spoke, with full recognition of his "temerity," before a packed house: "Never had [the public] been more numerous or more tightly squeezed together on the steps of the amphitheater."[109]

The suppression of the historical lectures was only an intimation of the more serious political meddling in the instruction of the faculty of medicine that was to come. In 1868, Victor Duruy, the liberal-leaning and reformist minister of public instruction, was constrained by the pressure of the episcopal members of the academic council of the university first to annul a medical degree duly granted by the Paris faculty upon its acceptance of the candidate's thesis, and second to summon for official reprimand the professor who had sponsored the candidate. The

---

[108] "Conférences historiques de médecine et de chirurgie. M. Axenfeld – Jean Wier et les sorciers," *Union médicale*, June 22, 1865, p. 577. For biographical information and guarded uncertainty about Axenfeld's native religion, see "M. le Professeur Axenfeld," *Progrès médical* 4 (1876): 657. See AN: F[17] 6672, both for official authorization of the independent course in 1860 and for its syllabus.

[109] Axenfeld, "Jean Wier et les sorciers," in *Conférences historiques faites pendant l'année 1865*, pp. 383–443, passim, and esp. pp. 419, 440–42; and for quoted comments on the lectures, *Union médicale*, June 22, 1865, p. 577.

offending thesis was *Etude médico-psychologique du libre arbitre humain,* by P.-J. Grenier; and the student's sponsor, the president of his examining committee, was none other than Alexandre Axenfeld.[110] Grenier's essay, replete with homages to Auguste Comte and references to "the most recent works on cerebral physiology and mental medicine," elaborated the remarks about the nonexistence of free will contained in Axenfeld's Wier lectures. It then went on to explore the implications of the unfree will for "a penal philosophy" – namely, the indistinguishability on physiological grounds of criminals and criminal lunatics and the consequent eradication of responsibility among both groups.[111]

The disciplinary measures taken against Grenier were not permanent. He was able to retrieve his investment in a medical education and to become a licensed physician by speedily producing another thesis, this time on an ideologically neutral subject.[112] But the *affaire* Grenier aroused civil libertarian indignation in the opposition press and brought forth measured protest from the two psychiatric journals then published in France. Both journals, acknowledging an impetuously "juvenile" quality in the thesis, praised it nonetheless for its "generous" aspirations and criticized the unsavory clerical and political machinations that had brought it into the limelight. "How dare the clergy forbid it?" asked the *Journal de médecine mentale;* and the *Annales médico-psychologiques* characterized the whole episode as illegitimate state interference in the internal workings and pedagogical functions of the faculty of medicine.[113] And while Grenier bowed to the force of circumstance, he was neither broken nor silenced. He appended to a new edition of his second thesis his correspondence with the chief instigator of all his troubles, Monseigneur Dupanloup, the Bishop of Orléans. He was, he announced proudly to the Second Empire's most prominent spokesman for religious conformity and a state-supported church, a free thinker (*libre penseur*) and a materialist, just as his father, a village doctor in the Périgord, had been. He believed that the political revolution in France was not yet over and hoped for a social revolution as well. He wanted Dupanloup to know that at the Paris faculty teachers and students alike laughed at the "scientific censorship exercised over medical theses as a weak concession" to the bishop's demands. It was laughable that "the word 'positivism' is manfully ban-

---

[110] Paris: Thèse de médecine, 1867. The examining committee is listed on the verso of the title page.

[111] P.-J. Grenier, *Etude médico-psychologique du libre arbitre humain,* 3d ed. (Paris: Delahaye, 1868), pp. 26, 28, 30, 88, 102–3.

[112] Grenier, *Du ramollissement sénile* (Paris: Thèse de médecine, 1868). It is possible that this seemingly innocuous topic was intended by Grenier as a sly comment on the brain-softening senility of the officials who had punished him.

[113] Examples of the press response are cited in *Annales du Sénat,* Vol. 10, p. 4. For reviews of the Grenier thesis, see Delasiauve in *J. de med. ment.* 8 (1868): 203–7; and Durand (de Gros) in *Ann. m.-p.,* 5th ser., 1 (1869): 189–93.

ished from official language," that "at the sound of the words 'materialism' and 'organicism,' the Vice-Rector is either petrified with astonishment or overcome with sanctimonious indignation."[114]

The initial acceptance of the Grenier thesis by the professoriate was
one of the danger signals that led clerical forces in France – already gal-
vanized by Duruy's project to extend state facilities for female secondary
education and thereby to encroach upon a traditional clerical bastion – to
gather over 2000 signatures on a petition to the Senate expressing alarm
over the materialistic tendencies informing the instruction at the Paris
Faculty of Medicine.[115] The result was an extended debate on this subject
on the floor of the Senate during the spring of 1868. Several members of
the upper clergy participated, united in their horror that endorsements
of "irreligion" could be permitted in a state-run institution of higher
learning. Representing the diametrically opposite viewpoint, that of latitudinarian laissez-faire, was the literary critic Sainte-Beuve, himself a
former student at the Paris Faculty of Medicine. In a long and spirited
speech, he argued that the quest for scientific truth, even if it led the
investigator to adopt philosophical materialism, must, in the modern
nineteenth-century world, be kept entirely free and separate from the
sphere of politics and law; in the latter sphere, he said, ultimate questions were irrelevant, and Benthamite calculations of utility sufficed as
criteria. For a legislative assembly such as the Senate to busy itself with
the philosophical implications of medical instruction was not only inappropriate but also smacked of the sad futility of Satan and his band of
fallen angels in Milton's *Paradise Lost*, who, banished to a solitary hill,
talked of free will and man's final destiny in a tortuous conversation that
was *sans issue*.[116]

The outcome of the debate was confused and ambiguous. The ballot
taken at the end of May effectively quashed the petition, some two-
thirds of the senators voting that it not be sent back to the government –
that is, that no credence be given to the factual accusations it contained.
But at the same time Duruy, as minister of public instruction, was forced
to make concessions to the clerical party. His speech during the debate
assigned (in violation of his own personal beliefs) an official philosophy – Cousinian spiritualism – to the university and stipulated that
professors conform to it both in their public lessons and their printed
writings.[117]

---

[114] See Grenier, *Du ramollissement sénile du cerveau*, 2d ed. (Paris: A. Delahaye, 1868),
dedication and letter to Dupanloup, pp. 6–8, 12.

[115] See Jean Maurain, *La politique ecclésiastique du Second Empire de 1852 à 1868* (Paris:
Alcan, 1930), pp. 838–39; and Jean Rohr, *Victor Duruy, ministre de Napoléon III: Essai
sur la politique de l'instruction publique au temps de l'empire libéral* (Paris: Pichon &
Durand-Auzias, 1967), pp. 165–71.

[116] *Annales du Sénat*, Vol. 10, pp. 14, 18, 20.

[117] Ibid., p. 103; and Maurain, *Politique ecclésiastique*, p. 864.

It should be noted that while medicine as a whole was under Senate investigation in this debate – Sainte-Beuve, for example, contrasted "Catholic-vitalist" and "heretical-experimentalist" definitions of fever – the specialty of psychiatry, dealing most directly with the mental aspects of human life, proved to be particularly vulnerable to charges of subversion. This was evident in the frequent allusions to the Grenier affair (the errant thesis was described by proclerical speakers as "atheistic and materialistic" and "incredible, attacking all the moral and religious prerequisites of society"),[118] as well as in an allegation that a doctor at the Salpêtrière had mocked an inmate for wearing a Virgin Mary medal and that such insults to religion were routine occurrences at that institution.[119] The Salpêtrière incident (or malicious rumor) was a kind of leitmotif of the debate: Sainte-Beuve conveyed to the Senate Charcot's personal declaration that "it was a pure invention"; and letters from Charcot and other Salpêtrière psychiatrists – Auguste Voisin, Moreau de Tours, Trélat, Delasiauve – were read into the official record as testimony that the allegation was a "lie" and a "calumny" and that respect for the religious practices of patients was the rule at the asylum.[120]

During the second half of the Second Empire, then, the psychiatrists were caught, as in a vise, between the liberal critique symbolized by the *affaire* Sandon and the more politically powerful (but less emotionally wounding) clerical critique symbolized by the *affaire* Grenier. Nor did the latter sort of beleaguerment immediately end or even diminish with the fall of the Empire in 1870. In its opening years, the Third Republic was painfully unsure of its political identity – republican largely as an accident of history, actually controlled by monarchists and anti-Communard proclerical upholders of what was called "the moral order." And so, during these years, the Paris prefect of police maintained a spy in the medical faculty of the capital.[121] His assignment was to cover the law faculty as well; but the vast majority of his reports concerned the medical faculty, indicating his judgment that more of the seditious data he sought could be garnered there.

The spy who went under the name of "Cujas" was an almost daily auditor of medical school classes from 1873 through 1876. Mingling among the authentic *carabins*, or medical students, he sized up their political mood and also sifted through the presentations of their professors for evidence of those "materialistic" doctrines that so keenly inter-

[118] *Annales du Sénat*, Vol. 10, pp. 3–4, 19.
[119] Ibid., Vol. 7, p. 78.
[120] Ibid., Vol. 10, pp. 18, 63.
[121] This practice seems to have ceased during the bona fide republican phase of the republic; the police archives on student surveillance for the 1880s and early 1890s are confined to newspaper clippings and official documents originating in the police bureaus.

ested his superiors. Instruction in *maladies mentales* particularly attracted him. Of a course in this subject he wrote, several days before its opening,

> I warn you in advance of this fact [the imminent opening], seeing that this subject matter, this burning (*brûlant*) terrain, will, despite all prudence and reserve in the professor, sooner or later rouse loud complaints from the proclerical forces (*les Jesuitières*) in the quarter. I will attend this course.

He did, and found it filled with "entirely pure materialism, not that gross, brutish and bestial materialism, but that studied scientific materialism that seduces you, that captivates you by the quasi-irrefutable proofs which it furnishes on its own behalf."[122] Charcot figured frequently in Cujas's reports. The affection and intellectual respect which the *maître* commanded among the students was noted,[123] as was the "purest materialism" which "marked all [of Charcot's] lessons on geriatric medicine (*les maladies des viellards*)" at the Salpêtrière,[124] and the anticlerical jokes that could spring spontaneously to his lips during his clinical instruction on nervous illness at the Salpêtrière:

> To a perfectly natural question of the professor [Charcot], the patient replied, "I saw the devil with two parish priests at the Botanical Gardens (*Jardin des Plantes*)!" The entire audience burst out laughing. The professor added, "That is a very characteristic group," [and] a new smile underscored these words of Monsieur Charcot.

Cujas also supplied a vignette of the political proclivities of Charcot's students. Leaving this particular lesson, they came upon the placarded proclamations of MacMahon, the president of the French republic, who was the obvious puppet of the monarchical Orleanist faction. The *carabins* began to chant "in chorus, 'There is the prose of our famous Mac. There is someone who ought to be in the Salpêtrière!' "[125]

The constantly probing, critical gaze of Cujas and the content of his secret police reports indicate the general government attitude toward psychiatry in the mid-1870s; but psychiatric beleaguerment also took more palpable forms. In 1874, all clinical instruction in psychiatry at the Paris municipal asylums was suppressed, a ban not lifted until 1876. The measure "irritated" and "stupefied" professors and students alike; it was, as Cujas recorded, vigorously denounced by Lasègue, and "the majority of the students think that it is the clergy who were at the root of this interdiction. . . . I will keep my eye on

---

122 APP: B^A24 52047, February 24, 1875 (no.39); February 28, 1875 (no.41).
123 Ibid., November 27, 1874 (no.374); October 27, 1876 (no.279).
124 Ibid., December 20, 1875 (no.361).
125 Ibid., January 17, 1876 (no.14).

this affair, which, given the circumstances, could well take on disquieting proportions."[126]

The anticlerical partnership

What a relief, then, for psychiatrists to be rid of the Empire and the antirepublican republicans of the "moral order"[127] and to find instead at the helm of the state a group of politicians whose values matched their own. The positivist method that provided the underpinning of Charcot's work on hysteria (and of the work of the Parisian psychiatric community generally)[128] had unmistakable political connotations – which is of course why the very word "positivism" had been, in Grenier's phrase, "manfully banished" from the official vocabulary of the Second Empire. Confining itself to the observed regularities in the relations among phenomena and shunning all talk of ultimate causes, infused with the spirit of the Comtean "law of the three stages," in which the third stage, positive science, replaced both theological and metaphysical explanation, positivism connoted anticlericalism – distrust or even detestation of the Catholic Church as a retrograde force militating against both scientific and social progress. Now the generation of republicans which had gestated in opposition under the Second Empire and had finally come into their own in the late 1870s were, in stark contrast to most of their Romantic counterparts of the 1840s, saturated with positivism and anticlericalism. This was most emphatically true of their leaders, men like Emile Littré (once Comte's chief disciple), Jules Ferry, and Léon Gambetta.[129] The result, when the Third Republic was finally "conquered by the republicans" in the late 1870s, was a close and utterly natural ideological fit between the political regime and the psychiatric profession. Ideological affinity readily translated itself into organizational terms: More intimately connected to the government than at any time since the Revolution, the psychiatrists now formed part of a tight network of republican politicians and scientist–politicians. The cast of characters, pared down to

[126] Ibid., March 20, 1874 (no.49); March 21, 1874 (no.50). On the lifting of the ban, see "Incident au Conseil général," *Révolution,* November 14, 1876, a clipping conserved in APP: B^A 65 134100 R.G. no.15; and "Rétablissement des cours cliniques dans les asiles d'aliénés," *Progrès médical* 4 (1876): 559.

[127] See their own use of "the reign of the moral order" to mean the period when "scientific studies, especially those of a medical nature, were not at all favored." *Progrès médical* 4 (1876): 559.

[128] See, e.g., the Comtean assumptions and vocabulary in Moreau de Tours's assessment of the state of the "science of mental maladies" in *Traité pratique de la folie névropathique (vulgo hystérique)* (Paris: Germer Baillière, 1869), pp. v–vi.

[129] See John Eros, "The Positivist Generation of French Republicanism," *Sociological Review,* n.s. 3 (1955): 255–77; and Louis Capéran, *Histoire contemporaine de la laïcité française: La crise du seize mai et la revanche républicaine* (Paris: Rivière, 1975), pp. 31–36.

the four main protagonists, was Gambetta, Paul Bert, Charcot, and Désiré-Magloire Bourneville.

Paul Bert, professor of physiology at the Sorbonne (and Claude Bernard's direct successor in this post), edited the science column – devoted to *vulgariser sans vulgariser* – of the newspaper *République française*, founded by Gambetta in 1871. He served jointly as minister of public instruction and minister of religion when Gambetta finally succeeded in forming a cabinet in 1881.[130] Charcot, though not a political actor, was clearly politically affiliated, entertaining Gambetta at his soirées on the boulevard Saint-Germain; called to Gambetta's bedside as a consulting physician during the politician's fatal illness; and even the father-in-law of Gambetta's political ally Waldeck-Rousseau.[131] Making up for Charcot's tendency to retire behind the scenes politically was Bourneville, the consummate hybrid psychiatrist–politician. Originally a student of Charcot, he popularized Charcot's work by publishing his lectures and founding the *Progrès médical* in 1873 to serve as the journalistic organ of the Salpêtrière school – thus playing the "bulldog" role that Thomas Huxley played with respect to Charles Darwin. A small, bearded, feisty, and irritable man, "his face as red as his politics," as one contemporary described him, Bourneville was temperamentally predisposed to court controversy. Holding a post as chief psychiatrist at Bicêtre, he served simultaneously as a member of the Paris Municipal Council from 1876 to 1883 and then sat for two consecutive terms (1883–1887) in the Chamber of Deputies, where he held Louis Blanc's old seat from the fifth arrondissement of Paris.[132] He was also active in the free-thought (*libre-pensée*) movement, which drew recruits almost entirely from the urban popular classes.[133] Three of these four men – Gambetta, Charcot, and Bourne-

---

[130] *Revues scientifiques publiées par le journal "La République française" sous la direction de M. Paul Bert*, Vol. 1 (Paris: G. Masson, 1879), p. 1; Bellanger et al., *Histoire générale de la presse française*, Vol. 3, p. 222; *Journal officiel*, November 15, 1881, p. 6346.

[131] Georges Guillain, *J.-M. Charcot: His Life, His Work*, trans. P. Bailey (New York: Hoeber, 1959), pp. 25, 32 n5; Henri Thurat, *Gambetta: Sa vie, son oeuvre* (Paris: Bibliothèque des Communes, 1883), pp. 404, 406–9. Some indications of the familial ties between the Charcots and the Waldeck-Rousseaus can be found in Waldeck-Rousseau, "Lettres à sa mère," Vol. 4, 1888–89, Bibliothèque de l'Institut, Ms. 4564, e.g., nos.41, 116. The only source I have found that credits Charcot with articulating political views (even in private) is the obviously biased Daudet, "Charcot ou le césarisme de Faculté," which reports (p. 284) Charcot's view of the French Revolution "in the conventional colors of Michelet and Quinet," his horror at Taine's likening the Jacobins to crocodiles, and his frequent "mutterings against 'the nobles,' their 'privileges' and 'habits of caste.' "

[132] J. Noir, "Bourneville, 1840–1909," *Progrès médical*, June 5, 1909, pp. 293–94; and for the quotation, Horace Bianchon, *Nos grands médecins d'aujourd'hui* (Paris: Société des editions scientifiques, 1891), pp. 35–36.

[133] Bourneville, *Etienne Dolet: Sa vie, ses oeuvres, son martyre* (Paris: Au siège de la Libre-Pensée du Ve arrondissement, 1879); *Congrès universel des libre-penseurs tenu à Paris du 15 au 20 septembre 1889, Compte-rendu officiel* (Paris: Dentu, 1890), p. 16,

ville – were, as was typical of Gambetta's entourage, parvenus, issues of those *nouvelles couches* whose ascension on the social ladder Gambetta promised as part of his democratic-republican political program.[134]

From this political-psychiatric nexus came, in the 1880s, an almost feverishly active collaboration which had three major consequences: the laicization of the Paris asylums and hospitals; the establishment of an academic chair in the diseases of the nervous system; and finally, the politicization of the hysteria diagnosis. Each of these three will be considered in turn.

The program of the newly republicanized Republic was dominated by an anticlerical crusade, and the psychiatrists of the Salpêtrière school participated in it enthusiastically. They did so for complex and multifaceted reasons: genuine intellectual conviction; their recent experience of clerically inspired meddling; their wish to demonstrate solidarity with the regime (all the more important because they had been consistently vilified by the liberals in the 1860s); and finally, their need for a pragmatic strategy of professional self-assertion. After all, their boundary dispute with the church, exacerbated by the ambiguous nature of the moral treatment and perpetuated by the terms of the 1838 Law, had never been resolved to their own satisfaction. Hitherto they had cautiously muted their anticlerical complaints, no doubt calculating that they had more to lose than to gain by provoking an outright confrontation with the church. But in the late 1870s and 1880s, the time was ripe for such a confrontation. Coincident with the effort, led by Jules Ferry in the national legislature, to wrest education from clerical control came the parallel effort, led by Bourneville at the Paris Municipal Council, to laicize the public hospitals.[135]

When the republicans came to power, fully two-thirds of the Paris public hospitals and hospices were employing religious sisters as nurses.[136] It was to destroy this near-monopoly that on Bourneville's initiative, the Municipal Council and the Assistance Publique jointly

which lists Bourneville as one of the delegates; Pierre Lévêque, "Libre Pensée et Socialisme (1889–1939)," *Mouvement social*, no. 57 (October-December 1966): 103.

[134] On the social background of Gambetta and his cohorts, see Theodore Zeldin, *France, 1848–1945*, Vol. 1 (Oxford: Clarendon Press, 1973), pp. 610–21. Zeldin includes Bert among the parvenus, but the latter's social class origins were considerably higher; see, e.g., J.-M. Mayeur, *Les débuts de la Troisième République* (Paris: Seuil, 1973), p. 100. Charcot's father was a Paris carriage maker of modest means; Bourneville's was a petit bourgeois property owner in the department of the Eure.

[135] Bourneville sometimes made the analogy explicitly; see, e.g., his remarks in the Chamber of Deputies, December 17, 1884, reprinted in the Bourneville pamphlet collection *Laïcisation de l'Assistance Publique: Discours et conférences, 1880–1890* (BN: R. 10960), 1884 pamphlet, p. 28.

[136] Speech of the minister of the interior in the Senate debate of December 19, 1885, reprinted in Bourneville, *Laïcisation*, 1886 pamphlet, p. 98.

established in 1878 the first "schools for laic nurses" designed to mold a new, self-conscious occupational group equipped, in Bourneville's words, with "professional knowledge." Located at Bicêtre and the Salpêtrière, the schools furnished models for those subsequently established at other hospitals in the capital and gave inspiration to similar laicizing efforts in the provinces.[137] In 1879, Bourneville embarked upon a full-scale battle, denouncing the nursing sisters publicly[138] and calling first for a severe reduction in the number of hospital chaplains and then for their total suppression. This program of complete hospital laicization was carried out in Paris in 1883, when the Municipal Council threatened to withhold funds from the hospitals unless they complied. The program was justified by its advocates on several grounds – as tangible support for the "scientific method" against the "metaphysical spirit"; as a safeguard for freedom of conscience; as an acknowledgment of the principle that in a republican regime "public welfare is different from Christian charity and is a national service which must be carried out in the civil sector."[139] Hospital laicization became synonymous with the name of the psychiatrist Bourneville, who even earned for his pains the antisemitic vituperations of the extreme right-wing propagandist Edouard Drumont. (The latter equated all anticlericalism with "Jewishness.") As Drumont put it in his bestselling tract *La France juive*, Bourneville had replaced the "compassionate and disinterested sisters" with salaried "harpies."[140]

Bourneville's laicization project expressed perfectly, and in a single gesture, both his support for the integrity of the republic – he depicted the nursing congregations in the hospitals as islands of self-government dangerously immune to administrative jurisdiction[141] – and his intention to prosecute openly the longstanding boundary dispute between medicine and the church. But what of an even more obvious project of the same sort, attacking the provision of the 1838 Law allowing clerical asylums to fulfill the official function of departmental asylums? The clerical asylums had shown no signs of withering away after

---

[137] See Dora B. Weiner, "The French Revolution, Napoleon and the Nursing Profession," *Bull. Hist. Med.* 46 (1972): 300; for the quotation, see *Laïcisation*, 1880 pamphlet, pp. 4–5; and on instances of provincial asylum laicization, ibid., 1884 pamphlet, p. 24.

[138] See, e.g., *Laïcisation*, 1880 pamphlet, pp. 10–23. The failings enumerated – medical ignorance, inattention to medical duties, insubordination to medical authority – are the familiar ones enumerated by early nineteenth-century physicians and psychiatrists; but Bourneville's tone is much more vitriolic.

[139] Louis Capéran, *Histoire de la laïcité républicaine: La laïcité en marche* (Paris: Nouvelles Editions Latines, 1961), pp. 86–93, quoting from speeches delivered at the Hôtel de Ville.

[140] Edouard Drumont, *La France juive: Essai d'histoire contemporaine*, 43d ed. (Paris: Marpon & Flammarion, 1886), Vol. 2, pp. 539, 541.

[141] *Laïcisation*, 1880 pamphlet, p. 19.

1838 but rather, once integrated within the national system, had held their own with remarkable constancy. As can be gleaned from official government figures for the years 1865, 1874, and 1889, there were sixteen of them, together accounting for between 17 percent and 18.5 percent of the lunatics interned at the expense of the departments.[142] From the republican anticlerical perspective, this arrangement was a kind of running sore – public monies annually diverted to the support of the religious congregations and to the undermining of scientific psychiatry. Predictably, Bourneville did try to rid the 1838 Law of this most odious provision; but here, uncharacteristically, his efforts failed.

The effort to reform the 1838 Law had been ongoing ever since the liberal outcry of the 1860s against arbitrary internments. The first bill for revision, coauthored by Gambetta and deposited in 1869, simply vanished with the fall of the Empire a year later.[143] In 1872 the effort at revision was resumed, again to no avail, by the physician and democratic-republican deputy Théophile Roussel. A decade later, the project was picked up by the government, which presented a bill to the Senate. The latter chose a commission, headed by Roussel, to study it. With a sense of fairness and a concern for the welfare of the insane which transcended the politics of anticlericalism, Roussel deliberately – and contrary to the wishes of the government – retained the clerical asylums that functioned in a public capacity. He believed that they were generally sound, had shown themselves conscientiously reponsive to the criticisms of the inspectors-general of lunatic houses, and were in any case certainly preferable to the lunatic quarters in public hospices on which many departments would have to rely if the clerical asylums were legally precluded.[144] It was 1887 before the Senate finally discussed and approved the Roussel commission's version of the bill and sent it on to the Chamber of Deputies.

Bourneville now entered the picture as rapporteur for the commission of the lower house appointed to study the bill, and as might be ex-

---

[142] The figures for 1865 and 1874 are found in Constans, Lunier, and Dumesnil, *Rapport général sur le service des aliénés en 1874*, Tables I.C. and I.E., pp. 506–7, 510–11. The clerical asylums are not explicitly tabulated, but, as can be inferred from the authors' comments (pp. 76, 78, 181), they form the vast majority (16 out of 18) of the institutions listed in Table I.C. as "asiles privés faisant fonction d'asiles publics." The figures for 1889 are found in Annexe No. 3934, *Annales de la Chambre des Deputés: Documents parlementaires*, Vol. 29, pp. 427–29.

[143] A. Mairet, *Le régime des aliénés: Révision de la loi de 1838* (Paris: Masson, 1914), p. 62. The onus of the Gambetta-Magnin bill was the ease with which the 1838 Law permitted incarceration in a lunatic asylum; ironically, in light of Gambetta's later pro-psychiatric stance, it placed much of the blame for this legislative defect on the lobby of *aliénistes* under the July Monarchy.

[144] Roussel explained himself publicly on this point; see *Annales du Sénat: Débats parlementaires*, Session extraordinaire de 1886, Vol. 17, pp. 254–55. For the legislative vicissitudes of the bill, see Mairet, *Régime des aliénés*, pp. 62–63.

pected, he displayed none of Roussel's judicious tolerance. The version of the bill prepared by the Bourneville commission was another two years in the making, and when it appeared it proposed to remove the clerical asylums from the national system on two grounds: They were medically inferior institutions, guided predominantly by considerations of profit (the various asylums run by the congregation of the Bon-Sauveur of Caen were branded as "veritable commercial exploitations"); and they had the lamentable effect of maintaining the entrenched clerical biases of certain regions of the country. It had become clear with time, said Bourneville, that contrary to the arguments of the legislators of the July Monarchy, the choice of whether to build a public asylum or use a clerical one was not dictated simply by the financial resources of a department. Many "rich departments" under the sway of the church had opted for treaties with clerical asylums, while many "relatively poor departments have . . . imposed sacrifices upon themselves in order to have their [public] departmental asylums."[145]

Despite the fact that on the insistence of Bourneville and others the chamber had in 1887 voted the revision of the 1838 Law an "urgent" matter,[146] the version of the bill prepared by the Bourneville commission faded into oblivion, never even becoming the subject of formal legislative debate. During the next decade three more bills for revision, all favoring abolition of the official status of clerical asylums, met similar fates, making various degrees of headway through the legislative process but ultimately languishing before that process was completed.[147]

How can we explain the failure of this particular anticlerical measure while others rode, with more or less ease, the crest of the anticlerical wave? The key factor is that removal of the clerical asylums from the public system was but a single clause in these bills for the revision of the 1838 Law. Other clauses typically included protection of the civil liberties of the allegedly insane by making the initial bureaucratic-cum-psychiatric decision for internment only provisional and subject to ratification by a local tribunal; special facilities for the criminally insane; and expanded facilities for the education of idiot children.[148] Such multifaceted bills could easily get caught in a political tug-of-war: The bureaucrats of the Ministry of the Interior, in particular, were prone to resent the partial loss of their prerogatives through the suggested new internment procedure.[149] The general congestion and self-paralysis that

---

[145] Annexe No. 3934, pp. 426, 429.
[146] *Annales de la Chambre des Deputés*, Session ordinaire de 1887, Vol. 3, pp. 485–86.
[147] See Mairet, *Régime des aliénés*, pp. 63, 93–106.
[148] See the comparison of the Roussel and Bourneville bills, Annexe No. 3934, Articles 1, 19, 38, pp. 434, 438, 441, and Bourneville's long discussion of the needs of idiot children, pp. 430–32.
[149] On this last point, I have adopted the interpretation of Nye, *Crime, Madness, and Politics*, p. 232.

characterized the legislative process under the early Third Republic no doubt also contributed to the repeated stillbirth of projects for the revision of the asylum law.[150] Bourneville had been, as ever, a stout-hearted defender of government anticlericalism, but even his immense energies could not, in this instance, overcome the forces for inertia in the parliamentary system.

A professional corps which had fostered the anticlerical aims of the regime with such impressive energy deserved to be its beneficiary. In the 1870s the one conspicuous lack in the professional accoutrements of the new specialty remained its exclusion from the university. Even after the professors of the faculty voted to establish a chair in mental maladies, the state evinced little eagerness to implement the measure. That vote was taken at the beginning of 1876, and since the republic of the "moral order" had not yet given way to the republic of positivist anticlericalism, a subversive air still clung to psychiatry in official circles. In the summer of 1876, the young left republican Georges Clemenceau forced the issue in the Chamber of Deputies. As a graduate of the Paris medical faculty (where he had found a sympathetic mentor in the Comtean professor Charles Robin, known as the "gendarme of materialism"), Clemenceau was an appropriate representative of that particular political-scientific mentality so important to the success of psychiatry at this historical moment. He called attention to the fact that no budgetary allotment had yet been made for the chair – which, continuing to adhere to the already defeated line of the psychiatrists, he called a "chair in insanity and diseases of the nervous system." Accompanied by applause and shouts of approbation from the benches of the left, and with supportive interventions by his fellow deputy Paul Bert, he stressed the importance of clinical instruction in psychiatry and pointed out that it required only the "miserable sum of 13,000 francs" – surely an insignificant amount for a chamber which had seen fit to retain in the budget "a sum of 241,000 francs for the theological faculties, even while agreeing that there were no students there." Clemenceau's budgetary motion passed; but two years later the chair, its title correctly shortened to the one voted by the faculty, had still not materialized, and an irate Clemenceau again raised the issue on the floor of the chamber.[151]

The government finally brought the chair into existence in 1878. But at the same time it sought to vitiate its impact by naming as its occupant a minor *aliéniste*, Benjamin Ball, a man in his early forties. "He appears to lack authority," sniffed the editorial in the *Gazette des hôpitaux*; he is "yet to win his spurs," said the one in the *Progrès*

---

[150] For this characterization, see Zeldin, *France, 1848–1945*, Vol. 1, pp. 584–86.

[151] *Journal officiel*, Vol. 213, July 29, 1876, pp. 5665–66; Vol. 230, November 23, 1878, pp. 10911–12. On Clemenceau as medical student, see David Robin Watson, *Georges Clemenceau: A Political Biography* (London: Eyre Methuen, 1974), pp. 21, 28–29.

médical, which also compared Ball to a "common rabbit" which the government had substituted for an elegant "wild hare" in concocting its "stew."[152] Ball was timid and pliable, as shown by lectures in which he dodged the question of the philosophical affiliations of psychiatry and was able "to please everyone."[153] Bourneville, never known for self-restraint, heaped sarcasm upon him, calling him the ministers' "favorite, their dearest Benjamin."[154] There was, in other words, little attempt on the part of the Salpêtrière school to hide its disappointment over the fact that Charcot had not been chosen for the chair.

Gambetta's assumption of the post of prime minister, however, led to an immediate rectification of this situation. Less than two months after the formation of the Gambetta cabinet, and on the recommendation of Paul Bert, Gambetta's new minister of public instruction and religion, a chair in the diseases of the nervous system, funded from the national budget, was created at the Paris Faculty of Medicine by a decree of January 2, 1882; another decree of the same date named Charcot as the first occupant of the chair. It was, as Charcot put it, the *consécration universitaire* that he had devoutly and publicly wished for since 1870.[155]

The logic, both political and personal, behind this move was obvious. Paul Bert was a thoroughgoing positivist in his own physiological researches; furthermore, he saw positive science as an intrinsic element of "a truly democratic conception of our social order" and was dedicated to revamping the "University of France, inheritor of Jesuitical methods [which] have reduced scientific instruction to sterility." His professional and intellectual kinship with Charcot was patent; both men were members of the Société de biologie and occasionally collaborated on presentations there.[156] And Bert used the science section of the *République française* to publicize Charcot's work on hysteria and the work of other members of the Salpêtrière school, as well as research on altered states of consciousness (dreams, somnambulism, suggestion), which had a compelling interest for both Bert and Charcot. Under Bert's direction, the science section also ratified the notion of a gradated continuum between sanity and madness and the appropriation by the field of psychiatry of the intermediate "neurotic" conditions.[157]

---

152 *Gazette des hôpitaux,* January 23, 1877, p. 65; *Progrès médical* 7 (1879): 401–2.

153 *Progrès médical* 7 (1879): 920.

154 Ibid. 5 (1877): 794.

155 *Journal officiel,* January 4, 1882, p. 34; Charcot, "Leçon d'ouverture," p. 315.

156 *Revues scientifiques,* Vol. 1, pp. 1, 4. For Charcot's membership in the Société de biologie, see Guillain, *Charcot,* p. 8. Bert served as president of the organization; see "Discours de M. Paul Bert, Président perpétuel de la Société de biologie" (Paris: Cusset, n.d.). An example of Bert–Charcot collaboration is described in "Sensations et perceptions colorées," *Revues scientifiques* (1879): 97–103.

157 Charcot's discoveries about hysteria are discussed in "Sensations et perceptions colorées" (1879), pp. 98–100; and "Folie et miracles" (1880), p. 333. The work of

The title of the new chair created for Charcot – "diseases of the nervous system" – was the most powerful ratification of that notion and that appropriation. The earlier chair, held by Ball and ultimately named "mental pathology and diseases of the brain (*encéphale*),"[158] reflected the "traditional" psychiatric focus on the varieties of full-fledged insanity. Charcot's chair, by contrast, mandated a focus on the *névroses*, those less severe varieties of mental pathology which, in its vote of 1876, the professors of the Paris faculty had deliberately sought to exclude from the purview of the psychiatric specialty. The academic appointment Gambetta bestowed on Charcot, then, officially sanctioned both the territorial expansion of psychiatry and the intensive study of hysteria.

In this expansion of their scientific domain, the psychiatrists probably found compensation for the somewhat disappointing outcome of their boundary dispute with the clerics. Bourneville had set in motion the process of dislodging the religious corporations from their traditional nursing function in the public asylums; but his failure to secure revision of the Law of 1838 meant that clerical asylums would continue to compete with public ones for patients interned at the public expense. The appropriation of hysterics and other *demi-fous* diminished the importance to psychiatrists of this incomplete monopoly over the asylum system, because by making thinkable and eventually feasible the office practice of psychiatry, it pointed the way beyond the asylum.

In the republican politics of anticlericalism, the refurbished and conceptually refined disease entity hysteria also played its part: The diagnosis became politicized. Because Charcot had laid down the immutable laws of hysterical seizure, the identifying marks of hysteria were now thought to be unambiguous. Furthermore, since the laws were universal, they applied to past eras as well as to the present. The drive to demonstrate the positivist universality of the hysterical syndrome led the Salpêtrière school to its investigations of male hysteria and also to its predilection for what the positivist physician and republican politician Emile Littré had dubbed "retrospective medicine" – that is, the reinterpretation of past phenomena, misunderstood in their own time, accord-

Charcot's student Charles Féré is described in "La famille névropathique" (1885), pp. 92–102. Altered states of consciousness are the subject of "Du somnambulisme provoqué" (1881), pp. 369–78; "Les rêves" (1884), pp. 11–18; and "La suggestion" (1885), pp. 182–88. Intermediate psychopathologies are affirmed in "Des maladies mentales qui lèsent la volonté et de la nature de celle-ci" (1884), p. 102. All citations refer to volumes of *Revues scientifiques*.

158 See the extract from the *Journal officiel*, April 24, 1877, giving the decree for the establishment of the chair, as reprinted in *Ann. m.-p.*, 5th ser., 17 (1877): 470.

ing to the categories of medical science.[159] What sorts of past phenomena were thus reinterpreted as hysterical? They were invariably those phenomena originally construed as religious in nature: demonic possessions, in which individuals become vessels of the malign forces of evil; and privileged intercessions of the forces of the divine, most notably mystical ecstasies.

These two types of religious experience translated with ease into aspects of the hysterical experience as defined and dissected by Charcot. When one period of the four-period *grande attaque* occurred in isolation or assumed a marked preponderance, four different "varieties" of hysteria resulted. Said the *maître:* "The second period will give birth to the demoniacal variety, the third period to the ecstatic variety." The second period of *grands mouvements* included those violent and hideous contortions – arms and legs flailing, mouth agape and tongue hanging out, pupils of the eyes darting in all directions, hair pulling, chest beating, ripping of clothing – which made the patient appear to be a "wild beast" possessed by the devil. (Plate 7.) The *attitudes passionnelles* of the third period included a bodily rigidity in which the patient could remain for hours or even days, motionless and absorbed in silent contemplation; this was the religious ecstasy of the mystics. Since the posture of "crucifixion" was part of the repertory of the third period, the patient might believe herself to be reliving Christ's ordeal on the cross. The ecstasy was nourished by the hallucinations which abounded during the third period. Visual hallucinations became beatific visions, aural ones became personal communications from the supernatural realm.[160]

The Salpêtrière school thus had the tools for its particular kind of "retrospective medicine." Charcot himself, always drawn to the iconography of hysterical attacks, produced, with one of his students, a volume in which paintings and engravings dating from the fifth through the eighteenth centuries and purporting to depict cases of demonic possession being cured or exorcised by saints were used to furnish, on the grounds of the postures represented, incontrovertible

---

[159] E. Littré, "Un fragment de médecine retrospective," *Philosophie positive* 5 (1869): 103–20. Charcot and Richer cite Littré's article in *Démoniaques dans l'art*, p. vi. While the label was new, the practice was not. Leuret, e.g., had argued for the existence of homicidal monomania by pointing out that under the names "lycanthropy" and "possession" it had been recognized in earlier eras; and Esquirol had cited him approvingly on this point. See Leuret, *Fragmens psychologiques* (Paris: Crochard, 1834), pp. 113–14; and Esquirol, "Mémoire sur la monomanie homicide" in *Maladies mentales*, Vol. 2, p. 834 n1. But what was a passing reference among the Esquirol circle became an intensively cultivated genre among the Salpêtrière school.

[160] *Démoniaques dans l'art*, pp. 91–109; p. 103 for the sentence quoted. This aspect of Charcot's teaching is also contained in a general textbook, A. Axenfeld and H. Huchard, *Traité des névroses*, 2d ed. (Paris: Germer Baillière, 1883), pp. 946–48.

proof that these demoniacs were really hysterics.[161] Beginning in 1883, Bourneville edited a series of nine volumes under the title "Bibliothèque Diabolique"; in each volume, the evidence in some early modern text describing instances of possession and ecstasy, usually in convents, was reinterpreted to prove that the religiously fervent individuals involved had been suffering from hysteria. Bourneville made similar arguments about contemporary instances of the same phenomena. For example, his brochure on a devout and highly publicized young Belgian woman who, in the 1870s, had begun to exhibit stigmata culminated in the chapter heading, "Louise Lateau is an hysteric: clinical demonstration." (Hemorrhages, it turned out, were yet another symptom of hysteria; and while the ruptured blood vessels were most often in the stomach, lungs, or uterus, they were sometimes just beneath the skin, giving rise to the putative stigmata.)[162]

Clearly this redefinition of the supernatural as the natural was secularizing in impact and in intent. The redefinition of the supernatural as the natural-*pathological* went further and had the effect of debunking religion; it was consonant with the frenetic crusade for laicization that marked republican politics in this era. Charcot's work in this genre tended to be forbearing and coolly objective: In the centuries before the "conquests" of modern science, "contemporaries could not help but give . . . [a] supernatural interpretation" to hysteria; but they had left written and pictorial records of "a hidden reason" beneath "that apparent incoherence," and so in spite of themselves had resoundingly affirmed Charcot's positivism.[163] Bourneville's tone was much more strident: Sixteenth-century clerics had "used the [hysterical] delirium" of a nun in the convent of Mons to "lend support to the doctrine of the Real Presence . . . and to the cult of saints"; at a time when Catholicism was being challenged by Calvinism, they "exploit[ed] public ignorance and superstition" in accordance with "all the self-interested traditions of Catholicism."[164] Even in his own day, Bourneville said, the politically retrograde wanted to "abuse the credulity of the people to inspire – or, on occasion, to impose – belief in miracles" and hence to keep the people intellectually undeveloped and politically subservient. To insist that Louise Lateau was a *stigmatisée* instead of an hysteric was to run afoul of the great joint tradition of science and the French Revolution.[165] Perhaps the epitome of the politicization of the hysteria

---

[161] Charcot and Richer, *Démoniaques dans l'art.*

[162] Bourneville, *Science et miracle: Louise Lateau, ou la stigmatisée belge,* 2d ed. (Paris: Delahaye, 1878), title of Ch. 3 and pp. 26–27.

[163] *Démoniaques dans l'art,* pp. vi, 109.

[164] Bourneville, preface to *La possession de Jeanne Fery, religieuse professe du couvent des soeurs noires de la ville de Mons* (Paris: Delahaye & Lecrosnier, 1886), pp. iv–v. This volume, originally published in 1584, is part of the Bibliothèque Diabolique.

[165] Bourneville, *Science et miracle,* p. 1.

diagnosis was a newspaper cartoon on Bourneville's 1883 campaign for the Chamber of Deputies: The "Radical Republican Socialist" candidate was depicted as chasing away the nursing sisters by hurling at them pamphlets from a shelf labeled "Bibliothèque Diabolique."[166] (Plate 6.)

The hysteric-demoniac equation – which can be regarded as the politicized hysteria diagnosis – was not just a jeu d'esprit of the Salpêtrière school but one of its constant preoccupations and an integral part of its public image. A visitor to Charcot's consulting room at the Salpêtrière in the mid-1880s saw "on the walls photographs, primitive Italian and Spanish paintings representing saints in prayer, ecstatics, convulsionaries, demoniacs – the great religious nervous-disease (*la grande névrose religieuse*), as they say at the asylum."[167] A peripheral member of the school, writing in 1880 in the *Revue des deux mondes* (the periodical that was de rigueur for educated Frenchmen), entitled an article designed to introduce Charcot's hysteria concept to those readers "The Demoniacs of Today." His central message was that "among the patients locked away in the Salpêtrière, there were many who would have been burned in former times, whose illness would have been taken for a crime. The study of this illness, in the present and in the past, is a sad and instructive chapter in the history of human thought."[168] So widely known was this aspect of Charcot's teaching that it made an appearance in Huysmans's antipositivist novel of the occult, *Là-Bas* (1891). Says the fictional character Des Hermies after reviewing the contentions of Salpêtrière psychiatry, "There remains this unanswerable question: is a woman possessed because she is hysterical, or is she hysterical because she is possessed? Only the Church can answer. Science cannot."[169]

Charcot's hysteria concept was a powerful interpretive device. The schematic point-by-point, gesture-by-gesture correspondences which it established enabled it to effect a smooth transformation of religious meaning into scientific meaning, a transformation which took on the air of a victory. This hysteria concept was a kind of capsule of the eighteenth-century Voltairean mentality, of the assault upon the clerical world view by the scientific world view. In the Salpêtrière literature on demoniacs, as in Axenfeld's 1865 lectures on Wier, the clerical world view was depicted as both intellectually and morally inferior: It was prerational and cruel, whereas medical science was rational and humane. (Thus it is not surprising to find that Bourneville reprinted Wier's writings on sorcery as part of the Bibliothèque Diabolique and

---

[166] AAP: Collection Bourneville, no.646, Liasse 2.

[167] Alphonse Daudet, "A la Salpêtrière," *Chronique médicale* 1 (January 1898): 15.

[168] Charles Richet, "Les démoniaques d'aujourd'hui," *Revue des deux mondes* 37 (1880): 340.

[169] J.-K. Huysmans, *Là-Bas*, trans. K. Wallace (New York: Dover, 1972), Ch. 9, p. 141.

that he saw the "retrospective medicine" of Charcot and his disciples as the lineal descendant of the historical essays of Axenfeld.)[170] Hysteria, then, implicitly contained within itself all the rudiments of an anticlerical campaign.

It is tempting to wonder whether the anticlerical potential of hysteria was apparent to Charcot before he embarked upon his investigations of the disease and whether that potential even influenced his choice of hysteria as a subject for research. Both speculations are certainly possible. After all, as early as the 1730s a French physician, Philippe Hecquet, had shocked the clergy by asserting that the convulsions then wracking certain Parisian Jansenists – as well as the alleged demonic possession of the Ursuline nuns of Loudun and the "trembling" of pious Huguenots in the Cevennes during the seventeenth century – were not miraculous but hysterical in nature.[171] Charcot was acquainted with Hecquet's text,[172] whose argument had been rehearsed even in nonmedical books of the early nineteenth century.[173] Indeed, so commonplace does the association seem to have been between hysteria and extreme forms of religious experience that in eighteenth-century England John Wesley was moved to volunteer a preemptive assessment that his Methodist converts beset by uncontrollable paroxysms were *not* hysterical – that he "had seen many hysterical fits . . ., but that none were like these."[174] The association could be made without fanfare in mid-nineteenth-century France. In 1848, a woman in the department of the Bas-Rhin attracted public attention by the allegedly miraculous visions which had enabled her to predict the revolutionary events of that February; the government-appointed cantonal physician pronounced her an hysteric.[175] In asserting the hysteric-demoniac equation, Charcot and his school drew upon an already existing tradition. Their innovation was to prove the equation with positivist rigor and to publicize it on a wide scale.

The popularization of the hysteria diagnosis and related "nervous" conditions served the anticlerical cause in a second, less explicit way. It helped to sever the close traditional bond between women and priests, which nineteenth-century French anticlerical republicans had always

[170] Jean Wier, *Histoires, disputes et discours*, 2 vols. (Paris: Bureaux des Progrès médical/Delahaye & Lecrosnier, 1885); and Bourneville's preface, Vol. 1, pp. i–ii.

[171] Philippe Hecquet, *Naturalisme des convulsions dans les maladies de l'épidémie convulsionnaire* (Soleure, 1733), pp. 8, 176, 193–94.

[172] Charcot, *Leçons sur maladies du système nerveux*, Vol. 1, pp. 303–4, 336–37.

[173] See, e.g., Henri Grégoire, *Histoire des sectes religieuses*, new ed., Vol. 2 (Paris: Baudouin, 1828), pp. 140–43.

[174] Robert Southey, *The Life of Wesley and the Rise and Progress of Methodism* (New York: Duyckinck, 1820), p. 123.

[175] "Hallucinations religieuses dans un état d'extase. Prédictions," *Ann. m.-p.*, 1st ser., 12 (1848): 367–73.

found so odious,[176] and to replace it with a dependency on the medical profession. "Women must belong to science, or else they will belong to the church," the republican politician Jules Ferry had warned in a speech of 1870.[177] Ferry was arguing for the expansion of public secular education for girls, which would purge their minds of dogma and superstition and insure that, as mothers, they would raise broods of little republican citizens. But another way to make women "belong to science" was to habituate them to thinking of their bouts of emotional distress as medical conditions falling within the purview of the physician, rather than as moral failings or spiritual crises requiring the guidance of the priest.

The novel *Madame Bovary* (1857), whose title character was widely regarded by nineteenth-century critics as an hysteric (although Flaubert gives no precise name to her malaise),[178] illustrates that, at midcentury, Frenchwomen typically looked to two sources of relief from such vague troubles as pervasive unhappiness, light-headedness, and heart palpitations. Emma Bovary's maid Félicité likens her mistress's condition to that of a woman she had known in another town who was "so sad, so sad, that to see her standing on the threshold of her house, she looked like a winding-sheet spread out before the door." The illness (*mal*) of this woman, Félicité continues, was "a kind of fog that she had in her head, and the doctors could do nothing about it, neither could the priest."[179] As Emma's own condition worsens, the same double counsel is sought: Her husband summons medical personnel to her bed, and she turns to the local priest. Psychiatrists of the period noted as well that women suffering from this indefinite and unnamed *mal* typically had recourse to both "their confessors and their physicians."[180] But as the medicalization of emotional life progressed, and the label "hysteria" (or "neurasthenia") became more firmly affixed to this female "fog in the head," the choice of counselor became clearer – and the new

---

[176] The seminal text in this regard is Jules Michelet's *Le prêtre, la femme et la famille* (1845), reprinted eight times before 1875. See the astute discussion of this theme by Theodore Zeldin, "The Conflict of Moralities: Confession, Sin and Pleasure in the Nineteenth Century," in Zeldin, ed., *Conflicts in French Society: Anticlericalism, Education and Morals in the Nineteenth Century* (London: Allen & Unwin, 1970), pp. 13–50.

[177] Quoted in Louis Legrand, *L'influence du positivisme dans l'oeuvre scolaire de Jules Ferry* (Paris: Rivière, 1961), p. 118.

[178] On Madame Bovary as hysteric, see the 1857 review of the novel by Charles Baudelaire in his *Oeuvres complètes*, Vol. 4 (Paris: Conard, 1925), p. 404; and Richet, "Démoniaques d'aujourd'hui," pp. 345–49. Flaubert, conversant with medical terminology both as the son of a physician and as a victim of convulsive seizures, probably agreed with this assessment, for he regarded Baudelaire's as the only satisfactory review of his novel; see Francis Steegmuller, *Flaubert and Madame Bovary: A Double Portrait*, revised ed. (Chicago: University of Chicago Press, 1977), p. 339.

[179] *Madame Bovary*, trans. P. de Man (New York: W. W. Norton, 1965), p. 78.

[180] See Henri Huchard, "Caractère, moeurs, état mental des hystériques," *Archives de neurologie* 3 (1882): 194, quoting here from B.-A. Morel's *Etudes cliniques* (1852).

clarity no doubt pleased psychiatrists and leaders of the early Third Republic alike. The anticlerical republican politician Jules Simon even tried to help matters along by coauthoring a guidebook for mothers on the rearing of female children. He stressed the importance of regular medical attention (and the avoidance of "charlatans") and the young girl's vulnerability to *malaises nerveux*.[181]

The approach to hysteria as an instrument of anticlericalism that has been pursued here is not intended to exhaust all the functions and meanings which gave that diagnostic category such prominence in France at the turn of the century. It seems clear, for example, that the intensive cultivation of the diagnosis also served as an instrument in the politics of gender – a view of the matter held, interestingly enough, by members of the nascent French feminist movement of the day. They discerned in the diagnosis a new form of male domination, finding suspect Charcot's disproportionate concern with the meticulous clinical description of hysteria and speaking caustically of his "sort of vivisection of women under the pretext of studying a disease for which he knows neither the cause nor the treatment."[182]

Nor, even more obviously, do the anticlerical uses of hysteria in France explain its contemporaneous thriving in countries where crusades against the church were not a distinctive feature of national politics. In the absence of detailed research about the epidemiology of hysteria elsewhere and about the stake that different national medical professions may have had in the diagnosis, I can only reiterate and expand upon the suggestion made at the opening of this chapter that the salience of hysteria in the French psychiatric community was likely a seminal factor. Association with the name of Charcot, one of the world's foremost neuropsychiatrists whose initial reputation had been based on sober and solid studies in pathological anatomy, made hysteria "scientifically respectable," writes a historian of the fin-de-siècle German medical scene.[183] Indeed, Charcot had an international audience not only at his Salpêtrière lectures but also among the medical reading public. His lectures on the diseases of the nervous system, which Bourneville began to publish in France in 1872, started appearing in translation in Germany as early as 1874 and in Britain and America in 1881. A later volume of these lectures, translated by Sigmund Freud – and, unlike its French counterpart, bearing the word "hysteria" in the title – was published simultaneously in both Leipzig and

---

[181] See Jules Simon and Gustave Simon, *La femme du vingtième siècle*, 21st ed. (Paris: Calmann Lévy, 1892), pp. 353, 360.

[182] C. R. [Mme C. Renooz], "Charcot dévoilé," *Revue scientifique des femmes* 1 (1888): esp. 245. The article also seeks to expose Charcot's hostile and condescending attitude toward women entering the medical profession.

[183] Hannah S. Decker, *Freud in Germany: Revolution and Reaction in Science, 1893–1907* (New York: International Universities Press, 1977), p. 78.

Vienna, thus encouraging its greater diffusion throughout the German-speaking medical world.[184] In a brief confidential letter addressed to an unnamed cabinet minister, Bourneville requested that Charcot be appointed to the Legion of Honor in time for the 1889 Exposition, citing among the credentials of the *maître* the numerous foreign translations of his works. In addition to the German ones prepared "a long while ago" – "an exceptional thing" in this time of intense Franco-German rivalry – and those translated into English, were their "Russian, Hungarian, Italian and Spanish" counterparts.[185] Through such translations Charcot's "schemas," the strikingly simple representations of pathological nervous conditions that he abstracted from the accumulated data of clinical experience, "educated all the physicians of Europe"; and the particular constellation of scientific, professional, and political forces that had succeeded in making hysteria *la question palpitante du jour* in France could readily influence the medical culture of other countries.[186]

Michel Foucault has seen the efflorescence of hysteria – the "hysterization of women's bodies," as he calls it – as one of four great strategies by which modern society at once increased its knowledge of human sexuality and developed a meta-structure of power over it.[187] In our own discussion, in which the sexual aspects of hysteria have been largely ignored,[188] the accumulation of scientific knowledge about hysteria has also been linked to power, but power with a different aim and power whose institutional agencies are more explicitly and narrowly defined: the power of a profession, in collaboration with a like-minded political regime, to further its interests at the expense of the clergy; and conversely, the power of that political regime, ideologically aided and enhanced by science, to secularize French society, to remove from the nation-state the rival authority of the church. For certainly the "human sciences" – not only Salpêtrière psychiatry but also Durkheimian soci-

---

[184] See translator's preface in Charcot, *Neue Vorlesungen über die Krankheiten des Nervensystems in besondere über Hysterie*, trans. S. Freud (Leipzig & Vienna: Toeplitz & Deuticke, 1886), p. iv. The volume of 1874, translated by Dr. B. Fetzer, was published in Stuttgart.

[185] AN: F^{17} 20385, Charcot: Dossier de carrière, letter of July 5, 1889.

[186] On the "schemas" and their pan-European dissemination, see Pierre Janet, "J.-M. Charcot, son oeuvre psychologique," *Revue philosophique* 39 (1895): 577. Hysteria is called the "question palpitante" in Pierre Giffard, *Les grands bazars* (Paris: Havard, 1882), p. 157.

[187] Michel Foucault, *The History of Sexuality, Volume I: An Introduction*, trans. R. Hurley (New York: Vintage, 1978), pp. 103–5.

[188] They make a complicated story: the role of sexuality in hysteria was alternately accentuated and deemphasized several times during the nineteenth century before it was given pride of place in the Freudian concept of hysteria. In Charcot's hysteria concept, there is a constant undercurrent of sexuality – for example, in the eroticism of certain *attitudes passionnelles* of the third period – but it is never canalized into theory.

ology – were pressed, willingly, into the service of the early Third Republic in its efforts at national integration. Psychiatry was used first, and largely for purposes of destroying remaining clerical strongholds; sociology came later, and was used for reconstruction, the creation of a "civic and laic morality" to replace the discarded religious morality of Catholicism. If, at the fin de siècle, more Frenchwomen than ever fell ill with a condition called hysteria, their illness was in part a political construction.

Conclusion

In the priest, as in the psychiatrist (*aliéniste*), there is always something of the examining magistrate.

— Marcel Proust

THIS wry observation of Proust's narrator might be read as an epitome of the historical development traced in this book. By the opening of the twentieth century, the psychiatrist, an insecure newcomer not long before, had been tacitly accepted as a full-fledged member of the company of professional men. He appears here flanked by the cleric and the judge, the two traditional authority figures with whom he had waged his most strenuous nineteenth-century boundary disputes in France, and with whom he now coexisted in a relationship of fundamental parity.

But Proust is primarily interested in highlighting a common characteristic that links the three authorities; and that is relevant to us as well. He points to a certain kind of professional prying, a quest for the truth not in what individuals say about themselves, but in what they can be made to reveal unintentionally. Indeed the passage that culminates in the quotation above sounds uncannily Foucauldian in its emphasis on the *visual* modality of such truth seeking. The narrator is seated beside the deathbed of his grandmother opposite a distant relative who belongs to a religious order. He notices that the cleric has "joined his hands before his face like a man absorbed in a painful meditation. . . . I saw that he had left a tiny space between his fingers. And at the moment when I turned my gaze away from him, I perceived his sharp eye (*oeil aigu*), which had been taking advantage of the screen provided by his hands in order to observe if my grief were sincere."[1]

In this book, the similarly "sharp-eyed" psychiatrist, whose classification of diseases by their visible signs is his stock in trade and his claim to

---

[1] Marcel Proust, *Le côté des Guermantes* in *A la recherche du temps perdu*, Vol. 2 (Paris: Gallimard-Pléiade, 1954), p. 339.

378

power, has been a familiar figure. Certainly the description fits Charcot, who, it will be remembered, noted with pleasure the willingness of his outpatients to be "minutely and curiously observed."[2] It was his "talent for observation," the "minutiae of his descriptions," and the "stubbornness with which he placed the smallest detail under scrutiny" that admiring contemporaries identified as "the method of Charcot."[3] Thus when doubts were expressed late in his career about the apparent omnipresence of hysteria, Charcot simply and haughtily dismissed any suggestion that his observations or the labels he affixed to them might be faulty. "To those who would reproach me for talking about hysteria all the time, I will reply – even before offering a more complete explanation – with this line from Molière. 'I say the same thing because it always is the same thing.' I declare it, and nothing more."[4]

If the bid for power through psychiatric knowledge has seemed more blatant in Charcot than in his early nineteenth-century predecessors, some of that difference must be ascribed to a difference in the tone of the historical era itself. From the beginning the psychiatric enterprise in France had required contact with the government, and from the 1820s there had been some contact with the general public as well. But by the fin de siècle, the political and public world that French psychiatrists entered was open, democratic, and raucous. Mass movements had begun to flourish under the aegis of republicanism and universal suffrage; the press had expanded massively; science had been popularized on an unprecedented scale. Hence features of French psychiatry already evident in the days of Pinel and Esquirol were greatly accentuated under the early Third Republic, and in some cases even swept up in a kind of carnival atmosphere. The theatrical elements of the moral treatment, confined within the walls of a hospice or sanatorium by Pinel and Esquirol, became the theatricality of Charcot's Friday lessons, where patients in nervous crisis and hypnotic trance were exhibited before an avid audience including artists and litterateurs as well as physicians. When Charcot lectured on tremors, for example, the afflicted patients appeared wearing headdresses decorated with long plumes, whose distinctive, feathery vibrations illustrated the different varieties of the pathology.[5] Charcot's supporters welcomed the weekly spectacles, but his detractors explicitly mocked their crude theatricality, speaking of the

---

[2] Charcot, "Leçon d'ouverture," *Progrès médical* 10 (April 29, 1882): 316. Quoted in Chapter 9 of this volume.

[3] See Pierre Janet, "J.-M. Charcot, son oeuvre psychologique," *Revue philosophique* 39 (1895): 572.

[4] Charcot, "La foi qui guérit," *Revue hebdomadaire*, December 3, 1892: 112–32, quotation on p. 123.

[5] Charles Féré, "J.-M. Charcot et son oeuvre," *Revue des deux mondes* 122 (1894): 415.

"Salpêtriens . . . climbing on stage like mountebanks, striking the gong and the tom-tom."[6]

Similarly, the interest of the early psychiatrists in the physiognomy of insanity – Esquirol's personal collection of plaster casts of the faces of lunatics; his commission to the artist Gabriel to sketch the inmates of the Paris asylums (Plate 2); Georget's parallel commission to the painter Géricault to depict the monomaniacs (Plate 3) – became under the supervision of Charcot, and with the benefit of the new technology of the camera, a giant and often grotesque archive of the iconography of nervous illness, extending now to bodily postures as well as to facial expressions, and much of it published (Plates 7, 8). The polite respect accorded Pinel and especially the well-born Esquirol as psychiatric patrons was transformed, in a national climate of infatuation with science, into Charcot's celebrity status. And finally, the government policy with which psychiatry naturally affiliated itself was not, as under the July Monarchy, a genteel campaign in a well-managed legislature chosen by a severely restricted suffrage, but a popular-based anticlerical crusade stirring up raw emotion. In short, a psychiatry that had always gravitated toward the state now allowed its style to be shaped by a new politics and a new public life; and that broad style, clashing with the expected sobriety of scientific endeavor, underscored its extra-scientific involvements.

Yet another feature of the Salpêtrière school tends to place in a suspicious light the power that accrued to Charcot as "sharp-eyed" master classifier – the relative attention given to classification and to therapy. So frequently did contemporaries level the charge that Charcot was far more absorbed in labeling than in treating his patients that his students regularly mentioned and responded to that charge in the spate of commemorative essays that appeared after his death in 1893. How many times, exclaimed one student, had he found himself in the middle of a discussion of Charcot's work when the gauntlet was thrown down by the remark, "You cultivate hysteria at the Salpêtrière, you don't cure it."[7]

But if he conspicuously deemphasized therapy, saying little about it in either his teaching or his scientific writings,[8] Charcot could not ignore it. His most sustained discussion of that subject, a quasi-popular

---

[6] See Antoine Imbert-Gourbeyre, *La stigmatisation, l'extase divine et les miracles de Lourdes: Réponse aux libres-penseurs,* 2d ed., 2 vols. (Clermont-Ferrand: Bellet, 1898), Vol. 1, pp. viii–ix. The gong and tom-tom were used to produce a startling noise that would induce catalepsy in hypnotized patients.

[7] Gilles de la Tourette, "Le Professeur J.-M. Charcot," *Revue hebdomadaire* 15 (1893): 616. See also Levillain, "Charcot et l'école de la Salpêtrière," *Revue encyclopédique* (1894), p. 109; and Féré, "Charcot," p. 422.

[8] Féré, "Charcot," p. 422.

article on faith healing that appeared only eight months before his death, is of special interest here. It brings our narrative full circle, for it shows Charcot picking up some of the oldest strands of thought in the century-long development of psychiatry in France. The article, like so much of the activity of the Salpêtrière school, was a response to religious life in France, in this case the flourishing miracle cult at Lourdes. The novelist Emile Zola, an aggressive partisan of the positivist method, had visited Lourdes in 1892 during the annual national pilgrimage and had contributed to an English periodical his impressions of the miraculous cures occurring at the Marian shrine there. They were, Zola said, an expression of that human "hankering after the lie," that need to cling to hope in the face of despair that forms the "foundation of all religions." The same periodical now solicited Charcot's views on this timely subject. First published in England, the resulting article appeared in quick succession in two French journals, one for the general educated public and the other for medical specialists.[9]

Following the model set by his naturalistic appropriation of religious ecstasy and demonic possession, Charcot sought to explain the cures at Lourdes in rational scientific terms. But while retrospective diagnoses of mystics and demoniacs as hysterical had unmasked those supposedly religious experiences and given the psychiatric practitioner a critical distance from them, Charcot's interpretation of miracle cures had a very different outcome. To be sure, the same positivist apparatus was brought to bear: "The therapeutic miracle has its determinism, and the laws which preside over its genesis and evolution are beginning to be known." But more gentle in his assessment than Zola, Charcot cast no aspersions on these cures, even while noting their often transitory nature. Rather, he frankly admitted that he had long been emulating them, seeking to "fathom, insofar as possible, the mechanism of their production in order to make use of its power." The cures worked, he had learned, within certain fixed parameters: only on patients who were trusting, credulous, and "as we say today, suggestible," and only on those diseases which exploited the "power that the mind possesses over the body."

With these remarks, then, Charcot brings us back to that therapeutics of psychophysiological reciprocity first codified by the Idéologues, or more accurately, back even further to the "medicine of the imagination" to which eighteenth-century French physicians lent habitual but

---

[9] See n. 4. Charcot refers to the involvement of Zola, called only "un littérateur célèbre," in "Foi qui guérit," p. 112. Zola's 1892 comments on his trip to Lourdes are quoted in the preface to the English translation of his novel *Lourdes,* trans. E. A. Vizetelly (Chicago & New York: F. Tennyson Neely, 1894), pp. v–vi. In addition to appearing in the *Revue hebdomadaire,* Charcot's article appeared in the *Archives de neurologie* 25 (1893): 72–87.

only informal credence. For unlike the Idéologues (and their early nineteenth-century psychiatric successors), whose formulations confidently
integrated this psychosomatic "mechanism" into science, Charcot depicted it as a valid part of the medical *art* that nonetheless still largely
eluded the rigors of medical *science*. "Do we know everything about
this supernatural domain which contributes in the highest degree to
faith healing and whose frontiers every day recede as a result of scientific attainments? Certainly not." And he joined to this acknowledgment Hamlet's comment that "there are more things in heaven and
earth . . . than are dreamt of in your philosophy."[10] Charcot has afforded us an unaccustomed, poignant glimpse of himself here; he appears without the armor of his positivist certainties, humble in the face
of the unknown. So anomalous was this public posture for Charcot
that one of his students called the article on faith healing "curious."[11]
But another, recognizing the article as an expression of some of Charcot's typical if little-known attitudes, declared his mentor "an empiric
in therapeutics" – that is, a healer with a hint of the charlatan, making
use of improvised, unscientific techniques.[12]

Unexpectedly and obliquely, then, the theme of consolation – of that
once religious and now secular balm which operates on the troubled
spirit – finds its way into the work of the last of the great nineteenth-
century French psychiatrists, linking him more firmly than would initially appear to the therapeutic tradition of Pinel and Esquirol. Charcot
usually took pains to play down, perhaps even to conceal this theme; yet
his 1892 article on faith healing had announced it as a constant in his
medical practice. The clearest appreciation of this aspect of Charcot's
work and public persona was given by the novelist Jules Claretie, who
had regularly attended Charcot's clinical lessons in the 1880s and 1890s[13]
and who, as a venerable member of the Académie française, commemo-
rated the tenth anniversary of Charcot's death in an essay entitled
"Charcot the Consoler." With a decade's hindsight, the 1892 article on
faith healing seemed to Claretie the most salient item in Charcot's corpus, and the Salpêtrière master now appeared as the leader of a vast
surrogate religion. He was "the embodiment or personification of our
epoch. The century of neurotics found its physician in him. In those
years just passed, dedicated to pessimism, all neurasthenic Paris paid

---

[10] Charcot, "Foi qui guérit," pp. 112–14, 131–32.
[11] Janet, "Charcot," p. 600.
[12] Féré, "Charcot," p. 422. As Féré explains his use of the term *empirique*, Charcot the
therapist (as opposed to Charcot the scientific researcher) "set little store by the
deductions of the laboratory, preferring remedies that had proved themselves in
human medicine."
[13] He even appears among the acolytes surrounding Charcot in Brouillet's famous painting; see Levillain, "Charcot et l'école," p. 113 (picture caption).

tribute to this great Parisian, . . . this apostle. . . . They came to the Salpêtrière as to a novena."[14]

This book has shown how French psychiatry developed from the amalgamation of several rather disparate elements: a bureaucratic function first sketched out by enlightened absolutist administrators and, given the continuity of bureaucratic forms in France, realized during the nineteenth century; the appropriation of a priestly function by a new medical specialist equipped initially with a populist ideology; and the elaboration of the scientific function of classifying phenomena. Perhaps even more far-reaching than the social repercussions of psychiatry's incarcerative institutions have been the social and cultural consequences of the interpretive framework provided by its classifications. Taken by psychiatrists into the courts of law, where it could transform criminality into monomania; into the doctor's private consulting room, where it might turn spiritual distress into mild hysteria; and even to the cemetery, where it tried to eradicate the sin of suicide and replace it with a morally neutral mental disease,[15] this interpetive framework also entered ordinary, nonscientific discourse. If Tocqueville saw his total absorption in the writing of *Democracy in America* as a monomania, so Flaubert and Mallarmé experienced their writing blocks as bringing them to the verge of hysteria, and the young Barrès perceived his negative attitude toward life as a symptom of neurasthenia[16] – instances of an importation of psychopathological categories into the lay description of feeling states that would, in the twentieth century, be intensified by the popularity of psychoanalysis.

Full discussion of the ramifications of this mode of psychiatric interpretation would be beyond the scope of this study. But it should be apparent that the power to classify, claimed by and granted to the psychiatrist, is one of the most basic, indeed primordial of social powers. Before he became himself a master classifier, Sigmund Freud implicitly recognized this fact through his encounter with Charcot. He reported that Charcot, "not a reflective man [but] a man who sees," had touted the unparalleled satisfaction of the mental labor he called "practising nosography" and that he made the rounds of the Salpêtrière wards to survey his own handiwork, the "clinical facts for the greater part named

---

[14] Jules Claretie, "Charcot, le consolateur," *Annales politiques et littéraires* 21 (September 20, 1903), pp. 179–80.

[15] See, e.g., Delasiauve, "Suicide et sépulture chrétienne," *J. de med. ment.* 8 (1868): 376–78.

[16] For Tocqueville, see Chapter 5 of this volume. For Flaubert, see the letter to Louise Colet of April 8, 1852 in *Oeuvres complètes de Gustave Flaubert*, Vol. 2 (Paris: Club de l'Honnête Homme, 1974), p. 179. For Mallarmé, see the letter to Henri Cazalis of February 18, 1869 in Stéphane Mallarmé, *Correspondance*, Vol. 1 (Paris: Gallimard, 1959), p. 301. For Barrès, see the journal entry of "décembre 1896," *Mes cahiers* in *L'oeuvre de Maurice Barrès*, Vol. 13 (Paris: Club de l'Honnête Homme, 1968), p. 73.

and defined by him." The dominion of the great, sharp-eyed French psychiatrist reminded Freud of nothing less than "the myth of Adam, who must have experienced in its most perfect form that intellectual delight so highly praised by Charcot, when God led before him the creatures of Paradise to be named and grouped."[17]

---

[17] "Charcot" (1893), trans. J. Bernays, in Sigmund Freud, *Collected Papers*, Vol. 1 (London: Hogarth Press, 1924), p. 11; and trans. J. Strachey in *Standard Edition of the Complete Psychological Works of Sigmund Freud*, Vol. 3, pp. 12–13. I have combined elements from both translations.

Appendix

The Esquirol circle: core membership
(arranged by order of birth)

Note about sources: Except where otherwise indicated, information about paternal occupation has been taken from birth certificates. Information about dates of formal attachment to the Salpêtrière as a salaried intern (*élève*) comes from AAP: Salpêtrière, Registres d'appointements, 1814–25 (2K1-2K12); these *registres* begin with the year 1814 and the one for 1821 (2K8) is missing from the holdings of the Archives. Information for which no source is identified comes from Semelaigne, *Pionniers*, Vol. 1.

1. DELAYE (Jean-Baptiste)
    b. August 16, 1789 in Saint Clement les Mâcon, a parish bordering on the town of Mâcon (Saône-et-Loire)
    Father's occupation: *maître cordonnier* (master shoemaker)
    Baptismal certificate: Archives départementales de Saône-et-Loire
    Initial enrollment at Paris Faculty of Medicine: 1815 (AN: AJ^{16} 6762 no. 224)
    Thèse de médecine (Paris): 1824
    Attached to Salpêtrière as *élève en 2ème classe:* 1819–20; as *élève en 1re classe:* 1822–23
    First full-time post: chief physician of the lunatic service, hospice de la Grave, Toulouse, c. 1828

2. RECH (André-Pamphlye-*Hippolyte*)
    b. May 31, 1793, Montpellier
    Father's occupation: *avocat* (lawyer)
    Birth certificate: Archives municipales de Montpellier (paternal occupation not given)
    Thèse de médecine (Montpellier): 1814
    First full-time post: chief physician of the lunatic quarters, Hôpital Saint-Eloi, Montpellier, 1822
    Source: L. Dulieu, "Le Professeur Rech," *Monspeliensis Hippocrates,* no. 33 (1966).

3. FALRET (Jean-Pierre)
    b. 7 floréal Year II (May 26, 1794), Marcilhac-sur-Célé (Lot)
    Father's occupation: *propriétaire* (property owner)

Birth certificate: Mairie de Marcilhac-sur-Célé
Initial enrollment at Paris Faculty of Medicine: 1811; first four
inscriptions taken at Montpellier Faculty of Medicine (AN: AJ[16]
6757 no. 296)
Thèse de médecine (Paris): 1819
Attached to Salpêtrière as *élève:* 1815
First full-time post: founded *maison de santé* for the insane at
Vanves, near Paris, with Félix Voisin in 1822

4.   VOISIN (Félix)
     b. 9 brumaire Year III (November 19, 1794), Le Mans
     Father's occupation: *tapissier* (tapestry- or rug-maker, upholsterer)
     Birth certificate: Mairie du Mans
     Initial enrollment at Paris Faculty of Medicine: 1815 (AN: AJ[16] 6759
     no. 141)
     Thèse de médecine (Paris): 1819
     First full-time post: founded *maison de santé* for the insane at
     Vanves, near Paris, with Jean-Pierre Falret in 1822

5.   PINEL (Scipion)
     b. 2 germinal Year III (March 22, 1795), Paris
     Father's occupation: physician (father was Philippe Pinel)
     Initial enrollment at Paris Faculty of Medicine: 1813 (AN: AJ[16] 6759
     no. 295)
     Thèse de médecine (Paris): 1819
     Attached to Salpêtrière as "surveillant des aliénés sous les ordres
     de M. Esquirol": 1820 (AAP: Procès-verbaux du Conseil général
     des hospices civils de Paris, Liasse 65)

6.   GEORGET (Etienne-Jean)
     b. 20 germinal Year III (April 9, 1795), Vernou-sur-Brienne (Indre-
     et-Loire)
     Father's occupation: *marchand meunier* (miller and dealer in grain),
     but oral tradition depicted him as a poor *cultivateur* or peasant
     farmer (René Semelaigne, *Les grands aliénistes français* [Paris: Stein-
     heil, 1894])
     Birth certificate: Mairie de Vernou-sur-Brienne
     Initial enrollment at Paris Faculty of Medicine: 1813 (AN: AJ[16] 6760
     no. 31)
     Thèse de médecine (Paris): 1820
     Attached to Salpêtrière as *élève:* 1817–19
     First full-time post: *médecin surveillant* at Esquirol's *maison de santé*
     in Ivry

7.   TRÉLAT (Ulysse)
     b. 22 brumaire Year IV (November 13, 1795), Montargis (Loiret)
     Father's occupation: *notaire publique* (notary)

Birth certificate: Mairie de Montargis
Initial enrollment at Paris Faculty of Medicine: 1813 (AN: AJ^{16} 6761 no. 90)
Thèse de médecine (Paris): 1821
First full-time post: physician of the lunatic quarters, Salpêtrière, 1840 (obtained by *concours*)
Between receiving his medical degree and 1840, Trélat abandoned his medical career for political activism.

8.   MITIVIÉ (Jean-Etienne-Furmance)
b. 11 brumaire Year V (November 1, 1796), Castres (Tarn)
Father's occupation: *négociant* (wholesale merchant)
Birth certificate: Archives municipales de Castres
Thèse de médecine (Paris): 1820
Attached to Salpêtrière as *élève:* 1815
First full-time post: codirector with Esquirol (his uncle) of *maison de santé* in Ivry, 1824
Source: Ch. Loiseau, "Eloge de J.-E. Mitivié," *Ann m.-p.*, 5th ser., Vol. 8 (1872).

9.   CHAMBEYRON (Antoine-Marie)
b. October 9, 1797, Lyon
Father's occupation: *boulanger* (baker)
Birth certificate: Archives municipales de Lyon
Initial enrollment at Paris Faculty of Medicine: 1818 or 1819 (AN: AJ^{16} 6428 records Chambeyron's second *inscription*, taken in the first trimester of 1819)
Attached to Salpêtrière as *élève en chirurgie:* 1823–June 1825; as *élève de médecine de la 1re classe:* June 1825
First full-time post: Chief physician at the asile Saint-Méen at Rennes, 1835

10.   BRIERRE DE BOISMONT (Alexandre-Jacques-François)
The family name was officially changed from "Brierre" to "Brierre de Boismont" in 1863, but the physician had used the latter throughout his career
b. 27 vendémiaire Year VI (October 22, 1797), Rouen
Father's occupation: *vivant de son revenu* (living on his income)
Birth certificate: Archives municipales de Rouen
Initial enrollment at Paris Faculty of Medicine: 1821; first two *inscriptions* taken at Rouen (AN: AJ^{16} 6763 no. 201)
Thèse de médecine (Paris): 1825
Frequented service of Pariset at the Salpêtrière after 1825; met students of Esquirol there and was integrated into the circle through the Sunday luncheons
First full-time post: resident physician at the *maison de santé* Sainte-Colombe in Paris, 1825

11. LEURET (François)
     b. 10 nivôse Year VI (December 30, 1797), Nancy
     Father's occupation: *boulanger* (baker)
     Birth certificate: Etat-Civil, Ville de Nancy
     Initial enrollment at Paris Faculty of Medicine: 1816; last ten *in-scriptions* taken at Nancy (AN: AJ[16] 6763 no. 76)
     Thèse de médecine (Paris): 1826
     First full-time post: physician at Esquirol's *maison de santé* in Ivry, c. 1828

12. CALMEIL (Louis-Florentin)
     b. 22 thermidor Year VI (August 19, 1798), Yversay (Vienne)
     Father's occupation: *juge de paix* (justice of the peace)
     Birth certificate: Mairie d'Yversay
     Juge de paix existed as a position only during the period of the Revolution; Calmeil *père* was also *avocat* (lawyer) and *propriétaire* (property owner); see Ritti, "Eloge de Calmeil," *Ann m.-p.*, 8th ser. 6 (1897).
     Initial enrollment at Paris Faculty of Medicine: 1818; last five *in-scriptions* taken at Poitiers (AN: AJ[16] 6762 no. 110)
     Thèse de médecine (Paris): 1824
     Attached to Salpêtrière as *élève en 2ème classe:* 1822
     First full-time post: medical inspector of the health service at Charenton under Esquirol, 1825

13. FOVILLE (Achille-Louis)
     b. 7 thermidor Year VII (August 6, 1799), Pontoise (Val d'Oise)
     Father's occupation: Foville was an illegitimate child of a Norman family which could trace its noble lineage back to the fourteenth century. His mother, Marie-Louise Foville, was thirty-five years old when she gave birth to him at an inn in the village of Pontoise. The birth certificate, in which the declaration is made by the innkeeper's wife, makes no reference to a father and describes the mother as "residing in Rouen" and "en route from Rouen to Paris, having been surprised by the pangs of childbirth while in this commune." The document also records that Foville *mère* was "living on her income" (*vivant de son revenu*) in Rouen.
     Birth certificate: Mairie de Pontoise
     Initial enrollment at Paris Faculty of Medicine: 1818 (AN: AJ[16] 6762 no. 138)
     Thèse de médecine (Paris): 1824
     Attached to Salpêtrière as *élève en 1re classe:* 1822–24
     First full-time post: chief physician at the asile Saint-Yon in Rouen, 1825

14. BELHOMME (Jacques-Etienne)
b. 1800, Paris
Father's occupation: former carpenter (*menuisier*) who opened a *maison de santé* for the insane in Paris, rue de Charonne. (For an indication of the family's circumstances, see Belhomme's petition concerning four missing *inscriptions:* "Forcé par les malheurs du tems de ne prendre ses premières inscriptions, ses parens ayant une famille nombreuse à soutenir . . ." [AN: F^{17} 2177, letter of July 4, 1822])
Initial enrollment at Paris Faculty of Medicine: 1819 (AN: AJ^{16} 6762 no. 125)
Thèse de médecine (Paris): 1824
Attached to Salpêtrière as *élève en 1re classe:* June 1823–24
First full-time post: assumed direction of his father's *maison de santé*, 1824

15. BOUCHET (Camille)
b. 10 brumaire Year X (November 2, 1801), Poitiers
Father's occupation: *propriétaire* (property owner)
Birth certificate: Mairie de Poitiers
Initial enrollment at Paris Faculté de médecine: 1818 (AN: AJ^{16} 6764 no. 2)
Thèse de médecine (Paris): 1827
Attached to Salpêtrière as *élève de la 1re classe:* March 1824–25
First full-time post: chief physician of the lunatic quarters, hospice of Nantes, 1833

16. CAZAUVIEILH (Jean-Baptiste)
b. 11 pluviose Year X (February 3, 1802), Salles (Gironde)
Father's occupation: *cultivateur* (peasant farmer) according to birth certificate; *propriétaire cultivateur* (property owner and peasant farmer) according to marriage certificate of Cazauvieilh *fils*, 1829, Liancourt, Archives départementales de l'Oise
Birth certificate: Mairie de Salles
Initial enrollment at Paris Faculty of Medicine: 1820; first seven *inscriptions* taken at Bordeaux (AN: AJ^{16} 6764 no. 58)
Thèse de médecine (Paris): 1827
Attached to Salpêtrière as *élève de la 1re classe:* 1825
First full-time post: physician at the hospice of Liancourt (Oise), 1827

17. MOREAU DE TOURS (Jacques-Joseph)
b. June 2, 1804, Montrésor (Indre-et-Loire) according to *dossier de soutenance de thèse*, AN: AJ^{16} 6767 no. 127. No birth certificate found for that date and place; a birth certificate for Joseph Moreau (whose parents were married at Montrésor) found for 12 floréal Year XII

(May 2, 1804) at Loché-sur-Indrois, commune of the canton of Montrésor, near the town of Montrésor (Archives départementales d'Indre-et-Loire).

Father's occupation (on birth certificate): *cultivateur* (peasant farmer)

Initial enrollment at Paris Faculty of Medicine: 1827; seven inscriptions taken at Tours beginning in 1823 (AN: AJ[16] 6767 no. 127)

Thèse de médecine (Paris): 1830

Intern at Charenton under Esquirol: 1826

First full-time post: physician of the lunatic quarters, Bicêtre, 1840 (obtained by *concours*)

18. ARCHAMBAULT (Théophile)
   b. February 19, 1806, Tours (Indre-et-Loire)
   Father's occupation: *propriétaire* (property owner)
   Birth certificate: Mairie de Tours
   Frequented Esquirol's service at Charenton in informal capacity
   First full-time post: adjunct physician of François Leuret at Bicêtre, 1840 (obtained by *concours*)

19. BAILLARGER (Jules-Gabriel-François)
   b. March 25, 1809, Montbazon (Indre-et-Loire)
   Father: *propriétaire* (property owner)
   Birth certificate: Mairie de Montbazon
   Initial enrollment at Paris Faculty of Medicine: 1827; first *inscription* taken at Tours (AN: AJ[16] 6774 no. 475)
   Thèse de médecine (Paris): 1837
   Intern at Charenton under Esquirol
   First full-time post: physician at Esquirol's *maison de santé* at Ivry (also Esquirol's personal secretary)

Bibliographical note

The strong connection between nineteenth-century French psychiatry and the state and Paris municipal bureaucracies translates into rich archival sources for the historian.

At the Archives Nationales in Paris, the main resource is the F^{15} series, Hospices et secours. It contains numerous cartons (especially 3899–3919) detailing the demands upon the prefects made by the Ministry of the Interior during the first half of the nineteenth century to build and staff facilities for lunatics and, eventually, to implement the Law of 1838. The prefects' replies reveal a great deal about local conditions for the insane and often include relevant portions of the minutes of the Conseil général of the department. Also of great value are the F^{17} series (Instruction publique) and the nineteenth-century archives of the Paris Faculty of Medicine, housed at the Archives Nationales as part of the AJ^{16} series. The folio registers of the minutes of the meetings of the medical faculty professoriate (especially AJ^{16} 6232, 6256–57) and those of the meetings of the Commission de l'Instruction publique (especially F^{17*} 1764) enabled me to trace the debates surrounding the entrance of psychiatry into the curriculum of the premier institution of medical education in France. The individual records of students at the Paris medical faculty (especially AJ^{16} 6759–74) provided biographical information about members of the Esquirol circle. Finally, the meticulously cataloged AJ^{2} series documents the national asylum of Charenton during its early decades.

At the municipal level, the archives of the Assistance Publique de Paris are indispensable to any reconstruction of the history of psychiatry in the French capital. In the early 1970s, the Assistance Publique inventoried the old records kept at each of the hospitals under its jurisdiction, removed these records to a central depot, and made them accessible to researchers at its reading room on the rue des Minimes. These records include over two thousand registers from Bicêtre and the Salpêtrière, beginning with the early eighteenth century and covering the inmate populations and virtually every aspect of institutional management and finances. For purposes of this book, I have made selective use of the nineteenth-century registers on newly admitted patients

(Salpêtrière 6Q2 and Bicêtre 6Q2) and on the salaries of medical personnel (Salpêtrière 2K1). Also among the archives of the Assistance Publique are the minutes of the Conseil général des hospices et hôpitaux civils de Paris, the board that governed the Paris public welfare system, including Bicêtre and the Salpêtrière, from the Napoleonic period on. The Collection Bourneville is a set of newspaper clippings concerning the political career of the Bicêtre psychiatrist D.-M. Bourneville during the early Third Republic.

The reports of the police spy "Cujas," deposited at the Archives de la Préfecture de Police de Paris (B^A 24–25), provide eyewitness accounts of lecture courses at the Paris Faculty of Medicine and clinical lessons at the hospitals in the 1870s; they include comments on such psychiatric *maîtres* as Charles Lasègue and J.-M. Charcot.

While the F^{15} series at the Archives Nationales offers a window on psychiatric affairs in the provinces, more detailed information about that subject requires use of local archives. In preparing this study, I have consulted only those of the Asile Saint-Méen in Rennes, a collection now housed at the Archives départementales d'Ille-et-Vilaine.

If archival material about psychiatric institutions is abundant, manuscript material from the pens of individual psychiatrists is in short supply. The letters of Dr. Antoine Chambeyron among the archives of the Asile Saint-Méen are the richest source of this kind that I uncovered, and even they fall within the category of official correspondence. But precisely because Chambeyron was so embattled, his letters to the local hospital administration tell us a great deal about his day-to-day professional life. Two cartons of letters to the minister of the interior requesting medical posts in public asylums (AN: F^{15} 3914–15) shed some light on psychiatrists' careers. Extant correspondence of a personal nature by psychiatrists is very rare. Philippe Pinel's nephew Casimir published large and interesting portions of the founding father's letters to his family; these appeared in the *Gazette hebdomadaire de médecine et de chirurgie* in 1858 and 1859 and were also subsequently published as a book – Casimir Pinel, *Lettres de Pinel* (Paris: Masson, 1859). I found in the Bibliothèque Historique de la Ville de Paris one personal letter by Esquirol, which turned out to be unremarkable. Some of the letters to his son by Antoine-Emile Blanche, Paris psychiatrist and *maison de santé* proprietor, can be found in the Bibliothèque de l'Institut de France, but their relevance to the subject of this book is minimal.

In the absence of more first-person documentation, obituaries – usually written by students and close colleagues – can be good sources of information about psychiatrists' personalities. One invaluable tool is René Semelaigne, *Les pionniers de la psychiatrie française avant et après Pinel*, 2 vols. (Paris: J.-B. Baillière, 1930–32), which offers biographical and intellectual portraits of some seventy-five nineteenth-century psychiatrists together with exhaustive bibliographies of their writings. A study of Pinel and longer sketches of Esquirol, Ferrus, J.-P. Falret, Félix Voisin, and Georget than are found in *Pionniers* comprise Semelaigne's *Les grands aliénistes français* (Paris: G. Steinheil, 1894). An additional feature of these works is that Semelaigne, the third generation of a Parisian psychiatric family and the grandson of Casimir Pinel, has peppered them with anecdotal lore.

As a general rule, the psychiatrists discussed in this book were quite prolific and publishêd both articles and monographic treatises. A few of them – for example, Esquirol, J.-P. Falret, Baillarger – brought out retrospective collections of their articles during their own lifetimes. Esquirol's *Des maladies mentales considérées sous les rapports médical, hygiénique et médico-légal*, 2 vols. (Paris: J.-B. Baillière, 1838) is the most comprehensive of these. But since Esquirol could not resist revising and updating his articles for republication, the collection is a primary source in its own right and does not obviate the historian's need to consult the articles in their original versions.

Psychiatrists' articles are found dispersed among numerous journals. The main nineteenth-century French psychiatric journal, cited throughout this study, is the *Annales médico-psychologiques*, founded in 1843 and still being published today. Before it came into being, articles on "psychiatric" subjects were accommodated in other periodicals, such as the *Décade philosophique* (1794–1807) and the *Journal général de médecine*; even after 1843 many general medical journals continued to include psychiatric materials on occasion. A second psychiatric journal, the *Journal de médecine mentale*, lasted only a single decade, from 1861 to 1870. The *Annales d'hygiène publique et de médecine légale*, founded in 1829, quickly became a forum for articles on forensic psychiatry and for statistical studies of asylum populations. The work of Charcot and his Salpêtrière school typically appeared in the *Progrès médical* and the more specialized *Iconographie photographique de la Salpêtrière*.

Particularly in the first half of the century, psychiatrists frequently made some of their most important statements in articles written for multivolume medical dictionaries, a genre that represented the continuation of the eighteenth-century encyclopedic tradition. Hence the *Dictionaire des sciences médicales*, 60 vols. (Paris, 1812–22) and the *Dictionnaire de médecine*, 21 vols. (1821–28) figure prominently among the sources for this study. All nineteenth-century French candidates for the doctorate in medicine prepared theses at the conclusion of their medical educations; a full collection of those written at the Paris Faculty of Medicine can be found at that institution's library and (since the theses were required to be printed) at the National Library of Medicine in Bethesda, Maryland, as well. Some of the theses have functioned as key texts in this study, notably Esquirol's 1805 *Des passions considérées comme causes, symptômes et moyens curatifs de l'aliénation mentale*.

Printed government documents shed important light on the history of French psychiatry. Many of those bearing on our subject were conveniently gathered together and republished during the early Third Republic – Ministère de l'Intérieur et des Cultes, *Législation sur les aliénés et les enfants assistés*, 3 vols. (Paris, 1884). Volume 3 contains the legislative debates over the Law of 1838, which can also be pieced together from the *Archives parlementaires*. Important ministerial reports on public assistance from the period of the constitutional monarchy, which include discussion of the insane, are J.-H. Laîné, *Rapport au Roi sur la situation des hospices, des enfants trouvés, des aliénés, de la mendicité et des prisons* (Paris: Impr. royale, 1818) and A.-E. de Gasparin, *Rapport au Roi sur les hôpitaux, les hospices et les services de bienfaisance* (Paris: Impr. royale, 1837). As state bureaucratic agencies became more specialized with respect to the care of the insane, reports too became more specialized; see the long and thorough survey by inspectors-general of lunatic services Constans, Lunier, and Dumesnil, *Rapport à M. le Ministre de l'Intérieur sur le service des aliénés en 1874* (Paris: Impr. nationale, 1878). The municipal administration of Paris made contributions of its own to this genre – for example, B. Desportes, *Compte rendu au Conseil général des hospices et hôpitaux civils de Paris sur le service des aliénés . . . pendant les années 1822, 1823 et 1824* (Paris: Impr. de Mme Huzard, 1826) and the plan for a model asylum, first published anonymously in 1821 and then republished several years later under Desportes's name, *Programme d'un hôpital consacré au traitement de l'aliénation mentale pour cinq cents malades des deux sexes* (Paris: Impr. de Mme Huzard, 1824).

The secondary literature on the history of modern French psychiatry is growing steadily, and any list of works I present here is sure to be out of date before long. To begin with the more general studies, Henri Baruk's *La psychiatrie française de Pinel à nos jours* (Paris: Presses universitaires de France, 1967) offers a succinct overview of the various theoretical currents. Henri F. Ellenberger's massive *The Discovery of the Unconscious: The History and Evolution of Dynamic Psychiatry* (New York: Basic Books, 1970), which is not confined to France, traces the development of mesmerism and hypnotism, which although initially peripheral to psychiatry bore such important fruit at the end of the nineteenth century. The same subject is treated with a national focus in Dominique Barrucand, *Histoire de l'hypnose en France* (Paris: Presses universitaires de France, 1967). Klaus Dörner has explored the crystallization of psychiatry in three countries – England, France, and Germany – in *Madmen and the Bourgeoisie: A Social History of Insanity* (Oxford: Basil Blackwell, 1981), a translation from the original German edition of 1969. Essays on France are included in two recent multiauthored collections, *Nouvelle histoire de la psychiatrie*, edited by Jacques Postel and Claude Quétel (Toulouse: Privat, 1983) and *The Anatomy of Madness: Essays in the History of Psychiatry*, edited by W. F. Bynum, Roy Porter, and Michael Shepherd (London: Tavistock, 1985).

The founding moment of French psychiatry has received a great deal of scholarly attention. Gladys Swain scrutinizes the myth surrounding Pinel's role as founder and "chain-breaker" in *Le sujet de la folie: Naissance de la psychiatrie* (Toulouse: Privat, 1977). Marcel Gauchet and Gladys Swain treat the period 1800–1810, with an emphasis on Esquirol and on the genesis of the asylum, in a highly philosophical work, *La pratique de l'esprit humain: L'institution asilaire et la révolution démocratique* (Paris: Gallimard, 1980). Dora B. Weiner has enlarged the known Pinel corpus through her discovery of a new manuscript, published both in English translation and in French as Philippe Pinel, *The Clinical Training of Doctors: An Essay of 1793* (Baltimore: Johns Hopkins University Press, 1980). In addition to making available a large number of Pinel's early published articles, Jacques Postel's *Genèse de la psychiatrie: Les premiers écrits de Philippe Pinel* (Paris: Le sycamore, 1981) also includes a newly discovered Pinel manuscript.

An important sociological synthesis of the period 1790–1860, which saw the asylum come to ascendancy, is Robert Castel, *L'ordre psychiatrique: L'âge d'or de l'aliénisme* (Paris: Minuit, 1976); it is complemented by Castel's "Le traitement moral: Thérapeutique mentale et contrôle sociale au XIXe siècle," *Topique*, no. 4 (1970). Using quantitative methods, Claude Quétel prepared a *thèse de troisième cycle* on an important clerical asylum of our period, "Le Bon Sauveur de Caen: Les cadres de la folie au XIXe siècle," Paris-Sorbonne, 1976. He has published some of his results in a two-part article, "Garder les fous dans un asile de province au XIXe siècle: Le Bon Sauveur de Caen," *Annales de Normandie* (1979). Other local histories of psychiatry heavily based upon archival sources include Colin Jones, "The Treatment of the Insane in Eighteenth- and Early Nineteenth-Century Montpellier," *Medical History* 24 (1980); Giordana Charuty, *Le couvent des fous: L'internement et ses usages en Languedoc au XIXe et XXe siècles* (Paris: Flammarion, 1985); and two studies of a fascinating episode of psychopathological "contagion" in an Alpine village in Savoy – Catherine-Laurence Maire, *Les possédées de Morzine, 1857–1873* (Lyons: Presses universitaires de Lyons, 1981) and Jacqueline Carroy-Thirard, *Le mal de Morzine: De la possession à l'hystérie, 1857–1877* (Paris: Solin, 1981).

A concise treatment of a tangled subject of critical importance to nineteenth-century psychiatry is José M. López Piñero, *Historical Origins of the Concept of Neurosis*, trans. D. Berrios (Cambridge University Press, 1983). Hysteria was the late nineteenth-century neurosis par excellence, and it has understandably received a good deal of scholarly attention. Ilza Veith, *Hysteria: The History of a Disease* (Chicago: University of Chicago Press, 1965) offers a survey from the ancient Egyptians through psychoanalysis. Jean-Marie Bruttin confines himself to France and to a much narrower time period in *Différentes théories sur l'hystérie dans la première moitié du XIXe siècle* (Zurich: Juris,

1969). A recent work, emphasizing visual imagery, is Georges Didi-Huberman, _Invention de l'hystérie: Charcot et l'iconographie photographique de la Salpêtrière_ (Paris: Macula, 1982). Elisabeth Roudinesco devotes the opening of _La bataille de cent ans: Histoire de la psychanalyse en France,_ Vol. 1: _1885–1939_ (Paris: Ramsay, 1982) to the discovery of hysteria. In a different vein, Robert B. Nye's study of the late nineteenth century, _Crime, Madness and Politics in Modern France: The Medical Concept of National Decline_ (Princeton, N.J.: Princeton University Press, 1984) discusses psychiatry as part of a broad consideration of the pervasive definition of social problems as social "pathology" under the early Third Republic.

For both their empirical content and their powerful theoretical perspectives, the works of Michel Foucault occupy a special and central place in the historiography of psychiatry. _Folie et déraison: Histoire de la folie a l'âge classique_ (Paris: Plon, 1961) focuses on the seventeenth and eighteenth centuries, stopping just as Pinel arrives on the scene; it should be read in the original, since the English translation, _Madness and Civilization,_ is based on a substantially abridged French edition. _Moi, Pierre Rivière, ayant égorgé ma mère, ma soeur et mon frère_ . . . (Paris: Gallimard/Julliard, 1973) contains primary sources and a collection of essays bearing on an early nineteenth-century case of parricide and, more generally, on the emergence of forensic psychiatry. _Discipline and Punish: The Birth of the Prison,_ trans. A. Sheridan (New York: Pantheon, 1977), perhaps Foucault's most important work from the viewpoint of the historian, situates psychiatry among a group of "disciplines," rooted in the Enlightenment, that Foucault regards as underpinning the modern liberal state. _The History of Sexuality, Volume I: An Introduction,_ trans. R. Hurley (New York: Pantheon, 1978) construes the diagnostic category hysteria as a manifestation of modern "biopower" and is also methodologically significant for the historian for its sustained argument that "sexuality" is a historically constituted rather than a natural object.

The history of psychiatry is embedded in the larger field of the history of medicine. The rise of modern medicine in France, in its theoretical and institutional aspects, has been the subject of considerable recent research; I will confine myself here to some of the most salient and relevant titles. Erwin H. Ackerknecht, _Medicine at the Paris Hospital, 1794–1848_ (Baltimore: Johns Hopkins University Press, 1967) serves as an excellent basic reference. Foucault's contribution to this literature is _The Birth of the Clinic: An Archaeology of Medical Perception,_ trans. A. M. Sheridan Smith (New York: Pantheon, 1973). Jacques Léonard, probably the premier historian of French medicine writing today, produced a Sorbonne _thèse de doctorat d'état_ entitled _Les médecins de l'Ouest au XIXème siècle,_ 3 vols. (Lille: Atelier de reproduction des thèses, 1978), which can be mined with great profit. Also of value are his _La médecine entre les pouvoirs et les savoirs_ (Paris: Aubier Montaigne,

1981) and his collection of documents, *La France médicale au XIXe siècle* (Paris: Gallimard/Julliard, 1978). The Royal Society of Medicine, which functioned as the transitional link to a characteristically modern medicine in France, is the subject of Caroline C. F. Hannaway's "Medicine, Public Welfare and the State in Eighteenth-Century France: The Société Royale de Médecine of Paris (1776–1793)" (Ph.D. dissertation, Johns Hopkins University, 1974). Martin S. Staum's *Cabanis: Enlightenment and Medical Philosophy in the French Revolution* (Princeton, N.J.: Princeton University Press, 1980) is the intellectual biography of a pivotal figure with close ties to the founding generation of French psychiatrists.

The sociological literature on the professions is vast. A general orientation is provided by an anthology edited by Howard M. Vollmer and Donald L. Mills, *Professionalization* (Englewood Cliffs, N.J.: Prentice-Hall, 1966). Important recent works include Eliot Freidson, *Profession of Medicine: A Study of the Sociology of Applied Knowledge* (New York: Dodd, Mead, 1970) and Magali Sarfatti Larson, *The Rise of Professionalism: A Sociological Analysis* (Berkeley and Los Angeles: University of California Press, 1977). Andrew T. Scull conceptualizes the nature of the profession of psychiatry in "From Madness to Mental Illness: Medical Men as Moral Entrepreneurs," *Archives européennes de sociologie* 16 (1975). Although it is concerned with new academic disciplines rather than with the service professions, I have found the work of Terry N. Clark helpful; see his "Institutionalization of Innovations in Higher Education: Four Models," *Administrative Science Quarterly* 13 (1968) and *Prophets and Patrons: The French University and the Emergence of the Social Sciences* (Cambridge, Mass.: Harvard University Press, 1973). Gerald L. Geison, ed., *Professions and the French State, 1700–1900* (Philadelphia: University of Pennsylvania Press, 1984) is a collection of essays by historians which, taken together, address the issue of the "peculiarity" of professions in France.

The birth of the modern "human sciences," closely related to the rise of the professions, is treated by Michel Foucault, *The Order of Things: An Archaeology of the Human Sciences* (New York: Pantheon, 1970); Georges Gusdorf, *Les sciences humaines et la pensée occidentale*, Vol. 7: *Naissance de la conscience romantique au siècle des lumières* (Paris: Payot, 1976) and Vol. 8: *La conscience révolutionnaire: Les idéologues* (1978); and Keith Michael Baker, *Condorcet: From Natural Philosophy to Social Mathematics* (Chicago: University of Chicago Press, 1975).

Additional sources on all these subjects can be found in the notes to individual chapters.

Index